OPERATIONS STRATEGIES FOR COMPETITIVE ADVANTAGE

TEXT AND CASES

FIRST EDITION

OPERATIONS STRATEGIES
FOR COMPETITIVE ADVANTAGE

TEXT AND CASES

FIRST EDITION

E. C. ETIENNE-HAMILTON
University of Montreal

The Dryden Press
Harcourt Brace College Publishers

Fort Worth Philadelphia San Diego New York Orlando Austin San Antonio
Toronto Montreal London Sydney Tokyo

Publisher	Elizabeth Widdicombe
Director of Editing, Design, & Production	Diane Southworth
Acquisitions Editor	Scott Isenberg
Developmental Editor	Tracy Morse
Project Editor	Doug Smith
Art Director	Pat Bracken
Production Manager	Ann Coburn
Photo & Permissions Editor	Steve Lunetta
Marketing Manager	Kevin Cottingim
Copy Editor	Judi McClellan
Indexer	Kristina Sanfilippo DeVico
Compositor	G&S Typesetters
Text Type	10/12 Garamond
Cover Image	C. Fatta Photography

Address for Editorial Correspondence
The Dryden Press, 301 Commerce Street, Suite 3700, Fort Worth, TX 76102

Address for Orders
The Dryden Press, 6277 Sea Harbor Drive, Orlando, FL 32887
1-800-782-4479, or 1-800-433-0001 (in Florida)

ISBN: 0-03-0976685

Library of Congress Catalog Card Number: 93-072905

Printed in the United States of America

3 4 5 6 7 8 9 0 1 2   039   9 8 7 6 5 4 3 2 1

The Dryden Press
Harcourt Brace College Publishers

■ ■ ■ ■ ■ ■ ■ ■ ■ ■ ■ ■ ■ ■ ■ ■ ■ ■ ■

Dedicated to the memory of my maternal grandparents,
Marie Louisiana Royer and Albert William Hamilton
who taught me the value of education,
hard work, compassion and charity.

The Dryden Press Series in Management Science and Quantitative Methods

Preface

There is now absolutely no doubt that manufacturing/operations is one of the prime strategic functions of any business. Whether or not manufacturing/operations achieves its strategic potential and contributes to the competitive position of a business depends entirely on how it is managed. Without exception, when the manufacturing/operations function fails to significantly contribute to the creation of sustainable competitive advantage, it is a failure, not of manufacturing management, but of top management. The buck truly stops here! This book is an attempt to show that the strategic and competition oriented management of manufacturing/operations is a top management responsibility and to present the philosophies, concepts, management processes, tools and techniques that have been shown to be invaluable in the creation of a competitively useful production/operations function.

We have given top priority to the customer. In all successful companies, the customer is the heart and soul of the business. The business must exist for the customer or it will not exist at all. Production must perennially serve the customer or it will be a reprobate disservice to the business and its employees, owners, and society as a whole. All through this book, we try to bring the student, the manager, and the reader back to the customer as the very reason to be in any business. Companies that do not absolutely value their customers cease quickly to be of any value to any one.

This book is different from existing works in the field of operations strategy in some unique ways. First, the preponderance of customer concerns in the presentation of all the material sets this work apart from others. I have taken pains to show that even in basic tools and techniques like set-up reduction and Kanban, the need to satisfy the customer must be central to thought processes of those that implement and use them.

Second, I have not shied away from presenting the fundamental tools and techniques that the best managed companies of the world have used to create competitive advantage. My long experience in teaching manufacturing/operations strategy to undergraduate and graduate students and managers has taught me that there is a tendency to trivialize the importance of basic tools and techniques in the strategy formulation and implementation process. Sooner or later, the implementation of manufacturing/operations strategy must grapple with the problem of applying the most powerful tools, techniques and methods that are susceptible to increasing the efficiency and effectiveness of the manufacturing/operations function. Many top managers cannot ask the right questions of production personnel and consultants because they do not fully grasp the basic tools, concepts and techniques. Some see the implementation of these tools and techniques as an operational and not a strategic management problem. For example, the treatment of MRP-II and small lot production and Kanban may, prima facie, appear to be operational. But MRP-II is a set of operational tools and techniques with much strategic impact. MRP-II is the only credible and potent modern management technology that plans and controls production and materials in the rigorous execution of a customer service strategy. One cannot take the risk that students and managers would leave a course or training program in manufacturing/operations strategy without understanding the fundamental mechanisms, tools, techniques and processes of MRP-II and how these relate to its basic strategic mission. However, I take the view that when one is trying to build a World Class Manufacturing operation and to derive strategic leverage from operations, the distinction between the strategic and the operational becomes blurred. Top management must manage in such a way as to extract strategic advantage from operations, and this point has been emphasized throughout this work.

Third, this work places emphasis on the concept of symbiosis as a prime source of competitive advantage in production operations. The concepts, tools, techniques and approaches that can be exploited to create competitive advantage have a very high potential to reinforce and feed on each other. Manufacturing strategy formulation and implementation creates symbiosis between approaches, concepts, tools and techniques of production/operations management and exloits such symbiosis to the maximum extent possible. Fourth, the role of waste elimination in the pursuit of manufacturing/operations excellence and competitive superiority receives central attention. The relationships between competition, strategic positioning, and waste elminiation have been highlighted and elucidated in many areas. The message is clear: Waste elimination is now a meaningful and powerful concept of manufacturing/operations and corporate strategy and programs, tools and techniques that target waste should be viewed and managed as part of the process of strategy implementation and strategic change. Once again, the manager cannot and should not avoid dealing with and gaining basic understanding of the tools and techniques if he/she wants to do a thorough and credible job of managing manufacturing for maximum strategic impact.

The chapters on quality come after the ones that deal with the basic concepts on competition and strategic positioning and waste elimination for good reason. First, this is not a book on Total Quality Management (TQM). Manufacturing strategy formulation and implementation involves much more than attempting to apply a popular TQM approach or paradigm. TQM is only one component, albeit a critical one, of the manufacturing/operations strategy framework. Moreover, there is now broad consensus that waste elimination is more global than traditional TQM concepts since bad quality is only one type of waste, even if a very important one. In a certain sense, I am trying to shift the whole area of manufacturing/operations strategy and world class manufacturing away from a singleminded focus on quality and toward a more balanced consideration of all sources of competitive advantage in manufacturing/operations. This is a tall order, but I was constrained to try.

There is a very important reason why the chapter that deals with managing change in manufacturing strategy was placed at the end. My experience is that if this material is presented at the beginning of the course, students show a propensity to regurgitate the concepts when they are dealing with specific cases or issues in strategic change all through the course, rather than trying to come to their own independent understanding of what is involved in changing manufacturing strategy. Furthermore, the book takes the position that the implementation of the tools of strategic manufacturing and world class manufacturing is an integral, aspect of the strategic manufacturing management process. It is usually better to present students with all the concepts, tools and approaches and their attendant constraints and philosophies, before asking them to pull all than together into a comprehensive framework of strategic manufacturing change.

The cases presented are all based on real life, field experience in actual companies. Names, data and locations have been disguised to preserve anonymity, but the essential issues and problems that confronted the actual companies have been kept intact.

The field of manufacturing/operations strategy and World Class Manufacturing is an exciting one. More and more companies are coming to the realization that their survival depends on the capability to manage production as a premier strategic function. It is my hope that this work will reinforce that understanding and will be of help to the students and managers who wish to gain broader and deeper understanding of the issues and concepts involved.

Acknowledgements

Many people contributed to the production of this work. I would like, first of all, to express my sincere thanks and gratitude to all the companies that have engaged me as a consultant and given me the opportunity to test my ideas in actual situations. My thanks also go out to the numerous students and managers who were the first to listen to me both at the Ecole des Hautes Etudes Commerciales and in my training seminars. I have learned more from them than they from me.

I wish to thank the Ecole des Hautes Etudes Commerciales (HEC), University of Montreal, for granting me a sabbatical and some funding for preparing this work. It would not have otherwise been possible. I also received valuable typing and manuscript preparation support from HEC, and for that, I am grateful. But, in the typing area, my deepest thanks go to Fernande Perrault for her tireless efforts in helping meet the deadlines.

I would also like to extend my appreciation to Peter Arnold (Boston University), Ann Maruchek (University of North Carolina at Chapel Hill), Soumen Goush (Georgia Institute of Technology) and Craig Wood (University of New Hampshire) who reviewed the manuscript and offered many pertinent insights and helpful suggestions.

I am grateful to the staff at Dryden for the encouragement and support throughout the development of this work: Scott Isenberg, acquisitions editor; Doug Smith, project editor; Ann Coburn, production manager; Pat Bracken, designer; Kevin Cottingim, marketing manager; Tracy Morse, editorial assistant; and Sam Stubblefield, marketing assistant.

I would be negligent if I did not thank my maternal grandparents for having taught me a thing or two about life. To them I am eternally indebted and it is my hope that I will live up to all the expectations they had for me. Surely, one could not be blessed with any better.

Finally to my wife Deirdre who has unwaveringly supported and shown love for and confidence in me, I say, *"Thank you from the bottom of my heart"*. I also express thanks to my four children Mineke, Ruth-Anne, Camille and Albert who were happy to give up some of the time that belonged to them in order that I may prepare this work.

In the final analysis, I and I alone, am responsible for whatever errors are contained in this book.

E. C. Etienne-Hamilton
Montreal, Quebec, Canada
November, 1993

Table of Contents

Contents

Table of Contents

Managing for Zero Defects   261

Small Lot Production and Kanban   303

Managing Purchasing for Superior Performance   337

Managing Maintenance for Zero Breakdowns   378

CHAPTER 1

The New Competitive Environment for Manufacturing

The competitive environment for manufacturing companies has changed dramatically over the last few decades. Competition is deeper, tougher, and more persistent. Now more than ever, manufacturing companies have to explicitly manage to deal with competition. The key concept to emerge over the last decade is *globalization,* which is both the result and the cause of the new competitive realities. In order to understand globalization, one must come to grips with the issue of market scope as a prime determinant of competition intensity.

MARKET SCOPE

The severity of competition in a market is fundamentally determined by the number of viable competitors that are competing in the marketplace and their respective strengths. A market that has a large number of competitors each possessing adequate technical, human, and financial resources will be competitive. In that case, enough competitors can and will react rapidly, if necessary, to neutralize every credible competitive move made by any firm that seeks to improve its position in the market at the expense of the others. As the number of competitors increases, more and more firms attempt to improve their position, which puts pressure for continuous improvement on each competitor. The existence of a large number of high caliber competitors depends on market scope, that is, the vastness or geographical dispersion of the market. As far as management of an enterprise is concerned, market scope can be placed into three categories: local, national, and international or global.

The Local Market

A local market exists when supply and demand are brought into equilibrium by industrial and commercial activities that are confined to a particular region of a country. The nature of the product and transportation, distribution and the financial constraints limit the scale of operations so that it becomes infeasible or impractical to distribute the product beyond a limited geographical space. Nearly all companies emerge as competitors in local markets and their subsequent growth both facilitate and capitalize on the broadening of the scope of the market.

The National Market

Markets are national in scope when their products are manufactured and distributed within the boundaries of a given nation. The products can be produced anywhere within the country and economically transported to any region. Although transport and distribution inefficiencies may still exist within the country, tariff and nontariff barriers erected by government make national production and distribution relatively "efficient." In some circumstances, national tastes are so deeply entrenched that consumers are willing to pay a higher price for a product or service manufactured specifically to meet these tastes. The furniture market, for example, tends to be national in scope, even though companies like IKEA from Sweden are beginning to emerge as international competitors. Whether IKEA is being proactive in exploiting a latent trend toward internationalization (globalization) of the furniture market or whether it has made a strategic blunder is too early to tell. One thing is certain, however, pioneer international companies thrive on their ability to detect when a market is about to become global and attempt to capitalize on that trend.

The distinction between a local and national market becomes blurred when bordering nations are geographically so small that tastes and transportation and distribution networks cut across many nations. In that case, the national market is more appropriately viewed as a few nations in close proximity. In Europe, Eurasia, and Africa, there are many cases where the national market transcends more than one nation.

The International Market

When production can be undertaken anywhere in the world and the product can be economically distributed and consumed anywhere else, the market can be said to be global in scope. In this kind of market, imports and exports are high even for producer countries and there is a free flow of goods. These markets are also characterized by the existence of many producer countries and nearly every country is a consumer and importer. However, production tends to be concentrated in a few international production centers and further globalization multiplies these centers. Globalization brings these competitively robust production centers into head-on competition with one another, and the market retains its global structure as some centers decline but others emerge to replace them. Automobiles, pharmaceuticals, electronics, chemicals, petrochemicals, farm machinery, and civil aviation are all examples of global industries.

The comments that have been made up to this point would lead one to anticipate that competition intensity increases radically as one goes from a local to a national and then to an international market. Indeed, the global market represents the ultimate level of competition intensity. By definition a global market has many high caliber competitors. It is precisely the presence of these companies that gives the international market its unique character. The globalization of a market usually requires that companies that want to maintain their competitive position must become multinational or global in strategy, structure, vision, operation, and distribution. These multinational enterprises have demonstrable capabilities to mobilize huge quantities of human, technical, and financial resources. Eventually, a global market comes to be dominated by these large multinational enterprises which leads to progressive disappearance of local and national companies or in the latter being drawn into competitive dependency relationships with global corporations as their specialized suppliers or affiliaters. Local and national companies have a very difficult time competing in global markets except if they deploy highly specialized or focused strategies, or if they form strategic and technological alliances with other local or national companies. These companies must find some means of offsetting the overwhelming competitive advantages held by the large, global enterprise. The globalization of markets and the emergence and entrenchment of the multinational enterprise are thus parallel and symbiotically related phenomena.

THE GLOBALIZATION OF MARKETS

One can affirm unequivocally that there is a persistent trend toward deeper globalization of markets that are already international in scope and also toward the increasing globalization of local and national markets. Local and national markets are buckling and giving way to the globalization phenomenon that became entrenched in the 1970s and 1980s. The trend toward progressive and deepening globalization is probably irreversible because it is powered by fundamental, deeply entrenched social, economic, and technological forces which are restructuring the world economic system. It is enough at this point to underline a few facts that demonstrate the existence of the new competitive reality for manufacturing:

1. In 1960, the four American automobile manufacturers—General Motors, Ford, Chrysler, and American Motors—held almost 100 percent of the American car market and were unchallenged (some thought unchallengeable). Car imports were limited to such internationally recognized luxury

cars like Rolls Royce and Mercedes Benz. Today, imports and cars manufactured in the United States by foreign companies have taken more than 30 percent of the U.S. market. American producers since then have created production centers in Europe, Australia, and Southern Africa while Japanese and European manufacturers continue to expand production in the United States. The Japanese, in general, and Honda, in particular, are increasingly tightening their hold on the American market by building plants in the United States to satisfy North American demand for their cars. The Americanization of Honda is, in our view, a precursor to the Americanization of all the Japanese-based car manufacturers.

2. In the early 1960s, the electronics industry was completely dominated by U.S. manufacturers. Americans invented solid state electronics and created the modern electronics industry. Today, electronics manufacturing is done on a large scale in at least four Western European countries while Japan is a leading world producer. The Pacific Rim countries have emerged as important production centers for electronics products. Meanwhile, imports now account for over 75 percent of the U.S. market for consumer electronics products including television sets, VCRs, radios, stereo-recorders, and so on.

3. Before the 1970s, the service industries, particularly the hospitality sectors—restaurants, hotels, motels, and resorts—were shielded from the effect of international competition. Today, there are very large multisite, international chains in every aspect of hospitality. McDonald's is now making a strong bid for the markets behind the iron curtain.

4. The pharmaceuticals industry already had an international character as early as the 1960s, but severe government regulations delayed its total globalization. Due to the standardization of government regulations and the rapid diffusion of medical technology and use of pharmaceutical products, this market is on the verge of becoming a global one.

Clearly, something more than advanced technology is at work, because both high- and low-technology industries are succumbing to accelerating globalization. We now turn our attention to understanding the factors that are propelling globalization in virtually every industry of the world.

FACTORS PROPELLING GLOBALIZATION

Globalization of markets is intimately connected to humanity's march toward the global village. The world is shrinking fast. Countries and markets that were once thought to be unreachable are now no more than a few hours away. Cultures that were once thought to be unblendable are now being fused together. A smaller planet is making it possible for companies to produce for a world market. The factors that are causing the planet to shrink are also the same ones that are eliminating regional and national differences in tastes and needs. So both the physical and sociocultural/psychological barriers to international production and distribution are disappearing. The trend appears to be irreversible, coming from a natural development of human culture and the maturation of human settlements.[1]

Economics of Communication

Means of communication that are simultaneously more effective, less costly, and more powerful make the diffusion of information easier and more desirable. The educated elite of even the world's poorest countries can keep themselves abreast of what is going on in the world as a whole. Better communication makes it easier to market products on a global scale. The diffusion of technology is such that citizens in many poor countries owned VCRs before most people in the industrialized countries where they were invented had them. Rapid communication means that local demand and distribution are quickly influenced by international events.

International communication leads progressively to the homogenization of tastes, wants, and needs. The marketing of McDonald's hamburgers in Paris, the People's Republic of China, and the former Soviet Union and the large scale use of vaccines in developing countries are vivid manifestations of such homogenization. Almost every country in the world has television and/or radio, the two most powerful mass communication media. Information on any critical world event gets diffused worldwide in less than 12 hours.

Economics of Transportation

Modern transportation technology and large-scale transportation have generated substantial reductions in transport cost on a global basis. Containerization and multi-modal transportation are some innovations that drastically reduced transportation cost. International transportation is now so efficient that in many cases it costs less to transport a good between two countries that are far apart than between two cities within the same country. Transportation is now so efficient and rapid that a flower can be harvested in France in the morning, transported to the exchange in Holland, sold, delivered, and put in the flower shop in New York the very same day, at a price comparable to what it sells for in Paris. In most sectors of economic activity, transportation cost and effectiveness have ceased to be a barrier to trade.

---

[1]For example, a profound crisis has gripped communism in the 1990s. The iron curtain concept is rapidly becoming an anachronism.

Recognition of the Advantages of International Trade

Economic science has now firmly accepted the idea that healthy international competition energizes national economies. The protectionist wave that swept through the world between the 1930s and the 1960s lost its force once most economists recognized that most countries would benefit from international trade. Protectionism saps the competitive energy from national companies and causes them to become more and more inefficient and saddled with obsolete technology. Opening up to world competition forces weak competitors out and pushes the stronger companies to sharpen their competitive skills. The General Agreement on Tariffs and Trade (GATT), which was signed by nearly all United Nations member countries, provides for systematically reducing tariff barriers until they disappear during the 1990s. The new economic philosophy provides the theoretical foundation for GATT and drives the march toward liberalized world trade.

Economic Performance of Free Enterprise Economies

Free enterprise and liberalized trade are complementary economic philosophies. To the extent that free enterprise is proved to be a superior economic philosophy, it inexorably legitimizes liberalized trade. There is now absolutely no doubt that free enterprise results in more efficient production and distribution and more accurate matching of supply and demand. Central planning, a cornerstone of Marxist–Leninist ideology, has failed miserably. Free enterprise economies have outperformed their centrally-planned counterparts in every sphere of economic activity in every region of the world, regardless of the sociocultural milieu in which each is introduced. All of the countries that succeeded in industrializing their economies since the last world war—Japan, South Korea, Brazil, Israel, South Africa, Hong Kong, Singapore, Taiwan, to name the most outstanding—did so using the free enterprise philosophy. Central planning is crumbling with the Marxist–Leninist foundation that supported it. Trade becomes easier and more natural when most countries embrace free enterprise.

The world economy is also dominated by free enterprise economies and that in itself globalizes economic activity, competition, and trade. The world's largest and most dynamic economies are based on free enterprise. More and more the United States, Japan, Germany, France, and Britain among others are pulling smaller economies within their spheres of influence which are quickening the latters' pace of economic development and giving increased momentum to the entrenchment of free enterprise on a world scale.

Sustained Global Industrialization

Although poverty persists in many countries, industrialization is spreading across the world. International diffusion of technology, better education, and a more complete and tested body of knowledge on management of development means that more and more countries are becoming industrialized. No less than 40 nations are either classified as Newly Industrialized Countries (NICs) or are on the verge of attaining that status. Spreading industrialization broadens the demand for consumer goods, homogenizes tastes, and creates new international production centers. The four little dragons of Asia (South Korea, Taiwan, Hong Kong, and Singapore), the peripheral European states like Spain and Portugal, the two leading countries of Southern Africa (South Africa and Zimbabwe), and a few countries in Latin America and the Caribbean have all achieved some level of industrialization. These countries are now important markets for industrial and consumer goods, and they are all significant exporters of one consumer product or another.

In many cases, these countries have either joined existing well-established economic unions—Portugal and Spain joined the European Economic Community—or have come together to form new free trade organizations. An example of the latter is the Latin American Free Trade Area (LAFTA). The creation of regional organizations to promote free trade between nations that are in close proximity quickly transforms local and national markets into regional ones, moving them closer to globalization. The march toward complete globalization will accelerate as regional trading blocks unite to form even larger free trade areas.

The Rise of Japan

Japan's rise to world industrial prominence revolutionized the international competitive arena. Japanese industry has systematically increased its share of world trade in industrial and consumer goods since the early 1960s. Already, Japan has replaced the former Soviet Union as the world's second largest producer of industrial and consumer goods. Most experts agree that if present trends continue, Japan will replace the United States as the world's dominant economic power by the turn of the century. Japan obviously capitalized on increasing globalization, since without it, Japanese industry would never have had access to the technology it needed to develop. Moreover, the Japanese market for industrial goods, in the days when Japanese industry was in its infancy, was too small to absorb increasing domestic production. Japan needed a world market in order to develop. Structural transformation of its economy was brought about, not by import substitution, but by export creation.

Once Japan had established itself as a world-class competitor, however, that fact gave major impetus to globalization. This was so for many reasons:

1. At the outset, Japanese enterprise adopted a global view of the market. Western companies, and particularly U.S. companies, were drawn into a global war by Japanese industry. Because Japan was attacking on all fronts, U.S. corporations were bound to defend on all fronts as well. Over the last decade, however, western enterprises have realized that in global economic warfare, the best defense is an aggressive offense. This began drawing all North American corporations into the world arena.

2. Japan's emergence as an economic superpower gave convincing evidence that the West was about to lose its monopoly on technology. The United States stood a real risk of losing its technological leadership altogether. This emboldened other countries, particularly the Pacific Rim nations, to challenge the West. That accelerated the international diffusion of technology and created new centers of international production for industrial and consumer goods.

3. The Japanese experience also showed that neither massive investment in research and development (R&D) nor an abundance of natural resources was necessary for sustainable industrial development. From approximately 1950 to 1975, Japan was not an innovator. Japanese industry was developed on borrowed, copied, and licensed western technology. It became clear, looking at Japan, that competence in adapting existing product designs, the speed of product and process adaptations, and mastery of manufacturing know-how to make superior quality products at competitive prices and cost, were enough to give a company a decisive competitive advantage on world markets.

4. Japan demonstrated that efficient production and high quality were enough to neutralize transportation cost disadvantages and tariff barriers. Every national market in the world could be successfully served by production undertaken anywhere on the planet and cultural differences ceased to be an important barrier to the location and successful exploitation of manufacturing plants away from a company's home base.

So while Japan was astutely capitalizing on growing globalization, it was also contributing to broadening the opportunity that it seized. Eventually, of course, Japan like Britain and the United States before, will contribute inadvertently to the emergence of its economic rivals.

Other Factors

International organizations like the UN have fostered transnational contact and dialogue. Expanding educational opportunities in the West and the emphasis being put on education as an agent of economic development have brought floods of students from developing countries to North American and Western European universities. The resultant cross-cultural contact has produced business and political leaders that have a global perspective both in the West and in the developing countries. An engineer from Taiwan who studied in the United States automatically thinks of the U.S. market when he returns to his home country and develops a new product. He is no longer intimidated by the U.S. culture, because he received a substantial part of his education in the United States.

Globalization is also reinforced by the fact that the United States is the favorite country for students of developing countries who study abroad. These future business leaders receive instruction and become reasonably proficient in English, which is fast becoming the international language of business and technology. A common language breaks down communication barriers and makes for a free flow of ideas and technology. It also facilitates global marketing and distribution of products and services.

The global corporation came into being because of increasing globalization. However, global enterprises also contribute to globalization. When a company goes international, its success and growth will naturally lead it to spread its tentacles. Markets that are further and further away from the home base are targeted, entered, and exploited. Moreover, by virtue of the fact that the global corporation is operating in many national markets, it can more quickly spot emerging opportunities that other companies cannot see. As the number of global manufacturing companies increases, their suppliers of materials and financial and transportation services are themselves bound to create global organizations so as to support them. As more and more companies succeeded at managing global operations, they created a body of knowledge on how these enterprises should be managed and controlled. Thus, the new global corporations could avoid the blunders made by the pioneer companies. The forerunners to today's global corporations demonstrated that it was possible to effectively manage a company on a world scale, and thus encouraged more companies to become global competitors. This was bolstered by the fact that a global company has distinct advantages. These corporations have market flexibility to balance worldwide supply and demand since they can move their products from one national market to another as supply and demand conditions dictate. They can also optimize plant location in order to capitalize on favorable cost structures wherever they exist in the world. Global corporations have a better chance of having the lowest cost network of plants. They can move quickly to exploit an innovation in all their markets, thus maximizing the returns from R&D. Moreover, because they are closer to their markets, they are more able to respond to customer needs. All these advantages, and many others, mean that global companies will continue to benefit from and contribute to globalization.

COMPETITIVE REQUIREMENTS
OF GLOBAL MARKETS

Globalization is both a threat and an opportunity. Companies that develop the competitive muscle to stand up to international competition will emerge as

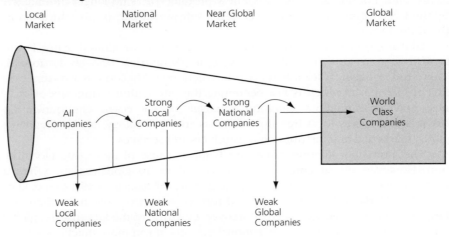

FIGURE 1–1 **The Filtering Effects of Globalization**

world leaders and will enjoy the benefits of access to a very large market. Those companies that are competitively weak will be driven to extinction by international competition. Globalization changes the fabric of competition in a market and imposes new and more exacting requirements on companies.

Figure 1–1 shows how a market evolves from local to international and what happens to companies that compete in it. Companies entering the market are looked at as going into a competitive tunnel. There are three phases in the tunnel which operate to screen out the weakest companies that survive to that phase. All companies enter the market, but only a few will emerge as world-class competitors, after market evolution from local to national to international has filtered out the weakest ones. A company may be a very strong national competitor but may not be able to do battle on a world scale. Some companies survive on the world market for a while only to be driven out by globalization. Massey-Ferguson of Canada is a company that emerged from being a strong national (Canadian) company and survived for a while as a global competitor. However, competition in the farm machinery market became so intense in the 1970s, that even Caterpillar faced a declining market share. Massey-Ferguson, the Canadian multinational, fared very poorly. It closed down numerous plants, received massive government subsidies, changed its corporate name to Varity Corporation, and moved its head office from Canada to the United States. It still suffered massive losses and has not yet regained its prior market position.

The model of Figure 1–1 suggests a few things. A company competing in an international market is doing battle with the very best of the world. Every world competitor would have gone through the filtering process that has been just described. One would naturally expect that the world's best are all producing superior quality. Evolution to an international market weeds out inferior quality products. Companies that cannot constantly improve quality fall victim to international competition. It is not surprising, then, that the globalization wave that began in the late 1960s was paralleled by a quality wave. Superior quality is the supreme requirement for competing in a global market. The customer in an international market can choose among a large number of high-quality products. Customers become aware of quality and are very sensitive to it. One very direct consequence of globalization, and it is the most natural one, is that quality becomes a clear competitive priority. Globalization naturally and unavoidably causes quality to improve. The global market functions in such a way as to force companies to produce ever higher quality levels. Quality came to the forefront of management thinking in the 1970s and 1980s because international competitive pressures were weeding out companies whose products were not up to world standard or were severely penalizing those companies that were lagging behind the world leaders. Corporations that are at the leading edge of quality technology in North America, and indeed in the world, are concentrated in purely global markets such as pharmaceuticals, farm machinery and equipment, paper products, electronics, and automobiles. Again, customers that can exercise choice from a large number of quality products soon become accustomed to shopping on the basis of quality.

The customer gives high priority to quality, but is not indifferent to cost. Precisely because the customer has a large number of products to choose from, he or she can pay more attention to cost or price. Customers know that they have power when a market is competitive. Competition operates to educate and inform the customer as to what constitutes a fair price for a given quality level. Global markets function to drive costs down to the minimum level that will keep competition healthy. Competition in a global market is very broad based. Competitors have access to all sources of cost advantage, because they can locate plants where cost structures are most favorable. The scale of the world market means that all competitors have access to economies of scale, from whatever source they may originate. Consequently, a global market is also dominated by the lowest cost producers. In order to survive in a global market, then, a company must produce superior quality and must maintain a favorable cost position. All the classical cost drivers such as scale economies, automated process technologies, learning-curve effects, and product standardization are available to all competitors in the market.

Globalization gives companies the best chance to maximize value for customers. Value means quality in relation to price. The pressure to maximize quality and minimize cost given the quality level, maximizes value delivered or available to the customer. One example in the automobile market will illustrate the point. Up to about the mid-1970s, Volkswagen in Germany was manufacturing world-quality cars in its chosen segments and the company was also cost/price competitive. The company's position as an international automobile manufacturer was good. During the late 1970s, two things happened to change the company's position. First, the Japanese made tremendous strides to improve quality. Moreover, the major Japanese manufacturers were also more efficient producers, so they were able to deliver better quality at a lower price in the same market niches where Volkswagen competed. Second, spiraling wage rates in West Germany during the 1970s and 1980s caused Volkswagen to become a relatively high-cost producer of cars in its market segment. Although the company's quality, in absolute terms, did not deteriorate and it still made world-level quality cars, an unfavorable cost position coupled with improved Japanese quality meant that it was no longer able to deliver acceptable value to its customers. Its market share tumbled and since the mid-1980s, the company embarked upon a massive restructuring program to cut costs. Volkswagen management became acutely aware that they had to find ways to keep the cost of their cars in line with major world-class competitors.

The Volkswagen example also illustrates the point that a company in a global market is often required to redeploy resources quickly so as to respond to competitive threats or opportunities. In international markets, response times are short because there are many world-class competitors that are able to quickly exploit a company's strategic weaknesses. Competitive flexibility, that is the ability to change competitive position quickly or to redeploy resources in response to competitive threats or opportunities, is now a key strategic requirement. Why this is so would not be obvious. The popular thinking is that global markets are dominated by large MNEs (multinational enterprises) which have divided the markets of the world among themselves using collusive agreements. However, this notion flies in the face of reality. We have seen that the international market epitomizes industrial and commercial competition and economic warfare. Oligopoly as an economics concept breaks down when considered within the framework of a global market. For example, the U.S. car market is still categorized as an oligopoly. But GM, Ford, and Chrysler are fighting the battle of their lives for survival. When one moves up to a world market, it takes only three or four national or regional oligopolistic markets and one has a competitive market. In the case of automobiles, the three oligopolistic markets in North America, Europe, and Japan link to form a fiercely competitive, global market. The concepts of monopoly and oligopoly appear to lose much of their significance when applied to a global market, because the free flow of goods, services, and technology between oligopolies stimulates healthy competition both within each oligopoly and at the international level. Flexibility is necessary because an international market is fundamentally pregnant with uncertainty. There are many and widely-dispersed competitors, each stretching to improve or entrench its position in the market. Breakthroughs are more frequent. The sheer number of competitive moves is such that they cannot be anticipated so as to plan preemptive attacks. The point must be emphasized: A global market is an uncertain one.

Companies survive in an uncertain market by constant improvement, innovation, and creative destruction. Constant improvement maintains the company's competitive edge, while innovation opens up new ways to create competitive advantage. Creative destruction means that the company seeks to be the active agent that drives its own technologies to obsolescence. The rationale is that market forces are constantly working to make existing technologies obsolete, irrespective of the actions taken by a company. Technological obsolescence is an ever-present reality in a competitive market. A company that does not actively try to improve on or even supplant its existing technology will be placed in a defensive, vulnerable position in the market. The more broad based the competition and the stronger the competitive strength and will of viable competitors, the stronger the imperative to improve on existing technology. A global market is a fertile ground for the development of competitors with the competitive will and the strength to attack a company's technological position.

Global markets belong to innovative companies. Innovation is the major agent of creative destruction and it also operationalizes continuous improvement. The global competitive arena stretches the company's ability to constantly create new products, processes, systems, methods, and management practices and to effectively harness these to take superior quality, low-cost products to market. Innovation is a company's response to actual or potential changes in the marketplace. The faster the pace of change, the more there is a need for the company to innovate. Consequently, both global markets and national markets that are rapidly moving toward internationalization, or local markets that are quickly becoming national in scope, make it imperative for a company to be an innovator. In a very important way, it is innovation that enables a company to keep pace with market evolution from local to national to global. The transition from a local to a global company is assured by successful innovation.

It has been noted that the global market is full of uncertainty. Innovations are also risky, uncertain ventures. However, Figure 1-2 argues that innovation is a proven strategy for dealing with uncertainty. Where future market and technological developments cannot be anticipated with reasonable certainty, the only logical response is to innovate. Innovation is both an offensive and a defensive strategy, because it can create a competitive edge for the innovator and nullify the advantage generated by a competitor's unanticipated competitive moves. Innovation creates surprises for competitors and prepares the company to deal with market-generated "surprises."

Globalization puts real power in the hands of the customer. The forces that are shaping the market are also shifting the balance of power in the customer's favor. Gone are the days when the so-called corporate giants could afford to be indifferent to their customers. No company, no matter how big, is indispensable, because the buyer can always find an equivalent substitute product if he or she searches diligently enough. Companies must genuinely

FIGURE 1-2 **Innovation and Uncertainty**

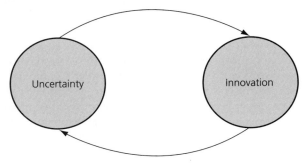

define their business as existing to serve the customer. The ability to serve the customer is now a critical requirement for long-term survival, no matter what the market.

Customer service, in the broadest sense, means that the company delivers consistently high-quality products, at the lowest possible cost and in the shortest possible time. The emphasis is on factual, verifiable performance of these three requirements. Corporations that are serious about customer service deliver everything they promise and promise nothing that they cannot deliver. The company must listen to its customers and solve customer-related problems with the utmost urgency, rather than be the problem or a major source of headaches for the customer. Consequently, the company must educate the customer at the same time that it is being educated by the customer. The flow of information between the company and its customers must be unfettered and must culminate in two-way influence.

The business must value each customer. All customers should be treated fairly and must be viewed as important to the business. A company that puts a premium on customer service does not categorize some customers as very important and others as not important. Customers classified as not important invariably get second class treatment. The choice for a high customer service company is between having or not having a particular customer. A company should value every customer with which it decides to do business. No customer is a tyrant, but every customer is king.

The ability to empathize with its customers and to demonstrate factually that it has genuine, deep concern for their well-being, is what sets the world-class company apart from the typical corporation. Thus, a business that puts a premium on customer service is customer oriented and conscious in everything it does. The business must exist for its customers, first and foremost. This is not a new slogan, but a competitive reality imposed by accelerating globalization. Businesses that exist for their customers will also be the most productive, efficient, profitable, and durable. The customer guards the door

Competitive Requirements and Market Scope					TABLE 1–1
Market Scope	**Competitive Requirements**				
	Quality	Cost	Flexibility	Innovation	Service
Local market	Moderately important	Important	—	—	Moderately important
National market	Important	Important	Moderately important	Moderately important	Important
Global market	Critically important	Critically important	Critically important	Critically important	Critically important

to survivability. Businesses survive and flourish when they create thoroughly satisfied customers.

Market Scope and Competitive Requirements

As a market evolves from local to global, the competitive requirements become tougher. The global market presents a company with the ultimate competitive challenge, because all five market requirements become critical success factors. Table 1–1 shows how the competitive requirements change as the market evolves. The classical trade-offs between quality, cost, flexibility, innovation, and customer service progressively evaporate. Trade-offs are replaced by symbiosis or interrelationships, whereby the performance of each competitive requirement must create better leverage to perform the others. This forces management to look very closely at the mechanisms and tools with which the critical success factors are performed. Symbiosis exists not between cost and quality, but between the alternative methods or programs for pursuing superior quality and low cost. Thus, just-in-time (JIT) programs which seek to eliminate waste by driving inventory levels down both require and result in lower defect rates which complement the effects of Total Quality Management (TQM) programs. A company that has well functioning TQM programs, which reduce process variability and increase worker expertise and participation in quality improvement, is in a very good position to implement JIT programs such as set-up and lot size reduction.

Globalization and the Competitive Value of Time

The realization that a company in a global market must achieve excellence on the five critical competitive requirements of Table 1–1 has created the need for a paradigm that links these requirements, resolves their apparent contradictions, and highlights the symbiotic relationship between them. The paradigm that has emerged over the last few years is Time Based Competition (TBC), and it is rooted in three related ideas. First, TBC is predicated on the notion that time is the most significant, overarching competitive requirement in any market, and that, at the most fundamental level, competitive superiority means the ability to do things faster than one's competitors. In support of that notion, proponents of the TBC paradigm produce extensive anecdotal evidence that shows that "time based competitors" such as Federal Express, Wal-Mart, Atlass Door, Thomasville, Citicorp, Toyota, Honda, Mazda and L. L. Bean, achieve superior performance on growth and profitability and sometimes come to dominate their respective markets.

Second, TBC makes a direct and strong link between time compression and improvement in the critical competitive requirements of quality, productivity/cost, innovation, flexibility, and service. Thus, as time is decreased, quality, flexibility, the pace of innovation, and customer service—shorter lead times and quicker response time in responding to customer requests—increase and there is a simultaneous decrease in cost. Consequently, by focusing on decreasing the single variable, time management simultaneously and inexorably raises performance of the five critical competitive requirements of quality, cost, innovation, flexibility, and service. Therefore, the key to improving competitive performance is to identify the major activities in sales research, development and engineering, procurement, production and distribution that add substantial amounts of time to the process of delivering goods or services to the customer, and to implement strategies and programs to compress time. In the TBC paradigm, time compression is the major mechanism for improving competitive performance.

Third, the whole organization must be made to focus on time as the major source of competitive advantage. This means that the company must be structured and managed to value time and the business vision and corporate culture must be designed to make time a competitive priority. A company is a time-based competitor when the drive to compress time permeates all its structures, strategies, internal processes, systems, and policies. In order to drive time into the crucial decision-making and organizational processes, TBC proposes that the performance measurement and reporting system include time as a significant measure of strategic and managerial performance.

As an emergent paradigm, TBC has much validity. Time is indeed related to most of the five competitive requirements of Table 1-1. Time reduction will inescapably result in improvements in cost, productivity, flexibility, service, and innovation. However, there are evidently markets where the relationship between time and quality is in fact the reverse of what is promulgated in the TBC paradigm. One could hardly argue for attempting to increase the quality of a fine French wine, Swiss cheese, Scotch whiskey, or traditionally cured ham by compressing the aging process. The quality of a

Rolls Royce, Lamborghini, or Mercedes Benz is dependent, in an important way, on the care, attention to detail, and time taken by the master artisans that are dedicated to the production of a masterpiece. A Steinway grand is among the very best pianos available anywhere because those involved in its creation take the requisite time to do everything right. Picasso would shudder at the thought that quality art could be produced by compressing time. And, there are clear indications that, at least on the factory floor and in research, development, and engineering, time compression can have a negative impact on quality. Case after case can be cited where very reputable pharmaceutical and automobile manufacturers have had to pay billions of dollars in civil litigation and product liability costs because they tried to cut corners and compress time in product development and testing. Quality takes time, so that the challenge, then, is to take no more time than is necessary and never to compress time to the detriment of quality.

Even in market segments where time is valued by the customer, such as rapid courier services, fast food restaurants, and the production and distribution of highly perishable products, it is only one component of product or service quality. McDonald's restaurants must produce and serve hamburgers fast, but customers also judge them, and rather severely, on product taste and consistency, service, courtesy, cleanliness, and ambience of the service environment. Federal Express is one of the most notable time-based competitors and it must deliver small packages in less than twenty-four hours. But customers also expect the service to be reliable and delivery and pick-up personnel to be courteous, and communicate an image of professionalism and a profound willingness to help. Time-based competitors attain competitive excellence by doing much more than simply managing to compress time. In adopting the TBC paradigm, management would be well advised to pay heed to the famous dictum of Ernest and Julio Gallo "and sell no wine before its time."

Despite these conceptual and philosophical shortcomings, the TBC paradigm is useful for three reasons:

1. It drives home the point that the severity and complexity of competition in a global market make it absolutely necessary to perpetually drive improvement on all strategic fronts simultaneously. It is not enough, in a global market, to perform competitive requirements better. A company faced with the reality of globally expanding competition, and that means all companies, sooner or later, must also be the fastest among the best. If time compression is part of an overall strategy to improve total manufacturing performance, then the fastest will also likely be the best.
2. It has elucidated and underscored the relationship that exists between time and the critical competitive requirements of cost (productivity) innovation, flexibility, quality, and service. Where the relationship exists in practice, management can drive broad improvement in competitive performance by focusing on time compression, although not to the detriment of other strategically important factors.

3. It has formalized time compression as a valid strategy for pursuing competitive advantage in manufacturing.

| Conclusion | The world's best companies have demonstrated that there is no inherent, irreconcilable conflict between the requirements imposed by a severely competitive market. The conventional thinking can be made to stand on its head if a company sets out to pursue excellence on all competitive fronts, simultaneously. The key word in global competition is excellence. Moreover a few leading corporations are changing the manufacturing equation in a fundamental way. Excellence in manufacturing comes about when superior quality is used as a weapon to drive costs down and when innovation and continuous improvement are agents for pushing quality up. Moreover, manufacturing excellence views innovation as the mechanism by which flexibility is sought. In an innovative corporation, technological change is a habit and innovation the norm. When this happens, change is viewed and dealt with as a way to avoid major long-term disruption, rather than being a disruptive force. A corporation that finds change disruptive is one that is placid and suffers from hardening of the arteries and organizational calcification. It has ceased to be driven by excellence and is definitely moribund.

How a company can pursue competitive excellence and market superiority on all fronts simultaneously will be the subject matter of subsequent chapters.

Case for Discussion

SPORTS EQUIPMENT MANUFACTURING (SEM), INC.

Mr. Brian Boulder, vice-president (finance) had just finished poring over the offer made by a leading competitor to take over the entire operations of SEM. He could not hide his disappointment and immediately headed for the office of his boss, Doug Carrington, to inform him of the bad news:

> My goodness, Doug, they are offering a price that is barely enough to cover the market value of the real estate that we hold. After eight months of trying to sell this company, that's the best we can do? Are things really that bad?

The Company

SEM was a major North American manufacturer of winter sports equipment with annual sales of over $70 million. Its product line consisted of skates, gloves, hockey equipment, ski boots, and other accessories. The company had risen from its modest beginnings as a family-owned business that manufactured ice skates to become a medium-sized company with a diversified product line. In 1978, the Carrington family, which owned 100 percent of the common stock, sold 51 percent of its holdings to a group of investors but retained a strong presence in the management of the company. Since its founding in 1962, the company had always been profitable.

SEM had built an enviable position as a highly innovative company with a very strong product line. It had cultivated and jealously guarded its reputation as a top quality producer. Many of the company's flagship products were endorsed and being used by some of the world's best professional hockey players and skiers. The company achieved its reputation as a quality producer by selecting only the best domestic sources of raw materials, by investing heavily in product design and testing, paying higher than average wages to attract and retain the best workers in the industry, and avoiding unnecessary investment in new production equipment in an effort to keep productivity high and production costs low. Because of their high-quality image, the company's products fetched a 15 percent price premium on the market. While some of its competitors would distribute other brands, particularly European manufactured products, to complement their product lines, SEM distributed only its own brand names, because it felt that it could not guarantee the quality of foreign products.

Trends in the Industry

Although nearly all of the world's production and consumption of winter sports equipment was done in Europe and North America, as early as 1975, Pacific Rim countries were beginning to enter the market. These new manufacturers started by focusing on the high-volume, easy-to-produce, labor-intensive products such as pads, gloves, and some ski boots, whose production could exploit their very low wage rates. They first gained a foothold in the market by becoming captive producers for the large department stores and sporting goods chains. Initially, these producers had built a reputation of supplying reasonable quality products at extremely low prices. For comparable quality North American products they offered a price advantage of between 20 and 25 percent.

The Pacific Rim producers had a distance disadvantage, but they were still able to quote lead times that were similar to those of North American producers. Countries like Taiwan, South Korea, the Philippines, Hong Kong, and Malaysia could rely on a massive pool of cheap labor, a disciplined, malleable work force, and an unconstrained industrial-relations and political climate to achieve unmatched manufacturing flexibility. Workers could be shifted from one operation to the next and could be called on to work long overtime hours if management decided that was necessary to meet a delivery date. The advantage in labor did not cause these producers to be complacent in adopting new and advanced process technology. Equipment manufacturers noted that the Pacific Rim countries were accounting for an ever-increasing share of their sales and some predicted that within five years they would become their biggest customers. By 1986, a major sports goods retail chain was sourcing more than 20 percent of its requirements from Asia up from only 5 percent in 1978. About 1985, SEM's most important competitor was taking a hard look at its North American operations in view of deciding whether it should shift sourcing to the Far East and by 1987 had apparently made a decision to start to use Asia as a major source.

Major Manufacturing Policies

The company's approach to process technology could be summed up in one phrase: *"Get every investment dollar out of existing equipment before investing in anything new, thus minimizing the investment required to keep the plant going."* The average life of equipment in the plant was 25 years and 95 percent was fully depreciated. Production was centralized in one area using three plants that were contiguously located. Physical proximity of the company's factories was thought to facilitate transfer of people, reduce fixed costs because of shared facilities, and facilitate supervision by top management. Each plant was supervised by a plant manager who reported to the vice-president of manufacturing, who in turn reported to the executive vice-president. Figure 1–3 shows the company's organizational chart as of the end of 1987. Four of the six top management positions were occupied by Carringtons.

In keeping with the personal philosophy of its founder and current president, Mr. Doug Carrington, SEM had always followed a policy of treat-ing its workers humanely. The company relied much less on immigrant labor than nearly all its competitors and paid wages that were considered high by industry standards. Standards for production workers were generally loose because the company had always operated on the premise that workers that are fairly treated would themselves produce to their maximum capa-bility. The plant manager admitted, however, that production standards had not changed in 15 years. Top management thought that the workers were producing as much and as fast as they could and any attempt to increase the production rate would probably have a negative impact on the industrial-relations climate, general employee motivation, and quality. Labor was 30 per-cent of manufacturing cost. The company's quality inspection program was reputed to be the most rigorous in the industry. Its 14 in-spectors working in its three adjacent plants had an average of 16 years direct production experience before they were named to their current positions.

Organizational Chart   FIGURE 1–3

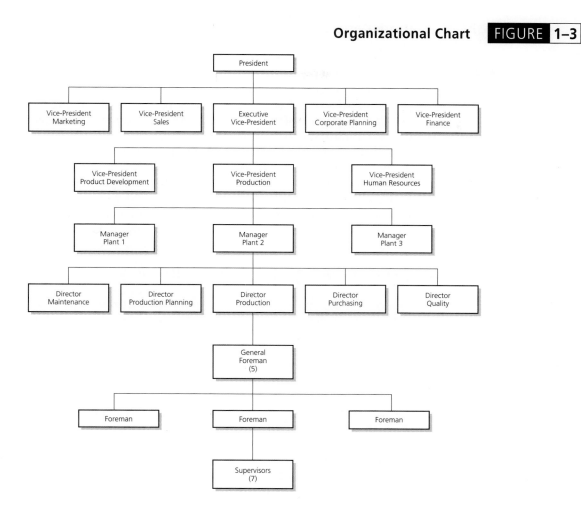

SEM manufactured all of its requirements because top management believed that this was the only way to absolutely guarantee the quality of its products. Raw materials accounted for 45 percent of manufacturing cost and were purchased only from reputable suppliers. Incoming inspection was thorough in keeping with the company's policy of rigorous quality control throughout all phases of the production process. All materials were purchased from domestic sources since the company had found these to be reliable. Even though top management recognized that these sources were not the lowest cost suppliers, it chose not to replace them for fear that lower cost sources could prove to be detrimental to quality.

Market and Financial Performance

In 1980 and for the first time in its history, SEM experienced a decline in its share of the market. Market erosion continued over the subsequent years, despite the company's efforts to arrest it. In the fall of 1986, the company announced an across-the-board cut in prices of 6 percent and mounted a massive promotional campaign aimed at shoring up sales. Promotional expenditure was increased from 3.5 percent of sales in 1985 to 6 percent in 1986. The new efforts were largely successful and the company experienced a small increase in its share of the market in 1986.

The impact on the company's profitability was, however, less than favorable. In the face of increasing manufacturing cost coupled with the cut in prices and the increase in promotional expenditure, the company returned a loss of $6.1 million in 1986 compared to a loss of $1.3 million in 1985.

The Company's Efforts to Return to Profitability

At the beginning of 1987, top management announced that it would cut its production work force of 630 by 10 percent thus saving $1.2 million a year. Plant management expected that there were enough remaining workers to produce the sales forecast for 1987. Managerial personnel and staff were also reduced from 310 to 260, a move that was expected to save $3.2 million per year. In addition, management decided to close one of the company's five regional warehouses and this would result in further savings of $1 million. The warehouse closing was thought to have very little negative impact, since it would only have the effect of increasing the lead time to about 17 percent of the company's customers by about one week.

During 1987, top management created an internal consulting group to identify other areas where costs could be decreased. The group identified production and materials planning and control as one area where substantial savings could be realized and recommended that the company implement an MRP-II system at a total estimated cost of $500,000. The group anticipated that the total savings from MRP-II would be about $900,000 annually once full implementation had been achieved. MRP-II was expected to take 18 months to implement. Top management approved the MRP-II project and implementation started in October 1987.

The company's market share decreased slightly in 1987, but the cost-cutting measures had a positive impact on its profitability. The net loss for the year was held to $1.6 million. The year 1988 saw a slight improvement to $1.4 million in losses. However, during that year it became clear to top management that the promise of MRP-II would not be realized. The project had fallen six months behind schedule and the cost to date had already reached

$650,000. Software modification, project consulting, and manpower training costs alone were already $104,000 over budget. The materials manager summarized the problems that plagued the MRP-II project in this way:

> Too much was riding on MRP-II. Everyone agrees that it is a valid tool and that we would have to implement it but the project was presented as a way to turn things around and to get significant results in the short term. The problems that the company faced were broader than mere business planning and control. There have been basic shifts in the market and the competitive situation and we failed to change our basic way of doing business to deal with them. Our competitors were much quicker to react than we were, and they are already reaping the benefits. It strikes me as significant that our major competitor started to make major changes at least three years ago. It cut production costs, closed unprofitable plants, acquired a small but fast growing company in the fitness shoes segment of the market, shifted, according to my estimate, at least 50 percent of its sourcing to the Far East, and cultivated novel relations with Asian suppliers. As they were doing these things, we continued to believe that we could compete in this fast changing market by doing cosmetic changes to our traditional way of competing.

The Decision to Sell the Company

In 1989, and against the advice of Doug Carrington, the new majority owners decided to sell the company and called in an investment banking firm to handle the sale. A detailed prospectus was prepared and sent out to a group of companies that competed in the same or similar markets to SEM and who would normally have an interest in buying it. Included in the group was SEM's major competitor, who put together a team composed of its own managers and some outside consultants to study SEM's operations and potential and to make recommendations as to whether it was a worthwhile investment. Within one month, the group had spent 35 working days studying SEM and prepared a report to top management in which it gave a recommendation against buying. After 8 months, top management of SEM received only one serious bid for the assets of SEM. It came from a real estate development company that was not part of the original group that was asked to submit a bid to buy SEM.

1. What are the forces that are shaping competition in SEM's business? Are these forces permanent or temporary?
2. What are the consequences of the new competitive environment for SEM's existing manufacturing strategy and market position?

Discussion Questions

3. Can the company grow and be profitable in that market? If no, why not? If yes, what is your justification?
4. How would you characterize the company's response to the new competitive situation? Why do you think the company reacted the way it did?
5. What should the company do?

References

Bartlett, Christopher A., and Sumantra Ghoshal, "Managing across Borders: New Strategic Requirements," *Sloan Management Review* 7, Summer 1987.

Business Week, July 9, 1984.

Bylinsky, Gene, "Japan's Robot King Wins Again," *Fortune,* May 25, 1987.

Dreyfuss, Joel, "Japan's Push in Pharmaceuticals," *Fortune,* July 20, 1987.

Drucker, Peter F., "The Changed World Economy," *The McKinsey Quarterly,* Autumn 1986.

Fallows, James, "Containing Japan," *The Atlantic Monthly,* May 1989.

Faye, Rice, "American's New No. 4 Automaker," *Fortune,* October 28, 1985.

*Industrial Vision for the 1970*s, Japan Ministry of International Trade and Industry, 1971.

"Japan's High Technology Industries," Long-Term Credit Bank of Japan, Tokyo, February 1984.

Knowlton, Christopher, "What America Makes Best," *Fortune,* March 28, 1988.

Kraar, Louis, "Korea's Big Push Has Just Begun," *Fortune,* March 16, 1987.

Krause, Lawrence B., "Has Korea's Economic Miracle Ended?" *Management Review,* March 1986.

Labich, Kenneth, "Boeing Battles to Stay on Top," *Fortune,* September 28, 1987.

Near, Janet P., and Richard W. Olshavshy, "Japan's Success: Luck or Skill," *Business Horizons,* November–December 1985.

Nomura Electronics Handbook, 1984, Nomura Securities Company Ltd., Tokyo, February 1984, 70.

Organization for Economic Cooperation and Development, OECD Science and Technology Indicators, OECD, Paris, 1984.

Porter, Michael, "Changing Patterns of International Competition," *California Management Review* XXVIII, 2, Winter 1986.

Sakai, Kuniyasu, "The Feudal World of Japanese Manufacturing," *Harvard Business Review,* November–December 1990.

Stalk, George, Jr., "Competing on Time," *The Free Press,* New York, 1990.

Stone, Nan, "The Globalization of Europe: An Interview with Wisse Dekker," *Harvard Business Review,* May–June 1989.

CHAPTER 2

World-Class Manufacturing: The Bedrock Concepts

Competitive pressure forces companies to exert themselves in order to survive and grow. The more intense the competition, the more a company must exert itself in order to maintain an acceptable market position. When competition is severe, only excellent companies survive. Competition weeds out weak or mediocre companies. Competitive excellence is now a central concept in management thought because it has been observed that a few companies thrive despite, or more accurately because of, competition. Moreover, those companies that flourish in severely competitive environments do not benefit from good luck or fortuitous circumstances, at least, no more than those that do not. Neither do they benefit from so-called comparative advantage in the broad economic sense. One often has the impression that these companies succeed in overcoming unfortuitous events—sometimes even cataclysmic ones—and also neutralize comparative disadvantage.

Management theory has always been preoccupied with what makes for excellence. The history of management is an exercise in trying to understand why some organizations, institutions, or societies perform better than others in designing, producing, and marketing goods and services. The definition of excellence kept changing and understanding was usually incomplete but the driving concern has always been the same: what makes some enterprises flourish while others, in the same markets or countries and having access to the same societal resources, slowly decay and eventually die? How is it that some companies that at one point in their histories were growing, dynamic, and prosperous come to lose their dynamism or capacity to survive and become moribund? The answer lies in the way these companies are managed. Enterprises succeed or fail because of management. A company does better than its competitors because it is managed better. Competitive excellence derives from managerial excellence.

Manufacturing excellence is honed out of managerial excellence. The notion that management ends at the entrance to the factory or at the organizational frontiers and lines of authority that demarcate the production function from the rest of the enterprise, is all too prevalent.[1] Of course, these boundaries or

---

[1] This is a strange notion because much of management thought was born in the factory environment. Even today, production continues to be a fertile field for developing, testing, and refining management theory and practice. For more on this, see Claude S. George, *A History of Management Thought* (Englewood Cliffs, N.J.: Prentice-Hall, 1972).

frontiers are purely artificial, created by the need to divide the organization into smaller, more manageable units. Over time, however, many managers came to view these boundaries as real, impenetrable barriers. The factory was seen as a separate, technocratic entity that was better left to technical people. Manufacturing excellence was seen as a technical and not a managerial problem. This view of production was nurtured in academia. In the 1960s, most business management schools in North America eliminated production management from their curricula, while churning out more and more MBAs steeped in financial analysis and portfolio management. The factory came to be seen as essentially a machine system that could be understood and managed only by technical experts. Top management in North America abdicated its responsibility for the factory and succeeded in starving it of much needed managerial talent. During the 1960s and 1970s, a very deep abnormality emerged from North American corporations. Some companies were designing and building the world's most technologically advanced and sophisticated factories but the products being turned out were not meeting customer expectations much less surpassing them. These factories may have been technologically advanced but they were dinosaurs with respect to the competence to serve a market and a customer. The idea that a company could do prolonged competitive battle without effectively managing the factory was ludicrous indeed. The production function mobilizes the lion's share of corporate resources, makes the product or service that is delivered to the customer, and most nearly represents the complexity involved in managing a total enterprise. A company exists to make products or services and to market them. Together, these are the complementary aspects of the very reason for a corporation to exist. The production function, because it is responsible for making what the company takes to market, executes a mission that defines the company's reason to exist.

Top management alone is responsible for endowing the company with the capability and wherewithal to relentlessly pursue improvement and manufacturing excellence over the long haul. *World-class manufacturing* is the culmination of such relentless pursuit of competitive excellence. A company has attained world-class manufacturing capability when it is able to compete effectively in a global market. Obviously, it is the globalization of markets that mandates the creation of world-class manufacturing operations and the philosophies, approaches, tools, and technologies to do it. The design of world-class manufacturing tests top management's ability to lead and mold the manufacturing organization and the company's capacity to learn, adapt, and innovate faster than most in the face of an intensely competitive global market.

The point cannot be overemphasized. Manufacturing excellence is nurtured by superior management. Superior performance in manufacturing comes from management excellence that penetrates the production function, viewing and managing it as an integral, indivisible part of the business. A company cannot have world-class manufacturing with worst-class management.

Neither can a company achieve competitive excellence when it tolerates mediocrity or even average performance in production. Manufacturing excellence emerges from excellence attained and sustained organizationwide. Manufacturing performance reflects and is reflected by the caliber of corporate management. Superior performance in manufacturing is totally a managerial concern and can be validly considered only against the background provided by the core concepts in management and competitive superiority.

THE HALLMARKS OF MANUFACTURING EXCELLENCE

A few basic characteristics differentiate the world-class manufacturing company from the average run-of-the-mill corporation. Research on managerial excellence has provided insight into what makes these companies unique. However, the specific issues relating to manufacturing excellence have received only scant and sometimes tangential treatment in research on excellence in management. Therefore, for our purposes, the general stream of research on managerial excellence will be supplemented, extended, and synthesized to deal with the unique character of the production function.

Global markets or those markets that are rapidly succumbing to globalization present a company with the ultimate competitive challenge. Nonetheless, a few companies in each of these markets are able to carve out and defend an acceptable market position for themselves. These are the world-class manufacturing companies and any serious observation will reveal that they are distinctive. Their distinctiveness exists along six crucial managerial dimensions. Collectively, these marks of excellence constitute the corporate culture and value system or the business philosophy. Culture and values exert a powerful influence on a company's competitive performance. As in the wider society, culture and values define what is acceptable and unacceptable behavior, and provide the wider social framework for motivating people. Anthropology tells us that humans cannot be studied and human behavior makes no sense except within the context of a specific culture and value system. Humans are homo sapiens, but their thinking, their inner self is essentially cultural. Motivation theory postulates that motivation systems exploit the norms and aspirations provided by the culture and value system. Human beings view the world and their place in it through the spectacles provided by their culture and value system. Culture defines what is legitimate or illegitimate and what are acceptable or unacceptable ways of behaving or engaging in social transactions. Values and culture lead to the "us versus they" vision that everyone adopts in a social setting.

All companies have a culture and value system. Fundamental values may be latent or patent, deliberately engineered or allowed to subconsciously evolve. Irrespective of the process by which it comes to exist, the corporate culture and value system determines how a corporation will develop and how well it will deal with the competitive challenges that it will inevitably face. One thing is known, however. A corporation's culture and value system is tough to change, just as larger societies tend to resist cultural change. The "us versus they" syndrome caused by the culture and value system is itself the greatest impediment to cultural change. The proof that the corporate value system changes slowly comes from the observation that nearly every world-class company cherishes a few powerful values whose origins can be traced 50 or even 75 years to the original founders or corporate heros. The value system changes slowly, except if a survival crisis brings about a revolution or if an individual with exceptional charisma emerges as the chief executive officer. Therefore, persistently and painstakingly nurturing the few fundamental values that will drive the corporation to competitive excellence is a crucial top management responsibility.

Customer Orientation

Companies that excel consistently over the long run are all deeply conscious of the customer. They see their very reason for existence as being to understand, serve, and create value for the customer. These companies view the customer not as a tyrant, but as a legitimate monarch and the customer's requirements, wants, and needs drive every activity undertaken by the corporation. The whole organization, from top to bottom has an overwhelming sense of responsibility to the customer. Customer consciousness and patent customer orientation permeate every organizational substructure and are deeply embedded in the corporate philosophy and value system. The world's best managed corporations come to understand their customers and try to understand them better and better. They stay close to the customer not in word and thought, but in deed and action. Customer service is not a platitude for broken promises for these companies, but rather a conscious, deliberate effort, backed by clear unequivocal action, to solve the customer's real or perceived problems. When a company is totally customer oriented, then the distinction between marketing and the other business functions becomes useless. The organizational barriers or the power politics that set marketing apart from and above the other functional groups crumble. They give way to mutual trust and a visceral sense of shared fate. Every function is managed as a marketing function.

Deep customer orientation, then, shows up as *total customer management.* The company sees its job as more than merely selling a product. A profoundly customer-oriented company views the sale as a small intermediate phase in the overall process to make and keep satisfied customers. Much effort and resources are invested in understanding the customer's needs before the sale and in preventing and solving problems that come up after the sale. The company is a problem solver for the customer. Total customer management also means that all business functions are deployed to anticipate and solve the customer's problems. The standard customer service department exists officially, but in the world-class company, it deals with and solves only a fraction of the problems that come up, because the whole business is involved with the customer. Excellently managed corporations structure and use the customer service department as one of many ways for dealing with the customer.

Competitive Spirit

Superior performance companies have a keen sense of competition. They are always on the look-out for new avenues to compete and are quick in detecting poorly served market niches. They behave as if the competition matters, which makes them deeply aware that they must earn the right to exist and serve the customer. Respect for other competitors protects these companies from becoming arrogant. Instead, humility and high regard for the competitive abilities of other noble competitors is the impetus that keeps them open, willing, and able to improve. World-class manufacturing companies, whether they be from North America, Japan, or Western Europe, work hard and relentlessly to carve out and sustain their market positions. Competitive spirit keeps the company striving and stretching to excel. Desire to compete and be the best is instilled in every employee which provides the motive force that motivates each individual to excellence. In the world-class organization, every employee is competing against himself or herself and against the best competitors.

The other side of competitive spirit is *entrepreneurship.* Manufacturing excellence is nourished by the freedom to take risks and explore new avenues for competitive improvement. Companies progress because they allow individuals to make bold, unpopular moves that challenge conventional thinking. Companies are created by entrepreneurs. They enter new markets with new products or new processes because they keep entrepreneurship alive. When organizational structures and processes prevent risk taking and stifle creativity, then the company is already well on its way to its grave. But the entrepreneur in the world-class company is not like a loose canon ball. Risk taking is encouraged, but it is also channeled into areas with the greatest competitive impact. This is a delicate operation. Top management has to create an internal organizational environment where individuals are free to undertake new ventures but guided by how management views the market and competition. Companies have dealt with this dilemma in various ways. Some implement a capital budgeting procedure that tolerates some budgetary leeway, or budgets that leak, thus making discretionary funds available to the internal entrepreneur. Others have a policy of spinning-off new divisions as new markets are opening up, thereby freeing new ventures from the stifling effects of an established bureaucratic organization. Still others nurture technology gatekeepers and project champions who can push new ideas to fruition even when there is overall organizational resistance or inertia.[2]

Search for Perfection

In the typical company, the notion that an organization should pursue perfection is viewed as both ludicrous and insane. The prevailing idea in most North American corporations is that excellence stops well short of perfection. Many CEOs readily accept average performance and even mediocrity because they are not in the habit of motivating employees to challenge the limits set by current notions of what is practical or impractical. The corporation, rather than being driven by the pursuit of a few competitive ideals, recedes back into a shell of pragmatism. The company's competitive performance is constrained by what is being or has been achieved rather than being driven by what could be achieved if the organization could break existing technological and competitive limits.

Excellently managed companies, on the other hand, are driven by the search for competitive perfection. They are never completely satisfied with actual or historical performance and are driven by the philosophy that there is always room for improvement. These companies and their employees are always searching for the perfect product, service, and production process. They are aggressively looking for ways to execute production activities perfectly and flawlessly. World-class manufacturing corporations want service without a hitch, production without errors, and products without defects. Top management manages the enterprise as if zero defects, zero inventories, zero breakdowns, and single-minute machine changeovers were a practical, attainable goal. Unlike their counterparts in the average, run-of-the-mill manufacturing corporation, they view perfection as an ideal to be aggressively, painstakingly, and persistently pursued. Their philosophy is that manufacturing perfection may not be attainable, but its pursuit is desirable and commendable. The whole notion of a performance standard, and how it should be computed and used, has been transformed by the search for perfection. If perfection is the ultimate goal, then the idea of a historical standard as normative, expected performance, is archaic, because any standard is obsolete by the time it is computed and agreed upon, and it thus cannot be validly used to gauge manufacturing performance.

It is this deeply ingrained belief that perfection must be sought that keeps the world-class manufacturing organization learning and stretching to improve

---

[2]For more discussion on these points, see Peters and Waterman, *In Search of Excellence* (New York: Harper & Row, 1972), 200–234. See also Allen, *Managing the Flow of Technology* (Cambridge: MIT Press, 1979).

further, long after the company has bettered its best and most competitors have been exhausted to extinction. Companies that have impregnated the corporate mindset with the desire to search for perfection have succeeded in creating a lasting challenge for all their employees. Search for perfection manifests itself in three ways:

1. *Mastery of the business fundamentals.* The basic requirements for success in the company's market are thoroughly understood, constantly communicated, and inculcated. The company can perfectly execute the business fundamentals because all employees are thoroughly trained in their part of the basics. When McDonald's Corporation sends employees to its Hamburger University for a few weeks so as to teach them how to prepare and serve hamburgers and to keep spotlessly clean surroundings, they are showing deep commitment to mastering the business basics. For some executives, McDonald's has gone overboard in paying attention to "insignificant" details. For McDonald's, however, maniacal attention to the business fundamentals is but the first step toward pushing the whole corporation toward competitive perfection and for teaching (putting into the psyche of) every employee, including those who prepare hamburgers, that every activity that performs customer requirements must be completely mastered.

2. *Habit of improvement and continuous improvements.* Companies that are searching for perfection keep looking for and finding ways to improve. A corporation that has nurtured desire to improve will always find ways to improve. A company starts to die the first time that top management tolerates the idea that even one activity cannot be ameliorated. Eventually, so many improvement projects will have been successfully implemented, that improvement becomes a companywide habit. One is struck by the fact that the world's best corporations keep improving their products and manufacturing systems year after year. Small improvements are being made in many different parts of the company on a daily basis. Improvement becomes the routine. Toyota Motor Company receives 750,000 suggestions for improvement from its employees every year and implements 40 percent of them. This means that roughly 1,000 suggestions for improvement are being implemented by Toyota every day, and the rate has been rising steadily over the last 10 years. Continuous improvement takes the company closer and closer to perfection.

3. *Experimentation/innovation.* To move forward, a company must generate, research, develop, and try untested ideas. The first company that has some evidence that a new idea has merit can reap the benefits of being the first to implement it. In order to maintain a competitive edge, a corporation must be fairly represented in the group of first-to-think-of or first-to-market or first-to-use or first-to-do companies. The information or insight upon which such "firsts" are based usually comes from experimentation.

Manufacturing excellence can be attained only if top management creates the internal environment—values, organizational structures, compensation and promotion systems, performance measurement, and evaluation policies—that will encourage people to generate and experiment with new ideas and also gives them the resources and authority to test and bring them to fruition, if possible. The experimenting organization usually has a pipeline of improvement projects in varying stages of maturity, as shown in Figure 2–1. One company president encouraged ongoing experimentation by reviewing the pipeline with every department head as part of the annual business planning process. Department heads were expected to have at least one project in each phase. Innovation is the twin sister of experimentation. In fact, innovation comes from successful experimentation.

The experimenting company is likely to be also innovative. As was explained previously, innovation is essential to survival in a global or globalizing market. Capacity and willingness to innovate is a hallmark of the excellent manufacturing organization. Innovation here refers not only to products, but also to processes, systems, management approaches, methods, and procedures. Innovation creates new ways of serving and creating value for the customer.

Companies that value experimentation and innovation not only generate new ideas, but are also quick to adopt innovations that come from outside. They are not afflicted by the Not-Invented Here (NIH) syndrome that sometimes comes with market and technical success. One is struck by the fact that despite long-term success, the world's best companies are able to remain quite open to the outside. Thus, the major innovations in production management over the last 25 years came from world-class manufacturers. Dr. Orlicky invented MRP-II[3] at IBM. Shigeo Shingo is one of the pioneers who invented JIT (Just-in-Time) at Toyota. Total Productive Maintenance (TPM) was also substantially developed at Toyota. Total Quality

FIGURE 2–1   **The Project Pipeline in an Experimenting Company**

---

[3]MRP-II, Manufacturing Resource Planning, is a set of management processes and tools for planning and controlling the business together with the production and materials function. MRP-II is invariably computer-based. For more on MRP-II, see Chapters 12 and 13.

Control (TQC) was developed in the United States but was refined by the leading Japanese manufacturing companies. World-class North American manufacturers were among the first companies to adopt JIT, and the Japanese approach to TQC and TPM. The best manufacturing companies are not only leaders in generating innovations, but are also quick in copying and adapting innovations made by others.

Total Quality Management

World-class manufacturing companies have an obsession for quality. Their motto is "quality, quality, and more quality." There is a never-fading commitment to push quality levels higher and higher. The commitment to quality is total, all-persuasive, and companywide. The business mission is defined, inculcated, and executed with the clear understanding that the company exists, first and foremost, to make and deliver a superior quality product. Product quality may be job 1, but total quality (i.e., quality achieved in all business activities) is the only job. Profit is a result which comes from perfectly executing quality as the company's most fundamental competitive mission, 100 percent of the time, all the time.

The loyalty to quality in a world-class manufacturing company surpasses mere commitment to excellence. It defines the very being of the enterprise. Obviously, competitive excellence comes naturally to companies that define quality as being the heart of the business. Compromises on quality are not tolerated and defects are promptly identified and expunged from the organization. Bad quality is like a virus which automatically triggers all the company's built-in mechanisms for its expulsion or rejection. Companies that are deeply customer oriented, value competitive spirit and entrepreneurship, and constantly search for perfection, have designed the organizational, and managerial processes that will attack bad quality virulently.

Competition and Strategy-Driven Production

Markets are competitive jungles and corporate strategy cuts a clear path through the competitive jungle. A clearly stated and systematically executed strategy is no guarantee of success but an absence of strategy is a guarantee of market failure. This is not the place to enter the debate on whether strategy is planned using managerial and market foresight, or whether it emerges progressively as top management deals with unforeseen circumstances. That debate will probably not be resolved in the foreseeable future and both sides are probably somewhat right. What is clear, even to the uninitiated is that companies that are succeeding are led by managers who have a clear idea of where they want to take the company and how they hope to take it to a desirable market position. The how's, that is to say, the specific actions that are designed to implement strategic intent, change repeatedly as market forces dictate and as experience reveals new insight. But the basic fact remains that excellently managed corporations have clear strategic missions.

Strategy is used to drive the production function, to give it a long-term sense of direction and competitive mission. In the world-class manufacturing company, the production function is continually executing a clear competitive mandate. Production is managed as a competitive weapon because it is explicitly linked with corporate strategy. In fact, the relationship between production and strategy in the best managed manufacturing corporations of the world goes beyond mere linking. Production strategy, policies, and programs are forged out of the company's basic strategic mission at the same time that corporate strategy is being molded by production competencies. The message that is emanating from the leading corporations in North America, Japan, and Europe is that production is either used to create competitive advantage or the company will have no competitive advantage at all. How well a corporation is deploying manufacturing resources to build strategic advantage is a good indication of how competently top management is able to deal with the complex problems involved in implementing strategy.

Total People Management

People are the stuff of which competitive excellence is made. Corporate excellence means human resources are selected, trained, coached, and deployed judiciously. Robots, machines, and software systems are all passive entities that must be created, implemented, and brought into action by people. World-class companies value and nurture their employees and stimulate them to use their creative potential. People are employed to use their creative capabilities first and foremost. The days when employees were valued mainly because of their dexterity or muscle power are all but over. Technology has overcome nearly all of the basic human frailties and has also increased the value of mental, perceptual, and creative abilities. The whole human being, and not just its physiology and anatomy, is critical to the modern corporation. The leading companies of the world today have recognized that and are managing the whole person as a thinking, perceiving, deciding, and acting entity. Companies that value the human being are also providing us with the most solid principles for managing people in an organizational setting.

SUPERIOR PERFORMANCE MANUFACTURING: THE BEDROCK IDEAS

The ideas presented thus far can be synthesized into a comprehensive framework that shows the fundamental factors that explain why some companies

Superior Performance Manufacturing Framework   FIGURE 2-2

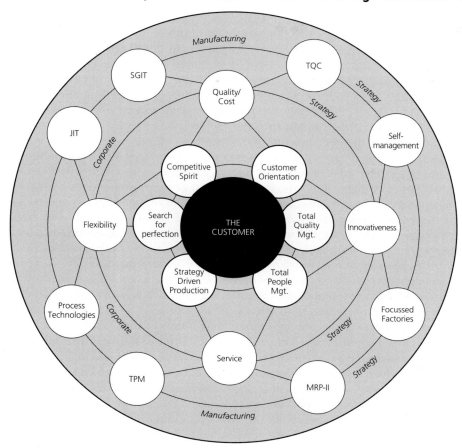

attain competitive superiority and how these factors interact. Figure 2-2 shows the model that emerges from the basic ideas discussed previously.

The Customer and Corporate Culture and Values

Managerial actions that produce lasting and sustainable competitive advantage or superior performance in manufacturing must be driven by the desire, if not compulsion, to satisfy the customer. All companies, past and present, that have achieved or are on the path to attaining competitive superiority have made the customer the heart and soul of the business. The largest and most successful corporations throughout history that allowed their success to cause them to lose their corporate humility and failed to bow to their customers, all lost their will to compete and their ability to drive improvement. The point cannot be overemphasized and neither can the case be overstated; there can be no enduring competitive superiority without the constant and permanent concern to attract, satisfy, and keep the customer. The business must exist for the customer and it must make total customer satisfaction its raison d'etre or sine qua non or else it will not exist at all, at least, not in the long run. When a corporation loses sight of its customers and fails to be totally imbued, even intoxicated, with the overwhelming desire to serve and create value for them, then that corporation has lost the very essence of its existence. Moreover, the customer does not become the heart and soul of the business by happenstance or coincidence. If it were so, competitive excellence and the attainment of strategic advantage would be a chance occurrence, and it definitely is not. The customer will be the heart and soul of the business only if management makes it thus. Consequently, the framework of Figure 2–2 suggests that management's most critical task, at least in a competitive market, is to make the customer the heart and soul of the business and to imbue the organization, through and through, with an unadulterated desire to satisfy the customer.

There is now broad consensus, both in theory and practice, that competitive excellence and superior performance in manufacturing can only be extracted out of a foundation of appropriate culture and values. But, if the raison d'etre of a business is to attract, create, satisfy, and retain a customer, then culture and values are appropriate only if they emanate from a successful interweaving of customer concerns into the fabric of the business. In effect, the overwhelming desire to create value for the customer is the quintessential value on which all other values hang or stand. Of what use are culture and values to the creation of sustainable competitive advantage if they do not flow out of the stuff of competition, that is, rivalry between firms for the customer's loyalty? Appropriate culture and values are, therefore, a projection of the reality that the customer is central to the business and is its lifeblood.

The culture and value system has six, symbiotically related, elements:

1. *Customer orientation.* A corporation that has made the customer's concerns the heart of its business is naturally and inescapably customer oriented and driven.
2. *Competitive spirit.* Businesses compete for the customer. Companies that believe customers make or break a business also work hard to attract and keep them. The will to compete is born out of the need to surpass other competitors in creating value for the customer as the sole basis for carving out an attractive market position. Only aggressive competitors can survive and flourish because only they will have the courage to commit the necessary resources to attack their rivals or defend their market position. The energy and motivation to commit large amounts of resources to retaining and attracting customers can only be sustained by the conviction that they are crucial to the business.

3. *Total Quality Management.* Customer driven companies quickly understand that customers demand, seek, and value quality. If customer concerns are omnipresent in the organization and are enmeshed in all structures and processes, then quality will also be everywhere. The striving to achieve and improve all facets of quality in all areas of the business is the essence of Total Quality Management which itself is born out of the overpowering desire to constantly increase value delivered to the customer.

4. *Search for perfection.* Globalization and competition, or the threat of it, empower the customer and drive the competitive or market requirements higher. Eventually, global competition will require that companies design, produce, and deliver near perfect products and services. Steinway and Sons refers to such a near perfect product in piano making as the realization of intelligent synthesis, while Mercedes Benz refers to its cars as the "ultimate driving machine." Although these characterizations have some promotional content, they express the idea that the challenge for the corporation in a global market is to create and build the ultimate machine and to design and deliver error-free service. Competitive markets empower customers who in turn push companies toward perfection. Companies that are managed to grow and prosper are also imbued with customer concerns and are driven, or rather drive themselves, to achieve perfection. World-class companies achieve the apparently unachievable and as a matter of course. They are able to constantly improve the products and services that were considered the best.

5. *Strategy-driven production.* Observation of the world's best managed companies suggests that manufacturing performance improves more readily and dramatically when the production function is driven by a clearly articulated corporate strategy and mission. When Xerox developed a clear corporate mission that enunciated the need to eliminate its cost and quality disadvantage in copiers, it not only set in motion the process to invent benchmarking, but also quickened the pace of implementation of JIT, SPC, supplier partnership, and Total Quality Management.

6. *Total people management.* In the final analysis, only people can improve a product, service, or production system and search for perfection. The motivation to excel or improve is a uniquely human trait. A company is customer oriented only if its employees are. Corporations can have no more competitive spirit than that which resides in the individual and collective consciousness of their employees. Concern for and preoccupation with quality are distinctly human in nature. And only people can embody the concerns and desires of a company's customers. The first time that a company tries to enmesh customer needs, wants, and concerns into its organizational and managerial processes and structures, it will immediately recognize that people are the critical agents for doing so. Consequently, such a company will manage, take care of, and nurture the whole employee. All companies that have reached competitive superiority

concretely demonstrate deep commitment to constantly improve the quality of their human resources.

CORPORATE STRATEGY

The corporate culture and value system, nourished by the desire to attract, retain, and create value for the customer, builds the organizational impetus to seek superiority in the performance of the five critical competitive requirements: quality, cost, innovation, customer service, and flexibility. Corporate strategy links these requirements to define a unique competitive position for the company. In a market that is local or national in scope, competitive position defines:

1. The competitive requirements on which the company will try to attain performance superiority and will emphasize in its efforts to be different from its competitors.
2. How the company will compensate for its weaknesses in the performance of the other competitive requirements.
3. The value the company creates for its customers, relative to its competitors.
4. The market share that will result from the company's overall, relative performance and the price it can extract from its customers.

In a global market, and given the particular market segment in which the company chooses to compete, the choice of competitive position is severely limited. The company must perform all the competitive requirements at an acceptable level. However, it can still attempt to go beyond its competitors in performing any one of them.

Corporate strategy links the five competitive requirements and unifies them into an appropriate strategic position in three ways:

1. Identification and specification of the key relationships and symbiosis between the critical competitive requirements.
2. Deployment of the relative amount of resources that are required to build the capability to perform the competitive requirements at an acceptable level.
3. Choice and implementation of specific policies, programs, systems, techniques, and tools that exploit symbiosis among the five critical competitive requirements.

The five competitive requirements are interrelated and are characterized by high levels of symbiosis. The recognition of these symbiotic relationships and the design of systems, technologies, and managerial actions to exploit and even enhance symbiosis, is one of the notable developments in manufacturing over the last two decades. It is the design of these systems, technologies and managerial actions that led to the conclusion that the five competitive requirements are not necessarily in opposition. Thus, quality improvement need not come at the detriment of cost. On the contrary, the reduction of defects can contribute significantly to lowering cost and advances in process technology, which increase productivity, also reduce cost. For example, advances in image reproduction technology in the fabrication of computer chips and automated chip testing process technology dramatically increased miniaturization and integration (i.e., the number of transistors that can be packed on a chip) raised productivity, increased microprocessor reliability, reduced defect rates, and decreased cost per chip. Process technology innovations have sometimes produced improved performance in flexibility, quality, and productivity or cost. The development of electric arc furnaces combined with innovation in continuous casting process technology decreased steelmaking turnaround times to one and one half hours compared to three to four hours for the traditional basic oxygen furnace. This increased one aspect of steelmaking flexibility because a minimill could produce more grades of steel in a given time and cut the delivery time to customers. The same two technologies radically increased productivity and reduced cost per ton. Nucor, one of the most heavy users of electric arc furnaces and continuous casting technology in North America, outperforms the integrated steel producers on productivity, cost, and lead time and is increasingly able to produce specialty steels of comparable quality in a market segment that was hitherto the exclusive domain of the integrated producers.

Corporate strategy also exploits symbiosis and creates linkages at the level of systems, tools, methods, techniques, and management approaches. For example, the implementation of Total Quality Management (TQM) usually results in the use of Statistical Process Control (SPC), Small Group Improvement Teams (SGIT), and vendor performance evaluation. SPC provides the means for systematic process monitoring which increases process reliability. As processes become more reliable, buffer inventories between processes can be reduced. Just-in-Time (JIT) reduces production lot sizes by reducing set-up times, which automatically reduces work-in-process inventories between processes. As JIT reduces production lot sizes, it compresses the quality feedback loop which enhances the effects of SPC. At the same time, Total Productive Maintenance uses SGITs as one of its key process improvement mechanisms. Information generated by vendor performance evaluation, one aspect of TQM, is used to certify vendors and move toward single-source procurement, a critical mechanism for improving both overall vendor performance and the quality of raw materials. Thus, by picking the right systems to implement and orchestrating their implementation, manufacturing strategy can unleash a chain reaction of managerial and organizational processes where one improvement program feeds and sustains a series of other improvement programs. If manufacturing strategy targets and successfully implements a sufficient number of systems, tools, techniques, methods, and approaches, it can create an explosion of improvement initiatives. The whole will surely be much more than the sum of its individual parts.

MANUFACTURING STRATEGY

Concrete actions chosen, mandated, or stimulated by corporate strategy and implemented in the manufacturing function give rise to the company's manufacturing strategy. Therefore, one cannot rigorously speak of manufacturing strategy unless production policies, programs, and systems are clearly and explicitly chosen to give effect to corporate strategic priorities. Manufacturing strategy links these policies, programs, systems, and actions into a systematic response by production to the competitive priorities chosen and communicated by the corporate strategy. Like corporate strategy, manufacturing strategy deploys available manufacturing resources to implement the actions that are designed to create specific competitive capabilities or skills. Manufacturing strategy binds the various production decisions and actions into a cohesive, consistent response to competitive market forces. The specific manufacturing programs highlighted are Total Quality Control (TQC), self-management, focused factories, Manufacturing Resource Planning (MRP-II), total productive maintenance (TPM), process technology choice, just-in-time (JIT), and small group improvement teams (SGIT). These have been selected because they are the latest and most advanced manufacturing management tools that were developed and are being implemented by widely acclaimed world-class manufacturing companies. However, the framework could be easily adapted to accommodate any tool that is deemed important to the pursuit of competitive advantage through manufacturing.

Corporate culture and values are the foundation upon which superior manufacturing performance stands. Incapacity to push quality levels higher or to drive costs down almost always means that the corporation has a weak value set or is being driven by the wrong values. When things go wrong with quality or service, they can invariably be traced back to a breakdown in the core values. A company does not put out bad quality because it has a few negligent employees or suppliers, since a company that is being driven by the right values will not select negligent employees or do business with lousy suppliers. This contrasts sharply with the perspective adopted by the typical manager. When there is a problem, management says, "fix it," which means that the focus is on the superficial, immediate manifestation of the problem rather than on the root cause. The approach to problem solving taught in most business schools and management seminars almost always attacks the peripheral causes rather than the root cause—the corporate value set. Invariably, the problem goes away only temporarily. For example, MRP-II will not be successfully implemented in a company that is not profoundly customer oriented. Total Quality Control can never take hold in a company that is not deeply committed to quality. JIT cannot be successfully adopted by a corporation that is not driven by the search for perfection. The companies that are today succeeding in implementing JIT, TQC, MRP-II, TPM, and other tools of superior manufacturing performance already have the core values well in place. It is noteworthy that companies that are already world-class are able to very quickly absorb world-class manufacturing concepts developed by other companies. In order to be successful, strategic change in manufacturing must capitalize on positive core values. Developing or nurturing the right values that can drive superior manufacturing performance constitutes the major facet of strategic change in production. But instead of this broad, value driven approach to production, most companies are afflicted with what can be called productivity myopia.

PRODUCTIVITY MYOPIA—FAILURE OF TRADITIONAL COST-REDUCTION STRATEGIES

The aggressive pursuit of cost reduction, while maintaining superior levels of quality, customer service and product innovativeness, is a requirement for competing in increasingly competitive and international markets. Customers usually seek to maximize the value they receive for the price they pay for a product or service. Companies that succeed in keeping their customers are those that increase or maintain the value that they deliver. Increasing value means one of three things: (1) increasing quality at the same price; (2) increasing quality faster than increases in price; or (3) maintaining quality levels while decreasing price. Any of these three scenarios requires either maintaining actual cost levels or decreasing costs relative to quality delivered. A company can always gain a competitive advantage by driving costs down without sacrificing quality and service, although it has to be emphasized that relative cost position is only one way to seek a competitive advantage. However, traditional cost-reduction strategies have generally failed to create the leverage over cost that a company needs in order to drive costs down consistently and continuously. This inability to achieve sustainable and long-term reductions in cost derives from a number of problems inherent in the way that costs are viewed, managed, and controlled in most companies.

The Labor Cost Blind Spot

The cost accounting systems in use in the vast majority of companies give a central role to labor cost control and reduction in the overall cost management effort. It is safe to say that every company that has even a rudimentary formal cost accounting system, tracks, measures, reports on, and pays close attention to labor cost in the budgeting process. Moreover, labor cost and time are invariably used as the basis for allocating overhead costs, even in companies where labor cost represents a very small proportion of total unit cost. Such a crucial role is almost never given to material or energy costs, even if these are the largest cost items in many situations. Material and energy use are rarely used as the basis for allocating overheads although their use more closely reflects the actual consumption of overhead items.

Emphasis on labor cost as the prime basis for cost management has gone beyond mere cost reporting and control. The cost budgeting process cannot be separated from the performance analysis and control environment that it creates for lower level managers. Companies do not set cost standards and measure and analyze actual performance simply for the sake of doing so. Invariably, there is some type of performance evaluation and review that comes from the monthly budgeting and reporting process. Whether top management intends it or not, the role given to labor cost in the overall cost control process communicates to middle-level managers the message that the control of labor cost is a critical priority. So, what started as mere cost control and reporting ends up shaping the environment for motivation and the behavior of middle-level managers. At the middle-management level, superior performance comes to be viewed as ability to control and reduce labor cost. By rewarding superior performance, top management ends up promoting those who have cultivated the knack to cut labor cost. Eventually, myopic emphasis on labor cost reduction comes to permeate the entire management hierarchy and managers become incapable of conceiving of cost management except in terms of the narrow issue of labor cost reduction and control.

Existing cost accounting systems make one crucial assumption that makes them virtually useless as instruments for broad, sustainable, and long-term reductions in cost. That assumption is a vestige of the period during which these systems were developed. The assumption is that labor cost is an important element of total unit cost so that leverage on cost could be created by focusing on controlling labor utilization. This assumption was probably realistic in the 1920s, when the birth of present day cost accounting systems took place in companies like DuPont and General Motors. The table below gives rough

Comparative Distribution of Unit Cost

	1920	1990
Labor	50%	15%
Materials	30	60
Overhead	20	25

estimates of the distribution of total unit cost in the 1920s compared with the 1980s and 1990s. Labor was clearly a significant proportion of unit cost with material and overhead costs together accounting for less than half of unit cost. The advances in industrial organization during the 1920s clearly focused on reducing labor cost, underscoring its perceived importance then in the pursuit of manufacturing efficiency. The development of the assembly line by Ford Motor Company and the development of work study methods by Frederick Taylor and the Gilbreths are two cases in point. Ford, Taylor, and the Gilbreths recognized the key role that labor cost reduction had to play in attaining production efficiency in their time.

However, technological developments since the 1920s with their implicit, if not explicit goal of reducing labor by massive mechanization have changed the structure of unit cost dramatically. Automation and mass production have created the situation whereby labor cost is less than 15 percent of unit cost in most companies. In many companies, labor costs that are 10, 8, and even 4 percent of unit cost are the norm rather than the exception. In fact, in the so-called labor intensive industries such as furniture manufacturing, labor is barely 40 percent of unit cost and decreasing.

The change in manufacturing cost structure away from labor and toward material occurred in such a way as to be imperceptible to the cost accounting methods of even the best managed corporations. Decrease in the importance of labor as a component of unit cost was not propelled mainly by technological revolutions but rather by progressive, incremental change that took place over decades. Individually, these technological changes are not sufficient to elicit changes in top management's view of strategic priorities and their response to competitive conditions. However, the cumulative effect of several decades of improvement in manufacturing processes, systems, and organization has made the old strategy of labor cost reduction useless. Yearly improvements in individual cost elements are too small to be identified as significant by the management accounting system, particularly when these improvements are buried into the averaging procedures of cost accounting.

However, when cumulated over a period of 10 or 20 years, these small changes are significant enough to warrant a change in management's view of cost and the choice of strategies for its reduction.

Erroneous Pursuit of Labor Efficiency

The prevailing assumption that labor is an important element of cost and that leverage over cost reduction can be gained by decreasing use of labor has shaped top management's myopic view of productivity. Even in the decades of the 1980s and 1990s when labor is likely to account for less than 10 percent of manufacturing cost, companies tend to emphasize labor productivity and efficiency in their drive to effect improvement in their strategic position on cost. In company after company, manufacturing efficiency is measured, expressed, and controlled in terms of output per hour or day, and cost accounting systems are replete with formulas for calculating and interpreting labor variances. What these companies fail to realize is that given the radical change in cost structure that has occurred since the 1920s there is very little strategic leverage that can be derived from labor cost reduction. As we shall emphasize later on, many items of waste and excess are individually likely to cost many times more than labor in the vast majority of manufacturing companies. This is the critical issue as far as aggressive cost reduction is concerned. Management can effect much more dramatic and strategically significant reductions in overall cost by pursuing waste elimination aggressively than by trying to reduce labor.

Mechanization to Replace Labor

Strategies to reduce overall cost are powerfully influenced by the assumptions that managers make about the structure and behavior of cost. It is therefore not surprising that the prevailing notion that labor cost reduction is an important aspect of cost reduction has affected the rationale for mechanization and the kinds of technological innovations that are likely to be adopted by companies. There is an almost universally accepted view that manufacturing efficiency improves as one substitutes equipment (capital) for labor in the manufacturing process. Labor substitution is used to justify most of the capital investment decisions of the majority of companies. Similarly, the built-in bias that management has about the significance of labor cost means that companies tend to be more receptive to new process technologies that reduce labor. Decades of using labor substitution as the rationale for adopting new process technology has created a kind of reflex action in workers that jobs are at stake once a new machine has been installed. Workers have a deep fear of mechanization, a fear which has been conditioned and nurtured by countless and predictable use of labor elimination as the rationale for mechanization. Unions have learned to capitalize on that fear to rally workers into resisting automation. Management is not blameless in the face of the current situation.

Widespread use of labor reduction as the main rationale for undertaking process innovation has seriously damaged the competitive position of many companies. Because labor utilization is already so low in most companies, engineers have to stretch labor savings calculations to the limit and adopt unrealistically low estimates of investment requirements in order for mechanization projects to satisfy corporate minimum rates of return. But this is a guarantee that investment decisions in new process technology will turn out to be "wrong" in retrospect. Moreover, management is confronted with a dilemma because as labor becomes less and less important in unit cost, it takes increasingly larger reductions in labor to justify these investments.

Strong emphasis on financial criteria, short-term payback calculations, and assumptions about labor that are evidently long outdated have discouraged managers from investing in process innovation and have sapped many companies of the ability to compete in increasingly competitive markets. Not only do these companies not improve labor productivity, the very thing they set out to do, but they also lose the most powerful competitive benefits of new technology such as increased quality, flexibility, and the creation of a companywide habit of improvement.

Ironically, the very same phenomena that block the search for improved competitive strength by way of new process technology have also stifled the initiative to improve existing but old equipment. The amount of labor that is needed to operate a piece of machinery is viewed as being determined by factors built into the design. Management tends to view labor savings as a one time effect that is reaped when the equipment is introduced. Major revamps of old machines are viewed to generate very little reductions in labor and are consequently thought not worth the effort. Besides, it is difficult, if not impossible, to achieve sufficient reductions in labor through a revamp of existing machinery to meet the return on investment goals of most companies. What is already difficult in the case of new equipment is virtually impossible when one is dealing with mature process technology. Companies have thus put themselves into a technological innovation trap created by the fact that they see reductions in labor as the main justification for investing in new process technology. The investment evaluation criteria that are in place in most companies both discourage process innovation and motivate management to "run the equipment into the ground."

Evaluation of improvement projects in existing old equipment must consider a broader range of factors other than labor cost reduction and, most importantly, must go at the heart of the economics of old process technology. As machines age, two things happen to reduce their overall cost effectiveness. First, there is general reduction in the capability to hold initial tolerances due to increased variability. Usually, there is no loosening of tolerances as the capability of the machine decreases but competitive pressures often result in tightening of product specifications. The true state of affairs is hidden by the fact that the machine can still make good products, even though the downside of that is higher levels of scrap. Higher scrap levels are thought to be "normal" for an older machine and acceptable quality levels in terms of standard defect rates are increased to reflect process aging. There is apparently no increase in the number of people needed to operate the machine, but the simple fact is that labor cost has increased substantially because the same hours are used to make fewer good products. Due to the fact that the cost accounting system rarely accounts for and reports on nonquality costs, the true situation is hidden from management. Consequently, the maintenance of process capability which is the main justification for investing to improve old equipment is not factored into the financial data used to evaluate major revamp projects.

Second, as machines age and little attention is paid to them, there is general reduction in machine reliability causing an increase in both planned and unplanned down time. Unplanned down time on new equipment is seen as unavoidable by virtually every manager in North America. When this attitude is transferred to old equipment it results in the defeatist notion that increasing levels of unplanned down time are entirely normal and acceptable and that the only feasible practical option available to management is to slow down the rate of increase. Once more, the visible amount of labor used does not change, although overall labor efficiency decreases in direct proportion to increases in the level of down time. Company after company in North America uses performance analysis and control systems to normalize higher levels of down time by making next year's standard last year's actual down time. In the absence of aggressive programs for improving old machines and strong preventive maintenance policies, increases in actual down time are systematic, predictable, and inevitable. Similarly, the standards for down time are increased year after year. The management information system used in conjunction with archaic assumptions about down time have robbed top management of the insight and incentive to make judicious investments. The consequence of these two phenomena and the technological innovation trap that they help create have sapped North American companies of the ability to aggressively deploy an overall cost reduction strategy by the astute exploitation of process technology.

THE GLAMOUR OF MASS PRODUCTION

By the time the United States emerged as an industrial power at the beginning of the twentieth century, it was widely accepted by economists and managers that major improvements in production efficiency are created by organizing manufacturing for mass production of standardized products. The advantages of standardization and interchangeability of parts were well documented and accepted with the work of Eli Whitney during the first half of the nineteenth century. During the latter half of the eighteenth century, the work of Adam Smith had provided the conceptual basis for support of the idea that hundredfold increases in production efficiency could be achieved by simply arranging factories to produce high volumes of identical products because of the effects of specialization. The invention of the assembly line by Ford provided concrete evidence that mass production could be achieved even in the context of automated manufacturing. Ford's assembly line demonstrated that not only can workers be specialized even when there is a large number of different tasks involved in putting a product together, but that these same workers can be made to work as a single, synchronized unit by using conveyors to link them together.

The world looked on in awe as the United States marched on to achieve unprecedented levels of production efficiency and technological supremacy. The United States had managed to organize production on a scale never seen before and it was not long before others were trying to replicate the U.S.'s industrial performance. Those who were busy studying the United States as a model for economic progress got hooked on the most obvious and appealing features of her industrial system. They saw a huge country meeting the needs of an enormous market for good quality, affordable goods, using the technology of mass production. It was not long before efficient production was associated with mass production and large lots. Production of high volumes of basically standardized products, the argument went, permitted reaping economies of scale in procurement, production, distribution, and marketing of goods. Large-scale production, it was argued, generated the cash necessary to apply technology intensively and to push automation to the fullest extent possible. Depreciation charges, other fixed costs, and change-over costs could be amortized over a large number of items resulting in significant reductions in per unit production cost and price. The era of mass production was born and the theories and models advocating its merits became entrenched in all standard textbooks on production management and, ultimately, in the minds of managers. The prominent position given to Henry Ford for inventing the continuous assembly line is one indication that managers saw in mass production the most powerful tool to pursue manufacturing efficiency.

RETHINKING LARGE LOT PRODUCTION

Wrong View of Costs

Over the last two decades a number of world-class manufacturing companies in North America, Japan, and Western Europe have reevaluated the arguments and assumptions that provide the rationale for large lot production. These companies have come to the realization that the premises on which mass production is based are questionable at best and downright wrong at worst. Production strategies, that are based on pushing large lot production in order to increase productivity and create leverage on cost, fail in the long run because they are not sustainable and in fact create a barrier against the achievement of sustainable, continuous improvement in a company's cost position. Countervailing arguments and premises have emerged that underscore the evils of mass, large lot production.

Cost reduction strategies that try to exploit the principles of large lot production start by classifying manufacturing costs into fixed and variable elements. Fixed costs are assumed to be insensitive to changes in the level of output for a given production unit. They are viewed to be given and determined when the production facility is being designed and built. Variable costs, on the other hand, are those elements of cost that vary in direct proportion to the level of output. The assumption is that variable costs are avoidable if production is not undertaken, while fixed costs are not. Herein lies the problem for most companies. By assuming that certain costs are fixed, management unwittingly nurtures the attitude that these cannot be reduced. Thus, the very designation "fixed costs" creates a barrier to their aggressive reduction. Fixed costs may not respond to changes in output but they can and are influenced by managerial action. What is at issue here is the choice of independent variable. In the conventional wisdom, the only independent variable that is used to classify costs is the level of output. So, to decrease these costs on a per unit basis, one can only increase output.

But the challenge to the accepted wisdom comes from the search for other powerful independent variables that can be used to exert leverage over the so-called fixed costs. Depreciation is a case in point. Absolute levels of depreciation are basically insensitive to changes in output so the conventional wisdom drives output up to reduce per unit depreciation charges. However, the absolute level of depreciation does respond to better management of maintenance. Therefore, with respect to the level of preventive maintenance and investment in improvement in existing equipment, depreciation is a variable cost. Another example will help make the case stronger. Production floor space and its cost have traditionally been viewed as fixed. As much as 50 percent of production floor space is used for WIP inventory. Progressive reduction in WIP liberates space that can be used to build other production units thereby reducing the cost of both new and existing production facilities. Space costs are relatively fixed with respect to volume of production but they are variable when viewed through programs to reduce WIP inventory.

Long-term strategies to reduce costs cannot proceed on the assumption that any cost is fixed. In the minds of many executives the fixed becomes the unavoidable which becomes the sacrosanct. Large lot production, by trying to reduce per unit fixed costs via increases in volume has made fixed costs sacrosanct, and has left many companies saddled with huge, inflexible factories built in the pursuit of economies of scale. Fragmentation of existing markets that come about as a result of individualization of consumer tastes has changed these large scale facilities into competitive dinosaurs. In today's fast changing, increasingly competitive markets, there is overwhelming strategic advantage to be gained from small scale, versatile, and flexible factories. Reduction in absolute fixed costs and overheads for a given level of output results in a reduction in the optimal scale of operations. That is to say, the challenge is to make the economic size factory progressively smaller by making it more fixed cost effective. Programs to slow down the aging of equipment, increase WIP inventory turns, reduce supervision by implementing self-management, to name only a few, make the optimum factory smaller.

Compromising Product Differentiation

Large lot production blunts one of the most powerful marketing weapons available, that is, segmentation. Every marketing manager recognizes that a market is not a homogeneous, undifferentiated mass of consumers, but rather a grouping of pockets of customers. Although the market as a whole shares the generic product need, one can always identify clusters of customers, referred to as segments, that have requirements that are variations around the basic need. The more these groupings or clusters are refined, the more they become internally homogeneous and also different from the other groups. The idea behind segmentation is that the marketer can create product offerings that more accurately meet the special needs of individual clusters, by differentiations of the generic product. Indeed, the deployment of a market position based on product differentiation must proceed from an accurate understanding of the true bases for market segmentation. By identifying market segments and their peculiar requirements, the company can dovetail product quality and features, price, promotion, and choice of distribution channel to the peculiarities of customer behavior that are germane to each segment. Product offerings that exploit valid bases of segmentation are more likely to create high levels of customer satisfaction and repeat sales.

Schematically, Figure 2–3 demonstrates the concept of market segmentation. The schematic highlights the powerful, strategic reason why markets should be segmented. Each niche has key success factors (KSFs) that are unique to it. A KSF is a basic product requirement, the performance of which is fundamental to growth, profitability, and survivability in the particular market segment. One should note that a company, in order to penetrate and

Market Segmentation and Key Success Factors (KSFs)  FIGURE 2–3

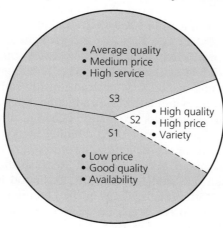

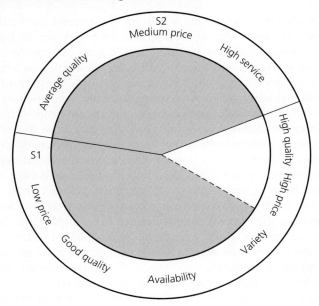

FIGURE 2-4   **Large Lot Production and Segmentation**

entrench its position in a market segment, must perform the key success factors of that segment. Execution of KSFs is the lever that controls a company's market position. Relative market shares reflect how well companies perform on the KSFs compared to their competitors. The KSFs represent product requirements that are valued by the customers and for which they are willing to pay. When viewed in this way, the KSFs become an important basis for judging both the accuracy of market segmentation efforts and whether any segment can be further segmented. When market segmentation is accurately done, there should be at least one KSF that is unique to each segment.

Traditional arguments used to justify and promote large lot production as a way to increase productivity and reduce cost run counter to the principle that segmentation/differentiation can be used to fine tune a company's market position. Often, no one market segment can provide sufficient volume to justify large scale operations and large lot production. So in order to achieve the volume necessary to make mass production economically justifiable, management broadens the segment scope by combining two or more market niches (Figure 2-4). The basis for segmentation becomes fuzzy and the array of KSFs of each enlarged segment becomes wider. Because the new market niche combines more than one true segment, the likelihood is high that the KSFs will be conflicting. Without clear focus in the definition of market segments, it becomes impossible to focus the production system to specialize on the execution of a limited range of market requirements. When such is the case, two things can happen: Either the production system produces a large volume of products that fit the exigencies of only one of the segments or a compromise product is placed on the market. In the first case, the company achieves a dominant position in one segment and fails in the other, giving a somewhat average market share in the broader, targeted segment. High sales in one segment compensate for dismal sales in the other. The second case scenario has as consequence that customers in neither true market segment are satisfied with a compromise product, leaving the company with mediocre sales overall. Either way, the company is vulnerable to competitive onslaught due to the fact that one or more of its true market niches are poorly served.

Marketing a compromise product in search of production volume to achieve large lot production sacrifices the company's market differentiation strategy on the altar of productivity and efficiency sought through economies of scale. The arguments that have been put forward above show that conventional ways of trying to achieve high production volumes will almost guarantee that the sought after volume will not be achieved. Worse yet, the production system becomes an impediment to the company's ability to achieve differentiation and to exploit the power that lies latent in segmentation. Production is not being used to create and sustain market advantage and the rationale of production management cuts against the grain of market evolution and the fundamentals of customer behavior. The trend in today's markets is for customers to demand an increasing variety of goods and services that enable them to express their individuality. Large lot production, on the other hand, forces customers into fixed consumption patterns and are modern day expressions of the famous Henry Ford dictum that "the customer can have any color car he wants, as long as it is black." It is interesting to point out that the same man whose genius invented the paramount large lot production tool, the assembly line, also abhorred the concept of product differentiation, reinforcing our view that the two are essentially incompatible.

Indirect Inventory Costs

Progress in lot size reduction over the last decade or so has revealed a very powerful relationship between production lot sizes and quality improvement. Companies that are achieving superior levels of quality and near zero defect rates have found that production lot size reduction contributes much more than a mere reduction in inventories. Rapid inventory turns and the savings in inventory costs associated with them, although they have significant financial impact, are a small part of the overall improvement in a company's overall competitive position that derives from lot size reduction. JIT's ultimate strategic mission is sustained, continuous quality improvement. Inventory reduction, while important, is only one mechanism by which JIT contributes to achieving total superior quality.

FIGURE 2-5 **Inventory Hides Quality Problems**

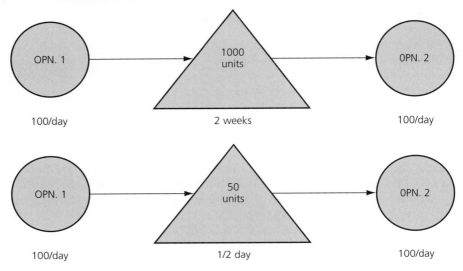

The relationship between quality and large lot production has two important aspects. The first is well captured by the principle derived from practical observation that inventory hides quality problems. The basis for this statement can be understood by referring to Figure 2–5. Assume that the lot size is 10 days production or 1,000 units. Because production is not synchronized, the 100 units per day are not transferred in small quantities to operation 2 for immediate processing, but are placed in inventory. Average WIP would be 500 units, or five days production. When processing at operation 2 begins, there are 1,000 units in inventory. Suppose the defect rate is 25 percent or 250 bad units. The worker at operation 2 will reject 250 units yet production will continue uninterrupted because the lot size of 1,000 cushions the impact of bad quality. There is no urgency to solve the quality problem. When the company strives to produce what has been sold using small lot synchronized production, high defect rates play havoc with delivery schedules and the urgency of quality problems are driven home continuously and in dramatic fashion.

Similarly, when the lot size is 1,000 units, WIP turns 52 times per year. Although this would be considered to be very good by most companies, one should note that when WIP turns 52 times there is up to two weeks' WIP inventory. The usual practice is for lot sizes to be processed through the operation on a first-come-first-serve basis, so that the current lot will be processed at operation 2 two weeks after processing began at operation 1. Defects introduced very early in executing operation 1 may be discovered two weeks after the fact, meaning that the quality feedback loop is two weeks. Not only is it too late to correct what caused the defects at operation 1—the entire lot was produced two weeks earlier—but it is also likely that the cause is no longer traceable. The large lot results in very slow feedback on quality and it is almost certain that quality problems cannot be corrected or traced to their source. The entire lot of 1,000 units would be affected by the quality problem at operation 1. Using a lot size of 50 or half a day's production reduces the feedback loop to one half day. There is a far better chance that the cause of bad quality can be identified and corrected. Moreover, correcting the quality problems early on when the first batch of 50 was being produced would increase the chance that the remaining 950 units would have been produced defect free. For subsequent batches, then, the production system would have operated in the preventive mode and defect rates for the entire 1,000 units would have been quite low, even if the first batch of 50 had a 25 percent defect rate. As we move toward small batch synchronized production, then, quality control strategy goes from slow feedback, defect correction to rapid problem identification and defect prevention. Companies that do large lot production will always find it difficult to achieve near zero defect rates.

Negative Impact on Customer Service

Large lot anticipatory production is often justified using the argument that it is necessary to have goods on hand to provide quick delivery to customers. Such is particularly the case when the lead time required by customers is less than the total production time for a typical batch of the item. If we designate the customer lead time by L_t and the total production time by C_t, anticipatory production is necessary when $L_t < C_t$. While this argument is a valid one, large lot sizes amplify the problem and increase the difference between L_t and C_t. Now one can look at this difference as the cost of providing customer lead times that are competitive. If we can reduce C_t sufficiently, it may be possible to provide the same level of customer service—shorter lead times— but at much lower cost. In fact, by sufficiently reducing C_t until it becomes smaller than L_t, that is $C_t < L_t$, competitive lead times can be achieved without anticipatory production and hence with no associated inventory cost. Production can be done on a make-to-order basis, thereby achieving the goal of making what has been sold.

Large lot and anticipatory production feed on each other in very insidious ways, and put a company into a vicious circle vis-à-vis the achievement of increasingly competitive lead times. In a competitive market, customer lead times are set by rivalry between firms. Individual companies attain a favorable competitive position by decreasing the total production time with the aim not of decreasing customer lead times per se, but of reducing the cost of serving the customer. The total production time can be divided into its three major components, queue time (Q_t), move time (M_t), and processing time (P_t) giving

TABLE 2–1

	Lot Size	
	100	**20**
Processing time	25 hours	5 hours
Queue time	<u>225</u> hours	<u>45</u> hours
Total time (hours)	250 hours	50 hours
Total time (days) at 8.0 hours per day	<u>32</u> days	<u>7</u> days

the simple formula $C_t = Q_t + M_t + P_t$. Q_t is the time spent by units waiting for their turn to be processed either because a machine is not available or because units from a prior lot or first units from the current lot are being processed. Observation tells us that the biggest contributor to Q_t is the lot sizing policy. But the key information that is gained from such a disaggregation of total production cycle time is that Q_t accounts for 90 percent of C_t. Increasing the lot size increases Q_t and magnifies the difference between C_t and L_t. For example, suppose a case where the processing time per piece is 0.25 hours, move time is negligible, and the percentage Q_t is 90 percent. Table 2–1 computes C_t, the total production cycle time when the lot size is 100 units as against 20 units, ignoring set-up time for the time being.

These data show that increasing the lot size from 20 to 100 units increases the total production cycle time from 7 to 32 days. Suppose the market is demanding a six-day lead time. The larger lot size would require 26 days inventory to offer reasonable service to customers. The smaller lot size requires only one day inventory. The lesson is that large lot production does not increase customer service, as is usually supposed, but only increases the cost of achieving competitive service levels.

THE SLOW PACE OF CHANGE IN NORTH AMERICAN MANUFACTURING

The competitive environment for manufacturing has been dramatically altered over the last three decades, spurred on by globalization and the restructuring of the world economy. Change continues at an unprecedented rate and thus deepens the threat to North American industry, calling for new strategic responses and novel approaches to managing production. However, North American corporations are slow in reacting to global competition and in adopting innovations in manufacturing management. The evidence that change is slow is widespread, but the following facts are enough to underscore the point:

1. Total Quality control (TQC), which is a set of proven tools and philosophies for rigorously assuring and improving quality, was developed in the United States in the early 1950s. However, TQC was virtually ignored by North American corporations until the mid-1980s, when it was reintroduced to North America after having been adapted and refined by the Japanese. The TQC pioneers such as Deming, Juran, and Feigenbaum were recognized in North America only after they had become household names in Japan.

2. Small Group Improvement Teams (SGITs) were part of the participative management movement that started in the 1950s. They were at first referred to as Quality Circles (QCs). The QC movement swept through North America in the 1950s and many major North American corporations attempted to implement QCs. But failure was widespread, and by 1970, the QC movement had all but died. North American corporations still have a tough time making quality teams work. By contrast, QCs spread quickly in Japan after their introduction in the 1960s, and there are currently about 3,000,000 quality teams involving about 20,000,000 workers in Japanese industry.

3. MRP-II began with the work of Dr. Orlicky at IBM in the early 1960s, which means that it has existed for about thirty years. MRP-II is a computer-based business planning technology. Because the modern computer is essentially an American invention, the early MRP-II pioneers thought that MRP-II would fit naturally in the North American corporate mindset. Currently, however, very few companies have a credible, effective, and strategically valuable MRP-II system, and most attempts at implementation fail.

4. JIT was invented at Toyota and was already well refined by the mid-1970s. Today, only a handful of North American corporations have succeeded in implementing JIT and none has achieved results even remotely comparable to those attained by Toyota, Nissan, or Canon.

The pattern of failure that characterizes the attempts by North American corporations to adopt TQC, SGITs, MRP-II, JIT, and other tools of modern manufacturing management, reflect a deep organizational malaise. These tools are not only the most advanced technologies available to a company that wants to push manufacturing performance higher; they have, as we have seen, very deep philosophical roots. Consequently, when a company fails in its efforts to implement these technologies, it is because its philosophical foundation and culture and value system do not provide the fertile environment in which superior performance is conceived, incubated, born, and nurtured to maturity. Failure to implement strategic change in manufacturing shows up as what we refer to as blocking-out (See Figure 2–6).

Most companies seldom attempt to change their manufacturing management approaches because existing organizational processes, attitudes, or

FIGURE 2–6 **The Blocking-Out Process**

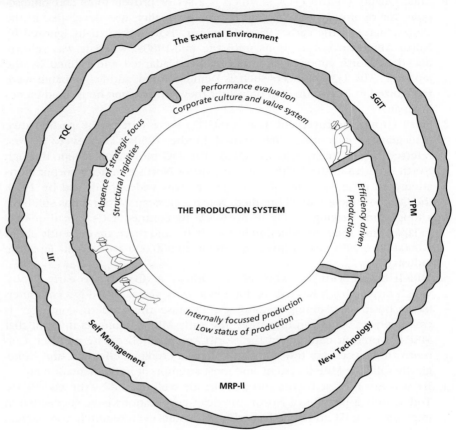

philosophies systematically block out new ideas and concepts. Classical blocking-out mechanisms show up as rationalizations as to why a new technology will not work or why the company is different from current successful users. Many managers harbor a latent "if it works, don't mess with it" attitude that prevents new concepts from being tested. The NIH (Not Invented Here) syndrome is also prevalent in historically successful corporations.

Manufacturing is particularly susceptible to block-out because of four reasons:

1. *The factory has traditionally been closed to competitive market forces.* In the past production management advocated that to be efficient, the factory should be shielded from internal and external environmental disturbances.

The factory may have been more efficient, in the narrow sense, but it became useless as a competitive weapon.

2. *The average factory resists experimentation.* Experiments are viewed as disruptive to the factory and are thought to lead to lower efficiency. Such is particularly true of mature, systemic production systems that have highly integrated and efficient processes, such as the petroleum refining, steel, and chemical industries.

3. *The average factory manager is not totally conscious of the customer.* Customer concerns stop at the door of the marketing function. Top management in most companies has not learned to look at the factory as a marketing weapon.

4. *Ideas are brought into a company by gatekeepers.* The young, dynamic, and innovative plant managers who are potential gatekeepers usually do not have the hierarchical clout that is required to push revolutionary ideas all the way to the top. The changes that these managers succeed in implementing tend to be cosmetic in nature, since profound cultural and philosophical change must be sustained by top management.

Blocking-out takes place because the corporate culture and value system, structural rigidities in the organization, internally focused production, absence of strategic focus in manufacturing, the low organizational status of production, and a production system that is driven by a myopic and narrow concept of efficiency erect a wall between the corporation and its environment that is tough to penetrate. Ideas do not flow freely into the company from the outside. The few ideas that manage to penetrate the existing organizational barriers take time to bear fruit because there is not a fertile ground for incubating and nurturing them. Figure 2–6 shows the blocking-out process in schematic form.

The mechanisms for eliminating blocking-out must eliminate structural rigidities, open up the organization and encourage, even promote, experimentation. Figure 2–7 summarizes the major points:

1. The walls of the organization must be softened up. The softening-up process is started and sustained by:
   - Organizational values that encourage experimentation, innovation, entrepreneurship
   - A fluid organizational structure
   - A market and strategy-driven production system that is deeply customer oriented

2. There must be robust gatekeepers that bring ideas in and assure insemination. Robustness is a function of hierarchical level, so organizational processes and values must facilitate top management involvement in manufacturing. Extensive training sessions and plant tours that are targeted at the top management group aid greatly in this endeavor.

FIGURE 2-7 **Eliminating Blocking-Out**

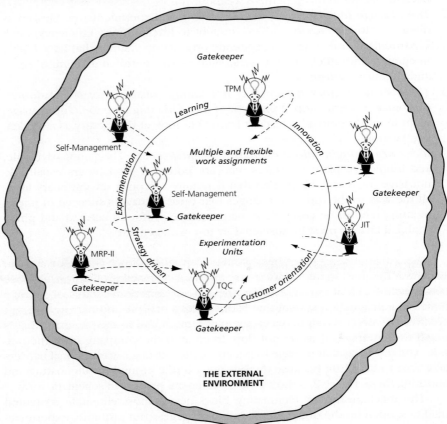

3. Internal fertilization must take place. Fertilization is brought about by intensive exchange of ideas on the inside. Extensive use of the team approach, cross-functional promotion, and multiple and flexible work assignments all increase the chance that fertilization will take place.

4. There must exist internal incubators where ideas can be grown to gestation. These incubators are nothing but organizational units or productive segments where ideas can be tested. The more such units exist, the more improvement projects that will be started and executed, and the greater the chance that some of these projects will take root.

In a very real sense, the dynamic and constantly improving manufacturing organization must open itself to the customer and to its external environment. It must be quick to adopt new ideas and concepts from the outside and must have the corporate humility that is essential to learning. It must identify, encourage, and promote managers who have a broad organizational and environmental perspective and who continually challenge the status quo.

ORGANIZATIONAL LEARNING

Continuous improvement is the result of constant learning. Companies, like biological species, must adapt to and learn to deal with the new challenges that come from their environments. Companies in competitive markets must always learn in order to survive and grow. The astute managers in sectors where competition is practically non-existent—regulated monopolies, para-public corporations in Canada and municipal (city) governments—find ways to entice their organizations to learn. Modern corporations have to learn faster because intense, global competition has quickened the pace of innovation and change. Organizational learning is the ability of a company to improve the core competitive skills that it has already acquired, to add to the core, and to delete skills that are dysfunctional. This is much more than individual learning. Individuals can learn, but that does not mean that the whole organization has learned as a result. The organizational collectivity itself must learn. Organizational learning must therefore involve not only the learning of skills by individual members, but also the ability to improve coordination and cooperation and to influence and pass skills and ideas on to others. The smartest organizations are not necessarily composed of the brightest and the best, if they are not able to cooperate with and to mutually influence each other. Similarly, a corporation composed of average people could exhibit high levels of learning if these individuals cooperate with each other and share their expertise. Four oarsmen preparing for a race would not generally have equal skills. One of them could row 25 percent faster than the others, but if he rows at his speed and ignores the other three, the team will lose. For the team to win, the best oarsman must cooperate with the other three, coordinate his efforts with theirs, learn to wait for them to catch up to his speed, and coach them to his level.

Managers can develop objective bases for judging whether organizational learning is taking place. Performance measures for monitoring all significant organizational activities and at all hierarchical levels should show year-by-year, even month-by-month, improvement. The learning curve or manufacturing progress function for new products and processes should show dramatic reductions in per unit cost or time that are at least comparable to industry experience. A company can use benchmarking to evaluate whether it lags, equals, or surpasses competitor firms in any significant activity.

The learning organization is designed. Companies that attain high levels of learning implement most of the following ten actions.

1. Build and nurture an environment where learning is valued. Train, promote, and reward people who demonstrate eagerness to learn.

2. Develop a solid, corporatewide mentor program.
3. Encourage experimentation and the testing of new ideas.
4. Create and support gatekeepers throughout the organization.
5. Make frequent and intensive visits of supplier, customer, and competitor facilities.
6. Benchmark excellent organizations, regardless of their sector of activity.
7. Create high aspirations. Constantly create new challenges.
8. Invest in innovation.
9. Forge partnerships with suppliers and alliances, joint ventures, and cooperative agreements with excellent competitors.
10. Enter into cooperative agreements with universities and other knowledge generating institutions.

Conclusion

Manufacturing excellence is honed out of an organizational philosophy, a corporate culture and value system, that makes the customer and customer satisfaction the central preoccupation. The value system must also encourage continuous improvement, search for perfection, experimentation, innovation and the search for superior quality. The production system in a world-class manufacturing organization is deeply conscious of the customer and is driven by the market and competitive strategy. This means that production must be open to the competitive forces that are shaping the market and the corporation must provide an environment where concepts from the outside will easily penetrate the organization, and will find a fertile setting where incubation can take place. Because people bring ideas and experiment with them, the dynamic manufacturing organization pays attention to people and taps their talent and creative potential. People are the agents of strategic change and continuous improvement. Any organization that does not motivate its members to excellence and fails in using them as creative, learning beings, will never achieve excellence. The core concepts in manufacturing excellence place top management at the center of the process. Only top management can effect the dramatic philosophical and cultural changes that are required if a company is to have a dynamic, continuously improving manufacturing organization. And only top management can nurture, refine, and deeply embed these values over a sustained period. Companies wallow in mediocrity because top management has failed to put in place the few core values that will drive them to continuously search for perfection.

Case for Discussion

EUROPEAN MASS TRANSIT INTERNATIONAL (EMTI)

The Advanced Manufacturing Projects team of EMTI had just presented its progress report on the World-Class Manufacturing project to top management.

The team had been formed one year ago and given the mandate to oversee the implementation of proven, modern concepts and approaches to managing production in EMTI's Small Equipment Division, the first phase of which was the application of JIT manufacturing. After one year of actively pushing and steering the introduction of JIT principles and techniques, the results were considered significant enough to warrant serious attention at the top management level. Set-up times had decreased from an average of 4.5 hours prior to the JIT project to 1.0 hour and work-in-process inventory had shrunk from $6.0 million to $0.84 million. Manufacturing lead times had gone from an average of 12 weeks to barely 10 weeks and on-time deliveries had increased from 78 percent to 92 percent. Moreover, the factory had surplus floor space of 25 percent from a state of congestion only one year earlier, even though demand had grown by 3 percent.

The Company, Its Culture and Strategy

EMTI was a large diversified transportation equipment company with annual sales of approximately $1.3 billion in 1988. Started by a group of inventors more than 30 years ago, the company had grown to become an international corporation with manufacturing operations in the United States, Canada, Europe, and South America. The Company was organized into six divisions, Bus Manufacturing, Small Aircraft, Special Aircraft, Mass Transit Equipment, Small Equipment Manufacturing, and Transportation Engineering and Consulting, with annual sales of $95 million, $320 million, $223 million, $580 million, $70 million, and $25 million, respectively. The Small Equipment Division manufactured small snow removal equipment used mainly by municipal governments and ski slope operators. Up until 1978, the company concentrated on the design and manufacturing of mass transit systems and snow removal equipment and had built a solid international reputation in these markets as a high-quality, innovative designer and producer of some of the best equipment available in the world. Sales grew very slowly during the last half of the 1970s due to cuts in spending by governments that were strapped with very high deficits and there was no prospect for improvement in the 1980s and 1990s. So although the company had shied away from diversifying outside of its traditional markets, it decided that diversification was necessary to maintain growth and profitability and to achieve its ambition as a major global corporation.

In 1985, the company diversified into aircraft manufacturing with the acquisition of a manufacturer of small jet aircraft that could be used either as a corporate jet or by major airline companies to service regional or feeder routes. Two years later, the company deepened its involvement in the aerospace industry when it acquired a manufacturer of specialty aircraft with annual sales of $180 million. Although EMTI had one of the largest pools of engineers in its industry, many observers and some members of the top management group doubted that the company could successfully enter a market that was so different from the company's traditional area of expertise. Despite these concerns and a very depressed aerospace market in the latter half of the 1980s, the company still managed to achieve modest sales growth between 1985 and 1988.

The entry into aerospace represented the most radical strategic and diversification move in the company's history. Civilian aircraft are among the most complex products to design, manufacture, and test, requiring the development, coordination, and deployment of highly diverse, first-rate, and innovative teams of engineers and technical people. All aircraft parts were designed and produced to rigid quality specifications and product testing and certification was severely controlled by the International Civil Aviation Organization with headquarters in Montreal, Canada.

EMTI had built a reputation as a hard-nosed, engineering-oriented, entrepreneurial company that was driven hard from the top. According to a senior vice-president,

> You cannot survive in this company if you do not have tremendous capacity to work hard, tolerate uncertainty and ambiguity, and be comfortable with the relentless pursuit of excellence. We are driven hard, not by decree from the top, but by example. Everyone here knows that top management asks nothing of us that they do not impose on themselves. We work hard, but the company makes it enjoyable by the monetary and nonmonetary rewards that we reap. You are encouraged to take risk and when it pays off you get full recognition for your efforts.

The company's entry into aerospace and transportation consulting exemplified its capacity to make bold entrepreneurial moves and succeed. The entry into aerospace came as a result of a decision by the former government owners of the aircraft division to privatize state-owned companies in an effort to reduce government intervention and a crushing deficit. EMTI jumped in with a ridiculously low bid on the assumption that very few companies would want to buy a money-losing aircraft manufacturer in a depressed market. The bet paid off, and EMTI acquired the aerospace division at less than the book value of the assets and government loan guarantees that amounted to 95 percent of the purchase price. The company's acquisition of the specialty aircraft manufacturer was done under similar and even more favorable conditions.

Top management liked to stress that the company had a unique culture which was commonly called the "EMTI way." When pressed to describe the EMTI way of doing business and its uniqueness, the vice-president of the small equipment division responded:

> First, we operate on the basis that every division or activity must be very profitable. We need profits to attract capital and maintain the confidence of our employees, suppliers, customers, and shareholders. That is why we

value change and innovation. Our managers must show a willingness to take calculated risks and to make bold moves. When we fail, we say, "win some, lose some." Second, we believe that in a fast changing market, time is critical, so we build structures that reduce delays. We cut red tape and push decision making close to where it will be implemented. At EMTI, we thoroughly despise bureaucracy and that is why we have broad divisional autonomy. At the same time, autonomous divisions readily cooperate with each other on major projects. We train all managers to set ambitious deadlines and to work so as never to miss them. That means we must value people, treat them fairly, and promote the competent. We want loyal employees who can take the heat and still not be discontent. Their sense of belonging must be so strong as to help them through the periodic failures. Third, our employees must be open and willing to learn. We give them every opportunity to train themselves thoroughly in their field of expertise or in what they think are emerging new areas. Finally, we do not compromise on quality, and that applies also to the quality of employees' expertise. We make the resources available and every employee is expected to perform to very high standards. We tolerate no excuse for mediocrity. And finally, we have the ambition to be a major global company and we are working hard to achieve that goal. It fits nicely with all the basic objectives that drive us.

That is the best way I can summarize the EMTI way, as it has influenced me over the years.

The Small Equipment Division (SED)

SED produced one of the core line of products on which EMTI built its reputation. In the early days of the company, SED accounted for 60 percent of sales and held a 35 percent share of the world market for small snow removal equipment. SED was one of EMTIs least integrated divisions with annual purchased parts of only $10 million. However, over the last 10 years, the division buckled under the strain of international competition, particularly from Canadian and Japanese manufacturers, and suffered a catastrophic erosion in market share from 35 percent to 15 percent of the market by the end of 1987. Gross profit margins shrunk from 42 percent of sales in 1980 to barely 25 percent in 1987. That same year, the division incurred a loss of $4.5 million on sales of $61 million.

In keeping with EMTI's long-standing philosophy of quickly abandoning unprofitable products and businesses, top management immediately served notice that it would get out of the market either partially or totally if the division did not become profitable within two years. Shortly after the announcement, the vice-president of the division took early retirement and John Mattingly was named to replace him.

Turnaround Initiatives

After extensive discussions with parent company top management, John was convinced that there was a strong desire not to abandon a traditional market of EMTI without putting up a fight. Top management thought that to buckle quickly under competitive pressure would send the wrong signal to competitors in the company's other markets that the company has little staying power. However, management was not willing to invest in the long-term viability of SED except if it had reasonable assurance that the division could be returned to a profitable, attractive position in the market. With the knowledge that he was not simply a caretaker for the smooth interment of the division, John created a committee headed by himself to evaluate the division's competitive potential and to come up with actions that could save it. In November 1987, the committee documented its findings and recommendations in a report entitled "The Manufacturing Rejuvenation Program." According to the report:

> The erosion of market share and the devastating consequences on SED's profitability derive from three related factors. First, over the last 10 years the division's product line has lagged behind its more aggressive and emergent competitors in terms of innovativeness, design improvement, and robustness. Customers were readily able to confirm that. Second, while our wages are comparable to those of our major competitors, our productivity has not improved as fast. We relied on our market position and quality reputation to pass these costs on to our customers, but as our competitors improved their quality our customers could perceive no difference in the performance of our products versus those of our competitors and were increasingly unwilling to pay us a price premium. We now have a 10 percent price disadvantage in the market. Third, we were not able to offer customers any better service that could compensate for our price disadvantage, and the competition is doing better than us in many ways. Our lead times are typically 10 to 12 weeks versus the 6 to 8 weeks quoted by our two major competitors. Finally, we have a much higher level of defects, twice as much inventory and 40 percent more space per unit of capacity than the best companies against whom we compete in this market.

The committee recommended an immediate increase in the level of R&D from 3 percent to 6 percent of sales and to invest $2.0 million to increase the level of automation over the next five years. Automation alone was expected to increase productivity by 5 percent per year. Because these projects were expected to generate benefits over the long run, the committee also recommended that the division invest heavily in the implementation of JIT manufacturing over the next three years. Because of the perceived impact of JIT on the fortunes of SED and the compressed time frame that was involved, its implementation would be spearheaded by a subcommittee headed by John Mattingly himself. It was estimated that the JIT project would reduce overall costs by 8 percent per year. In defining the JIT project, the subcommittee decided to place immediate emphasis on the radical reduction of set-up times, substantial decreases in inventories, particularly work-in-process inventory, workflow reorganization to cut factory space by 35 percent, a substantial reduction in manufacturing cycle, and continuous improvement teams at all levels.

Some members of divisional top management thought that the JIT project was too ambitious and represented a radical departure from the way the division was traditionally operated, while the majority, including John Mattingly, thought that JIT, as they understood it, represented nothing new for SED. The latter group thought that all the basic philosophies that supported JIT were already part of the EMTI way and that only the tools and techniques of JIT were new to SED.

In December 1987, the JIT project was formally launched. Within one year, the results had surpassed even the ambitious forecasts of the JIT implementation subcommittee. John decided to meet top corporate management to report on the division's progress to date because he was confident that time would show that SED had essentially achieved a lasting turnaround in its competitive position.

Discussion Questions

1. Describe and evaluate EMTI's competitive strategy.
2. What is meant by the EMTI way of doing business? What are its advantages and disadvantages? How does the EMTI way compare with the basic culture and values of today's highly successful companies?
3. Does the fact that SED has been losing market share and has been unprofitable for some time reveal anything about the EMTI philosophy? What challenges will top management be facing over the next few years?
4. Is divisional top management correct in asserting that JIT represents nothing fundamentally new to EMTI?
5. What is your evaluation of the success of the JIT project to date? What factors explain the results observed?
6. What should be the role of manufacturing in turning the SED division around?

References

"America's Best Managed Factories," *Fortune*, May 28, 1984.

Avishai, Bernard, and William Taylor, "Customers Drive a Technology-Driven Company," An interview with George Fisher, *Harvard Business Review*, November–December 1989.

Clark, Kim B., "What Strategy Can Do for Technology," *Harvard Business Review*, November–December 1989.

Curran, John J., "Companies That Rob the Future," *Fortune,* July 4, 1988.

Drucker, Peter F., *Innovation and Entrepreneurship,* New York: Harper and Row, 1985.

Feigenbaum, Armand, "Quality: The Strategic Business Imperative," *Quality Progress,* February 1986.

Gomory, Ralph E. "From the 'Ladder of Science' to 'The Product Development Cycle'," *Harvard Business Review,* November–December 1989.

Haas, Elizabeth, "Breakthrough Manufacturing," *Harvard Business Review,* March–April 1987.

Jaikumar, Ramchandran, "Postindustrial Manufacturing," *Harvard Business Review,,* November–December 1986.

Kets de Vries, Manfred F. R., "The Dark Side of Entrepreneurship," *Harvard Business Review,* November–December 1985.

Moser, Penny, "The McDonald's Mystique," *Fortune,* July 4, 1988.

Ramo, Simon, "National Security and Our Technology Edge," *Harvard Business Review,* November–December 1989.

Schonberger, Richard J., "Frugal Manufacturing," *Harvard Business Review,* September–October 1987.

Sellers, Patricia, "How King Kellogg Beat the Blahs," *Fortune,* August 29, 1988.

Stevenson, Howard H., "The Heart of Entrepreneurship," *Harvard Business Review,* March–April 1985.

Takeuchi, Hirotaka, and Ikujiro Nonaka, "The New Product Development Game," *Harvard Business Review,* January–February 1986.

Wheelwright, Steven C., and Robert H. Hayes, "Competing through Manufacturing," *Harvard Business Review,* January–February 1985.

Strategic Positioning for Superior Manufacturing Performance: The Manufacturing Mission

$\mathbf{A}$ few underlying forces are constantly at work changing the markets in which companies do business. All these forces operate to change and regulate the competitive situation. Increasing globalization is the dominant and powerful reality that every company must face. As markets become more global, competition increases in intensity, scope, and unpredictability, thus forcing the world's leading companies to sharpen their competitive skills. Top management of today's manufacturing companies must learn to deal effectively with competition. A company is created to survive, grow, and flourish as a going concern, which means that it must learn to be an effective competitor in the market place. Survival and growth are competition-bred concepts which convey the idea that there is a never ending battle for scarce resources. Competition and the threat of it force companies to exert themselves to compete in order to survive. A company must always earn the right to exist and to be selected to deploy scarce societal resources by being an effective competitor in a reasonably free and open marketplace. The rules of survival are defined and put in place by insidious forces unleashed by competition.

The literature on competitive strategy generally accepts the idea that a company that has an overwhelming position in a market can influence the rules of competition in its favor. Our view is that this is a misleading notion, since actions undertaken by any one company to influence the rules of competition in its favor are either nullified or legitimized by the very competitive forces that these actions are designed to shape. When the top management of a dominant company implements a competitive strategy that aims to influence or change the direction of market evolution, it is merely signaling that it has understood better than others where the market is inevitably headed. A company cannot change the rules of competition except in a way, and to an extent, permitted by the competitive forces actually or potentially at work. No one company, no matter how large or powerful, can take a market where it cannot or will not go. Companies are obligated to bow to the rules of survival and growth as dictated by the market or else pay a very high price, at least in the long run.

The most direct consequence of this is that corporate performance, in general, and manufacturing performance, in particular, are regulated by the fundamental competitive forces that are at work in the market. A company succeeds or fails, flourishes or declines, depending on how well it responds to and performs the requirements imposed by competition. The ability to design, structure, plan, control, and operate the manufacturing system so that it contributes significantly to the company's capability as an effective competitor is what sets the leading manufacturing companies of the world apart from the rest. Superior manufacturing performance hinges on the ability of top corporate management to mold the production function so that it responds effectively to and performs to the requirements imposed by competitive forces. Manufacturing excellence is nothing more and nothing less than the ability to deploy the production function as part of the corporate competitive arsenal. An industrial corporation cannot hope to attain world-class excellence and to survive and grow in the increasingly more difficult competitive environment that has been forged out of galloping globalization, unless manufacturing is made into a competitive weapon. The manufacturing function needs to be imbued with competitive mission and strategic purpose because it is a major agent for implementing and executing corporate competitive strategy. A production function that has not been imbued with competitive spirit and a very strong desire to respond to competitive forces, is nothing but moribund because no part of an organization can be driven to excellence unless competitive preoccupations have permeated its design, structure, and management processes.

Manufacturing excellence is forged out of a strong desire to compete effectively. Competition and the need to respond to it impel a corporation to pursue superior manufacturing performance. When the markets of the world open up, trade and nontrade barriers tumble down and consumers become more knowledgeable and demanding, then survival of the fittest becomes a day-to-day management reality. The fittest, in the world of manufacturing, are those few companies that achieve superior performance on quality, cost, delivery, and flexibility and have the versatility to keep performance at a superior level by constant improvement. Competitive strength or superiority and continuous improvement along key competitive dimensions go hand-in-hand. There is no conflict, not even neutrality, between continuous improvement as a world-class manufacturing concept and top management's responsibility for maintaining and enhancing the company's strategic integrity. In order to become a credible competitor in its market, a company must continuously improve its performance on the key competitive variables of cost, quality, and flexibility. Once it has achieved relative competitive superiority, a company must continuously improve so as to maintain its relatively superior position. A superior performer that fails to continuously improve its manufacturing performance will inevitably be displaced by other competitors that are better able to respond to the need to improve as dictated by the market. As a manufacturing management concept, continuous improvement is not another top management trap. Instead, it is the most basic requirement imposed by overpowering competitive forces. Where there is competition, there must be continuous improvement of manufacturing operations if a company is to survive and grow. The more intense the competition, the more persistent and significant is the improvement dictated by the market, and therefore, the quicker a company that fails to improve can lose its relative market position. When viewed from this perspective, continuous improvement is the most basic competitive requirement imposed on a company by competition.

CORPORATE STRATEGY AND MANUFACTURING PERFORMANCE

Corporate Strategy: The Fundamental Concepts

All companies, except those that are on a path to oblivion, must react to the competitive forces that are shaping and directing their markets. The struggle to survive and grow is paced by the actions that a company implements so as to respond to competitive threats or opportunities. Competition demands a corporate response and a nonresponse is in fact a very basic but dangerous reaction to the forces shaping the market. All it takes for a company to disappear from the market is for management to adopt a laissez-faire attitude toward actual or potential competition. A company's health and top management's confidence in its competitive position are measured by how vigorously the company responds to competition. The corporation's response as revealed by the actions formulated and implemented by top management is always based on an understanding, accurate or erroneous, of the direction and requirements of competition.

Top management is totally responsible for the health of the enterprise, its capacity to survive, grow, and flourish in its market. Management has complete responsibility for steering the company through the competitive jungle and to carve out an attractive place for it in the competitive arena. Management cannot eliminate competition, as we have seen. Top management's role is to create the wherewithal that will enable the company to survive and grow, despite the constant threat of competition, or better still, to thrive because of it. Managerial leadership must imbue the enterprise with competitive spirit so that the company will thrive on competition. Top management must provide the leadership and cultural framework that will bring the whole organization to view market competition as an opportunity. Sensitivity to and accurate understanding of competitive forces can be used to create the push for excellence and to challenge the company's capabilities. The point must be driven home that competition means survival of the fittest, thus creating the impetus for pursuing continuous improvement. It is extremely difficult for the chief executive officer to motivate an organization to excel in an environment where there is no competition. The large-scale inefficiencies of government bureaucracies and economic systems based on Marxist-Leninist philosophy can be traced directly to the fact that they are not held accountable to competitive forces.

Competition and its fundamental rule that only the fittest will survive force companies to seek competitive advantage. A company has a competitive advantage if it can, on balance, meet customer requirements as well as or better than other effective competitors in the market. The market compensates those companies that have competitive advantage. The struggle for survival in a competitive market hinges on the need to create better value for customers, thereby enjoying a competitive advantage. Companies survive and grow only to the extent that they can exploit or rely on some competitive advantage to create more value for their customers than their competitors can or are willing to do. This idea of competitive advantage forms the basis for defining corporate strategy and its key supporting concepts.

Competitive strategy is the process and the means by which a company creates a competitive advantage in its market. Strategy is a rational, planned response to competitive forces or the set of key management decisions that are designed to carve a favorable position in the marketplace. The process by which a company tries to maintain, enhance or entrench its market position relative to other competitors and the broad actions to implement critical management decisions that aim to do so, is the company's competitive strategy. In that sense, strategy is the deliberate effort, actions, and resource allocation that underlie a company's response to competition or the threat of competition. The need for strategy arises because there is competition and because a nonresponse, if it persists, will inevitably lead to the firm's disappearance as a viable, effective competitor. Survival is bred by competition and strategy is born out of top management's responsibility to formulate and implement actions that have the greatest potential to assure the firm's capability to survive, grow, and flourish in a competitive environment.

The search for competitive advantage is the raison d'etre of competitive strategy. Because strategy charts a long-run course for the company's survival and growth, the cultivation of competitive advantage must also be viewed as a process that takes place over the long run. Strategy changes over time in response to unexpected events, but each short-run change is an attempt to realign the basic strategy for the long run. No matter how frequent the short-term perturbations in the competitive environment, corporate strategy can only be based on management's expectations of how the market is likely to evolve over the long run. It cannot be otherwise because the critical decisions and actions that implement competitive strategy require radical shifts in resource allocation for product and process development, plant expansion, and the development of new competitive skill clusters, to name only a few. Strategy aims to implement the company's mission vis-à-vis the market. The concept of mission has the underlying connotation that the company is progressively, painstakingly, and persistently executing and pursuing a long-term objective.

Competitive advantage, then, must be sustainable for it to be any advantage at all. This rules out all advantages that derive from pure luck, created by short-term, unexpected market disturbances. Such advantages are fleeting and since they do not derive from a deliberately executed strategy, credible competitors who did not benefit from the temporary market situation are able to react quickly to nullify the disadvantage they suffered. The 1973 Arab oil embargo and the escalation in the price of gasoline gave Renault of France a temporary, fortuitous advantage in the market for small cars. However, the competitive reaction was swift and Renault reaped no permanent benefit from the short-term crisis. By contrast, the Japanese car manufacturers were already executing a strategy based on the mass production of small, high-quality cars. Their advantage derived from organizational capabilities that were developed over many years. They could sustain their advantage in the world market for small cars, because it came from technical, management, and production skills that were created and nurtured by judiciously chosen and executed strategic decisions. For example, Mazda (Toyo Kogyo) suffered debilitating decline in market share and profitability due to changes in the automobile market triggered by the 1973 oil crisis. The company's line of cars was based on the rotary engine which made them both fuel inefficient and environmentally undesirable. Moreover, Mazda was strapped with a very inefficient, integrated production system that was unable to produce cars cheaply. Productivity at Toyota was three times as high as that at Mazda while other measures of production efficiency told a similar story. Work-in-process inventory turns at Mazda were 17 compared with 150 for Toyota. The company did not have the capability to produce small, fuel-efficient, low-cost, high-quality cars which was precisely what the market was demanding. Every indication was that there was a fundamental shift in the market which would continue in the long run. Because some leading Japanese companies such as Toyota, Nissan, and Honda had the ability to produce what the market demanded, the new customer expectations were being legitimized and entrenched by the fact that a few companies were able to meet and even surpass their expectations. Despite the fact that some managers believed that customers were being too demanding and unreasonable, the competitive reaction and subsequent developments in the market proved that the customer was right and entirely reasonable. The Japanese share of the world car market was increasing steadily.

However, Mazda could not capitalize on the increasing attractiveness of Japanese designed and built cars. On the contrary, the company was losing market share and resorted to price cutting just to maintain sales. But price cutting could not be sustained for long since the production system at Mazda was not designed and managed to give the company a favorable cost position in cars. The core motor technology around which the company designed its cars and the production system it used to build them did not have the inherent capability to produce small, high-quality, relatively low-cost, and fuel efficient cars. Mazda could improve delivered quality in the short run by intensifying inspection and eliminating defective parts and cars before they got to market, but this would in no way change the fuel efficiency rating, environmental impact, or the overall cost of its cars. Mazda's marketing tactic of cutting price to sell cars was not sustainable over the long run.

The company needed to create a new strategic position by deploying resources to build the capability to respond to the new competitive reality. Mazda's survival depended on its ability to redesign its product line and production system to create a sustainable competitive advantage in small cars. Beginning in the mid-1970s, the company began to design cars based on the conventional engine and it also implemented a new production system (NPS). NPS was essentially Mazda's version of the Toyota Production System with synchronized production, JIT, zero defects, short cycle manufacturing, pull production, total quality control, and small group improvement activities, to name the most important elements. These changes more than doubled productivity and reduced work-in-process inventories and defects dramatically. The goal of NPS was to create lasting manufacturing skills and know-how that would enable the company to produce fuel-efficient, high-quality, and relatively low-cost cars, as a matter of course. The new customer requirements were to be met by a normal, even if disciplined, exploitation of the production system. Once the company had achieved an acceptable competitive position, the strategic decisions then focused on building the capability that would enable it to keep and, if possible, improve its market position. Only then would the company's competitive advantage be sustainable. NPS was fully implemented by 1980 and the production skills that it cultivated have given Mazda a sustainable competitive advantage in its market. Strategic change was fully implemented when it designed the ability to meet market requirements into all the company's systems, processes, procedures, and organizational units, and when the ability to produce what the market required became the dominant managerial and operating skills and know-how. One major goal of strategic management is to identify the crucial skills that will permit a company to have sustainable competitive advantage and to marshal the resources for the development, nurturing, and refinement of the requisite skills.

Dimensions of Competitive Advantage

Competitive advantage comes from the ability to create better value for customers and to sustain superior performance over the long haul. The strategy formulation and implementation process seeks to cultivate competitive advantage as the only sound basis for establishing a defensible and sustainable competitive position in the market. A competitive position that does not exploit an inherent competitive advantage cannot be defended. If a company does not have the ability to create better value for customers, it can only participate in the market for as long as it takes for normal competitive forces to signal to its customers that there is better value elsewhere, or for a competitor to launch an attack on its niche. This is the reason why the cultivation of sustainable competitive advantage is so fundamental to strategic management.

Value for customers can be appraised along two critical market dimensions, cost and differentiation. Customers buy products either because the price is low compared with other similar products or because these products have unique attributes that are valuable to the customers. Price is a marketing variable, but everyone recognizes that a company's ability to offer a low price is totally determined by its cost position; otherwise it is sacrificing some financial returns in order to protect its market position. Uniqueness makes the product different, in some perceptibly significant way, to the customer. Companies can combine cost and differentiation positions which gives rise to a number of possible but unique strategic positions in any one market. Companies have to constantly reevaluate their competitive positions in response to market signals on the success or failure of their current strategy. The emphasis on cost and differentiation and the mechanisms by which advantage is sought shift repeatedly. These shifts represent efforts by companies to establish unique market positions on cost and differentiation that exploit their existing competitive skills.

Low Cost

Cost is always a factor in a customer's decision to buy a product or service, even if it is not explicitly taken into account. All other factors that influence the purchase decision are traded off against cost/price, because cost is one basic parameter in any reasonable effort to evaluate value. We have seen that the ability to create value for the customer is the basic factor that determines a company's market position. Value may be evaluated by very formal means such as value engineering or analysis or may be judged by experience or gut reactions. Whatever the means used or its sophistication, rational behavior by the customer, the crucial assumption upon which competition is based, requires that value be evaluated. One is unable to judge value without some notion or estimate of cost. In a competitive market situation, then, low overall cost becomes a powerful lever for attracting customers and carving out an acceptable market position.

Low cost comes from superior efficiency. Cost represents the monetary value of the resources consumed in producing a good or service. Efficiency measures how well the transformation activities that were undertaken to produce the good or service were organized, coordinated, planned, controlled, and otherwise managed. The motivation to increase productive efficiency is driven by the need to reduce cost. The relationship between cost and efficiency means that low cost can be attained and converted into competitive advantage, if the company achieves the following four conditions:

1. Perform all value-adding activities more efficiently than its rivals.
2. Perform front-end activities, such as research, development, and engineering, in such a way that they enhance the efficiency with which downstream activities are performed. Thus, engineering for simplicity of design and manufacturability and process foolproofing contribute to cost advantage because they enable procurement and production to be more efficient.
3. Link into efficient suppliers, thereby using them as a source of cost advantage.
4. Eliminate all useless or nonvalue-adding activities.

Traditionally, economies of scale and market share were seen as the major sources of cost advantage. However, it is now known that large scale is no guarantee that costs will be low, because scale increases complexity and bureaucracy, which are major sources of inefficiency. General Motors is the world's largest car manufacturer but is far from being the low-cost producer in its markets, even after quality or class differences have been adjusted. Historically, much emphasis has been put on labor substitution and labor efficiency as means of reducing overall cost. Today, however, labor accounts for no more than 10 percent of overall manufacturing cost in most North American corporations. The last two decades have also seen the emergence of a few newly industrialized countries, such as Taiwan, Hong Kong, Singapore, South Korea, and Brazil, that have overwhelming comparative advantage on labor cost. Consequently, labor cost reduction is no longer a viable strategy for North American companies for gaining an overall cost advantage.

Every activity performed by an industrial or commercial enterprise is potentially a source of cost advantage. The first line of attack in a strategy to reduce cost is to identify and eliminate all competitively useless activities, that is, those that add to cost without creating value for the customer. Wasteful activities should be easy to eliminate once they are identified and viewed as waste, because there should be little valid justification for continuing to perform them. Once useless activities are eliminated, the second line of attack in the pursuit of an overall cost advantage is to identify those activities that add more to cost than they add to value. An activity is competitively advantageous if it allows the company to recoup more than the cost generated by it. Cost reduction would search for alternative ways to perform such activities more efficiently while conserving the market or competitive impact. Finally, the search for an overall cost advantage will bring the company to improve the efficiency with which all competitively useful activities are performed. This is a never ending process that tests the company's capability to respond to competitive pressures to reduce costs over the long run.

Waste elimination and continuous improvement programs are foundation world-class manufacturing approaches for implementing competitive strategies that aim to create an overall cost advantage. For any given quality level, costs are higher than the minimum that existing technology makes possible, mainly due to waste. The actual cost is the true minimum cost plus waste. Rigorous waste elimination is a cost-reduction strategy that strikes at the heart of what management of an enterprise is all about. Management is concerned, in a very important way, with the efficient deployment and utilization of resources for making marketable products. According to Barnard, efficiency together with effectiveness in resource deployment are crucial objectives of the enterprise.[1] Waste elimination tries to bring the actual cost of a product or service down to its true minimum. This is why the core philosophies of the Toyota Production System and subsequent variations adopted by such world-class manufacturing companies as Canon, Nissan, and Mazda, have such enormous competitive impact. Because they exploit the relationship between waste elimination and cost reduction, they have made the drive to eliminate waste and to continuously improve, a strategic, top management responsibility.

Waste elimination and continuous improvement necessarily involve the factory in an important way. Programs to remove waste drive costs down without sacrificing the company's existing differentiation position. The most profitable and sustainable way to achieve cost leadership is to remove all waste. In fact, strategies that seek to reduce cost without focusing on improving companywide efficiency through waste removal are both hard to implement and impossible to sustain. Waste removal is the most natural cost reduction strategy. Continuous improvement programs, on the other hand, aim at protecting whatever cost advantage has been engendered by the waste removal effort. Continuous improvement programs implement the company's response to the competitive pressure to maintain overall cost superiority. Cost advantage sustainability is thus the result of waste removal and continuous improvement programs that have been implemented and are functioning effectively.

Differentiation

Some companies base their strategic position on their ability to make the product or service unique. The generic product function is essentially the same, but the product is designed to meet the peculiar requirements or wants of a particular group of customers. All companies try to offer a somewhat different product from their competitors, except where the product is a commodity that cannot be differentiated, or where the market will not pay a price that makes differentiation financially attractive. The normal competitive

---

[1]Chester Barnard, *The Functions of the Executive,* (Cambridge, Mass.: Harvard University Press, 1968).

process in a free market motivates firms to differentiate their product offerings, because by so doing they have a better chance to carve out a favorable position in the market. Entrepreneurial activity and competition are complementary phenomena. Entrepreneurship feeds on competition and vice versa. Entrepreneurial activity is definitely highest where competitive forces are given free reign. Entrepreneurs, whether they work within an established corporation or are involved in creating and launching new enterprises, always seek ways to satisfy market needs that are not being satisfied by existing product offerings. Differentiation naturally results from this dynamic.

There are numerous ways to differentiate a product or service and the degree to which products differ along any one market criterion can be very small. Were it not for market forces, there would be uncontrolled proliferation of product offerings. However, for differentiation to make competitive sense, the company must be able to charge a premium that more than offsets the cost of differentiation. When differentiation has been taken too far, the customer cannot rationally evaluate the difference between the new product offering and those already on the market. There is unwillingness to pay for value that one cannot judge, so the customer refuses to pay a premium. The company is forced to withdraw the new product offering or reduce the price, thereby losing the advantage from further differentiation. The market effectively dictates the acceptable level of differentiation.

Products could be differentiated on quality, features, service, lead time, pre-purchase information, after-sales service, aesthetics, and so on. Like low cost, all organizational activities are potential sources of differentiation. A product can also be differentiated by using parts and services from suppliers that have unique competitive skills. The challenge is to exploit all sources of differentiation, paying attention to those that have maximum market impact. The pay-off from differentiation is acceptable as long as the company recoups more than what it costs to achieve the additional level of differentiation. Consequently, low cost and differentiation, although they are alternative sources of competitive advantage, are also symbiotically related. A company that is driving overall cost down on a companywide basis will discover more and more ways to profitably differentiate its product offerings. A company may be forced to limit its market niche to customers that can buy 1,000 units or more of a product, because its changeover cost is $2,000 per changeover. However, a set-up reduction program could reduce the changeover cost to $200 per changeover, making it feasible to market a variation of the product to customers who require only 100 units. Low changeover cost can make it attractive to dovetail the product to a particular, hitherto unexploited, market segment.

Superior Competitive Competence

Competitive advantage is sustainable, therefore, only if it comes from competitive skills and know-how that have already been harnessed by the company.

These skills are lodged in the hard and systems technologies that have already been mastered by the company as well as the managerial and operating know-how already held by management and lower-level personnel. People know-how and craftsmanship are the foundation competitive skills, since they provide the organizational competence to refine, improve, or acquire completely new but necessary skills. Competitive skills create competitive advantage and are consequently the major contributor to sustainability. That point must not be forgotten: Competitive advantage or the absence of it is not a chance occurrence, but rather results from deliberate decisions to develop and nurture the know-how that can be exploited to meet market requirements. A company cannot adopt an offensive or even defensive market position unless its existing know-how gives it the capability to perform the market requirements better or as well as its rivals. In a very real sense, companies win or lose in the market depending on how much competitive know-how they have and how fast they can change or improve their relevant skills when the market changes. Strategic change, or the reinforcement of an existing strategic position, inescapably means that resources are deployed to create new competitive skills or to improve existing ones. Competitive strategy succeeds or fails depending on how well it identifies what skills are required to serve the market and how effectively it marshals the resources and management effort to develop and nurture the necessary skills.

Sustainability comes from superior competitive competence or the mastery of skills that give the company the ability to perform crucial market requirements as effectively as or better than any other company in the market. Firms face repeated attacks on their market position as a normal consequence of competition. Even a clearly dominant leader in a market will be challenged from time to time, and this is a healthy situation. A company which has a market position that goes unchallenged eventually falls asleep and becomes very vulnerable to competitive assault. A company will be able to ward off a challenge or an attack, only if it has competitive skills that are as good as or better than any other viable competitor. The company must also have the capability to keep improving its execution of the crucial market requirements. Ultimately, then, top management through the strategy formulation and implementation process, seeks to equip the company with superior competitive competence. Strategy implementation achieves its managerial purpose when the company has been given the vital skills and know-how to execute the crucial market requirements as well as or better than any other viable competitor, and as a matter of course. The perspective adopted here makes the development and refinement of superior competitive competence the key top management responsibility.[2]

---

[2]The literature on competitive strategy uses the concept of *distinctive competence* to refer to this idea. However, distinctive competence conveys the impression that the ability to perform a particular market requirement is unique to the company. In fact, competitive skills are almost always shared by other viable competitors. Companies with superior competence will all come to share in the market.

Superior competitive competence has the underlying connotation that the skills harnessed by the company must be dedicated to executing variables that are valued by the customer. The company can have many different skills but there must be a set that gives it the capability to effectively execute the crucial market requirements. Competitive advantage comes purely from market-relevant skills. It is the ability to execute activities that are valued by the customer which makes a company competitively attractive and that allows it to carve out an acceptable market position. For example, an aluminum manufacturer could be particularly good at controlling pollution making it attractive to environmentalists or government. But unless it has sufficient skills in producing aluminum that meets customer expectations along such valued criteria as cost, quality, and variety, then it cannot survive for long in the marketplace. Some skills are useful in satisfying interest groups other than customers in the political bargaining arena, and this contributes to the company's well-being. However, survival and growth are assured by superior competence to execute market-valued requirements. Competitive skills and know-how are task specific. One major challenge of the strategic management process is to accurately read the market and to match the creation of competitive know-how with the crucial success factors imposed by the market.

Companies without superior competitive competence are destined to disappear. Competitive forces and the law of the jungle operate to weed out the weakest companies first, that is, those having no sustainable competitive advantage. Average companies will earn acceptable return on investment and may even enjoy growth during periods of very favorable market conditions. For instance, the late 1970s witnessed an incredible surge in the demand for microcomputers, and demand outpaced supply for almost a decade. For a time it appeared that any company that could make a microcomputer, any microcomputer, would find a profitable market for it. Companies without superior competitive competence did quite well and even flourished. The law of the jungle eventually took over once competitive forces had worked their way through that microcomputer market. Today, only the strongest companies such as Apple, Compaq, and IBM survive in this market. Superior competitive competence endows a company with the ability to survive through the toughest phases of market evolution.

Strengths and Weaknesses and Strategic Choice

The classical approach to competitive positioning advocates that a company's strategic position should be based on its strengths and weaknesses relative to the crucial market requirements as compared with its major competitors. The reasoning is that the company's strategic position should exploit its competitive strengths while avoiding market requirements that are in areas where it is competitively weak. The logic is simple and is apparently foolproof; capitalize on areas of competitive strength and avoid areas of competitive weakness. However, it is both dangerous and indefensible. Strengths and weaknesses, as we have argued, are cultivated and nurtured by the strategic management process and do not result from chance occurrences. A company that has weaknesses on crucial market requirements is insensitive to the needs of its customers or does not have the managerial acumen to steer the company in new directions. In any case, it shows that top management did not perform one of its most important strategic responsibilities, that of equipping the firm with superior competitive competence. Therefore, a company that has a weakness on any crucial market requirement also has a market position that it cannot sustain. A weakness in an area that is valued by customers is an open invitation to credible competitors to launch an offensive assault on the company's market position.

The evaluation of strengths and weaknesses must be a never-ending, proactive process if it is to provide information that is valuable for strategically positioning the company. Corporations that are not continuously reinforcing and creating strengths invariably get into trouble in a competitive market. Strategic decisions that have high potential to eliminate competitive weaknesses take time to implement and bear fruit which explains why many attempts at turning a company around fail. By the time actions taken to redeploy resources and eliminate competitive weaknesses begin to produce the desired results, the company's market position has been irreparably damaged by competitive attacks. Competitive strategy has to continuously prevent weaknesses from appearing in the company's market position, thereby maintaining superior competitive competence.

Market Segmentation

A company will have a favorable market position if it can perform the crucial market requirements as well as or better than any other competitor. It will be able to do that only if it possesses superior competitive competence. Companies can build superior competitive competence by linking the development of competitive skills directly to the crucial market requirements. But to avoid dilution of organizational effort and waste of scarce resources, top management must be able to accurately define the market requirements, since the latter are used to orient and guide strategy formulation, analysis, and implementation. The more clearly the market requirements are understood and the more precisely they are defined, the more accurately they can be targeted by the strategic management process.

Conventional thinking is that the crucial market requirements or key success factors should be defined at the level of the industry or broad market. Industry analysis to isolate the key success factors is a fundamental building block of most strategy formulation and implementation frameworks.

However, the view taken here is that the industry or market at large is too broad in scope to allow meaningful and precise enough definitions of the key success factors to be executed by the company. An industry is usually composed of a plethora of mini-industries just as a market can be divided into numerous market segments. It is very unusual to find companies that compete in an entire industry or broad market. Those that do invariably become huge, inefficient behemoths that are vulnerable to persistent attack by smaller, more versatile, and market-focused competitors. General Motors, Exxon, U.S. Steel, and General Electric come closest to competing in all segments of their respective industries. They have also been fighting tough battles to retain their dominance over the last two decades, and by all indications they are losing.

Markets can and should be segmented. The bases for segmenting a market vary from one market to the next, but the essential thing to note is that segmentation tries to divide the market into homogeneous groups of customers that have very similar or identical requirements and that behave the same way when buying the product. An analysis of customer needs and an understanding of customer behavior are the raw materials that can be used to meaningfully segment the market. Herein lies the problem for strategically positioning a company. Most managers do not invest the time and resources that are required to intimately understand customer needs and the critical aspects of buyer behavior. Consequently, many attempts at segmentation result in very general and blurred segment definitions that are useless as far as strategy formulation and implementation are concerned.[3]

Segmentation provides crucially useful information for deciding on an appropriate and sustainable market position. It can be used to identify markets within a market, so that the company can identify the key success factors (KSFs) that are unique to each segment. Competitive skills can be tailored to each segment, resulting in increased specialization, better focus, and improved chances for developing superior competitive competence on a segment-by-segment basis. Otherwise, the company is constrained to adopt a broadly targeted strategy, using a shot gun approach to the market. Competitive weaknesses cannot be validly evaluated at the level of the broader market, since general marketwide strength may mask visceral weaknesses in the ability to serve particular market niches. General Motors may have overall strength in the automobile market, but it had a tough time cultivating an acceptable position in the small car segment. All focused strategies and their implementation by way of focused factories require accurate and rigorous market segmentation. A company that has correctly segmented its market can dovetail its competitive skills to the KSFs of particular segments and thus

---

[3]For elements of industry analysis, see Michael Porter, *Competitive Strategy* (New York: The Free Press, 1980), 34–46; M. Porter, *Competitive Advantage* (New York: The Free Press, 1990), ch. 1, 7, 8; Wickham Skinner, *Manufacturing: The Formidable Competitive Weapon* (New York: John Wiley and Sons, 1985), 53–68

avoid being all things to all people. A company may have weaknesses when the whole market is considered. However, these weaknesses could disappear when its competitive skills are compared to the KSFs of a given segment, giving the company competitive superiority for that segment.

Market segmentation shows how the product or service should be differentiated in order for it to satisfy the requirements or needs of each segment. Differentiation is also based on segmentation. As long as the market can be further segmented, new ways of differentiating the product will emerge. In fact, companies that are pursuing a differentiation strategy rely on their acumen in market and customer behavior analysis to discover new, poorly-served segments. They then design products, production systems, and marketing programs to market unique product offerings to the new segments. There is no way to discover unsatisfied or poorly-served niches in a market except by segmenting it accurately. Any market can be segmented and every product or service can be differentiated. KSFs have absolutely no meaning, except with respect to market segments. A strategic position is precarious if it is targeted at an entire market or industry. Strategy is best deployed at the level of market segments. There is no such thing as KSFs of the electronics or automobile or steel industry. If one tried to list the KSFs for these broadly-defined industries, the list would be so long as to be totally useless for formulating and implementing competitive strategy. IBM does not, it cannot, compete in the electronics industry, but it competes in the business machines segment of that industry. General Motors is in the car market, only to the extent that it has many strategic business units (SBUs) that are deploying different strategies in different segments. GM's market position is blurred by the fact that it has not kept its various SBUs distinct enough and clearly focused on key market segments. KSFs can be accurately defined only when they come from precise market segments. A firm cannot validly position itself in an industry, only in a market segment. Superior performance in manufacturing comes from choosing the right segment and designing and managing the production function to perform the KSFs of the chosen segment. It will be shown later how this is fundamental to achieving a superior performance, focused factory.

Generic Strategies[4]

Companies can position themselves in a market along two general dimensions—competitive advantage and competitive scope. As discussed previously, competitive advantage can come from either low cost or differentiation. Broadly-targeted strategies mean that the company competes in all or most market segments. With a narrowly-targeted strategy, a company chooses to

---

[4]Porter, *Competitive Advantage*, 11–26.

FIGURE 3–1 **Generic Strategies**

COMPETITIVE ADVANTAGE

	Low cost	Differentiation
Broad target	1. Cost leadership	2. Differentiation
Narrow target	3A. Cost focus	3B. Differentiation focus

COMPETITIVE SCOPE

compete in a few, carefully chosen market segments where it has a definite and sustainable advantage on cost or differentiation. The result is the four generic strategies shown in Figure 3–1. The "differentiation" strategy exists when a company markets a unique product in each of all or most segments of the market. A company deploying a "differentiation focus" strategy markets a unique product in each of a few segments of the market. Similarly, a "cost leadership" strategy implies that the company is the lowest cost producer in each of most or all segments of the market, while the "cost focus" strategy means that the company has the lowest cost position in a few chosen segments. The generic strategies summarize the range of strategic options that can be exercised by a company in a competitive market situation.

Both broadly- and narrowly-targeted strategies present unique implementation challenges. The broadly-targeted strategies are the toughest to implement successfully, since they call for the company to be the absolute leader in the whole market either on cost or on differentiation. This may be possible in relatively homogeneous, unfragmented industries like steel and petroleum. But it is impossible for any company to be the absolute cost or differentiation leaders in an industry like electronics. Generally speaking, nearly all companies are constrained to follow some kind of focus strategy, and this is particularly so for companies that are striving to be the leaders, whether on cost or differentiation, in their chosen market segments.

Companies that are deploying broadly-targeted strategies fail to achieve cost leadership or true differentiation in every segment of the market. Their market positions become blurred because although there may be a clearly defined strategy and unambiguous competitive intent, these companies are unable to fully execute their formal strategies in the market. The development of superior competitive competence in every market segment taxes the company's managerial and financial resources until competitive skills become thinly stretched. Companies are constrained by their ability to develop superior competitive competence, not only to choose the type of competitive advantage they will seek, but also the market segments in which they will compete. The generic strategies are the extreme strategic choices that can be exercised by a company. Companies would be following a differentiation strategy not because they are competing in most segments of the market, but when the number of segments they compete in seems to set them apart from the average competitor. Thus, Philips can be said to be implementing a differentiation strategy, even if the company is not competing in most segments of the electronics industry, while IBM is deploying a differentiation focus strategy.

Focused strategies epitomize the problem of strategic choice, since they are the culmination of management's attempt to weed out nonviable strategies. The evaluation of which strategies are not viable calls for very thorough knowledge of the market and sharp insight to pick a strategic position that matches the market requirements with the company's competitive advantage. All segments of the market must be accurately pinpointed and described and the KSFs of each must be accurately expressed; focused strategies establish the company in the right segment. Top management also needs to have complete knowledge of the company's sources of competitive advantage before these can be matched with each segment's KSFs to determine which niche gives the greatest potential for fit between competitive advantage and KSFs. In addition, management needs to be knowledgeable about the competitive advantage of other competitors before it can conclude that its advantage in a particular segment actually derives from superior competitive competence. Focused strategies precisely exploit competitive advantage that is limited in scope and must zero-in on the absolutely right market segment. Successful focusers are bound to cultivate superior skill in understanding the market, their own competitive capabilities and that of other viable competitors. Without these, the risk that the wrong segment or competitive position will be chosen is very high. These requirements place a high premium on market and competitive intelligence. Successful focusers stay very close to their markets and keep a keen eye on the competitive moves of their competitors.

Continuous Improvement, Market Constraints, and Strategic Choice

Companies usually have to choose among alternative strategic positions. Strategic options exist because markets are far from homogeneous, which gives rise to market niches that have different KSFs. Market segmentation leads to the conclusion that there are many ways to survive and prosper in any market. As long as there are segments or niches, there will be strategic positions that are more or less appropriate to each. Strategic choice is primarily dictated by market constraints. However, if a company could muster all the skills necessary to adequately serve each market segment, the need for strategic choice would disappear. But this is not the case. The viable strategic options that can be followed by a company are severely limited by three basic factors: (1) the company's superior competitive competence, (2) the nature of its competitive advantage that is produced by its competitive competence, and (3) its degree of competitive flexibility. Superior competitive competence and flexibility are intimately related. Flexibility refers to the range of KSFs that can be successfully executed by a company or the number of different market segments in which it can effectively compete, over an extended period. Evidently, a company is not flexible if it has only one superior competitive competence. Flexibility is directly related to the number of superior competitive competencies that the company has. Therefore, competitive flexibility results from creating different superior competitive competencies. We differentiate here between competitive and operating flexibility. The latter refers to capabilities such as quick changeovers, ability to produce a high variety of products, and the capability to respond to volume changes. Of course, operating flexibility also contributes greatly to strategic flexibility.

The relationships between continuous improvement and strategic choice are shown in Figure 3-2. The impetus to improve the company's ability to execute crucial market requirements comes from competition and the constraints imposed by the market itself. Without competition there is no imperative to improve. The continuous improvement program is the company's ongoing, progressive response to competitive market forces. Continuous improvement that is sustained for a prolonged period is the critical source of

FIGURE 3-2 **Continuous Improvement and Strategic Choice**

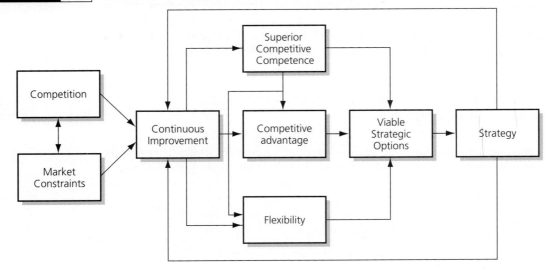

superior competitive competence, competitive advantage, and flexibility. Companies that keep improving all organizational activities will eventually come to have more than one superior competitive competence, which is what gives the flexibility to respond to varied competitive threats or to redeploy strategy. The viable strategic options open to a company are a function of superior competitive competence, competitive advantage, and flexibility. Companies with no superior competitive competence have few or no viable strategic options. These companies are left to choose among the poorest strategic alternatives available to competitors in the market, which guarantees that their competitive performance in terms of market share, growth, and profitability will be inferior.

Competitive strategy is what emerges when top management selects what it judges to be the best strategic option open to the company, and proceeds to implement it. Once deployed, strategy fuels and paces the continuous improvement program, placing the company in a perpetual, continuous improvement cycle, the key to sustaining superior performance in manufacturing. Top management, then, should formulate and implement strategy in such a way that it leads and facilitates the corporatewide drive to improve continuously. The point is that strategic management will be successful only to the extent that it provides a framework for and propels continuous improvement in manufacturing as well as in every other function of the business. The underlying thesis here is that the design of a continuously improving organization is a paramount strategic management responsibility. Continuous improvement is a mission to be vigorously pursued by the strategic management process. Too often, continuous improvement is dissociated from top management responsibilities and does not find a place or concrete expression in strategic plans. The crucial proposition put forward here is that continuous improvement is the medium through which superior competitive competence and competitive advantage are sought and perpetuated. The continuously improving organization begins and ends with corporate strategy.

The framework introduced in Figure 3-2 provides a fresh way to look at the cardinal principle in manufacturing excellence and how it relates to top strategic management. The achievement and maintenance of world-class manufacturing status involves systematically breaking the internal and external market and technological constraints that limit the viable strategic options open to a company. When most constraints have been broken or surmounted, the company has reached the ultimate in manufacturing excellence. A competitive position has been attained where the company can simultaneously follow all the major strategic avenues that are available in the market as a whole. All four generic strategies (Figure 3-1) become perfectly synthesized to form one single, overpowering competitive strategy. The company is the lowest cost producer and the most differentiated producer, which means that it is successfully deploying a large number of focused strategies. Such a company will be totally dominant in the broader market. It is the drive to achieve this ultimate strategic state which sustains the improvement effort and the search for competitive perfection. General Motors in the 1950s and 1960s came close to achieving that kind of competitive state. Toyota Motor Company is currently on the verge of achieving the competitive breakthrough that is envisaged here.

The ultimate competitive, strategic state, when it is achieved, is still temporary in nature. A company may have overwhelming competitive strengths to the extent that it comes to overpower its rivals. However, competitive strengths, no matter how overpowering it may be, cannot be permanent. Competitive market forces constantly operate to cause cracks to appear in a company's market position. Strengths become diminished and weaknesses are aggravated by improvement by other competitors. Competition works to make all companies work hard to earn the right to exist. This leads to a conclusion that can be sometimes very depressing to some managers—no corporation, no matter how large or powerful, can succeed in dominating its market over the long run, except if such a corporation is periodically redefined and reengineered by top management. Every major corporation will have to go through the process, sooner or later, of redefining itself and recreating the essence that made it great.

Every company, but particularly one that is very successful, must periodically redefine its market and business from scratch. It must evaluate and recreate the fundamental core technologies that it uses to serve its markets and must periodically remake, rejuvenate, change, or reanimate its foundation culture and values. Moreover, a successful company must periodically remake (reengineer) its entire manufacturing system—its fundamental manufacturing philosophies, systems, skills, and basic logic—for producing and delivering goods or services to its customers. And all successful corporations need to periodically reinvent ways to harness people and to define and create superior human resources. Competitive advantage has a strong propensity to evaporate when top management fails in its responsibility to periodically reengineer the corporation.

THE STRATEGIC MANAGEMENT OF PRODUCTION

Historically, top managers in North America and in the West generally attempted to implement strategic decisions on the assumption that manufacturing did not matter at all. The production function was seen to be at best neutral in the company's efforts to cultivate and defend an acceptable market position. Production was not seen as a function with strategic impact. The front line functions were thought to be marketing, first and foremost, finance, and sometimes research, development, and engineering (R/D/E). Production was cut out from the strategic management process, which resulted in a truncated approach to strategy formulation and implementation, as shown in

Production in the Corporate Strategy: The Truncated Approach

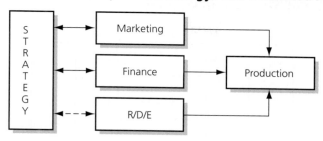

Figure 3–3. Production is not directly linked to the strategic core of the business, and it receives strategic signals and mandates indirectly from marketing, finance, and sometimes R/D/E, the functions which top management views as vital.

The fact that manufacturing is one step removed from the strategic core of the business has some severe consequences. The corporate strategy has lost the vital input of the function that accounts for the lion's share of corporate resources. Not only is the strategy formulation process impoverished, but there is also a strong possibility that manufacturing does not have the capability to execute the strategy. Many attempts at executing strategy fail because the manufacturing function has not been explicitly given the wherewithal to execute a clear strategic mandate. The truncated approach to strategy formulation and implementation usually means that manufacturing is responding to competitive demands that come not from top management, but from functions that have been traditionally viewed as strategic. These demands are often contradictory, which makes it impossible for production to be designed and managed consistently. Production lacks a clear strategic mandate that will give it the philosophical and authority base to make the necessary trade-offs among the conflicting demands of marketing, R/D/E, and finance.

In contrast, the leading manufacturing companies of the world are managing production with assumptions and philosophies that challenge the conventional approach. They have succeeded in completely integrating the manufacturing function and its peculiar demands and requirements into the strategic management process. They are successfully implementing their corporate strategies because they respect the quintessential principle that corporate strategy is executed, in a very important way, by the production function. Manufacturing is directly linked to corporate strategy and is managed as a prime strategic business function. Figure 3–4 shows the integrated approach used by the world's best manufacturing companies. All the business functions are exploited for competitive and strategic advantage.

FIGURE 3-4   **Production in the Corporate Strategy:**
The Integrated Approach to Strategy

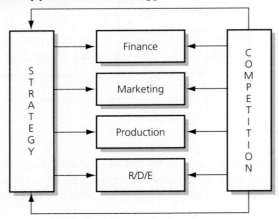

Some Fundamental Lessons

One can deduce six basic lessons from the way excellent companies manage production and link it with corporate strategy. These lessons provide the raw material for a framework for strategically managing production.

First lesson: The factors that give the world's best companies a competitive advantage in their markets are substantially based on aggressive, attentive, and systematic production management. Toyota, Canon, Sony, and Philips all have substantially production-driven competitive strategies.

Second lesson: A lasting advantage in the marketplace is cultivated on the basis of production and R/D/E. There are few, if any, circumstances where the marketing function alone can give a company enduring competitive advantage. Companies that stay close to the customer do so by paying attention to production.

Third lesson: The techniques and approaches that give a company decisive competitive advantage through its production system are simple and available to every company, whatever the cultural milieu. Total quality control (TQC), just-in-time (JIT), total productive maintenance (TPM), to name a few proven technologies, all emphasize perfect execution and mastery of basic management principles. The challenge is to place these technologies within the framework of long-term development of the manufacturing function.

Fourth lesson: The long-term and strategic development of the production function can only be done around a clear strategic mandate or manufacturing mission. The manufacturing mission must express the few driving concerns that are critically important to the company. It must be known and understood by all top functional managers.

Fifth lesson: The contribution of production to a company's competitive posture depends on the attention given to this function by top management. What characterizes management most in the world-class manufacturing companies is the attention given to production management and the devotion to manufacturing concerns. Top management is involved in manufacturing because it understands what makes the factory tick. When top management gets involved, manufacturing invariably performs its strategic mission.

In the world-class manufacturing companies in North America, Europe, and particularly Japan, people with a background in manufacturing are well represented in the top management group. The CEO in a typical Japanese manufacturing company more often comes from production than any other function, while in North America, company presidents are usually recruited from marketing and finance. When the CEO comes from manufacturing, production and its constraints and concerns are automatically integrated into the strategic management process. Top management must come to feel the heartbeat of manufacturing and to view it as a prime competitive weapon. Only then will they get involved in its ongoing management.

Sixth lesson: Where production is being managed for competitive advantage, so-called strategic decisions become completely intertwined with operating-level decisions. The distinction between strategy and operations becomes blurred or irrelevant. The operating actions are merely a phase or stage in the strategy formulation and implementation process.

Operations are naturally integrated into the strategic core. The very essence of operations is predicated upon the principle that production decisions execute strategic intentions. Companies that are at the leading edge of manufacturing excellence have liberated themselves from the notion that strategic change or the reinforcement of an attractive competitive position necessarily calls for radical, large-scale decisions that restructure the company from top to bottom or that acquire existing competitors. Upon close examination, most large-scale, revolutionary decisions do not change or reinforce a company's competitive position at all. Strategic leaps do take place, but they are infrequent. Instead, the world's best manufacturing companies depend on the cumulative effect of a large number of relatively small scale actions taken at the operating level to implement strategic change. Every action taken in operations is linked to strategy and made to contribute to the company's competitive position.

The new philosophy to the effect that operating decisions always have potential strategic impact is a revolutionary one. It changes the whole concept of strategy implementation as only involving broad decisions on backward or forward integration and general resource allocation. Strategy is also implemented by way of what appear to be mundane and small-scale actions. Thus, when Mazda took concrete steps to implement set-up reduction and small-group improvement teams, among others, it was implementing strategic change. The key is to make sure that all these small operating decisions have cumulative, competitive effects. This can only be done when they are all mission directed.

The idea that all production management activity must be executed to pursue a manufacturing mission is a powerful one. It argues that, like the corporation as a whole, the production function must be mission oriented, purposefully designed and managed. Furthermore, there must be a two-way link between corporate strategy and the manufacturing function. Corporate strategy determines manufacturing mission while the constraints, skills, and character of the production function must be taken into account when competitive strategy is being formulated and implemented. It becomes necessary, therefore, to explore all the significant ramifications of the concept of manufacturing mission.[5]

Manufacturing Mission: Defining the Concept

Market analyses and segmentation will have revealed the KSFs of each segment, while company analysis will have isolated superior competitive competence. The KSFs force the company to perform a few, customer-valued variables well, if it is to survive and grow. Manufacturing alone cannot execute all the KSFs. Some of these will be the responsibility of other strategic functions. The manufacturing mission is the set of key success factors of the company's market segment that are targeted by its strategy and delegated totally or substantially, to the production function. Figure 3–5 illustrates the concept. The market segment KSFs are distribution, quality, and delivery. Production has direct and substantial impact on the latter two, so they are the basis for formulating the manufacturing mission.

The manufacturing mission is the set of KSFs delegated to the production function. It represents what top management expects from manufacturing in terms of its strategic contribution. It specifies what production must do, not what it wishes to do, in order to be a competitive weapon. All decisions made in production relative to manufacturing system design, planning, control, and supervision must aim at accomplishing the manufacturing mission. As such, the mission is the principal driver of the production system and gives reason

---

[5]For more discussion on the role of operations in strategy formulation and implementation, see Skinner, *Manufacturing: The Formidable Competitive Weapon* (New York: John Wiley and Sons, 1985); S. C. Wheelwright, "Japan, Where Operations Are Really Strategic," *Harvard Business Review,* July–August 1981.

Defining Manufacturing Mission

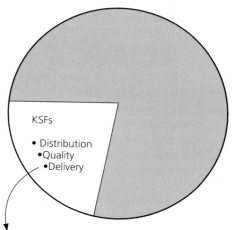

KSFs

• Distribution
•Quality
•Delivery

Manufacturing mission
• Achieve and maintain highest
  delivered quality consistent with price
• Achieve and maintain fastest and
  predictable delivery.

for existence to the factory. All world-class manufacturing companies have an explicit, formal manufacturing mission.

The concept of manufacturing mission has all the connotations of the religious and ideological meaning of mission. It expresses the idea that there are a few objectives whose accomplishment will be the dominant and continuous preoccupation of top manufacturing and corporate management. All production management activities and decisions should focus on the manufacturing mission. One major responsibility of the top production executive is to inculcate an accurate perception of the manufacturing mission in lower-level employees and to build a socialization process and organizational culture that indoctrinate all production employees in the manufacturing mission of the company.

One important consequence of deriving a market-based manufacturing mission is that corporate strategic changes necessarily require changes in the company's manufacturing mission. A strategic change does not become operational, unless it has been successfully deployed in the functions. It so happens that the manufacturing function is the toughest to redirect and reorient. Manufacturing policies and structure take more time to effectively change and implement than marketing or financial policies. Consequently, major strategic changes, to be realizable, must be placed within the time frame necessary to change the production system and to redeploy manufacturing resources.

The Role of Manufacturing Mission

In the way we have defined it, manufacturing mission is the key ingredient in the long-term orientation of the company's manufacturing function. The very concept of mission has the connotation of a long-term goal that will be systematically pursued by mobilizing all the available manufacturing resources. As a matter of principle, the concept of mission indicates objectives that can be achieved only in the long run. Although the basic manufacturing mission usually results in a series of short-term goals, these all derive from and should support the more enduring and critically important long-term objectives. Without a clear and explicit manufacturing mission, short-term decision making is not much more than operational firefighting. In other words, although short-term, operational goals and programs are an inescapable part of production management, they have more meaning and certainly make more sense, if they are placed within the framework of a manufacturing mission. That is, even the short-term programs implemented by the manufacturing function will be more consistent and coherent, if they reinforce the company's manufacturing mission.

It follows that the manufacturing mission is the strategic objective of manufacturing. It is that part of the company's strategic objective that has been delegated to the production function. In that sense, the manufacturing mission inexorably links production to the company's competitive strategy. By formulating manufacturing mission, top management is specifying explicitly how and to what extent, production is expected to support the company's approach to conquering the product market. At a different level, how well production executes the basic manufacturing mission is also a vital input in strategy formulation and implementation, since such performance may indicate how realistic strategy is, from the production point of view, or in what areas manufacturing competence needs to be improved.

Because it is the company's strategic manufacturing objective, the manufacturing mission is the major basis for evaluating the performance of production. How well the manufacturing function executes the basic elements of the mission is the best indication of how competently it is performing its strategic responsibility. The evaluation of manufacturing performance traditionally concentrates on short-term operating results to the detriment of sustainable, long-term goals. This partly derives from the absence of long-term objectives, in the first place. Without clear signals from top management, manufacturing executives have very little basis for orienting their activities with a long-term perspective and for marshaling resources toward the accomplishment of significant, sustainable results. The formulation and operationalization of a manufacturing mission constrains top production executives to think in terms of strategic performance.

Seen in this light, the manufacturing mission is the major input to the formulation and deployment of manufacturing policies and programs for continuous improvement. The manufacturing programs of a company should be designed and implemented to execute the manufacturing mission. A company's manufacturing policies and programs cover many decision-making areas, such as process technology choice, process R&D, TQC, JIT, and TPM. Without clearly stated long-term objectives, it is not likely that the decisions made by the typical top manufacturing manager would be consistent and coherent. With a manufacturing mission to guide decision making, manufacturing policies can have clear focus and managers can establish the right priorities. In cases where trade-offs have to be made—and it is clear that every major manufacturing decision will have to make some trade-off—the existence of a manufacturing mission helps managers in making the right ones.

The manufacturing mission can be looked at as the nexus between the company's competitive strategy and its manufacturing policies and programs. Programs and policies are chosen to build superior competitive competence so as to execute the manufacturing mission. The vital links are shown in Figure 3–6. According to the perspective adopted here, total quality control, just-in-time, total productive maintenance, self-management and the team concept, focused factories, cell manufacturing, and other world-class manufacturing concepts are practical ways to implement manufacturing mission. When manufacturing is managed strategically, these policies and programs—equipment and process technology, human resource management, quality control, production control and methods, procurement, production information system design, and production system structure—are all driven by the manufacturing mission. Efforts to implement JIT, TQC, TPM, and small group improvement teams (SGIT) are unlikely to succeed unless they emerge from a clearly-stated, strategy-derived mission. Manufacturing mission gives strategic and competitive meaning to all continuous improvement policies and programs. Otherwise, these programs are merely a hodgepodge of actions whose implementation will not survive beyond the initial interest associated with eye-catching acronyms such as TQC, JIT, TPM, and SGIT.

Specifying Manufacturing Mission Basic Principles

The analysis of the market and the company should culminate in a cogent and unambiguous statement of how the company should compete, from a production point of view. This is the idea of the specification of manufacturing mission, and it can be done on a formal or informal basis. In the latter case, there is no systematic effort by the top production executive to communicate the elements of the company's manufacturing mission to those executives that have responsibility for executing it. Subordinates form a perception of the critical aspects of the company's manufacturing strategy by interpreting the behavior of their superiors and peers and by observing the decision-making process over time. By the process of interaction and working together

FIGURE 3–6   **Corporate and Manufacturing Strategy and the Manufacturing Mission: The Vital Links**

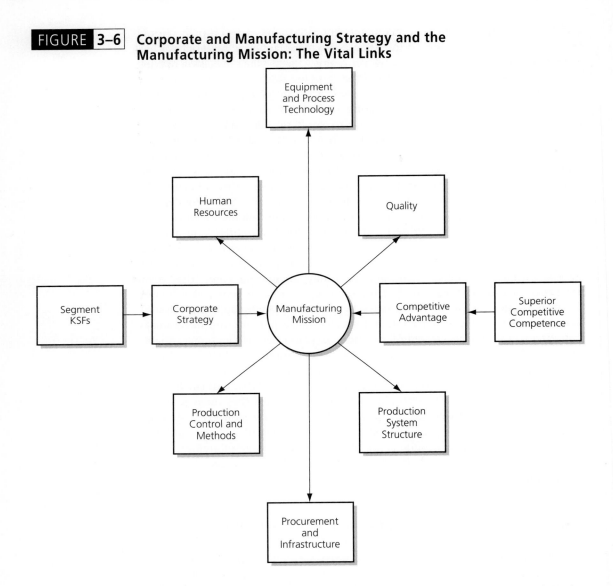

in groups, most managers come to understand and share values regarding the strategic issues confronting the company.

There are some inherent disadvantages to approaching specification and communication of manufacturing mission on an informal basis. First, the process of imbuing key managers with a sense of the company's manufacturing mission takes time and understanding evolves haphazardly. The manager is getting knowledge of the company's competitive priorities, piece by piece, and not necessarily at the opportune time. He or she has to wait long enough for a consistent pattern of behavior to evolve before developing any valid insight on the important aspects of production system design, management, and operation in the company. Moreover, there is no guarantee that the manager will have the right insight, since his or her interpretation of manufacturing management events, as they occur, is conditioned by past experience and individual preferences.

On the other hand, an informal specification of manufacturing mission has certain advantages. With no formal statement by which he or she can be bound, the manager feels more at liberty to exert influence on the company's manufacturing strategy. How fast the manager makes sense of and develops insight into an informally specified mission indicates how well he or she is filtering organizational information. A manager with good organizational perspective will be able to quickly isolate valid information from organizational noise. In addition, the speed with which subordinates develop accurate insight into the company's manufacturing mission indicates how consistent the company is in communicating and executing the fundamental elements of its manufacturing strategy.

A formal statement of the company's manufacturing mission is usually desirable. The development of such a statement can be facilitated by paying attention to a few powerful principles, as enumerated below:

1. *The trade-off principle.* As has been seen, the manufacturing mission is the set of paramount manufacturing tasks. There is a trade-off to be made, a price to be paid, in pursuing any task. The trade-off must be specified and evaluated for each task and a decision must be made as to whether that trade-off is tolerable. At least, top management must be fully aware of the trade-offs it imposes on the manufacturing system. However, we have seen that strategy must be deployed to generate sustainable, broad-based improvement in manufacturing performance so as to systematically reduce the number and severity of trade-offs that have to be taken into consideration when formulating and implementing manufacturing strategy. We have also seen that competition pushes companies to seek superiority in all key competitive requirements of the market. But, we also noted that competitive superiority can be maintained only if top management periodically re-engineers the company and recreates the essence that made it great.

   Thus, while companies that are driven by competition push hard to achieve overwhelming, broad-based competitive superiority, that very same competition is operating to force them to make trade-offs. Continuous improvement and constant learning only mean that the need to make trade-offs among competitive requirements and their concomitant manufacturing tasks will be a progressively less demanding strategic problem for the world-class company compared to its low performing counterparts.

2. *The principle of focus.* A production system can accomplish excellent results only if the range of tasks in the manufacturing mission is small. Focus means that the production system is a specialized strategic unit of the business. The manufacturing mission must be succinctly specified so as to accentuate a few dominant competitive priorities.

3. *The principle of external coherence.* The manufacturing mission should derive logically and directly from the company's competitive strategy. A crucial premise in the formulation and implementation of manufacturing strategy is that the link between corporate strategy and manufacturing mission must be developed and nurtured. The manufacturing mission is, in reality, a microcosm of the company's competitive strategy.

4. *The principle of internal coherence.* The design of the production system of a company is one of the most complicated tasks of top manufacturing management because of the large number of parameters that are involved. It is not surprising, therefore, that production systems are often plagued with design and operational inconsistencies. The problem of inconsistency in design and operation is exacerbated in two ways: (1) The initial design of the production system and its subsequent operation are done with no clear, strategic purpose in mind and (2) the evolution of the production system is allowed to follow its normal course, or the system is adapted haphazardly and piecemeal to changes in competitive conditions. An explicit manufacturing mission can minimize production system design inconsistency, if the mission itself has internal coherence. Viewed as a package, elements of the manufacturing mission should stand on their own as a single expression of the company's manufacturing priorities. When converted into manufacturing system specifics, the tasks should result in system characteristics that have few incongruities or anomalies. In other words, the various elements of the mission can be made to "speak the same language," when their design and operational ramifications are mapped out.

5. *The principle of functional integration.* The only reason for pursuing manufacturing mission is that its accomplishment will enhance and/or maintain the company's market position. In the final analysis, the successful execution of the manufacturing mission is judged by the customer. The manufacturing mission should be specified to integrate the needs of marketing with the constraints and capabilities of production. Effective execution of the manufacturing mission should significantly help the company meet the needs of the market, which is the ultimate test as to whether strategy is being successfully implemented in the manufacturing function.

Manufacturing Mission and Operating Focus

Operating actions easily lose focus and direction due to the large number of situations that have to be dealt with continually. The operations manager in a typical North American manufacturing company is constantly engaged in fire-fighting as he or she responds to one small-scale crisis after another. The plant operating environment is such that factory managers spend an inordinately large proportion of their working time solving short-term operating problems so as to keep the plant "up and running." Operating managers get so engross-ed with putting out fires, that they easily lose sight of their central responsibil-ity. The automatic, firefighting reflex that these managers develop to cope with the daily routine of factory management comes to impregnate their man-agement philosophy and behavior. Major decisions such as equipment replacement and major systems acquisition and implementation eventually come to be undertaken to solve immediate and pressing operating problems. These problems are tackled and solved one at a time, with no coherent logic or unifying mechanism. The large-scale manufacturing decisions come to be implemented piecemeal and the patchwork mentality that so often character-izes manufacturing management in North America takes over. Both long-term and operating-level decisions come to lose strategic focus and direction.

By adopting and thoroughly inculcating a manufacturing mission, corpo-rate management provides manufacturing management with a unifying force for all operating decisions. The manufacturing mission directs all production management decisions toward the company's competitive priorities. The short-term crises continue to be dealt with, as they should, but manufacturing managers will solve day-to-day operating problems without losing sight of the market and competitive exigences. A mission statement that is driven home repeatedly brings managers back to strategic objectives, every time they are prone to be led away by pressing daily problems. The seemingly unrelated decisions come to be viewed as having strong interrelationships when they are all driven by competitive priorities. A manufacturing mission statement forces production managers to look for and exploit symbiosis among the vari-ous strategic decisions, between strategic and operating decisions and among the operating decisions themselves. The result is clear focus on strategic and competitive priorities.

Evidently, then, the definition of the manufacturing mission and its inter-nalization by all significant corporate players, but particularly production man-agers, is the most basic prerequisite to the achievement of factory focus. The focused factory begins and ends with corporate strategy. As will be discussed subsequently, this makes the focused factory a tool for strategically managing manufacturing.

THE PROCESS OF FORMULATING MANUFACTURING STRATEGY

Figure 3–7 shows one of the seminal models of the process of manufacturing strategy formulation. Corporate strategy drives manufacturing strategy and in

FIGURE 3–7 Formulating Manufacturing Strategy

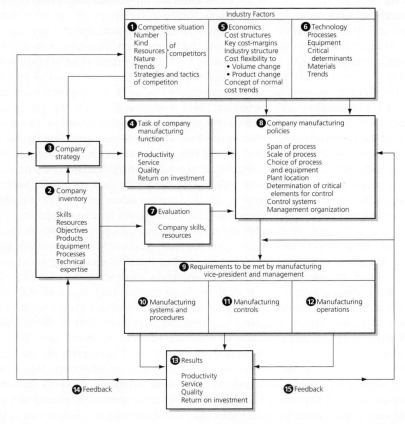

KEY

1. What the others are doing
2. What we have or can get to compete with
3. How we can compete
4. What we must accomplish in manufacturing in order to compete
5. Economic constraints and opportunities common to the industry
6. Constraints and opportunities common to the technology
7. Our resources evaluated
8. How we should set ourselves up to match resources, economics, and technology to meet the tasks required by our competitive strategy

9. The implementation requirements of our manufacturing policies
10. Basic systems in manufacturing (e.g., production planning, use of inventories, use of standards, and wage systems)
11. Controls of cost, quality, flows, information, inventory, and time
12. Selection of operations or ingredients critical to success (e.g., labor skills, equipment utilization, and yields)
13. How we are performing
14. Changes in what we have, effects on competitive situation, and review of strategy
15. Analysis and review of manufacturing operations and policies

Source: Skinner, Wickham, *Manufacturing: The Formidable Competitive Weapon* (New York: John Wiley and Sons, 1985), 65. Reproduced with permission

turn, is supported by it. The whole process culminates in the specification of requirements to be met by manufacturing and the design, operation, and control of the manufacturing function pursue these. Measurement of results and performance evaluation close the loop by providing feedback to the corporate strategy formulation process. When these concepts are applied, manufacturing is designed and managed with deliberate strategic intent and performance increases.

Conclusion

Manufacturing strategy must flow out of and mirror corporate strategy. Competition is the force that is driving corporate strategy and the pace and vigor of a company's response to competition is regulated by the intensity of competitive spirit created and nurtured by top management. Competition dictates that companies continuously improve their operations and their ability to perform market requirements. The fundamental goal of strategy formulation and implementation is the creation of sustainable competitive advantage. Sustainability requires that a company possess and maintain superior competitive competence which necessitates continuous improvement. Both corporate and manufacturing strategy must be deployed to create superior competitive competence and to maintain it by continuous improvement.

Corporate strategy picks and cultivates a strategic position. Companies can chose between three generic strategies: low cost, differentiation, and focus. The viable strategic options open to a company are limited by its strategic strengths and weaknesses vis-à-vis the requirements of the market. Continuous improvement programs reinforce and improve on superior competitive competence and open up the strategic options available to a company.

The formulation and inculcation of a manufacturing mission is a crucial phase of the process of deploying corporate strategy in the manufacturing/operations function. The manufacturing mission is the company's strategic manufacturing objective and is the nexus between the corporate strategy and the production/operations system. The mission drives the formulation and deployment of manufacturing policies and resources, establishes and communicates strategic manufacturing priorities, determines the choice and pace of implementation of continuous improvement programs, dictates, focuses, and serves as a frame of reference for all actions and decisions whose purpose is the creation and sustenance of competitive advantage. Production systems that are designed, structured, and managed for competitive impact must be and always are mission driven.

Case for Discussion

INTERNATIONAL AEROSPACE, INC.

Senior management of International Aerospace, Inc., (IAI) had recently initiated a complete evaluation of the company's competitive position as the first step to preparing it to compete in the aerospace market beyond the year 2000. The aerospace industry had gone through some massive changes over the last 15 years with the entry of the Airbus consortium which was challenging Boeing and other leading aircraft manufacturers in their traditional markets. Although IAI was a very small company by world standards, it too was facing severe competitive pressure from manufacturers in North America, South America, and Europe. Industry observers expected sluggish demand for airplanes for the remainder of the decade as a result of slow worldwide economic growth, depressed airline company profits, and severe overcapacity.

The Company

IAI was a manufacturer of small jet aircraft that was created by a European government over 20 years ago. Government was the sole shareholder up until 1985 when the company was sold to EMTI, a well-known manufacturer of mass transit equipment. The company's major product was a 24-seat jet aircraft that could be used either as an executive or corporate jet or by major airline companies to service regional or feeder routes. Sales had grown from $50 million in 1978 to $350 million in 1991. From 1978 to 1990, the company had cumulated losses of $180 million, $160 million of which were realized during the years prior to 1985. In 1989, the company made a profit of $1 million, its first ever. Profits were $3 million in 1990, but a depressed market lead to a loss of $5 million in 1991.

The company continued to maintain a very strong relationship with the government. From 1985 to 1991, it received R&D grants of about $20 million per year from the central government. Moreover, sales of aircraft to various government agencies totalled $120 million from 1985 to 1991. IAI also received export financing support from the central government in the form of low interest loans to finance export sales. For example, the company was recently awarded a contract of $95 million to supply an Asian airline company with seven airplanes. Ninety million dollars of the sale was financed by the central government at an interest rate of 2 percent, when the prevailing long-term interest rate was 10.5 percent. The president of the Asian airline company remarked that the availability of very low financing was a key factor in his company's decision to award the contract to IAI. Both the central and local governments gave generous grants to IAI to defray the cost of employee training and development. These grants totalled $2 million in 1991.

The Company's Competitive Position

Civil aviation aircraft are made to rigid quality specifications. All IAI aircraft had successfully gone through the rigid certification process mandated by the International Civil Aviation Organization (ICAO). The company had achieved the quality requirements at high cost. A recent quality audit had revealed that rejects accounted for 35 percent of material cost. In 1989, a major European aircraft manufacturer completed a quality audit of all its subcontractors and gave IAI's quality management system a pass grade. In a recent bid to supply four corporate jets to a large company, the IAI's price was 5 percent lower than that of its major competitor. However, the company's delivery schedule was four months longer.

IAI had a highly-qualified team of technical people. However, the company did not have the scale and resources to train and develop technical personnel as intensively as the major aerospace companies. Seventy percent of the company's engineers and technicians were recruited away from other aerospace companies. To attract these employees, IAI had to pay salary premiums of 20 percent.

IAI also lagged behind the majors in the use of advanced process technology. The company had 80 percent less investment per worker in Numerical Control (NC) and Computer Numerical Control (CNC) machines compared with the majors such as Boeing and Airbus, and 30 percent less compared to similar North American small aircraft manufacturers. The company had only recently started to experiment with JIT concepts and the implementation of a flexible manufacturing system (FMS).

Three years ago, the company launched the most ambitious development project of its existence, the design and development of a medium-range 65-seat jet aircraft. The aircraft was expected to be available for testing at the end of 1992 but as of the end of 1991, the project had fallen behind schedule by two years. In the meantime, competitors had overtaken IAI in their efforts to design and develop competing aircraft and some industry observers thought that the company had lost its early lead.

In 1989, the company started to implement MRP-II. At the time, MRP-II project team expected implementation to take two years at a cost of $1.5 million. MRP-II faced severe implementation problems and in one year, the initial project was suspended and a new team was formed to replan MRP-II implementation from scratch.

Initiating Strategic Change

The parent company had, from the beginning, found it difficult to build IAI into a lean and effective competitor in what was obviously a global market. Decades of depending on government support had, in the opinion of most top managers, created a bloated, slow-moving, inefficient bureaucracy that was ill-suited to the requirements of a competitive market. The parent wanted to integrate its own culture and philosophy into IAI but the latter's top management and technical staff resisted. IAI's engineers frequently remarked that EMTI makes very good buses, but they can't fly. EMTI management was unwilling to clean up IAI top management in the short term for fear that this would disrupt continuity of operations at a critical time in the subsidiary's development. They therefore opted to work closely with top management at IAI to do a joint evaluation and overhaul of IAI's competitive strategy, hoping to use the exercise to get a better understanding of how it should be positioned in its market and to effect necessary changes at the top management level.

Discussion Questions

1. What are IAI's competitive advantages and disadvantages? What are the sources of such advantages and disadvantages?
2. What are the advantages and disadvantages of IAI's long affiliation with government?
3. Can EMTI successfully manage a company that competes in a market that is so different from its traditional markets? If it can, what would it have to do to ensure success?
4. What does the MRP-II implementation failure tell you about the challenges that EMTI will face in bringing IAI to profitability?
5. Is the approach taken by EMTI to manage IAI's transition to a profitable, competition-driven company likely to succeed?

References

Coyne, Kevin P., "Sustainable Competitive Advantage—What It Is, What It Isn't," *Business Horizons,* January–February 1986.

Etienne, Eisenhower C., "Characteristics and Requirements of Product and Process Technology and Their Implications for the Strategic Management of Innovation," Administrative Sciences Association of Canada, Conference proceedings, June 1982.

Jelinek, Mariann, and Joel D. Golhar, "The Interface between Strategy and Manufacturing Technology," *Columbia Journal of World Business,* Spring 1983.

Porter, Michael E., "From Cpmpetitive Advantage to Corporate Strategy," *Harvard Business Review,* May–June 1987.

The Nine Mortal Wastes

$\mathbf{W}$e have already seen that competitive pressures in the marketplace require that companies, in order to survive and be profitable, must create increasing value for their customers. Furthermore, we have seen that increased value comes from increasing quality while keeping costs the same or keeping quality levels constant while decreasing costs or increasing quality faster than costs. While quality improvement and cost reduction can and do sometimes come from radical technological innovation, there are often more cost-effective ways to attain these two paramount objectives. In any event, total reliance on technological breakthroughs is likely to weaken a company's response to aggressive competition in the marketplace for two reasons: first, the company cannot totally control the outcome. The nature of a break-through is such that there is a slim chance of it occurring in the company's own facilities and there is no guarantee that when a competitor achieves a radical innovation, the company will be able to respond quickly enough to neutralize the threat. And second, many years will usually elapse between breakthroughs. During this time, companies that achieve progressive incre-mental improvement in quality and cost will have both assimilated the new technology and improved on it.

THE BASIC JIT PRINCIPLE

Constant, incremental improvement in quality and cost come not from mas-sive technological change that alters the production function, but from refine-ment and mastery of existing, known technology. World-class companies that have achieved sustained decreases in defect rates and unit costs have come to the realization that the actual cost of a product has two components, one that responds to qualitative changes in technology such as is produced by innova-tion of the breakthrough type and one that responds to better use of existing technology. For any given product,

$$\text{Actual cost} = \text{true cost} + \text{waste}$$

The true cost comes from trouble-free operation of the best technology available, and is a potential or target that must be rigorously pursued by management.

Large-scale technological innovation will reduce the true, potential cost. But, the critical barrier to attaining the true cost and thus exploiting known technology to the fullest is the level of waste that exists within the company. Any negative difference between the actual and true cost is waste.

Continual search for improvement, the daring to challenge conventional ways of doing things, comes from the conviction that waste is both extensive and pervasive. JIT is based on the idea that substantial improvement in a company's competitive and financial position can be gained through rigorous programs of waste removal. Actually, the motivation is more powerful than this. The philosophy behind JIT is that most companies can achieve more dramatic and rapid improvements in quality and cost by consciously managing to eliminate waste than by embarking on ambitious investment programs for new technology. Elimination of waste, because it is waste, is easier to achieve than radical change in equipment and process technology. Waste exists in many different forms and at every level in a company. By virtue of this, waste elimination can be used to mobilize the whole organization, from top to bottom. Virtually every employee, if given the right tools can identify some form of waste and design and implement programs for its reduction. Eliminating waste is a powerful way to install a self-management program for all employees and to create a companywide habit of improvement.

One fundamental principle in JIT is that all waste is bad. There is no acceptable level of waste. Waste elimination is the prime target of process improvement because all waste represents lost potential value to the customer. Maximum value for the customer exists when all waste has been eliminated and market forces regulate the price to the level that is needed to generate a fair return on investment. Because waste is a negative deviation from true cost, its level indicates how well a company has mastered existing technology. The true cost will never be known, because manufacturing management will never be an exact science and estimates of machine capacities and efficiency are, more often than not, subject to error. This being so, the only valid alternative available to a company that is serious about increasing value to its customers is to adopt programs to aggressively reduce waste. Many cases exist where managers were quite surprised at how much improvement was extracted from a machine, over and above the initial engineering estimates. An improved potential for the machine or system could be ascertained only after the fact. It is eventually discovered when one adopts the perspective that the only acceptable level of waste is zero and the company pushes very hard to attain that level.

When viewed in this way, waste reduction and eventual elimination become an integral part of the company's marketing thrust. Cultivating and nurturing the idea that waste creates a barrier to the company's ability to maximize value for the customer, and thus is lost potential for customer satisfaction, changes the underlying mission in the search for productive efficiency. The drive for productivity and efficiency in most companies is internally focused. Reduction in cost is sought in an effort to meet the reporting require-ments imposed by an archaic management information system or to imple-ment short-term, crisis-prone, turn-around strategies. Waste reduction in JIT, on the other hand, forces a long-term perspective in productivity improve-ment and cost reduction. By viewing waste elimination as a major mechanism by which increased value can be created for the client, JIT places customer satisfaction at the heart of the improvement effort. There is a one-to-one rela-tionship between waste reduction and value delivered to customers, since the price charged must ultimately cover the cost of waste in order to generate a profit. Every company is both a buyer and seller, and it should not be difficult to see that the price one pays to purchase raw materials and parts has an allowance for waste. The accounting system puts waste into the price paid to suppliers because the latter's costs include allowances for scrap, idle time, unplanned downtime, and other cost elements. This is one major reason why it is to the customers' benefit that suppliers adopt JIT.

THE NATURE OF WASTE

When first introduced to waste removal as a core JIT principle, few managers willingly admit that waste exists in their companies or departments. Yet the evidence that will be presented later will show that waste is a very large com-ponent of unit cost, greater than labor and even defect-free material cost in most cases. When one probes the thinking behind the way these managers react, one discovers that they inadequately understand what is meant by waste in JIT. People who do not believe that waste exists and is prevalent are not likely to do anything to eliminate it, while those who are confused about it are prone to implement ambiguous, misdirected waste-reduction actions. Managers who do not totally grasp what waste means dismiss JIT as wishful thinking and see programs to pursue zero defects, inventories, and downtime as thoroughly impractical. Alternatively, managers who accurately understand what JIT means by waste readily admit that it exists and can be substantially reduced, if not removed altogether. Evidently, to provide the impetus for waste removal and to create the right environment for motivating the pursuit of zero defects, inventories, and downtime, one needs to precisely understand what is meant by waste.

Imagine the following scenario. A company receives an order for a prod-uct to be delivered in five days. There is no work-in-process inventory in the plant, processes are physically integrated, there are no conveyors between operations so that the product is handed by one worker to the next as it is transformed. All the workers in the plant are completely trained, execute the methods with finesse, and are working by the principle "do it right the first time." Based on accurate estimates of the time required by each worker with no allowance for wasted motion or idle time, the total production time is eight hours. The company orders the parts from suppliers to arrive one day before the product must be delivered to the customer. The parts precisely meet specifications which were based on total customer requirements for the product. Eight hours before delivery is to take place the parts arrive, production begins and is executed without a hitch, with very little paper necessary. The workers, because they have mastered the methods and are quality and customer conscious, need little or no supervision. Given this scenario, a product that completely meets all customer specifications would have been made and there would have been a rock-bottom minimum consumption of productive resources. This product would serve as a benchmark for waste definition because it conforms to the vision of effective and efficient use of resources that is driving manufacturing performance in today's world-class companies. In JIT, waste is defined as any resource used over and above the strict minimum necessary to make good products. Zero waste means that the absolutely right product is made by doing it right the first time, using the right materials, methods, workers, and equipment. There would be no waste in the economy if all suppliers and customers applied these principles.

Every defect is waste and repairs only add waste to waste. There is no such thing in JIT as an acceptable level of defects or repairs. Repairs are simply the lesser evil when compared with throwing away a defective part or product, but an evil nonetheless. Herein lies the crux of the difference between JIT and conventional manufacturing. The latter defines acceptable quality as parts per hundred defective while the former defines the acceptable quality level (AQL) as zero defects. Toyota Motor Company is achieving defect rates of one part per million, yet defines that as waste.

Waste can also be viewed as whatever actions, managerial or operational, that do not add value to a product. Downtime, idle time, and inspection among others, come under this category. Quality managers find it practically sacrilegious to define inspection as waste. But one has to go deeper to understand what creates the need for inspection. People inspect products either because they have been designated as inspectors and must find work to do (after all, what is left for an inspector to do but to inspect) or because the production system cannot produce 100 percent good product. Inspection exists because the company has very little confidence in the production system's capability to "do it right the first time." When a company is achieving a defect rate of one part per million inspection becomes uneconomical and superfluous.

All excess is waste because it represents human, equipment, financial, and material resources that are available but not being used. Surplus machinery, human and material resources are often justified on the basis that they provide flexibility to respond to demand, capacity, and process variability. Excess resources are viewed as providing a buffer against inherent instability in both demand and supply. But, at a deep level, no excess is needed because anything that is a need must be immediately satisfied. When things are examined at a much deeper level still, it is noticed that excess resources do not provide for flexible responses to the market and production variability, but rather protect against the weaknesses of an inherently inflexible production system. Flexibility is the ability to respond to change and not a buffer against variability. Flexible production systems respond to market and product volume variability and do not buffer against them. The creation of surplus is the clearest admission that production and procurement are not managed to achieve a flexible response to the market. Buffers are an excess that waste resources in an effort to mitigate the severe adverse consequences of having an inflexible manufacturing system. Moreover, buffers deal with market and production variability at the wrong level because there is no effort to remove the source of instability. The response in JIT is to remove what is causing instability and thereby enhance the waste-reduction effort rather than have excess resources to buffer against variability.

Inventory is excess and therefore wasteful. The fact that something is in inventory means that it is not needed. An item that is in the warehouse or on the factory floor may be useful in the future but is certainly not needed today. And the basic question is, if it is needed why is it not being used or processed? In addition to being waste, inventory generates more waste and excess in space, obsolescence, internal transportation and all other resources that must be used to keep an item stocked. Goods are stocked not because they are needed now but because they may be needed in the future or simply because no one knows what to do with them. Inventory results when there is excess production and buying relative to the true requirements. Inventory violates the very essence of JIT, which is to make or buy materials when they are needed and in the required (always very small) quantities. The drive in JIT to reduce inventories comes from the realization that they are an excess and add no value to the product. On the contrary, inventory decreases value due to carrying charges and the indirect costs it imposes on the company.

The point must be underscored that waste consumes a significant part of the resources of an enterprise, and its removal is a major objective of manufacturing strategy. In conjunction with radical innovation in process technology, waste removal is of paramount importance to the pursuit of superior manufacturing performance and competitive advantage.

WASTE REMOVAL: THE GLOBAL VIEW AND KEY LINKAGES

Figure 4–1 presents a general view of a company's waste removal processes and how these are linked. Systematic waste removal starts with the competitive environment. Factors such as globalization, intense competition, or the

FIGURE 4–1   **Overview of Waste Removal and Its General and External Linkages**

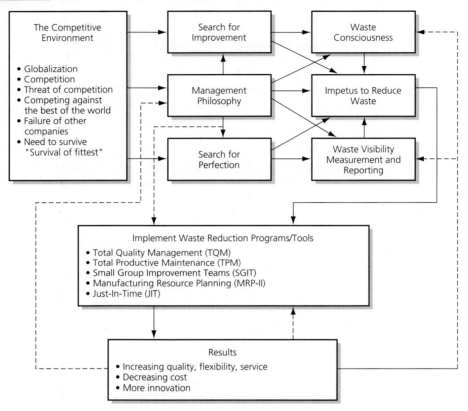

threat of it; the fact that in a global market, a company is competing against the best competitors in the world; the observation that even some good companies fail to match up to the requirements of an intensely competitive market; and the need to be the fittest in order to survive at all, propel the adoption or development of management philosophies that incorporate continuous search for improvement and perfection as organizational necessities. Appropriate management philosophies, search for improvement and search for perfection, coupled with waste consciousness and mechanisms to make waste visible, create the impetus to remove waste on a companywide basis. This impetus to remove waste, operating in conjunction with management philosophies that successfully manage organizational change such as worker empowerment and participation, worker training and free flow of communication and information, result in the implementation of waste removal programs and tools such as TQM, JIT, TPM, SGIT, and MRP-II. Favorable results from the implementation of these programs and tools provide positive reinforcement that strengthen the commitment to search for improvement and perfection, accelerate the impetus to remove waste, and encourage top management to liberate more resources to that end. Hence, when management reacts appropriately to the competitive situation by adopting waste removal as a key corporate mission, it can unleash a positively reinforcing cycle of improvement, where each action feeds on those that preceded it and, in turn, feeds subsequent actions.

The model of Figure 4–2 shows the critical linkages between the major waste removal programs and methods themselves. The numerous direct linkages are striking and they substantially explain the existence of very strong symbiosis between the various waste removal programs and tools, as noted in Chapter 1.

THE MOST PREVALENT WASTES

Companies that have achieved and are maintaining world-class, superior performance on quality, cost, delivery, and customer service have implemented systems and management approaches that identify and persistently reduce

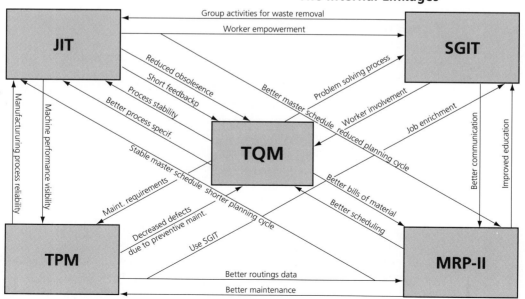

Waste Reduction Methods, Key Tools, Programs: The Internal Linkages   FIGURE 4–2

waste. The productivity machine in these companies is driven by the underlying principle that near-hundred-percent manufacturing efficiency is a practical goal that can be reached by converting all activities into value adding work. Waste must be completely identified and understood so as to give focus to the reduction effort. Any company will find only a few big ticket items are sufficient to mobilize the waste elimination effort for at least the first five years. These are:

1. Waste due to overproduction
2. Waste due to overbuying
3. Waste due to work-in-process (WIP)
4. Waste due to transportation
5. Waste of human resources
6. Waste because of excessive overhead
7. Waste due to bureaucracy
8. Waste in equipment and facilities
9. Waste due to bad quality (defects)

The above nine categories are not meant to be exhaustive and some companies will find that focusing on two or three is enough to launch their JIT campaign. However, each of these nine items is likely to require some action over the long term. One will also recognize that inventory mainly results from the three first items of waste; overproduction, overbuying, and WIP.

Waste of Overproduction

Producing more than what has been sold or is immediately to be sold creates inventories and is conclusive evidence that work was undertaken that was not immediately useful. Overproduction occurs either because known demand is produced ahead of time or because production is done in the hope that future demand will deplete what has been produced. There are many cases where producing a known future demand in advance is necessary to respond to seasonal fluctuation in sales. For a business that has a strong seasonal sales pattern, an overproduction strategy could be the least-cost option. However, one has to carefully evaluate the level of overproduction to see whether it is justifiable given the extent to which sales are seasonal. Moreover, significant gains in inventories and production efficiency can be gained by marketing actions aimed at flattening the peaks and filling up the valleys in the sales pattern. Anticipatory production should be the last strategy envisaged.

Overproduction of the second type, that is producing in the hope of selling is inexcusable. Labor could be deployed in much more useful work than to produce what might sell. Where this kind of overproduction exists, much better results can be achieved by investing a little bit more in market analysis so as to find out what demand is likely to be. If a company cannot develop a reasonably good idea as to what the demand for its products is likely to be a few months into the future, either it does not understand its market or the product is a very bad one. Overproducing cannot solve these problems, and it is counterproductive.[1]

Waste Due to Overbuying

Overbuying results from either buying too much (more than is immediately necessary) or buying too early. The first case, buying larger quantities than necessary, is usually justified on the basis that high fixed transportation and ordering costs as well as quantity discounts on large purchase lot sizes generate substantial savings. When examined closely, however, these arguments are found to have very little merit because they are based on false notions of cost. The decision to buy in large quantities is usually based on reflex action because purchasing managers have been conditioned into believing that, as far as delivered unit cost is concerned, a full truck is always better than a half-empty one, and that taking the maximum allowable discount always reduces costs. Other aspects such as inventory holding cost and the negative impact of inventory are often totally ignored. The performance analysis and control system used by most companies is also responsible for this kind of thinking. Purchasing managers are hardly ever evaluated on the basis of cost of holding inventory. A manager whose performance is evaluated using delivered unit cost to the exclusion of inventory holding cost, will buy in large quantities to minimize per unit purchasing and transportation cost. Compounding the problem, as was already pointed out, is the wanton underestimation of inventory holding cost coupled with the view that transportation and order processing costs are constraints that cannot be broken.

When examined on the surface, buying too early may appear to be a minor problem confined to the purchasing department. Upon closer examination one discovers that it often reveals that there are some deep organizational problems that have not been recognized, much less resolved. Inability to accurately time buying and delivery of materials to meet the delivery dates required by customers and incorporated in the master production schedule (MPS)[2] may indicate that production is unable to plan a realistic MPS and control its execution according to plan. Marketing sometimes puts pressure on

---

[1]For more discussion of the nature of waste and the importance of waste removal in improving manufacturing operations performance, see "Study of Toyota Production System from Industrial Engineering Viewpoint" (Tokyo, Japan: Japan Management Association, 1981); "Kanban Just-in-Time at Toyota" (Tokyo, Japan: Japan Management Association, 1985); "Ohno, Taiichi, Toyota Production System: Beyond Large Scale Production" (Tokyo, Japan: Japan Management Association, 1978).

[2]The MPS specifies planned weekly output of deliverable end items to meet promised customer delivery dates.

production to accept last minute changes in promised delivery dates, while rush orders and specials seem to be the rule rather than the exception. Poor, if any, communication of known future MPS changes to purchasing means that the full impact on materials requirements cannot be ascertained, or that precious procurement planning time is lost. The result is a master schedule that cannot be planned, controlled, and executed reliably and predictably, engendering deterioration in customer service. The end result, from a procurement point of view, is buying early to protect against unpredictable MPS changes. Overbuying reveals that there is poor communication of critical planning information between marketing, production, and purchasing, and that there is not a coordinated approach to executing customer lead times on the part of these functions.

Overbuying is also done to protect against unreliable vendor performance. Where vendors cannot execute reasonable guarantees of firm lead time, purchasing pads lead time to protect against worst-case delivery scenarios. The first reaction to poor lead time performance is to blame the vendor. But a buying company decides which vendors to buy from and controls the performance evaluation criteria that form the basis for continuing the relationship. There are very few markets where a company must do business with any particular vendors, and even in these few cases, adequate purchasing action to develop alternative, even if foreign, sources can influence the competitive structure of the supplier market. A well-planned and executed supplier development program not only broadens the supplier base but also stimulates existing vendors to improve their performance. As markets become more and more international in scope, the economic concepts of oligopoly (few producers) and monopoly (one producer) become increasingly archaic. Purchasing managers can no longer blame supplier market structures for tolerating inferior vendor delivery performance.

That competitive forces on a global scale have increased the amount of leverage even a small purchaser has over large, so-called oligopolists is well illustrated by the following real life case. A small Canadian manufacturer of glass products had historically bought all its glass requirements from three, very powerful North American producers. According to conventional economic theory, the glass industry in North America is a concentrated oligopoly, so the small manufacturer thought itself as able to do little to influence the three traditional vendors. Besides this, the company bought about $4 million worth of glass a year which was clearly not enough to enable it to make demands on its vendors. Lead times quoted by vendors were long, varying from eight to eleven weeks, depending on prevailing economic conditions and how much capacity rationing existed in the industry at any point in time. These very same conditions that caused long lead times also made them very unreliable and deliveries could be postponed by as much as two weeks. The company accepted this as the reality of doing business in a concentrated market. A defunct economic theory prevented the company from looking elsewhere, the reasoning being that the domestic, North American producers would be the most efficient and cost effective because they were huge companies that had substantial economies of scale. To further anchor the procurement department in its thinking based on traditional economic theory, purchasing people advanced the argument that even if some offshore suppliers could be found, whatever cost advantages they possessed would be more than offset by transportation cost. Long transportation time would also make lead-time length and variability more serious problems. The reasoning was cast in stone and all the arguments were developed to justify the path of least resistance— local sourcing.

Then, in 1987, the company president visited South Korea to try to keep abreast of new developments in equipment technology and came in contact with a glass manufacturer. He investigated the possibility of buying glass from the South Koreans. From all the answers received in response to his questions, the glass available in South Korea was equivalent in quality to what he bought in North America. But to his amazement, the South Korean supplier was willing to offer a six-week lead time. More amazing, though, was the price. Initial calculations revealed that he could purchase glass from South Korea and the landed cost to him in Canada would be 20 percent below the cost from North American sources. After an initial order confirmed initial expectations, he continued to do sourcing from South Korea. Lead time is still six weeks and reliability is near 100 percent. The point is that no matter what arguments are mustered to blame vendors for unreliable delivery, the ultimate and final responsibility for it must rest with purchasing. Poor delivery performance is caused by inadequate procurement policies and the fact that not enough attention is given to vendor evaluation, purchasing research, continuing vendor performance monitoring, as well as unquestioned acceptance of traditional arguments.

Waste Due to Work-in-Process (WIP)

The designation "work-in-process" is a misnomer. To be rigorously correct, WIP would be the pieces that are actively being processed at each operation and that would be entirely good, if that were all. What managers usually mean by WIP is whatever parts have not been completely transformed into finished goods and are found between the raw materials and end item warehouses. Actually, very little of what is referred to as WIP is in fact in process. Most WIP is not currently being processed at all, as illustrated in Figure 4–3. The system is making 12,000 pieces per year. Assuming raw materials, WIP, and finished goods turns that are 4, 6, and 3, respectively, inventories will be:

- raw materials: 3,000 pieces
- WIP: 2,000 pieces
- finished goods: 4,000 pieces

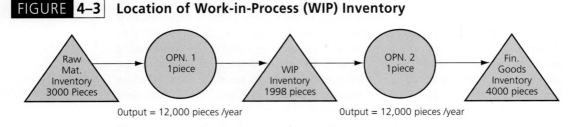

FIGURE 4–3   Location of Work-in-Process (WIP) Inventory

Note: When WIP turns six times, parts spend about nine weeks between the two operations in Figure 4-3, on the average.

However, the true WIP is only two pieces and to achieve this would be the primary goal in implementing JIT, one worker handing the piece he or she has just finished to the next worker who immediately starts to process it. So 99.9 percent of what is traditionally referred to as WIP is work that is not being processed, but just lying idle between two operations. Incidentally, some managers refer to WIP as "work in progress." One has to have a pretty warped sense of progress to admit that a part is making progress when it spends nine weeks between two operations that may be less than 20 feet apart, and the processing time itself is only 10 minutes per piece (2,000 hours per year divided by 12,000 pieces per year).

These considerations lead one to conclude that tremendous improvement in operating efficiency can be gained by managing to reduce WIP inventory. WIP is wasteful because the lion's share, 99.9 percent, is being held idle and spends many weeks with no value being added to it during that time. Therefore, the material has lost value via carrying charges and obsolescence for the time it spent idle. WIP also prevents JIT delivery to subsequent operations and its existence prevents synchronization and systematization of process flow. The WIP inventories represent stop points that have been inadvertently added to the flow, preventing processing from progressing smoothly and systematically. Rather than producing to meet the time requirement at the subsequent operation, upstream operations produce to stock. Considerable time is added to the transformation system, increasing factory lead times many times over. In the example given in Figure 4-3, time per piece at Operation 1 is 10 minutes, but the lead time for any part going from Operation 1 to Operation 2 is nine weeks. The remaining time is uselessly spent in queues, the waiting time percentage being 99.9 percent. Ironically, inventory is usually justified using the argument that they facilitate rapid delivery to customers. The data presented here show the opposite to be the case. WIP inventory adds uselessly to the lead time that can be promised to customers. Coupled with this is the demonstrable fact that WIP inventory hides in-process quality and machine reliability problems. Eliminating WIP inventory is a necessary first step in the pursuit of total quality, efficiency, and customer service.

Some fundamental but flawed operating policies explain the abnormally high WIP inventory that exist in North American industry. The push for high individual machine utilization even when there is a bottleneck in the production system is one most obvious cause. Managers strive for near 100 percent operating rates at individual machines because the performance review procedures that are used penalize them for idle time at individual work centers. For example, if the capacity at Operation 2 in Figure 4–3 fell to 500 units per month for one month instead of 1,000 units, the production manager would tend to still maintain full capacity loading at Operation 1, and WIP would balloon to 2,500 units after one month. This would be done to keep the labor utilization figures looking decent, although it is noteworthy that unless what causes the bottleneck is eliminated, actual output for the month will not exceed 500 units. Nothing is gained as far as output and customer service are concerned and much is lost due to higher WIP levels. It would have been best to reduce overall output to the level of the bottleneck until the problem is corrected. Continuing to load Operation 1 at the rate of 1,000 pieces per month shows better performance for machine center 1, but overall, the company loses. This also shows that process unreliability invariably leads to increases in WIP.

Furthermore, one should note that the scheduled output rate of 1,000 pieces per month is pushed through, disregarding a clear signal that this is no longer feasible. This is the famous push scheduling logic that is central to some production scheduling systems still widely used in North American companies. There is nothing in the scheduling or execution logic that will automatically shut or slow down Operation 1 when a breakdown creates a bottleneck. Large lot production compounds the problem because it only means that more is available to be pushed through. When all these factors are taken together, they explain the very high WIP inventories that exist in North American manufacturing companies.

JIT and Waste Removal

The most powerful set of tools available to the company that wants to bring about dramatic and continuous reductions in inventory is just-in-time. JIT is more than techniques. In its essence, JIT can be said to be one approach as well as a system for managing production and materials which emphasizes attacking quality and productivity problems on all fronts, simultaneously. It contrasts markedly with the partial and myopic approaches to increasing quality and productivity that have been the downfall of some leading North American companies. JIT defines quality in terms of people, machines, systems, materials, and all other productive resources. It outlines methods for constantly improving the effectiveness/efficiency with which these resources are deployed. More specifically, JIT can be defined using the schema of an input–transformation–output system as shown in Figure 4–4.

FIGURE **4–4**   **The Input-Transformation-Output System**

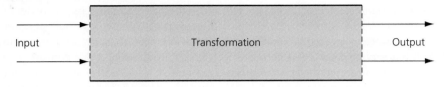

Every company, whether it produces goods or services is organized around such a transformation system. JIT means starting production of the finished product at the precise time to enable its on-time delivery to the customer, engaging materials in-process at the precise time to support production of the product punctually, and having just enough materials, in very small quantities, delivered at the precise time to engage them in work-in-process.

JIT is synchronized, stockless, continuous production, in a timed sequence, time-critical mode. In JIT, the crucial goal is to improve quality by eliminating inventory. The following schema (Figure 4–5) shows why this is so by comparing the level of inventory to the water in a lake where the problems are the rocks. As the level of water (inventory) increases, more and more problems become hidden thus precluding their solution by management action. Reduction of the level of water (inventory) must come from knowledge of what puts the inventory into a system as the most valid basis for knowing how to get it out. An expansion of the schema shows this. Inventory causes and is caused by a host of profound quality and operating problems that recur day after day in most companies. The problems are solved through firefighting, but the root causes are never eliminated. JIT tries to eliminate the causes by driving the inventory down, thus making the problems and their causes visible. For example, JIT does not try to reduce lot sizes by top management decree but by dramatically reducing the long set-up times which cause lot sizes to be large.

Waste Due to Transportation

Transportation can be placed into two broad categories. There is external transportation that links a company to its suppliers and customers, and internal transportation which links various stages in the company's own manufacturing and distribution system. Some transportation is unavoidable because industrial and commercial activity is geographically dispersed. Waste refers to transportation that is used beyond what is necessary and to costs that are sometimes hidden by logistic policies and procedures. Waste in external transportation partly derives from poor plant and warehouse location decisions

Manufacturing Performance Improving the Key Levers by Eliminating Inventory

FIGURE 4–5

What Puts It In	What Gets It Out
1. High set-up time	1. Reduced set-up time
2. Large lot sizes	2. Small lot sizes
3. Unreliable machines	3. High-process reliability
4. Poor in-process quality	4. Superior in-process quality
5. Poor vendor quality	5. Superior vendor quality
6. Unreliable vendor delivery	6. Reliable vendor delivery
7. Long production cycle times	7. Short production cycle times
8. Poor user-supplier coordination	8. Strong supplier/user coordination
9. Poor discipline and training	9. Thoroughly trained and disciplined workers
10. Complex process	10. Simplified process
11. Poor (zig-zag) layout	11. Direct, shortest route layout
12. Unreliable equipment	12. Reliable equipment
13. Poor planning/scheduling	13. Improved planning/scheduling
14. Underestimate the cost of inventory	14. True cost of inventory
15. No waste consciousness/visibility	15. Waste consciousness/visibility

and supplier choice. Plants, warehouses, and suppliers that are located far from markets can add substantially to transportation time and cost. Large transportation lot sizes and the unwillingness to question widely held views on the nature of transport economics exacerbate the problem. Transportation rate structures are not fixed but can be changed if managed with the goal of making small lot transportation both economical and rapid. One North American company managed to reduce its average transport lead time from two weeks to four days and transportation cost by 25 percent, while achieving transport lead time reliability that was greater than 98 percent. The key to this was to rethink long held ideas on transport efficiency.

Waste in internal transportation is more amenable to managerial action since it is created by factors over which the company has almost total control. Glamorous technologies such as AGVs (automatic guided vehicles) and high investment in conveyors in an effort to make internal transportation more "efficient" if not properly evaluated and implemented, only serve to hide waste and perpetuate it. The evidence is that excessive transportation results from a few basic decisions on plant structure and production strategy. The most important relationships are shown in Figure 4-6. The process begins when management decides to build a large plant in order to achieve scale economies and low cost. This creates high fixed costs which fuel large lot production and in turn generates high levels of WIP, raw materials, and finished goods inventories. When WIP is excessive, the space that it uses increases the distance between work centers that would otherwise be close or physically integrated. Transporting goods between these work centers requires conveyors. North American industry has glamorized the conveyor because it was seen as the key mechanism behind the unprecedented levels of production efficiency that were achieved by Ford Motor Company in the 1920s and 1930s. But conveyors are not the ideal because they are one stage removed from direct physical process integration. If one were to eliminate or

FIGURE **4-6**   **Major Causes of Waste in Internal Transportation**

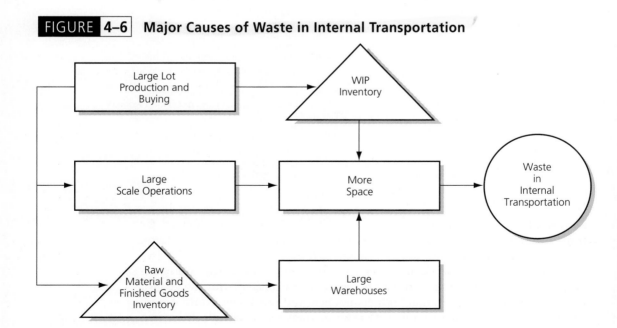

significantly reduce the WIP, very few conveyors would be necessary to achieve process integration. These same arguments hold for transportation within warehouses. Large warehouses mean more movement and AGVs can make a wasted activity more "efficient" but do not strike the problem at its core. One can hardly speak of efficiency until a uselessly created activity is first eliminated.

Waste of Human Resources

People are the most precious and versatile resource that any organization can have. No matter how much technology advances, that simple reality will never change and managers who do not internalize it will not be managers for long; either they will be thanked for their services and let go or they will drive their companies into the ground. There is broad consensus that the human resource must be judiciously used both for the well-being of the company and for that of society as a whole. Waste of human resources is the most terrible of all wastes for two crucial reasons. First, it is symptomatic of very deep management and productivity problems. People are the stuff of which organizations are made. Without people, the human essence, there can be no organized, coordinated, and deliberately thought through action. The human essence is quintessential in organization and management, and the spirit of a company emanates from the human spirit. Companies that tolerate, ignore, or do not try their utmost to eliminate waste in human resources are building their future on questionable premises, if they are building a future at all. A top management team that is not profoundly sensitive to the evils of human waste cannot be expected to provide the leadership to propel the drive for excellence companywide, and to persistently nurture and reinforce habit of improvement. This last phrase, by emphasizing the word "habit" recognizes that the continuous improvement effort is a human one.

Second, the quality of the human resource and how it is deployed is the motor, the creative force that drives and sustains all other waste reduction programs. In the final analysis, human beings eliminate waste. JIT motivates, prepares, and creates the mindset in people to reduce waste and gives them the tools, techniques, and concepts to do it. Unless the JIT tools are used wisely by people, waste reduction will never become an organizational reality. From the inception it must be emphasized that JIT is first and foremost a change in organizational culture, attitudes, philosophies, and vision, and human beings are central to all of these.

If nearly all managers recognize waste in human resources as bad, why does a company need the foundation principle in JIT to the effect that waste must be removed. The following anecdote, based on an actual case, will show the reason. The ABC company, a small manufacturer of household appliances, began in the early 1980s to face intense competition from foreign sources, particularly the Pacific Rim countries. These competitors were delivering products having the same or superior quality at prices that were 10 percent lower than what North American companies could offer. The new entrants on the market were fast developing a reputation as suppliers that never miss a promised delivery date. From all appearances, the Pacific Rim competitors were poised to annihilate the smaller North American manufacturers and even the larger competitors with entrenched market positions were experiencing erosion in market share.

ABC started to prepare to launch a defensive position to prevent real, after-inflation decreases in dollars sales, if not in market share. Its evaluation of its competitive position relative to the new competition immediately focused on labor cost due to the long-standing view that the Asian countries have a decisive labor cost advantage. The results of the analysis confirmed management in their thinking because it showed that the hourly wage rates in the relevant Pacific Rim countries were only one-tenth of the North American hourly rates. A massive short-term labor cost reduction program was implemented and a cost accounting system was installed. The company started to report on labor cost on a weekly basis, particular attention being paid to idle time as revealed by the idle time variances. Some improvement in labor utilization did take place, but not enough to slow down continued erosion in market share. The company folded its North American operations after three years and located in a Pacific Rim country.

The mistakes made by the ABC company are repeated on a daily basis by North American managers in many different industries. The company assumed that waste of human resources is the same as idle time. Its view was that workers must be kept busy producing. But being busy producing the wrong parts or products that are placed in inventory for six months is worse than being idle. Judicious use of labor does not necessarily mean eliminating idle time by pushing production but may simply require that we use the traditional "idle time" to do work that is much more valuable than producing to put in inventory. When labor cost is only 8 percent of unit cost, as was the case in ABC's industry, one cannot achieve labor cost parity with low-wage countries by eliminating 10 percent idle time. A 10 percent increase in labor productivity achieved by ABC only improved its labor cost disadvantage from one-tenth to one-ninth, and its overall cost disadvantage by 0.8 percent (10 percent improvement × 8 percent labor cost per unit).

While ABC was busy focusing on direct labor cost, it ignored some crucial facts relative to waste in human resources. Seventy-eight percent of all appliances completed in the factory had at least one defect that could have been detected and avoided by a well-trained, disciplined, and motivated labor force that was encouraged to "do it right the first time." These defects were repaired and the cost amounted to 35 percent of direct unit cost, or 44 times idle time cost. The plant employed 186 workers and 14 inspectors. The inspectors could not prevent defects, but the workers could. Inspectors were paid salaries that were 30 percent higher than what the average production worker earned. By paying those whose job it was to detect defects significantly more than the workers who could prevent defects, management sent a clear and powerful signal throughout the organization that defect detection is more important than defect prevention. The 14 inspectors together earned total salaries that were equivalent to 22 workers, or 3 workers more than what was lost in idle time. Better use of idle time to improve quality and reduce defects and inspection would have made extremely good business sense and could have been the beginning of a valid strategic response to foreign competition.

The issue of waste in human resources cuts much more deeply than what is revealed by simplistic notions of idle time and labor use variances. Workers in a factory can and should contribute much more than raw muscle power. People are creative, thinking beings that have an innate drive to excel and to surmount obstacles. Given the right climate, they can all become artisans, searching for perfection, seeking and rising up to challenges and being happy while doing productive labor. Douglas McGregor in *The Human Side of Enterprise* gave us some lasting ideas on human resource management that are still relevant and referred to today. McGregor made the observation that every manager makes a core set of assumptions about people which condition all managerial actions in human resource management. He placed these assumptions at opposite ends of a scale and called one set theory X and the other set theory Y.[3] Theory X views people as being innately lazy, irresponsible, shunning authority, desiring to be controlled and motivated by money. Managerial action requires close supervision and a strong authoritarian style. Management must give them production targets and they must be punished when these are not met. Theory Y takes the opposite view that people are innately industrious, they seek responsibility, authority, and autonomy and are internally motivated to look for challenging work. Managerial intervention must be participative and collaborative, rewarding people with recognition and other forms of positive reinforcement, and avoiding punishment.

Theory X provides the conceptual foundation upon which the old scientific management principles were based. Managers are paid to think while workers are paid to work. According to scientific management and its pioneer Frederick Taylor, productive activity could be scientifically organized, executed, and controlled with precise numbers. This is the basis for the labor variance report. When you make assumptions like those adopted by theory X and the scientific management movement, you get hung up on labor idle time and variance reports and ignore the real, significant issues. Theory Y shows the need to mobilize the labor force into creative action, to bring people to

---

[3]For more on theory X and theory Y, see Douglas McGregor, *The Human Side of Enterprise* (New York: McGraw-Hill, 1960).

use their creative, thinking potential to the full. You train and lead them to become masters of the craft of production and as they grow and improve, you delegate to them authority and responsibility for their work. In order for their work to be socially meaningful to them, you put them into cohesive work teams that will provide the support they need to tackle and solve the challenging problems that crop up in their workplace. You trust them with little, then with much and slowly but surely, they develop the craftsmanship to do work right the first time and solve an overwhelming majority of the problems that confront them. This is employee self-management in action, and every company that is achieving superiority in manufacturing has simply learned to do it better than its competitors. Waste in human resources is waste in using the creative power of the total human being individually and in a group setting. It is the most vicious and wasteful waste. Idle time is a nonissue or at least a very insignificant one.

Waste Because of Excessive Overhead

One thing leads to another and waste in human resources which emanates from erroneous concepts and practices in people management creates other types of waste. Scientific management and its partner theory X are based on the idea that workers must be externally controlled, closely supervised, and punished into conforming to standards set by an autocratic management elite. So, you need supervisors in large numbers to keep the span of control narrow. After all, if people are lazy, irresponsible, and apathetic, no one supervisor can control very many workers. And so, layers upon layers of line and staff are created in futile efforts to exercise control of the so-called uncontrollable, industrial worker. If the workers are lazy and irresponsible, then they must be driven to produce by an external force which management theory calls staff and supervisor. When management creates numerous levels of staff and supervision in an attempt to extract high levels of productivity from what it sees as an innately unproductive work force, it sets the stage for creating a vicious circle of self-fulfilling prophecies. More staff and supervision bear down on the work force which stifle the workers' creativity. Whatever creative energy is left is used to invent ingenious ways of warding off supervisors and staff, and workers get increasingly detached from their work. In fact, they come to hate factory work and surveys by industrial psychologists show them to be very dissatisfied. This confirms management's initial thinking that workers hate work so they increase supervisors and staff to tighten control, but productivity keeps falling in the next round of the cycle. When they are totally fed up, the workers get a union which deepens suspicion and conflict. By that time, the battle to build a productive, dynamic work force is almost lost, productivity is probably a third of what it should be and management and the union are locked into totally wrong assumptions about each other. Factory work becomes a punishment.

Waste in human resources leads to waste due to overhead. Overhead exists because top management is trying to put a head (supervisor) over a worker that it assumes has no head or simply does not know how to use it. The extent of waste due to overhead can be shown by data from an actual case, a small, North American company which manufactures molded plastic products. The company has sales totaling $45 million, employs 350 people, 80 of whom can be designated managers, supervisors, or staff. The span of control, the average number of people that reports to any one manager is 4. Now, a rule of thumb states that a manager can supervise anywhere from 7 to 25 people depending on whether the work being done by his or her subordinates is simple or complex. Plastic molding being simple work, the span of control should be closer to 25. The organizational chart for this small company is six levels deep, that is, there are five levels of reporting between the president and direct, production workers. It goes without saying that decision making is slow, there is excessive bureaucracy, and top management is having a tough time communicating its vision of the marketplace to production workers and to mobilize or motivate them to action. If the span of control was 25, the company would need only three levels in the organization resulting in a simple structure, little staff, rapid decision making and communication, and the president would be much closer to the heart of the factory.

Most North American companies are bloated with staff and top management is usually seven levels removed from production workers. And company presidents are ironically bewildered by their inability to understand the concerns of the factory and to make the factory understand them. One person, in a sarcastic remark on excessive use of staff by North American companies noted that the book of Hebrews in the Christian Bible mentions that Jacob died while leaning on his staff. Companies are dying every day leaning on staff, when they could thrive with lean staff. Managing using lean staff and the structural simplicity that comes from it is a distinctive characteristic of excellent companies. Excessive staff leads to complicated, multilayered organizational structures that make waste elimination impossible and in fact make waste invisible. Complex, multilayered structures erect barriers around work groups and make communication and coordination difficult. Many companies create staff whose only reason for existence is to coordinate and communicate with other staff. Companies that cannot effectively communicate a unified, meaningful corporate vision because there are too many staff fiefdoms will be unable to launch a coordinated companywide attack on their competitors.

Workers that are well trained, motivated, and encouraged to be autonomous do not need myriads of supervisors looking over their shoulders, just as assuredly as an experienced neurosurgeon does not need any supervision to faithfully and professionally expunge a brain tumor. The more workers are supervised the less they have time for productive, creative work. A manager who has to supervise four people in an eight-hour work day, must spend two hours supervising each and robs his subordinates of two precious hours of time that could be deployed creatively to do the job better. Dependence on staff is nurtured by latent prejudices that see workers as lazy, irresponsible, and unreliable. As the neurosurgeon needs no supervision because he or she has mastered the skills to do the job, so workers will need little or no supervision when management shows confidence in their creative abilities and trains them to become masters of the production crafts.

Waste Due to Bureaucracy

According to the now famous Parkinsonian law, work increases to fill the time allocated for it. The work undertaken may not be useful and may even create waste in other areas, but it will be done if there is available time. There is also a pernicious corollary to Parkinson's law which we have observed in practice. It is that the absolute amount of useful work decreases as the amount of useless work increases. If people are doing four hours of useful work when they have six hours time available, then they are doing two hours of useless or wasteful work. Now our corollary to Parkinson's law states that if you increase the time available for the same work to eight hours, which may be done by increasing the level of staff, then they will now do maybe three hours of useful work and five hours of wasteful work.

This brings us to a paramount observation. When a company increases staff, it makes more time available for work, and activity increases to fill that time. Now, it has been universally observed that staff naturally gravitate toward report writing, implementation of formal procedures and rules, documentation, paper manipulation, and the creation of committees. The formal bureaucratic structures that are natural to government and military organizations become embedded in the hitherto simple, informal, but flexible structures that have been the hallmarks of entrepreneurial organizations. The phenomenon can be called an entrepreneurial bureaucracy and it has become endemic to many companies, even those that achieved world-class status by having lean staff and flexible structures.

Some executives in the large entrepreneurial bureaucracies of today find relief in the fact that the organizations they have created are at least not as inefficient, wasteful, inflexible and stifling of human creativity as their public counterparts. This comparison is itself cause for deep concern, because just 50 years ago governments were much less bureaucratic and wasteful than they are today. Not too long ago, the only business of government was the conduct of foreign affairs via the diplomatic corps and the maintenance of a small army for national defense. Governments today have encroached deeply into private business. Bureaucracy tends to give more permanence to government but it causes companies to lose their innovative spirit and to disappear. Moreover, companies that have managed to eliminate bureaucracy will reduce waste and create more value for customers than those that do not. The customer will exercise his or her right of choice to punish companies that cannot react quickly to his/her needs. Bureaucracy leads ultimately to the demise of the enterprise.

Bureaucracy is waste. We have seen companies where managers spend better than half their time attending meetings and another big chunk of time filling out forms, writing, or reading reports. Companies today are awash in reports, memorandums, and procedural manuals. The new computerized management information systems (MIS) turn out very little information and mountains of data. One plant manager in a company that implemented a badly conceived MRP-II system received 720 pages of production and materials reports every Monday morning. When a consultant called in by the company asked him how he managed to study all these and still get enough time to do creative managerial work he replied that he never looked at them unless significant problems came up and that happened only once a month, on the average. At the end of every week the pile was thrown in the garbage. One wonders why the MIS department would generate 720 pages of reports, only a few of which were looked at once a month. The answer is simple: The MIS department must find work to do, and the most logical activity for such a department is report generation. If the company keeps adding MIS staff without taking a long, hard look at its rock bottom need, then it will get many more reports which will retrospectively justify the larger MIS department. The strangest thing is that the bureaucratic structures that companies have put into place create oceans of data and very little information. And going through data to get at the vital information takes time. There are numerous cases where executives spend days poring over volumes of reports written by staff in an effort to solve a problem and the information upon which the final decision is based was contained on a single page.

JIT aims to eliminate waste due to bureaucracy by simplifying everything. Simplify work methods, procedures, and practices to the extent that learning and memorizing them become natural. Reduce the information requirements for planning, controlling, and executing work to the bare minimum so that it can all be contained on a single card and can be assimilated at a glance. Simplify parts, routings, and operations so that scheduling can be programmed into the work itself, thus eliminating the need for computerized MRP-II scheduling systems that are complex. Make machines and operations mistake proof and provide for execution visibility so that workers can detect problems early or before they occur, thus making their correction and prevention easy. Select a few performance measures that strike at the heart of quality, cost, and efficiency and which are easy to capture, analyze, and understand for quick and direct feedback and preventive and corrective action. The JIT idea is that bureaucracy is the enemy of flexibility and speed of response to performance signals, and so, it must be significantly reduced, if not altogether eliminated.

Waste in Equipment and Facilities

Sophisticated capital budgeting techniques have been used in North America for a very long time. In his book, *My Years at General Motors,* Alfred P. Sloan[4] documented how these techniques were developed and refined by General Motors in the 1930s. The level of sophistication of the capital budgeting models used today would have overwhelmed even Sloan. What started at GM as an honest attempt to control and rationalize capital spending and to maximize return on investment became, since Sloan's days, an exercise in building elegant mathematical models to make capital budgeting scientific. A kind of new "Scientific Management Movement" has taken over and complicated the answers to a couple basic questions: (1) How much does the company need to invest in equipment and facilities so as to meet the requirements of the market? and (2) Will the return on that investment be worth the effort?

The so-called sophisticated capital budgeting procedures have not helped in reducing waste in capital resources and may have contributed to it. It may surprise most managers to find out that capacity utilization by North American industry averages about 70 percent. At the same time that companies are wasting 30 percent of facilities, management is preoccupied with justifying new investment in facilities on the basis that there will be near 100 percent capacity utilization and other questionable assumptions such as the useful life of the equipment will be ten years. When technology is changing rapidly, it is difficult indeed to find any piece of equipment that will not be relatively obsolete after five years, if there is not a strong preventive maintenance and revamp program. Figure 4-7 shows the factors that lead to waste in equipment. One should note that all these causes can respond to managerial action to eliminate them. This is a substantial waste for any company. Imagine the impact on the key financial performance parameters of a company, if its investment in equipment was cut by 30 percent. Depreciation charges and the total investment required to achieve the same sales level would decrease. Asset turnover, the breakeven point, and equipment related cost, such as maintenance, would decrease. Return on investment would show a substantial increase. The 30 percent could be deployed in other businesses to broaden the product line. Alternatively, a 30 percent increase in sales could be achieved with little or no capital expenditure. There are very few companies that would not double their profits if they increased capacity utilization by 30 percent.

Waste Due to Bad Quality

It has already been pointed out that the philosophy and approach to quality management that exist in North American companies encourage and normalize

---

[4]Alfred P. Sloan, *My Years at General Motors* (Garden City, N.Y.: Doubleday, 1964), ch. 8

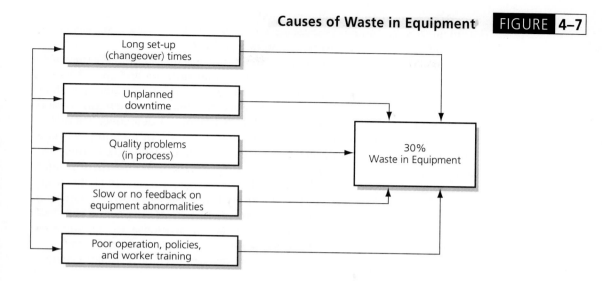

Causes of Waste in Equipment   FIGURE 4–7

- Long set-up (changeover) times
- Unplanned downtime
- Quality problems (in process)
- Slow or no feedback on equipment abnormalities
- Poor operation, policies, and worker training

30% Waste in Equipment

high defect rates. The concept of acceptable quality level (AQL), which is central to statistical quality control (SQC) including statistical process control (SPC), assumes that some level of defects, usually measured in parts per hundred, is unavoidable. Once one has understood what waste is, however, it becomes clear that every defect is waste. The only acceptable level of defects is zero and the only quality cost minimization strategy is rigorous prevention. When a defect has been produced, even 100 percent efficiency in correction cannot eliminate the waste caused by the defect. Without defect prevention, at the source, subsequent work may be excellent, but it is only added to a product that is already defective. That is worse than throwing good money after bad, it is throwing good money after no money at all. If a defect cannot be prevented at the source, the next best thing is to detect it as early as possible.

Continuous improvement, a cornerstone of world class manufacturing and JIT, means that defects are constantly being reduced to zero. The Kaizen principle asserts that zero defects, perfection, may not be attainable, but its pursuit is desirable in order to drive toward world-class excellence. This is why SQC and SPC often give disappointing results and cannot be the ultimate tools in managing to achieve superior quality. These techniques assume that defects are inevitable and they signal defects after the fact instead of signaling the coming of potential problems. Achieving near zero defects requires that the company control quality at the source, where it is created. The sources are people, processes, and supplier organizations. The JIT principles highlight the need to completely describe the work to be done, the requirements of the customer and subsequent processes and that workers be completely trained until they fully understand these. Moreover, processes must be maintained in superb condition and mistake proofed to prevent operation when there is a problem. Finally, suppliers must totally understand the quality requirements and must be partners in search of superior quality.

Defect correction is also flawed for another reason. A company that tolerates defects in its plant is likely to bring the same attitudes and approaches to the repair department. If the company is managing in-process quality with an acceptable quality level measured in parts per hundred, then the repairs department is likely to be achieving parts per hundred defective. Therefore, bad quality will invariably be delivered to customers. In addition, workers who know that there is a repairs department are likely to be lax in their attitude toward defects, further compounding the problem. Where there is not a total program for defect prevention, the repairs department is likely to get bigger. The same logic applies to inspection. It is waste because its rationale is defect detection and correction rather than prevention. Inspection will lead invariably to more inspection because workers subconsciously loosen up when they believe that defects will be subsequently screened out and repaired.

What is the extent of waste due to bad quality? Credible estimates suggest that bad quality costs in the typical North American company are equivalent to 25 percent of sales. If one considers the long-term negative impact of bad quality on a company's survivability, then 25 percent understates the true cost of defects. Companies that do not move quickly to deliver 100 percent good product to their customers, all the time, cannot survive the onslaught of foreign competition. This means that a company that sells $100 million annually is wasting $25 million every year because of defects. These figures look incredible but they are a very good estimation. There is hardly a company in North America that cannot double its profits and return on investment by reducing defects by 50 percent.

MAKING WASTE VISIBLE

Waste is extensive and costly and its elimination is not only desirable but necessary. However, waste is rampant because it is invisible. Invisibility is the enemy of waste reduction because a company cannot manage to eliminate what it cannot see, except if it is in the ghostbusting business. We assume here that very few managers are ghostbusters. Waste is usually difficult to reduce because the assumptions that managers make hide it. A company that boldly states that some waste is inevitable is not likely to do anything to remove it. The management systems managers put in place and the organizational structures they design hide waste. The standards used create waste invisibility because there is always an allowance for defects, breakdowns, and overhead embedded in them. Managers who take waste elimination seriously implement methods, procedures, systems, and practices that work to make waste visible. Visibility is the equal partner of all efforts to eliminate waste.

Some basic changes in the way a company is managed can create the requisite level of visibility to enhance waste removal.

Create Waste Consciousness

Managers who are deeply conscious of waste and its impact will naturally want to do something to reduce it, except if the company is already well on the road to disappearance. The factors discussed subsequently will all contribute to waste consciousness. The total conviction that waste exists, is extensive, and can be removed is a basic prerequisite. Waste consciousness can only be created over time, by constantly training, reminding, and presenting the facts to managers and employees. Communicating vital information is a necessity. Waste consciousness involves a resocialization process to create new attitudes, values, and philosophies in the minds of employees. Top management has a leading role to play because it is ultimately responsible for the socialization process and for communicating a unified, consistent set of shared values.

Reformulate Standards

Waste factors must not be buried in performance standards. These must be reestablished to show the true expected performance targets and the waste factors must be separated. The allowance for defects ought to be clear at a glance to everyone who has direct and indirect responsibility for achieving the standards.

Calculate and Report on the Cost of Waste

By separating waste factors from the true standards, management creates the potential for costing waste and reporting on it as a separate item. Costing is essential to creating waste consciousness. Managers always assume that there is not much waste in their companies. Putting a cost figure on waste, even if the estimate is off by a large margin, the absolute dollar figure is bound to shock even the most apathetic managers, because it is likely to be at least 25 percent of sales. Calculating waste indices as a percentage of sales or selective cost items will drive the point home that waste reduction can generate substantial financial returns to the company and create significant value for customers.

Set Improvement Targets

There must be a goal to improve every year and every month, no matter how much reduction has already been achieved. When management ceases to set higher targets, employees stop being challenged and some waste becomes normal. JIT is continuous, companywide improvement which requires that the goals be set higher all the time. It must be remembered that management will never know whether it can increase quality and efficiency, except retrospectively, after improvement has been achieved. Top management must always have and communicate total conviction that there is always room for improvement. Excellent companies motivate and lead employees to achieve what they initially thought was impossible. World-class management is the art of making the impossible happen before competitors. The ash heaps of history are full of companies that thought that superior quality or a better product was not possible. Their demise is a warning that in the world of global competition, companies that survive and thrive are those that constantly challenge their employees to improve.

Ever improving targets channel the drive toward the six zeros: zero defects, zero breakdowns, zero inventories, zero set-up time, zero paper, and zero capacity losses. These may not be achievable, but their pursuit is perfectly desirable. This is the motive force, the energizing idea in JIT.

Conclusion

There is now broad and strong consensus that significant waste exists in every activity undertaken by every corporation or organization. Waste is prevalent, adds significantly to cost and decreases the value that a company creates for and delivers to its customers. Traditional management philosophies and policies which define historical performance with respect to defects, downtime, overhead, human resources, inventory, and vendor related activities as acceptable, also perpetuate high levels of waste in most organizations. Because waste is an important part of overall cost, its identification and removal is a major element of any strategy that seeks manufacturing/operations excellence, competitive superiority and strategic advantage in any market. Managerial efforts to identify waste and its causes and actions that implement waste removal and continuous improvement programs are vital aspects of the formulation and implementation of manufacturing/operations strategy.

The impetus to remove waste has its genesis in the forces that determine the nature and intensity of competition in the market. Competition dictates that companies search for perfection and continuous improvement and forces management to adopt and implement policies that embody the exigencies of the competitive environment. Top management transmits this impetus to remove waste to the organization when it succeeds in creating waste visibility and consciousness and causes the corporation as a whole to abhor waste. Invisibility and unconsciousness are the archenemies of waste removal and provide the cover under which waste can continue to exist as a "normal" part of productive activities.

Because the impetus to remove waste originates in the competitive environment, waste removal is a never ending process. Competition is omnipresent and natural to all economic activities, at least in the long run. When a company has apparently succeeded in removing all waste, competitive market forces will define the new "waste free" performance as the new target to beat or standard to improve on. Sooner or later, some competitors will succeed in raising performance above the target or standard and will establish a new strategic performance benchmark. By so doing, they will have made it obvious to the market that significant waste exists. Moreover, the new superior performers will have contributed to the development or improvement of the tools that can be used by others to eliminate waste and achieve or surpass the new benchmark. Competitors that wish to protect or enhance their competitive advantage must either adopt or improve on these tools or else develop others that are superior to them.

Competition operates to make the existence of waste a constant reality, no matter how much improvement an industry has managed to achieve. Yesterday's efficient operations are today's wasteful ones, just as today's glamor factories and high performing production operations will be wasteful when compared to the superior performers of tomorrow. Top management's role is to keep alive within the walls of the organization, the market generated impetus to constantly remove waste.

Case for Discussion

ALUMINUM CORPORATION INTERNATIONAL (ACI)

Before you go further, let me make sure I understand what you are saying, Jim. If I get you right, you are suggesting that your best estimate is that a program of waste elimination could save this company upwards of $1 billion a year.

That is our best figure, Bob, and we ourselves had a hard time believing it. But after the task force spent several days checking the figures and assumptions, we had no choice but to accept the stark reality. That is why we came to the conclusion that the implementation of strong waste elimination programs is the best means by which we should seek to reinforce and increase our competitive advantage in the marketplace over the next five years.

If you are right, Jim, no one can argue about that. But I have a tough time believing that a company like ours, among the most profitable and progressive in its industry, that has always prided itself in its ability to innovate, develop people, and compete, can have so much waste within its walls. Jim, $1 billion is 20 percent of our total annual sales, you realize that, don't you?

The Company and Its Strategy

ACI was one of the world's largest producers of alumina, aluminum ingots, billets, and a variety of aluminum-based end products with sales in fiscal 1992 of $5.2 billion. The company was highly profitable and was always a favorite with both large and small investors. The company had consistently achieved an average return on investment of about 18 percent. It operated 35 aluminum processing plants in ten countries and four continents.

The 1992 annual report reaffirmed the company's historical approach to competing in its industry:

> While quality remains one of our key concerns and will continue to retain the attention of your top management, it is our firm belief that our company cannot sufficiently distinguish itself from its competitors simply by focusing on quality. Quality in our industry depends very heavily on process technology, and all our major process innovations can, in time, be replicated by our credible competitors. We should continue to place emphasis on reducing manufacturing cost per ton of metal.

The company was among the most vertically integrated in its industry. It owned virtually all the mines that supplied the raw bauxite used in its manufacturing operations and the ships and trains that transported the raw material. It manufactured a full range of end products from sheet metal for the automotive industry to aluminum foil for the consumer market. The company's own power plants supplied 60 percent of its energy needs at roughly half the cost of that bought from electric utilities. Aluminum smelters were voracious consumers of energy which accounted for 30 percent of unit manufacturing cost. ACI designed most of its process technologies. Its products included consumer goods and aluminum sold on organized commodity exchanges. Demand and prices varied with prevailing economic conditions. High fixed costs meant that profits varied with fluctuations in base metal prices.

ACI had always aggressively defended its market position. The company's market share gave it the ability to exercise some leverage over prices and to pursue economies of scale to their maximum. The company's large number of plants allowed it to reap substantial advantages in the development, testing, and implementation of new process technology. It had long been very successful in using the timing of new plant expansions to discourage competitors from encroaching on its market position. The company tried to bring new capacity on stream when forecast capacity utilization approached 95 percent.

The company also tried to roughly balance local production and demand in each of its principal markets and designed the sourcing network from its mines to minimize both inbound and outbound transportation costs.

The Waste Elimination Task Force

In March 1991, the corporate vice-president of manufacturing, fresh from attending a seminar on World Class Manufacturing persuaded top management to create a task force to do a preliminary evaluation of the potential impact of a waste elimination program on the company's operations. The task force identified five key areas of waste and compared the company's actual performance with what it thought was a reasonable target based on the best documented performance across a broad spectrum of metals processing industries. The comparisons are shown below:

	Comparative Performance	
Item of Cost	**ACI**	**Best Case**
Scrap metal losses as a percentage of sales	8%	1.0%
Losses due to unplanned downtime (% of sales)	7%	0.5%
Inventory turns per year	2.2	16.0
Investment in inventory	$1.5 bil.	$220 mil.
Spare parts inventory	$40 mil.	$15 mil.
Organizational levels	10	7
Cost saving from restructuring	—	$35 mil.
Inventory holding cost	28%	22%

calculate waste (handwritten)

Depressed world prices for aluminum in 1991 had forced the company to cut its R&D budget from $120 million to $80 million. Top management had recognized that such a drastic cut in R&D could hurt the company's process development effort, but it felt that it had no other viable option given the very unfavorable market conditions. It had therefore committed itself to restoring R&D spending to more normal levels as soon as conditions permitted.

Discussion Questions

1. Describe and evaluate ACI's corporate strategy.
2. What is ACI's manufacturing strategy? How well has it been working?
3. Evaluate the potential financial impact of a waste elimination program on ACI. What are the qualitative, nonmeasurable effects of waste elimination?
4. How do you explain the presence of waste in such a successful company as ACI?
5. Can waste elimination be a source of competitive advantage for ACI?
6. What would you do if you were the president of ACI?

References

Foster, George, and Charles T. Horngren, "JIT: Cost Accounting and Cost Management Issues," *Management Accounting,* June 1987.

Hiromoto, Toshiro, "Another Hidden Edge: Japanese Management Accounting," *Harvard Business Review,* July–August 1988.

Japan Management Association, *Kanban: Just-in-Time at Toyota,* Cambridge, Mass.: The Productivity Press, 1986.

Johnson, H. Thomas, and Robert S. Kaplan, "The Rise and Fall of Management Accounting," *Management Accounting,* January 1987.

Lenane, Dean-Michael, "Accounting for the Real Cost of Quality," *Quality Progress,* January 1986.

McIlhattan, Robert D., "How Cost Management Systems Can Support the JIT Philosophy," *Management Accounting,* September 1987.

Miller, Jeffrey, G. and Thomas E. Vollmann, "The Hidden Factory," *Harvard Business Review,* September–October 1985.

Ohno, Taichi, *Toyota Production System: Beyond Large-Scale Production,* Cambridge, Mass.: The Productivity Press, 1988.

Skinner, Wickham, "The Productivity Paradox," *Harvard Business Review,* July–August 1986.

Structuring Production for Superior Competitive Performance

Production systems, like the organizations of which they are an integral part, have structure. In management theory and practice, structure refers to the relatively enduring physical and social attributes of an organization and the patterns of relationships that link its various parts or subunits. Structure gives the organization its logical and distinctive, recognizable form that make it suited to its socioeconomic purpose. Structure reflects strategic purpose and facilitates the pursuit of the organizational mission. The structure of the manufacturing/operations function is not an end in itself but the means for pursuing the company's strategic ends. The structural characteristics of the manufacturing/operations function can either facilitate the execution of the manufacturing mission or it can be a hindrance to its accomplishment. Companies that are achieving manufacturing excellence and that are producing superior competitive performance endow their production/operations functions with favorable structural characteristics that are based on the concepts of factory focus, the focussing of the manufacturing organization, structuring production for JIT, and cell manufacturing.

FOCUSING THE FACTORY

It is now widely accepted that a plant that is focused to perform a narrow set of market requirements is competitively superior to a broadly targeted, general purpose one. The factory focus concept arose out of the need to convert production into a competitive weapon and to entrench manufacturing into the strategic decision-making process. Factory focus is a major element in the body of theory that links what goes on at the strategic level in the corporation to what goes on in the manufacturing arm of the business. Factory focus is a natural culmination of the introduction of strategic thinking to management of manufacturing operations. An analysis of Skinner's work in *The Focused*

Factory,[1] reveals that the factory focus concept synthesizes much of the critical issues that are involved in bringing strategic thinking to the production function.

In order to understand the meaning of factory focus, one must start with the strategy formulation implications of the concept. It will become evident from subsequent discussion that factory focus begins and ends with corporate strategy. Thus, the concept of factory focus requires that strategy formulation by top management incorporate the real and potential constraints, capabilities, and weaknesses of the production system into the choice of strategic variables. Given the state of technology and the competitive skills that exist in the production function, management will not achieve focus if it picks strategic variables that will be very difficult to achieve. Similarly, focus will be relatively easy if the competitive requirements exploit existing production system competencies.

Factory focus means that the production system is designed, structured, managed, and operated to achieve a known, limited set of manufacturing tasks. When these tasks are derived from strategy and are used as a catalyst to drive the entire manufacturing system, we talk of a manufacturing mission. The idea of manufacturing mission is in stark contrast to the ad hoc, unpredictable, short-term approach to manufacturing management that exists in many companies. Manufacturing mission implies that there is a long-term perspective and that production resources are marshaled toward the attainment of a strategic objective. The accomplishment of this strategic objective justifies the very existence of the production function of a business.

The central principle in factory focus is that a plant can give superior competitive performance only if it is designed and managed to execute the requirements of a single, narrowly defined market segment. When segment scope is limited and the factory is dedicated to only one market segment, then only one or two competitive demands are imposed on the plant.[2] Market segmentation and differentiation are matched by production system specialization. The one or two competitive demands that are imposed on the plant are thus likely to be consistent, coherent, and not in conflict one with the other.

---

[1]See Wickham Skinner, "The Focused Factory," *Harvard Business Review,* May–June 1974.
[2]When examined at a superficial level, the factory focus concept may appear to contradict the idea that competitive forces require that companies give superior performance on more than two fundamental competitive requirements. This is particularly true of the global market where companies must give superior performance on all five fundamental competitive requirements of quality, cost, flexibility, innovation, and service. However, there is no contradiction. Focus means that the factory must be exceptionally good at performing one or two competitive requirements over and above the minimum performance imposed by the market, but it must still achieve performance parity with other viable competitors on all the remaining competitive requirements that are not targeted by the company's focused strategy. How exacting performance will be on each competitive requirement, including the ones which the factory is made to focus, is determined by the scope of the market and competition, as discussed in Chapter 1.

The factory itself can be designed to have consistent and coherent structural and infrastructural elements that properly match the market requirements. The plant has a strategic focus and design logic that is easy to discern and evaluate. Production policies, programs, and technologies are selected and implemented to give the factory the potential to execute its clearly enunciated and tightly coherent competitive purpose and strategic mission. In a nutshell, the focused factory replaces the "one plant, many markets or competitive requirements" logic with a "one plant, one market niche or market requirement" logic.

The manufacturing mission must be explicitly derived from the market requirements that have been selected by corporate strategy. A corporate strategic position imposes requirements on the production function and these express the market requirements that production must successfully execute in order for the company to carve out and defend an acceptable market position. The factory focus concept requires that among all the objectives that can be used to drive manufacturing, the ones chosen must be an accurate, albeit partial, expression of the corporate strategy. Factory focus exists when the strategic priorities sought and executed by production are a mirror image of the company's competitive strategy. That is, manufacturing focus is strategic and competitive market focus operationalized in the factory. The focused factory is therefore a specialized production unit that is totally dedicated to the pursuit of strategic purpose.

THE TRADITIONAL GENERAL PURPOSE PLANT

In contrast with the focused, specialized factory, the traditional plant is designed and managed to be a general purpose production unit. The production system is not being managed to execute the strategic priorities of the business. The demands placed on the factory by the corporation are operational and short-term in nature, which means that they change often in response to short-term market and competitive pressures. The plant is being managed to achieve short-term operating goals that are usually couched in terms of efficiency and cost. There is invariably no effort to link what goes on in the factory with long-term competitive or strategic concerns. Rarely is the plant mission–oriented, and when it is, the mission itself results in conflicting strategic requirements being imposed on the factory. Four underlying factors explain why companies generally have general purpose, unfocused plants:

1. *Poorly defined market niches.* The market niche targeted by the plant is in fact composed of many pure segments, either because the basis of segmentation is wrong or because the company has poorly defined what business it is in. One company in the plastics molding subindustry segmented its market by classifying products as standard—whether the company had

its own standard molds, or nonstandard—whether the customer supplied the mold. The company recognized two market segments, when there were in fact five, if one used the end use as the basis for segmenting the market: automotive parts, food packaging, agricultural containers, household products, and hospital products. Each of these segments had unique requirements. The company had poorly defined segments because it defined itself as being in the plastics molding business and also because it used the wrong basis for segmenting its market.

2. *Failure by top management to recognize that different market segments impose different and often opposing competitive requirements.* For the plastics molding company referred to above, the requirements of the five market segments are listed below. Evidently, this company is competing in five very different market segments. The company would need five plants operated as separate organizational entities even if contiguously located, or shared the same physical space, but it had only one. It was using the same basic process technology, labor policies, buying organization, quality control system, production planning and control philosophy, and the same marketing program to compete in five quite different markets. The company has never achieved and cannot achieve competitive superiority in its markets. In every one of the company's segments, there are two or three focused competitors that are consistently outperforming it.

Market Segment	Competitive Requirements
Automotive parts	1. Super quality (precision and rigid adherence to customer supplied specifications)
	2. High lead-time reliability
	3. Rock-bottom costs for quality level
Food packaging	1. High quality (material purity)
	2. Low cost
Agricultural containers	1. Design robustness
	2. Timely delivery
Household products	1. Aesthetics
	2. Variety
	3. Rapid design change
Hospital products	1. Super quality
	Purity
	Rigid conformance to specifications
	2. Low cost
	3. High availability

3. *Failure of top management to recognize that changing the competitive profile of a production system is a tedious, long-term process.* The production system tends to have structural and cultural rigidities that take time to redesign and redirect. Simply changing a major process technology could take two to three years to plan and implement. Mastering the new process could take two years, which means that redeploying new technology could take five years or more. It is much easier to change market focus and to reformulate and redeploy strategy in the other strategic business functions such as marketing than to do it in production. Plants sometimes become unfocused because the factory could not keep pace with strategic change at the corporate level and in marketing.

4. *The company wants to be all things to all customers.* Top management takes this approach often to pursue growth, but sometimes because they do not know who the customer really is. Most companies, because they have not totally understood their market—its dynamics, structure, and future direction—hedge their bets by trying to please all customers. Of course, a company that cannot say no does not understand where its strength comes from. A company that has no competitive muscle is not confident that it is creating value for the customer and therefore serves him obsequiously. Servitude is not customer service, hence these companies are unable to create a group of loyal, respectful customers.

Conflicting requirements or vaguely defined, competitive demands mean that structural decisions such as process technology choice, process flow choice, and basic factory and work organization are not coherent or consistent. Without a clear manufacturing mission, the production system structure evolves according to prevailing pressures or in response to whatever process technologies, management systems, or approaches are currently in vogue. For instance, when JIT was in its infancy and in vogue, many companies undertook projects to dismantle machines, restructure layouts, and eliminate in-process inventory stocking points, in efforts to systematize flows, even if top management had never perceived JIT as a strategic tool. The scramble to restructure the plant to make it more amenable to the short cycle time manufacturing and pull scheduling approach of JIT did not emerge from a new sense of strategic direction at the top, but from superficial operating thinking at the bottom of the manufacturing hierarchy. The new JIT plants were a hodgepodge of conflicting design elements. For example, some factories had implemented flow systematization but could not use the pull schedule logic that fits with it because set-up times were still hours long instead of less than ten minutes.

General purpose, unfocused plants grow in patches or pieces as growing demand puts pressure on production people to find more space for additional capacity. The patchwork mentality reigns supreme when plants are not managed with clear strategic direction. Over time, the factory loses its basic logic, flows become jumbled and each section of the plant becomes distinctive in its own way. Each of these sections that was patched on becomes a "plant" that is pursuing operating objectives that are different from that pursued by the others and that have little to do with the company's strategic mission. Various sections of the factory are pulling in different competitive directions which guarantees that the company will be an inferior competitive performer. One company in the furniture market made a reputation producing high-quality, lacquered furniture. Market success brought growth and patchwork plant expansion. About 15 years after it first entered the market, the company had gone through seven plant expansions. At present, only the "finishing section" is rigorously pursuing a high-quality strategy. Other "sections" are driven to reduce labor cost or manufacturing through-put time or material cost or increase capacity utilization. The sections or "plants" have diverged from each other and most have slowly and surreptitiously abandoned the required strategic focus on quality.

THE FOCUSED FACTORY

Competitive Performance of the Focused Plant

The focused factory will always outperform its general purpose, unfocused counterpart. The reasons why this is so are simple, if not obvious.

The focused plant means that production is given strategic importance. Top management pays more attention to manufacturing when it designs and manages the factory as a strategic unit. From the viewpoint of top manufacturing management, implementation of the factory focus concept means that they are delegated strategic tasks and responsibilities that are based on analysis of the competitive skills and constraints of the particular production function. Thus, they are assured that the strategic manufacturing tasks are feasible and that their contribution to the strategic integrity of the firm is visible, known, and accepted to be significant.

Factory focus brings discipline to the production function, since applying the concept results in the formulation of a coherent set of policies that makes sense from a strategic and operational point of view. This eliminates confusion at the operating level and facilitates decision making by subordinates— lower level operations managers, factory foremen, production planners, shift supervisors. The focused plant is also a specialized production unit. Specialization breeds competence, which means that the factory can master the requirements of the market. In addition, focus gives the plant strategic purpose and competitive vision. The production function develops a sense of direction and this results in a highly motivated factory. As the saying goes, "if you know where you are going, you may not get there, but if you do not know where you are going, you will definitely never get there." Moreover, the focused plant is easier to design. It can be built to have a simple design and a lean structure. The plant can be designed and structured for maximum strategic impact.

A plant that is focused has small scale. It becomes easier to inculcate appropriate corporate culture, values, and philosophies that will propel the search for continuous improvement and competitive superiority. With clear strategic mission, small scale and simple structure, the factory is easier to plan and control. Poor performance on the competitive mission is easy to spot and correct. Small size and clear and coherent mission promote cohesiveness, common, uniform perspective, and shared fate. The focused factory has competitive, structural, and behavioral advantages that cannot be matched by a general purpose plant.

Factory Focus and the Management Hierarchy

The concept that superior performance results when a plant is designed and managed to perform a limited set of demands that emanate from a narrow market segment and a clearly defined corporate strategy, gives top management major responsibility for ensuring that the factory is focused (see Figure 5-1). The role of top management, however, must not be emphasized to the detriment of other managers who are lower down in the hierarchy. Top manufacturing management and operating management at the plant level also have a crucial role to play in bringing and keeping the plant in line with competitive priorities. The broad policy decisions that are made and implemented at the top management level are not enough to ensure that the plant will zero in on the right market priorities or that it will keep doing so. The nuts-and-bolts decisions that are taken on the factory floor may appear to be benign from a competitive strategy viewpoint. However, these decisions are repeated so often that their cumulative effect is to powerfully communicate actual, even if undesirable, priorities. Over time, these small-scale operating decisions can either blunt top management's ability to instill the company's manufacturing mission into the mindset of operating employees or completely change the strategic priorities as perceived or understood by the factory.

How operating level decisions and behavior can come over time to unfocus a factory, is well demonstrated by the following situations discovered during a one-day visit to a plant.

Company A manufactures high-precision metal parts for the automobile industry. The company has built a solid reputation as a supplier of superior quality parts and top management has repeatedly expressed the desire to guard their position as a quality supplier. The annual reports, formal statements by top management, and the resources devoted to cultivating competence in quality all reinforce it as the company's strategic and manufacturing

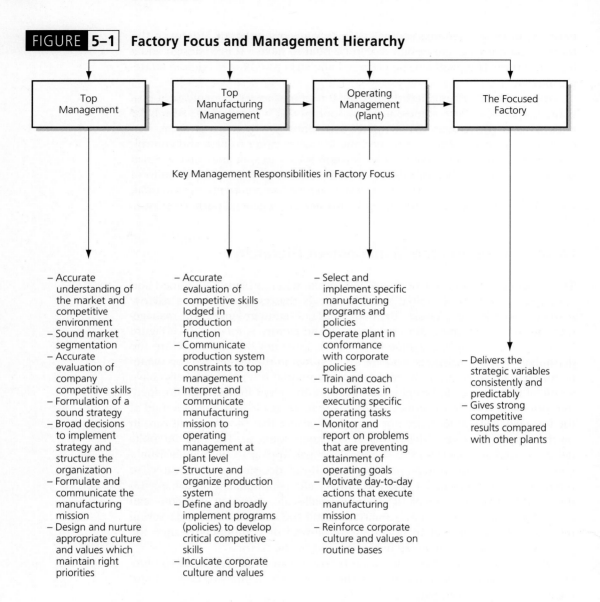

FIGURE 5-1 **Factory Focus and Management Hierarchy**

Top Management → Top Manufacturing Management → Operating Management (Plant) → The Focused Factory

Key Management Responsibilities in Factory Focus

Top Management
- Accurate understanding of the market and competitive environment
- Sound market segmentation
- Accurate evaluation of company competitive skills
- Formulation of a sound strategy
- Broad decisions to implement strategy and structure the organization
- Formulate and communicate the manufacturing mission
- Design and nurture appropriate culture and values which maintain right priorities

Top Manufacturing Management
- Accurate evaluation of competitive skills lodged in production function
- Communicate production system constraints to top management
- Interpret and communicate manufacturing mission to operating management at plant level
- Structure and organize production system
- Define and broadly implement programs (policies) to develop critical competitive skills
- Inculcate corporate culture and values

Operating Management
- Select and implement specific manufacturing programs and policies
- Operate plant in conformance with corporate policies
- Train and coach subordinates in executing specific operating tasks
- Monitor and report on problems that are preventing attainment of operating goals
- Motivate day-to-day actions that execute manufacturing mission
- Reinforce corporate culture and values on routine bases

The Focused Factory
- Delivers the strategic variables consistently and predictably
- Gives strong competitive results compared with other plants

mission. However, two situations at the operating level were dealt with in ways that could compromise the company's quality position in the long run:

Situation 1: A boom in automobile demand had doubled the demand for the company's products and had put a severe strain on capacity in the machining department. Under pressure to increase output, the machining department superintendent started to probe his employees for suggestions as to how to increase capacity in the short term. One young and creative employee who was with the company for about 18 months suggested that output could be substantially increased, if the feeding speed of the grinding operation was increased by about 20 percent. The superintendent accepted and implemented the suggestion even though some employees objected, because he saw no other way to increase production. Almost immediately, the defect rate increased from 0.5 percent to 4 percent. Within a month, the company started to receive complaints from customers and tried to deal with the problem by adding more inspectors in final inspection.

The decision to intensify inspection did nothing to attack the quality problem at its source. Moreover, it did not neutralize the message communicated to employees that quality is to be pursued only if this does not hinder the ability to meet market demand. This may prove to be devastating to the company's ability to nurture a strong quality culture, to instill continuous improvement as a survival necessity, to inculcate quality as the premier strategic objective, and to maintain quality superiority in the long run.

Situation 2: Demand pressures continued to intensify as sales kept growing by 25 percent per year. The company had a long-standing policy of doing two hours preventive maintenance on each machine after every 40 hours of operation. However, the company was now operating two shifts per day and capacity utilization was approaching 95 percent. New capacity was being planned, but it could not be brought on stream for at least 18 months. The company was desperate to find "breathing space" without adding a third shift. Plant management decided to liberate some capacity by cutting preventive maintenance to 0.5 hours per 40 hour shift, without ever considering the consequences of that decision on quality. Once more, the subtle message was communicated that quality can be somewhat sacrificed in order to increase sales volume.

In attempting to focus the plant, top management has to understand that there are exogenous variables over which the company has no or little control, and endogenous variables, which represent management's response to the external conditions. Factory focus depends on how well the external factors have been interpreted, how accurately the formulated strategy reflects the correct interpretation of the external factors and how precisely the endogenous, production factors mirror the strategy thus formulated. The responsibility for achieving factory focus is directly or indirectly shared by all major levels of management. In both situations described above management behavior at the plant level failed to reinforce a focused strategic position and, in fact, worked against it. Many plants become unfocused because situations like these occur repeatedly, day in and day out. Top management may be on top of the market and competitive situation but it is not in tune with what is going on in the factory.

Evidently, then, the broad strategic decisions that pick the company's product market, establish competitive priorities, allocate resources, and structure the organization and the factory, are a necessary crucial phase in achieving factory focus. But that is far from being the whole story. Management behavior at the lower levels as reflected in day-to-day operating decisions is equally critical. Top management needs to have a clear idea of what operating management behavior is required by competitive priorities and the manufacturing mission, and must constantly work to shape the behavior of lower level managers accordingly. The broad policy decisions need to be matched by appropriate operating policies at the plant level which can guide and instruct lower level managers as they execute their day-to-day tasks. Systematic, coherent, practical, and formal standard operating policies and procedures are indispensable for achieving and reinforcing factory focus at the plant level even if these must be prudently applied so as not to increase bureaucracy, stifle employee creativity, and excessively limit their discretion. It is also necessary for top management to receive continuous feedback from the plant for monitoring its performance on strategic priorities. Plant performance evaluation, within the framework of factory focus, is a strategic and not an operational task. Measures for evaluating plant operations must have strong bearing on the competitive priorities that are being pursued by the corporation. These measures must flow directly from the critical success factors of the market and how the company tries to position itself on these. Too many companies evaluate factory operations using measures that have little or no relationship to the company's strategic and manufacturing missions.

The Focused Factory as a Strategic Manufacturing Unit (SMU)

The problems associated with formulating and deploying competitive strategy in large diversified corporations, particularly the conglomerate, convinced many pioneers in management thought that strategy in these companies could be best deployed at the divisional level. Alfred Sloan at General Motors was an early advocate of the principle that top corporate management should exercise financial control at the center but should delegate responsibility for formulating and deploying strategy to divisional vice-presidents or their equivalent. Over time, the large diversified corporation came to be viewed not as a single, unified corporation that was deploying one competitive strategy, but a coordinated union of "corporations" each executing a more or less unique competitive strategy. The diversified corporation competes in many markets at the same time. Each market has distinctive requirements that call for particular strategic profiles. It is impossible for top corporate management to understand and master the full range of managerial skills that are required for effectively competing in a large number of markets.

A division of a large diversified company that has responsibility for formulating and executing competitive strategy for a specific product market is called a strategic business unit (SBU). Each SBU can stand on its own as a separate corporation and can be severed from the "family" usually with little or no negative consequences for the corporation as a whole. While it is true that there will always be some symbiosis between a given SBU and the rest of the corporation, symbiosis is usually not strong enough to, of itself, give the SBU significant competitive advantage from the link with the corporation as a whole. The SBU is, by definition, strategically, financially, and managerially self-sufficient. The SBU operationalizes the principle that for every unique product market, there should be one competitive strategy and one distinct organization that has clear responsibility and broad autonomy for choosing and executing that strategy.

The SBU concept has its parallel in the factory. The focused factory is a strategic manufacturing unit (SMU) because of the following:

1. It is a distinct, identifiable organizational unit that is administratively, if not physically, demarcated from the rest of the organization.
2. It has delegated responsibility for executing a specific manufacturing mission which comes from the competitive strategy.
3. It has a unique structure, its own process technology, and production policies.
4. It is managed to execute a clearly enunciated set of competitive priorities.
5. It is dedicated to serving a unique market segment, if not a product market.

Figure 5–2 shows the relationships between the market, market segments, competitive strategy, manufacturing mission, the SBU, and the corresponding SMUs for a company in the electronics components industry. The SBU in question produces high-quality printed circuits. The three SMUs and their manufacturing missions are also shown. SBUs permit a company to differentiate itself at the product market level. The manufacturing mission, as we have already seen, operationalizes a differentiation strategy in the plant. The design of focused factories or SMUs further fine tune the company's differentiation strategy in the plant. SMUs give the company the wherewithal to effectively produce the varied requirements of diverse market niches in a given product market.

Approaches to Operationalizing Factory Focus

Three different approaches are used by companies to focus their plants, based on the characteristics of the product and the product market. These are

1. *Cell manufacturing.* A cell is a semi-autonomous work group or machine center that is dedicated to producing a part or family of parts. Products

FIGURE 5–2 **Relationships between the Market, Competitive Strategy, and the Strategic Manufacturing Unit (SMU)**

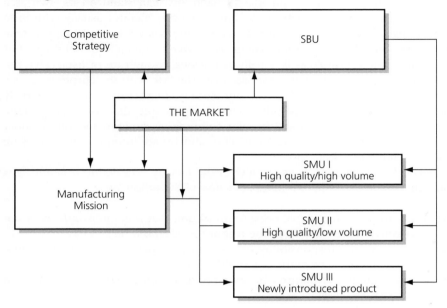

that are differentiated by one or two characteristics which are built into a major component are ideally suited to cell manufacturing. Each cell, by specializing on mastering the production of one part also meets the requirements of the market niche for which the product is made. That is, the part differentiates the product. A manufacturer of lawn mowers can achieve focus using cells, because there are only one or two parts such as the motor, the blade, and the control mechanisms that really differentiate the product. For example, dedicated cells that produce either electric or fuel motors give the company the capability to serve two niches of the market.

2. *Plant within plant (PWP).* The PWP is a factory structure which creates a specialized plant within a large dominant, and also specialized, one. It is suited to cases where one or two products are functionally similar to a standard line of products, but has many special features. Volume is usually too low to financially justify the creation of a wholly independent production system. Moreover, functional similarity between the standard and specialized product means that some resources such as equipment and control systems can be advantageously shared. The PWP is partially separated from the main factory both administratively and physically.

3. *One market segment, one plant.* This is the ultimate in factory focus evolution. Products are fundamentally different physically, functionally, and

on the basis of market requirements. Plants are separated from each other both physically and administratively.

As a company differentiates itself and implements a diversification strategy, it should evolve toward the one market segment one plant structure. Plants become dedicated, not only to particular products, but to market and strategic requirements as well.

Factory Focus and Market Evolution

The exogenous variables that influence market evolution—product innovation, product differentiation, and globalization—are characterized by change. These changes are more or less predictable and more or less persistent, depending on the nature of the product and the market, but they have to be dealt with. Factory focus must not only be achieved but it must also be maintained, which requires frequent and profound reevaluation of the environment (the exogenous variables), the corporate strategy, the manufacturing mission, and the parameters and structure of the production system. We insist here on profound reevaluation, because what may appear to be minor changes in the product market and technology could call for radical changes in strategy and manufacturing system design and operation.

The creation of electric arc furnaces to produce hot metal in a steel mill could appear to be superficial when compared to the traditional Basic Oxygen Furnace. However, when the electric arc furnace is considered in conjunction with continuous casting technology, radically new possibilities in competitive strategy and production system design emerge. Firms now have the possibility of competing in this industry on the basis of low cost, low product variety, short lead times, decentralized, nonintegrated, low-scale manufacturing operations, and high flexibility to respond to demand changes. These strategic choices were not attractive before the advent of the electric arc furnace and continuous casting technologies. The point is that changes that may not be individually very significant, may, when viewed collectively, alter the competitive fabric of an industry. Therefore, the very variables or targets that are being pursued by manufacturing management are changing, because these targets derive from a changing strategy.

A company, then, must do a periodic, systematic, and profound reevaluation of its manufacturing systems to find out whether each one continues to be a strategic manufacturing unit. The manufacturing audit is the tool for doing this. The audit evaluates the whole manufacturing organization from a competitive strategy perspective and draws a balance sheet of its competitive competence and strategic position. The manufacturing mission or missions are regenerated and confronted with the existing missions to bring out inconsistencies or irrelevancies that may have been generated by changes in the market. The manufacturing organization—structure, strengths, weaknesses, constraints, systems, and policies—is reevaluated from scratch in an effort to question its pertinence to the new market and strategic realities. The need for a periodic, full-scale manufacturing audit is a matter of common sense. Companies routinely perform at least one financial audit every year. It is only fitting that the manufacturing system which has major impact on financial performance should be critically evaluated periodically.

STRUCTURING THE MANUFACTURING ORGANIZATION

Companies typically perform a wide range of activities that are difficult to organize and manage as single, unitary production systems. Dividing up the entire activity set and structuring as many relatively homogeneous, smaller scale productive segments, increases manageability. A company's production activities can be organized by product or process resulting in a product-market-focused or a process-focused organization, as shown in Figure 5–3. The existence of many productive segments or plants, as opposed to one, means that there must be an appropriate level of coordination to ensure that they operate individually and collectively to advance the attainment of the company's strategic objectives. The role of central staff in such coordination is one of the key factors that differentiates the product-market-focused manufacturing organization from its process-focused counterpart.

The Product-Market-Focused Organization

In this type of structure, manufacturing activities are clustered around a product or product-market. Each product will have a plant or group of almost technologically identical plants that are dedicated to its production. Generally, plants have decision-making autonomy in areas such as process technology acquisition, product development, and labor training and development. Where the market, number, and scale of plants is large, the set of plants is usually organized as a separate, autonomous strategic business unit (SBU) with complete responsibility for all activities, including the development and implementation of corporate strategy.

Four conditions make it attractive to use the product-market-focused organization:

1. The market is highly segmented or differentiated which requires that plants be specialized by product-market.
2. The process technology is relatively simple, of low scale, creates low fixed costs and opportunities to reap substantial scale economies.

Structuring of the Manufacturing Organization   FIGURE 5–3

Product-Market-Focused Organization

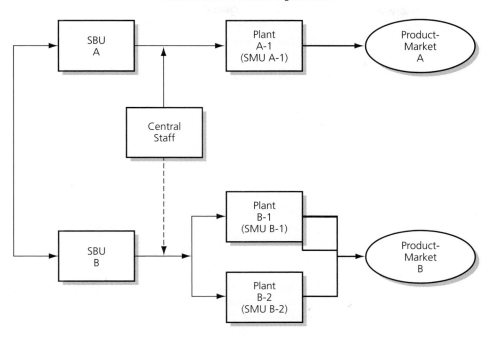

Process-Focused Organization

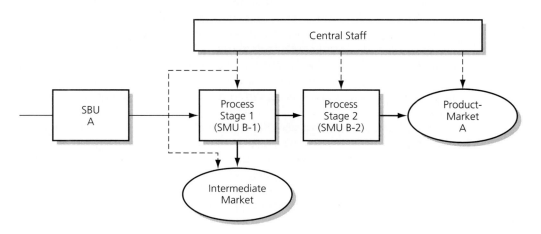

3. There is a shallow range of upstream activities.
4. There is a very effective supplier market that can be used to efficiently perform most upstream activities. In that case, the company can focus on performing only the activities that directly link it to the product-market. Nissan, Toyota, and some of Philips' international production centers are examples of companies that exploit this condition.

The product-market-focused organization offers three advantages:

1. The production system is in direct contact with the market, which fosters customer orientation and allows the plant to stay close to the customer. Management can easily decentralize decision making to the plant level because there is very little risk that customer orientation will be lost as a result. Performance measures can be market based.
2. Partial exit from any one of the product markets is easier since very few upstream facilities (plants) need to be sacrificed in so doing.
3. Decentralized decision-making authority, coupled with the fact that plants that produce for different market segments operate relatively independently of each other means that there is much less need for centralized coordination and the requisite staff to carry it out.

However, the product-market-focused organization can slow down the flow of technology, ideas, and information between the central organization and the plants or production centers. This can be damaging to the technological competence and innovative capability of the plants or production centers, particularly where these are not large enough to support the full range of R&D and engineering activities that are necessary to effectively compete in the product market and where there is some symbiosis between the core product and process technologies of the production centers. Because central coordination and control is relatively weak, it is difficult for the central staff to push technology and ideas across organizational boundaries and speed up intraorganizational transfers of technology. Such is particularly the case where the sets of plants that are serving different markets or segments are managed as SBUs.

Philips, the giant global manufacturer of electrical and consumer electronics products has designed a matrix structure that mitigates the negative effects of the product-market-focused organization on the flow of technology. The company designs and manufactures a diversified line of products, which includes radios, recorders, television sets, computer monitors, and light bulbs. Philips' matrix structure integrates two types of organization, national organizations and product divisions. A national organization has responsibility for managing all operations within a country. It can also be designated an international production center which means that it is the major source for Philips' worldwide requirement of a particular product. Cutting across the national organizations are the product divisions which coordinate Philips' worldwide strategy for specific products. The product divisions operate out of corporate headquarters in Eindhoven and in close organizational and physical proximity to the central R&D organization. Product concepts, initial designs and specifications, and breadboard versions are developed by product teams in the central organization. These are then transferred to the IPCs—the national organizations—for the development of actual prototypes, detailed specifications of mass production designs, and manufacturing processes. Because initial concepts, designs, and product specifications emanate from the central R&D organization and the process is coordinated by the product divisions, the IPCs can tap into the entire range of technological capabilities held by Philips. The flow of technology between IPCs is thereby accelerated.

The Process-Focused Organization

Figure 5–3 shows the essential elements of this type of structure. The entire set of activities from raw material processing to finished products is cut into distinct process stages and each is managed as a production unit. Each process stage produces the intermediate products that are fed into and further transformed by process stages that are located downstream. Each process stage adds value, accumulates cost, and can be managed as a cost center. Sometimes, process stages that are upstream of the final process can sell their output on an intermediate market. For instance, the pulp and paper industry is organized by process-chip production, pulp making, and paper making. However, integrated paper manufacturers sometimes sell pulp to nonintegrated paper manufacturers that further process it into specialty papers. In general, the process-focused organization is appropriate when processes are of very high scale and complexity and can be divided into distinct, identifiable phases. The process-focused structure is very prevalent in capital intensive commodity-type product markets such as metals, paper, and chemicals. Although the petroleum refining industry is process based or capital intensive, it generally does not use the process-focused organization because process integration is so tight as to preclude division into distinct phases. Petrochemicals, on the other hand, usually use process-focused organizations.

Despite the fact that breaking the operation up into smaller, homogeneous, process stages increases manageability, all these stages must operate as one in response to a single end product market. There must be tight control of cost and efficiency from one process stage to the next, because they must all function as one process. Consequently, the process-focused organization depends heavily on central staff to control and coordinate successive stages of the process in order to bring about discipline and cohesiveness in the execution of corporate policy and competitive strategy. Because some stages of the process are far removed from the customer and the direct influence of the market, it is difficult for production unit managers to have an accurate perception and global view of the competitive situation. Production segment managers in process-focused organizations tend to have an internal production system focus as opposed to an external market and customer focus. They have the propensity to adopt new process technologies and manufacturing systems that increase the efficiency of the segments that they manage, even if these are detrimental to the overall efficiency of the business. Conversely, they are prone to avoid adopting new process technologies and systems that may decrease a segment's own efficiency but that would raise overall efficiency. Moreover, where there is not a competitive market for the intermediate products, management must use some sort of formula for calculating transfer prices from one process stage to the next. This can distort performance measurement and evaluation of cost centers because no matter how sound a transfer pricing formula may appear to be, only a free, competitive market can determine the true value and price of a product or service. Transfer prices that are designed to recover full actual cost instead of target cost, further shield plant managers from the pressures to improve that are produced by the market and competition. For these reasons, the process-focused organization cannot give plant managers broad decision-making autonomy but relies on a central staff that can more easily develop a broad view of the business and competitive situation, in order to coordinate the various stages of the process. The goal is to make all the plants function as one unified process, as much as possible.

CHOOSING MANUFACTURING ORGANIZATION FOCUS

Figure 5–4 compares the two types of manufacturing organization on some important management variables. Neither is superior to the other. The choice of structure depends on the nature of the product, the structure of the market, the nature of the company's dominant process technologies, and the constraints and requirements of the production system. Whether a product-market or process-focused organization is most appropriate is largely dictated by the market and industry in which the business competes. A company that competes in the steel industry which produces a commodity-type product, using large-scale, process-intensive technologies that can be divided into distinct process phases, will most likely use a process-focused organization. Conversely, a company such as Black and Decker, which produces a wide range of consumer durables for a differentiated market, would usually use a product-market-focused structure. By extension, a company that produces for a differentiated product market but is characterized by high levels of backward integration, would use a hybrid structure that is partly product-market-focused and partly process-focused. Ford and Mazda, which produced their

Comparison of Alternative Manufacturing Organizations FIGURE 5–4

Differences between product-focused and process-focused manufacturing organizations:

	Product Focus	**Process Focus**
Profit or cost responsibility – where located	Product groups	Central organization
Size of corporate staff	Relatively small	Relatively large
Major functions of corporate staff	(a) Review capital appropriation requests (b) Communicate corporate changes and requests (c) Act as clearinghouse for personnel information, management recruiting, purchasing, used equipment, management development programs (d) Evaluate and reward plant managers (e) Select plant managers and manage career paths – possibly across product group lines	(a) Coordination with marketing (b) Facilities decisions (c) Personnel policies (d) Purchasing (e) Logistics – inventory management (f) Coordination of production schedules (g) Make versus buy, vertical integration decisions (h) Recruit future plant managers (i) Review plant performance, cost center basis
Major responsibilities of plant organizations	(a) Coordination with marketing (b) Facilities decisions (subject to marketing) (c) Purchasing and logistics (d) Production scheduling and inventory control (e) Make versus buy (f) Recruit management	(a) Use materials and facilities efficiently (b) Recruit production, clerical, and lower management workers (c) Training and development of future department and plant managers (d) Respond to special requests from marketing, within limited ranges

Source: Hayes, Robert H., and Roger W. Schmenner, "How Should You Organize Manufacturing," *Harvard Business Review,* January–February 1978, p. 112. Copyright © 1978 by the President and Fellows of Harvard College; all rights reserved. Reproduced with permission.

steel requirements in their own foundries prior to the mid-1970s (Ford once produced its own rubber from company-owned rubber plantations), use product-market-focused organization at the level of their assembly operations and process-focused organizations for upstream operations such as steelmaking.

STRUCTURING FOR JIT

Just-in-time, or the production of very small quantities of goods to meet weekly or even daily market requirements using very short manufacturing cycle time, is a major innovation in competitive manufacturing to have emerged over the last two decades. JIT is a major weapon for pursuing manufacturing excellence on quality, cost, lead times, and flexibility. The production system must be structured for JIT implementation. The principles to be presented here are some of the foundation concepts and mechanisms that, when applied, facilitate and accelerate progress toward JIT, zero inventories, and barely measurable defect rates. These concepts and mechanisms are the major levers that top management can pull to drive the waste removal effort. Four concepts or mechanisms have been categorized as such. They are load leveling, synchronized production, process integration, and set-up reduction. Some companies, due to industry specific factors, will be able to achieve more progress on all these dimensions than others and so will be able to accelerate JIT implementation. Others will have to work more painstakingly to redesign management systems that have been imposed by a given industry structure. Progress will be slower in the latter case. For example, load leveling is much more problematic for managers in the household appliances industry than for those in the personal hygiene sector of the pharmaceuticals industry, due to a much more pronounced seasonal sales pattern in the former sector. But managers who persistently try to do load leveling in household appliance manufacturing do achieve some degree of leveling and reap the benefits. As long as some progress is made in applying the four JIT levers, the company will reap good results in waste and inventory reduction and defect elimination. The vital point is that top management should never accept that progress cannot be made, no matter how unfavorable the industry peculiarities.

Load Leveling

The need for load leveling comes from the observation that unevenness is bad and variability leads to chaos. All biological systems operate to maximize homeostasis, or a steady state condition. Human beings as biological systems obey that rule and, in addition, engineer their social systems for stability and operational predictability. Managing a system that is steady is already difficult, so change and unevenness must be limited to what cannot be controlled or designed out of the environment. The more stability and evenness that can be created in the plant, the more management can aggressively push toward 100 percent efficiency. Unevenness is bad because it causes the system to expend valuable energy coping with change. Anyone who loves to walk will admit that it is much less tiring to walk on an even surface than on an uneven, rugged one, when the distances are equivalent. There is more physical stress and wear and tear on the muscles, and the walker spends vital physiological energy avoiding pitfalls or getting out when he or she falls into one. The same applies to a production system. The more evenness, the less the energy expended to produce a given output or the greater the output that can be produced for a given level of effort. To promote efficiency, improve quality, and reduce cost, management must eliminate waste (muda), inconsistency or unevenness (mura), and unreasonableness (muri). Unevenness not only makes it difficult to standardize and rationalize the operation but it also results from questionable management practices. Wild swings in production volume may come from a natural seasonal sales pattern, but they may also indicate that the company is sales driven and not really concerned with long-term customer satisfaction.

It is usual for demand to have some seasonal variability that is caused by natural consumption or buying patterns that are industry or economywide. Discernible peaks and troughs are evident when one examines sales volume over time. Wide swings in demand do not necessarily cause problems. It is the way that the company produces to meet the demand that is bothersome, because one is usually placed in a catch-22 position, as far as JIT is concerned. The company can decide to level production by absorbing the variability in demand through the creation of so-called seasonal inventories which are depleted when sales are higher than the stable, fixed production rate. As an alternative to inventory, the company could vary lead time, placing customers on back orders when demand is higher than capacity and substantially reducing delivery dates when demand falls below capacity. The first scenario creates inventories, while the second results in poor service during peak demand periods.

The opposite strategy to level production is to produce in congruence with the sales pattern by varying the production rate. This creates load variability and schedule instability, two factors that reduce productive efficiency. Variability is the sworn enemy of efficiency and defect-free production. When production volume is changing too much, plant management has a tough time pinning down the production schedule and they cannot optimize the production plan or organize workers and machine centers into a stable, predictable work pattern. Volume changes are disruptive to efficient production because they invariably require hiring, firing, and transfer of production personnel, which destroys employee morale, loyalty, and motivation. Managers find it difficult to invest heavily in training new or transferred personnel when they know full well that those they train will likely not be around for long. Workers who are constantly on the move will find it hard to become true production craftsmen because learning takes time, even for the simplest tasks. An employee can learn an operational task in a few days, but cannot in that time master the total job and sufficiently understand its intricacies and relationship to other jobs in the plant. The worker in an environment where there are frequent and important volume changes is robbed of the stability he or she needs to creatively look at and evaluate the job and what it takes to improve it.

Load leveling is a fundamental JIT condition. The goal is to create an environment where stability is the norm and schedule changes are few and far apart. Allowing the factory to fall into a normal, predictable work rhythm is what load leveling is all about. Factory management already has enough uncertainty to worry about without problems caused by load variability—unreliable vendor performance, machine breakdowns, absenteeism, just to name a few. Just coping with day-to-day changes saps energy, and diverts attention from the company's central mission to provide customers with 100 percent good quality products at competitive prices and minimum delivery times. By achieving some load leveling, management liberates energy that can be focused on the strategic mission.

When the load is level, capacity management is easy because progressive refinement of capacity plans will lead to matching supply and demand. The factory might overestimate capacity during one period and underestimate it the next, but as long as the production rate is predictable, the right balance between production and sales will be found. Once a capacity plan that meets the sales target is in place, production managers can zero in on bottleneck operations and search for the plan that maximizes capacity utilization. Difficulties in planning capacity are normally due to instability in the production rate. Poor capacity utilization also results from frequent product volume changes, because the bottleneck is a moving target. By stabilizing the production rate, bottlenecks remain fixed allowing them to be analyzed and eliminated or even used more effectively if they are the result of poor system design. When the factory is scheduled to a level load, overall plant efficiency and capacity utilization can be substantially increased by taking action to squeeze more output from the bottleneck operation. This can be illustrated by referring to Figure 5–5. Operation 2 determines the production capacity per day. At maximum system capacity, given the bottleneck, Operation 3 is producing at 60 percent capacity. Increasing its utilization to 100 percent or 250 units per day, does nothing to increase output or efficiency. Increased efficiency or utilization at either Operation 1 or 3 is a total waste. When Operation 2 is at full capacity, average systemwide capacity utilization is 78 percent. Managing the bottleneck operation to increase its capacity to 200 units per day raises average system efficiency or capacity utilization to 95 percent. Load leveling, by keeping bottlenecks fixed for a sustained period makes them visible and allows management time to improve on them. The pay-off is a large

FIGURE 5–5   Isolating and Managing the Bottleneck

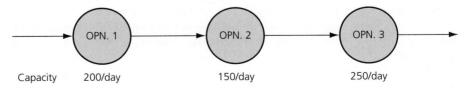

Isolating and managing the bottleneck

increase in total factory output resulting from a small investment at one or two bottleneck operations. And this increase in efficiency is real, because there is no commensurate increase in WIP and it is permanently sustainable.

Load leveling makes capacity balancing feasible and at the minimum necessary to provide competitive lead times with minimum WIP inventory. But where there are bottleneck operations due to capacity chunking, that is, different machines are available only in large "chunks" and capacity is not measured in equivalent units, then the best loading strategy is to plan for 100 percent utilization of the bottleneck work center. Other machine centers are then level loaded to the capacity of the constraining operation. WIP inventory can be squeezed from the system using this approach.

When the factory is not level loaded, every operation must have the flexibility to respond to large variations in demand. Flexibility to volume changes usually translates into excess capacity, particularly when volume increases are sudden. The plant that is not level loaded will never achieve near 100 percent capacity utilization and efficiency because it must have a large-capacity buffer. What many production managers refer to as flexibility is in fact surplus capacity and the wider the volume fluctuations the greater the excess needs to be. If there is not surplus capacity, uneven loads will dry up the bottleneck or minimum-capacity work centers, and the illusion of flexibility will quickly disappear.

Planning for a level load is a prerequisite to establishing a synchronized production flow, where the production rate at every work center is the same as and harmonized with other work centers. Variations in production rate cause WIP, but when output is the same at each operation, goods can flow nonstop, in continuous fashion, through the system. Whatever is produced at one work center can be immediately transferred for transformation to the next in line, because it is required work and it can be handled. A synchronous, continuous flow eliminates WIP, squashes idle time, and makes temporary production and efficiency problems visible. With level loading, the production at one work center automatically becomes the demand at subsequent work centers. The reverse is also true, that is, the production at a subsequent work center generates an equivalent demand at prior work centers. The production process is linked both backward and forward causing the system to stop when the production rate at any operation varies significantly from the norm set by the level load. Problem highlighting is built into the process itself and is an improvement on the Jidoka concept, where the problem must be seen by someone and action to highlight it requires human intervention.

If the production rate at each work center is similar and harmonized all through the process, then it does not matter whether the signal to produce comes from the first or the last operation, since individual processes are linked together both backward and forward. But the goal in JIT is eventually to make the system so trouble free and predictable that the factory can make what has been sold. Consequently, it will be better to use the last operation, which is closest to the customer order, to give a backward signal to produce. A level load and high system reliability would ensure that all prior processes can respond to the production signal, just-in-time. This is what is referred to as pull scheduling, and it results in dramatic decrease in WIP inventory. The forward-scheduling logic would create WIP when sales do not materialize or when there is a temporary capacity shortage at subsequent work centers. The pull logic, on the other hand, causes WIP to dry up and deepens the automatic stoppage effect. Pull by the last operation should not be envisaged where there is not some degree of load leveling because that would encourage surplus capacity at all operations.

Load Leveling in Practice

Implementing a level load policy is much less difficult than is imagined. The factors that prevent companies from level loading their factories are more often created by management policies and practices than imposed by unchangeable environmental forces. The forces that prevent a company from leveling production volume through the entire process are nurtured inside the organization. External conditions such as seasonal or cyclical demand patterns, although they determine how much leveling can be achieved, do not totally account for the wide fluctuations in production volume and employment that characterize production operations in North America. The major barriers are created by both marketing and production policy and the imperceptible interactions that take place between the two.

Marketing behavior is decisive in creating the attitude held by top management that the company cannot change or influence the sales pattern. Many of today's companies are still driven to maximize sales and market share at all cost. "Close the sale now" is the operative maxim and worry about quality, delivery promises, and cost reduction to show a profit, later. One company president who was the "best salesman that the company ever had" was totally convinced that sales were the basis for profit, so maximizing the latter, profits, absolutely required maximizing the former. After almost driving the company into the ground for two years trying to maximize sales, he was finally brought to his senses when he was reminded by the factory manager that there was an item between sales and profits that is ordinarily referred to as cost. Sales-driven, maximizing companies operate under the assumption that the company must follow the seasonal pattern because it is fixed by an unreasonable, tyrannical customer. That kind of customer will not and cannot be influenced to advance or delay his or her requirements.

Sometimes, particularly in the service industries, the demand is created by biological needs such as the need to eat, sleep, or recreate. Some manufacturing industries also have products the needs for which are temporal as exists in beverage and clothing industries. By contrast, however, most manufacturing

Smoothing the Sales Pattern

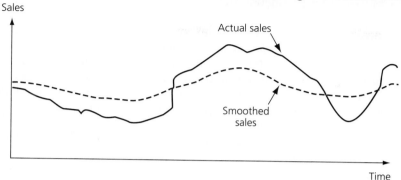

industries produce products whose demand can be advanced or delayed, within reasonable limits. The customer would be more than willing to make concessions to the manufacturing company, if superior quality, lower cost and reliable delivery could be guaranteed in return. Appropriate education can sensitize customers to the compromises involved and could set the stage for mutual understanding and long-term customer satisfaction, the surest way to achieve sustainable growth and profitability. Load leveling in the factory starts with marketing programs to achieve some smoothness in sales. Figure 5–6 depicts the nature of the problem. The natural sales pattern has some pronounced peaks and valleys. Specific marketing programs or ongoing customer education can smooth sales by making the peaks flatter and the valleys shallower. The graph also shows that it does not take a massive change in the demand structure to achieve reasonable and beneficial smoothness in sales. Shifting 10 percent of sales volume from peak to low demand periods, or 5 percent forward and 5 percent backward is sufficient for all practical purposes. Changing the demand pattern in this way requires that management tightly coordinate the marketing and promotion program with the production volume strategy. The marketing function must see that part of its role is to manage the customer in such a way as to permit the company to derive additional marketing leverage from production.

Uneven factory loading is also caused by generally-accepted production strategies and policies. Excess capacity creates the impression that the factory is flexible so top management really believes that large variations in sales can be accommodated at little or no cost. The simple fact is that the cost imposed by uneven loads such as low-capacity utilization rates, excessive WIP inventory, unreliable customer service, and inconsistent quality are severe, and can quickly eat up the margins on the small, short-term increase in sales generated by a chase-demand strategy. Large lot production adds to and aggravates the problem. It is known and can be easily demonstrated that producing end items in large lots amplifies the natural swings in demand. So, moving to implement small lot production helps a company to smooth the load placed on the factory.

Finally, production managers unquestioningly accept the idea that they must produce to meet an uneven sales volume because they feel powerless in the face of the sales driven strategies followed by their companies particularly when these strategies are formulated and pushed from the top. They have been conditioned by a corporate environment where the marketing function calls the shots and where sales people are the guardians of the company's strategic positioning. The politics of power in present day companies, except for a select few world-class corporations, are stacked against the production function. These companies may pride themselves into believing that they are marketing, customer oriented, but they are not. Total customer orientation and long-term satisfaction require that management use the factory to serve the customer. Trying to influence the sales pattern so as to promote efficiency, quality, and customer lead time reliability is an excellent way to create additional value for customers. Production managers should not allow themselves to be stigmatized as not being concerned with the customer when they express these views. On the contrary, it should be emphasized that these attitudes are ingrained in the minds of managers in every known world-class manufacturing company.

Flow Systematization

Production flow refers to the path or trajectory followed by the product as it goes through the transformation process. In some factories, the product follows a confused trajectory that causes it to zigzag through the plant, bypassing some work centers and alternately stopping and going like a repeatedly dammed, meandering river. The path is indirect and much longer than what is required by the underlying transformation process. In other factories, there is a direct, sequential flow from raw materials to the finished product. The path is visible and progression continuous. Even without theoretical concepts or empirical evidence, one should be able to see why a direct flow is more efficient. Flow systematization tries to create the direct, shortest route from raw materials to finished product.

Disorder in the work flow accounts for large increases in throughput times and WIP inventory. Plant layouts that are not based on a total view of all the operations required to make a product are likely to be haphazard and disordered. These confused layouts are responsible for the fact that products are uselessly carried long distances between operations that are far apart. Machine layout is not done to facilitate product handling and production flow, but rather to create space for WIP and to pursue an illusive flexibility. The result is that a product must skip one or more work centers before it gets to the right operation. Circular loops and flow backs are common features of the badly designed plant layout. In some factories these increases in transfer times account for up to 33 percent of production throughput time and also for a 75 percent increase in WIP inventory. Flow systematization is one way to effect dramatic reductions in throughput times and WIP inventory.

Inefficiency in production flow sometimes derives from piecemeal expansion of the factory. When capacity is needed at a bottleneck, management focuses on the work center affected and not on the entire sequence of operations. Additions to the plant are undertaken to relieve pressure on bottlenecks, one at a time, causing work centers to be split and dispersed throughout a growing factory. The factory's flow logic becomes blurred, even to those who actively participated in its design. Product routings become cumbersome due to the fact that there are many work centers for each basic operation. That fact aggravates the flow problem because now it is more difficult to balance capacity, giving rise to more bottlenecks. The only way out is to redesign the entire layout and production flow from scratch. Attempts at flow systematization will quickly reveal the magnitude of the problem that has to be solved.

Basic Flow Types

Production flows can conceptually be placed into four groups based on how close the path approaches the direct, shortest route through the transformation process. The two variables used for classification are continuity of operations and connectedness (i.e., the extent to which one operation is coupled or tied to upstream and downstream ones). The least desirable flow is the one that is random and uncoupled. As one increases the predictability and degree of coupling, one arrives at the ultimately efficient flow, where the path taken by the product is totally predictable and all operations are physically linked together.

Jumbled Flow

This is the classical job shop arrangement of the production process, where there is flow randomness and machine centers operate independently. There is no attempt to balance machine center capacity or to synchronize them with one another. Functionally similar machines are grouped together to form homogeneous work centers, hence the reason why the job shop is usually referred to as a functional layout. The sequence in which machine centers are located and their proximity to one another bear little or no relationship to the way in which physical product transformation takes place. The zigzag and sometimes circular work flow that is so prevalent in job shops derives from forcing a logical, continuous sequence of transformation activities to conform to a nonsequential functional layout. The jumbled flow is the farthest from the ideal, direct, shortest route path sought by flow systematization.

The widely held view that job shops have the inherent capability to efficiently produce highly differentiated, low-volume products must be critically reevaluated. Flexibility is not germane to machine functionality, the necessary criterion upon which the job shop-type plant layout is based. Job shops have traditionally been flexible because they use general purpose machines. Whatever can be done by a general purpose machine can also be done by an appropriate, well-selected group of special purpose machines. However, if specialized equipment were used in a job shop, there would be high levels of excess capacity and surplus machines. And herein lies the crux of the matter. Deploying special purpose machines in a job shop would have devastating consequences for efficiency and capacity utilization. Routings and production scheduling, already complex when general purpose machines are used, would become almost unmanageable. General purpose machines are not mandated by the fundamental, functional flow logic, but are used as a way to bring efficiency and capacity utilization up to tolerable levels. Despite widespread use of general purpose equipment, job shops have capacity utilization rates that are as low as 35 percent. This is the very high price that companies pay for designing job shops that will supposedly give them flexibility. Once more, this is an illusion. Any production system that sacrifices so much in efficiency and capacity utilization will be as "flexible" as a job shop. Jumbled flows result from fumbled layout designs.

Intermittent Disconnected Flow

This flow type has the general structure shown in Figure 5–7. The two operations that compose the transformation process are as close to each other as possible. However, the work being done at Operation 1 is not synchronized with that at Operation 2. For instance, if there are four products in the product line Operation 1 could be working on one production batch of product 1, while Operation 2 could be working on product 3. Operations 1 and 2, although they are both necessary to produce each product, are entirely decoupled (disconnected) from one another using WIP inventory. The flow is sequential but it is not the shortest trajectory between the two operations. Four additional, hidden time-consuming phases are added to the process. The processes cannot be physically linked until the WIP inventory is completely taken out. Operation 1 is not producing what Operation 2 requires but is producing to WIP. Shop queues and lead times are close to their maximum with the intermittent, disconnected flow. A breakdown or quality problems at Operation 2 does nothing to stop production at Operation 1. Similarly, all four WIP inventories will have to be depleted before a breakdown at Operation 1 causes Operation 2 to shut down. The intermittent, disconnected flow totally hides operating problems both upstream and downstream of troublesome machine centers. By progressively squeezing WIP out of the system, one can

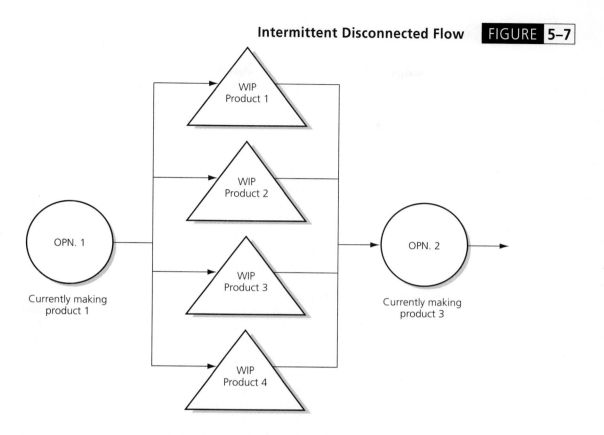

Intermittent Disconnected Flow FIGURE 5-7

move closer to process synchronization. Flow systematization results from continuously improving synchronization and increasing the low WIP inventory turns of the intermittent disconnected flow.

Intermittent Connected Flow

As shown in Figure 5-8 improved synchronization of the two operations means that they are always working on the same product at the same time, and there is only one product in WIP. The products are still cycled intermittently, or in batches. This simply means that a lot size of one product is produced and put in finished goods inventory, after which another product is produced. The products are intermittently cycled through the production process, but only one at a time. Operation 1 is still producing to WIP inventory, but a higher level of synchronization has cut WIP by 75 percent. One notices that there is a direct relationship between WIP reduction and product line differentiation. For example the synchronization needed to implement an intermittent connected flow would cut WIP by 90 percent if there were 10 products and by 99 percent if there were 100 products in the product line.

FIGURE **5–8** **Intermittent Connected Flow**

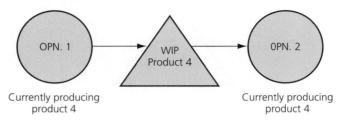

The reduction in WIP would also lead to dramatic reductions in queue and factory lead time. The flow is as direct as that of the intermittent disconnected flow, but the system has been brought closer to achieving the shortest path between raw materials and finished goods. The company that has achieved intermittent, connected flow is ready to push for the ultimate in flow systematization and process integration.

Continuous Coupled Flow

When the flow has been coupled, all intervening operations that do not add value to the product have been eliminated or reduced to what is needed to transfer units from one operation to the next. The sequence of work centers is totally determined by how transformation progressively takes place. All operations are simultaneously working on the same part and they are wholly dependent on one another. Successive processes are synchronized and tied to end item production. The flow is direct, with no backward loops as exists in the jumbled flow. The space and time path between raw materials and finished product is the shortest possible. WIP inventory is held at the level necessary to assure continuity of operations, given the transportation time between the various operations that comprise the production process. When there is a stoppage at any one operation, the whole system shuts down because the operations function like a single piece of equipment. Where conveyors are used to transfer work pieces, physical process integration can be attained by substantially reducing or eliminating these conveyors. Figure 5–9 shows the continuous coupled flow. Machine centers are the most natural that can be expected, given the way technology dictates that transformation should take place. One notes that the WIP does not decouple the operations but are used to physically link them. The role that WIP plays in the flow has been reversed.

Flow Systematization and JIT

Dramatic reductions in WIP inventory result from flow systematization. Depending on the number of products in the product line, one can achieve

Continuous Coupled Flow FIGURE 5-9

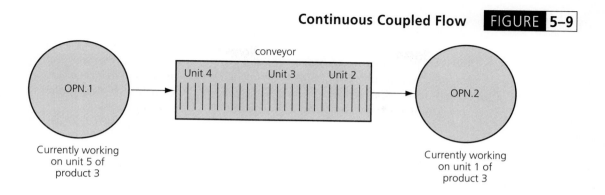

tenfold decreases in WIP by designing the flow so as to achieve the shortest path through the transformation process. The jumbled flow creates waste in movement, transportation, and queue times which can be driven to zero by structuring the flow to be more efficient. Considering that move and queue times often account for 80 to 95 percent of factory lead times, flow systematization can enable a company to offer much more competitive lead times to its customers.

Flow systematization is also the basic condition that must be met in order to achieve process integration. By physically integrating processes, a built-in Jidoka (Andon) mechanism, that is the stoppage of all work when there is a problem, is built into the transformation process. In some cases, WIP that was measured in thousand pieces was reduced to only a few. An integrated process is necessarily a balanced process because production volume automatically adjusts itself to the capacity of the slower "operation." So, the continuous coupled flow not only shuts down the whole system when the production is interrupted at any phase in the operation, but also slows or accelerates it automatically in response to moderate changes in demand. Increasing the throughput of the bottleneck operation instantly raises output systemwide.

Intermittent, decoupled processes have a negative impact on quality. Feedback on quality is very slow making it difficult, if not impossible, to trace defects to their source. When each operation in the flow is working on a different part, considerable time expires before the parts that are produced at one work center are used by subsequent work centers. By the time later processes are using the parts from previous operations, the latter would likely be working on a different product, robbing the first operation of the opportunity to prevent defects. The only alternatives left are either to repair defects at downstream work stations or to create a specialized repairs department for that purpose. In any event, the work center which produced defects did not have to repair them, which makes building quality consciousness difficult. By contrast, work centers in continuous, coupled flow operations are working on the same part, and are only a few parts removed from each other. Defects are discovered by the next downstream operation minutes after they are produced. The problem can be corrected so as to prevent defects on the remaining pieces. Continuous, coupled flow processes create an environment where defect-prevention strategies, such as repairing bad quality at the operation that produced it, can be actively and advantageously put into action.

Building Flexibility into Flow Lines

Prevailing textbook concepts present the flow line as an inherently inflexible production system just as they argue that flexibility is germane to the jumbled flow (job shop) arrangement. As in the job shop case, however, the generally accepted notion that flow or assembly lines are fundamentally rigid production systems is based on erroneous reasoning and misconceptions. The error lies in the failure to accurately differentiate between commonplace errors in line flow design and the foundation flow line concepts. Results achieved by some leading North American and Japanese companies in managing assembly lines created acute awareness that inflexible production lines result from design errors and operating constraints that result from flawed management principles and concepts. Flow lines are not inescapably rigid but flexibility must be designed into them. A line that is designed to be flexible definitely gives superior quality, cost, and lead time performance. It is possible to have a flexible response to the market in addition to superior efficiency and quality performance, the latter two being germane to the flow line.

Set-Up Reduction
Continuous, coupled flow systems have traditionally been used to produce high-volume, low-variety items because changeover times are so high as to make producing low-volume items inefficient. This is true where set-up times are extremely high. Therefore, drastic reductions in set-up times increase production line flexibility, making it economically attractive to produce low-volume items. The line is not inflexible per se, but the high set-up times induce management to dedicate it to high-volume standardized products. When management assumes that set-up times cannot be reduced, high-volume production becomes a permanent fixture of the flow line. If it takes eight hours for line changeovers, then the system is indeed inflexible, as far as product variety is concerned. High set-up times do not necessarily come with a flow line process. Job shops and continuous flow systems have an equal propensity to have long set-up times, but the general purpose machines used in most job shops assuage the problem, not by making changeovers easier, but by making them less frequent.

The evidence that has emerged from studying world-class manufacturers shows quite conclusively that 95 to 98 percent reductions in set-up times are entirely feasible. Toyota Motor Company has managed to reduce set-up times for some very complicated machines such as 800 ton hood and fender presses from 8 hours to 8 minutes. When such a specialized machine can be changed over in 8 minutes, one cannot talk about flow line inflexibility. On the contrary, an 8-minute changeover time gives maximum flexibility to economically produce a differentiated product line.

Flow Line Design

Four line designs are used in practice and their general structures are shown in Figure 5–10. The straight and L-shaped lines are the most prevalent but are also the least flexible. Workers have very little backward and forward mobility, making it difficult for them to help each other when problems arise or when there is a bottleneck. Straight and L-shaped lines discourage cross-training of workers and flexible work assignments. The U-shaped lines allow for both vertical (backward and forward) and lateral mobility and therefore provide far more flexibility than L-shaped lines. Most workers on a U-shaped line eventually come to master four different tasks. However, the U-shaped line, just like the straight and L-shaped, shuts off all production when there is a major problem. Parallel lines are as flexible as the U-shaped lines and also give better utilization. When one line is down, the other is likely to be running, so that the worst case scenario is a 50 percent reduction in output at any point in time. Line structure has a significant impact on flexibility and efficiency. Whenever possible, parallel lines should be used for maximum flexibility and capacity utilization. U-shaped and parallel lines also have positive motivational effects. Tasks are broadened—each worker does two—which reduces fractionation. Better face-to-face worker contact also contributes to a positive motivation climate.[3]

Repetitive Production

JIT originated in the consumer products industries of Japan such as automobiles and television sets. This had led some people to propagate the mistaken idea that JIT is only applicable to repetitive manufacturing situations. But while all the concepts of JIT are perfectly suited to repetitive manufacturing, the applications have gone well beyond these industries. Repetitive manufacturing creates the opportunities to have totally JIT companies, but a company can apply a substantial number of the JIT concepts even if it does not have repetitive production, and thus achieve substantial competitive leverage.

---

[3]Richard Schonberger, *Japanese Manufacturing Techniques: Nine Hidden Lessons in Simplicity,* (New York: The Free Press, 1982), 131–155.

FIGURE 5–10 Flow Line Designs

a. Straight line

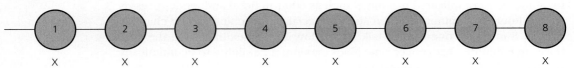

b. L-shaped line

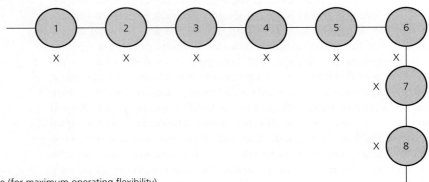

c. U-shaped line (for maximum operating flexibility)

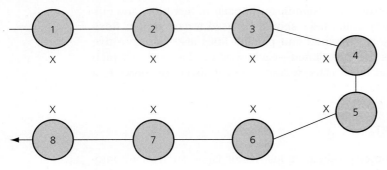

d. Parallel lines (for maximum operating flexibility)

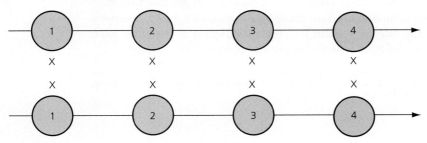

There are many reasons why JIT is more perfectly suited to repetitive manufacturing. Typically, in that environment, one is working with a standard product with standard and often interchangeable components and a predictable demand pattern. Consequently, it is easier to program production according to a reasonably fixed pattern and match the delivery of materials to that schedule. The learning process can be exploited to the maximum because the production environment is more stable and tasks, work methods, and shop floor design can be stabilized.

Basically, repetitive manufacturing offers the stability that aids in pushing a production system to higher levels of efficiency. In short, management can master nearly all the intricacies of the production system because of a stable pattern of problems and situations.

Repetitive production also helps in other ways such as the following:

1. The master production schedule can be stabilized and frozen, thus eliminating an important source of uncertainty and a cause of inventory. Once this is achieved, all other activities can be pulled by the MPS.
2. Repetitive production can be easily linked to repetitive, scheduled deliveries of very small lots of materials. Freezing of the MPS means that suppliers will have had enough advanced notice and planning information from the customer, which enables them to attain very high levels of delivery performance.
3. One can move easily to short-cycle manufacturing which helps in the rapid diagnosis of quality problems and the reduction of in-process batches.
4. The principle of $N = 2$, inspect the first and last piece of a production run, can be applied so as to minimize inspection while increasing quality levels.
5. The output of the system can be programmed and any deviation from scheduled output is a symptom of a problem.
6. Bottlenecks in the production system are predictable and action can be taken to eliminate them, thus increasing efficiency further.

The above comments mean that companies should try to exploit to the fullest-extent whatever repetitive production potential their production systems possess and they should also strive to increase that potential. In some cases, the product can be made in repetitive mode, but the potential is hidden from view because of the way management has chosen to respond to the market. In the name of the pursuit of growth, some companies try to compete in all segments of a given market, with the variations in product specifications that this involves, rather than focusing on standardizing the product by serving one or two niches. In other cases, a simple restructuring of the factory so that each subfactory is dedicated to one market niche, would greatly enhance the potential to move toward repetitive production. Even if the entire factory may not be amenable to repetitive production, certain sections of it could and these could be exploited by using a dedicated manufacturing cell. The point is that JIT and the systematic pursuit of manufacturing excellence require that the company exploit its innate potential for repetitive production to the fullest extent possible.

PROCESS INTEGRATION

Prior discussion indicated that there is a natural connection between flow systematization and WIP inventory reduction. WIP enables operations to function independently and intermittently. As these operations are synchronized and the flow is systematized, they begin to function as one process in near perfect harmony, thus eliminating the need for WIP. The results achieved by systematizing the flow and synchronizing production make it possible not only to make the operations *function* as one process but also to physically integrate them so that they *in fact* become one process. The aim is to design the plant in such a way that the many operations, although they perform different functions in the transformation system, are so harmonized and physically linked that they are one process in every other respect.

A physically integrated process is one that is perfectly balanced and operating in a pure just-in-time mode. Where the operations in a flow are physically tied together, there is perfect interdependence, so that the whole flow is interrupted once any operation stops. It cannot be any other way. Full process integration has not been achieved until the system automatically stops when any one operation ceases to function. Consequently, a physically integrated process must necessarily produce and transfer parts, just-in-time. A process (any one operation in the flow) cannot produce and transfer parts to itself, that is, to the physically integrated operations except just-in-time, one piece at a time. In that sense, constant improvement in the production system and materials flow to drive the plant toward JIT will culminate in a perfectly synchronized, integrated process where goods flow continuously or they do not flow at all. The production system will either operate trouble free or it will be in a shut down mode. This is the ultimate goal in JIT: All production is produced in a problem free environment because when there are problems, the entire system is down and when it is producing, there are no problems. The plant can now realistically deliver 100 percent good product. Like flow systematization, physical process integration minimizes WIP inventory and move times, and makes possible defect prevention since there is instantaneous feedback on quality. The process will also shut down when quality problems cannot be corrected "on the spot." The ability to build an automatic stoppage feature (Andon) in a process when there is a problem in a critical step in the search for continuous improvement and competitive superiority. Physical process integration builds that capability into the entire production system on line and is thus a potent tool of manufacturing strategy and the search for competitive advantage through manufacturing.

Phases in Process Integration FIGURE 5–11

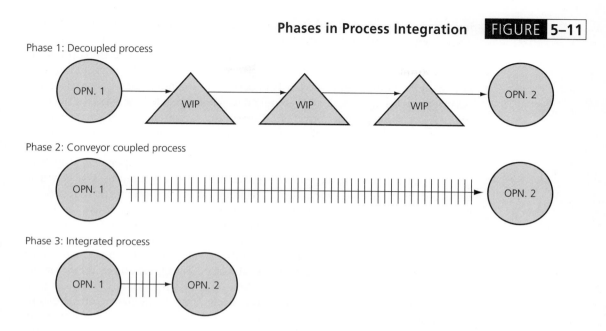

Phase 1: Decoupled process

OPN. 1 → WIP → WIP → WIP → OPN. 2

Phase 2: Conveyor coupled process

OPN. 1 →|||||||||||||||||||||||||||||||||||||→ OPN. 2

Phase 3: Integrated process

OPN. 1 →||||→ OPN. 2

Evolving toward Physical Process Integration

There are three distinct phases a production system goes through as it becomes physically integrated. These are shown schematically in Figure 5–11. The first phase is the decoupled, nonintegrated operation where sequential transfer batches of WIP are stored between the work centers. Inventory takes space, so the operations are far apart and there is neither flow nor volume interdependence. As WIP is reduced, the system evolves to the second phase, a conveyor coupled (integrated) process. The operations are still far apart, but they are linked by conveyor. An automatic conveyor would represent a somewhat higher level of integration, since the flow between the two work centers could be paced by the speed of the conveyor. Drying or choking up of the conveyor would indicate volume imbalance between the operations. WIP

Computing WIP Inventory TABLE 5–1

	Case 1	Case 2
Cycle time per piece	1 min.	1 min.
Distance between operations	60 ft.	60 ft.
Conveyor speed	20 ft./min.	30 ft./min.
WIP inventory (pieces)	3	2

inventory is determined by conveyor speed, the physical distance between the operations, and the cycle time at which the bottleneck operation is producing. Table 5–1 estimates WIP based on the data assumed. The third phase in process integration, a fully integrated process, is achieved by eliminating conveyors or reducing them to what is necessary to maintain the optimal distance between the operations. Space is reduced to what is needed for process functioning. All decoupling and "move" WIP inventory is eliminated when the operations are brought to close physical proximity. The conveyor can be eliminated when a worker can hand the piece that was just finished to the next worker. This is true physical process integration because if any one operation stops the entire system automatically shuts itself down. When Operation 1 is down it cannot deliver parts to Operation 2, which cannot continue to produce. Similarly, a stoppage at Operation 2 causes Operation 1 to stop because the problem operation cannot take the next part and there is no space for storing it. The processes become perfectly balanced also. If the cycle time at Operation 2 increases to two minutes per piece, (Table 5–1) then Operation 1 is producing too many parts which cannot be absorbed by Operation 2. The system chokes up. The only way to prevent choking is to slow down Operation 1 or eliminate the problem that caused the cycle time to deviate from the one minute standard. The latter would be the preferred approach. A stoppage at one operation liberates workers at other work centers to give help to fix the problem at the trouble spot. Feedback on quality is almost instantaneous.

Physical process integration permanently changes the production system structure so as to maintain WIP inventory and throughput times at the minimum levels attained by improvement activities. Unless the operations are physically integrated, there will be a tendency for the factory to revert to the old practices that gave rise to decoupled operations in the first place. By physically integrating processes, management designs the improvements made on WIP, throughput time reduction, and quality feedback into the physical, structural characteristics of the system. The efficiency and quality control parameters are built into the processes themselves and are not left to the discretion of workers and managers. Worker creativity is better used on tasks that truly require human judgment because they cannot be relegated to a machine or control system. Human talent is wasted every time it is used to solve problems or perform activities that are better done by machines.

GROUP TECHNOLOGY

Product Line Evolution

Nearly every company starts its business by producing and marketing a single, relatively undifferentiated product. Initially, the entire organization is focused on meeting the market requirements that will establish the product in the marketplace and give it broad acceptance. The production system is usually specifically designed to produce and deliver the market requirements of that one well defined product and the marketing criteria are narrow and well understood by production managers. All the key business functions such as marketing, production and materials, research and development, and finance are playing to the same very clear strategic drumbeat, and are dancing to the same competitive tune. Evidently, a product will not be able to challenge other existing, well-entrenched products and gain a foothold in the market unless there is a total, coordinated assault by all functions, which emanates from a clear, broadly understood competitive mission and unambiguous market requirements. Most products that succeed in achieving market acceptability must meet the criteria just mentioned.

Success in establishing an acceptable market position for the first product emboldens top management to seek broader market scope or coverage by modifying the basic product to meet similar market needs. The existing product is by now generating adequate profits that can be plowed back into research and development. Raising capital for related ventures is much easier when a company has a success story to build on. Moreover, R&D expenditures for adapting and differentiating the product are significantly lower, and the time required to go from design concept to product marketing is much shorter than for the first new product. The company has gained valuable manufacturing experience and production learning curve effects have started to push per unit manufacturing costs down to near parity with entrenched products. The peculiar marketing requirements are also better understood. The company can start to dovetail the marketing mix—the intrinsic product characteristics such as quality, form, fit and function, price, promotion program such as media choice and advertising budget, and the distribution channel for making the product available to customers—the four Ps—to well-defined and narrow market niches. All these factors and others lead inevitably to broader product differentiation.

Under pressure to keep responding to greater product differentiation, production expands plant capacity, adds machines, and creates production units haphazardly. While factory focus is almost automatic when one has to worry about only a single, well-defined product targeted to a particular market niche, product differentiation requires that focus be deliberately thought through and designed into the factory. And the broader the product line, the more managers must approach production system design with deliberation and clear strategic and competitive intent. Efforts to maximize sales and market share by increasing product differentiation cause top management to overlook the fact that the focused factory gives the company strategic marketing leverage from production. Single-minded emphasis on product differentiation with no parallel effort to differentiate at the plant level leads to unfocused production units, jumbled flows, and conflicting marketing demands being placed on the factory. Bringing together like products or parts with similar market and production requirements to form simplified, homogeneous, and tightly focused production units is the only way to restore order to the chaotic factory structure that is created by uncontrolled product differentiation. Group technology provides the mechanism for attacking the problem and provides some foundation data for process integration and cellular manufacturing, concepts that will be discussed subsequently.

What Is Group Technology?

Products or parts manufactured by a company, no matter how varied they may be, always have some characteristics in common. Group technology tries to find a logical basis for putting parts into like families, so as to design production systems that are better suited to the exigencies of each family. At one extreme, every company can be said to have a single family of parts or products, the common denominator being simply that they are produced by the same company. One will recognize, however, that this is a poor basis for grouping parts or products, because it rationalizes the status quo. It is also inconceivable that a company, except at its inception, will have products that all have the same marketing and production requirements. Some marketing mix and production system variation can usually be justified even for a narrow product line. No matter what the product, management can always find different ways to position it in the marketplace, which almost always means that some production factors must be designed, organized, deployed, and managed differently.

At the other extreme there is the possibility that each part is viewed as unique and requires a specially designed production unit. This is obviously not feasible for many reasons that are not necessary to delve into here. Group technology tries to find an acceptable middle ground between these two extreme positions by devising ways to group parts or products so that sufficient focus can be achieved without unmanageable production system differentiation.

How does a company know when it has pushed production system differentiation too far? The answer to this question is not as difficult as is imagined. As long as top management can conclusively pinpoint superior, customer perceptible performance on a key success factor that is produced by a specialized productive unit, then it has gained market leverage by further production unit differentiation. Group technology, by trying to answer the question how different from or similar a part is to others, tries to provide a sound basis for choosing the appropriate level of differentiation at the factory level.

Bases for Grouping Parts[4]

Four variables are normally used to group parts into families. The first which gives rise to the job shop-type system is process technology. All parts that

---

[4]We differentiate here between Group Technology as a logic and set of methods, concepts, and procedures for finding similarities between parts and products and Cellular Manufacturing, which exploits these similarities to create homogeneous, focused and high-performing manufacturing units called cells.

need similar machines to manufacture them are put together as one family and tend to be made in the same machine center. Part geometry is the second way for grouping parts. In this case, all parts are analyzed to see what common geometrical patterns exist, and those that are similar are grouped into a family. Metal fabrication shops find part geometry to be an effective way to form families, particularly when a CAD/CAM system is already in use. CAD makes details on part design quickly available and each part can be rigorously evaluated on screen before it is placed in one family or another. Material type is the third basis for grouping parts. Finally, parts can be grouped by process flow. The information for this will come from analyzing all part routings. All parts having the same or highly similar routings are grouped. Grouping by process flow is advantageous because it facilitates flow systematization and process integration.

Clearly, no one variable will be sufficient to accurately evaluate the similarity between parts or products. A first cut grouping using one variable could be sharpened by applying a second variable to the group that has been formed. The process can continue until little or no new additional information is generated. The main point is that appropriate structuring of the production system for differentiation and focus requires that some logical basis for grouping parts and products be found and applied.

CELL MANUFACTURING

Flow systematization and physical process integration feed on each other in symbiotically potent ways. These underlying JIT mechanisms can be collectively used to push manufacturing to even higher performance levels. They can be effectively used to design a cellular manufacturing structure, a production organization that integrates many bedrock concepts of superior performance manufacturing into a single small-scale production unit whose place in the large manufacturing system is clearly visible.

A cell is a small scale, clearly defined production unit within a larger factory that has complete responsibility for producing a family of like parts or a product. All machines and manpower needed to make the part or product family are contained within the cell, giving it some operational autonomy. Flexible worker assignments promoted by complete worker training are two important characteristics. Each worker is expected to master the full range of operating skills that are required by the cell. Systematic job rotation and training are therefore necessary conditions for effective cell development.

Self-management by the cell is aggressively promoted. The workers in a cell are encouraged to think creatively about production problems and are expected to come up with pragmatic solutions to these. They can seek advice and counsel from staff and plant management, but the problems are identified and analyzed by them and the solutions are entirely their own.

Workers implement and follow up on action plans to improve their work. Self-management is taken to the point where each cell sets improvement targets for itself and measures its performance against these. In addition, workers are allowed freedom to plan, coordinate and control their work, as long as they meet the volume, quality, time, and cost targets that are set plantwide.

By creating small-scale production units that are dedicated to produce a few similar parts, management increases work group cohesiveness. Each cell has only a few employees, typically less than 14, making interpersonal contact extensive. Strong human relationships are formed when all workers are part of a single, identifiable unit and are given operating autonomy and responsibility for a specific product. Workers are linked by the common purpose to continually improve the productive unit for which they are given significant responsibility. The self-management features that are built into cell organization tap the workers' innate need for responsibility and autonomy and give them the opportunity to exercise their creative potential in a pragmatic way. The cell structure keeps problems at a level where they are manageable even while workers are occupied with the operating task. For those problems that call for technical expertise beyond what workers can reasonably be expected to master, managers and production staff can be voluntarily called on to provide assistance. Cell manufacturing builds a cohesive subculture within the wider social environment created in the plant by top management.

Flexible work assignments tap the human drive to excel in a direct way. Employees are constantly learning new tasks, which keeps them challenged. Behavioral psychology is conclusive on the point that challenging work assignments keep employees motivated, satisfied, and highly productive. Job rotation within the confines of the cell introduce variety in work patterns, thus breaking monotony, which is recognized to cause absenteeism, quality, and productivity problems. Moreover, flexible work assignments contribute even more to work group cohesiveness and loyalty. Employees who regularly do the work done by other co-workers are more likely to demonstrate empathy and supportiveness when dealing with each other on the job. Workers are more able to offer encouragement and advice on how the work can be improved because they have experienced each job firsthand. Each worker can completely view and understand the tasks, responsibilities and mission dedicated to the cell by top management. Workers teach each other because "as iron sharpens iron, so shall one man sharpen another." The cross-fertilization process that emerges from this generates some truly creative ideas for work improvement. Cellular manufacturing is a tested way to eradicate the lukewarm, lackadaisical attitude that workers generally harbor toward one another's work in North American plants. Individualism and anonymity, nurtured by the wider society, are allowed to infiltrate the factory with severe consequences such as high absenteeism and dismal productivity. Industrial work can only be productively done in a work group setting. By energizing the work group, cellular manufacturing attacks industrial lethargy at its source.

Breaking the factory into small, homogeneous and cohesive productive units makes for easier production and quality control. Cells that are not performing according to volume and quality targets can be easily isolated, since the specific products or parts affected can be traced back to a single cell. The search for causes is made easy because the productive units involved are small. Quality parameters and control procedures are dovetailed to the particular requirements of the parts in question. Quality control activity is focused by production unit and part type which means that the cell can quickly master the quality requirements. Control is always enhanced when productive units are kept at minimum-required operating scale, a necessary condition for implementing cellular manufacturing.

When production is structured using cellular manufacturing logic, flow systematization can be rationalized. Group technology will reveal that different parts or products are more or less amenable to continuous, coupled flow. Some parts, because they are standardized, are common to many products and have very low changeover times, and thus, are quickly convertible to continuous, line flow production. Other low-volume, high-variety, and long set-up items can be managed to evolve toward a line flow much more slowly. Cells can be designed to exploit the characteristics that are peculiar to each part family and the flow can be "optimized" for each cell and for the group of cells as a whole. Flow systematization can be done one cell at a time, in order to avoid large scale disruptions in factory operations. The cells for which it is easy to systematize the flow provide rapid experience that can be exploited to tackle the big flow systematization projects later on. Cells that have been changed to line flow will invariably show superior performance on quality, throughput times and cost, providing the concrete evidence that enormous plantwide benefit can be attained.

Manufacturing cells give real production flexibility. Systematic job rotation and training in multiple skills make possible quick, flexible work assignments that can be used to alleviate bottlenecks anywhere they occur in the cell. Little or no additional training is required when workers have to be redeployed in response to volume or sales mix changes, since normal cell operation requires them to master all the skills internal to the cell. The goal is to make it routine for workers to learn new skills so that they can be easily transferred to another job within the cell or even to an entirely different production unit. Flexible work assignments create worker versatility without which there can be no real production system flexibility.

The work flow in a production system that is structured using cells is adapted to the unique requirements of each product or part. This allows the plant to produce high-volume, low-variety and low-volume, high-variety products simultaneously. The cell structure integrates both worker and product variety versatility into a single plant, giving it the potential to attain maximum production system flexibility. High factory focus can still be maintained. Cells can be designed around single products, product groups, unique parts, part families or at whatever level unique market requirements can be identified. For the same part, there may be one high-volume, standardized design and one low-volume customized design. Cells can be built for any of these, each focusing on the peculiar marketing or production requirements called for by each product or part type.

Cellular manufacturing makes self-management by workers a daily reality, going beyond the often faddish, mushy ideas propagated by some who are hooked on participative management. Some managers espouse participative management even while they harbor quite negative attitudes toward their subordinates' creative abilities. Cellular manufacturing takes the company beyond popularized participative management concepts to actual, ongoing, total employee involvement. It calls for radical changes in the way industrial work is designed, structured, planned, controlled, and supervised, a step that no top management can or will take unless it is deeply convinced that workers can master all aspects of their work. The decision to implement manufacturing cells can only come from a deep commitment to excellence and an overwhelming desire to permanently change the way the factory is viewed and managed. Too many executives believe that the factory and factory workers cannot be motivated to excel or that competitive excellence has nothing to do with production. The opposite is true. Corporate excellence must create excellence in the factory and a company cannot effectively compete until it has honed production into a corporate strategic arsenal.

When all factory employees are actively and continually bringing their mental capabilities to bear on job-related problems the sheer number of ideas generated are enough to energize the workplace. Ten employees in one cell who produce one idea each per week would have generated 520 suggestions in a single year. These are likely to be very practical ideas because production workers are so close to the job. Ideas instigate other ideas, giving rise to a continuous, almost self-sustaining chain reaction. Soon, there are so many that even if a small percentage are implemented the workplace would be revolutionized. As workers see their own creative output at work generating concrete results, they develop strong self-esteem and desire to succeed. They begin to challenge their own prior accomplishments and push even harder for improvement. The human need to achieve is fueled by concrete achievements that reinforce the drive toward excellence. Desire to excel and improvement action become tightly locked into the factory value system. Workers improve on the quality of their ideas as they become more proficient due to learning by doing.

There is conclusive evidence for these observations in some companies in North America. It has been noticed that there are very few good quality suggestions that come from the work force when a company starts an employee involvement program using small group improvement teams. There tends to be general skepticism at first because employees tend to view management's initial overtures as another employee participation gimmick. However, if management demonstrates that it is serious and persists in granting employees autonomy and responsibility for managing and improving their work, timidity quickly gives way to boldness. One company received a few suggestions from an entire team for the first six months of implementing an employee involvement program. Two years later, each team member was contributing two suggestions for improvement every month, bringing an annual team total to 192. The percentage accepted, which reflects their quality, went from 8 percent to 30 percent in just two years. True employee involvement unleashes the latent creative potential that every employee has and brings it to bear on problems in the workplace. Cellular manufacturing is the structural catalyst that starts, sustains, and contains the process.

Structuring the plant with manufacturing cells flattens the factory management structure and squeezes overhead out. Work group autonomy, worker versatility, and small group improvement activities all converge to drastically reduce, if not eliminate, the need for supervision. Cell manufacturing implements the idea that the work group should supervise itself. It also simplifies production planning and control, reducing planning and control staff. A work force that is motivated, trained and assigned specific clear responsibility for a product or part, does not need to be minutely supervised or controlled in order to do its job well. Complicated supervisory and control systems are required when workers have not been trained, motivated, and developed to be true production artisans.

Work group cohesiveness, which is reinforced by the cell structure, facilitates total people management. The cell can be more easily mobilized due to its small scale and mission focus. The cell is better able to exercise social control over deviant workers since it can more directly and immediately manipulate the social rewards and punishment system. The group can very quickly detect deviant behavior and can immediately withdraw social support from the worker who fails to conform. Similarly, a high performing group member is quickly visible and rewarded with esteem and respect from co-workers. Deviant behavior can be hidden from top management for a very long time, but it is visible to the small group. Consequently, management can work through the cell to instill the foundation corporate values, attitudes, and philosophies. Once these are internalized by key team members, the group itself will take over the socialization process to inculcate the values into the mindset of each worker. Corporatewide values are better communicated and instilled into daily work habits by small group processes. Top management is much too far, both spacially and socially, from individual workers to be able to interact with them intensively enough to permit these managers to significantly control the socialization process. Executives can shape corporate values and create an organizational environment for their sustenance and nurturing, but they cannot be reasonably expected to inculcate them into the minds of lower level employees. This must be left to the group, and cell manufacturing provides the conceptual framework for its implementation.

FIGURE 5–12 **The Organization as an Integrated Pipeline**

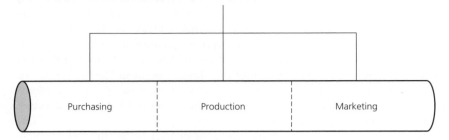

| Purchasing | Production | Marketing |

TOTAL INTEGRATION: THE PIPELINE CONCEPT

Process integration, small lot production that is driven by set-up reduction, and balanced uninterrupted production all contribute to a smooth continuous flow of product through the factory. Sales or marketing, production, and purchasing can thus be coordinated and orchestrated to function as a unitary, integrated input–transformation–output system. Such a system functions as a pipeline and attains maximum total resource productivity (see Figure 5-12). The ultimate goal of continuous improvement in manufacturing is to reduce lead times, WIP inventory, cycle times, process variability, downtime, and defects, to name a few crucial performance factors, until the whole company functions as a pipeline. Superior technical expertise contributes to the process of building this pipeline, but the fundamental skills that make it happen are managerial in nature. Technology, even if critical, must be harnessed by management in order for it to culminate in competitive superiority.

Conclusion

The choice of production system structure or configuration is an important aspect of manufacturing/operations strategy implementation. Structural decisions build competitive and strategic concerns, priorities, and constraints into the physical design of the production system. The structure of the production system also reveals the strategic intent that guided its deliberate design. The implementation of structural decisions creates the physical potential to pursue key strategic priorities but also bind or constrain top manufacturing management to a limited set of strategic options or avenues. Management cannot pursue competitive priorities that are beyond the physical capability of the production system.

The decision to focus the production system by designing, structuring, and managing it to execute a limited set of clearly defined competitive priorities is probably the most strategically significant structural decision that can be implemented by management. The focused factory is a mechanism of corporate and manufacturing strategy implementation because:

1. It calls for identification of clearly defined market niches and an accurate understanding of the key success factors of each.
2. It is based on a sound understanding of the unique capabilities that the production system must master in order to have the potential to contribute significantly to the creation of strategic advantage.
3. It operationalizes strategic choice at the level of the plant or operating unit by translating product and market differentiation into specialization at the level of the manufacturing/operations unit.
4. It requires consistent and coherent policies, philosophies and priorities at all levels of management and pushes these down to the factory floor.
5. It creates a production system that is driven by a strategic and manufacturing mission.
6. It simplifies the production system.

Other structural decisions, such as the focus of the manufacturing organization, cellular manufacturing, and structuring the production system for JIT, reinforce factory focus and further simplify the manufacturing/operations unit. They have also proved to be invaluable in increasing manufacturing and operations efficiency and effectiveness and in raising the level of competitive performance. Companies that excel in the marketplace are consistent in applying most or all of these concepts, but particularly factory focus, to design strategically significant production system structures.

Case for Discussion

NEW TECHNOLOGY CORPORATION (NTC)

Mr. Richard Osborne, president of NTC, was contemplating a restructuring of his company's operations to respond to a clear competitive threat. Since its founding more than eight years ago, the company's basic strategy, mission, structure, operating methods, and technology had remained basically the same. The entrance of a new competitor had made it necessary to rethink the company's approach to serving the market.

The Company

NTC was a medium-sized Canadian manufacturer of high-quality door windows and a limited line of sliding vertical and horizontal windows located in a small, semi-rural town with a very strong work ethic. Sales had grown from $800,000 in 1983 to $19.5 million in 1992, and total employment was currently 96. Profits in fiscal 1992 were $1.3 million. The company manufactured only high-quality door windows for the renovation market, but entered the new construction market with a full line of door windows in 1987. It added a limited line of sliding windows in 1988 in order to maintain a healthy growth rate.

The company's growth and development were based on the pursuit of three priorities:

1. To manufacture and deliver the highest quality door windows in the industry at the lowest possible price commensurate with that quality;
2. To achieve the shortest lead time in its market segment; and
3. To restrict growth to what the high-quality market segment and its competitive advantage would sustain.

The company's location meant that it could not readily recruit experienced staff from the local labor market and had to rely on its own training program to provide it with sufficient numbers of competent employees.

Organization and Major Production Policies

NTC had a very simple structure with one organizational level between the president and production employees. All employees saw Mr. Osborne as a friend and colleague rather than a boss. The president spent about one-third of his time on the factory floor talking to and coaching employees and, without exception, any employee could go into the president's office at any time. Mr. Osborne personally interviewed and selected every one of his employees, hiring those he thought were highly motivated and were likely to become loyal employees. NTC paid above average wages, gave employees generous performance bonuses, had no time standards, and all middle-level managers were referred to as coordinators.

The company made sure that every employee received at least four days of on-the-job training every year. Direct contact between the president and the employees and Mr. Osborne's natural penchant for coaching and encouraging his workers meant that those employees that stayed came to totally share Mr. Osborne's commitment to quality. Employee turnover averaged 4 percent per year compared to an industry average of 22 percent. This pleased Mr. Osborne because, in his words, "It takes at least two years to make a thoroughly quality-conscious employee."

NTC manufactured three basic products: external door windows, internal door windows, and normal sliding windows. Figure 5–13 shows the transformation process for each of the company's products. The line of external door windows was the company's key product on which its quality reputation was

Transformation Process FIGURE 5–13

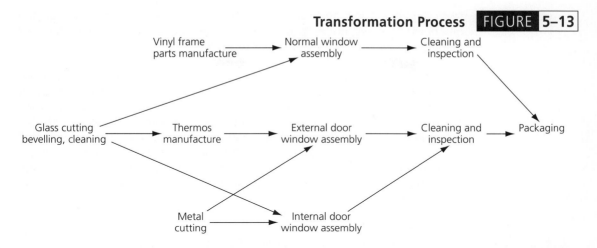

built and accounted for 60 percent of sales. Particularly critical to the quality of external door windows were the thermos manufacturing and the final cleaning and inspection operations. Therefore, the company used only the more seasoned, conscientious workers at these operations. The line consisted of 70 different end items with an average gross margin of 50 percent and an average daily volume of 700 units. Internal door windows consisted of 40 different items and accounted for 25 percent of sales, with a gross margin of 33 percent and an average daily volume of 300 units. Normal sliding windows were a very simple, standard product that was offered in 12 different options, had a daily sales volume of 950 units, a gross margin of 20 percent, and accounted for 15 percent of sales.

The company kept the three assembly operations physically separate but workers were often transferred between operations as the need arose, providing they had the minimum skill level required by the target operation. As the product line and sales grew, however, it was becoming increasingly difficult to match skill levels with the requirements of each operation. The three shared cells—glass cutting, metal cutting, and cleaning and inspection—were troublesome. Capacity utilization at the glass and metal cutting cells was approaching 100 percent and overtime was more than 20 percent during peak demand periods. That made it impossible for scheduled priorities to be respected. Mr. Osborne also wondered whether frequent transfers of personnel were affecting quality and worker discipline, particularly for door windows.

Competitive Threat

Two days after he started contemplating his options, Mr. Osborne received a call from his most important customer for external windows. Mr. Doug Barrett, president of ACE, had just received a promotional brochure and price list from Superior Doors and Windows (SDW), Incorporated. Going through the brochure, he could not help paying attention to one of the many assertions made by SDW:

> After many months of planning, we have added a complete line of door windows to our product line. We now have the most advanced plant in the industry and our employees are thoroughly trained. Our commitment to quality is total. We have a complete, autonomous factory dedicated only to the manufacture of door windows and so we are confident that we are the best in the industry. Our specialized factory means that we can unconditionally guarantee you the best quality at the best price and in the shortest possible time. Try us and you will discover that we mean everything we say.

Discussion Questions

1. What are the factors that explain NTC's market success?
2. Is the company's production system structure well suited to the competitive requirements of its market?
3. What should the company do to respond to the emerging competitive threat?

References

Ashton, James E., and Frank X. Cook, Jr., "Time to Reform Job Shop Manufacturing," *Harvard Business Review*, March–April 1989.

Dumolien, William J., and William P. Santen, "Cellular Manufacturing Becomes Philosophy of Management at Components Facility," *IE*, November 1983.

Greene, Timothy J., and Randall P. Sadowski, "A Review of Cellular Manufacturing Assumptions, Advantages and Design Techniques," *Journal of Operations Management* 4:2, February 1984.

Gyllenhammar, Pehr G., "How Volvo Adapts Work to People," *Harvard Business Review*, July–August 1977.

Japan Management Association, *Kanban Just-in-Time at Toyota*, Cambridge, Mass.: Productivity Press, 1986.

Japan Management Association, *Canon Production System: Creative Involvement of the Total Workforce*, Cambridge, Mass.: Productivity Press, 1987.

Kolchin, Michael G., and Thomas J. Hyclak, "Work Rules and Manufacturing Cells: A Case Study," *Technovation*, 9 1989.

Krafcik, John F., "Triumph of the Lean Production System," *Sloan Management Review*, 41, Fall 1988.

Sakai, Kimizasu, "The Feudal World of Japanese Manufacturing," *Harvard Business Review* November–December 1990.

Skinner, Wickham, *Manufacturing the Formidable Competitive Weapon*, New York: John Wiley and Sons, 1985.

Sugimori, T., K. Kusunoki, F. Cho, and S. Uchikawa, "Toyota Production System and Kanban System: Materialization of Just-in-Time and Respect for Human System," *International Journal of Production Research* 15:6, 1977.

Taheri, Javad, "Northern Telecom Tackles Successful Implementation of Cellular Manufacturing," *IE,* October 1990.

Teresko, John, "Group Technology: Shortening the Manufacturing Circuit," *Industry Week,* June 12, 1978.

6

Total Management of Total Quality: The Quality Wave

Beginning with the early 1970s, North American industry experienced a massive resurgence of interest in quality and its management. The trend continues today and is likely to last into the twenty-first century. The evidence that there is more attention being paid to quality is extensive and conclusive. Most business schools have now integrated some teaching on quality into their basic production management courses, both at the graduate and undergraduate levels. Engineering schools have done the same and some have gone as far as to make courses in statistical quality control and reliability engineering mandatory. The number of journals and popular magazines that are devoted to quality has increased dramatically over the last decade. At the same time, existing journals and magazines have increased the proportion of articles dealing with quality management. Prior to the mid-1970s, the American Production and Inventory Control Society focused its attention almost exclusively on MRP and MRP-II. Today, JIT and total quality control (TQC) have not only been integrated into its professional development program, but also take up significant parts of its key publications.

Significant change has also taken place inside many companies. A few have raised the status and organizational position of quality managers and staff, while others have substantially increased expenditures and activity on internal training. More and more companies are moving to make quality an ongoing part of organizational life by designing ways to get employees involved in quality improvement. This has created very strong demand for consulting services in quality management which is matched by new consulting companies emerging at historically unprecedented rates. And quality management gurus such as Deming, Juran, and Feigenbaum have now been placed at the forefront of management thought. Interestingly, the ideas for which Deming, Juran, and Feigenbaum are being hailed today were all introduced to managers in the 1950s. Something happened between the 1950s and the mid-1970s to change corporate attitudes toward quality.

Many reasons have been advanced for this revolution in thinking, but none stands more firmly than the Japanese phenomenon. Japan's rise to international industrial prominence was so rapid and profound that historians agree that there is no historical precedence to it. Japan achieved economic and industrial transformation at a rate and on a scale that were heretofore unseen in world economic history. No other nation has managed to transform its economy from being basically agrarian, weak, and inefficient to being the second largest industrial economy in the world in less than 30 years. Japan's industrial strength lies in products that are the marvels of technological progress: electronics, automobiles, machine tools, heavy equipment, and increasingly, pharmaceuticals and biotechnology. The extent of Japan's industrial progress and its importance for manufacturing management will be underlined by reviewing a few salient historical facts.

At the dawn of the twentieth century, Japan had a largely traditional economy, based on agriculture and fishing. Some manufacturing activity existed, but it was concentrated in the cottage and artisan industries. Production was entirely oriented toward satisfying a local unsophisticated market. Japanese products were hardly, if at all, exported to any other country. Japan was a very poor, unsophisticated feudal society, close to the very bottom as far as industrialization and economic development were concerned. For the Western economies and management scholars, Japan was little more than a culturally esoteric nation. A few, such as the United States and Great Britain, saw Japan as just one more little market for their industrial goods. At the outset, nonetheless, the Japanese showed themselves to be very open to Western ideas and to have a taste for Western industrial goods.

Already, however, a nascent industrialization was taking shape under the control of the Zaibatsu. These were very large, family-controlled enterprises that were forerunners to the modern day conglomerates. The Zaibatsu's economic potential derived from their control over extremely large land holdings, the cornerstone of an agricultural economy. Land conferred on the Zaibatsu families, not only economic, but also political and social power as well. Using land as a power base, the Zaibatsu came to totally dominate economic and political life in late nineteenth- to early twentieth-century Japan. Zaibatsu were not monopolies in the economic sense. They were societies and bodies politic within a loosely federated economic and political system. Before the war, a few Zaibatsu exercised total control over the Japanese economy, with four owning as much as 25 percent of Japan's invested capital. Each family Zaibatsu, such as Mitsui, Sumitomo, and Mitsubishi, controlled as many as 300 companies. The reader will note that these family names are still household words in modern Japan and elsewhere.

From the early 1900s to the 1940s, Japan made steady progress in producing industrial and consumer goods for the local market. By the time the second World War had ended, nearly every product known to the West was also available to the Japanese market, albeit in smaller quantities and lower quality. This was made possible mainly by imports but also by some local production. Japan's industrial transformation had essentially achieved "take-off." The initial progress increased Japan's confidence in its ability to master industrial production and in its capability to harness advanced technology. In fact, Japan became overly confident when in the 1940s, the nation decided to challenge the West, particularly the United States, for political and military control of the Far East. The resultant war was devastating for Japan when the Imperial Army suffered total and humiliating defeat at the hands of the United States. The results of the war brought home a clear message to the Japanese that their industrial and technological base was still substantially inferior to what existed in Europe and the United States.

These events persuaded the Japanese people in general, and the nation's leaders, in particular, that they should adopt a global view of markets and technology. What may be good for the local market and the technology that gave a company a local competitive edge, may not at all be good enough to compete internationally. Being the absolute best means being able to build world-class industrial systems and products. The most important barrier that Japan had to overcome was the fact that "made in Japan" was synonymous with inferior quality. The quality gap between Japanese products and those made in the West in the 1950s was huge. At that time, no western country paid any serious attention to the Japanese push to catch up with the West. Indeed, western countries, particularly the United States, were so unimpressed with the Japanese drive to industrialize, that western technology was made available to Japan on very generous terms. Japanese managers and engineers could freely visit western plants and were given almost limitless access to technology via loose licensing agreements. The United States was also totally confident that it could maintain or even widen its technological lead over Japan.

Japanese companies, on the other hand, became deeply conscious of the fact that even if cheap labor gave them some competitive leverage, the final and ultimate battle for world markets would be won on superior technology and quality. Managers in Japan saw superior manufacturing performance, and especially quality, as being absolutely essential to survival. Steps were taken to convey that conviction to the entire nation and to inculcate it into the mindset of every worker and manager. In 1956, the Japan Union of Scientists and Engineers, JUSE, invited Dr. W. Edwards Deming, a United States engineer with a background in statistical quality control, to give a series of lectures on quality. Deming's ideas were so enthusiastically received that up to this day the most prominent recognition given in Japan for quality excellence is called the Deming Prize. The first quality circle was registered in Japan in 1960, and the quality control magazine, *Gemba To QC* (Quality Control for Foremen) was launched the same year. The reader will note that although initial quality awareness started with JUSE and its engineers, the drive to quality superiority very quickly involved foremen and workers, those people who are on the factory floor and on the firing line. The Japanese quickly learned and applied the fundamental lesson that in order to achieve superior product quality a company must create quality commitment and excellence in the factory.

Intensive quality training and commitment continued unchecked. By the 1980s, there were over 3 million functioning quality circles in Japan which involved over 20 million workers in the continuous improvement of quality. The unswerving commitment to quality and the actions taken to improve it have resulted in perceptible and sustained improvement in the quality of Japanese products. So complete has been the turnaround in Japanese product quality that "made in Japan" is now the international symbol of quality superiority. Thus, in less than 30 years Japan went from copying quality control technology to being the nation whose approach to quality management is fast becoming the world standard. The fact that superior-quality performance is being achieved by the Japanese in virtually all industrial sectors is an indication that there are proven systems, technologies, and approaches that are being deployed with predictable results.

Simultaneous with the above developments and evidently propelled by visible and measurable increases in product quality, Japan experienced rapid increases in its share of the world market for industrial and consumer goods. For example, in 1974, Japan held 6.7 percent of the world automobile market compared with 6.7 percent for Germany and 84.1 percent for North America (the United States and Canada). By 1988, Japan's share had climbed to roughly 22 percent versus 3 percent for West Germany and 71 percent for North America. Moreover, 25 percent of domestic car production in the United States was done by Japanese multinationals and Honda America produced as many cars in its U.S. plants as it did in Japan. The consumer electronics industry in North America fared even worse under the Japanese competitive onslaught. The solid state transistor and its successor, the large-scale integrated circuit, crucial to electronics products, are both U.S. inventions. U.S. companies dominated their domestic markets and the world market in the late 1960s to early 1970s. Today, Japan holds 40 percent market share in semiconductors and the major consumer electronics products like VCRs and colored television sets are seldom manufactured in the United States and Canada. Japanese manufacturers are also poised to take a large part of the world market for the ultimate television product, high resolution television.

The fact that Japanese companies have enviable, deeply entrenched positions in the international market is now incontestable. It became equally clear by the early 1980s that superior product quality was the route by which their positions were achieved. Popular rationalizations that attributed Japan's growing prominence to low price, cheap labor, and protectionist policies at home were crushed by the overwhelming evidence that superior product quality was the decisive factor. Recent studies have shown that annual repairs per vehicle for North American produced cars are double the rate for Japanese produced cars. The mean time to fail or the duration of trouble free operation for television sets produced by North American companies is two years, while the corresponding figure for Japanese produced television sets is six years.

Faced with rapidly declining market shares and little prospect that the Japanese would relent in their competitive assault on an increasing number of markets, North American companies began to embrace quality as a survival necessity. Heightened interest was created by some leading world class manufacturers who were being humiliated by new and powerful competitors from Japan. Xerox, Harley-Davidson, General Motors, and Zenith, to name only a few, suffered substantial erosion in their once dominant market positions due to strong Japanese competition. There was no more denying that superior product quality was the factor that gave Japanese products a decisive competitive edge in the marketplace. In order to regain their former market positions or to at least arrest further erosion, worldclass manufacturers are being forced by competitive forces to improve the quality of their products until they achieve parity with competing Japanese products. This meant that more resources, attention, and top management effort had to be directed to quality.

The leading North American manufacturers soon began to require that suppliers perform to higher quality standards, starting a chain reaction that is now reaching third and even fourth level suppliers. This created the quality wave that was born in the early 1970s and continues to gain momentum. Paradoxically, however, most companies have joined the new quality movement because it is the latest management fad. They have joined the bandwagon without knowing what kind of wagon, who is driving, and what is its destination. Executives in these companies identify with quality issues at the very superficial level using a few slogans and popular catch phrases. There is not a deep, reasoned commitment to quality which flows from an accurate understanding that delivering a quality product is paramount to long-term customer satisfaction. But a few companies have come to understand that superior quality, far from being the latest management fad, is in fact an essential ingredient for success in markets that are increasingly becoming international in scope. As these companies succeed in defending their market positions and in some cases even strengthening their competitive posture, they give credibility to the quality movement. They also search for suppliers that have achieved or can be nurtured to quality excellence, further deepening the roots of the quality movement by extending it to third and even fourth level suppliers. Superior quality is quickly becoming integral to the corporate culture of the world-class manufacturers in North America and will eventually embrace a substantial proportion of companies. This is the absolute minimum condition that must be met before there can be any credible response by North American companies to the threat from the Pacific Rim countries.

THE BALDRIGE AWARD AND QUALITY PROGRESS

The creation of the Baldrige Award in 1987 and its subsequent administration by the National Institute of Standards and Technology (NIST) is having a significant impact on quality management and the commitment to quality in North American companies. The Baldrige can be awarded every year to a maximum of two companies in each of three categories: manufacturing, service, and small business. The award gives recognition to companies that have distinguished themselves in quality improvement, but results are only one of the criteria used to evaluate companies. Consideration is also given to the mechanisms, procedures, policies, management processes, and principles that produce quality results. The NIST examiners who are responsible for evaluating candidates for the award, look for evidence that the commitment to quality is deep and pervasive, and that sound quality management principles and technology are deeply entrenched in all of a company's organizational processes, culture, systems, and values. The concern is not necessarily measurable results, although positive results are a barometer of improvement in overall quality management, but on the permanence of the mechanisms that generate these results.

Table 6–1 shows the criteria used to evaluate companies that competed for the award in 1991 and the maximum number of points allocated to each criterion. While one could be in disagreement with the way the points are distributed, the choice of criteria is sound.

The Baldrige criteria capture the essential issues around which broad consensus has emerged as to how quality can be assured and improved. For example, some managers can contend, and validly so, that quality results (180 points) are important, but not more so than the human resource management practices (150 points) that are critical in producing these results. However, no one will argue that both sound human resource management practices and the realization of significant, measurable results are not essential ingredients of a total and effective quality improvement program.

Companies that compete for the Baldrige go through an extensive application and evaluation procedure. Xerox, the winner in 1989, claims that preparing its application cost $800,000. A group of examiners, experts in quality management, then rate each applicant using the Baldrige criteria. A few of the top scoring companies are selected for extensive on-site visits. During these visits, examiners pay particular attention to how well quality policy has been deployed by the company. Effective deployment has taken place when there is unity of quality purpose, commonality of vision, and consistency of values and attitudes throughout the organization, from top management to the factory floor and across all organizational functions. Quality deployment also means that the whole company is engaged in quality improvement and sound quality management practices, methods, processes, systems, and procedures are being used everywhere in the company. Quality deployment spreads the quality effort throughout the organization and sustains it with appropriate levels of resources. The Baldrige criteria and the way they are used to evaluate a company's quality improvement program provide managers with a set of clear criteria and tested guidelines for designing a quality improvement program.

TABLE 6–1	The Baldrige Criteria

1.0 Leadership (100 points)
    1.1   Senior Executive Leadership (40)
    1.2   Quality Values (15)
    1.3   Management for Quality (25)
    1.4   Public Responsibility (20)

2.0 Information and Analysis (70 points)
    2.1   Scope and Management of Quality Data and Information (20)
    2.2   Competitive Comparisons and Benchmarks (30)
    2.3   Analysis of Quality Data and Information (20)

3.0 Strategic Quality Planning (60 points)
    3.1   Strategic Quality Planning Process (35)
    3.2   Quality Goals and Plans (25)

4.0 Human Resource Utilization (150 points)
    4.1   Human Resource Management (20)
    4.2   Employee Involvement (40)
    4.3   Quality Education and Training (40)
    4.4   Employee Recognition and Performance Measurement (25)
    4.5   Employee Well-Being and Morale (25)

5.0 Quality Assurance of Products and Services (140 points)
    5.1   Design and Introduction of Quality Products and Services (35)
    5.2   Process Quality Control (20)
    5.3   Continuous Improvement of Processes (20)
    5.4   Quality Assessment (15)
    5.5   Documentation (10)
    5.6   Business Process and Support Service Quality (20)
    5.7   Supplier Quality (20)

6.0 Quality Results (180 points)
    6.1   Products and Service Quality Results (90)
    6.2   Business Process, Operational, and Support Service Quality Results (50)
    6.3   Supplier Quality Results (40)

7.0 Customer Satisfaction (300 points)
    7.1   Determining Customer Requirements and Expectations (30)
    7.2   Customer Relationship Management (50)
    7.3   Customer Service Standards (20)
    7.4   Commitment to Customers (15)
    7.5   Complaint Resolution for Quality Improvement (25)
    7.6   Determining Customer Satisfaction (20)
    7.7   Customer Satisfaction Results (70)
    7.8   Customer Satisfaction Comparison (70)

1,000 Total Points

Note: For a complete evaluation of the Baldrige, see Garvin, David A., "How the Baldrige Really Works," *Harvard Business Review,* November–December 1991.

Source: National Institute of Standards and Technology

The Baldridge has contributed to quality progress in North America in many ways. It has created heightened quality awareness and consciousness and has helped push quality to the forefront of strategic thinking. Some very reputable companies—Federal Express, Xerox, and the Cadillac Division of General Motors—have won the award and this has caused managers to increasingly make a direct link between quality improvement and competitive performance. Winners of the Baldrige are active agents in the diffusion of quality principles and technology because large numbers of managers, customers, and suppliers seek their advice and value their knowledge. The award is also helping in strengthening the emerging consensus around the vital quality issues as it becomes more evident that winners differ mainly in the way they implement their quality improvement programs and little on the core principles and concepts.

With its emphasis on leadership and the customer, the Baldrige has put the responsibility for quality improvement at the door of top management where it legitimately belongs and reminds managers that the customer must be central to the quality improvement process. We are progressively seeing the emergence of the foundation values and managerial principles upon which superior quality performance can be erected. And companies are quickly coming to understand that these principles are germane to any sound management philosophy and process.

The major criticism of the Baldrige comes from those who note that it does not predict superior market and financial performance. Federal Express still maintains leadership in its market but Xerox has not succeeded in regaining its prior market position. Cadillacs are not rated as the top cars in their class even though Cadillac won the award. The failure of Baldrige to predict market and financial performance could be explained by three factors:

1. The Baldrige criteria emphasize factors that contribute to long-term quality superiority. It could be that the award has not existed long enough to produce its true long-term effects.
2. All companies, including those that have world-class operations and which produce superior quality products experience deterioration in market and financial performance when there is a generalized slowdown in the economy.
3. The award measures the quality capability and progress of domestic companies. In global markets, these companies have to improve faster than their foreign competitors in order to sustain or strengthen their market positions.

However, as the number of recipients increases and NIST gains experience administering the award and sharpening the criteria, the Baldrige will continue to contribute to the impetus to manage quality as a prime strategic weapon.

WHAT IS QUALITY?

Quality has been defined in many different ways to serve diverse purposes. However, some care must be taken in choosing an appropriate definition because the way quality is defined by a company will partly influence how it is viewed, understood, and managed. The quality definition must have motivational impact and must also clarify the company's strategic quality mission in language that has meaning for all employees. It has been said repeatedly that superior quality is integral to manufacturing and managerial excellence. As a consequence, quality needs to be defined and conceptualized in terms that are beneficial to the drive to achieve superior performance in manufacturing.

Traditional Definitions of Quality

One popular definition states that quality is fitness for use. It comes from the legal concept handed down from British common law and reinforced by many civil litigation cases in North America and Europe. In the legal and consumer protection tradition, a product is bought for a specific, identifiable use and is to function acceptably while being used in the way that the customer originally envisaged. The manufacturer has the legal obligation to ensure that the product performs its designated function. Originally, the fitness for use concept only applied where the customer took reasonable care not to abuse the product. More recently, however, courts in the United States have tended to rule that the failure by the customer to exercise reasonable care does not exonerate the manufacturer from liability for defects that are found in the product. The manufacturer's responsibility is maintained in all cases except where there is obvious, wanton abuse by the consumer. In addition, the fact that the manufacturer used the best available technology, rigorously inspected and tested the product and otherwise took extreme care to prevent defects, do not exonerate it from product liability. Product paternity is rigorously and totally enforced in virtually all western countries.

The fitness for use concept gives a marketing orientation to product quality. The manufacturer is forced to anticipate all possible reasonable uses for the product and to do so from the customer's perspective. This can only be adequately done if there is an effort to study the consumer's need and to probe historical and future applications of the product. Moreover, the manufacturer has total responsibility for delivering defect-free products to the customer. The product quality focus must emphasize defect prevention because nothing exonerates the producer from liability when the product fails to function or causes bodily or psychological injury while being used. However, the fitness for use concept has one important flaw which is that it is abstract, general, and difficult to operationalize on the factory floor. Specifically, it is almost impossible for employees to be conscious of fitness for use when they are undertaking production activities. As a result, it cannot be used as a vehicle for motivating and sustaining the quality improvement effort because employees often cannot concretely identify with the use or uses to which the product will be put.

Partly to deal with the fact that fitness for use is an abstract, meaningless concept for most employees, an alternative definition of product quality has gained wide acceptance. According to this view, quality is conformance to specifications. A product is deemed to be good if it conforms to the specifications provided by the user. This definition has some unique advantages. First, it is relevant for both external and internal purposes. The specifications can come from the final customer to whom the product is delivered or from internal customers who use the parts that make up the product. Conformance to specifications is a "useful" concept for suppliers as well and its adoption led to the fundamental principle that the next operation or phase in manufacturing the product is the customer. Second, conformance to specifications places some responsibility on the customer to evaluate his or her needs and to translate these into adequate specifications. Efforts to accurately specify the product will sometimes reveal inadequacies in need definition and evaluation. Finally, the specifications that are used to define product quality also provide the basis for evaluating product conformance and for measuring and controlling quality.

Despite its obvious advantages, conformance to specification has some serious weaknesses. There is nothing in the concept that can be used to motivate quality improvement. For most managers and employees, conformance to specifications is a bland engineering concept that is difficult to bring alive in the factory or in any non-technical business function. Besides this, there is the very real danger that if appropriate care is not exercised, product specification becomes an exclusively engineering responsibility that progressively alienates customers, suppliers, and factory people, with the devastating consequence that conformance to specification provides very little basis for quality measurement, appraisal, and prevention. The question that must be constantly asked is whose specifications and by whom were they done? Unless product performance parameters are chosen in such a way as to assure companywide input and on the basis of full and precise understanding of customer needs and requirements, then conformance to specifications may be marginally useful or even counterproductive.

The concept may also block or retard the quality improvement process. Without companywide programs to challenge existing technology and to be innovative in studying evolving customer requirements, the specifications become the norm that is slowly viewed as being sacred. The organization can then become preoccupied with meeting the specifications rather than with improving product quality. Sometimes, managers will resist going beyond minimum acceptable product specifications on the grounds that this is more quality than customers paid for. Unwillingness to push beyond agreed to specifications means that the company never finds out whether it is feasible to make better product quality to more exacting standards, but at the same cost. The company does not experiment in quality improvement and cannot gain experience in pushing product quality to ever increasing levels. Quality may be conformance to specifications, but superior quality comes from challenging the specifications and the technology that bind the company to a given quality target.

As definitions of quality, fitness for use, and conformance to specifications both have a profound weakness that make them undesirable when a company wishes to launch a total, corporatewide attack on poor quality. The flaw lies in the fact that in these concepts quality is synonymous with product quality. Those who are propagating quality management ideas using these concepts invariably have in mind the quality of the thing or service that is delivered to the customer. The argument is that it is the customer who passes the ultimate decisive judgment on how well the company is satisfying his or her needs and that this can only be judged by the quality of the good or service that is delivered.

This position has much truth to it. A customer cares little about what goes on within a company, as long as the product or service paid for satisfies his or her needs. Even if the customer wanted to go beyond what is delivered, in most cases the exercise would be impossible and too costly. Judging the product or service is the only efficient and objective way to evaluate a supplier's quality performance. But one must admit that product or service quality is a partial index of total quality and a proxy for it, even if it is a good one. What may be adequate for the customer when deciding which product to buy is grossly inadequate when the concern is for building a sustainable, continuous drive toward superior competitive performance everywhere within a company. The point is that product quality is only one dimension of total quality, albeit an important one, and it results from achieving and pursuing quality in all operational and managerial activities. In other words, there is quality behind quality and managerial action is more neatly and directly focused, and likely to be more effective if targeted at the primary quality generation activities rather than the partial, myopic results that show up as product or service quality.

An Alternative Definition

Given the foregoing discussion, one can conclude that the quality concept must satisfy two key requirements. First, it must liberate quality management from the narrow product quality focus that is endemic to the traditional definitions of quality. The quality concept must have meaning to all managerial levels and to every function and activity within the company. That is to say, it must promote a true, total quality concept and emphasize total quality management from top to bottom in the management hierarchy. This is absolutely essential in order that the concept can be used as a vehicle for promoting managerial and operational excellence everywhere within the organization. On that view, total quality management is synonymous with the pursuit of world-class manufacturing and waste identification and removal. Searching for perfection and the drive to continuously improve efficiency are unquestionably total quality management principles. Second, the definition of quality that is adopted by management must make improvement central to quality if the company is going to have a reasonable chance of maintaining or solidifying its market position. From this vantage point, the only acceptable quality standard is an ever improving one and specifications must be challenged, tightened, and refined, ceaselessly. Producing to more and more exacting specifications is the new standard in the world competitive arena. Companies must not be willing just to meet the standards. They must demonstrate an ability to surpass the standards and maintain a competitive cost position while doing so.

The following definition meets the requirements for a sound, pertinent quality concept. Quality can be defined as the degree to which a necessary product, a thing, or an activity approaches perfection. The goal is perfection and the focus is any product, thing, or activity that is necessary or useful to the company. One needs to emphasize not only use, but equally important, usefulness. Quality and the pursuit of excellence are simultaneously enhanced when useless or wasteful activities or products are eliminated. The waste removal efforts that are integral to JIT are generically quality management activities. The standard to shoot for is perfection and the drive must be sustained until perfection is attained. Since perfection is practically not achievable, the quality concept given here propels improvement on a long-term basis.

When quality is defined in this way, everything that everyone does is totally a quality activity. Too often, quality management and control are carved out of normal work activities and are viewed as separate, distinct processes or procedures. Thus, a worker on the assembly line is said to first produce and does quality control subsequent to production by doing a quality check. Our definition, on the other hand, recognizes and emphasizes that the worker is involved in quality every millisecond that he or she spends on the job. Observing whether the worker accurately follows the work methods and whether or not he or she precisely executes the work motions like a master craftsman, validly falls within the ambit of quality management. Assuring that the worker is thoroughly trained, has the right tools to get the job done, and has a clean, orderly, and healthy work environment are also quality management activities. Helping the worker solve family problems, if he or she is in favor of it, and maintaining good physical and mental health contributes enormously to his or her ability to produce impeccable quality, and are therefore valid quality management concerns. The western idea that work life must be totally separated from private and family life may in the long run prove to be a hindrance to pursuing perfect quality. Companies that find innovative ways to reconcile the need to manage the worker as a total, indivisible human being and the right to privacy that is so ingrained in western democratic tradition will reap huge benefits from improved quality and efficiency. The list can go on, but the central idea is that all management is quality management. The search for perfection in an organizational setting requires that there be total management of total quality. As long as every single activity is not being planned, coordinated, executed, and controlled with complete perfection, then there is waste and room for improvement. The role of management is to steer the company, as a whole, toward perfection, that is, zero waste, zero defects, zero downtime, and zero inventories.

Quality Delivered to the Customer

Traditionally, quality has been viewed as the physical product or service that is delivered to the customer. In practice, however, the customer receives more than simply the good or service that he or she purchased. There is usually much information that is delivered to or received from the customer that must meet quality requirements if the quality of the product or service is to be thoroughly appreciated by the customer. The quality concept must be broadened to deal with these. Quality delivered to the customer has the following five elements:

Product quality. The customer is primarily concerned about how well the product meets his or her expectations relative to form, fit, and function. The only objective evidence that the customer has that the supplying company understands his or her needs and is dedicated to satisfying them is contained in the product and its performance. Superior product quality reflects the character of a manufacturing company. One hundred percent good quality product can only come from companies that are competently managed, 100 percent of the time. Shoddy products emanate from poorly designed, managed, and controlled organizations. Product quality projects a powerful image to customers that no amount of promotion and marketing gimmickry can change. The fact that every product that is shipped will result in a satisfied customer is the litmus test that a company understands and applies the marketing concept that long-term profitability comes from total customer satisfaction. To be acceptable, products must conform to customer requirements. A company should not deliver products that do not meet customer expectations, and if per chance it does, the situation should be rectified with urgency.
　　Product quality usually has six dimensions:
1. Fitness for use. The product satisfies the purpose for which it was bought.
2. Durability. The product has a useful and economic life that is commensurate with the price paid.

3. Maintainability. The product can be repaired when and if it does fail and at reasonable cost.
4. Reliability. This is the proportion of the time that the product is available for use. A related concept is the mean time to fail, or how long trouble-free operation lasts, on the average.
5. Appearance, form, finishing. These often reflect workmanship quality. Some products, such as sports cars have very stringent appearance requirements, while others, such as fashion clothing are bought almost exclusively on that criterion.
6. Uniformity. Products such as processed foods, drugs, and chemicals usually have to be uniform in content and appearance. Particularly in the pharmaceuticals and chemical industries, uniformity can greatly affect product performance.

When customers judge quality, they may focus on one or more quality characteristic. However, there is a tendency for the chain to be judged by its weakest link. The customer will often ignore a particular characteristic if it causes no problems. The moment that the quality characteristic starts to be problematic, it is usually used to pass absolute judgment on the quality of the entire product.

Quality of customer education. Designing and producing a quality product calls for some participation by the customer, who must accurately understand his or her needs and transmit them to the producer. The customer's experiences can provide information that can be very useful in improving product design and manufacturing. The customer can also contribute to quality by using the product more judiciously and by not pushing it beyond its design limits. Education will prepare the customer to make an active contribution to product quality. The customer exercises freedom of choice, but a producing company can create the right customer by appropriate education. The better the education the more the company is able to serve the customer and to receive some quality service in return.

Quality of information. Selling a product invariably involves an information exchange between the seller and the buyer. The buyer must provide the producer with the necessary product specifications and delivery schedule. The seller must provide the buyer with information on how the product is to be installed, used, and maintained, among other things. Errors in information can and often do contribute to products being delivered that do not conform to the buyer's expectations. When this happens, there is a quality problem, no matter how skillful the methods used to blame the other party. Faulty product documentation also contributes to a dissatisfied customer. An impeccable product that is delivered with documentation errors does not meet the customer's expectation. Total delivered quality necessitates that error-free documentation on product transportation, installation, operation, and maintenance be delivered as well.

Quality of after-sales service. The product must be supported in the field, particularly if it is designed for a long useful life. The customer should not be impressed when a durable product performs flawlessly for the first few weeks. Many a customer has been impressed with a new car for the first few weeks only to discover later that he or she bought a lemon. Superior quality requires consistent, predictable performance over the useful life of the product. A product that fails during use is not the ideal, but the next best thing is for it to be repaired quickly and perfectly when failure does occur. The product must be supported by the manufacturer during its useful life with the same care and vigor with which it was designed, manufactured, and sold. The after-sales service given by a company should reflect its quality philosophy and mission and should be executed with finesse and competence. Companies that are serious about quality are also executing after-sales service to rigorous and exacting standards.

Quality of need definition. The most basic marketing question that one can ask about any product is whether it satisfies a need. The need may be expressed or latent, real or imagined but the product is more likely to succeed if it is designed and manufactured to meet a need that can be described and specified. Since most companies sell to external customers, this marketing reality forces them to rely on information given by consumers in order to evaluate and specify the market need. The customer must be surveyed, probed, and otherwise analyzed for vital information which can be made available to those designing and manufacturing the product. No matter how serious the need analysis is, however, someone must translate the information and cues gleaned from the customer into a product concept and design. The need will be defined more or less accurately, depending on the extent to which those responsible for product development and design become thoroughly acquainted with the market need. Product designers should be so engrossed in understanding the requirements of the market that they subconsciously behave like the ultimate customer, actively and critically evaluating every product characteristic with a view to increasing value for themselves. When this happens, the development team can be said to have put on the mind and heart of the customer going beyond what can be done by mere market research. There is no doubt that market research that is well planned and executed can provide some information upon which to base product positioning strategy. Nevertheless, it is a poor substitute for intimate identification with the customer and the product by the development group. Product requirements must eventually be converted into specifications and features by technical people. They can approach that task as third parties who are trying to understand the customer by using information provided by another agent such as the marketing function or they can become the customer in order to understand the true needs.

Quality products can hardly emerge from inaccurate and fuzzy understanding of customer requirements, for the most fundamental quality characteristic is that the product as conceived and manufactured matches the need as it is actually experienced by the customer. Precise need definition takes place when product developers so closely identify with the customer that they become his or her advocates and totally feel the impact of every product characteristic. When this happens, the company has succeeded in creating a group that has adequate market and technological information which can be synthesized into a quality product design. A company cannot rely exclusively on market research to provide information to specify the product need. Market research data must be analyzed, evaluated, probed, and translated into product design requirements and all these processes are prone to error and distortion. Errors in understanding and translating market research data into product specifications are difficult to eliminate but their number and severity can be minimized by integrating the R&D and design groups into market research activities. Need definition will be accurately reflected in product specifications when product development is integrated with market research and need appraisal, thus bringing technical people closer to the customer and the market. Eventually, the product development and design team should be customer advocates and should begin to think and react like the customer. In fact, deep customer consciousness will have been created when the product development group thinks and behaves like the most demanding customers.

A company can only create and nurture such thorough customer consciousness if it is totally marketing oriented from top to bottom and across all the business functions. The company is in business to create and serve a customer and it will succeed in this most basic mission when every resource at its disposal is deployed to that end. Marketing orientation in the sense used here is much more than the recognition that the marketing function is an important one. A totally marketing oriented company, as has already been pointed out, will recognize that the marketing function as an organizational unit, is responsible for but a small part of the marketing effort. Complete customer orientation exists when those responsible for product research, development, and design behave like customers and the market generated information for defining the product need is not adulterated or distorted by organizational processes. Market research data must be analyzed, evaluated, probed, and translated and all these processes are prone to error and distortion. Need definition will be precise when the company succeeds in making customers of the product development group. Figure 6–1 summarizes the key ideas involved.

QUALITY AND STRATEGIC PERFORMANCE

The point has already been made and needs to be repeated that consistent, superior quality, delivered on a long-term basis, can only come from a rigorously

FIGURE 6–1 **Product Development and Design in a Completely Customer-Oriented Company**

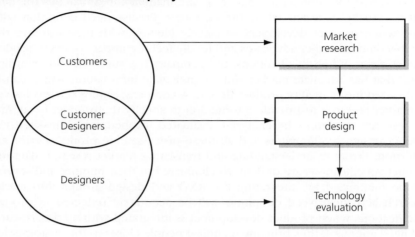

customer-oriented company. Indeed, strong emphasis on superior product quality epitomizes wholehearted commitment to customer satisfaction. The desire to push quality to ever higher levels can only be driven by deeply embedded, companywide commitment to the customer. Companies that achieve quality excellence recognize that it is important to deliver the right product to the customer at a competitive price. These same companies take the time and put in the effort that is necessary to accurately identify and understand customer needs and requirements. The commitment to quality can be no deeper than the loyalty to customer satisfaction. Quality and customer orientation go hand in hand and each is only an expression of the other.

World-class companies have now come to the powerful realization that superior product quality, given the price that the customer is willing to pay, is the ultimate if not the only strategic mission of a company. It is certainly the only strategic mission that is all-encompassing to the extent that the whole company must be mobilized in its execution. The quality mission is a potent unifying force for all the business functions, since perfectly executing it will require every organizational unit to give 100 percent performance. Responsibility for quality is so broad that no single business function can or should have total control over it. Superior product quality is the most natural, corporatewide, strategic mission. Quality superiority endures as the top competitive priority whose execution guarantees long-term financial health and growth even when there are massive revolutions in market structure and scope. Companies like Rolls-Royce, Mercedes-Benz, and IBM have all lived through market revolutions that have left economic history littered with the ashes of bankrupt rivals. Quality is the constant, perpetual strategic imperative, no matter how small or large the company or how broad or narrow its market scope.

Quality is the most prominent intrinsic product characteristic. Whether visible or invisible, it is always experienced by the customer and is usually aggressively sought by him or her. The customer measures quality, objectively or subjectively and uses it, in an important way to evaluate the producing company and the fairness of the price paid for the product. Customers invariably evaluate the trade-off between price and quality before they buy the product, which makes quality a key input in the decision to buy. The quality/ price trade-off is also used after the purchase to evaluate whether the producer delivered fair value. Quality, therefore, always impacts on customer satisfaction and is crucial in determining repeat purchases.

The activities involved in producing a consistently superior-quality product challenge a company's ability to compete in a competitive environment. It is not a coincidence that quality and the attention paid to it increase as competitive conditions become more severe. The reverse is also true. When the competitive environment deteriorates there is always a parallel and simultaneous reduction in product and service quality. Centrally planned economies, for example, have earned a reputation for producing inferior-quality products that cannot compete on world markets. Similarly when market forces are introduced in a planned economy, there is a resultant rapid increase in product quality. Quality superiority requires that a company master the essential product and process technology that are fundamental to the product. Technical excellence and production craftsmanship provide the discipline that is essential to producing high-quality products. Every company that has mastered quality also has solid technical resources and recruits, trains, and nurtures the best production specialists in its industry. The managerial or competitive challenge is to keep developing and maintaining the best technical and human resources in the face of rapidly changing technology as well as over the long haul.

Managerial and technical excellence, achieved on a companywide basis, that is, across all business functions and at every organizational level, is the foundation upon which quality superiority can be built. The ability to push product quality to higher and higher levels is what demarcates truly excellent companies from the mediocre ones. An internal corporate environment or value system that puts a premium on organizational and individual excellence provides the cornerstone for implementing a competitive strategy based on superior quality. Corporatewide excellence finds its most natural and practical expression in the quality of the products that a company puts on the market. Poor quality reveals corporate mediocrity, no matter how many slogans to the contrary that are repeated by top management. Companywide excellence must extend to suppliers, since purchased inputs comprise an important and increasingly larger share of total product costs. Excellent companies that are devoted to quality only do business with excellent suppliers that share their views and philosophies on quality. Supplier partnership can only be built on a common commitment to quality superiority and excellence by both users and their suppliers. A mediocre supplier that is not totally committed to quality improvement cannot naturally respond to the demands placed on it by a quality-conscious producer. Two companies that have radically divergent views on how important quality is to market success and long-term competitive viability have no basis for building a close partnership based on shared values, mutual trust, and confidence.

The Japanese Phenomenon

Japan's rise to world industrial prominence is further evidence that quality is an important strategic factor. Before the 1960s, Japanese industry was noted for producing inferior-quality goods. At that time, Japan was looked at as an imitator nation that could never pose any serious threat to western countries. The leading western industrialized countries totally dominated markets at home and abroad, from the simplest consumer goods to very complex industrial products. Made in the USA, Great Britain, or Germany was the international symbol for quality and industrial craftsmanship. From ship building to sewing machines, pharmaceuticals to tea cups, the West had absolute monopoly on industrial production. It appeared that the West had a stranglehold on world industrial markets and that other cultures like Japan would have to be forever content with begging for a few techniques here and there, copying whatever designs they could, and generally living as best they could off the crumbs from the tables of America, Britain, Germany, and others. Japan could perhaps carve out a niche for itself by producing outdated western goods for its own use and for the Asian markets.

But the Japanese leadership had already come to the conclusion that Japan could play a leading role in world industrial competition if it could change its quality image. A quality reputation, however, is made by producing quality over a sustained period. A lasting quality image is created when customers, after using the product repeatedly come to the conclusion, based on experience, that its quality is indeed superior and not mere happenstance. Japanese manufacturers, like anyone else who markets inferior-quality products, had earned their reputation and were paying a very high price for it in the battle for international trade. Contrary to the view held in some circles, a quality image cannot be created by sexy promotional programs. Quality reputations are built by quality products that emerge from painstaking attention to detail and to craftsmanship. The Japanese had learned that powerful lesson and were willing to make the investment in human resources and technology that was necessary to dramatically improve their quality.

The emphasis that Japanese companies have put on quality improvement has continued unabated since Deming's first visit, with concomitant, sustained increase in visible, measurable, factual quality. Today, made in Japan is indisputably the symbol of quality worldwide. While western manufacturing companies are measuring quality in parts per thousand defective, leading Japanese manufacturers are achieving defect rates that are barely measurable—one part per million (or billion) defective. There has been a revolutionary turnaround in Japanese quality over the last 25 years and it was clearly produced by specific actions such as worker training, employee involvement, and companywide allocation of quality authority and responsibility. These changes resulted from a change in the vision and attitude of top management. Japanese managers began to see quality as a company's foremost strategic mission, and thus liberated the creative talent and resources that were necessary for its long-term improvement and eventual mastery.

Simultaneous with these developments in quality, and certainly propelled by them was a predictable, profound improvement in Japan's position on international markets. The data speak loudly and clearly. From a struggling, weak position in the television market in the early 1960s, Japan has emerged in the 1980s as the world's largest producer and exporter of household television sets. Japanese manufacturers have driven North American producers from the VCR market and are now challenging the leading American companies such as Intel for dominance in large-scale integrated circuits. Indications are that they have also preempted entry by North American manufacturers into the high resolution television market, which most experts believe is the next revolution in household television production. In the early 1960s, the world motorcycle market was dominated by North American, British, and West German manufacturers. Today, only Harley-Davidson remains as a serious competitor after that company was almost driven to bankruptcy by Japanese competition. It is noteworthy that the incredible turnaround at Harley-Davidson was achieved when the company opened up and massively adopted Japanese manufacturing philosophies and approaches such as total quality control and JIT. Xerox, which epitomizes American strength in copiers, experienced humiliating reductions in market share from 60 percent to under 40 percent after Japanese manufacturers such as Canon, Sharp, and Minolta launched a competitive assault on the world copier market.

Numerous arguments have been put forward to explain Japan's success, some bordering on the ridiculous. When Japanese car manufactuers began to strengthen their positions in the world automobile market in the late 1970s, some experts found a convenient explanation in the 1973 Arab oil embargo and the rapid increase in gasoline prices that resulted from it. High gasoline prices were forcing consumers to switch to smaller, fuel-efficient cars. The trend, it was argued, naturally gave a decisive market advantage to the Japanese since they were already deeply entrenched in the small car segment of the market. Thus, the Japanese were benefiting from good luck and their increasingly favorable position had nothing to do with competitive acumen or the mastery of automobile design and manufacturing technology. Consequently, their competitive advantage would fizzle out, once the big three American automakers had enough time to downsize their product line or when oil prices decreased, in real terms, to pre-1973 levels.

Remarkably enough, both events took place, yet the big three North American automakers continued to lose market share to the Japanese. This revealed a fatal flaw in the reasoning that attributed Japan's success to fortuitous circumstances. It could not account for the fact that it was very broad based, affecting simultaneously industries such as steel, automobiles, consumer electronics, copiers, and heavy equipment. If Japan was successfully entrenching itself in the world car market because small cars, its traditional niche, were more desirable, what would account for its increasing market share in other industries that are very different from automobiles? Moreover, how is it that European manufacturers such as Renault and Volkswagen that had traditional expertise in building small, fuel-efficient cars, were unable to capitalize on the change in consumer preferences?

There is nothing magical about what Japanese manufacturers have achieved and no far-fetched reasons are required to explain it either. They became totally convinced that a shift was taking place in the international market, not caused by any oil embargo, but by natural competitive forces. Because markets were becoming international in scope, quality would become a premier strategic variable. They went beyond rhetoric and showed their deep commitment to quality by investing heavily in its development on all fronts—human, technological, and organizational. They persisted in their belief that the 1970s would usher in an era where consumers would demand superior quality and invested for the long haul. They consequently were prepared to sacrifice short-term financial results in order to invest in quality development. Customers are now voting for Japanese products with their dollars because these products constantly achieve the highest delivered quality commensurate with what the customer sees as a fair price. Television sets designed and built in Japan have mean times between failure (MTB), the average time that a set will give trouble free operation, that are twice as high as North American produced ones. Similarly, electronics components made in North America have defect rates that are higher, by orders of magnitude, than those made in Japan. Any company or country that manages quality as the foremost strategic weapon and pays long-term attention to it, will achieve similar quality levels and will also come to have a dominant competitive position in its market.

Superior Quality and the Bottom Line

Concern for final financial results is natural to top management. In a competitive arena, companies must attract capital and to do so, they must generate acceptable financial returns to compensate for the risk that investors are willing to take. The argument is not whether top management should be preoccupied with the bottom line, because in the final analysis, a company must be profitable in order to be viable. Rather, the issue revolves around how much emphasis should be put on the bottom line and whether financial performance should not be judged using a long-term perspective. There is also the question as to how much emphasis should be put on profit versus the factors that create profit, such as quality and innovation. Whichever way one views these issues, it is evident that North American managers are too preoccupied with short-term financial results while they tend to pay lip service to quality. Performance criteria, such as continuous improvement in quality, are far more useful for judging overall top management effectiveness than are short-term profits. The attention given to profits as a measure of corporate performance is not matched by emphasis on quality, because western management thinking generally does not view quality as the major source of profits. On the contrary, North American corporate philosophies nurtured by some archaic concepts of quality economics have tended to blur the relationship between quality and profits. Given the cultural context, increased accent on quality will come about when the right relationship between quality and profitability has been established. Managers who are concerned about improving the bottom line will naturally pay more attention to quality, if it can be shown that superior quality is the best mechanism for achieving sustainable, healthy financial returns.

Quality Costs

Early attempts to understand the economics of quality started by identifying and classifying so-called quality costs. Feigenbaum's classification is among the earliest and best known. He placed these quality costs, as he referred to them, into four categories, namely, prevention, appraisal, internal failure, and external failure. Prevention costs, as the name suggests, are those that are incurred to prevent defects, such as inspection and test design, and planning. Appraisal costs are created by the need to evaluate conformance to specification and these are born by actually executing test and inspection. Internal failure costs are created when a purchased part fails after incoming inspection or when an internally manufactured part or product fails before delivery to the customer. External failure costs result from a product that fails or malfunctions during use by the customer (user).[1]

There are two problems with the whole concept of quality cost. First, a look at all four cost categories reveals that they all exist because defects are produced. These costs would be entirely eliminated if no defects were produced,

---

[1] A.V. Feigenbaum, *Total Quality Control* (New York: McGraw-Hill, 1983).

that is if the entire company "built it right the first time." Consequently, what most managers refer to as quality costs are in fact the costs that result from not making quality every time, all the time. The so-called quality costs are non-quality costs, for want of a better expression. Hence, at the outset, a very powerful distortion was introduced into quality control economics and the attitudes that were nurtured by it. Managers, because they never heard about anything called quality profits but were always reminded about quality costs, developed the biased, erroneous perception that quality imposed cost penalties on a company. Budgeting procedures, with their built-in bias toward cost minimization, reduction, and avoidance, reinforced the attitude that the quality delivered should be the minimum that one can get away with. Budgetary pressures to reduce or contain costs either constrained investment in quality development and assurance and, in some cases, even reduced it. Quality, like research and development and innovation, became an unwitting victim of an ill-conceived financial control system. Financial performance evaluation and reporting rather than contributing to long-term financial health became an impediment to it by unintentionally restricting investment in quality, the prime strategic factor in the company's competitive arsenal.

Quality tends to get serious attention when customer complaints reach crisis proportions. Top management usually goes into action on quality when they are threatened with lost business from a very important customer or when product warranty costs spiral out of control. The basic motivation is to reduce or avoid costs and not to create permanent strategic leverage from quality. The budgeting process in conjunction with the conventional idea that quality costs money have conditioned management behavior in a potent way. Quality cost reduction strategies get primacy over long-term investments for sustained quality improvement. Top management is operating in a reactive mode, solving short-term, quality-related financial crises rather than aggressively leading their companies to produce ever higher quality levels. Most companies are not purposefully working to increase customer satisfaction with quality. Instead, they are always inventing ways to minimize dissatisfaction. Too many North American companies are being dragged, kicking and screaming, into taking action on quality.

Second, once the so-called quality costs were identified, it was inevitable that some effort would be made to understand how they behave in relation to quality. One framework that is still very popular among quality control professionals is shown in Figure 6–2. C_p, C_f, and C_t are prevention (appraisal), failure, and total costs, respectively. The quality level can be increased, but this increases prevention and appraisal costs. However, more rigorous prevention and appraisal reduce defects thereby reducing internal and external failure costs. The total cost curve has a theoretical minimum point and a corresponding optimal quality level. The company has no interest in pushing quality beyond the optimal level because that would worsen its financial situation.

Quality Cost Trade-Off  FIGURE 6-2

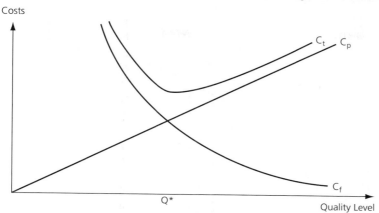

The subtle argument is that quality should be improved only up to a certain point. Any effort to go beyond that optimal level wastes resources and adds cost uselessly.

The idea that there is an optimal quality level beyond which a company should not seek to go was further entrenched into quality control technology by the schema presented in Figure 6-3 which is widely used in standard books on quality. The reasoning behind the schema is as follows. As the quality level is increased, costs increase exponentially because preventing defects becomes more and more difficult. The reader should note that the cost curve in Figure 6-3 mimics the total cost curve in Figure 6-2 when one goes beyond the optimal quality level. But there is not a corresponding increase in price, because, as the argument goes, there must be a practical limit to the price the consumer can or is willing to pay. Theoretically, there is a quality level where the difference between the cost and revenue curves is maximized. A company that is behaving rationally and is seeking to maximize profits, so the argument goes, should not push quality beyond the optimal level shown as point Q_1^* in Figure 6-3.

Management attitudes toward quality has been long influenced by the arguments presented in these schematics. Few quality control specialists have questioned their conceptual foundations. The simple fact is that an optimal quality level exists only on paper and has no basis in reality. They are purely theoretical constructs and no one, to our knowledge, has ever come up with a shred of evidence that supports the assumptions behind the cost and revenue curves presented in Figure 6-3. These concepts are appealing to the analytical mind, but offer little to guide hard quality decisions. No company that we know has ever found that magical optimal quality level. It is truly amazing

FIGURE **6–3** **Quality, Cost, and Revenue**

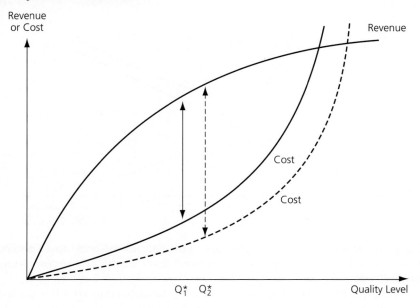

that a theory that was never tested and could not be shown to predict reality could influence quality professionals the way these concepts did.

Quality management technology developed in the West, because it defined an optimal quality level based on erroneous cost and revenue relationships, froze quality improvement in time. Companies that were doing well financially and were able to attribute their performance to good quality thought they had achieved the optimal level. Because the theory told them that pushing quality higher would result in marginally higher costs and, simultaneously lower revenues, they were discouraged from investing further in quality improvements. The theory was wrong for many reasons. First, even if the revenue and cost functions had the general form shown in Figure 6-3, their parameters cannot be computed precisely. The most important quality (nonquality) cost item is external failure cost which cannot be estimated in practice. Who can put a reasonable figure on the lost sales, goodwill, and long-term profits that is occasioned by one product that fails during use by the customer? Product failure is likely to be so costly that prudence would seem to dictate that a company always try to prevent defects and surpass customer expectations. Competitive forces operate to compensate the company that always does a little bit more.

Second, the exponentially increasing cost curve ignored the managerial imperative to increase the effectiveness with which resources are utilized.

There is nothing incompatible between cost reduction or avoidance and increasing quality. If the resources deployed in quality could be used more effectively, then the company could deliver higher quality at lower cost. The dotted cost curve in Figure 6–3 shows increased quality management effectiveness and efficiency, allowing the company to give higher quality at lower cost. However, a corporate attitude that drives management to manufacture products that surpass customer expectations whenever possible has little to do with quality costs per se. On the contrary, it flows naturally from a deep commitment to total customer satisfaction. Companies are driven to excel in quality when top management has effectively created and nurtured a corporatewide attitude that quality is quintessential to long-term survival. They perceive failure costs to be astronomical because poor quality impacts negatively on what they have defined to be their very reason to exist, namely, to deliver and support a superior-quality product.

The market vision and the role that quality plays in customer satisfaction "create" high failure costs. The same goes for quality cost effectiveness. When a company puts a premium on quality and manages it as the strategic mission, then nonquality costs are automatically perceived as high. The view that quality is costly derives from poorly understanding the role that it plays in customer satisfaction. Conversely, companies that view quality correctly easily come to understand that it is nonquality that costs whereas quality generates profit. These same companies, because they put ongoing emphasis on quality, learn to master it and reap the benefits of experience, experimentation, and learning by doing. By these processes, they come to get more quality for less. Companies that do not push hard to improve quality are not likely to improve "quality" cost effectiveness. Neither are they likely to come to harness the marketing power that comes from constantly improving quality and surpassing customer expectations.

An Alternative View: The Mount Fuji Effect

Quality improvement need not cause costs to increase exponentially or even increase at all. The only way that higher quality would mean ever higher costs would be if the company never learns and never becomes proficient at designing and building quality. One would have to assume that all organizations make the same mistakes over and over again and never learn from them. Besides this, know-how and technology would have to be frozen in time, with no gain from technological innovation. There would have to be no progress in processes, products, management systems, and methods. The people who build products would have to be incapable of building on experience so as to improve workmanship. This is contrary to everything one knows about the leading manufacturing companies of the world which prove to be remarkably versatile, demonstrating extreme capacity to learn and improve on products,

 **6–4**   **The Mount Fuji Effect**

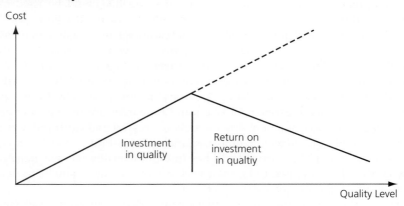

processes, and methods. Capacity to learn and to capitalize on experience are hallmarks of world-class manufacturing companies. The now famous manufacturing progress function (learning curve) and the experience curve have been proved to exist in every industry. Manufacturing organizations can be designed and managed to learn and improve on their know-how.

The quality cost function shown in Figure 6–4, popularly referred to as the Mount Fuji effect illustrates the point that a company ought to be able to learn and become increasingly effective at producing quality. One can refer to it as the quality progress function. A company starting from a base quality position where there is not much emphasis on quality would have to invest heavily for some time in order to achieve a quality turnaround. Crucial organizational structures, managerial processes, philosophies, vision, mission, and attitudes would have to change. Massive investment in employee training and orientation would have to be made. Organizational inertia created by years of managing quality as a low-priority item would have to be overcome, which would require heavy investment. At the same time, little returns would result because significant improvement in quality takes time. Quality is a discipline that must be learned and craftsmanship takes time to develop. Accordingly, quality cost increases.

Adopting a short-term perspective and projecting the quality cost curve would lead management to believe that the only way to increase quality is to keep increasing cost. However, the short-term increase in costs are mainly an investment, because they create structures, procedures, and attitudes that have a lasting effect on quality. When management persists in investing in these quality foundations, the company slowly starts to master quality and becomes more effective at producing it. Eventually, the cumulative impact of the investment starts to be felt and the critical mass is reached. Quality costs relative to revenues, begin to decrease. The long-term perspective leads to the opposite conclusion that relative quality costs decrease as one increases quality. This is the power of the long-term view in quality management. What at first sight appears to be bad in the short run is in fact very good in the long run.

Quality Is Profitable[2]

Crosby's dictum that quality is free is a significant improvement over the archaic idea that quality costs money. It comes from the recognition that what are referred to as quality costs are in fact the cost of producing defective products. These costs are totally avoidable if a company can maintain defect-free, trouble-free operations. They can at least be dramatically reduced when defect rates approach the one-part-per-hundred thousand level. Crosby's idea is that a company that emphasizes doing it right the first time corporatewide will reap higher quality at no additional cost since it costs nothing to do it right the first time. Because better quality can come at no extra cost, quality is profitable since better products are likely to fetch a premium on the market or capture a better market share.

One can very easily demonstrate that quality is profitable. Every major international corporation that also has a solid reputation for superior product quality usually achieves a return on equity and market share that is substantially above the average for its industry. Companies like IBM, Digital Equipment, Mercedes Benz, Rolls-Royce, Toyota, Frito Lay, Boeing, Maytag, Sony, DuPont, to name only a handful, are household names in their respective markets and have solid reputations for making superior-quality products. They all have dominant positions in their markets and are among the most profitable companies anywhere. Economic history is replete with companies that disappeared because they marketed shoddy products—Lada in its efforts to market automobiles in North America, Electrohome in television sets, for example. There is no company, to our knowledge, that went into bankruptcy because it had a superior-quality product or because its product surpassed customer expectations. Despite overwhelming evidence to the contrary, some quality managers still harbor the view that a company can produce too much quality.

Further evidence that superior quality has a strong, positive impact on profitability comes from work done by the Strategic Planning Institute. As part of its effort to document how different management strategies impact on the competitive performance of a company, the institute regularly conducts surveys of about 200 different companies representing approximately 2700 business units. The work that interest us here has to do with the relationship between a company's relative quality position and its performance on a few crucial performance indices such as return on investment (ROI), return on

---

[2]Philip Crosby, *Quality Is Free* (New York: The American Library, 1980).

FIGURE 6–5 **Impact of Relative Quality Percentile on Return on Investment and Return on Sales**

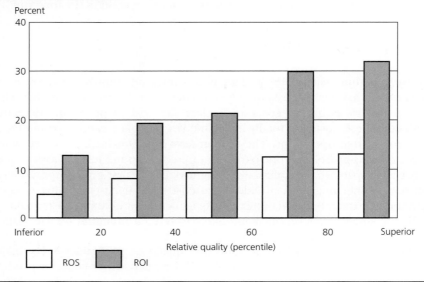

Source: PIMS data base.

sales (ROS), and market share. These results are published under the acronym, PIMS, profit impact of market strategy.

The PIMS methodology is straightforward. Key product attributes, excluding price, were first identified. Managers were then asked to indicate, subjectively, the relative quality of their products compared to competing ones, by attaching a scale from 1 to 10 to each product attribute. Products that were rated high on the most important attributes would receive a high relative quality score. Then attempts were made to relate these quality ratings to the key performance parameters. Figures 6–5 and 6–6 show the results of the PIMS analysis. Companies whose products have been evaluated as inferior have an average ROS of 5 percent and an average ROI of 12 percent, whereas those that received a superior-quality rating have an average ROS of 13 percent and an average ROI of 32 percent. Moreover, there is a systematic increase in ROS and ROI as relative quality performance increases. The data in Figure 6–6 confirm the relationship between quality and market share. Companies that have high-quality ratings also have dominant market shares. These results confirm the anecdotal evidence discussed earlier that superior quality increases a company's financial and market position in a rather dramatic way. A company can almost triple its ROI and ROS by moving its quality performance from inferior to superior. In addition, a superior quality product will come to dominate its market, as the market share data demonstrate. Quality is a prime strategic weapon.

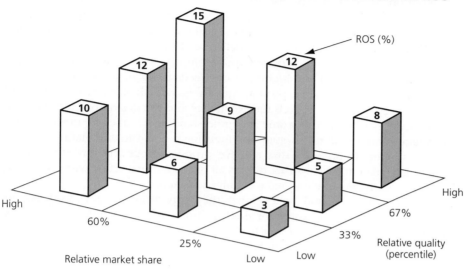

Impact of Relative Quality Percentile and FIGURE 6–6
Relative Market Share on ROS

Source: PIMS data base.

The PIMS data were also used to draw some conclusions on other issues. No relationship was found between relative quality and relative cost position. In other words, high quality did not result in high cost. This challenges the concept that increasing quality increases costs. However, there was a direct correlation between quality and price. Companies that had the highest relative quality also had a relative price that was 8 percent higher than those with the lowest relative quality. Combined with the economies of scale that come from a higher market share, this would explain the impressive ROS results that were achieved by the highest relative quality companies. Superior quality contributes to high financial performance in three ways. First, there is no additional cost created, so that reduced defects decrease marginal production cost. Second, superior quality reduces overall cost by enabling a company to reap economies of scale in R&D, production, marketing, procurement, and distribution that comes from a larger market share. Third, a company receives a substantial price premium when it markets a superior quality product.

Conclusion

According to the extensive anecdotal evidence and the PIMS results, quality is very strongly related to every crucial strategic performance variable. However, as we have already argued, product quality is only the result, the culmination of the pursuit and achievement of excellence in a company. Superior quality as the Japanese experience and the history of world-class North American corporations have shown, does not happen overnight. One should not be fixated on product quality, for doing so would be to confuse the ends with the means. The right focus is to go deeper and to examine quality behind quality; the management philosophies, attitudes, vision, processes, and policies that drive a company to excellence. One needs to understand the processes, practices, and programs that companies implement so as to push attained quality higher and higher. There needs to be an acute awareness that behind measurable, visible product quality is a particular organizational culture that reinforces the search for excellence and the desire to achieve perfection. One needs to also come to understand that superior quality is the product of mastering technology and focusing it on a variable that is valued by the customer. Companies that achieve product superiority are deploying a total management process that directs all organizational effort with singularity of purpose, the goal being total customer satisfaction.

Many managers still believe that they can make shoddy products but design sexy television promotional ads to build a positive quality image. The evidence suggests that it cannot be done this way. The lesson is that the company must create the quality and the quality will create the image.

Case for Discussion

ONTARIO COPPER PRODUCTS (OCP), INC.

Integrated Household Appliances (IHA), Inc., OCP's largest customer, recently audited its major suppliers, and had informed OCP that serious weaknesses were discovered in its operations. IHA expected its suppliers to implement result generating actions within the next six months. Otherwise "we will have to revoke your status as our supplier."

The Company, Its Products and Operating Environment

OCP was an old, well-established Canadian manufacturer of various copper wires, tubing, pipes, and rods. Sales in 1992 were $30 million, 40 percent of which was exported to the United States. The company's products are used in the manufacture of various industrial and consumer products, of which electrical appliances were the most important. Sales to household appliance manufacturers were 65 percent of total sales in 1992. The company has held a dominant position in the Canadian market since the early 1950s and was also a supplier to some leading U.S. companies.

Copper wire used in appliances must be produced to tight tolerance relative to metal purity and uniformity of diameter. OCP found it increasingly difficult to meet the specifications of its customers. Its facilities were run down and the work force was composed of workers who had spent an average of 15 years with the company and most had never been retrained. Five years ago, a young metallurgical engineer freshly hired by the company had suggested that the nature of the product and the operations were very conducive to the application of Statistical Process Control, but the suggestion was never studied by the company. Historically, the internal defect rate was 16 percent and about 4 percent of shipments were returned by customers. Per unit manufacturing cost was composed of 14 percent labor, 16 percent energy, 40 percent materials, and 30 percent overhead. Gross margins were about 30 percent of sales.

OCP was a technically oriented company that was driven hard from the top. Promotion to top management had always been from within and the last four presidents had an average of 25 years service with the company before they assumed that position. According to one insider, "We have a strong tradition in our company, and to survive you must be totally loyal to it. This is a tough business and it would be difficult for an outsider to be comfortable in here." The fact that OCP was unionized, most managers thought, made it difficult to improve operations. The prevailing view among senior management was that the union practiced featherbedding, created restrictive work rules, made excessive wage demands, and resisted innovations that could improve productivity. The union, on the other hand, saw management as being inept, inconsiderate, authoritarian, and using strong arm tactics to bully workers. OCP had lost 45 days to strikes and walk-outs over the last 10 years.

The Customer

IHA was a leading U.S. based manufacturer of small household appliances, lawn mowers, and small tools with sales of over $3.5 billion in 1992. The company had built its reputation as an innovative, technology and market-driven manufacturer of some of the most robust products in the industry. The company was also an innovator in factory and distribution management approaches. For example, it was one of the first to develop and successfully use MRP and quickly followed that with MRP-II and Distribution Requirements Planning.

IHA was among the first North American companies to test, adapt, refine, and implement JIT manufacturing concepts, cell manufacturing, small group improvement teams (SGIT), and statistical process control (SPC). The company had proved itself as an able competitor and fought hard to defend its market from foreign competition. It was largely successful in beating back increasing competition from Japan, Western Europe, and the Pacific Rim countries, as evidenced by the fact that while most U.S. manufacturers suffered an erosion in market share between 1976 and 1985, IHA managed to increase its overall share of the market.

Top management was convinced that its emphasis on superior quality, high levels of customer service and on the need to drive costs down through improved efficiency and superior technology, would help IHA retain and defend its market position. But 70 percent of its part numbers and 55 percent of its per unit manufacturing cost was accounted for by purchased items. IHA purchased $3.6 million of product from OCP in 1990. In 1991, it decided to manage supplier quality as rigorously as it managed quality in its own plants. The decision was taken to implement a complete supplier certification program as a first step toward identifying weak ones and eventually recertifying the one or two best suppliers per part. In communicating the new policy to existing suppliers, management asserted:

> Within the next two years, we will buy only from the two best suppliers in our industry. All our suppliers must be able to supply 100 percent good product, 100 percent of the time.

Moreover, IHA tightened its definition of good product and cut the tolerances on all parts in half.

Quick Review of Quality Management at OCP

Ms. Diane Fulton had been named plant manager barely six months ago. As she reflected on the new customer requirements, she noted a few things that might be useful. Since her company started selling to IHA 20 years ago, they had always delivered what the customer requested. OCP obviously did a lot of defect screening and from time-to-time the customer returned a batch of product that did not meet the specifications. But OCP had always replaced the defective products at no cost to the customer. Besides, OCP's experience was no different from that of other suppliers. The quality management procedures used at the plant had not changed in recent years, but they were no worse than what her competitors were doing. She also noted that nearly all the employees were very positive about a half-day seminar on quality that was conducted recently in the plant, the only one ever given to the production workers. Although quality was never the business of production workers, OCP always managed to hold a fair share of the market and make a decent profit.

It would be tough to change the plant and she was wondering whether it was worth the effort. Maybe she could write off IHA as a customer and seek out new ones. Everyone was talking about total quality management (TQM) these days, but she was not sure it was not a new slogan for the same old way of doing business. In any event, she was sure that it would cost about $500,000 per year over the next five years to implement TQM concepts and she would have to invest in new equipment and systems at a total cost of $2.4

million. That would cut deeply into her reported profits and her annual bonus would vanish. Her young engineer had promised that SPC would eliminate defects, would only cost $25,000 to implement, and would require little change in the way the plant operated.

Diane Fulton was sure that she was on the path to finding a solution to the problem when the sales manager bolted into her office. He had just read in the newspaper that OCP's second largest customer was contemplating starting a vendor certification program.

1. Where are the pressures coming from in OCP's business?
2. Are the requirements imposed by IHA reasonable? Can OCP afford to ignore these requirements?
3. What are the fundamental elements of OCP's approach to quality? In what ways are they different from what prevails in today's world-class manufacturing companies?
4. What are the major barriers to strategic change and quality improvement at OCP? How would you deal with these barriers?
5. If you were Diane Fulton, what actions would you take to put OCP on a strong competitive footing?

References

Box, George E. P., Ragu N. Kackar, Vijay N. Nair, Madhav Phadke, Anne Shoemaker, and C. F. Jeff Wu, "Quality Practices in Japan," *Quality Progress,* March 1988.

Business Week, Special Bonus Issue, "The Quality Imperative," 1991.

Crosby, Philip B., *Quality Is Free,* New York: McGraw-Hill, 1979.

Deming, Edwards W., *Quality, Productivity, and Competitive Position,* Cambridge, Mass.: Massachusetts Institute of Technology, Center for Advanced Engineering, 1982.

Feigenbaum, A. V., *Total Quality Control,* New York: McGraw-Hill, 1983.

Garvin, David A., "Quality on the Line" in *Unconditional Quality, Harvard Business Review,* Paperback, 1991.

Garvin, David A., "Competing on Eight Dimensions of Quality," *Harvard Business Review,* November–December 1987.

Groocock, J. M., *The Chain of Quality,* New York: John Wiley and Sons, 1986.

Juran, Joseph M., and Frank M. Gryna, Jr., *Quality Planning and Analysis,* New York: McGraw-Hill, 1980.

Main, Jeremy, "The Curmudgeon Who Talks Tough on Quality," *Fortune,* June 25, 1984.

Main, Jeremy, "Detroits Cars Are Really Getting Better," *Fortune,* February 2, 1987.

Reitsperger, Wolf D., and Shirley J. Daniel, "A Comparison of Quality Attitudes in the USA and Japan: Empirical Evidence," *Journal of Management Studies* 28:6, November 1991.

Laying the Foundation for Superior Quality

The world's best managed corporations, those that have achieved quality superiority and competitive distinctiveness, share many traits. One such mark of distinction is the persistence with which they produce superior and consistently improving quality over a long period. There are very few newcomers or fly-by-night companies among the world's best competitors. All, or nearly all of them have a long, uninterrupted history of making superior-quality products that customers are willing to buy and will continue to buy. While the products of today are far better in many cases than those of the past, the fact remains that the old and long dead products were, in their day, the best in their class. Henry Ford's Model T car is obviously a dinosaur, a patently inferior product, compared to the best cars made by Ford Motor Company today. But the Model T was one of the best cars available on the market in its day.

What is striking about companies that reach world-class excellence in quality is that while markets, customer requirements, technology, and production methods change, they are able to keep the attention to quality and the ability to deliver it constant. These companies are able to absorb enormous changes in all aspects of their business while maintaining constancy of purpose and performance relative to quality. The changing technologies, tools, and methods for putting quality into the product are like the four walls and the roof of a building. They can be dismantled, redesigned, rebuilt, and refined as many times as necessary, to conform to changing customer tastes and requirements. But the foundation upon which the buildings are erected is so strong that it will outlast even the best designed and erected building. The strong foundation means that the company does not have to start afresh every time markets, technologies, and tools change. Because it has the rock solid foundation, the company is always one step ahead when it must rebuild the building to adjust to new realities in the marketplace.

What most people see when they look at the superior quality companies are what is obvious and visible, the four walls and the roof. Thus, Ford Motor Company was hailed for the assembly line, just like Toyota is being hailed for JIT. And so, managers today who are striving to emulate the world's best competitors are trying to implement JIT, TQC, and TPM at breakneck speed. If we look deeper, however, we will discover that the key to quality superiority lies in the foundation ideas. Unless the foundation ideas are well in place, the push for quality superiority is like erecting an elaborate and "strong" building on a hollow foundation. Lasting quality superiority starts with a rock solid foundation. The difference between the best companies and even the above average ones lies in the foundation quality concepts. We will now elucidate the few powerful ideas that differentiate superior quality companies from the others and will consider how companies can build the foundation for quality superiority. It is not surprising, then, that companies that are already producing superior quality are invariably the first to master whatever new quality improvement tools and technologies that are developed.

IN SEARCH OF THE FOUNDATION OF QUALITY SUPERIORITY

Lasting quality superiority can only be erected on a solid foundation of core management concepts. In the long search for these core concepts, no three individuals stand out more than W. Edwards Deming, Joseph M. Juran, and Philip Crosby. We will now review their work as a basis for gaining insight into the nature and role of these concepts and as a prelude to outlining the managerial and organizational foundation of quality and superiority and lasting quality improvement in the modern enterprise.

W. Edwards Deming and Quality Leadership

The Japanese quality movement started with a series of lectures by Deming in 1956. He was categorical in his message to Japanese leaders: Japan would receive respect from the West only when the quality of Japanese products matched or surpassed that of those in the West. Deming's initial focus was on the use of scientific methods, particularly SPC, to control processes, analyze and search for causes, and improve quality. He found a very enthusiastic audience among the ranks of Japanese business leaders, managers, and particularly the Japanese Union of Scientists and Engineers (JUSE). Within a few years of the first Deming lectures, JUSE had launched its Statistical Quality Control and Quality Control for Foremen (Gemba To Quality) courses. By 1960, just four years after Deming arrived, the Japanese Quality Circles movement, which was instrumental in diffusing quality management technology all through the ranks of industry, was born. The Japanese honored Deming by naming their highest annual award for quality the Deming Prize.

The Deming philosophy (approach, paradigm) has five core elements.[1] The first and foremost is managerial leadership from the top. Deming is

---

[1]W. Edwards Deming, *Quality, Productivity and Competitive Position* (Cambridge, MA: Massachusetts Institute of Technology, Center for Advanced Engineering, 1982).

insistent and forthright in asserting that top management is totally responsible for the company's quality performance. Quality will improve only when top management changes its attitudes and values, manages quality by example, and creates the environment where employees must and will be willing to improve quality. The profound changes that are necessary to unleash the process of sustainable and significant quality improvement can only start at the top.

But neither top management, nor workers can improve until they have proven, tested knowledge. The strong emphasis on knowledge, the second element of the Deming philosophy, is unique among the leading quality experts. Doing one's best is not good enough; managers and workers must acquire the *deep* knowledge of quality technology, principles, methods, scientific tools, human behavior, the market, customer requirements, and manufacturing processes on which to base actions that are likely to lead to mastery of quality. Management must acquire the sound knowledge that quality management requires and must see to it that all employees acquire it as well. Quality does not just happen but is *made to happen* by the application of tested, rigorous scientific knowledge. Only workers who know the job and have thoroughly mastered it to become experts and craftsmen, can make and improve quality.

The third element of the Deming philosophy is the requirement that workers be thoroughly trained and motivated to use their knowledge. Continuous and thorough training are prerequisites to quality superiority and continuous improvement. Workers will be motivated when top management creates the proper environment where creativity can flourish by driving out fear. The old command and control mentality with its emphasis on punishment instills fear and blocks creativity and desire to learn. When management drives out fear it creates an environment where workers will freely exercise creativity and will be willing and ready to learn.

The fourth element of the Deming philosophy centers around the tools and methods that can be used to apply the knowledge base to solve real quality problems and facilitate continuous improvement. Deming places much emphasis on two of these: (1) The plan-do-check-adjust (PDCA) problem-solving cycle and (2) SPC. Because of its scientific rationale, SPC receives much attention in the Deming philosophy. The PDCA cycle is simple and is shown schematically in Figure 7–1.

The Deming philosophy has a unique conception of the nature and causes of quality problems and management's role in their eradication. Deming contends that 85 percent of all quality problems derive from common causes that is, factors that exist throughout the company. Because these causes are widespread, they can only be attributable to common policies and practices that top management has put in place, and therefore, workers have no control over these. Common causes are systemic in nature and they can be eliminated only by management action to change the policies and practices that give rise to them. Quality problems due to poor vendor selection policies and criteria, poor worker training and a deficient motivational environment, or the

The Deming Problem-Solving Cycle   FIGURE 7–1

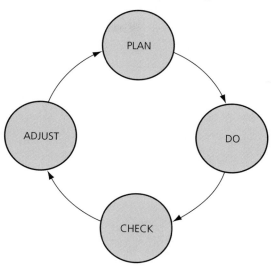

failure to properly maintain equipment, or to provide tools and manufacturing processes that are adequate to get the job done, all fall under the umbrella of common or systemic causes and they all emanate from ineffective managerial actions. Special causes, on the other hand, are the responsibility of the worker who is directly responsible for a task or operation. A worker who fails to stop a machine when it malfunctions is an example of a special cause.

Deming's view is that SPC was the most powerful tool that could be used to systematically analyze and differentiate between the variation in product parameters that are attributable to systemic as opposed to special causes. Variation is always present in a process, so the question for quality management is when is variation acceptable or unacceptable. The SPC chart in Figure 7–2 shows how acceptable and unacceptable variation can be statistically defined. As long as the product or part parameters fall within the upper and lower control limits, the process is in a state of statistical control, and no action is required on the part of the worker. Once the parameters fall outside of the control limits, a special cause is at work and some action should be taken to remove it and bring the process back into a state of control.

Systemic causes explain the difference between the upper and lower control limits. The underlying quality level can be improved only as these systemic causes are eradicated. Since these causes arise throughout the company, it takes concerted action at the top management level and in process design, research and development, and improved maintenance policies to eradicate them. Once basic improvement has been achieved, the SPC chart would detect it and reestablish the new limits that could be used to identify unacceptable variation due to special causes. Deming's thinking is that SPC is the major tool

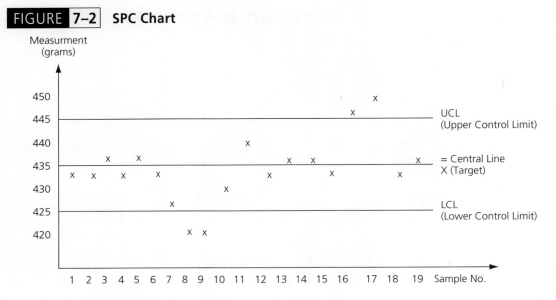

FIGURE 7–2 **SPC Chart**

of quality improvement because it gives a scientific definition of acceptable and unacceptable variation and pinpoints which is due to systemic causes that call for broad managerial actions and which is due to special causes that demand worker intervention.

While SPC is a valid quality management tool, more and more companies are questioning the importance attached to it in Deming's philosophy. The Japanese, in particular, were initially very enthusiastic and loyal users of SPC but have recently started to move away from making it a central aspect of their quality management programs. Increasingly, companies are coming to realize that they cannot rely on SPC to push defects to near zero. The culture and value system that put a framework around the use of SPC are more crucial. Deming himself has been moving away from his initial emphasis on SPC and is now giving more prominence to managerial leadership as a crucial determinant of quality superiority.

Deming's fourteen point program for improving quality, shown in Table 7-1, is the fifth element of his philosophy. These points clearly have much more to do with the general management issues than SPC.

Joseph Juran and the Breakthrough Sequence[2]

Except for Deming, no other individual has influenced modern quality management more than Juran. His approach has many unique aspects that set it apart

---

[2]Joseph Juran and Frank M. Gryna, *Quality Planning and Analysis* (New York: McGraw-Hill, 1980).

Deming's 14-Point Program	TABLE 7–1

1. Create constancy of purpose for improvement in product and service.
2. Adopt the new philosophy.
3. Cease dependence on mass inspection.
4. End the practice of awarding business (to suppliers) on price alone.
5. Constantly and forever improve the system of production and service.
6. Institute modern methods of training on the job.
7. Institute modern methods of supervising.
8. Drive out fear.
9. Break down barriers between departments.
10. Eliminate numerical goals for the work force (because most of the changes that are necessary to achieve these goals are not the responsibility of the worker but of top management).
11. Eliminate work standards and numerical quotas. They cause the worker to put priority on quantity instead of quality.
12. Remove barriers that hinder pride in work of hourly workers.
13. Institute a vigorous program of education and training.
14. Create a structure in top management that will push every day on the above 13 points.

from Deming's philosophy. The starting point for Juran is a commonly accepted definition of quality which he defines as "fitness for use," a definition which comes from the legal principles of British common law. A product is of acceptable quality if it is fit for the use for which it was acquired. By defining quality in this way, Juran makes the customer key to the understanding of quality and to the search for ways to improve it. In Juran's thinking, a product goes through a series of sequentially connected phases, each contributing to its fitness for use. The distinct phases identified by him are design, process development, vendor selection and relations, manufacturing control, inspection and testing, distribution, customer relations, and field service. These phases are sometimes referred to as the total quality control (TQC) cycle.

Each phase presents unique challenges, constraints, and opportunities to the achievement of fitness for use. The key to understanding quality and improving it lies in the ability to break each phase up into its constituent elements and to measure the impact of each on the quality of the product. Juran advocates extensive use of statistical analyses to aid the process. One of the hallmarks of the Juran approach is the emphasis on the costs of quality and how these behave as a function of the quality level. As quality increases, failure costs decrease, but appraisal and prevention costs increase. There is a point where the total costs of quality are minimized, and management has no

FIGURE 7–3 **Juran's Anatomy of Quality Problems**

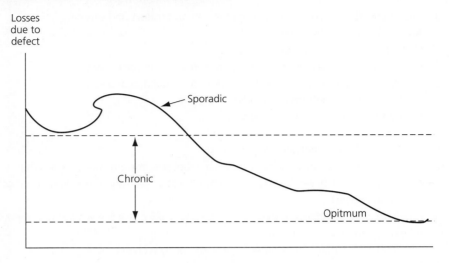

interest to push the quality level beyond this optimal point. In other words, quality is limited by the cost to achieve it and the price that the customer is willing to pay. As we will see later, emphasis on the concept of an optimal quality level, if not carefully done, could discourage managers from pushing, for ever increasing quality.

The company has to adapt its search for improvement to where it actually was on the path to the optimum: This search and the supporting actions have been classified into three phases, as shown in Figure 7–3.

1. Breakthrough projects: In the early phases of a company's quality progress, there are many opportunities for breakthrough projects that effect dramatic reductions in losses due to defects. These projects are geared to solving chronic quality problems, 80 percent of which can be solved by management intervention. Workers themselves only account for 20 percent of chronic quality problems.
2. With the design and implementation of a sufficient number of breakthrough projects and with appropriate control mechanisms to prevent the recurrence of problems, the company can reach the optimal quality level where losses due to defects are minimized. No more breakthroughs are likely at this point, and the focus of the quality program shifts to maintaining all the gains generated by the breakthrough sequence.
3. At the optimal quality level, the company is ready to enter the control sequence where it sets appropriate standards, measures quality constantly, provides feedback to signal sporadic or reemerging problems and takes

appropriate corrective action. Juran advocates using the annual quality audit to set objectives for quality performance, search for causes and design action programs that would eradicate these. The quality audit is different from day-to-day quality control in that the former involves top management in the control sequence.

Philip Crosby and "Free Quality"[3]

Prior to Crosby's emergence as a leading thinker in the modern quality movement, the notion that higher quality could only be attained at increasingly higher cost was well entrenched in the minds of practicing managers and experts. The work of Juran, in particular, was predicated on the concept of an optimal quality level as conceptualized in his cost curves that purport to show how total costs behave as a function of the quality level. Juran thought that there was a quality level beyond which it made no economic sense to go, because the penalties for doing so were very severe. Total costs increased exponentially as the company tried to push the quality level above the optimum.

Crosby took issue with this central postulate of the Juran thesis. Crosby took exception with the notion that quality is costly and suggested the alternative conceptualization that quality was free and it is only poor quality—the failure to meet customer requirements—which is costly. To reinforce the concept, Crosby developed the quality maturity grid that shows how a company's quality management capabilities evolve through five distinct phases, the nature of each phase and, above all, the cost of quality (nonquality) as a percentage of sales. Table 7–2 summarizes the quality maturity stages on six critical dimensions. Crosby's argument is that by managing the company and taking it from Stage I to Stage V, top management produces a return that is equal to 17.5 percent (20% − 2.5%) of sales, an amount that is more than enough to justify the investment in a more extensive quality effort.

Crosby also outlines a fourteen point program (Table 7–3) for implementing total quality management and for moving the company systematically toward Stage V. There are some striking differences between the Deming philosophy and Crosby's approach. In particular, the idea of a zero defects day and the setting of measurable goals are in diametrical opposition to points 10 and 11 of the Deming fourteen point program. However, Crosby's approach can stand in its own right as a lasting contribution to the discovery of the foundation concepts of quality improvement and superiority. We will now draw on these ideas and others to develop a basic framework of the foundation concepts of quality superiority.

---

[3]Philip Crosby, *Quality Is Free* (New York: McGraw-Hill, 1979).

TABLE 7-2	Crosby's Quality Management Maturity Grid				
Measurement Categories	**Stage I: Uncertainty**	**Stage II: Awakening**	**Stage III: Enlightenment**	**Stage IV: Wisdom**	**Stage V: Certainty**
Management understanding and attitude	Fails to see quality as a management tool.	Supports quality management in theory but is unwilling to provide the necessary money or time.	Learns about quality management and becomes supportive.	Participates personally in quality activities.	Regards quality management as essential to the company's success.
Quality organization status	Quality activities are limited to the manufacturing or engineering department and are largely appraisal and sorting.	A strong quality leader has been appointed, but quality activities remain focused on appraisal and sorting, and are still limited to manufacturing, and engineering.	Quality department reports to top management, and its leader is active in company management.	Quality manager is an officer of the company. Prevention activities have become important.	Quality manager is on the board of directors. Prevention is the main quality activity.
Problem handling	Problems are fought as they occur and are seldom fully resolved; "firefighting" dominates.	Teams are established to attack major problems, but the approach remains short term.	Problems are resolved in an orderly fashion, and corrective action is a regular event.	Problems are identified early in their development.	Except in the most unusual cases, problems are prevented.
Cost of quality as percentage of sales	Reported: unknown Actual: 20%	Reported: 5% Actual: 18%	Reported: 8% Actual: 12%	Reported: 6.5% Actual: 8%	Reported: 2.5% Actual: 2.5%
Quality improvement actions	No organized activities.	Activities are motivational and short term.	Implements the 14-step program with full understanding.	Continues the 14-step program and starts Make Certain.	Quality improvement is a regular and continuing activity.
Summation of company quality posture	"We don't know why we have quality problems?"	"Must we always have quality problems?"	"Because of management commitment and quality improvement programs, we are identifying and resolving our quality problems."	"We routinely prevent defects from occurring."	"We know why we don't have quality problems."

Note: This chart is adapted from Philip Crosby, *Quality Is Free*, 32–33.
Source: Artemis, March, and David A. Garvin, *A Note on Quality: The Views of Deming, Juran and Crosby* (Boston, MA: Harvard Review Paperback, 1991), 28. Reproduced with permission.

Crosby's 14-Point Program

TABLE 7–3

1. **Management commitment.** Top management must become convinced of the need for quality improvement and must make its commitment clear to the entire company. This should be accompanied by a written quality policy, stating that each person is expected to "perform exactly like the requirement, or cause the requirement to be officially changed to what we and the customers really need."

2. **Quality improvement team.** Management must form a team of department heads (or those who can speak for their departments) to oversee quality improvement. The team's role is to see that needed actions take place in its departments and in the company as a whole.

3. **Quality measurement.** Quality measures that are appropriate to every activity must be established to identify areas needing improvement. In accounting, for example, one measure might be the percentage of late reports; in engineering, the accuracy of drawings; in purchasing, rejections due to incomplete descriptions; and in plant engineering, time lost because of equipment failures.

4. **Cost of quality evaluation.** The controller's office should make an estimate of the costs of quality to identify areas where quality improvements would be profitable.

5. **Quality awareness.** Quality awareness must be raised among employees. They must understand the importance of product conformance and the costs of nonconformance. These messages should be carried by supervisors (after they have been trained) and through such media as films, booklets, and posters.

6. **Corrective action.** Opportunities for correction are generated by steps 3 and 4, as well as by discussions among employees. These ideas should be brought to the supervisory level and resolved there, if possible. They should be pushed up further if that is necessary to get action.

7. **Zero defects planning.** An ad hoc zero defects committee should be formed from members of the quality improvement team. This committee should start planning a zero defects program appropriate to the company and its culture.

8. **Supervisor training.** Early in the process, all levels of management must be trained to implement their part of the quality improvement program.

9. **Zero Defects Day.** A Zero Defects Day should be scheduled to signal to employees that the company has a new performance standard.

10. **Goal setting.** To turn commitments into action, individuals must establish improvement goals for themselves and their groups. Supervisors should meet with their employees and ask them to set goals that are specific and measurable. Goal lines should be posted in each area and meetings held to discuss progress.

11. **Error cause removal.** Employees should be encouraged to inform management of any problems that prevent them from performing error-free work. Employees need not do anything about these problems themselves; they should simply report them. Reported problems must then be acknowledged by management within 24 hours.

12. **Recognition.** Public, nonfinancial appreciation must be given to those who meet their quality goals or perform outstandingly.

13. **Quality councils.** Quality professionals and team chairpersons should meet regularly to share experiences, problems, and ideas.

14. **Do it all over again.** To emphasize the never-ending process of quality improvement, the program (steps 1–13) must be repeated. This renews the commitment of old employees and bring new ones into the process.

Note: This summary is adapted from Philip Crosby, *Quality Is Free* (New York: McGraw-Hill, 1980), 132–139, 175–259.
Source: Artemis, March, and David A. Garvin, *A Note on Quality: The Views of Deming, Juran and Crosby* (Boston, MA: Harvard Business Review Paperback, 1991), 29. Reproduced with permission.

THE QUALITY CULTURE AND VALUE SYSTEM

When one adopts a broad perspective and sees quality as a total concept, encompassing all useful organizational activities, then it becomes evident that there is no qualitative difference between the drive to constantly improve quality and the push to achieve world-class excellence. Superior quality is nothing but a concrete manifestation of excellence achieved and maintained across a broad spectrum of managerial activities. This being the case, the foundation concepts promulgated by Peters and Waterman in *In Search of Excellence*[4] are very useful in any attempt to understand how product superiority can be achieved and maintained as an ongoing organizational experience. These authors underscored the point that excellent companies have an organizational culture and value system that sets them apart from mediocre, run-of-the-mill corporations. Excellent companies nurture a corporate culture and value system that makes them unique and distinctive. The distinctiveness lies in the fact that the culture and value system is deliberately designed, nurtured, and promoted to make excellence and its pursuit normal and deeply embedded in all organizational processes and activities. Managerial and organizational energies are channeled toward excellence and perfection. These excellent companies have built-in value systems that shape individual attitudes so that mediocrity is defined as deviance, excellence is inculcated into the managerial psyche, and perfection is accepted as an entirely desirable, even if not feasible, mission.

Similarly, superior product quality results from a corporate culture and value system that makes product superiority germane to survival. Companies that produce superior quality consistently and predictably have succeeded in building and nurturing a quality culture and value system that makes quality improvement and heightened concern for quality, a permanent aspect of organizational life. The drive for excellence finds its ultimate expression in the companywide obsession with quality that one finds in the outstanding, world-class companies. There seems to exist, in these companies, a natural organizational compulsion to improve quality and to challenge the quality limits. Heightened, widespread concern for quality has become a permanent aspect of organizational life. It is perfectly natural and normal, in these companies, for every worker to think, act, plan, and execute quality, and to be motivated to painstakingly search for perfection. Poor quality is defined to be very abnormal and its existence anywhere within the company or at the supplier level is managed as a profound crisis. Quality is integrated into all managerial, supervisory, and operational activities, from the complex and daunting to the simple and mundane. These unique, world-class companies have forged a

---

[4]Thomas Peters, and Robert H. Waterman, Jr., *In Search of Excellence: Lessons from America's Best-Run Companies* (New York: Harper and Row, 1982).

deep, broad and lasting corporate consensus that superior quality is the means for achieving survival, growth, and profitability in the marketplace. What is striking about companies that achieve and sustain superior product quality is their distinctiveness. They have a way of thinking about quality and of executing it on a daily basis that sets them apart from the typical company. They are different and their uniqueness is visible, evident and striking. Companies like Mercedes-Benz, IBM, and Frito-Lay have quality as their superior competitive competence.

The quality culture and value system must be so profoundly embedded into the corporate structure that it can only be created and sustained by top management. Chester Barnard in *The Functions of the Executive*[5] makes the point rather forcefully that the chief executive officer must be the architect of the corporate culture and value system. It can be no other way. Values and culture so condition human behavior and are so fundamental to the achievement of cooperative effort, that it is difficult to see any other agent having responsibility for their creation, propagation, inculcation, and regeneration, if need be. Culture and values are the raw material, the binding agent, that holds organizational life together. Sociologists have long told us that cultural homogeneity and shared values act as powerful magnets that bring human beings together into social contracts. Shared values make behavior more predictable and eliminate the anxiety and stress that can come from social interaction. Social proximity is less threatening when there is one culture and core values that are accepted by all parties to the social contract. The chief executive is the ultimate motivator, leader, and organization builder, and these are crucial to the management process. By designing and nurturing the quality culture and value system, top management provides the looking glass through which the entire company will view all quality-related issues. Moreover, the culture and value system provides the organizational framework for solving quality problems for the short and long term. Quality is managed and controlled strictly within the framework provided by the quality culture and value system. This is the quality fact of life. Quality problems are viewed, understood, and solved using the assumptions, priorities, and organizational processes that are legitimized by the shared values that are peculiar to the company. Top management, because it is responsible for inciting and channeling appropriate human action in an organizational setting must create the value set upon which such action is based. The creation of the quality culture and value system requires profound and pervasive changes in organizational structure and mission, and affect the very character of a company in an important way. Maintaining the value system, once it has been steered into being, calls for strong organizational discipline to keep the value set unique in the face of market

---

[5]Chester J. Barnard, *The Functions of the Executive* (Cambridge, Mass.: Harvard University Press, 1968), Chapter 5.

FIGURE 7–4   **The Quality Culture and TQC**

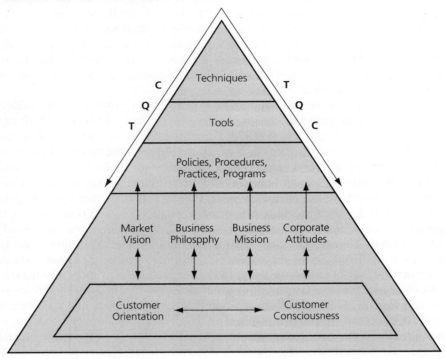

and technological revolutions. Only the chief executive has the requisite positional authority to intervene in an organization so profoundly and persistently.

Organizations are contrived social systems. They are designed, structured and purposefully perpetuated. The value set, which is the organization's lifeblood, must also be created purposefully. The culture and value system impart "reason to be" to an organization, since it is what makes social interaction possible, in the first place. How an initial, very limited set of values gives rise to an organization and subsequently becomes extensively elaborated is not a question that can be dealt with here. Trial and error undoubtedly play a major role in that elaboration process. Whatever the mechanisms at work, the conclusion is irrefutable; every company has a value set that successive top managements have dared to create and embed into the structure, processes, problem-solving mechanisms, and practices that they relegate to the lower echelons.

Figure 7–4 schematizes the key elements of the quality culture and value system and how they relate to other quality-control concepts embodied in what is commonly called total quality control (TQC). The value set is presented as the bedrock, the foundation, upon which all quality management activities must rest. Many companies attempt to implement TQC without taking the time and devoting the resources that are necessary to create the value set that sustains all meaningful quality control activities. This is like building a house on a foundation of sand. TQC, as a coherent set of quality policies, procedures, tools, and techniques can be used to its potential only when the environment that supports it is appropriate. Regardless of how much effort is put into TQC implementation, the probability that it will fail is very high unless the quality culture and value system has been designed specifically to facilitate and motivate long-term mastery of quality. Evidently also, TQC implementation is natural where the value set makes superior quality a competitive imperative.

The quality culture and value system have four symbiotically related components: (1) market vision, (2) corporate mission, (3) management philosophies, and (4) corporate attitudes. When these components are appropriately defined and blended into all managerial processes, they exert overwhelming influence for effectively designing and implementing the TQC system. The argument here is that companies that create the right corporate value set will inevitably successfully implement and use TQC. Furthermore, the right quality culture provides the learning environment where TQC concepts will be refined, improved on, or even changed, if the need arises.

Market Vision

How a company views its market exerts a powerful influence on its dedication to quality. Corporations that are driving hard to improve quality and maintain product superiority look at their market in quite specific ways. First, these companies adopt a long-term market view. They are responding to short-term market changes, but on the whole, they try to anticipate how the market will evolve over the long run. Their basic assumption is that when one takes the long view, markets always evolve to be radically different from what they are today. What gives the company a competitive advantage in the short term will always turn out to be a disadvantage, or at least neutral, over the long haul. Companies that are in business to maintain quality excellence are always very busy preparing for tomorrow's market requirements. Today's market is always a fait accompli. The strategic errors that will drive a company into the ground tomorrow, are always made today, just like present success always derives from preparing for market changes many years in the past.

Second, competition is taken to be omnipresent and all powerful. Competitiveness is the driving force behind the quality effort. Top management is acutely aware that competition is present and that no one company can hope to dominate its market for long, except by hard work and astuteness. Companies that achieve dominant market positions and thereby attempt to use it to eliminate the competition, always end up being annihilated by competitive market forces. World-class companies try to constantly improve quality because there is visceral conviction that the company's strategic viability absolutely depends on it. Competitive market forces drive quality to ever increasing levels and those companies that are achieving impeccable quality are simply obeying the dictates of the market. World-class companies are imbued with a fiercely competitive spirit.

Third, these companies view increased globalization and its consequences as normal market evolution. Globalization is seen not as a threat to survival but as an opportunity to expand and exercise competitive leadership on a much broader scale. International competition rather than forcing a progressive company to seek relief by way of government protection serves as the spark to ignite it into action. The knowledge that the competitive battle is being waged against the best the world has to offer propels action to increase quality. Top management willingly accepts the challenge to motivate the organization to higher levels of quality excellence.

The relationship between competitive scope and quality is clear. Product quality is the highest in markets that are international in scope. As a market evolves from being a local or national to an international one, there is always a significant and discernible increase in product quality and across many niches. The anecdotal evidence suggests conclusively that when a market globalizes and produces competitive disruption, the companies that get into trouble first are those that are weak on product quality. Electrohome in household television sets and Massey-Fergusson in farm machinery and equipment are classic examples of companies that were driven into bankruptcy by global market forces. Neither company could have been said to be producing a world-standard quality product when they got into trouble. Companies that survive the destabilization caused by globalization are those that manage to get their quality levels high enough, quickly enough. Globalization operates to purge inferior quality out of the market.

Market vision is created or nurtured at the top by the chief executive. Company presidents generally manage and exercise leadership based on their market view. This may be done either consciously or subconsciously, but it is always true that how a manager views the world or his or her weltanschauung will totally influence how he or she behaves in response to global events and, in point of fact, determines whether that manager will perceive these events at all. Managerial leadership carries with it the necessary connotation that the chief executive shapes the mind set of key subordinates and eventually the whole company to conform to his or her view of the market. The market vision could emerge at lower levels in the company, and it sometimes does. Nevertheless, in order for it to shape competitive strategy and mobilize the entire company into action, the market vision, and only one market vision, must be thoroughly embraced by the chief executive officer. A president can hardly exercise leadership over people whose visions of the market are different from his or her own, when that very same market controls the factors that make for competitive success or failure.

The appropriate market vision, then, must be forcefully asserted and communicated. Successful company presidents seize every opportunity whether it be formal or informal, to state, refine or improve the company's market vision and to incorporate it into the thinking of lower level managers. The chief executive must be constantly alert to vital cues that may indicate whether the right market vision is being adopted by subordinates. In addition to routine positive reinforcement on a recurring basis, the promotion system can be used to ensure that those who are in key management positions share the company's market vision and that they themselves are coaching subordinates to embrace it.

The Business or Corporate Mission

Managing for short-term results has caused a terrible inversion of priorities in most companies today. The short term has replaced the long term and the blind search after profits has replaced genuine commitment to excellence. Profits from quality became so sweet that managers soon forgot that the sweetness came from painstakingly cultivating a quality image on the basis of sweat, tears, and toil. The fruits tasted better than the planting and pruning, so executives began to want the fruits without the labor. The ends were worshiped far beyond the means. Executives who were going to be around for only a few years started finding it impossible to work hard to cultivate profits in the long run. John Maynard Keynes' dictum that "in the long run we are all dead" started to strike management as advice against worrying about the long run. Indeed, it even implied that it is foolish to think long term. But Confucius had warned the Asians that "if no thought is taken of the future, then disappointment is near at hand." In a rather bizarre twist of events, Keynes' long run no longer lasts a lifetime, due to accelerating technology. Company presidents who thought that they would not have to deal with the long run were finding out that they were without a job and a company to run by the time they were 50 or even 45 years old. The short-term game caught up with North American managers.

The mission is to provide a superior quality product. It is to constantly improve quality until it is mastered. The mission is and can only be to develop a totally satisfied customer that comes back for the product, repeatedly. A company should see itself as being in business forever and to serve the customer for just as long. When company presidents see the business mission as quality, they manage for the long term, and the short-term profits automatically take care of themselves. The paradox of management is that companies that pursue quality perfection relentlessly and pay less attention to profits are the most profitable while those that are most concerned about profits are the least profitable. Superior quality is the only corporate mission that makes sense, particularly given the new realities of global markets, the toughest competitive arena ever faced by industrial and commercial enterprise.

Business or Management Philosophy

Organizations are concrete, rational, social systems that are purposefully designed. Their existence requires voluntary contractual relationships between people. But their concreteness masks the fact that they are based on powerful ideas that reflect the visionary thinking of their creators. A company executive is like a master architect who uses a design to give concrete expression to abstract thought processes, the powerful ideals that drive organizational action. This is what we refer to here as the business philosophy. It is the set of ideals that top management is trying to concretely express, like the master architect, as day-to-day organizational action. The world's greatest corporations were put into place by the founders who had a potent business philosophy that made the company distinctive from its inception.

A company that is driving quality to perfection has a business philosophy which embraces quality comprehensively. Quality must be a core idea in the business philosophy, so that, at the outset, the company is defined to be in the quality business. The chief executive officer is responsible for forging such a philosophy where it does not already exist. Companies that do not make quality germane to their business philosophy will have difficulty sustaining improvement over the long haul.

The world's best corporations are naturally managed by people who are deeply committed to the profit motive. But profit is not seen as enough reason for a company to exist. Profit is viewed as compensation for having executed a mission that is even more basic. The company is in business to create and serve a customer and to increase customer satisfaction. By analogy, the company exists to make the best quality product commensurate with the price that the customer is willing to pay. Quality is the only valid reason for a company to exist. Even if the company makes a short-term profit but product quality is inferior, then management defines this as failure to execute the corporate mission. The objective is to deliver 100 percent good quality, 100 percent of the time.

Quality is not job 1, but the only job. When a company adopts the philosophy that quality is job 1, it is showing tolerance to the idea that some compromises can be made on product quality, as long as it gets top priority. If quality gets 60 percent attention while cost gets 40 percent, quality is still job one. How much emphasis is placed on quality will vary depending on how many other jobs there are. Quality is the only job is the ideal that will push the drive to achieve perfection. Companies that define quality as the only job and take the pains to communicate that idea, inculcate it into daily work practices, and constantly coach and coax all employees into accepting it, will have no difficulty driving product quality higher and higher. Employees must come to work every day to make quality, only quality, and nothing but quality. That is the business philosophy of the best companies that the world has to offer. Everything else is mediocrity by a different name.

Corporate Attitudes

Quality is a human discipline. Technology systems and programs help to amplify human effort, but superior quality is, above all, produced by, with, and through people. The evidence for this is incontrovertible. Even a superficial examination of any company that has a reputation for quality will reveal that there is unshakable respect and concern for people in everything it does. When one probes very deeply one finds that competitive superiority exists in tandem with superior human resources. The ability to recruit, retain, and develop highly motivated and creative people is what challenges the best companies. Simply stated, they have learned how to manage human resources better than competitive laggards. Human resource development is undertaken specifically to inculcate the right corporate attitudes.

The corporate mind set must be shaped to accept constant improvement. People who do not believe that things can and should always improve are hardly predisposed to making the effort to improve. Perpetual, long-term improvement must be wholeheartedly sought. The personnel socialization process must be deployed to create a habit of improvement. People must be so accustomed to improving quality, that it becomes an ingrained habit. When this is part of the corporate attitude, quality improvement becomes automatic, because employees are always dissatisfied with the quality status quo.

As a corollary to habit of improvement, the whole company must also be totally engrossed by the idea that perfection, although it is not achievable, is an entirely legitimate goal. People who are driven to excel, seek perfection and are thrilled as they get closer and closer to it. Management is at its finest when it has created the environment where people will aim to be the best that they can be and when they think they have gotten there to motivate them to aim higher, to try to be better than their best. The operative maxim is that there is always room for improvement. The giants of international competition repeat the incredible feat of always improving what is already the best product in the world. When the desire to better one's best becomes an obsession, then the company is on the road to quality excellence.

Quality can be mastered. A few exceptional companies set out to master quality, and in the process learned that zero defects can become reality. Most North American companies are measuring quality in parts-per-hundred. The world's best are measuring quality in parts-per-hundred-thousand or in parts-per-million, in some cases. There are companies that are on the verge of achieving defect rates of one-part-per-billion. Now, this is not actually zero defects, but most people will agree that it is tantalizingly close to it. When a company is achieving virtually zero defects, then one can say that quality has been mastered and the monster has been tamed. For some companies, quality is predictably bad. The goal in pursuing superior quality is to make the product predictably perfect, surpassing customer expectations nearly every time.

Once a corporation has driven home the idea that zero defects is the goal, then the corresponding attitude that perfect quality requires total prevention becomes easy to cultivate. Defect prevention is the only valid strategy for achieving zero defects. The corporate quality culture and value system must be designed to propagate and reinforce the idea that defect correction is both wasteful and ineffective. It is wasteful because it can be avoided and does not constitute a value-adding activity. It is ineffective because a company that is correcting defects will quickly find that the defect correction activities are themselves plagued with the same errors that create poor quality in the first place. A company that is relying on correction is definitely passing defects on to customers. The prevailing company attitude will always be internalized by those who are repairing internal failures. The more defects that are produced internally, the greater the number of defects that are being passed on to customers, regardless of the investment made in repairs and defect identification. This is the defect paradox and it explains why defect prevention is such a powerful strategy.

All work must be planned, controlled, and executed to do it right the first time. As one person said, "If you have time to correct it you have time to do it right the first time." And you would have saved all the hassles involved in looking for, analyzing, and correcting the error. It is possible for employees to have the discipline to execute their work mistake free, provided that they are trained, sensitized, and constantly encouraged to do so. Some managers, however, hide behind the adage that to err is human. While this is wholly true, one also notices that the more people accept that mistakes are inevitable, the more mistakes they make. Conversely, when people refuse to bow to the idea that mistakes are normal, there is always a dramatic reduction in the number of mistakes. The accident rate for passenger automobiles is much higher than that for passenger airlines and the error rate for check processing by banks is barely measurable. The number of defects in the typical car is very much higher than that in a typical jet airplane when both are delivered to the customer. When errors or defects are understood to be disastrous, the defect rate goes down significantly. The managerial challenge is to mold corporate attitudes in such a way that employees come to see every defect as a disaster.

Attitudes can be inculcated, shaped, and reshaped. Otherwise, the achievement of quality superiority would be little more than a random process, which it definitely is not. On the contrary, companies that achieve world-class quality excellence deliberately set out to do so while those that adopt a laissez faire approach never progress beyond mediocrity, if they progress at all. World-class companies are unique in their abilities to develop and maintain positive quality attitudes. Some companies such as Harley-Davidson and Chrysler avoided financial catastrophe by achieving revolutionary changes in corporate attitude toward quality. However, creating the right attitudes takes time and effort. Attitudes are deeply embedded in the human psyche. They are subconscious mental processes that make behavior almost automatic.

The Four Forces Shaping Corporate Attitudes toward Quality   FIGURE 7–5

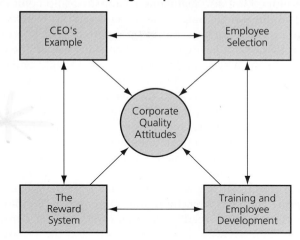

Corporate attitudes toward quality are shaped by four fundamental forces, as depicted in Figure 7–5. Very significant, and often overlooked by managers, is teaching by example. CEOs are too prone to pay lip service to quality and do not take the time to provide concrete examples of concern for quality to their subordinates. A bad example, or a wrong cue can wipe out hours of speeches and volumes of memos, policy statements, and training manuals, in an instant. The CEO provides quality leadership and shapes the quality mindset by practicing quality in the normal course of exercising his or her duties. Employees are looking to the CEO for coherence, consistency, and singlemindedness of quality purpose. The reward system must also reflect and be buttressed by the quality mission. Employees should advance because they do quality work and have completely adopted the quality mission as their own. Each employee selected for advancement must reflect the corporate attitude toward quality and must embody the company's quality mission. Bonuses, pay incentives, corporate perquisites, and other rewards must be consistently tied to superior quality performance. The reward system must be designed and applied to shape the right and discourage the wrong attitudes toward quality. One small company rejected the most educated, experienced, and articulate employee for the newly created position of Director of Quality Assurance, because he was not the most exemplary in terms of quality attitudes and ongoing achievement in his work.

Training and personnel development activities are a crucial vehicle for inculcating and shaping the right attitudes toward quality. Corporations that are known for their superior quality also train intensively at all organizational levels. Their training programs are also quite varied and have become permanent aspects of the managerial process. Training has been integrated into the job itself. Superior quality requires corporatewide craftsmanship, which must not only be developed but also maintained. Craftsmanship comes from formal off-the-job and on-the-job training so as to cultivate know-how. Employees will, by the dint of their common sense and experience, develop work-related skills. However, there is no guarantee that such skills will be the ones that are crucial to the company. A systematic training program will hone employees in skills that are useful for the future, and can also be used to create the attitudes that enable employees to use these to the maximum and to want to improve on them. There is evidence that the typical German and Japanese company is giving 20 hours of training to each employee every year. The corresponding figure for the average North American company is 4 hours.

Training creates a favorable climate for motivation because employees see it as valuable to them personally. It also demonstrates corporate commitment to the individual and his or her well-being, since training dollars are invested for the long term. The company, by training intensively, conditions employees to accept change more readily. An employee who is constantly being trained becomes acutely aware that improvement and the progressive refinement of know-how are critical to survival in the marketplace.

Personnel selection, because it provides the raw material with which the training activities must work, also plays a key role. The goal is not to select employees that already have the appropriate attitudes per se. Because so few companies are producing superior quality, there are correspondingly few employees in the labor force whose attitudes have already been shaped adequately. Personnel selection will have executed its mandate if selection policies, criteria, and activities identify and recruit people who have the potential to be changed by the training program.

THE BASIC PREREQUISITES

Quality starts and ends with the customer. Businesses that have attained quality superiority have learned to take care of their customers. A company cannot make much quality progress unless it has made the customer the driving force. Companies that are achieving long-term, continuous improvement in quality possess two enduring characteristics: (1) customer orientation and (2) customer consciousness.

Customer Orientation

The philosophy that a business exists to create and satisfy a customer is a radical departure from the short-term preoccupation that dominates management thinking in so many North American corporations. The new philosophy has served to put customer orientation at the heart of business decision making. Managers are beginning to realize that customer orientation is much more than the periodic drive to push sales. Most marketing people also harbor the erroneous view that a company is customer oriented when marketing "calls the shots." Behind this viewpoint is the belief that no other function can or should defend the customer's interest and that only the marketing function can be customer oriented. In reality, most marketing functions are not customer oriented. Short-term pressures to increase sales, often at the risk of reducing quality; unwillingness to refuse an order even if it is clear that the delivery schedule cannot be realistically adhered to; the widespread practice of classifying customers as A, B, C and giving the As more attention than the Bs and Cs, all compromise total customer orientation. When the marketing function wants to call all the shots, then it has not fully grasped what its mission is and what it takes to keep customers satisfied. A marketing function that is customer oriented very quickly comes to understand that the entire company must be in the business of creating and keeping the customer. The marketing function is not even the major contributor to customer satisfaction, even if it has an important role to play. When top management accepts the position that the company must be driven by the marketing function, the whole company ceases to be customer oriented and quality deteriorates. Excellence in quality invariably results from total corporatewide customer orientation.

Customer orientation is cultivated by the policies and practices that are put into effect by top management. Customer satisfaction through total quality must be placed at the heart of the business mission as defined, communicated, and promoted. When critical functional objectives are derived from this mission, these too must be carefully specified so that customer satisfaction via quality is the core idea. The business mission and its functional ramifications must be thoroughly known and understood by all employees. Every organizational unit and employee must understand that they are exclusively in the business to satisfy customers. The business mission must be promoted and propagated until there is absolutely no doubt that the customer is king, even if not tyrant. This sets the stage for making the business customer oriented in its very essence.

Customers' requirements must find concrete expression in all productive activities. These requirements must be clearly expressed often so that employees would come to understand them completely. Moreover, workers should be trained and encouraged to ask for clarifications when any requirement is ambiguous. Too many workers are called upon to perform tasks about which they do not understand why and how they relate to the final customer. The factory worker is not assembling a product. Rather, the worker ought to recognize that he or she is serving the customer in a very important way, right there on the assembly line. This gives much more meaning to production tasks and increases the self-esteem and motivation of production workers.

Employees who are kept informed about market developments come to see the need to respond to changes in the marketplace. They also develop sensitivity to customer requirements. Management tends to keep lower level employees, particularly those in the factory, in the dark about what is going on in the market. Market research information tends to be coveted by top management and marketing people. And these very same managers lament the fact that factory people do not identify with marketing concerns. How can they when the information upon which good understanding of marketing concerns can be based is seen as belonging to a privileged few? Factory workers can and will accurately understand customer demands when the information that can sharpen their understanding is made available on a regular basis.

Similarly, information on customer complaints, inquiries, and products returned due to defects should be widely publicized within the company. For employees to accurately understand how serious it is to produce bad quality, they must see how it impacts on the customer and how the latter reacts to poor quality. One company decided to put defective products or an adequate sample on display for all employees to see. A chart showing the number of customer complaints over time can be displayed prominently, while letters of complaints from customers can be posted all over the plant. Some companies have created cross-functional and multilevel teams to discuss and analyze customer complaints and to propose actions to eliminate the problems that cause these. One company has pushed these ideas quite far by requiring that all supervisors, and eventually workers, if possible spend some time—about 10 weeks—working in the customer service department. Surely, there is no better way to come to understand how serious bad quality is, short of being the customer, than to be the one who has to deal directly with customers when there is a problem. When supervisors and production workers start to feel the heat from customer complaints, they will learn to take quality seriously.

All these policies and practices aim at building customer awareness and create an organization that empathizes with the customer. When all employees become acutely aware that everything they do must be done to promote or create customer satisfaction, then the company has achieved true marketing orientation and is not just paying lip service to it. Every person in the organization must come to understand that the customer is the ultimate arbiter of their performance. Only then, is the company being managed to achieve customer satisfaction. This is one prerequisite to creating a company that has the potential to achieve quality excellence through continuous improvement. Customer orientation must cut deep and broad into the organization if the company is going to have the stamina to rise up to the challenges and surmount the barriers that thwart efforts to improve quality even when it appears, prima facie, impossible to improve.

Customer Consciousness

Continuous, sustainable improvement which culminates in quality superiority is a natural consequence of deep, companywide customer consciousness. A company is deeply customer conscious when all organizational units, and indeed all employees, are constantly and acutely aware of the customers and their needs, likes, dislikes, concerns, and requirements. The whole business must be customer focused, and customer requirements must be permanently visible to the entire organization. Although these requirements are expressed differently depending on the organizational function or unit, the basic fact remains that companies that are profoundly customer conscious find ways to keep the requirements of their customers perpetually visible to all employees. The customer must be put at the heart of the business, while the company constantly monitors the customer's heartbeat. When the customer sneezes, the company catches a cold, so to speak. Small changes in customer behavior or requirements which are wholly imperceptible to the average company are quickly detected and responded to by companies that have deep customer consciousness. A company that pays obsessive attention to every detail of the customer's requirements and tries hard to respond to them is demonstrating profound customer consciousness.

The customer must be the heart and soul of the business. Every organizational unit must come to think, perceive, and behave like the customer. All employees, whether they be management, technical, marketing, or plant personnel, have to adopt the role of customer advocate, defending and promoting the interest and well-being of the company's customers. Some may see this as promoting divided loyalty, pitting the employee against the company. The opposite is in fact true. In progressive, customer-conscious companies, the customer is the business and there is no antagonism between the interest of the customer and the well-being of the supplier company. Any adversarial relationship between a company and its customers is unhealthy and undesirable. It indicates that either the company or its customer, or both, have not come to the essential understanding that the rules of survival overwhelmingly favor both suppliers and customers that cooperate with and support each other.

The deep customer consciousness that powers continuous, sustainable improvement in quality is not a chance occurrence. On the contrary, customer consciousness is deliberately created, nurtured, and reinforced by companies that set out to excel in the marketplace. Without exception, companies that succeed in building an enviable, enduring competitive position manage the organization to give primacy to the customer. Whereas most companies define their businesses around the thing—product or service—they produce, customer-conscious companies define the business around the customer. The company is defined as being in the business of creating and keeping satisfied customers, rather than producing a good or service. The good or service is viewed as the means by which the company pursues the ultimate end—a completely satisfied customer.

Quality must be redefined and its execution must be done so that the customer becomes central to all quality improvement efforts. The quality concept must be broadened to liberate it from the narrow, product focus. Most companies that are embracing TQC still emphasize total product quality, as if the product were the only thing that the company delivers to the customer. Customers receive more than a mere product or service from their suppliers. They also receive information, advice, training, after-sales services, and psychological support that are vital parts of the bundle of attributes that is often referred to as the product. In order to instill customer consciousness in the organizational mind set, companies need to emphasize the total quality concept referred to as quality behind quality, by putting quality responsibility, authority, and accountability into every facet of organizational life. In that sense, quality is not conformance to specifications, since that definition leaves open the issue of how and by whom specifications are formulated. Corporations that are making the customer central to quality mastery and improvement define quality as the perfect design and execution of all activities that create value for customers. Quality is total conformance to customer requirements. Therefore, the building and nurturing of a profoundly customer-conscious organization by top management requires it to design organizational structures, mechanisms, and processes for putting the voice of the customer in all managerial, technical, and operating activities carried on by the company.

The marketing vision must also be broadened so as to unshackle it from the narrow functional focus that has been traditionally adopted and promulgated by North American managers. Customer satisfaction is the mission of the entire enterprise, and so, the marketing mission must be broadly defined and distributed on a corporatewide basis. On that basis, any activity or job that does not contribute in a concrete, identifiable way, to customer satisfaction is probably useless and is most likely a waste. Putting responsibility for customer satisfaction into every job is the necessary first step to build corporatewide customer consciousness. Making every employee accountable for customer satisfaction is the key to cementing and deepening corporatewide customer consciousness, and for putting the customer at the heart of the business. As a bonus, these actions put the employee's heart into the job and contribute to job satisfaction and worker motivation, because the employee can link what he or she does on a day-to-day basis to the quintessential competitive mission of creating and keeping satisfied customers. Customer and job satisfaction are thus symbiotically related facets of the competitive challenge to achieve product superiority through continuous improvement in quality.

Consequently, no matter where defects are discovered or complaints originate, they must be dealt with, in some way, by the activity or employee that caused them. The quality feedback system must channel complaints and data on defects to those responsible for the problem that gave rise to them, and action to correct the problem must involve the employee or employees responsible. All operating, technical, and managerial employees must be made to deal with and respond directly to customer complaints and defects. In the past, companies have made the error of having repairs and customer service departments that deal with defects and complaints from customers. While these have their place, they shield the employee from direct responsibility for customer satisfaction, if they are the only means for dealing with customer complaints. Companies that want to build customer consciousness as a powerful motor of quality improvement, cannot allow feedback on defects and complaints to stop at the repairs, after-sales-service and customer service departments. Doing so exonerates the worker from responsibility for customer satisfaction and removes the ultimate form of quality accountability. Where there is no responsibility and accountability, there can be only irresponsibility and indifference, which result in inferior-quality products being sent to the market.

BUILDING THE CUSTOMER-RESPONSIVE ORGANIZATION

The Voice of the Customer

Responsiveness to customer needs and requirements are basic to any quality improvement effort. Companies are responsive to their customers' needs and requirements only to the extent that they are customer oriented and are characterized by deep customer consciousness. In companies where these two prerequisites are met, the customer is solicited for suggestions, ideas, and concerns. Customers are probed and questioned with a view to discovering their true needs. The customer is genuinely listened to because the information that he or she provides is used to improve the product, its design, and the way it is manufactured. Customers know they are listened to when they see visible, measurable improvements in quality or cost that are the result of feedback that they provide to the supplier company. Not all quality or cost improvements are the result of direct customer feedback, since the supplier can sometimes anticipate customer requirements or concerns. However, it is difficult to say that a company listens to its customers if at least some improvements in product quality or cost cannot be traced directly to customer reactions. The ability to listen and respond to the voice of the customer indicates willingness to improve on and master quality. It also shows that there is corporate humility which leads the company to admit that there is always room for improvement. Companies stop listening and responding to their customers when they have come to the arrogant conclusion that no one can show them how to make their products better.

The customer's voice must be made to permeate all activities that are involved in designing, testing, and manufacturing the product. This is easy to do when the enterprise is small. In the old artisan or craftsman system, which was the epitome of small scale enterprise, the craftsman was president, marketing person, design engineer, purchaser, and production worker. All the functions and hierarchical levels of a business enterprise coalesced into one function and were embodied in a single individual, the craftsman. There was total and direct contact between the artisan and the customer so customer feedback was complete and instantaneous. All information given by the customer and assimilated by the artisan was immediately and totally incorporated into all activities involved in designing and making the product. The capacity of the customer to influence product quality was limited by an ability to communicate his or her needs, concerns, and requirements to the artisan and to the latter's ability to understand and assimilate the feedback that the customer was transmitting. No coordinating mechanism or formal feedback tool was needed to listen to and respond to the customer's concerns. There was total integration between all business activities and between the enterprise and its customers, because the artisan—owner, worker, buyer, designer, seller—was the integrating agent. This was the ideal state as far as listening and responding to the voice of the customer is concerned, and it is shown in Figure 7–6.

The modern corporation has a structure that is much more complex than the artisan business. Due to its large size, geographic dispersion, and sometimes wide competitive scope, present day corporations are often structured along functional lines. Functionalization is necessary so as to keep organizational units manageable and the span of control reasonable. Moreover, structuring the company using classical business functions allows organizational units to specialize in executing one activity set such as production, sales, finance, or R&D. Functional cohesiveness increases.

On the other hand, functionalization leads to parochialism and a general loss of the corporatewide perspective. Employees begin to defend narrow functional interests, often to the detriment of the business as a whole. What may be good for any one function may be devastating for the corporation as a whole. In the absence of a strong corporate philosophy that discourages or inhibits parochialism, functional heads and their subordinates spend much time and energy in corporate jockeying. Eventually, one function comes to

FIGURE 7–6   **The Voice of the Customer in a Small or Artisan Enterprise**

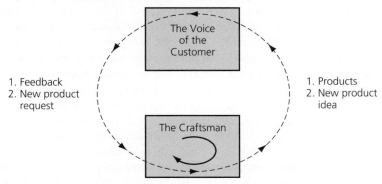

The Voice of the Customer in a Complex Organization FIGURE 7–7

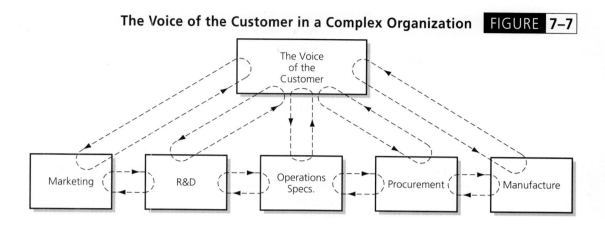

dominate the corporate power structure and imposes its view of the business on the company. This sets the stage for armtwisting, persistent interfunctional conflict, and mistrust. The customers' needs become entangled in the web of corporate politics and the business loses its customer focus. The single biggest problem caused by functionalization, as far as listening to the customer is concerned, is that coordination between the customer and the producing company and between the business functions is made infinitely more complex. It is no longer natural or easy for the company to accurately understand customer requirements and to transmit them systematically across all the business functions. Management must deliberately intervene to build the organizational processes, communication channels, and coordinating mechanisms that will cause the company to listen and respond to customer requirements. These ideas are shown in Figure 7-7. Organizational processes, communication channels, and coordinating mechanisms that establish vertical linkages between the business functions and the customer, and that forge horizontal linkages between the functions themselves, have to be put in place. Evidently, designing these processes, channels and mechanisms to enable the company to listen and respond to the voice of the customer is a major challenge confronting top management of present day, complex, industrial corporations.

The Flow Influence

Building a customer responsive organization involves much more than designing structures to speed the flow of information between the company and its customers and across the various business functions. While a smooth flow of high-quality information does help the organization to better understand customer requirements, it is not the most fundamental aspect of customer responsiveness. The information flow is only one indication that a business is trying to listen to its customers. More decisive is what happens to the information that the company receives. Information may be received and transmitted to all functional groups, but subsequent R&D, procurement and production activities may be failing to use it to improve quality and broad competitive performance. Surveys and other means of getting feedback from customers may create the image that the company is a responsive one. However, the perception thus developed will be short lived, unless customers see that the concerns they express result in concrete improvements in product quality, cost, and other performance criteria.

Customer responsiveness means that customers are exercising real influence over quality and other business activities. Figure 7-6 and 7-7 underscore the view that customer responsiveness shows up as a flow of influence vertically between a company and its customers and horizontally across all the business functions. Customers know that they have exerted influence on quality when they can see concrete design ideas, changes, or product features that make the product better suited to their requirements. Influence can also flow in the other direction, from supplier to customer. For example, a customer may agree to change how a product is specified or used so as to maximize its actual quality impact. Or the supplier may educate a customer on the value of new products or product ideas. Similarly, as each function is responding to customer requirements, it is shaping the way functions that are upstream and downstream respond to these. At the same time, each function's understanding of customer requirements and actions taken to respond to them, are shaped by the viewpoint and constraints of the other functions. The result is an interlocking chain of influence that forges a corporatewide consensus on the precise needs of the customer and the best way to satisfy them. Vertical influence exerted by the customer and the supplier on each other assures that customer requirements are accurately understood by the latter. Horizontal influence exerted by each function on all the others ensures that these requirements will be accurately and uniformly transferred across the functional interfaces. The product or service which emerges out of the company will more likely match the customer's expectations. Figures 7-6 and 7-7 illustrate the principle that both the capability to produce to exacting quality standards and the capacity to continuously improve quality over the long haul, depend on the company's ability to transmit and respond to the voice of the customer throughout its organization. The flow of information is important, but better quality will not result, if the information is not digested and acted upon by the whole company and used to improve the product cost or quality.

The Determinants of Customer Influence

How much the company listens and responds to the voice of the customer, or alternatively, how much the customer influences whatever activity the company performs as part of its market mission—product research, development, design, manufacture, sales and distribution, after-sales service— depends on how thoroughly the foundation quality concepts have been operationalized and honed into place. Both vertical and horizontal influence flow naturally from actions to implement the foundation quality ideas outlined in Figure 7-4. Nevertheless, customer orientation and deep customer consciousness are preponderant. If the company is thoroughly customer oriented and deeply customer conscious, then it will give primacy to understanding and satisfying customer requirements. The customer will not only be allowed to influence the quality improvement effort, but the company will also aggressively solicit the customer's viewpoint and will integrate it into all productive activities. Customers will be used as a major source of innovative ideas. In addition, when customer orientation and consciousness permeate all functions of the business, then there is very likely to be interfunctional empathy, mutual trust, give and take, and a very high chance that there will be broad consensus on how the product, if not the whole organization, can be made better. The corporate will prevails over disparate and narrow functional interests. Implementation of the foundation quality concepts means that the corporate will totally reflects and is molded by the will of the customer.

Additional measures can be taken to strengthen interfunctional influence and to make it an integral aspect of the organization. Management policies and organizational structures that intensify interfunctional interaction and coordination also promote interfunctional influence. Although heavy interaction increases the potential for conflict, customer orientation and deep customer consciousness make for positive conflict resolution. Intensive interfunctional interaction eventually reduces functional barriers to communication. This leads to a smooth information flow between the functions, the development of corporatewide consensus on quality issues and stronger interfunctional cooperation and coordination. By these processes, the company learns to better manage activities that cut across many functions and that give rise to interface problems. Severe communication and coordination problems between functions are a major hindrance to innovation and quality improvement. Poor coordination and communication increase the time it takes for a company to convert an idea into a new product, process or quality improvement program.

Interfunctional influence can be built into the organization using the matrix-type structure and cross-functional quality improvement teams.[6] Both these approaches promote interfunctional influence by way of the organizational structure. The matrix organization is shown in Figure 7-8. Innovation

---

[6]For more discussion of the culture and values requirements of the matrix structure, see, Christopher A. Bartlett, and Sumantra Ghoshal, "Matrix Management: Not a Structure, a Frame of Mind," *Harvard Business Review,* July–August 1990.

FIGURE 7-8   **The Matrix Structure**

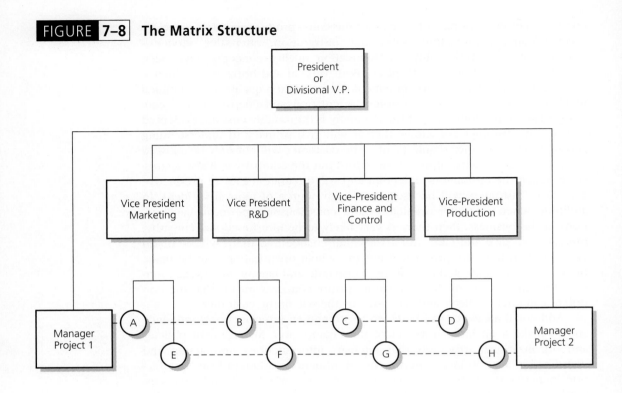

projects are executed in the functions using functional specialists. However, interfunctional coordination is assured by managers who are responsible for the whole project and can bring the corporate perspective to bear on decisions that plan, control, and execute it. Project managers serve as the focal point for all communication and information relative to the project, and they can assure that all relevant information is promptly and widely disseminated across all functions. The result is less interfunctional conflict and rivalry.

Matrix organizations possess some critical weaknesses that have prevented their wide adoption by companies. First, they are designed to deal with situations where large scale, innovation projects are numerous. The matrix structure gave companies the organizational flexibility to handle many major innovation projects simultaneously. Project organizations could be quickly assembled as new projects came on stream. Once projects were completed, the organization was easily dismantled and specialists refocused their energies on purely functional activities. However, most of the activities that are involved in quality improvement, are very small scale and are undertaken continuously and permanently by the company. Their scale does not justify either a designated project manager or any significant, temporary change to the organization. Second, although the matrix structure reduces interfunctional conflict, the dual authority structure on which it is based generates another type of conflict. Companies using the matrix structure have discovered that it generates a high potential for conflict between project management and the functional heads. Project managers are accountable for the key performance parameters of quality, cost, and time, but these are substantially controlled by the priority that the functional heads assign to each project. The matrix structure makes project managers responsible for project performance but does not give them the requisite authority for bringing projects to fruition. In addition, the functional specialists are placed in a position where they report to two superiors, project management, and the functional heads. A healthy balance is rarely found in practice, which means that one or the other of the superiors becomes the de facto boss. Consequently, matrix organization structures are likely to give poor results if the customer responsiveness that comes from implementing the foundation quality concepts does not already exist in the organization. The formal matrix structure, in and of itself, can do nothing to enhance the flow of interfunctional influence and build consensus and foster cooperative spirit. The structure is only an outline of top management's intentions. The formal structure must be vivified by systems and interpersonal relationships that facilitate communication, the flow of information and influence. Moreover, consensus will emerge from the matrix structure only if the supporting culture, shared values, organizational mores and vision incorporate consensus as a fundamental requisite to the management process. In the absence of these interpersonal relationships that are forged by corporate and quality culture and values, a formal matrix structure invariably becomes dysfunctional by aggravating interfunctional conflict and mistrust. Many companies have failed to get any benefit out of matrix management concepts because they did not pay attention to the supporting culture and attitudinal requirements of the formal matrix structure. Others such as Philips and Unilever have orchestrated matrix management into an art form and have used it to cause corporate vision to proliferate through the global organization and to deploy policy worldwide.

The second way to build interfunctional influence into the organization is through quality improvement teams that are linked vertically and horizontally throughout the organizational structure and which cut across functional lines. Figure 7–9 shows such a structure. Quality teams are integrated using an individual who acts as a linking pin with teams that are higher up in the hierarchy. Cross-functional teams bring together employees that work in different functions or departments, thus broadening the problem-solving perspective of the teams and the scope of the problems that they can handle. The linking pin facilitates free, vertical flow of information. The cross-functional teams which also incorporate the linking pins disseminate information laterally. Consensus develops both vertically and horizontally and according to the corporate will, since all teams converge at the top of the hierarchy. Vertical influence exerted by the customer on each function gets converted into lateral interfunctional influence by the cross-functional teams. Vertically-linked, cross-functional teams are permanent organizational units that facilitate the

FIGURE 7–9 **Vertically and Horizontally-Linked Quality Improvement Teams**

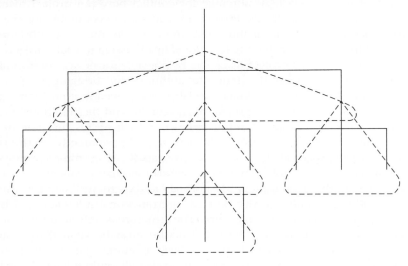

development of corporatewide consensus on customer requirements and other quality issues. They are ideal for tackling the numerous small-scale projects and problems that are a necessary part of any program for continuously improving quality over the long run.

Quality Function Deployment: The House of Quality

The task of designing and manufacturing products that satisfy customer requirements and tastes is a major challenge for companies that compete in today's competitively tough markets. The voice of the customer must infiltrate all activities that are involved in designing and manufacturing the product. The functions need to be tightly coordinated and there must be smooth and effective communication and influence between the various functional groups. A few companies have pioneered in the development and application of tools that aim to coordinate the functions that are developing products. These same tools keep the functions focused on customer requirements. One of these tools is quality function deployment (QFD) or the house of quality. It originated at Mitsubishi's Kobe shipyard site in 1972 and is today used by leading companies such as General Motors, Ford, Toyota and Digital Equipment. QFD is one aspect of the overall management process known as *policy deployment*, which refers to the extent of propagation of quality activities in a company. The first dimension of policy deployment deals with pushing the company's vision, mission, and customer-oriented value down from top management to the factory floor, thus making the entire company customer

Japanese/U.S. Engineering Change Comparison: The Impact of QFD FIGURE 7–10

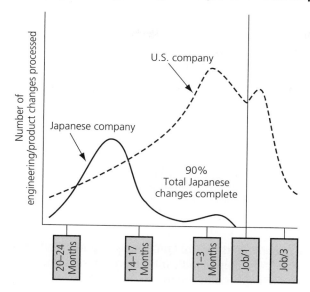

driven. The second dimension of policy deployment creates programs and activities for continuous quality improvement throughout the company and liberates the necessary resources to support them. Policy deployment is successful when quality improvement activities are an important part of the responsibilities and tasks of all employees and reach deeply and broadly into the fabric of the organization.

QFD operationalizes policy deployment in the creation of new products. It is a set of planning and communication procedures and processes that coordinates the organizational units that design and manufacture a product. Its purpose is to keep attention focused on customer requirements and preferences as the product evolves through ideation, design, and production. QFD operationalizes product attributes that customers desire and expresses them as information that can be understood by and is relevant to each discipline or function that is involved in creating the product. It provides a mechanism for interfunctional planning, communication, and coordination and for giving the central place to customer requirements. QFD isolates and highlights key product quality characteristics that are valued by the customer and keeps all development and manufacturing activities focused on them. It is also a tool for systematically defining customer needs and tastes and for translating these into specific, often measurable, product and process characteristics.

Figures 7–10 and 7–11 show the impact of QFD on product quality and cost. Toyota Motor Company experienced a dramatic decrease in overall start-up costs after they introduced QFD as shown in Figure 7–11. Start-up costs

Reduction in Overall Start-Up Costs

January 1977 (100%)

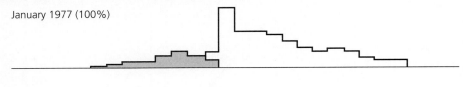

April 1984 (39%)

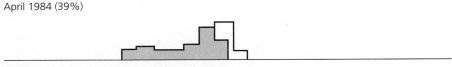

☐ Preproduction cost (operator training, etc.)
☐ Start-up cost (loss)

declined to 39 percent of their pre-QFD levels. Figure 7–10 shows that Japanese manufacturers are doing significantly fewer design changes after production begins than their U.S. counterparts without QFD.[7]

QFD is the overall concept that is used to describe the process by which a company converts customer requirements into appropriate technical, control, or operating requirements for each stage of product development and manufacture. Five key concepts define the QFD process:

1. *Customer attributes.* These are the desirable characteristics of the product expressed by customers in their own language. Customer attributes are identified by market surveys, user experience with the product, comparison with competitive products, government regulations, evaluations by consumer protection groups, and feedback from sales people.
2. *Counterpart characteristics.* They are the customer requirements translated into quality specifications in terms appropriate to design, testing, procurement, and production activities. The counterpart characteristics specify quality for the final product, from the customer's viewpoint.
3. *Product quality deployment.* This identifies and specifies all activities for converting the customer attributes into final product characteristics. The aim is to plan all work that must be done so as to make sure that counterpart characteristics accurately reflect and are based on customer expressed requirements or attributes.
4. *Deployment of the quality function.* This is the process undertaken to assure that customer attributes, that is, the quality specifically desired by

---

[7]L. P. Sullivan, "Quality Function Deployment," *Quality Progress,* June 1986, 39.

customers, are achieved throughout design, parts procurement, process planning, and production. Activities involved in deployment of the quality function involve much more than QFD, and rely on the entire total quality management effort.

5. *Quality tables.* The various matrices used to systematically steer the product development effort so that customer attributes become the final product characteristics.

The mechanical aspect of QFD is executed using four key documents:[8]

1. Overall Customer Requirement Planning Matrix which translates customer attributes into counterpart characteristics. It provides a way of going from generally expressed customer requirements to specific, measurable, and controllable final product characteristics.
2. Final Product Characteristics Deployment Matrix derives critical component characteristics from the final product characteristics specified in the planning matrix.
3. Process Plans and Quality Control Charts specify the critical product and process parameters and also checkpoints, or phases in product development and manufacture where these parameters are best verified and controlled.
4. Operating Instructions identify activities, operations, or tests to be performed by plant and other operating personnel to assure that all critical quality parameters are being built into the product.

QFD is only one among the many tools available to a company that wants to build products that satisfy customer needs and tastes. It is one way to force those responsible for product specification, design, and manufacture to respond to the voice of the customer. QFD is not a panacea for all the quality problems faced by a company, but should rather be looked at as one part of the corporatewide quality improvement program. QFD itself must rest on the foundation quality concepts, and in fact flows naturally from them. It presupposes that the organizational arrangements such as interfunctional teams, customer orientation and deep customer consciousness, which give rise to interfunctional influence, are already in place and working. QFD also presupposes that the company has the ability to forge corporatewide consensus on what constitutes quality and how best it can be realized. Therefore, QFD is one way to further refine and reinforce customer responsiveness. The evidence for this point of view is very strong. Nearly all the companies that have implemented QFD or are driving hard to implement it are in severely competitive global markets. QFD users are all in industries where it has become competitively mandatory to respond effectively

---

[8]See L. P. Sullivan, "Quality Function Deployment."

and unambiguously, with a high degree of certainty, to increasingly stringent quality requirements. These companies are all stretching themselves to the limit to improve what are already world-class quality products and have strong, distinctive quality cultures. QFD can only be used effectively by companies that have designed organizations that listen and respond to the voice of the customer. When the foundation quality concepts are in place, QFD becomes one more weapon that a company can use to attack quality problems.

ACCELERATING THE PRODUCT DEVELOPMENT PROCESS

Traditionally, products progress through the development process one phase at a time and in sequential mode. Although sequential product development and design requires little coordination between the different disciplines or groups that are developing a new product, it is very inefficient and time consuming. Absence of coordination promotes dysfunctional conflict and prevents groups that are downstream from benefiting from the ideas and knowledge generated upstream. It also gives rise to a number of backward loops in the development process as the product designs or concepts are sent back to a prior phase for further work because the upstream phases did not take into account the constraints or information available at downstream phases. Problems with the work done by groups located upstream are only discovered when downstream groups are well advanced in their work. The nature of sequential processing and the backward loops that it gives rise to are shown in Figure 7–12. Some companies try to deal with the problem by using a coordinator to facilitate the flow of information between the technical disciplines or functions that are involved in product development. This improves the process somewhat but does not result in any dramatic change.

FIGURE **7–12** **Sequential Product Development Process**

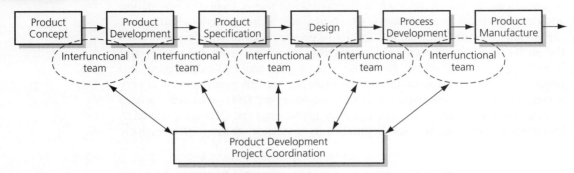

FIGURE 7–13

Improving Response Time in New Product Development—Mechanical Transmissions

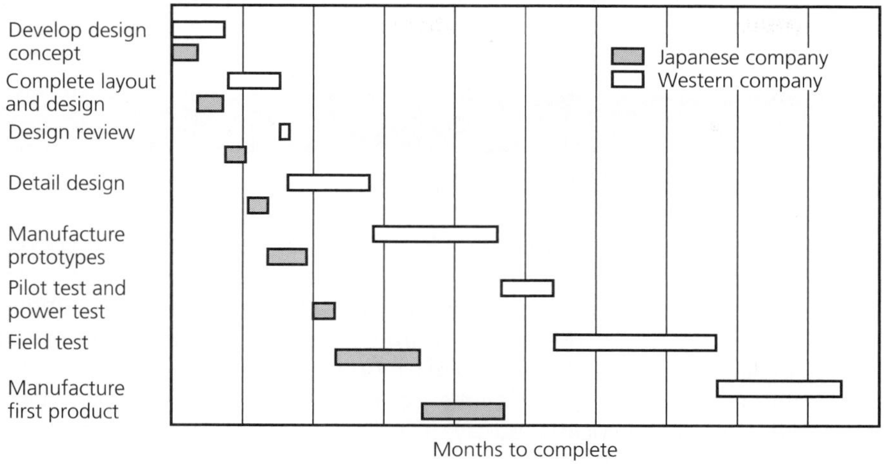
Develop design concept
Complete layout and design
Design review
Detail design
Manufacture prototypes
Pilot test and power test
Field test
Manufacture first product
Japanese company
Western company
Months to complete

Source: Stalk, George, Jr., *Competing against Time,* The Free Press: New York, 1990, 118. Reproduced with permission.

A more effective way to compress the time involved in product development is to use the concept of concurrent engineering by doing parallel execution of successive activities as much as possible. Downstream groups receive vital information to start their work as soon as enough valid data is available. Upstream groups receive feedback on possible downstream constraints and problems before they have completed their work. Coordination is still necessary, but it is facilitated by a freer and constant flow of information. Figure 7–13 compares the two approaches. Concurrent engineering can halve the time it takes to design products and take them to market. That means that the company can receive feedback from the market much quicker and can accelerate the process of improving the product.

Conclusion

The foundation quality concepts are the cornerstone of any corporatewide, long-term quality improvement program. They determine a corporation's capacity to absorb new technologies and tools that are designed to improve quality. They also determine how naturally increasingly higher quality levels will come to a company. The foundation ideas give the corporation the capacity to listen and respond to the voice of the customer and the ability to put in place mechanisms, processes, and organization structures that are the hallmarks of a customer responsive organization. Hence, the capability to push for zero defects or to implement any tools and techniques that drive defect rates down, come from the foundation quality concepts. These simple facts must not be overlooked in the long and hard search for quality superiority.

Case for Discussion

ONTARIO COPPER WIRES (OCP) (B)

Ms. Diane Fulton, plant manager at OCP, a Canadian manufacturer of copper wire and related products, had decided that she had to act quickly to improve quality in her plant. One month ago, an important customer had implemented a new vendor certification program and the customer's audit had given OCP a failing grade. OCP had six months to improve its quality and meet tightened customer specifications. As a signal of what appeared to be a new trend in North American industry, a second customer was contemplating implementing vendor certification. Ms. Fulton decided that now was the time to act.

Actions Initiated to Improve Quality at OCP

Within two days of deciding that she should respond to the new customer requirements for improved quality, Ms. Fulton called a meeting of all her managers and supervisors to explain the new quality realities to them and to solicit their input on how the situation could be dealt with. Bringing people together to discuss and exchange ideas was a rare occurrence at OCP, and the atmosphere at the meeting was initially tense. However, people soon settled down and began to discuss the issues frankly.

At the meeting it was decided to create a steering committee to develop and propose a complete action plan for implementing TQM at OCP. The steering committee was given the mandate to identify actions that could be taken immediately. Within two weeks of receiving its mandate, the steering committee had recommended that the following actions be implemented.

Defect measurement, costing, and reporting. Presently, we are only identifying a material as defective if it absolutely fails to meet specifications. Materials that are reworked and subsequently meet the specifications, are not considered as defects although they add to cost. No one knows how much bad quality is costing us and we have no method for reporting on it. Good cost figures will tell us if reducing defects is really worth the effort and investment.

Training. We clearly need to train our employees more. For a start, every employee should receive a minimum of 100 hours training on the new concepts, methods, and techniques of quality management. Formal quality training should be bolstered with continuous, on-the-job training so that our employees know their jobs and the quality requirements thoroughly. We must work with the union to design and implement a solid training program and the workers must know that training is not a way to eliminate jobs but to help them to develop marketable skills and to be competitive.

Inspection. We should intensify our inspection procedures so as to be able to meet our customers' requirements better. It is our view that we should add two more full-time inspectors to the five we currently use as a temporary measure. Eventually, all employees should be trained to take over inspection related to the quality of their work.

Group meetings. Employees should be encouraged to meet once per week to discuss and solve quality problems and to share information about their work. Weekly meetings would be costly in time but we believe that the increased quality and reduced waste that result from the ideas that are produced will more than compensate for the lost time.

Statistical Process Control. We should proceed to implement SPC as soon as possible. We estimate that the software and hardware can be procured at a cost of $28,000. Training costs will amount to about $33,000 because we will need to train all our engineers, technicians, and workers. SPC could dramatically improve our ability to meet our new customer requirements because it will help us detect early the processes that are starting to produce defects. We believe that SPC will eventually help us reduce defects from the current 20 percent to about 4 percent.

Ms. Fulton's Reaction to the Committee's Recommendations

Ms. Fulton immediately gave the committee the mandate to implement all the recommendations and approved the necessary budget. Within three months, most of the recommendations had already been or were well on the way to being implemented. Within four months, the company had all major processes being monitored with SPC and defect reporting had started. Six months after OCP launched its quality improvement project, and after three months of defect costing and reporting had been compiled, Ms. Fulton had asked the project manager to make a presentation on progress to date. Defects had gone down to 19.7 percent from 20 percent and costs had decreased from $7.5 million to $7.4 million. The project manager was about to show his excitement when Ms. Fulton interjected:

Rob, I do not think you understand how far we have to go. At the rate we are improving, it will take us fifty years to be able to meet the new customer requirements. I do not have to tell you that by that time we will be out of business and you will be out of a job.

Discussion Questions

1. Evaluate the actions taken by Ms. Diane Fulton to implement strategic manufacturing change at OCP.
2. What is the role of culture and values in the improvement process? Did the initiatives taken by OCP management reveal full recognition of that role?
3. Are the results of the initiative taken so far satisfactory?
4. Can/should the pace of improvement at OCP be quickened? Why or why not?
5. If the pace of improvement can and should be quickened, how would you proceed to do it?
6. Does OCP have a good foundation for radical and sustained quality improvement? If yes, what are your reasons? If no, how should Diane Fulton proceed to put it in place?

References

Bartlett, Christopher A., and Sumantra Ghoshal, "Matrix Management: Not a Structure, a Frame of Mind," *Harvard Business Review,* July–August 1990.

Deming, Edwards W., *Quality, Productivity and Competitive Position,* Cambridge, MA: Massachusetts Institute of Technology, Center for Advanced Engineering, 1982.

Hirsckhorn, Larry, and Thomas Gilmore, "The New Boundaries of the Boundaryless Company," *Harvard Business Review,* May–June 1992.

Peters, Thomas J., and Robert H. Waterman, Jr., *In Search of Excellence: Lessons from America's Best-Run Companies,* New York: Harper and Row, 1982.

Skinner, Wickham, *Manufacturing the Formidable Competitive Weapon,* New York: John Wiley and Sons, 1985.

Managing for Zero Defects

Competitive market forces are putting relentless pressure on companies to produce ever increasing quality at the lowest possible cost. This translates into a need to constantly reduce defects. Because competition cannot be expected to abate, companies that are responsive to competition are imbued with strong competitive spirit and are driven by deep customer consciousness to naturally adopt a quality mission that incorporates zero defects. Moreover, the level of defects being produced by a company is always symptomatic of the quality problems that remain unsolved and reflects its current state of mastery of quality. Continuous improvement which is mandated by competition and the need to create increasing value for customers—the only basis for long-term customer satisfaction and retention—naturally embraces zero defects. Top management's responsibility, first and foremost, is to equip the company with the capability to reduce defects systematically and progressively, and then to sustain the resolve to push them to zero. The philosophies, policies, technologies, tools, and practices for doing so have been developed, refined, tested, and applied by the world's most competitively robust corporations and are now available to any company that wants to pursue zero defects.

ORIGIN AND NATURE OF ZERO DEFECTS

The U.S. military was faced, in the 1950s, with the task of assuring high product reliability even as these products become increasingly complex. Reliability studies had shown that product reliability decreased rapidly as the number of components increased. With the development of increasingly sophisticated weapon systems, the number of components in any one system mushroomed. Consequently, assuring reliability became a huge problem. The relationship between product complexity and reliability is easy to demonstrate. Suppose a simple product has two components each with a probability of failure equal to 90 percent. If the product fails when any one component does not function, then product reliability is 81 percent (90% × 90%). Now, suppose that same product is redesigned with four components, each having the same reliability as before. Then, overall product reliability falls to 65.61 percent (90% × 90% × 90% × 90%).

Product reliability can be increased by duplicating critical components and connecting them in parallel. When any one component fails the others will continue to function normally, thus preventing a component failure from becoming a product or system failure. This strategy is called redundancy and is widely used in products or systems where extremely high reliability is crucial. The human body, a most wonderful system, incorporates the redundancy principle extensively. It is not surprising that it is also one of the most reliable systems around.

However, redundancy has a down side to it, because if the individual components have lousy reliability the number that is required in order to achieve a target reliability increases, and the product becomes bulky. Bulkiness can also cause components to interfere with one another, thus decreasing the benefits of redundancy. For example, if the target reliability is 99 percent and individual component reliability is 90 percent, then two components are needed. But if individual component reliability drops to 80 percent, then three are required. Component reliability has decreased by 11 percent but the number required to maintain target system reliability has increased by 50 percent. Although redundancy works, it is a strategy of last resort, because it complicates product design and does not attack the reliability problem head on.

One needs redundancy because the components are unreliable, in the first place. The greater individual component unreliability, the more redundancy that is required to achieve reliable products. In the illustration used above, the target system reliability can be achieved with one component that has a 99 percent reliability. Material cost would be reduced and the design simplified, with a commensurate decrease in assembly and test cost and no loss of reliability. Alternatively, if two components were used as before, reliability would increase to 99 percent for the product. Evidently, increasing individual component reliability is the much better strategy.[1]

The dynamics of this problem lead to the conclusion that increasing component reliability dramatically improves both product reliability and cost. Since component reliability is strongly influenced by defects, it was not long before design engineers identified defects as the major cause of product unreliability. Zero defects (ZD) was born out of this environment, where there was a managerial imperative to make increasingly sophisticated products absolutely reliable and at the same time cost effective. When target product reliability approaches 100 percent, say 99.99 percent, then the requirement is for 100 percent component reliability, which gets translated as zero defects.

Zero defects (ZD) therefore is not an objective, since objectives, in the managerial sense, are practically attainable. Rigorously, one cannot attain zero

---

[1]The calculations to show this are simple: Three components, each having an 80 percent reliability, give an overall reliability computed as follows:

$$R = 0.8 + (0.2 \times 0.8) + (0.2 \times 0.2 \times 0.8)$$
$$= 0.992$$

defects, because one part per ten million defective is still not zero defects. Some managers have created a stumbling block to the quality improvement effort by insisting that since zero defects cannot be achieved, any program that seeks to achieve it is a pipe dream. However, the mathematics and the management do not agree on this point. One part per ten million is not mathematically zero, but it is practically, hence managerially zero. But the biggest managerial rationale for zero defects is that it is a powerful motivator that keeps the organization stretching to attain perfection. Zero defects also creates a corporate vision that the ultimate goal is to deliver a perfect product that totally meets or surpasses customer expectations. By insisting that the goal is zero defects, top management drives home the message that quality is the only priority and must be mastered. Zero defects thus serves to shape the right corporate attitudes toward quality. Every defect is waste and there must be sustained improvement in quality as long as the company is in business. When defect rates are one per thousand, zero defects will motivate the company to aim for one per ten thousand. Upon achieving a one-per-ten-thousand defect rate, then the target will change to one per one hundred thousand. As long as there is one defect anywhere in the company then there is a motivation to try to remove it.

Conventional thinking on ZD has obviously missed the essential point that it is first and foremost a mechanism to focus the improvement effort. Figure 8–1 shows the concepts that are key to understanding ZD as a management strategy and processes for operationalizing quality improvement, manufacturing strategy, continuous improvement, and waste elimination. The main impetus for ZD comes from the foundation quality concepts, which define quality to be one of the key strategic success factors of the business, and customer orientation and deep customer consciousness as the necessary prerequisites to the pursuit of quality superiority. Companies that do not see quality as strategically crucial and do not make the customer the heart and soul of the business, will have difficulty embracing ZD and sustaining the drive to eliminate defects. A strong set of corporate values that make quality a competitive imperative and essential to long-term customer satisfaction also embolden and motivate managers to rigorously pursue zero defects.

Two other key concepts that strengthen the managerial and operating rationale for total defect elimination have emerged over the last two decades. They are also shown in Figure 8–1. Takumi, or the perpetual search for improvement, keeps the organization trying to attain perfection. Every defect is imperfection and is an indication that quality has not been totally mastered. Every defect has a root cause that can be identified, eliminated, and prevented from recurring if the organization has been designed and structured and is managed to learn from experience. Without the philosophical power that Takumi unleashes, zero defects will be looked at as pie-in-the-sky stuff, a pipe dream. Waste elimination is the other concept that drives ZD. Management is

FIGURE 8–1 Zero Defects: A Managerial Perspective

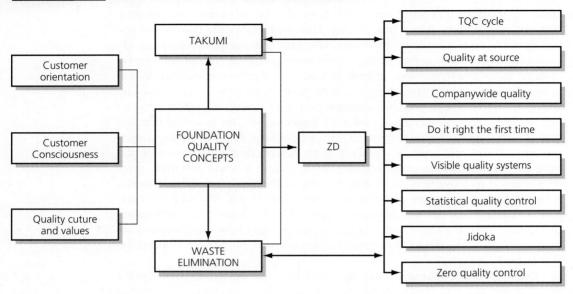

seen as being responsible for assuring effective and efficient use of all corporate resources. Effectiveness and efficiency are at their maximum possible levels when there is no waste. So waste elimination is, in a fundamental way, what management is all about. All defects are wasteful, hence, waste elimination provides the impetus for isolating and eliminating defects. Waste will be completely eliminated when there are no defects, that is, all managerial and operational activities are executed defect free. Takumi and waste elimination energize ZD.

The right side of Figure 8–1 shows the eight programs that operationalize the ZD effort by bringing it to life in day-to-day operations. These programs take ZD from its philosophical base and put it in specific work activities that actually try to remove defects. Takumi and waste elimination provide the philosophical and motivational base that can be used to create the right organizational environment for implementing specific ZD programs. ZD links the top management responsibility for nurturing the quality culture and value system with lower level management responsibilities to achieve specific, measurable, and always improving quality objectives.

Takumi and waste elimination have already been exhaustively dealt with. The remaining discussion will deal with the action-oriented dimensions of ZD and how they operate and reinforce each other in the pursuit of managerial and competitive excellence and in the implementation of corporate and manufacturing strategy and continuous improvement.

The Total Quality Control Cycle FIGURE **8–2**

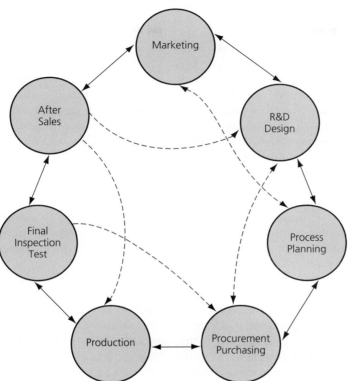

THE TQC CYCLE

It has long been recognized that a product goes through distinct stages as it progresses from an abstract idea to a problem solving artifact. These stages have been customarily referred to as the total quality control (TQC) cycle, which is shown schematically in Figure 8–2. As conceived originally, the TQC cycle showed a product going through a rigorously sequential process. However, it is now known that the process involved in creating a product, although basically sequential in that there is discernible progression toward the final product, is characterized by numerous feedback and hop-skip loops as downstream activities are anticipated from data generated two or even three phases upstream. For example, process planning tries to deal with product manufacturability and this traditionally strictly followed R&D and design activities, when a prototype product was available. However, it is now known that the earlier one thinks about and incorporates manufacturability concerns into the process, based on market research data, for example, the quicker the product can be brought to market, the more likely it is to succeed. The product development cycle is thus better seen as a progressive, but iterative, process.

The TQC cycle brings home the idea that there must be a total quality management process that links every phase in product development. Every phase builds on and uses data generated by all previous phases. In turn, each phase generates data that is useful for subsequent phases, making the cycle a continuous, linked input-output chain. No one phase controls the process, making interfunctional and coordinated organizational processes crucial to realizing total quality. One can say quite matter-of-factly that coordinating mechanisms that create interfunctional symbiosis, free flow of information, and mutual understanding are more crucial to quality development than the perfect execution of any one phase. The best design that cannot be manufactured except with excessive defects may satisfy design engineers, but it certainly does not advance the company's quality position on the market. Rigorously assuring quality will always require strong coordinating and integrating organizational mechanisms to promote unity of purpose, free flow of information, and interfunctional commitment to quality superiority.

Historically, in North America, defect reduction or removal has always been associated with product inspection and testing. Defect elimination is usually viewed as being unavoidable, while top management subconsciously accepted the idea that the plant had gotten as far as it could in preventing defects. Some managers had come to the conclusion that the production problem was solved, implying that manufacturing technology had been pushed to its practical limit. Therefore, any reduction in the level of defects passed on to customers could only result from more rigorous product testing and inspection. A few chief executives saw the factory as a headache, a real beast that was impossible to tame. Failure to understand the plant drove top management further and further away from it until the conclusion was reached that the factory was the real villain at the root of bad quality and management could do very little to change that state of affairs. The only way, company managers argued, that one could have an acceptable level of defects was to create a police force of inspectors to patrol the factory. Inspecting bad quality out was adopted as the only viable defect reduction strategy.

Inspection as a strategy to reduce defects was bound to fail because it assumed that the factory was the major, if not only, source of bad quality. The reality is, however, that defects can be introduced anywhere in the TQC cycle. One company that manufactured paper making machines started a project to trace defects to their source. To management's surprise, errors in design and blueprint preparation accounted for 90 percent of all defects that were discovered after the product was assembled. Another company was able to trace 35 percent of defects to bad quality delivered by suppliers (procurement in the TQC cycle). Inspection and test to screen out defects is also a questionable strategy for at least two reasons. For one thing, the inspection and test procedures themselves are likely not to be 100 percent effective, which means that where the company relies heavily on inspection and test to reduce defects, poor quality will always be passed on to customers. For another, inspection and test is very ineffective as a cost reduction, value maximization strategy. Identifying a defect does not eliminate the waste, but only throws good money after bad. Depending on what phase in the TQC cycle the defect is introduced, the waste in value added prior to defect detection at the inspection and test phase could be a substantial proportion of total product cost.

Defect control procedures must be instituted before and after each phase in the TQC cycle to ensure that the output produced by each phase is defect free and that what is being built into it is also the right quality. Instead of inspecting quality out, the strategy is to build quality in. And this means that quality must be a dominant concern at every step of the TQC cycle since both good quality and defects can be introduced anywhere in the cycle shown in Figure 8-2. The TQC cycle shifts the emphasis from "inspect bad quality out" to "put good quality in," in the first place. Rather than the passive, reactive response that characterizes traditional strategies that are based on inspection and test to assure quality, the TQC cycle advocates an aggressive (active), proactive approach to defect reduction and eventual removal.

The TQC cycle also liberates defect prevention and quality assurance from the narrow, product focus that is conditioned by much quality control technology. The excessive product focus that associates quality with a tangible thing is the main reason why Total Quality Control technology has penetrated neither the service sectors nor the service activities of manufacturing firms—customer service, repairs and maintenance, personnel administration, after-sales service—in any significant way. After all, marketing produces or deals with very little that is tangible, when it is contributing to product realization. But, the information and ideas that emanate from marketing are crucial to building quality in. The TQC cycle highlights the fact that even these intangible phases of product development must be controlled to first prevent and then filter out defects. A product may be a tangible thing, but its ideation emerges from purely intangible, abstract processes, and information is created, transformed and used all through its development. Quality designs emerge from quality market and technical data, just as surely as quality during production requires defect-free designs and blueprints. A few companies use a design qualification team to evaluate design integrity before blueprints are released to the factory. Production can then proceed with very high assurance that the designs themselves are not a source of defects during process planning, procurement, and production.

QUALITY AT SOURCE/QUALITY OF SOURCE

The TQC cycle reinforces the view that quality is built in or put into a product by the series of activities that bring it into existence. There is no other way to create quality and the unusual emphasis placed on inspection, test, and repairs is wide off the mark. Inspection and test may reveal that a product does not meet quality expectations, but that very fact is clear proof that these are not quality creation activities. Inspection and test only confirm that quality is present or absent, after the fact. Reliance on these activities is at best a temporary measure and at worst an admission that the quality creation functions themselves—market analysis and need evaluation, R&D and design, process planning, procurement, production—cannot be managed to achieve acceptable quality standards, predictably. Repairs also add costs that are nearly all avoidable, if not totally so. Of course, the inspection, test, and repairs activities can be quality ones, in the sense that they can do the job assigned to them with near perfection thus eliminating the need for products to go through repeated backward loops before they are delivered to the customer. Otherwise, they are best seen as the lesser of two evils, the worst one being product failure during use by the customer.

Quality is better controlled at the source activities, where it can be rigorously built in. The source activities are those which if executed perfectly will result in 100 percent good product, thus vitiating the need for inspection, test, and repairs. The product that comes from the factory would be the minimum cost one, given current technology. Rigorously controlling and assuring quality at the source (sources) is simultaneously a quality-maximizing and cost-minimizing strategy. It creates quality, thereby helping avoid waste due to defects and repairs and nonvalue-adding activities such as inspection and test. At the source, one can totally prevent bad quality from being produced. A defect prevention strategy always requires that the sources that are creating defects be isolated and evaluated and that the abnormalities that are causing these defects be eliminated. In addition, nonrecurrence of the causes can only be assured by understanding and mastering the sources and total integration quality into their normal operation. One cannot prevent defects, except at the sources. Everywhere else one tries to control defects will always be either detection or correction, but not prevention. Because zero defects is compulsorily based on prevention—it in fact requires 100 percent prevention effectiveness—it can only be validly operationalized at the sources. Anything else can only provide information to help management judge the extent to which the prevention strategy, and consequently zero defects, is being attained. This in itself is a useful contribution, but not the strategically desirable situation.

All the phases of the TQC cycle except inspection and test are sources of quality. For defects to exist, they must be introduced by the source activities. Good quality, like bad, comes from the source because inspection can only provide feedback to the source to correct defects or try to prevent them. The action is still source controlled. No matter how much feedback is given, there will be no improvement in quality if the source functions do not have the potential to produce good quality. A separate inspection function is required only if the source functions do not have the wherewithal to evaluate whether

or not the data or parts received from prior source functions meet requirements. Due to the fact that the inspection and test function exists to provide
feedback, it is desirable that it be integrated into the source activities, as
much as possible. Feedback, in that case, would be more accurate because
employees at the source should, as a minimum, know the requirement for the
task they themselves execute. The TQC cycle may lead one to overlook the
fact that inspection and test need not be a separate function and are indeed
more effective when integrated into the source activities, if this is feasible,
because feedback would be more direct. Inspection would thus occur and
exist in good symbiosis with the value-adding activities. Quality at source
could be reinforced with inspection by the source—source inspection.

We have argued that quality is built in and made and that a few major
sources, mostly within the company, exert considerable leverage over the
outcome. Quality does not just happen, but is made to happen at the places
and by the functions that create it. The factory, which is the place where
most value is added by the producing company must, contrary to traditional
wisdom in North America, have significant responsibility for product quality.
The factory is also the final battleground, the last frontier between the
management mission to deliver quality and the quality itself. All information,
materials, and processes that are deployed in the quality effort, converge on
the factory floor. Underscoring the factory's importance in making quality is
the fact that every company that has a reputation for product superiority also
pays attention to manufacturing. The Japanese revolution in quality started in
and is still going on in the factory, after more than 30 years of unrelenting
effort. German world-class manufacturing companies, indisputably the European leaders in quality management, pay undivided attention to making quality on the factory floor. Harley-Davidson in its bid to gain strategic advantage
on both quality and cost gave the plant major responsibility for quality. Failure
to see the potential in the factory or to strategically realign the organization to
raise production's strategic status is a major stumbling block to achieving
quality superiority by most North American companies. Rhetoric that pur-
ports to boost factory morale and lip service admission that the plant is an
important quality source will not change the strategic reality in most companies. Organizational structures need to change to give equal prominence to
production as to marketing. Top management has to develop an irrevocable
commitment to production as a strategic quality source and that commitment
must be made to permeate the entire organization. Fundamental shifts in organizational power must take place to make manufacturing an equal partner in
strategy formulation and implementation. Manufacturing vice-presidents must
be listened to and their advice must be sought and implemented. The promotion system, traditionally biased in favor of those with a marketing (function)
and finance background must give an equitable chance to those that cut their
teeth in production. Such is the reality that company presidents need to create in their companies.

It goes without saying that quality at source necessitates quality of source. Quality is built and made means that it takes people, equipment, and systems that can get the job done. Although technology and systems are important, people are paramount. Technology and systems are dumb objects, until activated and exploited by people. Nonetheless, ensuring that the right equipment and systems exist and that these have been designed specifically to deliver quality is a necessary fall out from the quality at source principle. Worker training to provide the best qualified, disciplined, and quality craftsmen in the business is a prerequisite. We have already emphasized that all superior quality companies are distinctive in their personnel selection and development policies. They select much more carefully and rigorously, train more completely and intensively, compensate their employees better, and provide for a much richer, meaningful work life than their run-of-the-mill counterparts. All this is done to achieve quality of source. These excellent companies do not neglect the technology and systems. They invest more in R&D, do more internal process development, are innovative and have better equipment and system maintenance policies than the average company in the same or similar industries.

DO IT RIGHT THE FIRST TIME

Zero defects means that all work is planned and executed without mistakes or errors. Mistakes can be avoided or at least significantly reduced, if appropriate measures are put in place to try to prevent them from occurring. Most errors or mistakes on the job are due to sheer carelessness or inadequate training and tools. The proof that mistakes can be driven to near zero levels is that they are in fact at that level in activities where making them would be devastating to the customer, such as in delicate, radical surgery. Cardiovascular surgeons and neurosurgeons do not make many errors.

Do it right the first time can be seen as a theme around which the company can rally in an effort to reduce errors to virtually zero. The accent is on "do," which implies that the execution activities such as product design and production have a central role to play. "Do" also means that mistakes are controllable at the source, by those performing the work. Mistakes are made or "done" and do not just happen. Even so-called accidents are rarely caused by fate but instead result from human error interacting with natural phenomena. Workers who set out not to make mistakes wholly succeed while those who adopt the fatalistic view that they cannot be avoided end up making a lot.

The "right" in do it right the first time accentuates the fact that there are standards against which all work can be judged. In performing work, there are right ways and wrong ways. The company should select one right way, one standard, and train workers to be thoroughly knowledgeable about it. The best work methods should be developed and the training program ought to make these clear, precise, and deeply ingrained in the work practices of employees. The organization should enforce the standards scrupulously so that do it right the first time becomes synonymous with "do what has been decided." Employees are free to experiment and innovate on work methods, and they should be encouraged to do so, as long as they can differentiate clearly between experimentation and the performance of usual work. When employees do find innovative ways to improve on work methods, then the new methods should become the new right way, and all should stick to it.

"Do it right" puts the human being in the driver's seat, which is how it should be. In the final analysis, technology and systems do not produce quality, people do. As was pointed out previously, machines and systems are passive, unthinking entities that can only be brought to life by human beings. Sure enough, people need to have adequate tools in order to do it right. But it is the human element that intervenes somewhere in the product realization or TQC cycle to define what is right and to ensure that all actions—human, machine, and systems—are executed to conform to the standard. "Do it right" means that the company has the right people, tools, systems, methods and processes, the right need information, product designs, and parts from suppliers. That is to say, all phases in the TQC cycle must be planned, executed, and controlled to a known, agreed upon set of quality standards even if these standards are being continually pushed higher and higher.

Sometimes, however, a company may find itself in the situation where it cannot say with confidence that it has the right standards everywhere in the product realization cycle. This is quite normal and is, in retrospect, a desirable situation because it reveals that the organization is somewhat dissatisfied with the status quo. All improvement actions, in a certain sense, emanate from some level of dissatisfaction with actual results and the methods by which they are pursued. "Do it right" necessarily means a constant search for that ultimate right way to conceive of, design, and manufacture a product so that there is no waste in materials, information, or time while the product meets exacting customer quality requirements. That ultimate "right" way is impossible to find, theoretically at least, but the search for perfection and continual improvement to eliminate waste keep world-class companies driving hard to find it.

Do it right the first time means that there should be only one attempt at each task and it should succeed every time the task is repeated. If it takes two tries to perform an activity properly, then the people responsible have not mastered the task or the tools are not adequate for the job. Every attempt to do the task over and above the first one is correction and therefore wasteful. The principle, that if there is enough time to correct—and there always is—then there is enough time to do it right the first time, is a truism. Suppose the standard time for an operation is 20 minutes, but the worker produces a defect which takes 5 minutes to correct. Then, allowing 25 minutes to do the job, but emphasizing getting the right quality the first time would add nothing to the total time. On the other hand, adding some more time would cultivate quality discipline and save waste in materials. Also, there would be a much lower risk that defects would be passed on to subsequent operations, permitting a much smoother operation flow. The possibility exists that more time consumed at earlier operations could be recouped by better efficiency at later ones. All correction, no matter how mundane and insignificant is waste, no amount of rationalizations can change that simple fact. A company is on the road to quality excellence when this simple principle has been driven home to every employee, embedded into the corporate mindset, and enmeshed into every method, system and organizational policy. Do it right the first time must be embraced as the corporate battle cry declaring all out war against defects.

COMPANYWIDE QUALITY

Companies that have made quality the cornerstone of their competitive strategy have marshaled all organizational resources toward its improvement and eventual mastery. They have found ways to make quality the central business of every organizational unit. Devotion to quality and its improvement is shared by all functions and these in turn mutually support each other in pursuing the quality mission. There is equal emphasis on quality no matter what the function or the activity being performed. Quality is omnipresent and is the only strategic priority for every function. It is the common spinal cord that runs all through the organization's social and technological fabric. The few companies that manage quality using these ideas call this companywide quality, meaning that every business unit is being managed to achieve quality superiority in its area of organizational responsibility, whether it be R&D and design, marketing, production, procurement, logistics, or any logical subdivision of these.

Companywide quality will culminate in a quality control cycle that starts and ends with top management, after going through all organizational units and activities. The control loop has five fundamental phases, as shown in Figure 8–3. When a company is managing quality for results, there will be rigorous and diligent control at all stages in the control cycle. There will be clear allocation of quality responsibility and authority; clear, realistic, and agreed upon quality objectives throughout the company; specific, goal-oriented, action plans; a solid measurement system for monitoring results, a well thought through reporting system for providing companywide quality feedback.

Responsibility, authority, objectives, and accountability in quality matters need to be widely distributed in the organization. Employees have responsibility, first and foremost, to do quality work, no matter what job they have been assigned. The current practice in personnel management is to provide a task description that gives each employee responsibility for a particular task. Quality responsibility is usually not formally assigned, if assigned at all. Employees

A Quality Control Cycle   FIGURE 8–3

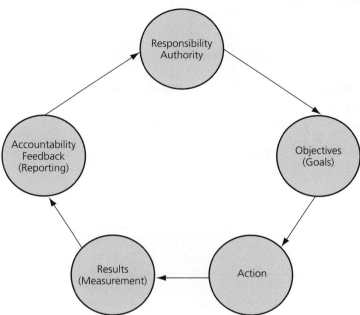

either tacitly assume that they have some responsibility for quality or they are sensitized to it by informal procedures and interaction with supervisors. Under these circumstances, the extent to which employees feel responsibility for quality depends wholly on the supervisors, and not on the basic corporate management system. The depth of commitment to quality would be quite variable, preempting a coordinated attack on problems relating to it. Figure 8–4, on the other hand, argues for assigning specific, clearly-defined quality responsibilities across the organization and from top to bottom in the hierarchy. Responsibility needs to be matched by authority so that those who have major responsibility also have the authority to back up their actions and carry out the tasks assigned to them.

Nowhere is this need to match responsibility and authority more critical than in the plant. As we have seen, the factory is a significant source of quality and has major responsibility for ensuring that the product coming out from the factory is defect-free and in conformance with or surpasses customer requirements. The nature of a manufacturing enterprise is such that the production function cannot but have major responsibility for quality, although this is rarely formally recognized by companies. Sometimes top management recognizes the plant's role and formally assigns major quality responsibility to it but does not put control mechanisms in place to assure accountability.

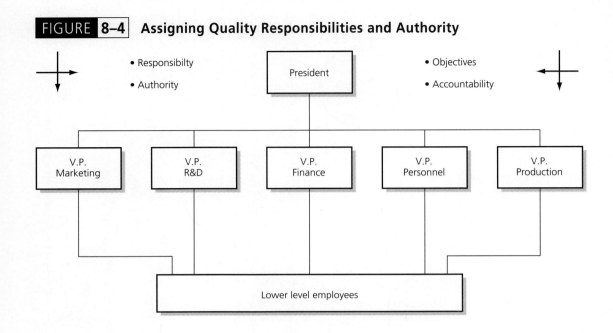

FIGURE **8-4** **Assigning Quality Responsibilities and Authority**

- Responsibilty
- Authority

President

- Objectives
- Accountability

V.P. Marketing

V.P. R&D

V.P. Finance

V.P. Personnel

V.P. Production

Lower level employees

Moreover, responsibility is usually assigned to higher factory management with no effort to make it filter down the organizational hierarchy to reach the workers on the factory floor, those who are really executing quality on a continuing basis. Where quality responsibility is unambiguously assigned throughout the manufacturing organization, there is often the added problem that factory managers feel they do not have the authority that will allow them to influence quality actions in a way commensurate with the responsibility they have for it. When the crunch comes, these managers feel they get the heat but their views are subject to veto by powerful players in marketing, R&D and engineering and quality control. The historical distribution of actual, as opposed to hierarchical, power in North American companies has tended to work against production managers. Organizational charts reveal, for example, that production vice-presidents have as much power as their marketing or R&D-engineering counterparts. The reality is, however, that marketing vice-presidents influence the company's strategic direction much more than production vice-presidents. The following case illustrates the dilemma that is often faced by company presidents and how organizational distortions in authority and responsibility adversely affect quality progress.

Houseware, Inc., manufactures household appliances, particularly refrigerators. The outside body of each refrigerator is shaped from steel that must meet some rigid specifications. One of these is that the sheet metal must be clean and free from any oxidation so that the outside of the appliance can be smoothly painted and also permit the paint to hold fast for the product's useful life. Defects on the metal surface, especially oxidation spots, would cause the paint to peel off quickly and the appliance would soon start to rust. This means that the sheet metal supplier must have very good steel rolling and scrubbing facilities and must be able to exercise severe control over the metallurgical properties of the steel during manufacture. The company usually bought sheet metal from three steel producers, and there were very few complaints in the past. The vice-president of purchasing had clear responsibility for assuring that materials delivered by suppliers satisfied the company's quality requirements. The vice-president of production was also held responsible for outgoing quality. This was official company policy.

During one of the company's recent peak selling periods, the spraying department noticed anomalies in the sheet metal from a major supplier. After some trouble shooting, it was determined that the supplier's scrubbing operations were not thoroughly cleaning the surface of the sheet metal. If the materials that were recently delivered by that supplier were used, major rust problems would appear in the refrigerators during use by customers. The normal lead time on sheet metal was eight weeks and the last shipment from the supplier who was having quality problems accounted for 20 percent of raw material inventory. Replacement material could not be acquired in time to produce the sales forecast for the peak season, except at a price that was 35 percent higher than normal. Supplier lead time would be three weeks, instead of eight, which meant that the company would lose 20 percent of peak period sales. If this happened, there would certainly be a loss for the current fiscal period, because peak sales accounted for 60 percent of annual sales.

The company had, over the last three years, launched a vigorous company-wide campaign to make quality the number one priority and to give production a key role in quality decisions. The official policy was that purchasing was responsible for ensuring that incoming materials satisfied rigorous quality requirements. The vice-president of production officially had "total" responsibility for the quality of products leaving the plant, as far as production related defects were concerned. The vice-president of production, fearing that continued use of the defective material would result in inferior products that would damage the company's quality reputation, decided to stop using the material in question. He was also concerned that continued use of the defective material would send a confused signal to workers and to the rest of the company and asked purchasing to return it and to buy from the alternative high-priced source. Purchasing obviously concerned about the materials budget impact of such a move, argued for using the material and for waiting to see if problems later developed with the product. The warranty program already in place could be used to replace the "few" products that might be affected in a few months time. The cost would be much less than replacing the defective material now at a cost that is 35 percent higher, particularly because the company would still lose 20 percent of its peak sales. Besides, he argued, the warranty program only covers 12 months and most problems are not likely to develop during that period.

The vice-president of production was unmoved and asked for a meeting with the vice-president of marketing and the president to discuss the problem and decide what should be done. The president listened to all the arguments but was particularly struck by the fact that the company's sales could suffer so much leading to a loss for the current fiscal year. He praised the vice-president of production for being so quality conscious but declared that it was absolutely necessary that the company meet its sales and profit budget for the current year. Production was instructed to use the defective material and they did after much grumbling. It was clear to everyone that production was responsible for outgoing quality, but that when the crunch came, it did not have the power to veto decisions that compromise quality. The widely accepted notion that failure to meet the sales and profits budget for one year is a corporate disaster confers incredible informal power on marketing and on those who can show that the decisions they propose will prevent sales from sliding in the short term.

Quality responsibility is taken seriously when those involved are accountable for quality results. That calls for clearly-defined, measurable quality objectives that can be used to regularly evaluate performance. Like responsibility and authority, accountability and objectives must permeate the entire organization, from top to bottom and across all functions. Objectives serve as the basis for evaluating quality progress and their repeated use to measure employee and management performance communicates the message that they have quality responsibility. The statement that everyone is responsible for quality makes no one responsible for it until everyone is held accountable for accomplishing some measurable quality objective or objectives. I have visited well over one 100 plants in North America. In almost all cases, top factory management is evaluated against both cost and volume objectives. More than three quarters use productivity objectives—standard time per piece—to judge individual performance on the factory floor. But among these factories, no more than four have been assigned clear, measurable quality objectives by top corporate management. Fewer still—less than three—have assigned specific quality objectives to production workers. In other words, fewer than 4 percent of the companies involved had formally assigned quality responsibility to their factories and could make them accountable for quality by evaluating performance according to agreed upon objectives. Less than 2 percent of these companies had, by top management action, pushed quality responsibility to production workers, those who are executing quality every day. The surprising thing is that top corporate management in all the companies visited were very quick in declaring that quality was an important strategic factor, and they did it in all sincerity. But the formal distribution of authority and responsibility and the mechanisms for assuring accountability were absent. Quality progress can only be evaluated against a clear benchmark of concrete, significant, and ever improving objectives. People whose performance is not evaluated using quality objectives are far from likely to feel responsible for its continuous improvement.

Setting Objectives for ZD

Realistically speaking, the ZD program cannot start trying to achieve zero defects immediately. ZD is a long-term, progressive, and continuous improvement effort. Achievable objectives should be set in the short term and they should be used to steadily guide the company to virtually zero defects. The principles enunciated by management through objectives are applicable to the zero defects context. Objectives must be realistic, that is to say, they must be achievable within the time frame envisaged. Unrealistic objectives are either demotivating or are quickly dispensed by employees as a pipe dream or another management ploy to muscle ever higher levels of productivity from the factory, or in popular parlance to squeeze the last drop of juice from the orange. Another consideration is whether objectives should be easy to achieve or should be ambitious so as to challenge the improvement effort. Corporate philosophies on that issue vary widely. Some companies prefer setting targets low so as to maximize the chance that they will be met, allowing individual motivation free play in influencing how much they will be surpassed. Others set difficult to achieve objectives that will make employees stretch, using the objectives themselves as a motivational tool. Arguments both for and against each strategy can be found, and which one will be favored depends heavily on the personality and managerial philosophy of the CEO. Some executives believe that employees can be coaxed into giving their best, relying on voluntary performance to strengthen cooperative effort. Others believe that employees will not give their best unless the reward system drives them to do so. The debate on this issue will not be settled in the foreseeable future.

A quality objective, in order to be realistic, must have some relationship to the current reality. Very high current defect rates would tend to favor ambitious goals both because failure to improve quickly would create a quality crisis and because abnormally high defect rates mean that there are obvious, easy to eradicate causes of defects. As defect rates approach zero, it becomes increasingly difficult to reduce them further. However, a company might not want to be ambitious initially, but may rather want to set modest, easily achievable goals. The argument here is that initial successes, even if modest, confirm that progress is feasible, motivating employees to want to experiment further and try harder. Nothing succeeds like success and one failure tends to attract another.

Goal setting should involve those who will be working to achieve them, as much as possible. The manager or supervisor is counselor, suggesting alternative goals and leading employees to accept that they can do better, if they truly can, or convincing them to set a lower less ambitious target according to their own judgment of their potential. But employees should always accept the goals adopted as their own. When this happens, goals become an internalized, powerful motivating force. Very few employees will insist that they can achieve an objective and not do their very best to bring it to fruition. Quality objectives are organizational, in the sense that they are used to motivate and judge corporate progress on defect elimination. But they are also profoundly personal, since they will mobilize the attention and effort of individual people, eight hours a day for an entire lifetime.

Although quality goals start at the top, because they have strategic implications, they must be made to cascade down the organizational hierarchy. Some companies set and keep them at the top, leaving the filtering down to haphazard, informal processes. Others set them at the bottom on the belief that quality goal setting is too mundane an activity to be dealt with by top management. Companywide quality and the need to create a corporate assault on defects argue for having them impregnate every organizational unit. All quality goals must be set at the top first and systematically distributed throughout the corporation. Organizational functions and units will be called on to contribute a larger share to defect reduction based on an evaluation of how much they are contributing to the current defect rate and how much leverage they have over defect prevention. Figure 8–5 illustrates the idea. Evidently, goal distribution must be based on an exhaustive defect cause analysis, function by function. The company must know where defects are coming from and how difficult it will be to eliminate the causes.

Goal setting for defect reduction should express constantly improving targets. There is no absolute, acceptable level of defects. The goal is to drive them to zero. Management, particularly at the upper echelons, must lead the organization to search for always decreasing defect rates. The goal setting exercise should be viewed by top management as an opportunity for it to inculcate the right attitudes and to communicate the corporate quality philosophy. When properly done, goal setting can be used as a management mechanism to steer the company toward continuous improvement and to incite it to aim for perfection. Goals give employees something to aim for, permitting them to focus improvement activities. In the context of world-class manufacturing, goals are not mere goals. They are mechanisms and tools to motivate, to communicate management's vision, and to drive the search for excellence. They also create unity of purpose when they are all linked to one strategic objective, as was explained previously. Goals form the basis for evaluating performance and for rewarding those who are achieving excellent results. They reveal those individuals or units that are not performing as expected, thereby allowing management to formulate corrective action. A realistic quality goal that is accepted and internalized by all employees is vital to motivating pragmatic quality improvement action. Goal achievement boosts self-esteem and confidence and is partly its own reward. Our experience is that

Distributing the Overall Defect Rate FIGURE 8-5

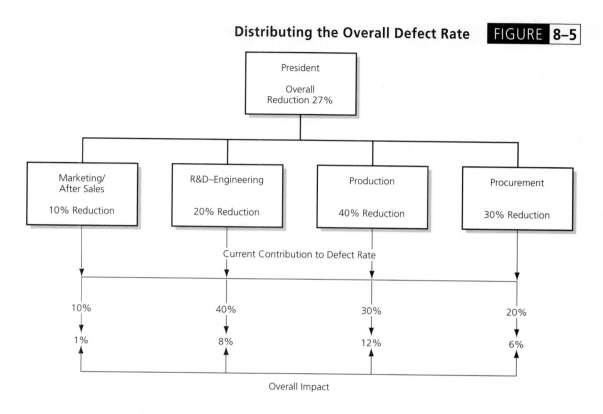

when top management fails to exercise quality leadership there is always an absence of clear, strategic quality objectives at the top and little goal directed actions throughout the organization. Leadership to strive for quality superiority always culminates in goal-directed action and invariably imbues the corporation with a strong sense of purpose in quality improvements.

Defect Measurement and Reporting

Progress toward zero defects must be constantly evaluated. There is no room for random guesswork in the tough competitive environment that exists today and will continue in the future. Top management must know, beyond a doubt, whether the company is making progress in defect elimination. Performance evaluation requires goals. But equally important, it requires defect measurement and reporting. The very notion of zero defects implies that they are measured and that there is knowledge as to their magnitude. Whenever a company begins to be deliberately managed and led toward quality superiority, top management will recognize the need to have a formal defect measurement and reporting system. It provides feedback to top management so that it can judge whether the strategic quality mission is being successfully executed.

Defect measurement takes two forms, one subjective and the other objective. In subjective defect measurement, the company knows customer requirements, but whether or not a product conforms to these depends on subjective judgment. Product classification is a judgment call. A human being must look at the product, turn, touch, smell, or taste it, and decide, without any formal measuring system, that it is good or bad. The alcohol content of a bottle of vintage wine can be precisely calculated, but whether or not it tastes good is a matter of taste. And as the old Latin saying goes, "De gustibus non est disputandem" (we cannot argue about tastes). When the lady inspector on the television commercial assertively declares "They don't say Haines until I say they say Haines" she is expressing the essence of subjective defect evaluation. Although we cannot argue about tastes, we can agree on them, if there is consensus on what it is we are looking for. Subjective defect evaluation, to be valid, requires that the person doing the evaluation build strong intuition about what quality is. The level of intuition—a kind of sixth sense, so to speak—that is called for can only come from experience and thorough training. Above all, however, the one evaluating quality must put on the heart and mind of the customer. He or she must smell, feel, sense, taste, and see like the customer. As we said before, that kind of identification with customer needs can only develop in a company that is totally customer oriented in every aspect of its business. So, it has to be reemphasized that there can be no sustainable quality progress without complete customer orientation and deep customer consciousness.

Objective defect evaluation uses measurable quality specifications to measure conformance to customer requirements. Objective measures include weight, chemical composition, length, strength, and other established methods to categorize products. Although these variables are amenable to precise measurement, they are still prone to error since they must be measured using instruments or tools operated by people. Tools may be wrongly calibrated, poorly maintained, and erroneously operated. Without proper care and discipline, employees have been known to make errors in registering quality date. Whether measures are subjective or objective, therefore, does not reduce the key role that people play in product classification. Subjective evaluation calls for employees to be trained to sense quality. Objective evaluation requires that they be trained to operate, maintain, and calibrate measuring instruments and to read and interpret data. Intensive training is indispensable to achieving quality superiority, no matter what the specific quality action is or where it is executed.

The quality control loop is closed with the reporting system. Reports ought to be simple and based on the goals set. They should be designed to provide direct and visible evidence as to whether goals are being achieved. Conclusions relative to whether progress is being made in defect reduction should be evident from the reports with no secondary data transformation being necessary. The reports should speak clearly and precisely on every quality objective accepted. These comments argue for liberally using charts and graphs in reporting on quality, because they make for both parsimony and simplicity, key characteristics of any management reporting system. Simple reports can be produced quickly and frequently, providing intensive and punctual feedback. Feedback that is temporarily far from the quality event is not much useful as an aid to problem identification and diagnosis. This has significant bearing on the locus of defect control, to be discussed subsequently. Suffice it to say, for the time being, that the locus of defect evaluation and control should be as close as possible to the source producing defects.

VISIBLE QUALITY SYSTEMS

Upon entering a factory that is producing excellent quality as a matter of course, one is struck by the visible evidence that it is being managed to that end. The workers, equipment, and internal factory environment reflect quality discipline. The most dramatic aspect is good housekeeping. Orderliness, a place for every thing and every thing in its place, is the rule of law, and contrasts sharply with the general disorder that reigns supreme in so many factories. Cleanliness is not only preached, but practiced. Excellently managed plants demolish the image of the typical factory as a place that is cluttered with dust, grease, and junk. Most of these plants that are super clean are not in electronic component manufacturing operations that have often been bragged about in the media, as being cleaner than surgical rooms. Instead, they are the usual nuts-and-bolts factories that make all the conventional products. The difference lies in the fact that the search for perfection has been so deeply ingrained in the corporate mindset that it affects the quality of the work environment also. The discipline to do quality work extends itself to the physical environment where work is done. Sloppiness and untidiness are but indirect reflections of general laxness and a lackadaisical attitude. The old English proverb which says that cleanliness is next to godliness shows the link between a clean factory and the search for perfection. Another adage, order is heaven's first law, obviously carries the connotation that orderliness indicates that perfection has been nearly attained. Cleanliness and orderliness provide visible evidence that the factory is being managed to execute perfect quality.

Canon, the camera and office equipment manufacturer, uses the parlor factory concept to promote orderliness and cleanliness. When one understands what a parlor is, one begins to grasp the extent to which a few companies at the cutting edge of international competition are devoted to companywide excellence. The parlor, in western tradition, is a super clean, meticulously ordered room where special guests are entertained. Originally also, the parlor was a business establishment, elegantly furnished to resemble a private living room. The original parlor catered to the sophisticated tastes of the landed gentry and ruling classes in Europe. It had to be designed, operated, and kept to reflect cultural sophistication. Canon wanted to have immaculately clean and orderly factories that created a positive, sophisticated work environment. A livelier work place, it reasoned, would stimulate creativity and motivation. The parlor factory concept conveys the philosophy that the factory must be so clean and orderly that workers could feel comfortable entertaining their most prominent guests right on the factory floor.

Signal systems are a good way to implement quality visibility. Several electronic devices can be used to detect machine malfunctions and to emit visible feedback to operators so that processes can be shut down. Jidoka techniques implement quality visibility, but rely mainly on workers to judge whether there is a malfunction and then to stop the process. The more sophisticated signal systems will detect malfunctions or products that do not conform to requirements and give a signal, or preferably, will stop the operation. Signal systems can be designed to detect machine malfunctions the moment they occur, and usually, before any defect has been produced. Nearly every machine can be equipped with signal systems for at least a few critical quality parameters. These devices are frequently very cheap, providing a cost effective way to prevent defects at the source.

Quality visibility is enhanced by measures undertaken to publish performance results throughout the organization. Employees who know that the company is measuring and reporting on performance come to be sensitive to quality issues. Constantly disseminating information on target versus actual defect rates makes employees aware of the targets, performance relative to goals and the actions that are being implemented to improve quality. The very fact that they are kept informed about quality results, communicates the message that defect reduction is their business. Moreover, it also cultivates the attitude that every employee has some impact on defect elimination. Quality problems become visible when results are made available to all. Most people will automatically try to associate the results that are presented to them with ongoing quality management actions or perceived problems. They try to intuitively and mentally explain the results they observe, based on their own work experiences.

Defect display is just one way to publish poor quality results. Employees can very easily identify with the situations that gave rise to the defect. The quality brass tacks are not hidden behind some abstract data. They are right there in front of their very eyes. The defect can be seen, touched, or analyzed, whatever it takes to truly understand and appreciate it. Nothing will grip a worker's attention more than to have access to a sample of bad quality. For if a picture is worth a thousand words imagine what is the value of the real object. The same goes for exceptionally good quality. Displaying superior quality product brings superior quality to life. Employees can form a concrete image of what the company means when it refers to good quality. A company that extensively displays both good and bad quality is making a double learning experience available to its employees. It is telling them what to avoid by displaying defects and what to aim for when it showcases good quality.

Visible quality systems condition employees to think constantly about quality and to put it in their work habits. Companies that use visible quality systems extensively are putting workers and managers in a work environment where it is very normal to think about quality and how to plan and perform work better. Craftsmanship must become a habit. The organization needs to be immersed in and swamped by quality issues. The company needs to be gripped by the single-minded purpose of eliminating defects. There must be a proliferation of defect removal ideas, concepts, and ongoing actions. Zero defects must be everywhere and must be known and seen to be everywhere. This is the goal of visible quality systems.

STATISTICAL QUALITY CONTROL (SQC)

What Is SQC?

North American industry, using work done by Dodge, Romig, and Shewhart, pioneered the use of statistics in quality control. For a very long time, quality control technology relied very heavily on statistical analysis to inspect incoming and outgoing materials and also to maintain control over internal processes. Those who were eager to see management become the new science embraced statistical tools very enthusiastically. The period from 1930 to about 1965 saw wide scale use and development of statistical tools in quality control. The U.S. military gave credibility to statistical quality control and helped entrench it permanently into quality management technology. With its now famous military standards tables and quality control procedures, the U.S. military almost literally imposed statistical quality control on North American industry. Contractors and subcontractors have to follow the guidelines that are contained in formal documents such as MIL STD 105-D, if they wanted to do business with the U.S. military. Many contractors and subcontractors to the U.S. defense department were from glamour industries like advanced electronics, weapons systems, shipbuilding, and aircraft manufacturing. They included companies at the frontiers of advanced technology. It was natural, therefore, that they gave credence to and totally legitimized statistical quality control. When Deming went to Japan in 1956, he went armed with the favorite statistical techniques, and for years, Japanese industry faithfully learned and applied statistical quality control. In an effort to demonstrate how far behind the Japanese the North Americans had fallen, the observation was made that the average foreman in Japan had ten times more training in statistical quality control than the average North American industrial engineer.

Statistical quality control (SQC) is normally divided into two parts. The first, acceptance sampling, tries to develop sampling plans for incoming and outgoing inspection. The aim is to provide the inspector with statistical information upon which to base the decision to accept or reject an incoming or outgoing lot. An appropriate sample, *n,* is taken from the lot, *N.* The sampling plan specifies in advance, what should be the sample size, *n,* and what is the acceptance number, C. The sample is extracted, inspected, and the number of defects is noted. If the number of defects is less than or equal to C, the lot is accepted without 100 percent inspection. Otherwise, the lot is rejected which means that every unit is inspected, if the test is not a destructive one. The lot is returned to the supplier where the test is destructive or where the agreement between the customer and the supplier specifies that it could be. This is not the place to delve into the statistics behind acceptance sampling. It is enough to state that every plan, that is a sample size, *n,* and its corresponding acceptance number, C, is chosen to respect given probabilities of accepting a bad lot and rejecting a good one.

The second part of SQC is statistical process control, (SPC). The goal in traditional SPC is to provide feedback on the state of the process, that is, whether it is functioning normally or not. The ideal situation exists when all products come from processes that are in control. The characteristics of samples of products coming from the process are used to evaluate whether it is in a state of control. The state of the process is inferred from the quality characteristics of the products that emanate from it, using well-known statistical models.

Products coming from a process will display some variation along key quality characteristics. If one weighs boxes of breakfast cereals that come from the weighing operation, one will find that although the target weight is 450 grams, there will be a variation around the acceptable weight. This will happen, even if the process was in control and functioning normally. There is random variation in product characteristics due to imperfect technology or random causes that are either not well understood or are impossible or too costly to eliminate. Of course, the more process design improves and the process operating conditions are understood and controlled for, the less random, unpredictable variation in product characteristics there will be.

SPC computes upper and lower control limits for each product quality characteristic that one wishes to control. The standard formulas for doing this are available in most basic texts on quality control.[2] When the UCLs and LCLs are placed in a convenient form for displaying feedback on the process, one gets the well-known control charts. Figure 8–6 shows two examples of SPC charts. The first is applicable to cases where quality can be evaluated objectively, that is, the characteristics can be measured using a standard measurement system, and is called a control chart for variables. The second chart can only be used for subjective quality measurement, when quality can only be evaluated by someone's subjective judgment. In this latter case, the product

---

[2]See, for example, A. V. Feigenbaum, *Total Quality Control* (McGraw-Hill, 1983), ch. 14.

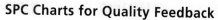

SPC Charts for Quality Feedback   FIGURE **8–6**

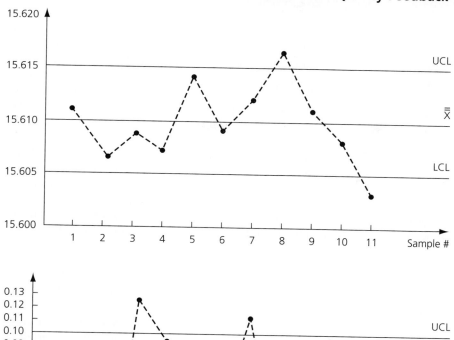

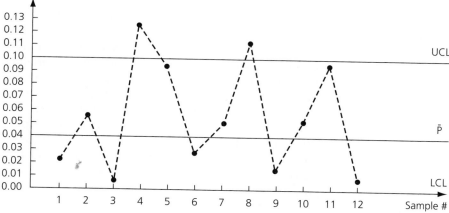

attributes, whether it is good or bad, are used to evaluate quality. The control chart for attributes is more of a defect reporting mechanism than a tool for controlling the process that is generating the defective products.

SQC and Defect Removal

At the time it was developed by Dodge, Romig, and Shewhart, SQC represented a major revolution in quality control and defect reduction in North

America. Inspection, hitherto a very informal, almost haphazard, process could be systematized and formalized. It could also be executed to look for agreed upon variables and to respect decision criteria, such as the acceptable quality level, the probability of accepting a bad lot and of rejecting a good one that the company could live with. Everyone in the company could control quality using the same numbers, assumptions, and criteria. At least there was some potential to get consensus on what it was the company wanted to control and how. SQC requires that there be some agreement on vital quality characteristics and how they should be measured and controlled. Some effort had to be made to understand the requirements and on measuring, or at least evaluating, conformance to them.

SQC contributes in an important way toward creating a quality feedback system. The statistical tools were designed to give feedback. Their use at least provides management with the ability, albeit limited, to know how well the company is doing in controlling or reducing defects. In many North American companies today, the formal feedback that management receives on quality comes from the information generated by SQC. The company can know, even if after the fact, whether it has problems and where. Statistics gave the company the potential to pinpoint problem areas and to trigger the search for causes. Quality problem visibility was enhanced by SQC.

The biggest contribution that SQC makes to defect removal is that it creates quality consciousness. Designing the sampling plans and control charts force those responsible to think through the requirements, the product characteristics, the process capability and the methods for making the product and controlling its quality. Repeatedly using the plans and charts generates heightened awareness of quality and quality issues. The feedback provided by SQC contributes to employee and supervisory discipline, because the fact that some performance is tracked conveys the message that the company pays some attention to quality. SQC feedback, although limited, builds and reinforces accountability when problem areas are probed, investigated and analyzed. By isolating the areas that are producing defects, SQC brings some focus to the quality improvement effort.

SQC changes the motivational climate and communicates a shift in corporate priorities. That is why companies that have no formal quality control procedures in place experience dramatic reductions in defects when they introduce SQC. The Hawthorne effect accounts for most of the decrease. SQC causes employees and managers to pay a bit more attention to quality. Interest is heightened by the novelty of the statistical tools, which in themselves create an atmosphere of high science, expertise, and sophistication. The quest to learn the new statistical tools motivates employees by challenging them. The Hawthorne effect tells us that if management shows interest in what employees do, that fact alone stimulates productivity. Any action is better than inaction and SQC implementation is action that conveys the message to employees that someone, somewhere in the company, is thinking about quality improvement.

Naturally, companies that were serious about quality adopted SQC and long before those which were not. The Japanese totally embraced it, and were even spellbound by the newly acquired tools. Major world-class manufacturers in North America embraced SQC wholeheartedly. Many people attributed Japanese success in quality to the fact that they were very advanced in using statistics, particularly SPC. When in the late 1970s, Fuji-Xerox was achieving defect rates of less than one part per one hundred thousand, lower than what Xerox was achieving in the United States by an order of magnitude, many experts attributed the difference mainly to the fact that Fuji-Xerox was using SPC extensively. And the people at Xerox in the United States, in an effort to match the results attained by their Japanese affiliate, pushed hard on SPC and were aggressive in helping their own U.S. suppliers implement it. Many observers identified SPC as contributing enormously to a quality turnaround at Xerox. SPC was and is still being touted as a major world-class manufacturing tool.

The statistical theory upon which SQC is based imparted an aura of scientific rigor to it. Quality control specialists did not have to rigorously defend their ideas because the statistical formulas were long proven. In the late 1970s and early 1980s, nearly all world-class manufacturers had or were adopting SQC, particularly SPC. Many well-known, world-renowned North American manufacturers were requiring that vendors implement SPC if they wanted to maintain their status as certified suppliers. Adopting SPC soon became an end in itself, rather than a tool. Company after company saw in SPC the solution to nearly all their quality problems. SPC became a panacea and it was implemented with little regard to the foundation quality improvement ideas such as the quality culture and value system, or how it related to the total defect removal effort. A few companies are now realizing that SQC/SPC was oversold. Companies that were getting results from SQC/SPC were doing so because they did much more than SPC. They had laid the foundations for superior quality and had created companywide quality responsibility and accountability. SQC/SPC was a very small part of the total quality effort, even if it did make a contribution.

THE INADEQUACIES OF SQC/SPC IN ZD

SQC Is Feedback Quality Control

The various SQC tools use some sampling procedure to judge whether quality is acceptable or unacceptable. Products are inspected or tested, after they have been produced or after the operation being controlled has been executed. SQC is based on after-the-fact inspection and evaluation of quality, and is therefore a feedback mechanism. By definition, then, SQC accentuates defect correction rather than prevention. The best that SQC can do is to give the basis for taking some action, to prevent additional defects from being produced, at a given point in time. SQC is mainly defect correction. An acceptance sampling procedure signals whether corrective action should be taken on a lot of materials while SPC provides the information that can be used to judge whether corrective action should be taken on a process. Defect prevention is only incidental to the SQC procedures and methods.

SQC gives feedback on the level of quality that has been produced. Feedback is useful if it comes very soon after the occurrence of bad quality and also if it stimulates prompt corrective action. The time that elapses between the occurrence of a defect and its detection by the feedback system is the quality feedback loop and can partly be designed into the SQC procedures and methods themselves. Sample sizes and the time interval between samples are important SQC parameters for controlling the feedback loop, and their role has been strongly emphasized in classical quality control technology. Small samples taken frequently are generally advocated when reasonably timely feedback is required. However, other factors such as lot sizes, the staging of inspection stations, and the role of the operator in inspection and quality are now known to have much more impact on the length of the quality feedback loop than the sampling procedure used. Moreover, no matter how timely feedback is, it is useless unless it triggers appropriate corrective action and statistical procedures are basically neutral in that regard. Whether or not feedback will be followed by swift action to eliminate what is causing bad quality depends on managerial or organizational factors such as prevailing attitudes toward quality, management policies, work force training and involvement, quality consciousness, and reward systems, which have little or nothing to do with SQC. Feedback systems can contribute to improving the effectiveness of defect correction, but they are much less useful for defect prevention.

The quality feedback loop is illustrated in Figure 8-7. The process shown has four operations, each having a three minute cycle time, which means that the total processing time is twelve minutes. The current lot size is 400 pieces and lots are inspected using a sample extracted when the entire lot has been processed. Queue time is assumed to be 60 percent, which is on the low side since queue time is 80 percent or more in practice. Using these data, the quality feedback loop is five weeks, which means that defects are signalled at the final and only inspection station five weeks after they have been produced at Operation 1. The calculations are as follows, if a 40 hour work week is assumed.

$$\text{Total processing time} = 400 \text{ pieces} \times 1/5 \text{ hours/piece}$$
$$= 80 \text{ hours}$$

$$\text{Q-time} = 60\%$$

$$\text{Processing time} = 1 - \text{Q-time}$$
$$= 40\%$$

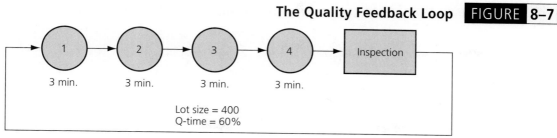

The Quality Feedback Loop FIGURE 8–7

Lot size = 400
Q-time = 60%

5.0 weeks

Total time = 80 hours/0.4
= 200 hours
= 5 weeks

One should note that this is a very simple operation with a relatively short time per piece at each operation.

The results show one very powerful reason why SQC and all quality control systems that rely on feedback to correct defects cannot be relied on to reduce defect rates to near zero. Based on the data shown in Figure 8–7, defects are discovered five weeks after they are produced, making it virtually impossible to isolate and correct the problem that caused them. The production system may have been already rescheduled to produce a different product by the time the quality control system has given feedback on the state of the prior batch. The entire lot could have been defective and the information to judge its quality would be available too late to prevent at least some defects from being produced. For SQC to give reasonable results, the feedback loop needs to be drastically reduced.

Reducing the Quality Feedback Loop

Quick feedback contributes to the effectiveness of the defect correction program. In SQC, the speed of feedback is improved by decreasing both the sample size and the time interval between samples. Although this approach helps, it is not the most effective way to improve the speed of feedback. For example, reducing the sample size by one half in the problem illustrated in Figure 8–7 has no impact on the feedback loop. However, reducing the time interval between samples by taking a sample once the first 200 units are produced instead of waiting for the entire lot of 400 reduces the feedback loop from 5 weeks to 2.5 weeks.

Figures 8–8a and 8–8b on the following page show two ways to effect dramatic reductions in the feedback loop. In the first case, the feedback loop is reduced from 5 weeks to 5.3 hours when the lot size is reduced from 400

FIGURE 8–8a **Impact of Lot Size Reduction on the Quality Feedback Loop**

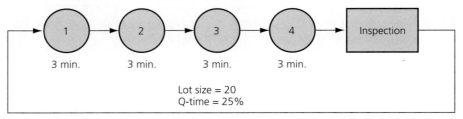

Lot size = 20
Q-time = 25%

5.3 hours

FIGURE 8–8b **Impact of Multiple Inspection Points on the Quality Feedback Loop**

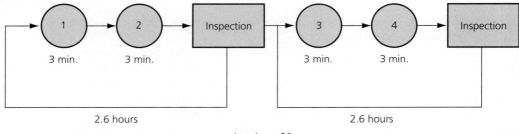

Lot size = 20
Q-time = 25%

to 20. Companies that have been successful in implementing small lot production have been able to reduce lots to 1/40 of their original sizes. Therefore, the lot size reduction illustrated in Figure 8-8a is entirely feasible. Reducing the lot size decreases both the total processing time and the Q-time percentage, which means that the feedback loop shrinks at a faster rate than the lot size. Figure 8-8b places inspection points after Operations 2 and 4. The result is that the feedback loop shrinks further from 5.3 hours to 2.6 hours. With a 2.6 hour feedback loop, not only is there a better chance that defect problems can be traced to their source but causes can also be eradicated early enough to prevent further defects.

The fundamental conclusion that can be drawn from Figures 8-8a and 8-8b is that even as a feedback tool, the effectiveness of SQC greatly depends on lot sizes and the positioning of inspection points. Furthermore, defect correction progressively becomes defect prevention as lot sizes approach one and inspection is built into the operation. When the lot size is one and the worker is responsible for inspection, feedback is instantaneous. In such a case, defects can be quickly corrected and their causes promptly eradicated making it possible to produce the remaining subsequent units in a problem-free environment.

SQC Standards Invariably Get Frozen in Time

Sampling plans for controlling the quality of incoming lots are usually chosen to assure that four performance criteria are satisfied. These criteria are

1. The acceptable quality level (AQL), which is the percentage defective or lower than lots should have for them to be judged good.
2. The producers' risk, α or the probability of rejecting a good lot, that is, a lot that meets the specification for AQL.
3. The lot tolerance percentage defective (LTPD), which is the maximum percentage defective a lot should have.
4. The consumer's risk, β, which is the probability of accepting a bad lot that the sampling plan should assure. β is also the probability of accepting a lot that contains a percentage defective that is equal to or greater than the LTPD.

Similarly, SPC computes upper and lower control limits for each process based almost exclusively on samples extracted from units produced by the processes. Some care is taken to systematically eliminate samples that appear to be outliers or indicative of a poorly controlled process. Once AQL, α, LTPD, and β factors and the SPC control limits are established, they become the norms for judging the quality of incoming lots and abnormalities in process functioning.

Over time, then, the SQC criteria and limits become the quality norms or standards. They come to be viewed as absolute, even sacrosanct, performance objectives and those responsible for quality become convinced that performance is acceptable once it satisfies the SQC parameters. Indeed, SPC theory suggests that repeated use of the SPC charts accompanied by systematic elimination of the outliers lead to process control with a standard. Mature users of SQC find that quality performance becomes frozen in time, if they do not put in place other quality programs to stimulate improvement. There is nothing in the SQC tools themselves that will motivate the organization to challenge the norms or the standards that employees have grown accustomed to. SQC is not an improvement tool, so it cannot be a major weapon to drive the company toward near zero defects. Excessive reliance on SQC may have the opposite effect and block progress toward zero defects.

Low Defect Rates and SQC Effectiveness

Statistical quality control and its supporting tools give questionable and meaningless results in low defect rate environments. The basic tools of acceptance sampling and control charts were developed decades ago, when defect rates

| TABLE 8–1a | **Acceptable Quality Level (Defect Rate) and Sampling Plans** |

AQL	LTPD	α-risk	β-risk	Sample Size	Acceptance No. of Defects
0.10	0.20	0.05	0.30	54	9
0.08	0.15	0.05	0.25	115	14
0.04	0.10	0.02	0.20	134	10
0.01	0.05	0.02	0.15	148	4
0.001	0.03	0.01	0.05	149	1
0.001	0.02	0.01	0.01	436	2

| TABLE 8–1b | **SPC Charts for Varying Proportion Defective (Defect Rate)** |

Sample Size	Proportion Defective		Standard Deviation (σ)	LCL (-3σ)	P	UCL ($+3\sigma$)
100	4/100	0.040	0.019596	0	0.040	0.0987
100	2/100	0.020	0.014000	0	0.020	0.0620
250	8/1000	0.008	0.00563	0	0.008	0.025
500	4/1000	0.004	0.00281	0	0.004	0.012
1000	1/1000	0.001	0.00095	0	0.001	0.004

were measured in several parts per hundred. They are not precise enough to give the information needed to control, much less prevent, defects in contexts where one part per hundred thousand or one part per million is the norm. The data in Tables 8-1a and 8-1b demonstrate the basic weaknesses inherent in the SQC tools. As Table 8-1a shows, the sample size increases rapidly and the acceptance number, C, decreases as defect rates approach the one-part-per-thousand defective level and the α and β risks are controlled at 0.01, the sample size is 436 and the acceptance number is 2. The information says that 436 units should be inspected to find out if the sample has two units defective. Inspection becomes long and tedious, which means that the information it produces probably comes too late to be useful for preventing defects. Because the defect rate is one per thousand, the company must inspect 2000 units or approximately five samples, in order to discover two defects. Similarly, had the defect rate been one per one hundred thousand, 200,000 units would have to be inspected in order to find two defects. Inspection, in these cases, is evidently a waste of resources. Better results

The Weaknesses of SPC FIGURE 8–9

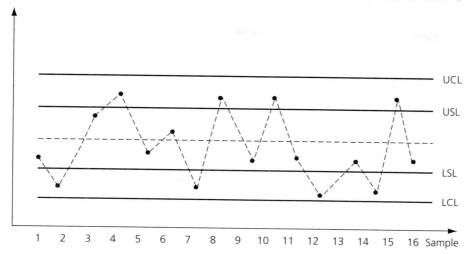

would be attained if these resources were used to control or prevent defects at the source, that is, before-the-fact rather than after-the-fact, inspection.

Table 8-1b shows an analogous analysis for the case where SPC is the tool being used. The data show the control limits for different sample sizes and defect rates or proportion defective. The upper control limits are always substantially higher than the average defect rates, p. The SPC chart is showing that the process is under control during periods when the actual defect rate being produced is two or even three times the normal average proportion defective, an evidently unacceptable situation. The defect rate will be higher than the average proportion defective roughly 50 percent of the time. There is no imperative to eliminate the source of these defects because the SPC chart categorizes them as normal.

Two basic weaknesses of SPC can be evaluated using Figure 8–9. UCL and LCL are the upper and lower control limits while USL and LSL are the upper and lower specifications limits, or what are usually referred to as the tolerances. The chart shows that the process is in a state of statistical control, but half the samples have mean characteristics that are outside the tolerance. The process is producing a large proportion of defects, as far as the product specifications are concerned, but the SPC chart says that the process is functioning normally. The process does not have the capability to meet the tolerance without defects. Statistical process control computes control limits based on the existing or historical quality levels that the process has demonstrated that it is capable of producing. Customer requirements do not enter into the choice of control limits. As shown in Figure 8–9, the tolerance compared with the control limits only determine the probable defect rate.

Moreover, the SPC chart simply shows that a process is or has just been out of statistical control. What plant personnel do with the information is quite another matter. Those who have been beguiled by the apparent "scientific" principles of SPC tend to see it as an end in itself, rather than a tool for reducing defects. However, the search for causes of process out-of-control conditions is the crucial phase of using SPC. Unless the company has the wherewithal such as small group improvement teams to probe, find, and eliminate the problems that are causing a process to go out of control, then SPC is a totally impotent tool.

SPC gives some information that can be used to bring processes into a state of statistical control. The crucial phase in defect reduction and zero defects is to improve the process once it has been brought under control. The goal is not to bring the process under control, but to improve it until the statistical control limits are inside the customer's (user's) tolerances. The critical weapon in defect elimination and prevention are the attitudes and practices that eradicate what is causing defects. Continuous improvement programs bring the process under control and keep them there. They are also the only way to reduce process variability and increase process capability until the statistical limits are smaller than the tolerances.

SQC and all feedback systems cannot be used to drive defect rates close to zero. They must be backed up with source inspection if they are to be reasonably effective. Source inspection of suppliers, work methods, practices, and materials identify and correct problems at the source, where there is maximum potential for eradicating the causes of poor quality and for preventing defects. SQC has a good set of tools for reducing defects and most companies will find them useful to begin with. But the goal is to make the classical SQC tools redundant by continuously improving quality and moving to implement systems that rigorously prevent defects.

DEFECT PREVENTION SYSTEMS

Successive Checks (SUCS)[3]

Feedback systems can contribute significantly to defect prevention if they are designed to detect defects very soon after bad quality has been produced. Inspection must take place very close to the operation and after few units have been produced. Successive checks or inspection by the immediately succeeding worker meet both requirements. Inspection is limited to one or two quality criteria that can be quickly and easily appraised, but which have a strong

---

[3]For a full discussion of SUCS and SECS, see Shigeo Shingo, *Zero Quality Control: Source Inspection and the Poka-Yoke System* (Productivity Press, 1986).

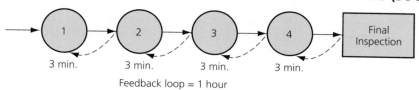

Successive Checks (SUCS) FIGURE **8–10a**

If we assume a lot size of 20, as in Figure 8–8a and 8–8b, the feedback loop for SUCS is 1 hour, computed as follows:

$$
\begin{aligned}
\text{Number of pieces processed} &= 20 \\
\text{Time per piece} &= 3 \text{ Min.} \\
\text{Q-time is virtually zero} \\
\text{Feedback loop} &= 60 \text{ Min.}
\end{aligned}
$$

In SECS, feedback is instantaneous.

impact on overall quality. Wherever possible, all pieces are inspected, that is, the norm is 100 percent inspection. Where successive checks are used, feedback is direct and almost instantaneous, which makes for both rapid problem identification and diagnosis, and also stimulates quick action to eradicate what is causing poor quality. A worker that sees a part returned to him by the fellow worker downstream feels morally obligated to take action to fix the problem. SUCS uses the group or social contact on the job to motivate employees to respond positively to feedback on quality. In addition, SUCS reinforces the basic modern quality control principle that the customer represents the next operation whose quality requirements must be met. SUCS gives the internal customer, the next operation, a voice in quality assurance. Figure 8–10a diagrams SUCS.

One difficulty has served as a barrier to widescale implementation of SUCS systems by North American corporations. The factory subculture in most companies in North America is designed to discourage workers from passing negative judgment on the work of their colleagues. This attitude is a throwback to the days when deep, permanent conflict between management and workers was the norm. Management personnel and plant employees functioned like two separate and distinct organizations, each having its own unique value set. Management often placed "stool pigeons" among plant personnel so as to identify and eliminate the so-called troublemakers. In time, factory employees came to look at colleagues that passed negative judgment on their work as "stool pigeons" who were on management's side. Workers in many plants in North America still harbor such attitudes toward colleagues who evaluate their work. Consequently, many creative workers are reluctant to pass judgment on the work of a fellow worker because they fear being isolated and ostracized by the larger work group.

Management should not assume that employees will naturally accept the responsibility for evaluating the quality produced by a co-worker. The way that the factory has been historically managed ensures that workers will resist the implementation of SUCS systems. Factory management styles in North America have tended to create deep mistrust between management and workers and have generally failed to build cohesive work groups that encourage mutual help, high employee involvement, self-development, and continuous group learning. Top management must anticipate and explicitly deal with the behavioral issues that are involved in any attempt to implement a successive checks system. Workers must be allowed, even encouraged, to express all their fears and concerns about the SUCS program, and these must be all dealt with frankly and openly. Extensive training and education is indispensable. Voluntary participation in work groups and the implementation of successive checks at any particular work station help eliminate the suspicion that there is a hidden agenda. SUCS should be designed and promoted as a tool for positive feedback and the goal should be quality improvement. There should be rewards for quality improvement, never punishment for failure to improve.

Self Checks (SECS)

Feedback is instantaneous and promotes defect prevention when workers are formally assigned the responsibility for inspecting their own quality. In that case, inspection is not a separate activity, but is rather built into the work methods and task descriptions at each operation. Quality is built, controlled and verified at the source, where mistakes are made and where quality is in fact created. Self checks recognize that even the best workers will and do make mistakes, but by building inspection into the work itself, errors do not get translated into defects for the subsequent operations. SECS are based on the observation that most mistakes do not become defects if they are promptly identified and corrected. Figure 8–10b shows the SECS system schematically. Products are passed on to the next operation only after they have undergone the mandatory inspection. Products that have errors are corrected at the producing work station. The problem that is causing defects are also immediately corrected.

The principles for designing and implementing self checks are the same as those for successive checks. However, SECS are both easier to implement and have higher motivational impact because they are not affected by the fears associated with SUCS. Workers usually do not resist the idea that they should have responsibility for their own quality and many are very favorable to it. SECS broaden worker involvement and autonomy, enrich the job, and instill pride of craftsmanship in factory employees. SECS communicate the subtle but powerful message that quality is an integral part of every job. Long-term use of self checks develops workers who have quality discipline and deep quality consciousness.

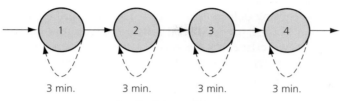

Self Checks (SECS)   FIGURE 8–10b

Feedback loop = 0 hour

Management attitudes and philosophies are the biggest barrier to implementing an SECS program. Most managers simply do not have the confidence that production workers can be taught to control their own quality or should be trusted to do so. The notion that plant employees are wholly untrustworthy, lazy, sloppy, and need to be closely supervised is still prevalent in North America. The assumptions of theory X and Taylorism lie hidden deep in the opaque recesses of the managerial mind, even when management overtly espouses the virtues of worker autonomy, involvement, and self-management. The armies of inspectors, staff, and technicians that are a standard fixture in the quality organization and hierarchy are convincing evidence that management does not have the confidence that workers can undertake full responsibility for the quality of their work, even if they are trained to do so. Unless management unshackles itself from the archaic principles of Taylorism, it will be unable to unleash the creative power of workers in the search for zero defects.

Early Warning Systems, Jidoka and Feed Forward SPC

Machines do not suddenly break down and defects seldom appear without warning. And when processes begin to produce defects it is because basic process operating variables such as temperature, pressure, and normal process deterioration caused by wear and tear have been allowed to drift outside of acceptable limits. Changes in the quality characteristics of inputs that are not adjusted for when the machine is being operated also cause the process to produce defects.

Early warning systems signal factors or problems that are known to cause defects at a particular process as far upstream of that process as possible. The basic goal is to correct the problem or situation before it impacts on the process or to adjust the process or operating method to cope with the identifiable variable. For example, the grinding time applied to a metal part can be increased or decreased to adjust for metal hardness. Experienced operators intuitively do this. Early warning systems can be combined with Jidoka—stop all work when there is a problem—to build a rigorous defect prevention system. Signals can be fed to downstream operations which try to adjust for the anticipated defect generation condition. The first time that the adjustment does not produce the desired quality, the whole process is stopped and the condition that is causing defects is removed. The same principle can be used to statistically control the process. Feed forward SPC adjusts process parameters not when characteristics of the product being made by the process go out of control, but when the input characteristics deviate significantly from ideal specifications. Feed forward SPC is extensively used in paper making operations. The process operating parameters such as roller speed, pressure, and temperature are adjusted not on the basis of the quality of the finished paper, but on the basis of the quality of the pulp. Feed forward SPC is the only statistical quality control tool which can prevent defects.

Machine Foolproofing and Poka Yoke[4]

Mistakes that are not promptly corrected will lead to defects being produced. One cannot prevent human beings from making errors, but machines can be designed so that they will not function unless they are operated properly or unless the right material is fed into them in the right way. Hundreds of foolproofing devices have been designed and tested, and this is not the place to detail them. Devices that prevent errors in machine functioning or operation are called Poka Yoke. They are often very inexpensive to design and install and instantly and automatically give zero defects, except on the rare occasions when the Poka Yoke device itself fails. Companies that want to produce near zero defects must implement an extensive foolproofing program, with the goal being to foolproof every machine that is amenable to being so designed or improved. Operations that have been foolproofed usually produce 1 per 100,000 defective, as a matter of course. In any event, defects produced by these machines can invariably be traced back to upstream operations. So, when successive and self checks, signal systems, Jidoka, source inspection, and feed forward SPC have been complemented with an extensive foolproofing program, the whole production system can attain defect rates of 1 per 100,000 or better.

Conclusion

The organizational will to reduce defects to near zero is born out of the corporate culture and value system and is sustained by the foundation quality concepts and the two supporting concepts, Takumi and waste elimination or Kaizen. Statistical quality control, while useful in reducing defects to the 1 per 100 or 1 per 1000 range, cannot be relied on to achieve zero defects. The pursuit of ever increasing quality requires that a company look for ways and technologies to reduce defects to barely measurable levels. Defect prevention

---

[4]Poka Yoke is a Japanese word which means mistake proofing.

systems become mandatory for those companies that want to achieve quality superiority. ZD is no longer a pipe dream, but a competitive necessity that has been brought about by the market forces born out of expanding globalization. World-class companies convert ZD into a practical production reality, and also make it one aspect of their competitive distinctiveness. The courage to think in terms of zero defects reflects strong competitive spirit and a penchant for challenging the competitive limits. It also indicates an overwhelming desire to motivate the organization toward the highest competitive ideals. Managers who implement programs aimed at reducing defects to zero stimulate their subordinates to push existing technology to its limits and to develop alternative technologies for bringing defect rates down. These managers implicitly communicate the idea that quality can and should always be improved. Adoption of zero defects as a corporate mission is tantamount to accepting the basic business principle that the company must deliver ever increasing value to its customers.

Case for Discussion

PLASTIC CONTAINERS, INC. (PCI)

Background

PCI started producing plastic tubing for the New England maple syrup industry in 1971. By 1985, it had added containers for the fishing, agricultural, food and beverage, automobile, and medical care industries. Sales were $62 million and profits $3.7 million in 1991. The company had 320 employees and a reputation as a high-quality, innovative, and service-oriented company. PCI was Q-1 supplier to a big-three car manufacturer. In 1983, the company started exporting its products to the Quebec maple syrup industry and the fishing industry in the Canadian maritime provinces.

The Process

PCI used the high-precision, semi-continuous injection molding process, in which plastic resins are injected into an automatically preheated mold with pressure and temperature kept constant during the injection cycle of 15 to 45 seconds. Once injection was completed, the mold was cooled with cold water, after which the product was automatically dislodged. The semi-finished product was either stocked or was sent directly to the printing department where the appropriate customer's labels were printed.

Emerging Competition

The competitive situation was getting difficult. The car parts segment was facing tough competition from manufacturers in South Korea and Japan. The South Koreans were particularly aggressive, offering customers a 20 percent price advantage and very good quality. The agricultural products segment was in decline as a result of declining North American catches and an increased penetration of the fish industry by foreign vessels. The medical segment was steadily losing market share to offshore manufacturers in Puerto Rico and Mexico as the quality of their products increased. While PCI held a clear advantage on quality, the gap between it and producers in Mexico and Puerto Rico was narrowing. Net profit margins decreased from 9 percent in 1986 to 6 percent in 1991.

The Innovative Climate at PCI

PCI had earned its reputation as an innovative company. It was one of the first plastic container manufacturers to implement statistical process control and to try to apply total quality control concepts throughout its organization. The company named a vice-president of quality in 1978 and developed a quality manual in 1979. It was at the forefront of its industry in using MRP-II in 1982, which helped decrease inventory from $7.6 million in 1982 to $5.2 million in 1984. On-time deliveries went from 72 percent to 96 percent during the same period. PCI installed AGVs in 1985, one of the first companies in its industry to use that technology. AGVs increased overall productivity and decreased throughout time and in-process inventories by 3.5 percent, 8 percent, and 30 percent respectively. In 1986, the company started implementing JIT concepts and had achieved a 60 percent reduction in set-up times within one year. JIT took hold quickly at PCI mainly because the company had encouraged decision making by consensus. In 1987, PCI became the first in the United States to use a Japanese supplier to produce some of its molds. Compared to U.S. fabricated ones, Japanese molds were 28 percent cheaper, were delivered in 9 weeks instead of the usual 12 taken by U.S. manufacturers, produced containers to one-half the tolerance and almost never cracked. Off-tolerance products and cracked molds accounted for roughly 55 percent of defects. The company was however reluctant to become entirely dependent on the Japanese for its supply of molds.

Responding to the Competitive Threat

Top management at PCI was determined to defend its market position and in 1990 started the process of searching for appropriate responses. Management soon realized that it would have to drive all costs down and push defect rates to near zero, be able to quote delivery times of one week instead of two, and increase productivity by 5 percent per year for at least the next five years. All the programs implemented so far would have to be intensified and innovation in processes, systems, methods, and products would have to be accelerated.

There was broad consensus among top management on the actions contemplated by the company. However, there was a sharp disagreement between the vice-president of production and the vice-president of quality as to how best to pursue zero defects. The vice-president of production thought that defect reduction depended largely on worker skill, motivation, discipline, and pride of workmanship. Process technology design and robustness were secondary. The best process, she intimated, could do little to drive defects to near zero, if the workers were not willing and able to use it. The vice-president of quality, on the other hand, argued that process engineering and design was the key factor in driving defects down and cited the experience with the Japanese molds to back his position.

Top management at PCI was eager to move into action to reinforce the company's competitive position. It had, however, never proceeded with actions that have such deep repercussions on the company's fortunes without broad consensus among the group.

Discussion Questions

1. How would you describe the competitive situation in PCI's market? What are the forces that are shaping competition?
2. Describe and evaluate the company's response to the competitive situation?
3. How can reliance on Japanese mold manufacturers impact on PCI's competitive position? Should the company increase its reliance on Japanese mold manufacturers?
4. What is the role of process technology versus worker management in pursuing zero defects?
5. What should PCI's top management do about the disagreement between the director of quality and the director of production?

References

Clark, Kim B., and Takahiro Fujimoto, "The Power of Product Integrity" in *Unconditional Quality,* Harvard Business Review Paperback, 1988.

Crosby, Philip, *Quality Is Free,* New York: McGraw-Hill, 1980.

Deming, Edwards W., *Quality, Productivity and Competitive Position,* Cambridge MA: Massachusetts Institute of Technology, Center for Advanced Engineering, 1982.

Ealey, Lance A., *Quality by Design: Taguchi Methods and U.S. Industry,* Dearborn, Mich.: ASI Press, 1988.

Feigenbaum, A. V., *Total Quality Control,* New York: McGraw-Hill, 1983.

Groocock, J. M., *The Chain of Quality,* New York: John Wiley and Sons, 1986.

Hauser, John R., and Don Clausing, "The House of Quality," *Harvard Business Review,* May–June 1988.

Juran, Joseph, and Frank M. Gryna, *Quality Planning and Analysis,* New York: McGraw-Hill, 1980.

Reicheld, Frederick F., and W. Earl Sasser, Jr., "Zero Defections: Quality Comes to Service," *Harvard Business Review,* September–October 1990.

Taguchi, Genichi, and Don Clausing, "Robust Quality," in *Unconditional Quality,* Harvard Business Review Paperback, 1988.

Small Lot Production and Kanban

For reasons discussed previously, Western companies, following the practices developed by the major North American manufacturers, have established large lot production as their manufacturing strategy. However, evidence has been presented that large lot production is inefficient and creates many problems. Its converse, small lot production, raises manufacturing performance to hitherto unachievable levels. Small lot production contributes to superior quality, cost, and delivery performance and results in large-scale improvement in production efficiency and effectiveness.

JIT aggressively pursues small lot production as an important manufacturing objective. The goal is not to achieve small lot production by decree, because top management cannot mandate that lots be small if it does not create the organizational environment and make the appropriate tools available for reducing lot sizes. Rather, the JIT objective is to manage the parameters, philosophies, and attitudes that create large lot production so that small lots become progressively more economical to produce. The last point must be emphasized. JIT seeks to make small lots financially, operationally, and strategically attractive. Small lots must make perfect strategic and marketing sense with respect to quality, cost, delivery, and flexibility. Only when this has been done can one say that manufacturing performance has been absolutely improved and the company's strategic market position has been better entrenched. JIT tries to reduce lot sizes until small lot production becomes the natural state, the accepted practice. The limit is achieved when the economic production lot size is one unit. The JIT goal is to create strategic, marketing, and operational advantage by drastically reducing production lot sizes. The improvement effort is directed toward attacking the constraints, attitudes, and philosophies that make large lot production attractive.

CHAPTER 9

SMALL LOT PRODUCTION AS MANUFACTURING STRATEGY

Large lot production is based on three premises. The first is that set-up times are high and add significantly to product cost. Secondly, it accepts set-up time and cost as absolute constraints. The reasoning is that if set-up time can be at

FIGURE 9–1 **The Operational and Strategic Links of Small Lot Production**

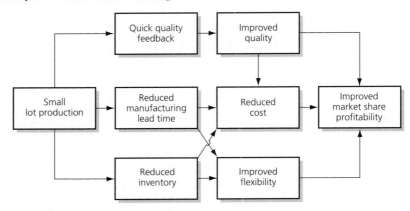

all reduced, the investment to do so would be higher than the savings generated. The third premise is that the only way to achieve reductions in set-up cost that can be perceived by customers and influence their buying behavior is to increase lot sizes to a level that will drive per unit set-up cost to almost zero. Large lot production is thus one element of an overall manufacturing strategy that pursues low cost as a strategic objective.

The reasoning behind large lot production as an element of manufacturing strategy is erroneous. Although set-up times are high, they are not an absolute constraint and can be reduced dramatically and with very little investment. Moreover, the hidden costs of large lot production are rarely considered in evaluating its validity as a component of manufacturing strategy. As was noted previously, large lot production increases inventory and obsolescence, lengthens manufacturing lead times, decreases quality and the potential for pursuing a product differentiation strategy, and reduces manufacturing flexibility. Small lot production is based on a completely different rationale.

The model of Figure 9–1 also underscores the operational and competitive value of systematic time compression and reinforces the conceptual validity of the time-based competition (TBC) paradigm. As set-up time is compressed, quality and flexibility increase and manufacturing lead time, inventory, and cost decrease. All these improvements improve the company's market share and profitability.

SET-UP TIME: THE VILLAIN IN SMALL LOT PRODUCTION

Companies generally maximize production lot sizes in an effort to drive per unit set-up cost close to zero. In so doing, they ignore very important countervailing costs such as inventory carrying charges, longer manufacturing cycle, and customer lead times, and costs associated with quality problems that are hidden by inventory. These companies are, on balance, adding costs by increasing lot sizes rather than decreasing them. Large lot production that is undertaken to reduce per unit set-up cost is a very costly production strategy. Often, there is no other logical basis for deciding on the lot size except that it minimizes per unit set-up cost. Long set-up times, in addition to conditioning managers to think in terms of large lot production and providing the rationale for increasing lot sizes, also decrease flexibility. The flexible production system must be able to switch production quickly in response to short-term fluctuations in demand and to changes in the product mix. Long set-up times are a major obstacle to quick market response. The design of a flexible production system requires that product changeover times be a negligible part of total production time.

The fundamental premise of small lot production is that set-up times and cost can be dramatically reduced by concerted and well-conceived managerial actions. Moreover, the experience of many companies, both in North America and Japan, shows that when all the benefits of small lot production are taken into consideration, well-targeted, set-up reduction programs can significantly ameliorate a company's competitive position. Small lot production is now widely accepted as a valid and potent building block of a company's manufacturing. The strategic and operational links that it fosters can extend deeply and broadly into any set of programs that aim to implement corporate and manufacturing strategy. The most important of these links are shown in Figure 9-1.

The Lot Sizing Model

A few companies try to take inventory carrying charges into consideration by applying the well-known economic order quantity model. Developed in the 1920s, the model attempts to optimize the costs associated with the lot size decision by modeling how total set-up costs and total inventory costs behave as lot sizes vary. The basic model is shown schematically in Figure 9-2 on the following page. As the lot size, Q, is increased, the average inventory, and therefore the total inventory holding cost, also increases. Similarly, increasing the production lot size decreases the number of set-ups and the total set-up cost, TSC. All costs are expressed here on an annual basis. Adding the two costs, THC and TSC, gives the total annual costs, TC, associated with any lot size. The total cost curve is minimized at Q*, the economic order quantity (EOQ), or optimal production lot size. It can easily be shown that the formula for computing Q* is given by the following expression:

$$Q^* = \sqrt{\frac{2 \times D \times S}{h}}$$

where

$\quad$ D = annual demand for the product or part
$\quad$ S = set-up cost to launch one lot
$\quad$ h = annual holding cost per unit
$\quad$ Q* = optimal batch size

FIGURE 9–2 The Lot Sizing Model

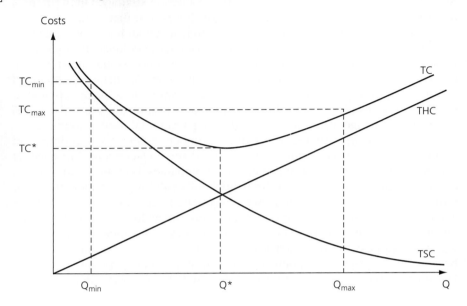

Given the cost parameters, no other batch size can give lower inventory cost. Although the EOQ model oversimplifies reality, it at least tries to incorporate two countervailing costs in the lot size decision. Hence, its application will give far better results than blindly pursuing large lot production so as to dilute set-up costs only. If management tries to produce the maximum lot size Q_{max} in order to reduce per unit set-up cost, then total costs, TC, increase substantially from TC_{min} to TC_{max}.

One should also note that if management tries to decrease lot sizes by mandate, without changing the fundamental cost structure, then the direct costs increase as is indicated by the model when the production lot size is reduced to Q_{min}. The indirect inventory costs will improve, but the overall cost position will not decrease as dramatically as if the cost structure is changed, thereby making small lots optimal. Q_{min} is a smaller lot size and may be better than Q^* when other, nonmeasurable costs are considered, but it is not an optimal lot size. But if one can drive the cost parameters lower as in Figure 9–3, and make Q^*_a the new optimal lot size, then, absolute superior performance will have been achieved. The nonmeasurable costs will have been decreased in tandem with the measurable direct costs incorporated in the model.

Figure 9–3 also gives some insight into how set-up cost reduction can be used as a major lever for achieving small lot production. Rather than arbitrarily increase the lot size in pursuit of reductions in per unit set-up cost, which

The Logic and Effect of Set-Up Cost Reduction   FIGURE 9–3

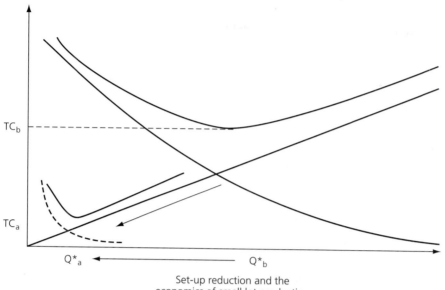

Set-up reduction and the
economics of small lot production

ironically add to total costs, one can drive set-up cost down and make small lot production economical. Driving the set-up curve down by more effective change-over management and continuous improvement reduces the economic lot size from Q^*_b to Q^*_a. The new, much smaller, lot size is economic, given the improved cost structure. The total cost associated with inventory has been reduced from TC_b to TC_a. A real, measurable, sustainable increase in financial and operating performance has been achieved as opposed to the artificial, illusory reduction in cost—per unit set-up cost—that comes from increasing the production lot size. Like the results achieved through set-up cost reduction, JIT attempts to make small lot production attractive by changing the underlying cost structure and exploiting the true economics of production lot sizing.

Promoting Small Lot Production via Set-Up Reduction: An Illustration

Table 9–1 gives some data that can be used to illustrate the concepts presented here. The lot size for each case, before and after set-up reduction, can be calculated using the simple EOQ formula. Before set-up reduction,

$$Q^* = \sqrt{\frac{2 \times 1800 \times 300}{6.00}}$$

$$= 450 \text{ units}$$

After set-up has been reduced from 3 hours to 0.08 hours or 5 minutes,

$$Q^* = \sqrt{\frac{2 \times 1800 \times 8}{6.00}}$$

$$= 70 \text{ units}$$

All the remaining calculations are shown in Table 9–1. They can be used to evaluate the impact that a change like the one presented can have on the performance of the business.

DERIVING STRATEGIC LEVERAGE FROM SMALL LOT PRODUCTION

The Operational Impact

The most obvious impact (as shown in Table 9–1) is the reduction in measurable inventory costs from $2550 to $420, for a $2130 saving. While this may

TABLE 9–1	Before Set-Up Reduction	After Set-Up Reduction
1. Annual demand (units)	1,800	1,800
2. Unit price (cost)	$20	$20
3. Inventory holding cost (%)	30	30
4. Inventory holding cost per unit (2) × (3)	$6	$6
5. Set-up time (hours)	3	0.08
6. Set-up cost per hour	$100	$100
7. Set-up cost per set-up (5) × (6)	$300	$8
8. Lot size, Q* (units)	450	70
9. Average inventory (units) (8) × 1/2	225	35
10. Number of set-ups (1) ÷ 8	4	26
11. Total annual holding cost (9) × (4)	$1,350	$210
12. Total annual set-up cost (10) × (7)	$1,200	$210
13. Total annual cost (11) + (12)	$2,550	$420

appear to be modest, it would generate a substantial cash flow when extended to all products and parts. If the product described in Table 9–1 is representative for a company that is producing 100 different products and parts then it would reap savings totalling $213,000 annually, on a permanent basis, by reducing lot sizes to the extent done in the illustrative example. Again, if one considers the product used in Table 9–1 to be an average one, such a company would be generating approximately $6,000,000 in sales and $300,000 in net profits assuming a net profit margin of 5 percent. The cash flow generated by small lot production is almost equal to the entire annual profit. Superior cash flow performance in this case derives from improvement in inventory turns. Again taking our example to be representative of what can be achieved companywide, overall inventory turns would go from 8 (1800 ÷ 225) to 51.4 (1800 ÷ 35). Some world-class companies have demonstrated that it is entirely feasible to turn inventories 100, 200, or even 300 times per year.

Higher inventory turns mean less obsolescence because how fast inventory turns over measures how long materials and products are kept before they are used, and therefore, how likely they are to deteriorate. Before set-up reduction, in our example, an item was being kept in inventory for 13 weeks on the average, before being used or sold. With small lot production, the time an item is held shrinks to 2 weeks, a clear improvement particularly for highly innovative or fashion sensitive, short shelf life items. One can immediately see that market-forecast inaccuracy creates few problems when small lot production is the norm. When a product is being scheduled for production four times a year or every 13 weeks, there could be visceral forecasting problems. For one thing, demand must be forecast for at least 13 weeks in advance, as opposed to just 2 weeks as in our example. Any marketing manager knows that forecast accuracy will be much better when the forecast horizon is shrunk from 13 weeks to 2. For another, forecast error can be more easily accommodated when small lot production is practiced. Where a product is being scheduled four times a year, production can be normally adjusted to demand every 13 weeks. During that period stockouts invariably result if demand is greater than forecast and excess inventory occurs when demand is less than forecast. For the two-week, small lot production cycle, production can be adjusted to demand every two weeks and forecast error is a minor problem. Small lot production makes it easy to adjust production to demand. Figure 9–4 shows the idea. The difference between production and demand is great for large lot production but almost negligible when small lots are the standard. Small lot production gives the flexibility to respond to a changing sales pattern and to cope with the inevitable forecast errors. Too many so-called MRP-II gurus in North America clamor ceaselessly for better, near-perfect forecast from marketing without recognizing that the production system must also be made flexible enough to execute a forecast that is bound to be erroneous. As the Chinese sages have said "prediction is a very difficult art,

FIGURE 9–4a **Large Lot Production Strategy**

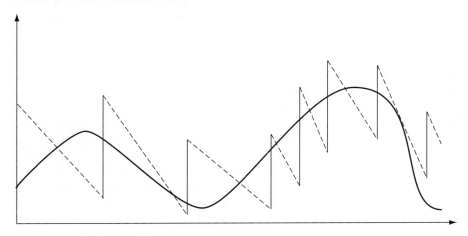

FIGURE 9–4b **Small Lot Production Strategy**

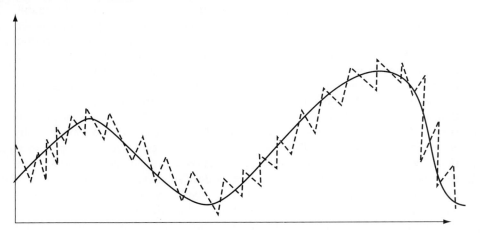

especially with respect to the future." Difficulties created by erroneous forecasts are as much a production as a marketing problem. Herein lies a fundamental problem with MRP-II. It is almost exclusively a planning and control tool and was not designed to deal with execution problems on the factory floor. Plans are to be executed, otherwise they are useless. Small lot production, by way of set-up reduction, modifies the execution system and gives the potential to flexibly execute plans and sales forecasts.

Changeovers are more frequent in small lot production which increases set-up learning. Set-up personnel are more likely to master changeovers and to do it right the first time, if they do them very often. A positive cycle is created whereby set-up time reduction improves learning which further helps to decrease set-up time. There have been cases where merely increasing changeover frequency without applying any major set-up reduction tools and techniques have generated incredible results. One major North American manufacturer of personal hygiene paper products started a JIT implementation project. One particular machine in the plant required eight hours to changeover, and no reduction was achieved in the prior ten years. When asked why they needed eight hours to do the changeover on that machine, set-up personnel gave the usual, automatic response, "it has always been this way." Changeovers on the machine were done every six weeks, that is, the production run was six weeks demand. Production planners decided, arbitrarily, to do changeovers every week in a desperate effort to start progress toward small lot production. After four months, to everyone's great surprise, the average set-up time went down to three hours, for a 63 percent reduction. Companies that start to do small lot production can come to develop it into an art form.

Lower set-up times mean better machine and capacity utilization. The data in Table 9–1 show a 10-hour saving due to set-up reduction from 4 set-ups at 3 hours each to 26 set-ups at 0.08 hours each, for a 0.5 percent increase in capacity assuming that there are 2,000 hours of capacity per year. Again this may appear to be negligible but for a $50,000,000 company, it is equivalent to being able to increase sales by $250,000 without additional physical capacity.

Strategic Marketing Impact

Significant lead time reduction can be derived from small lot production, and this is well born out by Table 9–1. One will recall that the lead time that can be promised to customers is given by the formula,

$$L_t = Q_t + M_t + P_t$$

where,

L_t = lead time
Q_t = queue time
M_t = move time
P_t = production time per batch (lot)

Ignoring move time, since it is usually negligible, assuming that the Q_t percentage is 90 percent as in most cases where large lot production prevails and 20 percent for small lot production, and that time per piece is 0.10 hours, one

TABLE 9-2	Lead Time and Small Lot Production		
		Lot size = 450	Lot size = 70
Total production time		45 hours	7.0 hours
Q-time percentage		90	20
Q-time		405	1.8
Total lead time		450 hours	8.8 hours
Lead time (days)		56 days	1 day

arrives at the following results as shown in Table 9–2. The lead time has been shrunk from 56 days to 1 day. If customers tolerated a 56-day lead time before and the product can now be made in 1 day, the selling company can literally make what has been sold, just in time. The producer has a 55-day margin to plan and schedule production, buy materials, and still be in a position to deliver on time. Besides, a much shorter lead time can be easily accommodated, permitting the producer to vary the lead time so as to smooth production. Flexible lead times, production leveling, and very low inventories are all related and compatible.

Market niches that were hitherto considered too small can now be profitably exploited. Using the data in Table 9–1, and assuming demand to be 360 units per year, gives 31 units as the lot size. The set-up time per unit equals 0.17 minutes or 10 seconds which is 60 percent lower than the per unit set-up time when set-up time is 3 hours and the lot is 450 units. One company had a similar experience. The company makes injection molded plastic products for both industrial and household use. The set-up time for the typical injection machine is about 4 hours. For a long time, the company had designed and tried to market a small line of specialty household products but the demand seemed to be too low to make the venture profitable. By implementing a set-up reduction program, machine changeover was reduced to 15 minutes, making it attractive to produce the specialty items on a purely make-to-order basis. After only 3 years, specialty items account for 6 percent of sales and 11 percent of profits. Set-up reduction allows the company to systematically change from make-to-stock, anticipatory production to a make-to-order, just-in-time strategy. The production system, which usually is a barrier to achieving product differentiation becomes a tool for increasing product variety and broadening market scope.

But the biggest impact of the set-up reduction presented in Table 9–1 is that much inventory has been squeezed out, thereby increasing problem visibility. Machine reliability and in-process defects create crises in the system, putting pressure on managers and workers to solve them, once and for all. When there is little or no inventory, problems that went hitherto unnoticed

Lot Sizes and the Feedback Loop   FIGURE 9–5

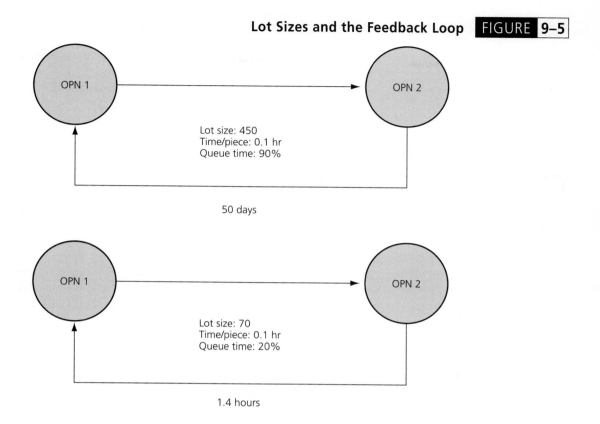

Lot size: 450
Time/piece: 0.1 hr
Queue time: 90%

50 days

Lot size: 70
Time/piece: 0.1 hr
Queue time: 20%

1.4 hours

now shut the entire production system down, which makes the existence of a problem visible to all, even to the most apathetic worker. Plant managers can no longer hide inferior machine maintenance practices and poor quality workmanship under mountains of inventory. Based on the example in Table 9-2, the production time for the entire batch is 7.0 hours and the queue time is 20 percent. A defect that is produced at one operation is discovered 1 day later as opposed to 56 days for the case where the lot size is 450. This makes it possible to quickly identify and correct the problem and produce some units trouble free. Even without flow systematization and process integration, substantial defect reduction would be realized. Figure 9–5 compares the feedback loop for two lot sizes. Reducing the lot size reduces the feedback loop from 50 days to 1.4 hours. In the latter case, only 14 units would be produced before the problem becomes visible, while in the first case, the entire lot would have already been produced and the first unit would have been completed 50 days before. Clearly, rigorous defect prevention requires that small lot production be the norm.

TABLE 9–3	Hood and Fender Press Comparison (800 ton press)			
	Toyota	**U.S.A.**	**Sweden**	**W. Germany**
Set-up time	8 minutes	8 hours	4 hours	4 hours
Set-ups per day	3	1	—	1/2
Lot size	1 day	10 days	1 month	—

TABLE 9–4	Set-Up Reduction at Jidosha Kiki Corp.		
Set-Up Time	**1976**	**1977**	**1980**
>60 min.	30%	0	0
30–60 min.	19%	0	0
20–30 min.	26%	10%	3%
10–20 min.	20%	12%	7%
5–10 min.	5%	20%	12%
100 sec.–5 min.	0	17%	16%
<100 sec.	0	41%	62%

Some Accomplishments in Set-Up Reduction

The data on which the illustrative example in Table 9–1 is based reduced set-up from 3 hours to 0.08 hours (five minutes). The reduction factor is 36. At first sight, such a decrease may appear to be totally unrealistic, but when viewed against the background of what some leading, world-class companies have achieved, they are seen to be entirely feasible. Table 9–3 shows that Toyota has reduced set-ups by a factor of 60 when compared with its North American counterparts. Table 9–4 which gives the results for Jidosha Kiki Corporation in Japan is even more impressive. In just four years, the company was able to so dramatically reduce machine changeover time, that 78 percent of set-ups took less than 5 minutes and 62 percent less than 100 seconds. It should also be emphasized that Toyota is changing over the same machine as its North American competitors, but in 1/60 of the time. A North American automobile manufacturer, by doing one 8-hour set-up every 10 days, loses 1 hour of productive time per day. Toyota could produce a similar product six times per day, and yet have better equipment utilization and higher productivity. WIP inventory at Toyota would also be much lower, and the company would reap all the benefits of small lot production. Toyota turns WIP inventory 300 times per year, while the average North American company can barely achieve 30 turns. Small lot production enables Toyota to drive costs down, while improving quality and flexibility.

Set-Up Reduction Principles and Technology

The drive to reduce the set-up time (and thus cost) of an operation aims at the ultimate objective of doing set-ups in a single minute. When this goal is achieved, the production system can economically operate in a one-piece-at-a-time mode, where the production lot size at each phase of the operation is one unit. Each worker can physically hand each unit to the worker at the succeeding operation, and production can be done continuously, one piece at a time. Conveyors and most other transportation equipment can be a practically eliminated except where the product is too bulky or complex to be manually transferred from one operation to another. Physical process integration can be envisaged. Eliminating in-process inventories saves factory space that is usually used for stocking parts between operations, the major reason why transfer equipment is needed. In addition to the above positive effects, single minute set-up allows the company to economically pursue a mixed-model processing strategy, since the changeover from one model to the next is negligible. The following table shows that a production run of 1000 for five models is more economical than a run of 1000 for a single model when set-up is reduced from 90 minutes to the single-digit level. This would considerably reduce set-up time per unit:

	Before Set-Up Reduction	Single Digit Set-Up
Set-up time/set-up (minutes)	90	9
Production run	1000	1000
No. of models	1	5
No. of set-ups	1	5
Total set-up time (minutes)	90	45
Production/Model (units)	1000	200
Set-up time/Unit (minutes)	0.09	0.045

The groundwork for set-up reduction is laid by first applying tested general management principles. Set-up reduction must be sustained over the long haul, and this requires that management cultivate the vision, attitudes, and organizational philosophies that will give impetus to the project. There is a radical shift in attitude and manufacturing strategy and policies that is called for by any meaningful, long-term set-up reduction program and techniques and their application cannot bring about such change. Set-up reduction technology comes alive when the appropriate managerial principles are well understood by key operating managers. The technology is important but the management processes, attitudes, and philosophies are paramount. Toyota Motor Company started changing its view on set-ups as far back as the early 1960s. Nearly 30 years later, the push for set-up reduction continues unabated, even though most changeovers are well within the single-digit range. The foundation principles were solid, and so, they withstood the wear and tear of time. Too many managers and JIT experts overlook that quintessential point.

The Basic Principles

Single-digit set-up (SDS) is the goal. Kaizen, systematic and continuous waste elimination, and Takumi, the perpetual search for improvement and the pursuit of perfection are the motive force. Companies that are attaining massive decreases in set-up nurture an internal environment where the search for excellence is valued and they bring their employees to view quick changeovers as a vital aspect of competition and customer-driven improvement. Managerial action to achieve single-digit set-ups is fed by the desire to challenge the conventional wisdom that changeovers are long and cannot be reduced. Anyone will admit that it takes boldness, courage, and an incredible drive to excel to push changeover times from 8 hours to 8 minutes and to still have the ambition to aim higher. And a top management that nurtures the motivational environment that sustains such an endeavor has learned how to tap the limits of human creative potential. When the organizational value system is right, the technology will be harnessed. If the technology is not available, then it will be created by that very same organization, as long as it is humanly possible.

Building on Kaizen and Takumi, there are a few steps that every company will have to go through to make set-up reduction an integral part of the overall improvement process:

1. *Recognize that set-up time, no matter how short, is a problem.* In most companies, set-up is viewed as normal and set-up personnel are classified as productive labor. The surest way to kill any attempt to reduce the time required to do changeovers is to classify them as necessary, normal, and cast in stone. The reality is that long set-ups, because they are a major cause of inventory and its attendant negative impact on quality and the pursuit of excellence in production/operations, are a significant strategic problem for many companies. Moreover, high set-up times result in lost production time and limit the range of products that can be economically produced by the

plant. It is also evident that by forcing management to lengthen production runs so as to make the cost penalty associated with set-up bearable, long set-ups increase the lead time that a company can reasonably promise its customers. The first step in set-up reduction is for management to recognize and define long set-ups as a significant problem. This is the view of set-up time adopted in JIT and this is what motivates and sustains the drive for its eventual elimination by world-class manufacturing companies.

2. *Evaluate the strategic and operational impact of set-up reduction.* Even a modest attempt to do this will reveal enormous strategic leverage from a systematic set-up reduction program. Some advantages are qualitative in nature while others, such as the reduction in inventory levels, can be quantified. There are two levels to this analysis. The first will use actual set-up times, actual performance on important dimensions such as manufacturing lead time, the quality feedback loop, capacity utilization, and per unit set-up time and compare these with estimated performance using a target for set-up time based on the improvement in set-up time reduction that JIT companies are experiencing. This analysis will show management that the project is worth pursuing beyond the purely academic level and will be a major catalyst for implementing a small pilot study. At the second level, an actual department is selected for implementing a set-up reduction program. Typically, such a department should be small to ensure program manageability and should have good potential for set-up reduction. At the end of the pilot study, there should be conclusive evidence that set-up reduction is feasible and would result in substantial strategic and operational advantages.

3. *Observe, study, and describe set-up procedures and practices.* The initial dramatic reductions in set-up time invariably come from eliminating flaws in set-up procedure and practices. These reductions can be as high as 90 percent. Inconsistencies and flaws in procedures and practices usually derive from their piecemeal development and absence of standard operating instructions to be followed by set-up personnel. In the very few companies where these standards exist, there is no follow-up and periodic retraining to reinforce adherence to them. Methods for studying set-up procedures range from informal, instantaneous observation to the more sophisticated filming of key set-up personnel with movie cameras.

4. *Identify activities that have high potential for improvement.* These could be those activities that account for the biggest chunk of total elapsed set-up time, which could be made visible using pie charts, or those activities that, at first sight, appear to have high potential for improvement.

5. *Establish objectives for set-up improvement.* The basic Kaizen principle in JIT recognizes the need to emphasize improvement of the operation. Generally speaking, it is desirable to aim for modest improvement initially, except where major flaws in existing set-up management justify an ambitious objective. There is not likely to be improvement in set-up execution,

unless there is a clear improvement objective. In accordance with management by objectives, the participation of set-up people and employees facilitates the drive toward set-up reduction. A modest initial objective helps employees internalize the fact that set-up reduction is feasible.

6. *Describe, document, train set-up personnel to use and implement new set-up procedures, and monitor results.* The critical point is the training of employees in the new procedure. To facilitate this without disrupting continuity of operations, it is often desirable to reserve time outside of normal working hours for practicing the new procedure. This also reduces the pressure put on employees who are learning new techniques and practices.

7. *Do follow-up and continual training to keep the momentum going.* Reporting mechanisms should be put in place so as to monitor progress and ensure that gains are permanently maintained. Small group improvement activities to broadcast and share achievements build a supporting culture for long-run progress. Set-ups have a tendency to become long if they are simply left alone. Striving for improvement is the only way to counteract inertia and retrogression.

SINGLE MINUTE EXCHANGE OF DIE (SMED)[1]

Toyota Motor Company with assistance from Mr. Shigeo Shingo pioneered the search for techniques and procedures that can reduce set-ups to the single digit range. SMED comes from the conviction that it will be eventually possible to achieve changeovers in one minute. SMED evolved from a set of well-defined and tested practices for achieving sustained and substantial reduction in set-up time. The basic practices have been well documented by Shingo and others. SMED is based on many years of experience in set-up reduction and is a systematic, logical, and scientific method for achieving it. Before we proceed to discuss the three basic SMED principles, it is worthwhile to define the two supporting concepts, inside exchange of die (IED) and outside exchange of die (OED). OED is made up of those set-up elements/activities that are done while the machine (process) is still producing parts. IED, on the other hand, are those activities that are performed when the machine or process is stopped. The critical step in set-up reduction is to make sure that the actual IED activities are those that are totally necessary, that is, the machine is stopped only when it must be in order to execute necessary IED activities. Set-up preparation and planning activities such as set-up tool and parts requisition and transportation (movement) are legitimate OED activities. However,

---

[1]Shigeo Shingo , *Toyota Production System from Industrial Engineering Viewpoint* (Japan Management Association, 1981), and *A Revolution in Manufacturing: The SMED System* (Tokyo, Japan: Japan Management Association, 1983).

most companies stop the machine even before the set-up preparation work is complete due to poor set-up planning and scheduling.

The difference between OED and IED can be fully grasped by using the Indy 500 as a reference point. Current technology and the rigors of the race require that the driver come in from the track for changing tires and refilling the gas tank. Now imagine the following scenario. A driver comes into the changing bay, and the lone set-up man is not present. A one-half hour search finds him in the coffee lounge taking a break. He continues to drink his hot beverage, which takes 15 minutes and walks to the service area to find out what's the problem. After inspecting the car for another 15 minutes, he comes to the conclusion that a tire change is warranted. He goes to the parts area and discovers that there are five different tire types and he spends 5 minutes, searching for the right one. He then makes his way with the tires and the tools that he thinks he needs to do the job. On arriving at the service bay with the tires and the tools he starts to make the change, one tire at a time. Upon installing the fourth tire, a "quick" inspection shows it to be defective. The three tires have taken him 2 minutes each to change, for a total of 6 minutes. He goes back to the parts area for another tire, consuming another 5 minutes. The fourth tire is changed, 2 more minutes have passed, and he is all set to give the go signal when someone reminds him that the tank needs to be filled as well. The whole process is repeated, and with luck—a lot of luck—the changeover will be completed in 2 hours, by which time the whole race would be over.

This description may appear to be an exaggeration, but it accurately describes what takes place in almost every North American manufacturing company. The race is not the Indy 500 but the battle for world market dominance. The task is not changing tires but machine set-up. North American companies are locked into a gruelling battle for world markets and are increasingly getting going when the race is already over. Industries where North American enterprise were once the juggernauts, such as electronics, textiles, clothing, steel, automobiles, pharmaceuticals, and petrochemicals, are falling like dominos under the onslaught of better Asian and European companies. The changeover time and how it is planned, controlled, organized, and executed reveals managerial acumen or organizational sclerosis.

What actually happens in the Indy 500 is as follows: There is a team that enters the race and it includes the driver and all of his or her support people. Based on the best technical information, the team knows how many laps will expire before a changeover is required. They also know how much time is required to prepare and execute the changeover. At the appropriate time, and before the driver comes in, they go through the changeover drill. All parts and tools are checked, once, twice, three times. There is specialization of function, one person for each basic task. When everything is ready in the service bay, the driver comes in, and with perfect coordination and synchronization, the entire activity set-up is executed in 8 seconds. All preparation was done

FIGURE **9-6**   **OED vs. IED**

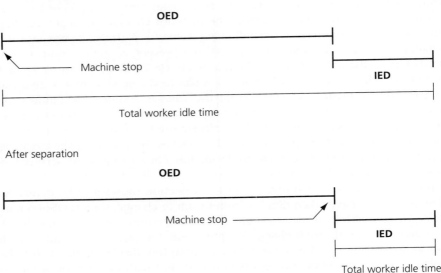

prior to the changeover. These are the OED activities. The 8 seconds are the IED tasks. Craftsmanship brought to bear on the problem reduces the time by orders of magnitude. The 8 second time results from knowing what is to be done, mastering how to do it by practice and training, tight planning and control, and then absolute coordination and execution without a hitch. What this does for the Indy 500 team, SMED aims to do for set-ups.

The SMED Principles

SMED technology can be distilled into four core principles that have evolved from the practices developed and applied by Toyota. They were designed to highlight and attack the inefficiencies that result in long set-up times.

Separate OED from IED

The basic idea is shown in Figure 9–6. All OED activities are bunched together and are executed separately from all IED tasks, even if they are done by the same person. Machine availability and worker productive time are both increased.

Separating IED from OED involves studying the set-up procedure phase by phase and element by element so as to classify these as to whether they are preparatory to the set-up or are an integral part of the set-up itself. The goal here is to group all OED activities together so that these can be isolated and screened from the set-up and performed prior to machine stoppage. In the vast majority of cases, the set-up time can be reduced by up to 60 percent by this simple bunching of OED activities and their performance prior to machine stoppage. One should note that the total set-up time is the same, but only the IED activities result in unproductive labor and machine time, which represent the real cost impact of set-up time. The time spent by set-up personnel is a fixed cost which is negligible compared to unproductive machine and labor cost. In JIT, the guiding principle is that idle time is waste and should be avoided as much as possible. The separation of IED from OED is one of the first moves in the elimination of idle time of production workers caused by poor set-up planning.

Set-up planning is the key to eliminating unproductive time caused by OED activities. In most companies, the standard practice is to begin all set-up activities after the last piece of the current production run has been produced. The impact on unproductive time is shown in Figure 9–6. The SMED practice, on the other hand, is to time production of the last piece so that it coincides with the end of the OED activities. This can be done if execution of the OED activities begins well before production of the last piece. The result is that unproductive time is limited to the IED activities by overlapping OED activities and production of the last pieces of the current run. This arrangement is entirely feasible since production and set-up are usually done by different people, thus allowing the OED activities to be executed while the last few units are being produced.

Move IED to OED

IED activities stop production while the OED ones do not. Therefore, it is absolutely essential that steps be taken to convert IED to OED. The methods used to bring this about are as varied as the machines involved. However, they all involve preperformance of some IED activities, leaving only what cannot be done in advance to postmachine stoppage. Moving IED to OED can reduce set-up time by as much as 20 percent. Some useful ideas follow:

1. *Premounting as many parts as possible.* A set-up may involve attaching ten different parts to each other and to the machine. Some premounting could create two subassemblies that can be hooked to the machine, making the IED much shorter.
2. *Using rollers and platforms to facilitate die mounting.* It requires minor engineering modifications of machines, tooling, and fixtures so that IED set-up elements can now be performed while the machine is still running. For example, by providing an extra platform on a punch press and equipping it with rollers, a die can be placed at the appropriate level without stopping the machine.
3. *Preheating dies for trial shots on die-casting machines.* This reduces the heating time after the die is set and also reduces the number of units scrapped before good quality is produced and production begins in earnest.

Make IED More Efficient

Once the IED activities have been reduced to the bare minimum, steps can be taken to improve the efficiency with which the true IED activities are executed. Vital information is provided by repeatedly studying, observing, and analyzing IED to uncover flaws in methods and procedure. A company which has arrived at this stage should seriously consider further describing, documenting, and filming the set-up activities. Major actions to improve IED execution include parallel execution by a team—the four tires in the race track example are replaced simultaneously while gas is being put into the tank—and mistake proofing (foolproofing) jigs and fixtures to eliminate error. Mistakes result in duplicated effort and wasted motion. Training set-up personnel so that they totally master the changeover is vital to efficiently executing IED activities. Performing IED more competently so that it becomes a craft will reduce set-up time by an additional 10 percent.

Eliminate Adjustment

It is not unusual for adjustments to consume 5 to 7 percent of IED, so that by eliminating them, one can achieve further reduction in set-up time. Adjustments should be separated from settings. Settings are the first position the tool is placed in, while adjustments are the fine tuning that takes place after setting. A machine could be equipped with gauges, for example, so that the setting and adjusting are integrated, thus eliminating the adjusting altogether. When a machine has been equipped for automatic setting and adjusting, one-touch set-up becomes feasible.

Applying the four core SMED principles could help a company achieve a 95 to 97 percent reduction in set-up time, and at this stage, nearly every set-up would have been reduced to the single-digit range. Small lot production would then be fully operational giving WIP turns of 150 or more. Further mastery of changeovers can then only come about by engineering and selecting machines that are either designed to be easily changed over or to require no set-up at all. In the latter category one would find FMS's (flexible manufacturing systems) and CNC (computer numerical control) machines. These systems allow "changeovers" to be machine programmed and commanded, allowing switching from one product to the next to be done automatically. Set-up time is zero and does not require that labor be used in the process. Parts in an FMS can be scheduled in purely mixed-model mode and the schedule itself can be changed in seconds.

SDS-SMED and Repetitive Production

Consistent quality and very high efficiency are the hallmarks of continuous, uninterrupted production. As management constantly improves and fine tunes the production system, the factory will naturally evolve toward the stability, consistency, and predictability that characterizes repetitive production.

Small lot production is an intermediate phase. Production lot size reduction is in itself movement toward more repetitive production. A product that has an economic lot size that covers demand for six weeks is being produced intermittently. Cutting the lot size down to one day's demand represents a big improvement toward repetitive production. When set-up time has been reduced to the single-digit range so that the process can be "kanbanized" and production takes place six or even ten times a day, then production is essentially repetitive. Attaining SMED usually means that production can be done one piece at a time and the system need not differentiate between different options of the same product. A one minute set-up is as short as the shortest cycle time in many assembly operations, so that the changeover appears as just one more operation. Where this has occurred, the system is repetitive. The entire differentiated product line can be treated as one standardized product. Single digit or one-touch set-ups can be productively done by production workers, further making them an integral, undifferentiable part of the operation. Single-digit set-ups (SDS) and SMED allow a company to implement repetitive production in hitherto intermittent, large lot operations. The company can simultaneously reap the benefits of standardization and differentiation. SDS merge standardization and differentiation into a powerful, production-deployed, competitive strategy.

INVERTING THE SCHEDULING LOGIC

Companies that have progressed to single-digit set-ups (SDS) or single minute exchange of dies (SMED) can use that expertise to create more strength in manufacturing operations. One place that SMED can be very advantageously used is in production scheduling. The scheduling system is usually isolated from the execution in traditional production management practice, since those who are preparing the schedule are different from those who are executing or producing to meet it. In addition, the scheduling systems in general use have no production or quality control mechanisms built into them, thereby making them useless in creating problem visibility and in performance improvement. The scheduling system in JIT is explicitly integrated with execution and it is designed to exert automatic control on production and quality, by making schedule execution problems visible. Moreover, the scheduling logic in JIT will implement the Andon (automatic stoppage) principle or Jidoka (manual stoppage) when there is a problem in the scheduling mechanisms themselves.

The Push Scheduling Logic

The traditional scheduling system applies a push logic in developing and executing the schedule. The central concepts on which the push schedule is

FIGURE 9–7   **Push Scheduling Logic**

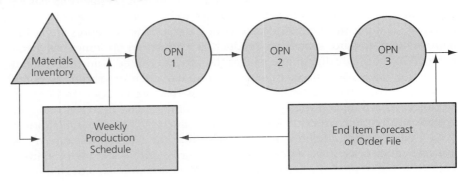

based are shown in Figure 9–7. An end item sales forecast or order file is converted into a weekly production plan, often referred to as the master production schedule (MPS). Before the MPS is released to the factory for execution, its validity is verified by evaluating whether estimated capacity and materials requirements will be available for every week in the schedule. Capacity requirements for each work center are estimated on a weekly basis. If capacity and materials are judged to be sufficient for each week in the schedule, it is sent to the plant for execution. Schedule formulation and execution are separated organizationally and conceptually. Organizational separation exists because the people who formulate the schedule are not responsible for its execution and the process usually does not have an instantaneous feedback and automatic adjustment mechanism that ties the two together. There is conceptual separation because the schedule formulation time frame is totally different from the execution time frame. This latter point is crucial to understanding the fundamental weaknesses of the push scheduling logic.

When the schedule is capacity validated, the scheduler looks at available weekly capacity at each work center. The assumption is that if weekly capacity is sufficient, the schedule is doable. Based on anticipatory production thinking, the schedule is released starting with the first operation with the expectation that it will be executed or "cut" one phase at a time. The schedule will be "pushed" through Operation 1, then Operation 2 and 3 in perfect, uninterrupted sequence, the scheduler expects and herein lies the problem. The MPS is planned using available weekly capacity for all machine work centers, but it is executed on an hour-by-hour basis, one work center at a time. If the prior estimated available capacity for all work centers materializes on an hour-by-hour basis in each work center, there will be no problem and the MPS will be executed as planned. But this is evidently totally unrealistic. Work center capacity varies hourly due to defects, different work center efficiencies, and other problems, which make a schedule that is planned on a weekly basis wrong when one looks at what is dynamically taking place every hour during actual execution in the plant. When a bottleneck or any other capacity-reducing problem occurs at any work center, the schedule is still pushed through, which causes WIP to increase. Pushing a planned schedule through just because it was planned and even though it cannot be realistically executed solves not a single problem and creates many. Where a bottleneck exists, no amount of pushing, or even shoving for that matter, will make the schedule come out, and is likely to create nervousness which causes quality and efficiency to deteriorate. The push scheduling logic has no built-in control mechanism to shut the production system down when there is a problem—the Andon or Jidoka principle—and cannot dynamically adjust the schedule to an ever changing execution situation. So, push scheduling fails to exploit four important avenues for improving an operation. It is neither sound production control nor good execution. Furthermore, it does not aid in making execution problems visible and creates WIP inventory. In addition production is scheduled on an anticipatory basis, which is counter to JIT. Pushing the schedule through produces in anticipation that there will be a need instead of producing when the true need exists at the final operation (OPN 3).

The Pull Scheduling Logic

The ingredients that are necessary to implement a pull scheduling logic are shown in Figure 9–8. The goal is to eliminate the weaknesses of the push schedule by tightly integrating scheduling with execution and building automatic adjustment and stoppage (Andon/Jidoka) mechanisms into the process. As usual, a planned schedule is created, and its validity is determined by

Pull Scheduling Logic   FIGURE **9–8**

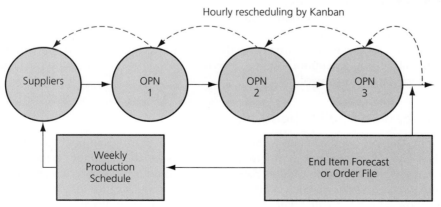

Hourly rescheduling by Kanban

estimating anticipated, available weekly capacity for all work centers. The schedule is simply used to put into place enough capacity to produce the sales forecast or order file. Schedule execution, on the other hand, begins just-in-time, when the need for shipping the customer or warehouse order is felt at the last operation. At that moment, a small quantity of parts is pulled from Operation 2 and Operation 3 emits a production signal using Kanban. The pull signal on Operation 2 is an order for it to replenish the small quantity of parts that have just been used, and to do this, it in turn must pull a small quantity of parts from Operation 1, which becomes an order for that work center to replenish the inventory that has just been pulled.

Pull scheduling adjusts the MPS to hourly execution realities on the shop floor as follows: Suppose the MPS had planned 100 units per hour on the expectation that the minimum capacity at all work centers will be 100 units per hour, that is, the estimated planned capacity at the bottleneck operation is 100 units per hour or 4000 units per week, assuming a 40-hour work week. Now, if a problem at Operation 3 temporarily reduces available capacity to 50 units per hour, then that operation can only pull 50 parts from Operation 2, since execution starts when parts are pulled through by Operation 3, the 50 units are the production order for Operation 2. To produce an order of 50, Operation 2 must pull 50 parts from Operation 1, which become the production order for that operation to replenish 50 parts. The capacity at Operation 1 may be 100 per hour and 125 per hour at Operation 2, but at that specific point in time and based on a real execution constraint, all three operations are producing 50 units per hour. The pull schedule has automatically adjusted to the actual execution potential, no matter what the plan. Some might say that this is wasteful, but it is actually the most efficient way to produce, given the problem at Operation 3. Producing 100 units per hour at Operations 1 and 2 solves nothing, because production cannot exceed the capacity at the bottleneck operation. No matter how much pushing is done, only 50 units will be produced until the problem is solved. Push scheduling would only add 50 units per hour to WIP inventory. The pull logic slows down the process to create idle time at Operations 1 and 2, making the bottleneck problem visible and liberating workers at these two work centers to help quickly solve the problem at Operation 3. Inverting the scheduling logic perfectly integrates scheduling and execution with powerful consequences for manufacturing performance and control.

Kanban and Pull Scheduling

Pull is the logic and Kanban is the regulating mechanism. Kanban is so vital to the scheduling process in JIT that it is necessary to accurately understand what it is, how it works, and its role in the scheduling and execution system.

Kanban means visible record and its goal is to make the just-in-time production schedule totally executable and visible to those who are executing it.

A Sample Kanban Card FIGURE 9–9

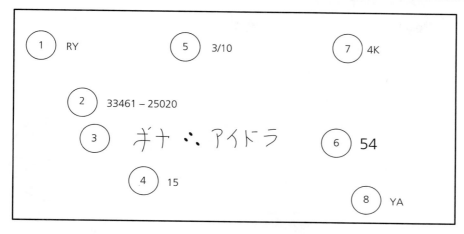

Legend:
1. Automobile model   5. Kanban number/Total number of Kanbans
2. Part number   6. Stock location area
3. Part descripton   7. Preceeding operation
4. Container capacity   8. Succeeding operation

This is absolutely essential to the pull logic. The realities on the plant floor are changing so dynamically that it is impossible to have any meaningful, realistic schedule that is generated by a computer or other "external" scheduling system. The schedule must be continually built and regenerated by the execution system and it must be physically visible to all who are executing it. Kanban is a physical, visible signal which provides incontrovertible proof that a specific quantity of a specific part must be immediately produced. Production activity control and schedule adjustment by hourly rescheduling is paperless. Figure 9–9 shows a typical Kanban card.

Kanban traditionally referred to a small card that was hanged on containers for in-process parts to indicate the need to produce another batch. In practice, any method that constantly and dynamically adjusts the schedule based on actual execution constraints and makes the instruction to produce visible is referred to as Kanban. Also, the word has come to refer to both the card and the standard container for stocking parts on the factory floor. When there are a few standard parts, containers can be dedicated and a pure pull scheduling system can be used. However, a way must be found to use each container for many different parts when the variety is high. The generic Kanban system, to be discussed more fully later, achieves this by putting a little anticipation (push) in the pull schedule and producing just a little bit ahead of time.

FIGURE 9–10 **Flow of Kanban**

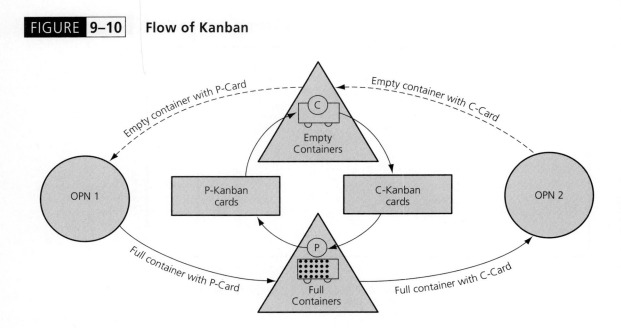

There are two types of Kanban systems: (1) Single card Kanban; (2) Double card Kanban. The latter is the most interesting, so we will focus on its description and evaluation. In this system, there is a conveyance Kanban, which authorizes the worker to transfer a container of parts from the parts' stocking area to his or her work station, and a production Kanban, which signals to the worker at the prior (feeding) work station to start producing a container of parts. In JIT, it is recommended that each container have a capacity equal to 1/10 the daily production rate. By implication, each container is turning over ten times in one day which represents a very rapid WIP inventory turnover. The diagram in Figure 9–10 shows how the flow of parts and cards works between two operations to regulate the scheduling and execution system.

Computing the Number of Kanbans

The number of Kanbans that are released in circulation is one of the critical parameters of the process, since in conjunction with the container size, it dictates the maximum level of in-process inventory. In the two-card system, one can calculate the number of production Kanbans and then match these with the same number of conveyance Kanbans. Similarly, the number of production Kanban cards equals the number of containers.

The formula for computing the number of Kanbans is simple, Let,

Y = number of Kanbans
D = demand per unit of time
T_w = production queue time
T_p = production time per container (batch)
K = container capacity
a = safety factor of no more than 10% of container capacity

Then:

$$Y = \frac{D\ (T_w + T_p)\ (1 + a)}{K}$$

Normally, Y is kept fixed, so that any increase in demand would require that T_w, T_p or a decrease, so as to accelerate production and this would be recognized as an improvement. Sometimes, when the system is producing in steady state, the manager could deliberately reduce the number of Kanbans so as to force cracks (problems) to appear in the system and effort can be directed to solving these. Such deliberate change in Y is a means of testing how much employees have mastered their jobs and is a key way of maintaining improvement. The formula for the number of Kanbans is designed to program just enough WIP inventory into the process to keep production going while the next small batch is being produced. The WIP just covers the time parameters $T_w + T_p$, which are the production lead time between the two operations that are being regulated by Kanban.

Kanban Dynamics

The following data will be used to illustrate the quantitative aspects of Kanban dynamics.

Demand per hour, $D = 60$
Container capacity, $K = 30$
Waiting (set-up) time, $T_w = 0.25$ hours
Production time, $T_p = 0.75$ hours
Safety (variability) factor, $a = 0.0$

Given these data, the number of Kanbans is computed using the formula given above.

$$Y = \frac{D\ (T_w + T_p)\ (1 + a)}{K}$$

$$Y = \frac{60\ (0.25 + 0.75)\ (1 + 0.0)}{30}$$

$$Y = 2$$

TABLE 9–5	Simulating Kanban

	0	1	2	3	4	5	6	7	8	9
Demand (pull by succeeding work station)		60	60	60	30	30	30	90	90	90
Production (preceeding work center)	60	60	60	60	30	30	30	90	90	90
Receipt (stock point)		60	60	60	60	30	30	30	90	90
Inventory on hand	60	60	60	60	60	60	60	00	00	00

Note: Theoretically, and without the control exercised by Kanban, inventory would be 90 units. But this is actually, physically impossible since there are only two containers with a total capacity of 60 units.

Table 9–5 simulates the system by systematically varying the demand (pull) by the succeeding work center and tracing the effect on the prior work center and on WIP inventory.

The data reveal a few things about Kanban that have already been alluded to. The ideal state for the system exists when the demand or withdrawal is steady at 60 units per hour. When demand is constant, the WIP inventory is 60 units. When demand falls to 30 units, WIP inventory is still at 60 units. However, when there is a sudden withdrawal over the planned 60 units as happens when demand goes up to 90, the WIP inventory dries up. If demand remains at the higher level for a sustained period and production does not increase, then there will be a shortage. A fall in demand causes idle time at both operations. Ironically though, a sudden increase in demand that comes soon after a decrease causes idle time at the pulling work center. The analysis reinforces conclusions arrived at before on the conditions for operating Kanban effectively. There must be either high-process flexibility, a smooth demand, or some combination of the two. Production leveling and flexibility increase the extent to which JIT can be promoted.

The same data can be used to show how Kanban works as the regulating mechanism, the heart beat of the system. Suppose steady state operations have been reached with the two Kanbans calculated before, but management wants to push the system to a superior performance level by pulling one Kanban out of circulation. The most direct and visible effect is that the maximum WIP inventory goes down to one Kanban or 30 units. The pulse of the system must adjust to the one Kanban constraint whose effect can be traced through the formula. Putting $Y = 1$ into the model, one gets:

$$1 = \frac{60 \, (T_w + T_p) \, (1 + 0.0)}{30}$$

and therefore,

$$T_w + T_p = 0.5$$

The lower Kanban level forces the system to produce at double the former steady state rate. Forcing the system to respond faster stresses it and causes cracks to appear at the weak spots. Problems will emerge and once these have been solved, a new higher performance steady state will have been achieved. Kanban is not only a regulating mechanism but also a lever that can be used to propel and sustain the improvement effort. Moreover, Kanban also makes any deviation from the operations plan clearly visible by either drying up WIP, shutting down the process flow or creating idle time. Deviations from a plan must be planned or else they will show up as problems.

For Kanban to be used effectively, then, three essential conditions must be met. These are quick response time, economic small lot production, and load leveling. Unless the prior operation can respond quickly when a sudden withdrawal causes the system to dry up, machine utilization will be atrocious. Economic small lot production is the only way to justify the very small batches that are used in a pull system. Set-up reduction controls this condition. In principle, one should not envisage implementing Kanban and pull scheduling until set-up times have been reduced to the 20 minute range. Load leveling is necessary to prevent the wild swings in demand which cause drying up to take place. Nevertheless, the absolute minimum condition is economic small lot production.

Kanbanizing High-Variety Production

Pull scheduling and Kanban program can fine tune the execution system once acceptable stability has been achieved. Improvements in the flow and the process, coupled with load leveling make possible very high levels of efficiency by stabilizing the production system. Any level of stability, once achieved, can be programmed into the system using Kanban and pull logic. From this perspective, Kanban conserves whatever stability has been achieved by making all execution problems such as bottlenecks, low productivity, idle time, poor in-process quality, and poor scheduling, visible when there is a deviation from the steady state plan. Repetitive production gives the stability that Kanban requires while high-variety production does not. High product variety invariably means demand instability, schedule variability, and erratic pull by the last operation. Besides, the principle that each part must

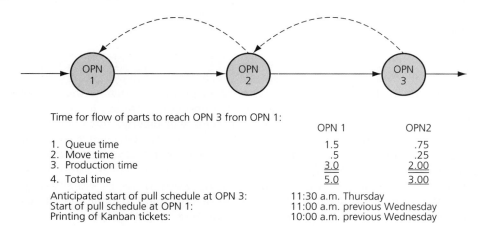

| FIGURE | 9–11 | **Generic Kanban** |

Time for flow of parts to reach OPN 3 from OPN 1:

	OPN 1	OPN2
1. Queue time	1.5	.75
2. Move time	.5	.25
3. Production time	3.0	2.00
4. Total time	5.0	3.00

Anticipated start of pull schedule at OPN 3:   11:30 a.m. Thursday
Start of pull schedule at OPN 1:   11:00 a.m. previous Wednesday
Printing of Kanban tickets: 10:00 a.m. previous Wednesday

have its own container and unique Kanban card is impossible to apply in practice if there are many part numbers. High-variety production is not amenable to the rigid operating discipline that is required by Kanban.

Some companies have recognized that and have tried to at least partially "Kanbanize" high-variety production. They have successfully adapted it to cases where production is not fundamentally repetitive. In that context, the very large number of parts precludes each part having its own, dedicated containers. A way must be found to use containers flexibly for more than one part. This is accomplished by forecasting (anticipating) the pull schedule and then sending feedback back up to the first and subsequent operations. These can start to build the part just in time to arrive at the final operation to execute the pull schedule. Kanban tickets can be electronically printed to flow with the parts from the first operation. Figure 9–11 shows how the system would work. Generic Kanban does some push and pull and executes the schedule in near just-in-time fashion. Generic Kanban can be looked at as an intermediate phase in the evolution of high-variety production to repetitive production. The final, repetitive production phase can be implemented after products and parts have been standardized or the production system is broken up into small, focused factories, each producing a limited product line.

Kanban as a Management Tool

In order to understand the true function of Kanban in JIT, it helps to go beyond the mere mechanics and examine the managerial impact. Kanban programs the production system to deliver and produce in JIT mode. Without Kanban and the few rules that create the discipline for its use, controlling production to achieve JIT would present horrendous supervision problems. Kanban automatically creates a signal to produce, so no external schedule follow-up and supervision is required, once the basic parameters are set and the operating rules are adhered to. Deviations from the plan are made visible, so plant management can leave the process to function, until the system itself signals that there is a problem either by revealing idle time at one operation or by stopping the entire system.

Push scheduling logic requires managerial action to adapt to small deviations, but Kanban automatically adjusts the schedule within the limits programmed into it by the safety factor. No rescheduling is called for until the system is shut down. Plant management need not worry about fine tuning the schedule themselves. And since adjustment to small deviations is constant and automatic, fewer large changes to the schedule will be necessary. Sometimes a major rescheduling effort is called for because small deviations were not attended to and their cumulative effect becomes intolerable for the system.

Kanban is a production order and a work order release program. It tells the prior operation what to produce, how much, and in what sequence. Except in very rare circumstances, Kanbans must be processed in rigid sequence. The release is also done at the time required to enable the parts to be delivered to the pulling operation, just-in-time. Therefore, Kanban schedules the operation automatically and dynamically and controls critical operating parameters such as set-up time (T_w), production time (T_p), and WIP inventory. The ability to slow or shut down the operation when there is a problem is the ultimate improvement mechanism. Kanban simplifies and implements very high-level production scheduling and control mechanisms without the bureaucratic structures that come from computerized systems such as MRP-II and production control staff. Production control is in the heart of the factory, under the very noses of every single worker. Kanban is to the production system what an automatic pilot is to an aircraft. You put information on the destination, the flight trajectory, and weather conditions into the system and it will take over the control of the aircraft. When the problems become too severe and need human intervention, an alarm (signal) goes off and the human pilot takes over. As long as the deviations are small and the general schedule has not changed, then Kanban will pilot the system without managerial intervention.

Conclusion

Small lot production and Kanban are powerful tools for implementing manufacturing strategy. Small lot production unleashes a chain reaction of cause and effect relationships that drive improvements in cost, lead times, quality, and flexibility and which culminate in an improved and sustainable market position. Kanban is one of the most potent mechanisms yet designed for exercising tight control of the factory floor, for stimulating continuous improvement and for conserving the gains already made. Many North American companies were slow in adopting small lot production and Kanban because these tools are not couched in the glamorous concepts of corporate strategy. The operational bases and simplicity of small lot production and Kanban, while not beguiling to "strategic thinkers" in corporations in North America, nevertheless have potent strategic ramifications. When a company implements these tools, it sets the stage for creating symbiosis between operations and strategy and for exploiting a web of operational and strategic interrelationships. Strategy is effectively deployed in day-to-day operational activities on the factory floor.

Case for Discussion

KANBAN AT NEW TECHNOLOGY CORPORATION (NTC)

NTC is a Canadian manufacturer of high-quality door windows and sliding vertical and horizontal windows. Sales and profits in 1992 were $19.5 million and $1.3 million, respectively. The company's strategy pursued three competitive priorities:

1. Produce the highest quality door windows in the industry;
2. Deliver the best value to the customer by achieving the lowest cost commensurate with that quality;
3. Seek to grow as fast as the market and its strategic advantages will allow.

Recently, the company started to implement a number of management innovations aimed at improving its performance. The company had implemented MRP-II, TQM, and was in the process of implementing JIT. After these changes, defects went down by 36 percent, throughout time by 20 percent, unit manufacturing cost by 7 percent, inventory turns improved by 30 percent, and productivity increased by 2.5 percent. Sales for the fourth quarter had increased by 25 percent over the corresponding 1991 period. NTC was attracting the attention of competitors and customers. The company, for the first time, received 15 requests for plant tours in the first quarter of 1993.

There were three products in the product line. External door windows were offered in 70 different variations and had a daily volume of 700 units. There were 40 different options of internal door windows and daily production was 300 units. Sliding windows were a standard product offered in 12 different options and were easy to manufacture.

In implementing JIT manufacturing, the company focused on reducing set-ups and kanbanizing operations in the three cells where sliding windows were made. It was thought that these cells were the ideal places to experiment with and learn to apply JIT concepts and to see if the benefits could be substantial. Management decided to physically separate these cells from the rest of the operation, to reorganize the work flow to make it short and direct, and to transfer some of the best workers to the cell to work with plant engineering on developing JIT manufacturing.

Within three months, average set-up times in the three cells went from 25 minutes to 2 minutes and the company designed and started to use Kanban cards to schedule the cells. The MRP-II generated shop schedule increasingly became useless because production orders were coming out of the cells much faster than MRP-II could monitor and report on their progress. The typical lot size was reduced from 200 to 2 windows. Space requirements were cut in half, in-process inventories were reduced from $6,000 to $120, the cycle time per piece was reduced by 8 percent, and the defect rate was reduced from 6 percent to 0.5 percent. The production coordinator suggested that the whole operation could be scheduled one piece at a time, and the company could enter the make-to-order replacement market for sliding windows, a segment that was as large as that for door windows.

Dick Osborne, president of NTC, was convinced that the company should move fast to extend JIT manufacturing and Kanban to the whole company because he believed that his team had achieved a strategic revolution. Persuaded that NTC's experience so far would make the task easy he authorized his coordinators to take the necessary steps to implement JIT plantwide and to kanbanize all remaining manufacturing cells.

1. Describe and evaluate NTC's manufacturing strategy? What is the role of JIT in that strategy?
2. Why did Kanban JIT work in the cell for sliding windows?
3. Are the improvements in performance achieved significant enough to have competitive impact? Why or why not?
4. How difficult will it be to kanbanize the remaining cells?
5. What recommendations would you make to Mr. Dick Osborne?

Discussion Questions

References

Japan Management Association, *Kanban Just-in-Time at Toyota: Management Begins at the Work Place*, Cambridge, MA: Productivity Press, 1986.

Japan Management Association, *Canon Production System: Creative Involvement of the Total Workforce*, Cambridge, MA: Productivity Press, 1987.

Neil, George, and Jim O'Hara, "The Introduction of JIT into a High Technology Electronics Manufacturing Environment", *IJOPM* 7,4, 1987.

Ohno, Taiichi, *Toyota Production System: Beyond Large Scale Production*, Cambridge, MA: Productivity Press, 1988.

Raia, Ernest, "Just-in-Time USA: Journey to World Class," *Purchasing*, September 24, 1987.

Shingo, Shigeo, *A Revolution in Manufacturing: The SMED System,* Tokyo: Japan Management Association, 1983.

Zipkin, Paul, H., "Does America Need a JIT Revolution?" *Harvard Business Review,* January–February 1991.

Managing Purchasing for Superior Performance

Companies that attain and maintain competitive excellence achieve sustainable superior performance in all of the business functions. The entire spectrum of business activities is managed to create maximum value for the customer. Key competitive requirements are executed to near perfection by every business unit, while all the business functions are tightly coordinated and purposefully deployed to deliver a united attack on the market. The pipeline concept provides an excellent representation of this. The business is structurally differentiated but the coordinating mechanisms, culture and value system, fundamental competitive mission and motivational climate operate to make the company work as a holistic, integrated, competitive entity. Inter-functional cooperation replaces the constant jockeying for political position that characterizes most companies. Mutual trust and respect by all functions replace historically cultivated mistrust and denigration of some functions by other, "more strategic" ones. In today's ferociously competitive business environment, all functions are strategic and each should be managed to achieve its strategic potential. A business function that is responsible for a mission or activity set that is not strategic should be dismantled and all the activities ought to be performed by outside suppliers who can manage and execute them with strategic impact.

Few business functions have been denigrated and relegated to a position of strategic insignificance more than purchasing. By whatever measure one chooses to evaluate it, purchasing has historically been managed, structured, and compensated as a strategically inferior business function. Better than 75 percent of North American businesses still do not have a vice-president of purchasing and materials or its equivalent. More than 45 percent of North American companies have structured procurement so that the top purchasing manager reports to the manufacturing vice-president or its equivalent. In most companies the highest organizational level that can be reached by the best procurement manager is the director of purchasing level. In my consulting with dozens of North American companies and some Fortune 500 ones, I have never met a company where someone with a strong background in procurement ever became president. Every other function had contributed to the presidency, except purchasing. Less than 1 percent of companies in North

America have employees in procurement or related functions that are members of professional associations dedicated to developing and promoting purchasing education. As far as can be ascertained, not a single company president belongs to any such professional association.

In this chapter, we will present the key concepts of procurement management that can be used by a company to manage purchasing as an element of an effective manufacturing strategy and to derive superior performance from it.

KEY ISSUES IN STRATEGIC PROCUREMENT[1]

Vendor's Impact on Competitive Performance

The low emphasis that top corporate management places on procurement is surprising, given the strong impact that vendors have on a company's strategic position. Purchased materials account for between 55 to 85 percent of unit cost in the typical manufacturing company, and there is a discernible upward trend in the percentage over the last 20 years. On the average, materials account for 60 percent of unit manufacturing cost. Roughly 60 percent of a company's unit cost is generated by vendors. Most chief executives are busy trying to effect cost reductions in their plants, forgetting that major leverage on cost exists in the plants of their suppliers. A competitive strategy that seeks to create a cost advantage must reach into supplier companies if it is to succeed. Low overall cost for the producing company requires that vendors also establish a low cost position. Alternatively, a company that wishes to gain a low-cost position is under an absolute obligation to seek out and do business with low-cost vendors. One would have a tough time finding a company that managed to cultivate a low-cost advantage despite sourcing from high-cost vendors.

Material cost as a percentage of total cost has shown a strong historical tendency to increase, and there are fundamental structural factors at play which guarantee that this will continue to be so for the foreseeable future. Many raw material sources are depletable or are renewable at very high cost. Scarcity will exacerbate and is likely to be prevalent during the twenty-first century. The laws of supply and demand are bound to interact to exert persistent, upward pressure on material cost. The rate of resource depletion will accelerate as more and more countries develop a diversified industry base. When India, China, South America, and Sub-Saharan Africa will have achieved structural transformation of their economies in the twenty-first century, the demand for raw materials will multiply by a factor of ten, because of that fact

---

[1] For more discussion of the strategic issues in procurement, see Ravi Veukatesan, "Strategic Sourcing: To Make or Not to Make," *Harvard Business Review,* November–December 1992.

alone. The best scenario is that there will be ferocious competition for less and less raw materials. Even the so-called renewable resources, such as hydro-electricity, will be put under severe strain as their normal consumption approaches and surpasses the rate at which they are rejuvenated. Canada is abundantly endowed with hydroelectric potential, but there is a physical limit to how much hydroelectricity can be produced by that country. Increasingly, therefore, the low-cost strategic ball game will be played in the courts of vendors under the leadership of the procurement function.

Like cost, quality is influenced by vendors in an important way. A company cannot improve on the quality delivered by its vendors except at great expense and effort. One can argue that vendor quality cannot be improved by in-coming inspection, since inspection merely confirms the quality that already exists in purchased materials. Defects are better prevented by the vendor because that is where it can be done both cheaply and effectively. Vendor facilities are a major source of quality. One company spent seventy cents of every sales dollar on purchases and 82 percent of the parts that were in the final product were from outside sources. Assuming that vendors managed quality only as good as that company and that there was no in-coming inspection to filter out bad parts, roughly 82 percent of the defects in the product would be produced by vendors. There is a direct and strong correlation between vendor quality performance and the quality delivered to customers. Vendor quality enters the product through the parts that they supply, and in-coming inspection is not likely to be 100 percent effective in capturing vendor-produced defects. A company's in-coming inspection is likely to be no more effective than its own final inspection. Moreover, companies that are serious about quality are not likely to do business with mediocre suppliers.

Toyota Motor Company has received worldwide acclaim for its quality. One would be tempted to conclude that Toyota quality is built in Toyota factories. But when one looks at the facts closely, one notices that Toyota spends eighty cents of every sales dollar on purchased parts. Intuition would lead us to conclude that 80 percent of Toyota quality is made or assured by Toyota vendors. Toyota's factories are in fact responsible for a very small share of the overall quality results. The strong emphasis that Toyota puts on developing very strong, quality-conscious suppliers and on insisting that all suppliers deliver 100 percent good quality every time, attests to the fact that they believe that vendor impact on per unit product cost, through purchase costs, is as high as vendor influence on quality. The same is true for every world-class manufacturer. Companies that are being managed to produce superior quality generally do business with suppliers that produce superior quality. Companies that analyze returns from their customers to find out the origin of the defects find out that suppliers that are weak on quality account for more than their fair share of defects. Apparently, despite a company's best efforts, supplier-produced defects find their way into the final product roughly in proportion to the share of total defects delivered by each supplier.

Vendor delivery performance also greatly affects the company's own delivery performance. Most late deliveries by manufacturing companies are occasioned by late deliveries of parts by vendors. The problem is aggravated by the simple fact that if only 1 percent of all vendors deliver late, then all orders will be shipped late. A product that is made with 1,000 parts, 60 percent or 600 of which are purchased, cannot be shipped on time if only 1 part is delivered late. One cannot ship a product on time with 99.9 percent on-time parts. They must all be on time. Unreliable vendor deliveries are a major headache for most companies, due to this simple dynamic. Companies tried to deal with the problem by creating huge raw materials and parts inventories, only to find out that higher inventories encouraged vendors to be more unreliable. The higher inventories imposed severe cost penalties and insidiously caused quality to deteriorate. What started as simply delivery unreliability soon became a quality, cost, delivery, and inventory problem, all perfectly intertwined. When management tried some quick fixes such as across-the-board cuts in inventory, the problem simply metamorphosed and became more insidious than before. The best managed North American companies, taking their cue from world-class manufacturers in Japan, began to realize in the 1970s that the only way out of that quagmire was to manage total vendor performance. Vendors must deliver 100 percent good quality product, on time and at competitive prices. Some of the world's best companies invented JIT, which is one way to simultaneously attack quality, cost, delivery, inventory, and inflexibility. Following their lead, world-class companies in North America were quick to adopt JIT.

The False Promise of Vertical Integration

Reliance on vendors is likely to increase as the diversification and vertical integration mania of the 1970s and 1980s fizzles. Companies that undertook massive vertical-integration projects because they thought that these would give them better efficiency and greater control over material sources, soon discovered that they were drifting away from their core businesses. They gained increased organizational control over raw materials in that supply was assured. But they could not manage the new businesses as well as companies that specialized in them. Vertical integration also complicated the business and added several layers to the organizational structure. Managing a new, even if related, business diluted top management attention and led to the bread and butter business units being somewhat neglected. Top management had failed to "stick to the knitting" and did not focus its energies on those aspects of the business where it had accumulated all its experience and know-how, and where the company had made its name. Somehow, some chief executives thought that they could master a new business in 2 or 3 years when it took them 25 or 30 years to carve out a niche in the core business.

Most companies that made bold vertical integration or diversification moves by acquiring existing corporations got into trouble operating both the existing and the new business units. By the mid-1980s, diversification and acquisition mania was replaced by frantic efforts to divest everything except the core business. The key words in the late 1980s were divestment, restructuring, and downsizing. The concern is to create smaller, meaner organizations with lean and flat structures. The old multilayered pyramidal structures are fast being replaced with flatter ones where there are five or less levels between the chief executive officer and production workers.

Deintegration and divestment to create a simpler, more focused business is a necessity if a company is to have the versatility, flexibility, and quick-footedness that is called for by the new global competitive environment. Deintegration makes sense both economically and strategically. Highly integrated businesses are tough to control, extremely difficult to motivate, and hard to give unity of purpose. Size, beyond a certain point, creates inertia. A football player at 120 pounds is much too light. But at 450 pounds, he is definitely too heavy to move around swiftly and respond to the strategic signals and moves from the quarterback. The lean production system uses the minimum level of physical facilities, little overhead, a simple process with the minimum number of process stages that are required to compete in the product market, and has an inventory level that is measured in hours or days, instead of months. Vertical integration works against these basic principles. Vertical integration calls for maximum levels of physical facilities and processing stages as the company takes over more and more of the activities that could be performed by suppliers and also uses more staff to coordinate the additional number of process stages. Moreover, a larger number of process stages inescapably means more inventory to decouple them.

Make versus Buy

The decision as to whether a company will produce its own requirements of a part or material or whether it will use outside sources is the most fundamental in the strategic management of procurement. Historically, companies in North America have shown a preference to manufacture as much of their requirements as possible. Managers reasoned that the make option resulted in lower cost, less risk, and better control over quality and delivery. In some cases, companies produced their own requirements in an effort to protect innovations, manufacturing practices, and proprietary technology. However, the advantages attributed to internal sourcing are not automatic and it has some very important disadvantages such as the tendency for the company to tolerate less than excellent performance on the part of its own plants and the general reluctance to close down an inefficient or ineffective operation, in addition to the disadvantages mentioned previously. Toyota buys much more of its requirements than GM, but outperforms it in the car market. Intel has done extremely well as a focused producer of microprocessors for computer manufacturers. The problem of developing and managing the supplier relations that accompany the decision to buy is no more complex than that involved in managing a set of plants. The decision to buy has some other powerful advantages:

1. Suppliers can be an important source of innovation and new technology.
2. Suppliers serve as gatekeepers. Because of their links with other suppliers and final producers, suppliers are in a unique position to keep customers abreast of developments in both the supplier and end product market.
3. Suppliers pass the advantages of focus, small scale, and specialization to their customers in the form of lower overall cost, higher quality, more flexibility and lead times that are often lower than a company's own manufacturing lead time.
4. Because they support more than one customer, suppliers can achieve both the economies of scale and the steep learning curves that they can use to drive costs down.

Strategic Procurement and the Global Supplier

As markets become more global in scope and companies deploy global strategies, customers are pulling their suppliers into the international competitive arena. This phenomenon further accelerates the pace of globalization and creates a pool of capable suppliers that can support the global strategies of their customers. A company is a global supplier when it can capably and effectively supply customers across a large number of national boundaries. Without effective global suppliers, many companies could not deploy global strategies because they would find it difficult to design and manage the network of plants that such a competitive strategy requires. Reliance on global suppliers means that companies can avoid designing and managing vertically integrated operations on a global scale. Dependence on global suppliers offers a company some distinct strategic advantages:

1. The company is buying from suppliers that it has evaluated and tested in other markets, usually its home market. Supplier capability is assured.
2. A strong customer/supplier relationship already exists. Using the supplier as a global one further reinforces the relationship.
3. It extends the superior performance of the supplier in one national market to all national markets that the customer enters. The competitive advantages that the supplier offers can be quickly propagated across the customer's entire network of plants.

4. Global suppliers reduce part of the uncertainty that customers face as they extend their global reach.
5. The global supplier is probably the most cost effective. As the customer broadens the scope of its activities, it creates scale economies in R&D, production, logistics, distribution, and marketing for the supplier, part of which can be passed on to the customer. The customer also reaps some economies of scale in supplier selection, certification, and a stronger partnership.

In the past, the dominant growth strategy for a supplier was forward integration toward the product market. Today's preferable strategy is to become a preferred supplier to a global corporation, or a company that is poised to become global, in one national market and extend the relationship to all markets where the customer has a presence.

Divestment and deintegration will only increase reliance on vendors. An increasing share of unit product cost will be accounted for by purchased materials. Vendors' quality, cost, and delivery performance will have increasing impact on overall company performance. Strong vendors will increasingly be necessary in order for a company to achieve strategic leverage over a wide variety of competitive variables. Procurement will have to be integrated into strategic business decisions.

QUALIFICATIONS OF A GOOD VENDOR

On the whole, companies choose their vendors and decide whether to continue doing business with them. A company that has bad vendors has no one to blame but itself; good vendors don't grow on trees but are developed by the buying company. Vendors are chosen, supported, encouraged, and motivated to be good by their customers. Vendor choice is a crucial management activity, particularly in the light of the foregoing discussion. Companies that are being directed to competitive excellence have very clear ideas as to what are the characteristics of a good vendor, and they go through great lengths to assure that vendors conform to their expectations before they start to do business with them. Vendor selection is taken very seriously by the best North American manufacturing companies. Over the years, these same excellent companies have pinpointed what it takes to be a good vendor.

Excellent companies are also the best vendors, since every company is both a buyer and a seller. Buying is nothing more than the flip side of selling. Companies that put a premium on excellence and quality superiority, as we have argued, are profoundly customer oriented from top to bottom and across all functions and organizational units. Such companies stay close to the customer, listen to him or her, and strive to meet, and better yet, surpass his or her expectations. These very same qualities make a company an excellent vendor. Before deciding to do business with a vendor, the first basic question that must be answered is "to what extent is customer orientation entrenched in the fabric of the vendor's organization, its culture and value system, its business philosophy and vision, and in employee attitudes?". Excellent vendors are committed to and apply the concept that the company exists to create and retain a customer and that the goal is total customer satisfaction. Once these philosophies and attitudes are deeply embedded into the organization and there are programs and policies for refining and operationalizing them, then all other requirements for a good vendor naturally fall into place. The prevalent notion that vendor evaluation is an exercise that can be dispensed with quickly using a competitive bid and the "Yellow Pages" is a managerial travesty with dire consequences. A buying company that is serious about competitive excellence will try to understand the guts of the vendor's business by examining the foundation concepts upon which the vendor organization stands.

Integrity, honesty, and humility flow naturally from a sound business philosophy and a solidly honed culture and value system. A company that sets out to maximize value for the customer will conduct business above board, will have no hidden agendas, and will frankly admit mistakes when they are made and before they are made public, if discovered. Attempts to cover up errors that impact negatively on customers are a sure give away that management has not made service to customers the heart of its business. Recalls that come late and after threats from regulatory agencies, defective products that are reluctantly pulled from the market, and product test results that are glossed over, concealed or even deliberately altered, all reveal enormous cracks in a company's commitment to total customer satisfaction.

Innovativeness, desire to improve, and a fiercely competitive spirit come naturally to vendors that put emphasis on satisfying the customer. Innovation is stimulated by the will to increase value for customers and to keep doing so as long as the vendor is in the chosen market. Companies become the best by being innovative, and they innovate to keep their position among the best competitors in the market. A vendor that stops innovating very quickly loses the ability to keep delivering the best quality at the lowest possible price. How a vendor got to be among the best is instructive only to the extent that it reveals that it will most likely continue to be among the best. Products that were yesterday at the cutting edge of technology and represented breakthroughs in quality when they were first marketed are today relegated to the ash heaps of history. Similarly, products that today epitomize quality superiority will tomorrow be useful only as museum pieces, if at all, unless they are constantly improved or "destroyed" by innovation. Companies that are in business for the long haul will only choose vendors that will likely be in business in the long run. Innovation, the desire to improve, and competitive spirit are the fuel that keep a companies burning with the passion to excel and to be the best.

Excellent vendors, then, pursue quality improvement with relentless zeal. They drive hard to try to surpass customer requirements and will sometimes lead their customers in quality improvement. Excellent vendors are not dragged into quality improvement kicking and screaming. On the contrary, they begin to search for ways to make a new product better, as soon as they have started to market it. They will not put a new product on the market until they are certain that its quality is beyond reproach. And when they commit the occasional error, they are quick to correct it and to pull the product off the market, if need be. The first question a company should ask about a vendor is not whether the price is low, but whether all its resources are marshaled to produce to exacting quality standards all the time and every time.

SUPPLIER PARTNERSHIP

The Concept

World-class companies depend on world-class suppliers so they can deliver superior quality, on time and at favorable prices. Worthy suppliers help their customers compete, instead of working against them. Suppliers who have understood what their business is all about go all out to help their customers develop and sustain competitive advantage in the marketplace, because a company that does not have strategic advantage that can be sustained will not have a supplier for long. Excellent suppliers support and reinforce the competitive thrusts of their customers wholeheartedly, recognizing that this is what they are in business to do.

At the same time, a quality supplier must be rewarded when the job is done right. The rewards are invariably monetary, based on price, but they can be much more. The good supplier has the right to a fair price, one that will generate a profit. Good suppliers have earned the right to descent profits that will enable them to invest in quality and cost improvement and cultivate competitive advantage that will be passed on to their customers. A fair price is not a favor that is granted to the supplier but is compensation for work well done. Beyond price is the long-term guarantee and also an increasing share of the customer's business. There can be also other nonmonetary rewards such as access to technology and information.

Suppliers and customers are locked into a symbiotic, mutually beneficial competitive relationship, where each helps the other compete, and each encourages and motivates the other toward excellence. At least that's how it should be. The adversary, arm-twisting relationship that so characterizes supplier/customer relations in North America must give way to cooperative, mutually advantageous business dealings. Management must begin to recognize that no one but the competition gains when a company uses corporate economic power to suck the supplier dry. Companies that use arm-twisting to extract unfair concessions from their suppliers are damaging their own long-term viability. In supplier relationships there is really no such thing as a free lunch. Fleecing the supplier is like a boomerang—it turns back on you.

Supplier partnership establishes long-term, mutually beneficial relationships with suppliers, and turns it into a source of competitive advantage. The partnership concept recognizes that the strengths and distinctive competence of suppliers can be utilized to full potential by the customer company only if there is a closely, tightly coordinated organic relationship between the supplier and user organizations. The usual relationship founded on arms-length transactions with suppliers conducted on a more or less frequent basis stifle information exchange. In extreme cases, information is deliberately distorted in an attempt to improve one's bargaining position. When there is little or distorted information that flows between supplier and user, the two have difficulty communicating their vision of the competitive situation to the other party. Cases exist where one party does not believe true information given by the other, due to mistrust and suspicion. Information that is divulged, in that case, is interpreted as a bluff in a classical game of poker. Suppliers and users are playing poker with each other when they could do much to help each other. Supplier partnership builds a relationship between supplier and customer that makes it easy and normal for both parties to lay all the cards on the table, except in rare circumstances such as where trade secrets must be protected

The best managed corporations in the world are increasingly viewing their suppliers as belonging to a larger family of companies. Such is particularly true of the leading Japanese companies. One hears of the Sony, Mazda, and Toyota families, emphasizing the close, organic relationship that exists between these companies and their suppliers.[2] The competition is not between Toyota and General Motors or Ford, but between the Toyota family of companies and General Motors or Ford. The world-class companies in Japan

---

[2]The relationships are particularly strong within the commercial and industrial groupings referred to as Keiretsu. These are clusters formed when companies come together to nurture and exploit strong commercial ties for competitive advantage. There are two types of Keiretsu: (1) The horizontal Keiretsu centered around a large general trader (sogo shosha) or a bank, (2) the vertical or supply Keiretsu formed by the strong cooperative links between a large industrial corporation and its smaller suppliers. Cohesiveness and a clear nucleus of control are the most basic differentiating characteristics of a Keiretsu. Other characteristics include (1) closed boundaries that exclude non-member companies from benefiting strategically from the bond, (2) the promotion and pursuit of a dominant, general objective, (3) joint consultations and general policy-making, (4) pooling of resources, expertise, and competitive information, (5) clear hierachy of power and influence in the case of a supply (vertical) Keiretsu, (6) ownership ties based on the fact that the dominant company owns between 2 and 5 percent of the stock of the smaller ones (suppliers in a vertical Keiretsu), (7) the dominant bank holds between 5 and 10 percent of the stock of member companies, (8) high concentration of buying and selling within the group.

For more discussion of the nature of the Keiretsu and how it operates, see Angelina Helou, "The Nature and Competitiveness of Japan's Keiretsu," *Journal of World Trade,* vol. 25, No. 3, June 1991.

have united with their suppliers to do battle on a world scale. They view an attack on the flagships of the families such as Toyota, Mazda, and Sony as an attack on all members, including suppliers. They have promoted cooperation and esprit de corps within the family that assure free information flow and openness in their dealings with each other, although they are closed to outsiders whom they define as the common enemy. With technological, financial, and managerial assistance, they are helping each company in the family to help every other one compete and so strengthen the market position of the family.

By contrast, the leading North American manufacturing companies are fighting two battles, one against their suppliers and one against their major competitors, the Japanese families of companies. North American companies go to great lengths to try to maintain their distinctiveness and independence from their suppliers. Multiple sourcing, that is having many suppliers for the same part, is designed to reduce dependence on suppliers and to play one supplier against another with a view to reducing price. The North American view is that a company needs to have multiple sources so as to reduce dependency on any one supplier and promote price competition. The logic behind this philosophy is flawed because a company cannot reduce its dependence on suppliers except by eliminating them and producing the material itself. This is called vertical integration and its effectiveness as a strategy is now questionable. Multiple sourcing does not eliminate dependence, but instead makes the buying company dependent on many average suppliers.

Figure 10–1 outlines the key elements of the supplier–partnership concept. The goal is to derive strategic leverage from suppliers, which is a must given the impact that vendors have on a company's own quality, cost, and delivery performance. A company cannot have maximum impact on the market without exploiting the competitive strengths of its suppliers to the fullest extent possible. The ability to use supplier organizations in this way requires that unique, cooperative relationships be formed with suppliers. When these relationships reach their ultimate expression and the customer and its supplier still maintain their identity, one has a partnership. A world-class supplier or a supplier that has potential to be world class, will show no recalcitrance toward the partnership concept. How readily suppliers accept the partnership concept is a strong indication of how prepared they are to face up to the challenge to become world-class vendors.

IMPLEMENTING SUPPLIER PARTNERSHIP

Mutual Dependency, Shared Fate, and Mutual Confidence

Buyer and vendor must develop a sense of shared fate and recognize that mutual dependency is a reality that cannot be eliminated in the present day

FIGURE 10–1 **Elements of the Supplier–Partnership Concept**

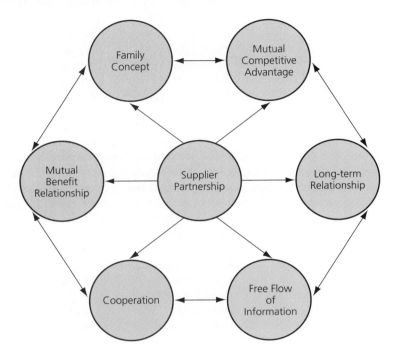

marketplace. As competitive conditions toughen and technology becomes more complex, the need for cooperation deepens. Increasingly, the ability to survive will require that a company use all the weapons in its competitive arsenal to their full potential. Strong vendors are one such potent weapon. The first step toward implementing vendor partnership is for vendor and buyer to become completely convinced that mutual dependency is germane to doing business in a competitive market. A company cannot be large enough that it will not have to depend on vendors. Top management in both the vendor and customer organizations have to internalize the philosophy that in the final analysis their companies succeed or fail together.

This means that a company must have full confidence in the capability of all its vendors, without exception. When a buyer knows that its vendors have the capability to perform well on all performance criteria, there is much less concern about having alternative sources. Multiple sources are often justified on the basis that it promotes healthy competition among vendors to the benefit of the buyer. More likely, however, companies buy the same part from many suppliers because management is not absolutely convinced that all vendors have the capability to meet all requirements and to keep improving performance. Management will have difficulty accepting mutual dependency or shared fate unless vendors have demonstrated the ability to perform to exacting, superior performance standards. Adequate mechanisms and procedures for rigorously evaluating vendor capability need to be put in place, and their application must be a normal part of the management process.

Ad hoc supplier evaluation done using data provided by a few business references or gleaned from published government sources and trade journals, are grossly insufficient. The days when purchasing people would evaluate a supplier by pondering for one hour over a few files or by making a few phone calls to some "contacts" are long gone. Evaluating vendor capability so as to implement supplier partnership is very serious business that must be executed professionally and on the basis of exhaustive supplier research. Supplier evaluation ought to culminate into supplier certification or decertification. The eventual goal is for the company to do business only with suppliers that have been selected by a strict certification procedure.

Vendor capability highlights the need to go beyond mere performance criteria such as price, quality, and delivery. Vendor capability evaluation puts every aspect of the vendor organization under the microscope: the management culture and value system, the strengths and weaknesses of each function, the organizational structure, financial policy and structure, personnel policies, marketing policies, strengths and weaknesses of the existing process technologies, technology policy, to name only a few. The magnitude and depth of the tasks to be accomplished in a meaningful vendor capability analysis call for expertise that is well beyond what exists in the typical purchasing department. Vendor capability analysis is best done by a multifunctional, multidiscipline team dedicated to that purpose.

In addition to widely available data on a potential vendor, the buyer has to use information produced by its own certification team. One popular instrument for generating the required information is a questionnaire designed to that end. These questionnaires range in length from 3 or 4 pages to over 25. Questionnaires are filled by the certification team during an extensive visit of vendor facilities. Depending on the complexity of vendor operations, these visits have been noted to last up to two days. The questionnaire approach is useful because it forces the buyer to decide, in advance, what it is looking for in a good vendor and also necessitates firsthand observation of vendor facilities. The questionnaire can be used to pinpoint to a vendor that has been decertified or that has not achieved certification weak areas that must be improved in order to gain certification. In a very real sense, the questionnaire documents the characteristics that the buyer is looking for in a vendor and provides a framework for developing a consensus on vital procurement issues that affect both parties.

For the world-class company, vendor certification is an ongoing process that aims to implement supplier partnership. Because it is a time consuming activity, the buyer can set a time frame—two years, for example—during which all vendors will be evaluated for certification or decertification. During the time period set, every vendor is evaluated at least once. Subsequent to these initial evaluations, another time frame, say five years, can be established for executing ongoing vendor capability analysis. In the interim, special evaluations can be scheduled for vendors that are performing below expectations. Ongoing performance evaluation provides vital information for scheduling initial, special, and ongoing vendor capability analyses. Common sense would dictate that initial evaluations should first focus on those vendors that are currently performing below expectations and then slowly extend to the progressively better ones. When evaluations are being repeated as a normal, ongoing process, the worst performing vendors should be tackled first, thus focusing attention on where the procurement problems currently exist. Ongoing vendor performance evaluation signals whether vendor capability should be reviewed more quickly than is called for by the normal time frame for repeated capability analysis. That is to say, vendor capability is periodically evaluated, whether or not performance is acceptable. The ongoing performance results only serve to advance or delay its timing.

The complete process which culminates in vendor certification or decertification is shown in Figure 10–2. One notes that vendor certification, in companies where vendors are being utilized to their maximum strategic potential, is driven by the realities of the competitive situation and the strategic requirements of the buyer. Supplier partnership embraces issues that are deeper, broader, and strategically more critical than mere buying. Good buying contributes to a company's operational and financial well-being, but it does not deal with the hard competitive realities. Strategic procurement will go beyond buying to understand the competitive requirements that must be met by suppliers, will specify vendor qualifications, and choose ongoing vendor-performance criteria that flow directly from the strategic position, strengths, weaknesses, and constraints of the buyer. Supplier certification should help the buying company identify, choose, and maintain a strong relationship with vendors who can execute specific key success factors to near perfection. The buying company ought to know quite clearly what competitive variables, such as quality, price, and delivery, it wants the vendor to execute excellently and whether the vendors chosen have the capability to perform to expectations. In order to be able to deal with these aspects of strategic procurement, the company must understand its market intimately, and must have a clearly defined, deliberately chosen, strategic position in the marketplace. Companies that do not have a clear competitive posture are certainly not in a position to communicate clear strategic requirements to their vendors.

One should also note that vendor-capability evaluation uses information from three distinct sources: (1) secondary sources, published data such as that from trade journals, manufacturers' indexes, and the like, (2) primary data

The Vendor Certification Process    FIGURE 10–2

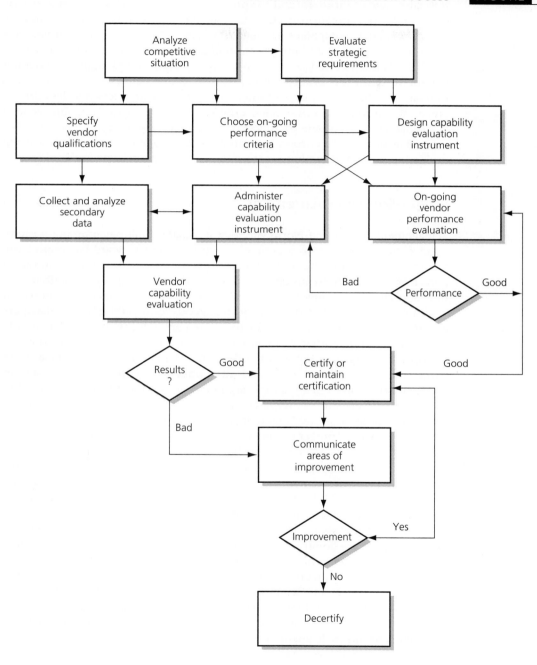

generated by the buyer's own capability evaluation instrument such as questionnaires and plant tours, and (3) primary data generated by ongoing, day-to-day, vendor-performance evaluation of which the famous demerit system is one type. When companies are merely buying, they put heavy emphasis on secondary data. As they implement strategic procurement and supplier partnership, data generated by vendor-capability analysis and rigorous, ongoing vendor-performance evaluation become more crucial to vendor-capability evaluation, while secondary information sources assume less and less importance. When vendor-performance criteria used to evaluate ongoing vendor performance are chosen to reflect competitive requirements and are also derived from a clear corporate strategy, then ongoing vendor-performance evaluation only serves to bolster the strategic procurement process.

Single-Source Procurement

Management practice in North America has made multiple sourcing a sacrosanct concept. Numerous arguments have been put forward to support the view that a company should have more than one source for each material or part. However, all these arguments hinge on the economic rationale that multiple sourcing is the only means of maintaining healthy competition between vendors and thus assures the most advantageous terms to the buyer. Managers also think using many suppliers for the same part reduces the risk that supply will be interrupted either by unanticipated events. The buying company in a multiple-sourcing situation is not dependent on any one source and can have bargaining leverage over each and all suppliers to extract concessions on price, delivery, and quality so the argument goes. Free and fair competition has always been the centerpiece of North American economic thought. Antitrust legislation in the United States and the anticombines laws in Canada are all designed to prevent concentrations of economic power and to break up companies that are deemed to be big and powerful. All this is done to maintain a healthy competitive environment and to eliminate the super-profits or economic rent that monopolistic and oligopolistic market structures are believed to create. Multiple sourcing is based on arguments that are carried over to the procurement function from microeconomic theory.

What may be sound reasoning when viewed from the microeconomic perspective breaks down when applied to the procurement function. Multiple sourcing may promote price competition between a few suppliers and reduce the risk of supply interruption. But it also imposes some severe disadvantages on the buying company when one considers all facets of the total procurement cycle. First, multiple sourcing is not necessary to maintain a fair competitive price and it may in fact exert no influence on price at all. The idea that multiple sourcing will guarantee the lowest possible price contradicts economic theory. Price is regulated by market forces prevailing in the entire industry regardless of how many suppliers a company chooses to have. What impact would it have on price if a company chooses to buy from 6 out of 100 companies in a perfectly competitive market? Obviously none. Buying from only one supplier in a competitive market would have no impact on the prevailing price either. Similarly, what would change, from a price viewpoint, if a company buys from two out of four suppliers in an oligopolistic market structure instead of from only one? Nothing would change. Price would be dictated by the external market conditions, no matter what sourcing policy was adopted. In a perfectly competitive market, buying policy cannot influence price, while in an oligopolistic market, the buying company can only affect price by choosing the best oligopolist.

As for the other variables such as delivery, the buying company will have the best conditions, by choosing the best supplier and not by having many suppliers. We have argued before that competitive conditions push companies to increase quality, and some suppliers are more aggressive than others in leading the market as a whole to improve quality. So, as far as quality is concerned, the best conditions are assured by market structure and how aggressive particular companies are in responding to competitive conditions. The buying company gets the best quality by choosing the best, most quality-conscious vendor. The number of vendors is insignificant. Whichever way one examines the critical issue, vendor performance has nothing to do with multiple sourcing, but is instead determined by the ability to judiciously nurture and motivate the best supplier. Supplier partnership and vendor certification play a decisive role in that regard.

Multiple sourcing improves supply continuity, but it is not the best strategy for doing so. One excellent supplier that gives a 99 percent delivery reliability is better than three average suppliers, each of whom can only perform to a 60 percent delivery reliability. In the latter case, the overall delivery performance is 93.6 percent $[.6 + (.6 \times .4) + (.6 \times .4 \times .4)]$. But the 93.6 percent delivery figure is not assured. Companies use a multiple sourcing policy to increase supply continuity on the assumption that other suppliers can make up for the shortage when one supplier is experiencing problems. Such is not always the case, particularly because the average supplier usually does not have the flexibility to respond quickly to unexpected increases in volume. Moreover, an average supplier almost always has difficulty executing a tight delivery schedule which is precisely what is called for when the buying company must shift orders from a supplier who is having problems to other sources. The inadequate capabilities that cause a supplier to be average or poor are the very ones that are likely to cause poor delivery performance and supply interruption. The factors that make for poor supplier performance can neither be eliminated nor mitigated by wantonly increasing the number of vendors.

Multiple sourcing, then, does not strike at the heart of supplier performance and does not aim to eliminate the causes of poor performance. The goal in multiple sourcing is not to improve supplier performance on quality, cost, and delivery, but to find strategies to cope with it. As a procurement policy, multiple sourcing represents management resignation vis-à-vis supplier problems that are deemed to be unsolvable. There is an attempt to cover up mediocre supplier performance by having multiple sources. The irony is that procurement problems multiply and become more severe as one increases the number of suppliers. The effort needed to deal with, supervise, and follow up on unreliable suppliers puts a strain on procurement resources. With little time available to deal with long-term, strategic procurement issues, the company reverts to focusing on the short-term, pressing needs. The company ends up doing much buying and very little, if any, procurement. The purchasing department comes to exist for the sole purpose of dealing with one short-term buying crisis after another. Companies that are doing multiple sourcing cannot cope with the issues that are involved in implementing supplier partnership except if they substantially increase the resources devoted to procurement.

Companies that are managing procurement so as to utilize vendors to maximum competitive advantage are fast moving to implement single-source policies. They systematically reduce the number of suppliers per part until they are buying one or an entire family of parts from a single, certified source. Ideally, there will be one supplier per family of parts when single sourcing is fully implemented. However, a rigorous single-source policy is a long-term target that may take decades to implement, so that one should anticipate a progressive evolution toward full, single-source procurement. Systematic reduction in the supplier base ought to be one goal of the overall continuous improvement effort. Despite the long-term nature of the task, many North American companies have achieved impressive results in paring down the supplier base. Xerox managed to reduce the number of its suppliers from about 3000 to 300 in less than two years. The company must be given recognition for achieving such dramatic results. However, the progress the company made partly reflects the fact that single sourcing is now a mature, proven concept. Companies no longer need to rely on experimentation and trial and error in trying to implement single sourcing. Moreover, North American companies have much leverage for reducing the number of suppliers because multiple sourcing was historically pushed to the very ridiculous extreme. Management insecurity caused companies to increase the number of suppliers well beyond what was needed even to satisfy the rationale upon which multiple sourcing was based.

Single-source procurement has numerous advantages over traditional multiple sourcing. To begin with, doing business with much fewer suppliers liberates time and resources that can be used to improve the quality of the relationship with vendors. More time can be spent to deal with suppliers and to supervise them, with no increase in staff or other resources. Time and resources saved can be redeployed to deal with long-term procurement issues. A company that cuts its supplier base in half can double the effort put on, and the attention given to, any one supplier. Vendors can be more closely supervised and purchasing control increases appreciably. Suppliers whose performance is not meeting expectations can be very quickly isolated and steps can be taken to work with them to correct the problems. Reducing the number of suppliers also means that more time can be spent to evaluate supplier capability, a necessary first step to the implementation of supplier partnership. Procurement resources can be reallocated so as to increase effectiveness. Considerably more time can be spent to ensure that the suppliers selected have the potential to perform adequately, thus minimizing subsequent procurement problems. Where a rigorous certification process is implemented, ongoing problems are the exception and not the rule. Vendor certification reduces procurement problems because it selects suppliers who are likely to be high performers. Management, by implementing supplier certification, creates a positive cycle of continuous improvement in supplier performance. A rigorous certification program operates to reduce day-to-day procurement problems, which in turn allows more time and effort to be devoted to bolstering the certification program. Single sourcing gives the company the potential to initiate such a continuous improvement cycle.

Single sourcing simplifies procurement considerably. There is less paperwork due to a reduction in the number of orders, invoices, and accounts payable. Paperless purchasing can be realistically envisaged when one is dealing with a few, highly competent suppliers. The computer and control system required to electronically link buyer and supplier are greatly simplified when there are few suppliers to deal with. Supplier evaluation and supplier performance tracking, review, and reporting are also easier. Rather than report infrequently on the performance of a large number of suppliers, the buyer can evaluate and review performance of a few suppliers intensively and extensively.

In this vein, the buying company can function with a more predictable, stable supply pattern. Fewer vendors facilitate vendor and transportation scheduling and this results in both delivery reliability and savings in transportation costs. A complex supplier network makes vendor scheduling quite difficult, if not downright impossible. With little chance for vendor scheduling, it is not possible to plan transportation so as to maximize transport equipment utilization or to arrange for haul backs. The reduction in transport costs that results from haul backs and better vendor scheduling is one important cost-reduction effect of single-source procurement. In addition, a more predictable, stable, and efficient transportation system permits the buying company to reduce both in-transit and warehouse raw materials inventories. As a company implements and evolves toward single-source procurement, there is always substantial reduction in inventory investment and transportation cost, with simultaneous improvement in delivery reliability.

As a company reduces the number of suppliers, the amount bought from each must necessarily increase. The supplier reaps some important cost advantages from this, the major one being that plant utilization increases. Some of the cost advantages can be passed on to the buyer, usually in the form of quantity discounts and price breaks. Single and not multiple sourcing may be the way to the fairest price, given the prevailing market structure.

A supplier that has been certified as the only one with whom the buying company will do business will attach very high value to the relationship and will generally try to protect and improve it. The buying company comes to be viewed as a most valuable customer who must be helped and supported. The buyer gets special, favored treatment. Suppliers in a single-sourcing relationship tend to bend over backwards to support their customers and to satisfy their requirements. By selecting a supplier as a single source, the buying company expresses full confidence in the vendor's ability to perform impeccably. Few suppliers would do anything to violate that confidence.

The certification process that leads to eventual single-source procurement itself ensures that the supplier will have the best quality available on the market. Certification assures quality, not by inspecting products when they are delivered, but by assuring that the company has quality suppliers. Quality is best assured by making sure that one has the best vendors. Vendor certification not only controls quality at the source but in addition controls the quality of the source. Control of source is by far the most effective and efficient strategy for achieving quality superiority. Vendor certification, a necessary precondition for single-source procurement, weeds out bad suppliers and motivates the best to improve, thereby guaranteeing that the buying company will have continuously improving quality. The role of single sourcing in the continuously improving procurement cycle is shown in Figure 10–3. The schema shows that supplier partnership, vendor certification, superior performance procurement, single sourcing, and continuous improvement in vendor performance are all mutually supporting, interlocking concepts.

Managing Evolution toward Single-Source Procurement

Managers who are accustomed to buying from multiple sources and come to view it as a way to assure supply security react very negatively to single sourcing as an alternative procurement policy. The idea that a company can come to rely on a single vendor for a family of parts is absolutely shocking to most managers, particularly in North America. The first reflex reaction is to propose a plethora of reasons why single sourcing cannot work. When confronted with the evidence that the best manufacturing companies have either implemented or are now implementing single-source procurement, these managers can quickly give many reasons why their own companies are different from every conceivable company that has successfully implemented the single-source concept. Most first negative reactions to single-source procurement come from culture shock, mainly because the concept originated in Japan, which is culturally very different from North America. Japan's cultural

The Continuously Improving Procurement Cycle   FIGURE 10–3

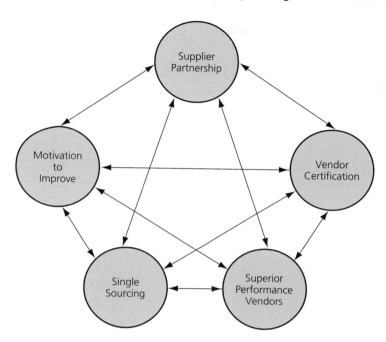

uniqueness is frequently used by managers in North America to explain why single sourcing will not work here. Procurement management in the West has always had difficulty accepting and dealing with mutual dependency between buyer and vendor. The North American psyche stubbornly resists the idea that buyer and vendor mutually depend on each other for their survival. Shared fate is accepted only with reluctance by people who from childhood have been socialized to cherish and fiercely defend their independence. "I am monarch of all I survey" is the North American operative maxim.

The best way to deal with the culture shock that single sourcing imparts is to plan for a progressive but systematic reduction in the supplier base while assuring and even improving vendor performance. Systematic, managed evolution toward single-source procurement exploits the known fact that where there are more than two vendors in a group, some will always perform better than others. A few vendors will consistently perform better than the group as a whole. By isolating the few that already give better-than-average performance, and buying exclusively from them, the company automatically increases overall buying performance. The company improves procurement effectiveness by weeding out the below-average performers. Furthermore, by eliminating the poor performing vendors the company also sends a powerful

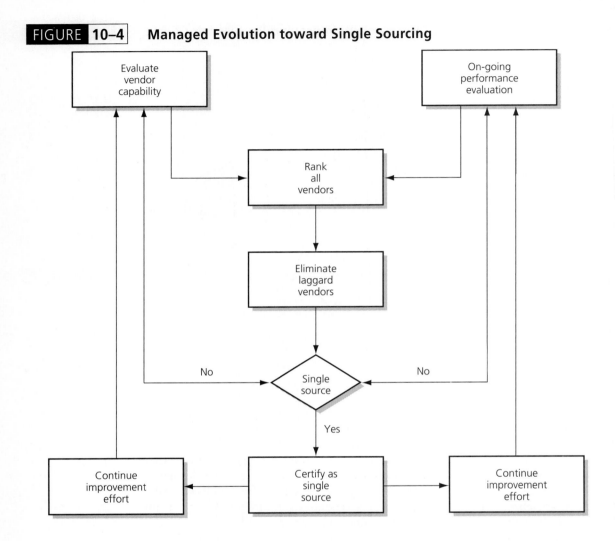

FIGURE 10–4   **Managed Evolution toward Single Sourcing**

signal that it will no longer buy from vendors who do not contribute positively to its ability to compete. That in itself is sufficient to motivate the few remaining better suppliers to push harder to improve quality, cost, and delivery performance.

One company uses the information generated by vendor-capability analysis and ongoing supplier-performance evaluation to manage and direct the evolution toward single, certified sources. The broad outlines of the procedure are shown in Figure 10–4. The capability analysis and ongoing performance evaluation were used to rank vendors. After this initial ranking all but the best two or three vendors for each part were eliminated, reducing the supplier base from 500 to about 200. Ongoing vendor evaluation continued and after 18 months, another capability evaluation of all vendors was done. Once more, the information from the capability evaluation and ongoing performance evaluation were used to rank all vendors and to eliminate the weaker ones. The results were that the company had reduced the supplier base to 120, with 30 suppliers being certified as single sources. The impact on procurement performance was dramatic. Purchasing department time devoted to order processing was cut in half. The defect rate of purchased items went from 3 percent to 0.5 percent. Supplier on-time delivery went from 82 percent to 96 percent and purchased-parts inventory went down by 65 percent. The company's goal is to buy 50 percent of its parts from certified single sources within three years. The message here is that dramatic improvements in procurement performance can be reaped well before pure single-source buying has been achieved. Furthermore, even if a company might never have a single source for each part family, the very fact that it is managing to implement single-source buying raises procurement performance considerably. Single-source buying is one potent mechanism for implementing continuous improvement in procurement.

Zero Inspection

Supplier partnership and its supporting mechanisms such as vendor-capability evaluation, vendor certification, and single sourcing all aim at guaranteeing superior quality by selecting quality suppliers to begin with. The philosophy behind this is that in procurement, like in production, product quality, delivery reliability, and low cost reflect the competence of the total organization that is responsible for them. Procurement must be managed so that the buying company probes deeper than the obvious quality manifestations and examines quality behind quality. The focus is shifted from the output, effects, or symptoms to the built-in philosophies, attitudes, programs, procedures, and systems that are driving quality in the supplier organization. This is the quality-at-the-source concept applied to procurement. Failure to evaluate the quality potential and capabilities that exist or can be made to exist in the supplier organization leads the buying company to waste much effort and valuable resources in trying to improve quality after the fact. A supplier that has not designed quality into all facets of its organization will be unable to perform to high standards in the short term except by scrapping a high proportion of defective products and passing the cost on to the buyer. Neither will such a supplier be able to sustain quality improvement in the long run, except if it takes the time and invests the resources necessary to cultivate quality excellence. The most effective and efficient way to assure quality is to control it at the source, in the supplier organization, where quality is created.

In-coming inspection is a widely used strategy for assuring quality of purchaser materials. But it is the least worst option for assuring that high-quality materials are provided to the factory. It is based on the archaic attitude that quality can be inspected into a product. As a quality-assurance procedure, in-coming inspection is bound to fail, because it does not concentrate on putting quality in at the source. Moreover, lower overall defect rates can only be attained at higher cost, where the buyer depends heavily on in-coming inspection. The vendor must eventually recoup the cost of defective materials, and the only party that can possibly pay for it is the buyer. Companies always pay for bad quality produced by their suppliers, and this is why the buyer has a deep, vested interest in selecting capable sources and in helping certified suppliers to improve on and master quality. Both vendor and customer gain when they cooperate to ameliorate quality. The buyer reaps the competitive advantages that come with quality superiority such as a higher ROI, a better market share, and more vibrant sales growth. The buyer will also likely compensate a supplier that is improving quality with a secure and growing share of business. The buyer similarly benefits by getting a higher quality at a lower relative cost. The mutually derived benefits only serve to cement and foster the partnership relationship.

Reliance on in-coming inspection, except in very rare cases where it is mandated by government regulation or required by public institutions such as the military, shows that the buyer does not have confidence in the quality assurance programs, procedures, and capabilities of the vendor. In-coming inspection is a nonconfidence vote, a lie detector test that is given to a suspect who swears that he never committed the crime. The old Russian proverb says "trust but verify," but most companies are verifying when it is much too late for verification to make much difference. Verification should be done at the source, when it can be used to prevent bad quality and avoid cost. Although managers deny that in-coming inspection is a nonconfidence vote, the evidence suggests that it is. If it is not, why is it that suppliers who have a history of delivering high-defect rates are inspected more rigorously and more frequently than those whose defect rates are relatively low? Why do companies that thoroughly evaluate vendor capability and have an effective supplier-certification program do much less in-coming inspection than those that do not? Vendor-capability analysis which leads to certification gives the buyer absolute confidence in its vendors, and promotes the mutual trust that is necessary to building a strong partnership with suppliers.

The need for in-coming inspection reveals that the supplier is failing to do it right the first time, and is relying on a defect filtering process in order to meet minimum quality standards. If the vendor rigorously applies the principle that work must be done right the first time and is successful in so doing, then there will be less need to inspect purchased materials. Actually, the situation is worse than this. A buyer who can justify in-coming inspection as a strategy to control the quality of materials is implicitly admitting that the vendor is oriented toward defect correction. Moreover, if in-coming inspection is financially justifiable, then it means that the vendor has not even successfully implemented a good defect filtering mechanism. Such a vendor is indeed a very long way from building the internal quality management discipline that will produce superior and increasing quality. In that case, any reasonable supplier capability analysis and certification program would reject a vendor like this, at least in the short term. The supplier has the responsibility to deliver 100 percent good product, all the time. The need for any level of in-coming inspection is a clear indication that the vendor is somehow failing to execute its quality responsibility. A company that inspects purchased materials is doing work that can be avoided, if the supplier is serious about quality.

Suppliers should be selected, developed, and managed so that zero in-coming inspection becomes the norm. Materials should be consistently almost defect free, thereby making it both practical and cost effective to deliver them right to the factory for immediate use, except in the exceptional situations where government regulations mandate that they must be quarantined. In-coming inspection is not needed if purchased materials have barely measurable defect rates. Supplier quality management procedures should be so effective that in-coming inspection becomes a waste. When defect rates are less than one part per hundred thousand, then there can be no valid reason for continuing in-coming inspection. At that level of defects, ten lots of 10,000 units each would have to be inspected before a single defect could be found. Suppose the sample size that is used to inspect each lot is 100. Then, the company would inspect 1000 units to try to find one defect. The one defect in the total number inspected of 1000 would represent a 1 per 1000 defect rate, which is far superior to the overall defect rate achieved by most companies. Under these circumstances, in-coming inspection is like trying to find a needle in a haystack. These arguments further reinforce the position that the only reason why companies do in-coming inspection is that vendor quality has historically been unacceptable.

Zero in-coming inspection is not unrealistic. Some managers view it as a pipe dream, but it is not. Pharmacies and hospitals generally do not sample test the products that they buy from pharmaceutical companies. The large grocery chains buy from food processing companies and put articles on the shelf without any in-coming inspection. In both pharmaceuticals and food processing, quality is critical and defects could be catastrophic to the customer. Precisely because of this, regulatory authorities have imposed severe quality-control procedures on the manufacturer. Poor-quality products that are sent to market can drive these manufacturers into bankruptcy almost overnight. Therefore, it makes extremely good business sense both from a regulatory and strategic point of view for the vendor to produce impeccable quality every time. Buyers have confidence in the product being delivered because they know that the producer has implemented very rigorous quality-control procedures. Quality control and defect prevention programs at the source vitiate the need for in-coming inspection. Zero inspection is the norm and the experience is that the system operates excellently.

What the regulatory and competitive environment have done for quality in pharmaceuticals and food processing, top management must do in industries where these factors are not as overpowering. Top management in the supplier organization has to make all employees come to see zero defects as a survival necessity and build the quality-control systems, programs, and procedures that can make products that are defect free. Buyers will naturally come to have high confidence in a supplier when the latter habitually delivers products that have barely measurable defect rates. A world-class supplier will deliberately set out to manage quality so that the in-coming inspection procedures of the customer become useless. The buyer has no need to inspect materials that are made by suppliers that are attaining near-zero defects. The new challenge in procurement, then, is to buy only from suppliers that are attaining near-zero defects.

Vendor-capability analysis and the supplier-certification process provide the data upon which the decision to implement zero inspection can be based. A vendor capability evaluation that culminates in a supplier being certified gives the proof that the company should have total confidence in the ability of the certified vendor to meet or surpass superior performance standards, as a matter of course and with minimal supervision. A company that does not have that kind of confidence in its certified suppliers should reexamine its certification process. Absolute confidence in the supplier's competitive capability should be a natural consequence of a sound vendor-certification process. Otherwise, the process is flawed because it is certifying suppliers that are judged afterwards to be weak. Consequently, zero inspection, because it reflects total confidence in vendor quality, is one benefit to be derived from implementing vendor certification. The willingness to stop in-coming inspection is the acid test that the buying company trusts vendors to deliver superior quality. Reluctance to implement zero inspection reveals that the buyer trusts neither its certification process nor the ability of vendors to meet quality expectations.

Vendor-capability improvement and reduced in-coming inspection are parallel developments. Ongoing vendor performance evaluation will indicate whether the vendor's quality is improving and whether prior improvements are being preserved. The intensity of in-coming inspection can be reduced as vendor performance evaluation shows that vendors are making and preserving significant reduction in defects. The level of inspection can be reduced either by reducing the sample size used to inspect each lot or by systematically reducing the proportion of lots that are inspected. As an illustration, a company might inspect all lots coming from a supplier when the defect rate is three parts per hundred. If quality improvement brings the defect rate down to one part per hundred and it is being sustained at the new level, then in-coming inspection can be reduced by inspecting every third lot with the same sample size. Eventually, if improvements continue, inspection could be reduced to only the amount needed to periodically audit supplier quality. A supplier who has improved quality to the point where no in-coming inspection is necessary would normally be expected to be certifiable. Zero inspection is a subgoal of vendor-capability evaluation and vendor certification and is a natural offshoot of the supplier–partnership concept applied in practice. Total confidence in supplier quality vitiates the need for in-coming inspection.

SMALL LOT PURCHASING

Reevaluating Large Lot Purchasing

Purchasing managers in North America like to buy in large lots. Many have been conditioned to think that there is no other alternative but to buy two, three, four, or even six months' material requirements. Purchasing management practice has put forward numerous arguments to justify large lot purchasing, and most managers never stop to evaluate whether the traditional arguments make sense or to question and challenge the underlying assumptions. It turns out that the reasons advanced to justify large lot purchasing do not stand up to serious analysis. Large lot purchasing was designed for the competitive and technological environment of yesteryear and one would be hard pressed to justify it in today's business conditions.

Large lot buying is often justified using the argument that one can reap quantity discounts or price breaks. The supplier designs a price structure that reduces the per unit price as the lot size ordered is increased. What economic factors make it attractive for a supplier to do this? There are usually two that are significant. The first and the one openly admitted to by vendors is that high set-up costs make it uneconomical to produce and deliver in small batches. A large order, so the argument goes, makes it possible to dilute the per unit set-up cost and the savings can be passed to the customer as price breaks or quantity discounts. While this argument has some merit when looked at superficially, it does not stand up to rigorous analysis. It is now recognized that long set-up times, far from being cast in stone, are the result of poor set-up management practices. Simply put, high set-up times reflect production management inefficiency. Management can effect dramatic reductions in set-up times and push them to the single-digit range. Price breaks that charge a higher price for small orders are effective devices for making buyers pay for poor set-up management by vendors. There is no need for quantity discounts when set-up time has been reduced to the single-digit range, because the set-up cost would be negligible. Instead of charging a higher price for small orders, the supplier should be managing so as to reduce set-up time, thereby making small orders available at the lowest price in the pricing structure. A good vendor ought to have a long-term program to constantly reduce set-up times and whether such a program has been or is being implemented should be a factor in the decision to certify the supplier.

The second factor is more insidious and most suppliers never admit that it is a consideration. Long set-up times force the vendor to do large lot production. In order to be able to quote realistic and competitive lead times when the buyer wants delivery in small quantities, the vendor must either do small lot production with the high set-up time, or else cumulate a large number of small orders to get to the economic large lot. The first option increases the per unit cost and is dealt with using the discount pricing structure referred to previously. The second option increases the inventory held by the vendor who then has to bear the high-inventory holding costs. The vendor tries to avoid these costs by encouraging the buyer to stock the material. The way this is done is to design a pricing structure that encourages the buyer to buy in large lots. The astute vendor will try to come out ahead by making sure that the price reduction given to the buyer is much less than the cost of holding the inventory. In these arrangements, the buyer who is not alert invariably loses. For example, one company thought it advantageous to buy five months' supply of a material instead of one because there was a 3 percent price reduction for doing so. However, this meant that the inventory was held for an additional four months. At an estimated annual inventory holding cost equal to 30 percent, it cost the company 10 percent to stock the item for four months. The net cost disadvantage to the buyer was 7 percent. Most discount pricing structures are designed this way, to shift the burden of holding inventory onto the unsuspecting buyer. Whatever strategy is used leads to the same fundamental conclusion. Price breaks are designed to pass the cost of the supplier's inefficient set-up management practices onto the buyer.

Another popular argument used to justify the decision to buy in large lots is that it minimizes ordering and order-processing cost and paperwork. It is argued that there are a number of activities such as vendor selection, price negotiation, purchase order write-up, order follow-up, in-coming inspection, and receiving, that must be performed every time an order is placed. Large lots, so the argument goes, increase purchasing department efficiency by minimizing the volume of these activities. Upon closer examination this argument is identical to the one used by those who justify large lot production on the basis that set-up times are long. Large lot purchasing fails to attack the true source of purchase order processing inefficiency. If the purchasing department can find ways to process each order much more efficiently, there will be no compelling reason to buy in large lots. Besides, large lot buying may save time for the purchasing department, but it creates more problems than it solves and adds more cost than it reduces. Large lot buying increases inventory and all the problems associated with it.

Transportation cost economics are also used to justify large lot buying. Transportation companies usually have rate structures that give price breaks to customers that move full loads. There are severe cost penalties associated with transporting less than the full load, and the smaller the load, the more severe the penalty when transport cost is expressed on a per unit basis. On the surface, this may appear to be a valid reason to buy in large lots. However, when the cost associated with holding inventory is factored into the decision, smaller lots are found to be more economical in many cases.

The performance measurement and evaluation system exerted considerable influence on the decision by procurement people to seek reductions in price, order processing, and transportation cost, by increasing lot sizes. Procurement managers are invariably held accountable for purchase price, ordering, and transportation cost, but are very rarely measured using inventory turns or inventory holding cost. Moreover, once purchased parts pass an initial quality test, subsequent quality deterioration because materials are held in inventory for long periods are rarely imputed back to the purchasing department. In fact, inventory and nonquality costs are rarely computed, much less imputed to any department at all. The performance evaluation system drove the procurement department to maximize performance along the measures for which it was held accountable. Top management, by the way it chose to measure and evaluate purchasing performance, forced procurement managers to pursue their departmental self-interest to the detriment of the company as a whole. A manager whose performance is evaluated on the basis of price, ordering, and transportation cost to the exclusion of inventory carrying and nonquality cost, will automatically attempt to minimize per unit and transportation cost by maximizing lot sizes. Purchase lot size reduction will never be aggressively pursued, unless the procurement performance evaluation system used by a company is designed to make managers accountable for raw materials, inventory reduction, and nonquality costs. This is the absolute minimum condition.

The factors that influence the decision to buy in large lots are in fact variables that can be changed by managerial action. Small lot purchasing is feasible if management views these factors as constraints to be broken by managerial intervention. Both order processing and transportation costs can be radically reduced by management programs that specifically aim to reduce them. A few companies have been able to cut order processing cost and time to near zero by implementing advanced technologies such as EDI (Electronic Data Interchange). Some companies have reduced transportation cost by up to 60 percent, while simultaneously reducing purchase lot sizes by up to 75 percent and purchase lead times from several weeks to a few days. Figure 10–5 shows the relationship between order processing and transportation costs and purchase lot sizes. Management has considerable leverage over these costs and by driving them down, the constraints that make large lot purchasing necessary are broken or relaxed. Small lot purchasing becomes not only feasible but financially attractive as well. C_{O+T} is the total order processing plus transportation cost and C_H is the total inventory holding cost. As the

FIGURE 10–5   **Economical Small Lot Purchasing**

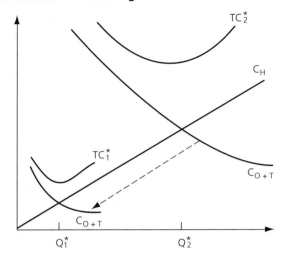

total ordering plus transportation cost is driven down, the economic purchase lot size goes down to Q_1^*, from Q_2^*. The associated total cost goes down from TC_2^* to TC_1^*. The principle is that procurement must be managed to make small lot purchasing economical.

Advantages of Small Lot Purchasing

Beyond the purely financial considerations, small lot purchasing makes sense for many reasons. As with small lot production, feedback on quality is quicker. The buyer is using each small lot more quickly and comes to discover defects sooner, even where zero inspection is the norm. For instance, suppose the policy is to buy twelve weeks' usage of a particular material or 6000 units. Because it is used at the rate of 500 per week, a few defects in the first 1000 will not cause any concern since there is always hope that the remaining 5000 units will have a low enough defect rate that will compensate for the higher than normal number of defects found earlier. By the time that one realizes that the entire lot is bad, several weeks will have passed and it may be much too late for the supplier to do anything about the problem that caused the defects. But if the policy is to buy one week's usage at a time, the few defects discovered early on will cause production people to get suspicious and maybe inspect all the remaining pieces. In any event, the entire lot will be used in only one week and the quality of the entire lot will be known in that time. The supplier can receive feedback on quality one week after the material was delivered instead of several weeks later, as is the case when large lot purchasing is the policy.

Push versus Pull Synchronized Procurement FIGURE 10–6

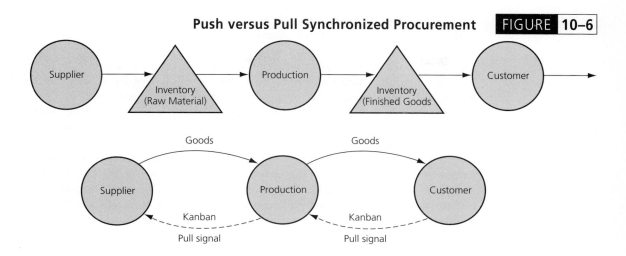

Small lots are essential to implementing JIT purchasing. The smaller the lots are, the closer buying can be matched with the material requirements generated by small lot, repetitive production. Purchase lot sizes can be reduced to the point that daily delivery of materials can be made directly to the factory floor, without passing through a raw material warehouse. All materials inventory are held as floor stock. Progress in purchase lot size reduction has enabled a few companies to pull materials from the delivery bay and into the plant almost continuously. The pull production system is thus extended to suppliers, where the signal for the supplier to deliver comes from a material pull signal emitted by the first operation in the user's process. Nissan Motors has implemented such a pull system to effectively synchronize the supplier delivery schedule with its own daily pull production schedule. Kanbans are generated by the daily material requirements of the first operation in Nissan's factories. The Kanbans needed are electronically computed and transmitted to suppliers on a daily basis, with no paper being involved. In this way, the supplier delivery schedule exactly matches Nissan's daily production schedule and material requirements. Figure 10-6 shows the typical push procurement logic based on large lot purchasing and the pull logic using Kanban signals to link buyer and supplier schedules. The push approach buys materials to put into inventory. As purchase lot sizes are reduced, the buffering inventory between supplier and user represented by the raw materials warehouse, shrinks. When raw material inventory has been reduced to just a few days' supply, the Kanban pull system can be used to synchronize production and procurement. Raw materials are pulled as needed from suppliers.

Purchase lot size reduction, then, is essential to synchronized production and procurement, and to linking the production schedules of the supplier and the user, which are the fundamental requirements of JIT purchasing. The resultant impact on raw materials inventories is mindboggling. Companies that were carrying two to three months' raw materials requirements in inventory are now carrying a few days' supply. It is now known that large purchase lot sizes are the major reason why raw materials inventories are inordinately high and inventory turns extremely low. Purchase lot sizes are usually much higher than they need to be because procurement managers cultivated the attitude that there was little that they could do to reduce order processing and transportation costs, beyond increasing lot sizes to capitalize on discount pricing and transportation cost structures. The large lot purchasing strategy solved nothing, but instead replaced order processing and transportation with inventory holding cost. It also created other visceral problems that left the company worse off. What was good for the purchasing department was very bad for the company as a whole. Purchase lot size reduction gives real gains in procurement effectiveness by pursuing absolute improvement in order processing and transportation efficiency. The resultant decrease in raw materials inventories and favorable impacts on quality eliminate associated costs without adding new ones, thereby reducing overall costs.

Waste Removal in Order Processing and Transportation

The guiding principle in manufacturing and competitive excellence is that waste elimination is the major source of productive efficiency. Real increases in order processing and transportation efficiency come from waste removal in these two areas. Small lot purchasing is practical, provided that the reduction in purchase and transportation lot sizes is propelled by real improvements in order processing and transportation efficiency. The continuous improvement process must zero in on waste in these areas.

Waste in order processing can be pinpointed only when the specific time-consuming and cost-adding activities involved are identified and analyzed. The following list of activities gives an idea as to what is called for by purchase order processing:

1. Need recognition
2. Purchase requisition preparation
3. Purchase requisition transmission
4. Purchase requisition verification by the purchasing department
5. Supplier choice and negotiation
6. Purchase order preparation
7. Purchase order transmission
8. Receipt and scheduling of the purchase order by the vendor
9. Vendor queue time
10. Vendor production time
11. Transportation time

Supplier Partnership and Certification and Lead Time Length

FIGURE 10–7

Lead Time Controllability	Lead time length	
	Short	*Long*

Controllable	1. Need recognition
	2. Purchase requisition preparation
	3. Purchase requisition transmission
	4. Purchase requisition verification
	6. Purchase order preparation
	7. Purchase order transmission
	12. In-coming quality inspection
	14. Receipt and stocking
	
	   *Supplier partnership
	   *EDI
	   *Kanban
		5. Supplier choice and negotiation
		8. Receipt and scheduling of purchase order by supplier
		9. Vendor queue time
		10. Vendor production time
		11. Transportation time
		12. In-coming quality inspection
		
		   *Supplier partnership

Noncontrollable		13. Quarantine requirements

12. Incoming quality inspection
13. Quarantine requirements (where applicable)
14. Receipt and stocking activities by the warehouse

The supplier lead time is the sum of the time taken by all these activities.

Figure 10–7 classifies these activities along two dimensions: (1) duration under normal circumstances and (2) degree of control normally exercised by the buyer over each. The major mechanisms for their elimination or for reducing the time consumed by each activity is also shown. The analysis shows that all the long lead-time activities and therefore those that add substantially to ordering cost, can be eliminated or drastically reduced by implementing supplier certification and the partnership concept. Supplier choice and negotiation, vendor queue time, and in-coming quality inspection, are either not necessary or take very little time, when a buyer has a group of solid, certified suppliers. The short but controllable activities can also be eliminated or significantly reduced by current technologies such as EDI or by JIT mechanisms like Kanban. A supplier partnership program also helps to make these short-duration activities more efficient or to eliminate them altogether. The conclusion is that order-processing time and cost can be reduced by 95 percent to 98 percent by a well-designed waste elimination program.

Waste in transportation is particularly prevalent in the North American context. The United States and Canada are respectively the fourth and the second largest countries in the world, geographically. Canada is a very sparsely populated country with a population density of about seven people per square mile. The continental United States and Canada cover a geographical area of some 6,600,000 square miles and four different time zones. Linking these two countries into a free trade area means that goods must be transported long distances to be taken to market. North American managers frequently use this physical fact to argue that efficiency in transportation comparable to what exists in Western Europe and Japan is not attainable here. Logistics managers in North America have become blind to waste in transportation because of the popularly accepted arguments.

While it is true that Western Europe and Japan have distinctive advantages in transportation efficiency due to their limited geographical areas and extremely high population densities, a North American company can do much to make transportation more efficient by identifying and eliminating waste. There are six prevalent sources of waste in transportation:

1. Waste in time: inefficient transportation increases lead time
2. Waste in inventory due to over-transportation
3. Waste in storage space when large lots are bought to capitalize on transport economies
4. Waste due to rush orders, by forcing a slow, inflexible transport system to deliver rapidly and respond flexibly
5. Waste due to bad quality because materials deteriorate when transport times are long
6. Waste due to internal warehouse transportation: a large warehouse requires many and longer moves to stock and pick materials

Once more, much improvement in efficiency can be made by attacking these wastes. A handful of North American companies have been able to reduce transport lot sizes by up to 80 percent, cut lead times from six weeks to four days, and reduce per unit transport costs by 40 percent, managing logistics so as to eliminate waste in transportation.

JIT distribution demands that the transportation system be organized and planned to efficiently deliver and pick up small loads. Route flexibility and the versatility to move different types of material using the same transport mode are essential. Multiple pick-ups and deliveries are a necessity. The transport system must be designed for quick response and delivery time, with no or little loss in transport efficiency. JIT companies need to have a quick transport rescheduling capability, which can be achieved if more attention is paid to logistics planning, supported by much more investment in transport management. The necessary conditions can be well met by an astutely designed and managed system based on trucking. JIT distribution companies invariably find out that trucking takes an increasingly larger share of their transportation requirements. Trucks can be designed for side loading which makes multiple pick-ups and deliveries practical. Nestable containers and scheduling for haulbacks give flexibility and versatility while simultaneously reducing cost and

	Time between Production and Consumption of a Pharmaceutical Product				TABLE 10–1

	Actual		Potential	
	Turns	**Days**	**Turns**	**Days**
Inventory level (manufacturer)	2	180	9	40
Inventory level (wholesalers)	4	90	12	30
Inventory level (retailers)	6	60	18	20
		330		90

time. Black and Decker has had impressive results by using trucks for repetitive, multiple deliveries and pick-ups of very small loads in JIT mode. Transport lead times, on the average, went down to days from weeks. Transport cost decreased by 30 percent in some cases mainly because of a 60 percent haul-back rate. More and more companies are proving that JIT distribution can be done even in North America and the gains are as impressive as in Japan or Western Europe.

High levels of distribution inventories increase the time between production of a product and its consumption or use by the customer. Table 10–1 shows how the inventory level affects the elapsed time between production and consumption of a pharmaceutical product. The calculations were done using two alternative scenarios, one based on the actual, approximate results for inventory turns and the other based on what an analysis showed could be achieved within two years by implementing JIT distribution concepts.

The existing inventory level held by the producer and the other intermediaries in the distribution channel meant that the product was being consumed by the customer 330 days after it was produced although this is a product whose shelf life is critical to its performance. Another interpretation is that the manufacturer is 330 days away or removed from its final customer. Any feedback that the producer receives from the market relative to product performance, product acceptance, the evolution of sales levels, and consumer reaction to extrinsic product characteristics such as aesthetics and packaging functionality, is at least 330 days late. For this reason, the company in question found it very difficult to forecast sales accurately, because the data on sales history at the retail level lagged actual sales at the manufacturing level by 150 days. JIT distribution, by reducing the inventory at each level in the distribution channel, would considerably reduce the time between production and consumption. Feedback on product performance and quality would be much more rapid and the company would be closer to its market and its customers. Inventory pushes a manufacturer further and further away from the end customer and from the heartbeat of the market.

TABLE 10–2	Impact of Ordering and Transportation Cost Reduction on Some Key Performance Parameters		
		Ordering cost $100	Ordering cost $4
Purchase lot size, Q, $Q = \sqrt{\dfrac{2 \times D \times O}{h}}$		1000 units	200 units
Total annual ordering cost		$ 2,000	$ 400
Total annual holding cost		2,000	400
Total transportation cost		30,000	18,000
Total cost		$34,000	$18,800
Average inventory		500 units	100 units
Inventory turns per year		40	200
Days materials held in inventory		9	2

Effects of Reducing Ordering and Transportation Cost: An Illustrative Example

Table 10–2 computes the impact of reducing ordering and transportation cost on a few key performance parameters such as inventory turns, days materials are held in stock, and total costs, including transportation cost. It has already been proposed, on the basis of the experience of a few leading companies, that 95 percent reductions in ordering cost are entirely feasible, given modern technology, a supplier partnership program, Kanban, and synchronized repetitive purchasing. The Black and Decker experience teaches us that transport costs can be reduced by 30 percent, using a well-organized, planned, scheduled, and controlled trucking system. Putting all these data together gives the calculations shown in Table 10–2. The demand for the item in question is estimated at 20,000 units per year, and the annual inventory holding cost is $4.00 per unit.

Applying the formula for the economic order quantity, Q, we have the lot sizes shown. The per unit transportation cost is assumed to be $1.50 and a 40 percent reduction reduces it to $0.90. The data speak for themselves. Reductions in ordering and transportation cost have a dramatic impact on procurement and distribution performance.

Conclusion

The concepts upon which superior procurement performance is based are neither numerous nor hard to implement. Once managers challenge the conventional thinking and formulate and operationalize a new vision of the role and impact of procurement on the company's competitive performance, they unleash the forces that sustain superior procurement performance. The new vision asserts that vendors (suppliers) are critical to a company's competitive success and should thus be managed as an integral part of a company's competitive strategy. That is to say, a company's competitive strategy is partially executed by its suppliers. A company can improve on what vendors deliver or can control for vendor weaknesses on cost, quality, lead time, flexibility, and innovation only at great cost. They can avoid such cost by choosing the right vendors and managing procurement to world-class excellence.

The effective execution of competitive strategy, then, requires tight coordination, cooperation, and mutual trust and confidence between customer and vendor. The concepts of supplier partnership, vendor certification, and single sourcing are but ways to operationalize the new vision of the role and impact of suppliers on the company's competitive position. The need is for managerial, as opposed to physical, integration of vendor and customer organizations. The purpose is to achieve tight strategic and organizational coordination of two autonomous but mutually dependent organizations. Such coordination does not require that the supplier and customer organizations be identical in culture and values. But it does suggest that there must be compatibility of culture, values, business philosophy, business mission, and market vision. Compatibility means that the supplier and customer can work together to pursue mutually beneficial strategic objectives while maintaining their corporate distinctiveness. Compatibility assures that supplier and customer can work closely together and yet maintain a state of healthy tension from which cross-fertilization of ideas and new ways of serving the market can emerge.

Every world-class company is unequivocally a world-class supplier and thus has the wherewithal to choose, manage, nurture, and retain vendors that help it compete in a global market. Management simply has to require that vendors perform to the same exacting standards demanded by the company's customers. The fact that a company is a world-class competitor confers on it the legitimacy to require superior performance from its suppliers. Acceptance of anything less than vendor excellence on quality, cost, service, and innovation is to vitiate the very principles and values upon which one's own success is based.

Case for Discussion

OUTDOOR SPORTS, INC. (OSI)

It was a year ago that we decided to start doing major sourcing from the Far East, so it is time to assess whether the policy worked as we had expected. Should we hold the line, strengthen our relationship with our Asian sources or increase our efforts to develop some more? Of course, that depends on the competition and the effectiveness of our new strategy.

The Company and Its Strategy

OSI was the U.S. affiliate of a large European conglomerate. The parent company competed in six different industries ranging from sports equipment manufacturing and distribution to petrochemicals and had sales of $4.2 billion in fiscal 1990. The U.S. subsidiary produced a variety of sports and fitness products such as skis, hockey pads and gloves, ski boots, poles, and jogging and hiking shoes, with sales of $145 million in fiscal 1991, and was operated as an autonomous business unit.

OSI was a relatively small player in a huge market and the company survived by being an aggressive competitor, exercising meticulous control over cost, emphasizing customer service, being quick to spot and respond to emerging trends, relying on a team of managers that were thoroughly knowledgeable about the industry, and maintaining a very lean structure. For example, the top management at OSI consisted of only four individuals and that same leanness was maintained right through to shop floor supervisors. A typical plant with 95 employees was managed by one manager and three supervisors. The company was among the most profitable in its industry, and had achieved that performance even as some competitors were closing plants. OSI quickly closed down unprofitable plants and opened or acquired new businesses related to the sports and fitness industry to quickly shift resources away from stagnant segments and into promising ones.

The Competitive Situation

Competition in the sports and fitness industry was fierce. The market was dominated by a few large companies such as Reebok and Nike that spent hundreds of millions of dollars on new product design, promotion, and penetration and support of distribution channels. Margins were high but product development and advertising and promotion costs cut deep into profits. By focusing on the more basic products and keeping promotion and development costs low, companies like OSI survived in the interstices of the market serving the less fashion-conscious, more value-seeking customers. OSI's net profit margin was 3 percent in 1991, a figure that was 33 percent higher than the average for companies of its size.

Income Statements ($00,000)			TABLE 10–3
	1990		**1991**
Sales	1280		1450
Cost of sales:			
Beg. inv. (raw mat. and in-proc.)	52		45
Direct labor	394		299
Manufacturing overhead	187		146
Purchases (raw mat.)	383		307
	1016		797
End. inv. (raw mat. and in-proc.)	45		32
Cost of goods manufactured	971		765
Beg. inv. (finished goods)	185		213
Purchases (finished goods)	35		237
	1191		1215
End inv. (finished goods)	213		200
Cost of goods sold		978	1015
Gross profit		302	435
Selling, admin., and other expenses		276	391
Net profit		26	44

Manufacturing and Procurement

OSI operated in what is commonly called the needle trades where cutting and sewing various materials constituted the bulk of the manufacturing process. These industries were labor intensive and were coming under increasing pressure from production in low-wage countries. Per unit manufacturing cost for the typical U.S. plant was composed of 40 percent labor, 40 percent materials, and 20 percent overhead, even if the bulk of U.S. manufacturing was concentrated in the lower wage southern states, and it was known that the industry relied heavily on undocumented workers that were willing to work for very low wages in sweat shop conditions.

Historically, OSI had manufactured all its requirements and located its plants reasonably close to its major markets so as to shorten its response time. Table 10–3 presents the financial statements for 1990 and 1991.

The company's purchasing department consisted of one manager who reported to the vice-president of production, two buyers, and one administrative assistant. Although OSI did no formal vendor certification, it had a long-standing policy of building close, long-term relationships with suppliers and cooperating with them to the maximum to solve mutual problems and assure superior performance. Lower than expected vendor performance did not automatically result in lost business for the supplier. OSI would first work with the supplier to solve the problem and would only end the relationship if there was strong disagreement as to what should be done or if several attempts to solve the problem did not produce the desired results. The company expected superior, constant or improving performance on cost, quality, and delivery, and constantly evaluated suppliers on these dimensions. As a result, the company's purchasing cost was well in line with what prevailed in the industry, even if OSI was a small company by industry standards.

International Sourcing

As early as 1987, it became clear to OSI management that the needle trades would have serious difficulty competing against low-wage countries. The company's wage rates, including benefits, averaged $11.50 per hour, compared to $0.75 an hour in many Asian countries. The actual cost advantage was much greater than this because these countries had virtually no restrictive labor laws, had weak or no unions, low rates of absenteeism, few government controls, low taxes, direct government support in the form of cheap infrastructure, and subsidized energy costs. In 1988, the company gave a few trial orders for finished goods to some suppliers in Taiwan, South Korea, and the Philippines and found that the landed cost was 25 percent lower than its own manufacturing cost and quality levels were comparable. OSI found these suppliers to be reliable, eager to learn, aggressive in seeking new business, and valued the relationship with their customers. Purchases from OSI's Asian suppliers were increased slowly until 1990 when OSI decided to redirect its sourcing.

The change in procurement strategy had four components:

1. A shift in buying of materials from domestic to Asian suppliers to the tune of $16 million;
2. Using a captive supplier in the Philippines to produce $4.5 million worth of gloves;
3. Buying a 30 percent interest in a small Taiwanese manufacturer and sourcing $6.3 million worth of pads from it;
4. Buying a plant in South Korea and using it to produce $9.4 million worth of jogging shoes.

The new procurement strategy had been fully in place for one year now, and Anne Brenton, president of OSI had called a meeting to evaluate its effectiveness and to decide if it should be reinforced. She summarized the issues raised in the course of the meeting:

I agree it has not been smooth sailing, but we are learning how to do business in Asia. As our friends in purchasing have argued, the domestic suppliers will respond and eventually eliminate the advantage that Asia has in labor and other costs. But the question is when and can we afford to sit by and wait for them to do so? Wages in Asia will catch up to U.S. levels, but can we realistically expect that to happen before 25 years. Japan has had a labor cost advantage since the 1920s and rapid industrialization since the 1950s has not wiped it out. Should we deepen our reliance on Asia and what are the consequences if we do? These are some of the tough questions, my friends, and we better come up with some good answers very fast.

Discussion Questions

1. How has OSI managed to survive in a market dominated by large companies?
2. What is the financial and strategic impact of the new procurement strategy?
3. What are the advantages and disadvantages of the new procurement strategy put in place by OSI? What is involved in "Learning to do business in Asia," and are there any competitive (strategic) advantages to be derived from such learning?
4. Should the company increase its reliance on the Far East? What would be the advantages and disadvantages of so doing?

References

Ansari, A., and Batoul Modarress, "JIT Purchasing as a Quality and Productivity Centre," *International Journal of Production Research,* 26, 1, 1988.

Ellram, Lisa M., "The Supplier Selection Decision in Strategic Partnerships," *Journal of Purchasing and Materials Management,* Fall 1990.

Newman, Richard G., "The Buyer-Supplier Relationship under Just-In-Time," *Production and Inventory Management Journal,* third quarter, 1988.

Sakai, R., "The Feudal World Japanese Manufacturing," *Harvard Business Review,* November–December, 1990.

Schonberger, Richard J., and Abdolhossein Ansari, "Just-In-Time Purchasing Can Improve Quality," *Journal of Purchasing and Materials Management,* Spring 1984.

Managing Maintenance for Zero Breakdowns

Most managers believe that breakdowns are inevitable. The corporate credo is that it is normal for a company to have a certain level of breakdowns and the unplanned downtime associated with it. An equal number of managers, both within and outside of the maintenance department harbor the attitude that the costs related to breakdowns are both unavoidable and insignificant. The way the vast majority of companies manage maintenance reflects these deeply entrenched attitudes, and the maintenance policies and practices adopted by these companies are guaranteed to give results that confirm and reinforce the prevailing attitudes. Maintenance has been inadvertently put into a vicious cycle of self-fulfilling prophecies that have "ghettoized" both the maintenance departments and the factories they are supposed to care for. If you cannot avoid breakdowns, then you will not manage to prevent them, and so you are bound to have them, which means that you were right that you cannot avoid them—this is the circular reasoning upon which much current maintenance policy is founded. Maintenance policy and issues have been couched in popular catch phrases that are as simplistic as they are dangerous. "If it works, don't fix it." "Stop it only when it stops." "We have to maximize up time, so patch it up as quickly as you can." "I do not care if you have to tie it with bailing wire, as long as you get it up and running fast." "We have a cost advantage because our equipment is fully depreciated." These popular phrases reflect attitudes that are nourished by wrong conceptions of maintenance issues and poor understanding of how far a strong maintenance program can go toward eliminating breakdowns.

A small but growing number of companies are questioning the old assumptions and the maintenance policies and practices that derive from them. Outstanding world-class companies in North America, Western Europe, Japan, and the other industrialized Pacific Rim countries are challenging the conventional wisdom on maintenance and breakdowns, and are discovering in the process, that it is reasonable to think in terms of zero breakdowns. These very same companies have come to realize that even though zero breakdowns are theoretically impossible to attain, the maintenance system can be designed and managed to achieve breakdown rates that are tantalizingly close to zero. The maintenance system is being used to push machine capability and reliability very close to their technological limits. Over the last decade, companies that are operating at the cutting edge of maintenance system design and management have discovered that breakdowns, far from being insignificant, impose some severe cost penalties, operating, and competitive constraints on a company. Maintenance is increasingly being viewed, designed and managed as a source of profits and competitive advantage. Changes in managerial thinking that have taken place over the last ten years have led top management in a few companies to conclude that breakdowns are inherently bad, and that there can be no acceptable level of breakdowns except zero.

THE STRATEGIC ROLE OF MAINTENANCE

Most managers trivialize the role of maintenance, seeing it as a set of strictly operational activities with no strategic impact. But, there is abundant evidence to the contrary. In some sectors, such as civilian air transport, medical delivery, electricity generation by public utilities, and the military, equipment reliability is critical and the maintenance function must be managed as a premier strategic instrument. In the process-intensive industries such as steel, petrochemicals, sugar and petroleum refining, and aluminum production, capital, fixed labor and overhead costs are a very high proportion of total costs. Equipment reliability affects output, productivity, and unit costs in a very important way, and maintenance management is vital to overall market success. Some of the most powerful technologies and management approaches that companies increasingly depend on to continuously improve their operations and achieve superior competitive performance depend on or presuppose an effective maintenance management system that assures equipment reliability. Notable among these are robotization, flexible manufacturing systems (FMS), JIT, and SPC. Robots and FMSs must operate predictably and reliably, or else high levels of downtime will wipe out the potential advantages that can be derived from them. JIT requires equipment reliability to attain JIT delivery and to expunge work-in-process inventories from the system. SPC can only lead to process improvement if maintenance uses it to identify the causes of unacceptable variation and systemic quality problems and then take maintenance related actions to correct these problems and prevent their recurrence. Figure 11–1 on the following page shows that maintenance, JIT, TQM/SPC, and key process technologies meet at some crucial interfaces.

We see once more that the goal of manufacturing strategy is to derive *strategic* and *competitive advantage* from *operations*. It is often a useless exercise to differentiate between the strategic and the operational. In the pursuit of manufacturing excellence, the operational is strategic, and corporate strategy must be deployed broadly in all operational activities. The Japanese

FIGURE 11–1 **Critical Interfaces That Underscore the Strategic Role of Maintenance**

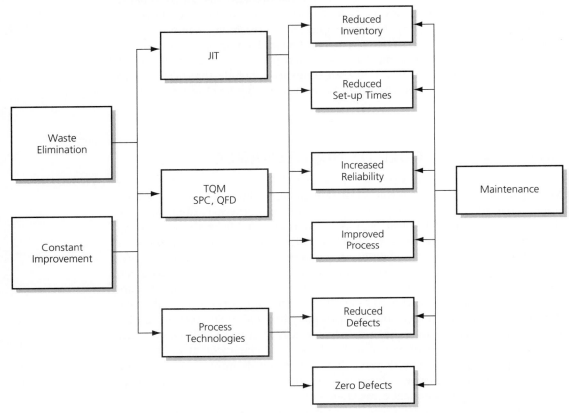

have done much to teach us this lesson and the best-managed companies in North America are fast learning it.

PROBLEMS CAUSED BY POOR MAINTENANCE MANAGEMENT

Breakdowns or Unplanned Downtime

Inadequate maintenance has a direct and visible impact on equipment availability, or what is commonly referred to as uptime. Downtime rates of 10 to 25 percent are usual in companies that pay scant attention to maintenance.

Equipment that is poorly maintained breaks down frequently causing work stoppages and disruptions in the work flow. It is not unusual to find plants where downtime and breakdowns are the norm and employees and managers have come to expect several work stoppages in any one day. Low machine availability is the standard in many companies, which partly explains why capacity utilization in North American plants averages about 70 percent. With 10 to 25 percent downtime so widespread, it is small wonder that those companies that are experiencing 5 percent downtime rates are seen as doing an excellent job of managing maintenance and see little need to try to improve. A 5 percent downtime rate looks impressive when a large number of plants have 20 percent downtime.

Historically, the management reporting system has also played a major role in sheltering the downtime problem from top management scrutiny. Companies generally do not compute and report on the direct cost of downtime. A handful attempt to report on direct downtime costs, but the available cost figures grossly understate probable downtime costs because the indirect costs are either overlooked, ignored, or assumed to be negligible. However, in most cases, the indirect costs associated with downtime are likely to dwarf the direct, easily measurable costs. One lumber manufacturing company was experiencing one hour of unplanned downtime per eight hour shift in a plant that employed 120 people. The average hourly wage was $6.50, so the plant accountant estimated downtime costs at $780 per day or $525,000 per year, because the plant worked three shifts per day. This company did a far better job than most in reporting on downtime costs. Nevertheless, the reported cost figures severely underestimated the true downtime costs. A more accurate analysis revealed that the indirect costs were much higher than the $525,000 direct cost figure. These costs are shown in Table 11–1 on the following page. The figures used by the company ignored the contribution on lost output because the plant was operating at "full" capacity. It also ignored the cost of defects, lost productivity during start-ups after breakdowns were repaired and the reduction in equipment useful life, all caused by frequent breakdowns. Top management, because it has the responsibility to approve the reporting system that is put in place, is ultimately responsible for the fact that the true cost of breakdowns is invisible or grossly understated, thereby shielding the downtime problem from appropriate action to eliminate its causes.

Breakdowns are largely avoidable and the evidence is conclusive that they are caused by weaknesses in corporate policies, attitudes, and vision that in turn shape and legitimize erroneous maintenance management policies, practices, and priorities. Machines that are managed so as to avoid breakdowns, breakdown much less often than those that are not. The human body is probably the most complex, sophisticated, and versatile machine known. It is fine-tuned to near perfection and has a degree of reliability that is mind-boggling, despite the severe punishment and maltreatment that it receives. Prior to the 1970s, medical science placed much emphasis on curative medicine to treat

TABLE 11–1	**Breakdown Cost Analysis**		
Direct cost			
Labor			$ 525,000
Indirect costs			
Lost contribution		$448,000	
Loss due to defects		180,000	
Lost productivity during start-up after breakdowns		120,000	
Estimated cost resulting from reduction of equipment useful life		190,000	
Other indirect costs		85,000	
			1,023,000
			$1,548,000
Indirect costs as a percentage of total downtime costs			66.08%

diseases. Since the 1970s, however, medical science has recognized that curative medicine has probably gone almost as far as it can in treating diseases. Preventive medicine is fast taking hold and is now recognized as a far superior strategy for maintaining good health. Morbidity rates are much lower for groups that emphasize prevention habits such as regular exercise, weight control, good eating habits, and avoidance of tobacco, excessive alcohol, and stress, than for those that do not. The evidence is that life expectancy can be increased by as much as 20 percent by following the guidelines prescribed by preventive medicine. Incapacity caused by serious illness can also be reduced to virtually zero or can be delayed until old age. Similarly, in the manufacturing context, breakdowns can be reduced to negligible levels and equipment useful life can be increased by 30 percent with a sound preventive maintenance program.

Modern jet aircraft are among the most complex machines ever built. Breakdowns and malfunctions are almost always fatal for the customer and devastating for the company's market image and competitive position. Regulatory agencies have imposed rigorous preventive maintenance programs on the passenger airline industry and compliance by airline companies is closely monitored. Accidents are thoroughly investigated by government agencies that are responsible for passenger safety. The breakdown rate is not zero, but it is not far from it. The average jet aircraft functions for 20 or more years without a breakdown or catastrophic malfunction. During these 20 years, an average aircraft would have flown for 40,000 hours with no breakdowns or malfunctions in flight. Any manufacturing company that achieves 2 hours downtime for just 2,000 operating hours, a rate much higher than what airline companies achieve, would have a revolution in manufacturing excellence. Deregulation of the airline industry in the United States by the Reagan administration put a severe squeeze on profits. Some companies tried to cut costs by postponing or reducing preventive maintenance. The results were quick and predictable. Equipment breakdowns, accident rates, and malfunctions in flight rose dramatically, confirming that the maintenance program was instrumental in avoiding breakdowns and malfunctions. Some world-class manufacturing companies in Japan and Germany are attaining uptime rates that are higher than 90 percent and there is a clear consensus that the maintenance program is the major contributing factor.

JIT production is impossible to implement in an environment where there are too many breakdowns. JIT delivery to the subsequent operation, including the customer, is wholly thwarted by unreliable equipment. Pull production scheduling, a cornerstone of the JIT mode of manufacturing, is not feasible if the equipment does not operate reliably and predictably. When production is triggered by the tightly synchronized pull schedule, the whole production schedule is thrown into disorder if any supplying operation cannot respond. Breakdowns prevent the supplying operation from responding punctually to the pull schedule. An operation that is frequently disrupted by breakdowns cannot be organized and controlled to produce to a continuous and synchronous production flow. Breakdowns create bottlenecks making it impossible to balance capacity and level the output (load) produced by the factory. Machines that break down frequently encourage management to place buffer inventories between operations in the hope that these will enable the factory to produce continuously. Buffer inventories cut against the grain of the fundamental JIT principle that inventories are bad and must be eliminated. It follows that zero breakdown maintenance is not only a cornerstone of any credible strategy to achieve superior manufacturing performance, but it is also necessary to implement full JIT production. Companies that are implementing JIT very quickly discover that unreliable equipment is a major barrier to their ability to tightly synchronize and integrate production.

Higher Defect Rates

Equipment that breaks down frequently can be a major cause of defects. Processes are known to deteriorate rapidly just before a malfunction causes a breakdown. Feedback statistical process control exploits the idea that unacceptable variations in product characteristics are directly traceable to variations in process functioning. Identifiable malfunctions in the process are rightly assumed to cause unacceptable variations in product parameters. A malfunction is nothing more than a defect in the process that can be isolated and corrected, and it means that the equipment is operating well below its potential. Machine operators find that it is difficult to operate the process to hold the tolerances during the slightest malfunction. It either takes more time to produce to the tolerances or the scrap level increases causing efficiency to be lower than the standard. It is a known fact that malfunctions, whether or not they culminate in breakdowns, are a major source of process variability, and consequently, a major cause of defects. Quality also suffers soon after a breakdown has been repaired, either because of fine tuning or because it takes time for the equipment or the operator to "work up to speed." Process variability tends to be high soon after a start-up and remains high until the process enters the steady state. Therefore, both the malfunctions that can lead to breakdowns and the breakdowns themselves contribute to higher than expected defect rates.

Longer Set-Up Times

Poorly maintained equipment takes more time to change over. Set-up personnel are generally part of the maintenance department, which makes it likely that inadequate maintenance management policies, practices, and procedures will show up in the way setups are viewed, planned, coordinated, and executed. Attitudes toward setup reflect the overall quality of the maintenance management environment. A company that tolerates having equipment that break down frequently is a company that will accept all the excuses as to why setups cannot be reduced. Managers that accept the idea that breakdowns are inevitable will never manage to reduce breakdowns and their companies are guaranteed to experience high losses due to downtime. These same managers reveal an attitude toward breakdowns that is nurtured, reinforced, or at least permitted by a particular corporate culture. That same culture and value system will nurture or reinforce the idea that long setups are the norm. In organizations, as in societies, things are usually interrelated in many subtle ways. Companies that tolerate mediocrity in any one business activity will end up tolerating mediocrity in all activities. The companies that are today driving hard to achieve zero defects are the same ones that are pushing for single digit setups and zero breakdowns. High breakdowns and long setups are inexorably linked because they have a common source—a corporate culture and value system created by top management which accepts yesterday's performance as the norm for today and tomorrow.

Poor maintenance also affects set-up times in a more direct way. When equipment is poorly maintained, it is not unusual for set-up personnel to find out, while setups are being performed, that certain parts are badly in need of repairs or have to be replaced altogether. If there was a rigorous preventive maintenance program, these parts would have been discovered during preventive maintenance when their replacement is planned or expected, and no undue work stoppage would take place. The time necessary to replace or repair the part cannot be avoided by a preventive maintenance program, but its replacement can be planned during a period where this would cause no stoppage or when the impact of such a stoppage would be least costly. Bad parts that are discovered during setups unnecessarily lengthen set-up time and cause disruptions to the work flow at a time most likely to have the most dire consequences on productivity, flexibility, and quality. Moreover, the fact that bad parts are discovered during setup means that they must be replaced on an emergency basis and this is bound to increase the time that it takes to replace them. Parts requisitioning must be rushed and the right part must be located. In a poorly designed and managed maintenance system, which is where breakdowns would be expected to be frequent, the procedures for identifying and requisitioning the right part is likely to be slow and inefficient. Because defective parts that are discovered during setups cannot be repaired or replaced as an external activity (OED) but rather as an internal activity (IED), they only increase the set-up time and reduce productive time, uselessly. The worst time to discover and replace defective machine parts, it turns out, is during set-up activities.

Low Equipment Efficiency Due to Reduced Speed

Reduced speed is a normal reaction to frequent breakdowns. Foremen and operators sometimes think that the equipment breaks down because it is driven too hard, so they naturally cut back on production when they perceive that breakdowns are abnormally high. Sometimes they are right as in the case when standard operating procedures for equipment operation are not followed. However, it often happens that the operating speed is too high, not because the equipment is inherently incapable of going fast but because it is poorly maintained. The output rate per operating hour can be maintained for old equipment, providing an appropriate maintenance program that takes the age of each machine into account is developed and implemented.

Machine operators also sometimes react to detectable or suspected malfunctions by slowing the equipment down on the assumption that if given enough time the malfunction will go away. A few employees use even more dangerous reasoning when they slow machines down during a suspected malfunction. They reason that the problem can be delayed until the next planned maintenance, if there is one, or transferred to the next shift, if they are lucky enough. These are very poor operating practices, but they are inadvertently encouraged by the philosophy that one should not stop the equipment until it stops, that it is morally wrong to stop production, and that one should not mess with the equipment as long as it works. The Jidoka or Andon principle (automatic stoppage or stop all work when there is a problem) is designed to combat and eventually eliminate these undesirable attitudes to maintenance.

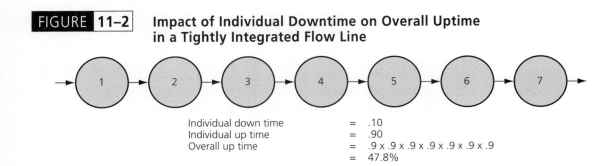

FIGURE 11-2   **Impact of Individual Downtime on Overall Uptime in a Tightly Integrated Flow Line**

Individual down time	= .10
Individual up time	= .90
Overall up time	= .9 x .9 x .9 x .9 x .9 x .9 x .9
	= 47.8%

Poor Worker Morale and Low Productivity

The equipment is the major tool that the worker uses to execute his or her assigned tasks. Equipment that frequently breaks down is frustrating to workers, particularly the conscientious ones, because it is difficult for them to establish a smooth work rhythm. Unreliable equipment interferes with worker productivity rather than being an aid to efficiency. Disruptions are devastating when the production system is organized as a flow line, because when one machine breaks down, the whole line must eventually be stopped. A flow line becomes virtually paralyzed as individual machine downtime rates approach 10 percent. The overall uptime rate for a tightly integrated flow line that has seven operations each with a 10 percent downtime rate is 47.8 percent, as shown in Figure 11-2. In the case shown, machines are down more than 50 percent of the time, cutting plant productivity to less than half its potential. On the assumption that the average breakdown lasts 30 minutes, there would be one breakdown every hour, or eight interruptions in an average work day. The impact on worker morale is bound to be devastating and work would be demoralizing in an environment like this, rather than being a source of pride, self-esteem, and challenge. Figure 11-2 shows the calculations for a simple flow line, with only seven processes. Most flow lines are much more complex than this, which means that uptime and productivity would be much lower. Poor worker morale is also likely to increase accidents, absenteeism, and decrease worker discipline generally, further exacerbating the downtime and productivity problem.

Workers cannot have confidence in the ability of top management to lead the company to competitive excellence and market respectability when the equipment to do the job does not run adequately. And they should not have confidence in the company's capacity to survive in a fiercely competitive environment that is regulated by unpredictable, external forces over which the company has no control, if the equipment that is totally within control creates major headaches for management. Thus, a company that is not succeeding in maintaining in impeccable working condition the equipment that it already has within its own operations will not be successful in creating or adopting major process innovations.

Mastery of process technology starts at the most fundamental level—the ability to operate and maintain an existing, known technology. Companies that are not able to maintain the equipment in near-perfect working condition have not really understood enough about their technology to be able to innovate and use it to strategic advantage. Inadequate maintenance quickly annihilates the competitive advantage that process technologies were designed to give. Many companies robotized their operations in search of cost, quality, and flexibility advantages only to see these washed away by numerous breakdowns and high downtimes. The maintenance system could not perform to the stringent requirements of advanced manufacturing technologies. The robotization craze of the late 1970s fizzled out in the mid-1980s, because robots did not deliver on their productivity, cost, quality, and flexibility promise. High downtime and low capacity utilization caused by poor maintenance were the major culprits. Workers know intuitively that a company that is not able to maintain and exploit existing processes is far from mastering the fundamental technologies that are important to its ability to survive. They rightly blame top management and lose confidence in its capacity to exercise competitive leadership. We have seen plants where top factory management became the laughing stock of production workers because the equipment could not be made to run properly and reliably.

Accelerated Aging of Equipment

Longevity statistics demonstrate quite convincingly that good health maintenance and disease-prevention practices contribute significantly to a long, healthy life. People that develop poor health maintenance habits and whose lifestyles are not oriented toward disease prevention are more susceptible to serious illnesses such as cardiovascular diseases and cancer. They also die much younger. The medical analogy is equally applicable to production equipment. Poor maintenance causes more serious and frequent breakdowns and accelerates the aging and mortality of machines. Old equipment that is well maintained can perform as good as brand new machines. A strong maintenance program can go very far in delaying the time when existing equipment will have to be replaced. A car that is poorly maintained might last only four years, while one that is well maintained might be good for six or seven years. An excellently maintained car could last eight to ten years. Excellent maintenance could increase equipment useful life by one-third.

The now famous bathtub curve has long been used to show how breakdowns vary over the life of a piece of equipment. Figure 11–3 shows the distribution which usually results. The frequency of breakdowns over time follows three distinct patterns. During the first phase, breakdowns are abnormally high as defective or weak components fail to function either at the

FIGURE 11–3   **The Pattern of Breakdowns over Time**

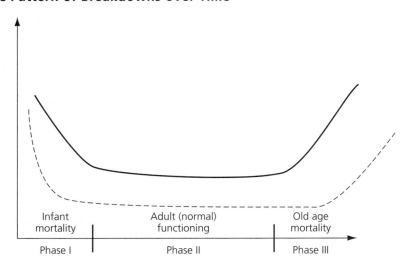

beginning of equipment start-up or soon thereafter. The equipment is said to be in the infant mortality period because malfunctions are caused by the failure of reasonably new components. After successful start-up, the equipment enters a relatively prolonged period during which normal levels of breakdowns are experienced. It must be emphasized that what are normal levels of breakdowns depend on the maintenance program in place. The equipment will function normally until old age sets in, causing the more robustly designed and manufactured components to fail. Breakdowns start to increase to abnormally high levels. Old age will eventually afflict every piece of equipment, no matter how robustly designed and well maintained. The aim in properly maintaining the equipment is to deepen and lengthen the bathtub, that is, to have a much lower mortality rate during adulthood (phase II) and to delay the onset of old age mortality (phase III). The equipment must be kept younger, longer.

Hard data on the relationship between maintenance intensity and equipment useful life are not forthcoming. However, practical experience suggests that a strong maintenance program that is executed with discipline can extend equipment useful life by 30 percent or more. Cases exist where equipment that was expected to last 10 years were kept productive and efficient for more than 20 years. Just a 20 percent increase in equipment useful life is enough to significantly improve a company's financial position. By investing more in maintenance and insisting that plant managers care better for existing equipment, top management can ensure that machines will keep operating at peak efficiency for many more years than originally expected. A solid maintenance program can do much to delay the aging and obsolescence of equipment thereby maximizing the value of the investment in plant and equipment.

The Six Big Losses

Breakdowns and the other ills caused by poor maintenance philosophies, policies, and practices impose losses that can be avoided. Inadequate maintenance causes waste and increased production performance requires that such waste be identified, targeted, and removed. Seiichi Nakajima[1] refers to waste in equipment resources as the six big losses that are formidable obstacles to equipment effectiveness. He categorizes these losses as follows:

Downtime:
1. Equipment failure—from breakdowns
2. Setup and adjustment—from exchange of die in injection molding machines, etc.

Speed losses:
3. Idling and minor stoppages—due to the abnormal operation of sensors, blockage of work on chutes, etc.
4. Reduced speed—due to discrepancies between designed and actual speed of equipment

Defect:
5. Process defects—due to scraps and quality defects to be repaired
6. Reduced yield—from machine startup to stable production

The categorization used by Nakajima is similar to the concepts discussed previously. Figure 11–4 shows how archaic maintenance philosophies, policies, and practices give rise to the six big losses in equipment effectiveness. The final result is that equipment and process technology is being used at half their potential in a large proportion of companies today. The six big losses have always been present but they have been, until recently, invisible to the management eye, covered up by a morass of old philosophies and assumptions, conventional wisdoms, wrong priorities, general laxness, and an archaic performance measurement and reporting system. Search for perfection, waste elimination, and continuous improvement concepts have uncovered the naked truth that these six big losses are in fact waste that need to be eliminated before a company can extract full value from its investment in equipment. Top

---

[1]Seiichi Nakajima, *Total Productive Maintenance* (Cambridge, MA: Productivity Press, 1984), 14.

FIGURE **11–4**   **The Six Big Losses Due to Inadequate Maintenance**

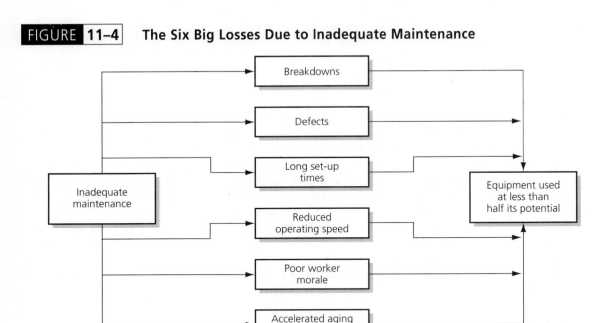

management will no doubt be flabbergasted to learn that it can double the output of existing facilities by changing the way it views and manages maintenance, that is, by managing it as a competitive tool.

Computing the Effect of the Six Big Losses: Overall Equipment Effectiveness (OEE)

The six big losses that reduce overall equipment effectiveness can be expressed as a simple, practical formula. Figure 11–4 shows all the pertinent relationships, which can be formulated as follows:

$$\text{OEE} = \text{availability} \times \text{efficiency} \times \text{quality rate} \\ \times \text{useful life index}$$

Availability is the time left for operating the equipment after breakdowns and setups. Efficiency refers to the rate at which the equipment produces output, compared to the potential while it is being operated. A machine that can produce 1 piece per minute should produce 60 pieces in one hour. If the machine produced 50 pieces during one hour of uninterrupted operation, then the operating efficiency is 83.33 percent. Operating efficiency can be calculated using the formula below:

$$OE = \frac{\text{ideal time per piece} \times \text{actual production} \times 100}{\text{total operating time}}$$

For the example referred to earlier,

$$OE = \frac{1 \text{ minute per piece} \times 50 \text{ pieces} \times 100}{60 \text{ minutes}}$$

$$= 83.33\%$$

Operating efficiency is affected by the operating speed and lower productivity caused by poor worker morale. The quality rate is 100 percent minus the defect rate. The useful life index represents the extent to which equipment have to be retired early because they were improperly cared for. If management believes that equipment useful life could be extended by 20 percent with a thorough maintenance program, then the useful life index is 80 percent.

The following data which are representative of a medium-sized manufacturing company can be used to show how much progress remains to be made in maximizing overall equipment effectiveness.

Average availability = 60%
Average operating efficiency = 85%
Quality rate = 96%
Useful life index = 90%
Overall equipment effectiveness = .60 × .85 × .96 × .90
OEE = 44%

The company could more than double equipment effectiveness and therefore useful output, by eliminating the six big losses. A company's ability to create value for its customers, to reduce the cost, and increase the quality of its product or service is thus substantially influenced by how effectively it manages maintenance. A doubling of output, as in the present case, would give any company the leverage to reduce prices while maintaining or even increasing quality.

The process technology is being exploited at its technological limit when overall equipment effectiveness is 100 percent or alternatively when the six big losses have been driven to zero (see Figure 11-5). The eventual goal is to reach 100 percent efficiency, but immediate and pragmatic ongoing action focuses on the six big losses as waste. Like all forms of waste, they must be identified, costed, reported on, and targeted with continuous improvement programs. Some of the six big losses such as long setups, reduced productivity

FIGURE 11–5 **The Six Big Losses and Overall Equipment Effectiveness**

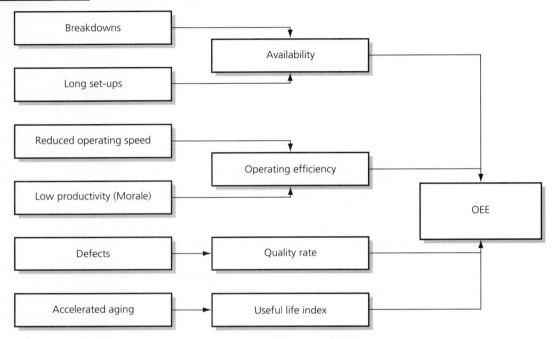

due to low morale, and defects will also be targeted by other waste-reduction projects. Targeting them with the maintenance improvement program not only brings maintenance people into the companywide process to pursue superior competitive performance but also creates some redundancy that reinforces, amplifies, and sustains actions taken elsewhere in the organization. These redundancies are useful because they reinforce symbiosis and anchor continuous improvement in the organization's procedures, processes, and practices and serve to instill waste consciousness and visibility.

TOTAL PRODUCTIVE MAINTENANCE (TPM): THE NEW PHILOSOPHY AND STRATEGY OF MAINTENANCE MANAGEMENT

Beginning in the mid-1970s, a new approach to managing maintenance was emerging in the leading world-class manufacturing corporations in Japan, Western Europe, and North America. It was referred to as total productive maintenance (TPM), and its explicit vocation was zero breakdowns. Today,

TPM has proved itself to be a major strategic tool, a tested process for embedding continuous improvement in maintenance activities.

Nakajima defines TPM in the following terms:[2]

> TPM is productive maintenance carried out by all employees through small group activities. Like TQC, which is companywide Total Quality Control, TPM is equipment maintenance performed on a companywide basis.

TPM is productive maintenance using total employee involvement as a supporting principle. The emphasis is on productive maintenance because TPM pursues the two critical productivity objectives, zero breakdowns and zero defects. Contrary to traditional thinking which regards maintenance as a productivity reduction activity, TPM views a well-designed and executed maintenance program as a productivity enhancement tool. The goal is to drive productivity close to the technological limit by removing the six big losses created by inadequate maintenance philosophies and practices (Figure 11–4). The six big losses also include defects. TPM and ZD complement each other in very direct and obvious ways. Product quality depends on the quality of the equipment and process technology. TPM, by aiming to eliminate process malfunctions, variability, and breakdowns enhances process quality and ensures that process functioning is not a source of defects.

TPM is the culmination of efforts to achieve total equipment effectiveness. Maintenance philosophies and policies evolved through four distinct phases as follows:

Stage 1: Breakdown Maintenance
Stage 2: Preventive Maintenance
Stage 3: Productive Maintenance
Stage 4: TPM

Data reported by Nakajima show that more and more companies in Japan are shifting from breakdown maintenance to TPM. The data are shown in Table 11–2. Over a period of only three years, the proportion of companies that had implemented TPM more than doubled from 10.6 percent to 22.8 percent, while the proportion doing purely breakdown maintenance went down by almost 50 percent, from 12.7 percent to 6.7 percent. TPM itself is being strengthened as more and more progressive companies replace basic preventive maintenance with predictive or condition-based maintenance. Predictive maintenance tries to identify vital signs or symptoms of equipment or process deterioration very early, even before they cause a malfunction, abnormal

---

[2]Nakajima, 1.

TABLE 11–2	The Four Developmental Stages of PM and the Current Situation in Japan		
		1976	**1979**
Stage 1	Breakdown maintenance	12.7%	6.7%
Stage 2	Preventive maintenance	37.3%	28.8%
Stage 3	Productive maintenance	39.4%	41.7%
Stage 4	TPM	10.6%	22.8%

Source: Nakajima, Seiichi, *Introduction to TPM: Total Productive Maintenance,* Cambridge, Mass.: Productivity Press, Inc., 1988, 10. Reproduced with permission.

process variation or breakdown. Sophisticated equipment diagnostic techniques are used to predict whether a breakdown is imminent and to correct the potential problem before it occurs. With predictive maintenance, a company can progress from zero breakdowns to zero malfunctions. Figure 11–6 taken from Nakajima[3], shows how TPM systematically improves on preventive maintenance and productive maintenance, and provides the framework for a complete definition of TPM:

1. *Maximize overall equipment effectiveness.* The six big losses must be eliminated. Since they are avoidable losses, TPM ultimately generates

FIGURE 11–6   The Evolution from Prevention and Productive Maintenance to TPM

	TPM Features	Productive Maintenance Features	Preventive Maintenance Features
Economic efficiency (profitable PM)	◯	◯	◯
Total system (MP-PM-CM)*	◯	◯	
Autonomous maintenance by operators (small group activities)	◯		

TPM = productive maintenance + small-group activities
*MP = maintenance prevention
PM = preventive maintenance
CM = corrective maintenance

[3]Nakajima, 12.

profits substantially higher than the additional investment required to implement it. The major investment is what is required to change management and employee attitudes. Once the right attitudes are in place, TPM becomes a natural source of long-term profits.

2. *Establish a thorough system of preventive maintenance.* TPM seeks zero breakdowns, malfunctions, and maintenance-related process variability. TPM adopts the philosophy and attitude that breakdowns, malfunctions, and process variability can be eliminated by a rigorous preventive maintenance program. Moreover, all the available evidence suggests that from a productivity, profitability, and equipment effectiveness viewpoint, it is far better to emphasize preventive instead of breakdown maintenance. (An ounce of prevention is still better than a pound of cure.) When bolstered by predictive maintenance, TPM takes breakdown and malfunction prevention as far as the search for maintenance excellence can take it. Preventive and predictive maintenance systems are designed and implemented to fit the entire useful life of every machine.

3. *Maintenance by all departments.* TPM challenges the conventional thinking that maintenance is a job for the maintenance department only. Such thinking promoted centralization of maintenance activities, alienated other departments such as engineering, production, procurement, and personnel that have a valid role to play in breakdown prevention and created organizational barriers to the free flow of vital information. TPM accepts the idea that the maintenance department alone cannot eliminate breakdowns. Maintenance concerns and breakdown prevention must be integrated into the thinking of all departments.

4. *Total employee involvement.* Maintenance responsibility has historically been delegated to the maintenance department. Top management hardly sees maintenance as part of its total corporate responsibility. A central philosophy behind TPM is that top management must be actively involved in the search for zero breakdowns. Final responsibility for shaping the right maintenance philosophies, policies, and practices rests at the top. Progress toward zero breakdowns challenges the technological, human, and managerial capabilities of a corporation. Top management has the critical role of leading the company and motivating all employees to accept and work relentlessly toward such an ambitious objective. Precisely because the ultimate objectives in TPM are zero breakdowns and zero defects, all employees, from top management to production workers, must be involved in some aspect of maintenance. The breakthrough in TPM comes not from technologies or techniques for executing maintenance or from mechanisms for improving equipment reliability, although these facets are important. TPM is a revolution in maintenance and the search for zero breakdowns because it defines overall equipment effectiveness as a crucial competitive objective and involves all employees, including top management, in the maintenance management process.

5. *Autonomous maintenance and small group activities.* Operator involvement to increase overall equipment effectiveness is unique to TPM. Operators are trained to take increasing responsibility for maintaining their equipment in perfect working condition. Some companies have developed the concept of operator proprietorship to refer to the fact that workers are not only responsible for using the equipment, but also to ensure that it is well maintained. Operator involvement is put in practice when workers are trained and mandated to do as much of the required preventive maintenance as they possibly can. Autonomous maintenance by operators enriches the task and serves as a powerful motivator. Small group activities to encourage mutual help and sharing of improvement ideas enhance and accelerate the process whereby operators come to have full proprietorship of the equipment and master execution of the preventive maintenance program. Small group activities make learning newly delegated maintenance activities easier and provide a social support system that reduces or eliminates anxiety at the beginning of TPM implementation. Small group activities that are designed to help implement autonomous maintenance by operators and to foster the pursuit of zero breakdowns is also peculiar to TPM. Consequently, TPM further complements the drive toward zero defects because it can exploit the quality team structure already in place.

Improved Breakdown Maintenance

The time lost to breakdowns depends on two factors, the number or frequency of breakdowns and the time taken, on the average, to repair a breakdown. TPM aims to reduce breakdown frequency to zero and is therefore the principle mechanism for improving equipment availability. However, sizeable decreases in breakdown frequency take time to bring about because TPM itself takes time to implement. Changing from pure corrective or repair maintenance to full TPM can take up to five years, even when there is strong support from top management. During the time that TPM is being implemented, particularly at the very early stages, companies can get quick results in improving overall equipment effectiveness by being more efficient in repairing breakdowns. For the data presented earlier, overall equipment effectiveness would increase from 44 percent to 70 percent, if availability increased from 60 percent to 90 percent. Experience with companies that have embarked on an intensive set-up reduction program confirms that set-up times can be cut by up to 90 percent in less than two years. If these set-up reduction activities are accompanied by efforts to make repair of breakdowns more efficient, equipment availability can be brought up to the 90 percent range in less than 18 months. It is easy to see how the JIT effort that seeks single-digit setups or single minute exchange of dies is reinforced by and reinforces TPM and overall equipment effectiveness. There should be no doubt, then, that a company that implements a sufficient number of the concepts that seek to attain superior performance in manufacturing creates a positive cycle of continuous improvement, where one improvement program feeds on and sustains other programs. Improved breakdown maintenance is thus an integral part of the TPM effort because shortening the time that it takes to repair breakdowns positively impacts overall equipment effectiveness, as long as breakdowns are greater than zero.

Setups, breakdown frequency, and breakdown repair efficiency interplay to determine equipment availability. The analysis shows that actions implemented to make breakdown maintenance more efficient can pay huge dividends in equipment availability and productivity. Generally, breakdown maintenance can be drastically improved by the implementation of the following simple ideas:

1. *Training of maintenance personnel.* This is a much neglected area, although it is easy to do, costs little, and has a demonstrably large impact on equipment availability and manufacturing efficiency. Maintenance personnel are among the most undertrained in today's factories. They are invariably left to themselves, to learn as much as they can, with little help or direction from management. Both formal and on-the-job training specifically geared to raising the skill level of maintenance personnel can contribute enormously toward reducing downtime by increasing the efficiency with which malfunctions are diagnosed and repaired. Maintenance personnel who are not well trained make costly errors in diagnosing and repairing malfunctions and frequently have to make two or three tries before they arrive at the right diagnosis or fix the malfunction. "Do it right the first time" applies equally to maintenance as to quality and it means that those doing the maintenance must be provided with the training that will enable them to do it right the first time. Poor training makes corrective maintenance a hit-and-miss affair for many companies, unnecessarily lengthening the time it takes to get machines up and running after a breakdown. Wrong diagnoses, replacing the wrong part, correcting a problem that did not exist, and simultaneously failing to correct the real problem the first time around, all contribute to corrective maintenance inefficiency, although all these problems can be eradicated by a sound training program.

2. *Invest in advanced diagnostics technologies.* Training sharpens the skills and judgment of maintenance personnel and gives them the capability to pinpoint the causes of failures and malfunctions as quickly as possible. However, human judgment and experience can go only so far in speeding up failure-cause analysis, particularly in the complex technological environment that characterizes modern factories. Human judgment can be greatly aided by well-chosen diagnostics equipment, especially in cases where the causes of failure are insidious and hidden from the five human senses. Much advancement in equipment diagnostics has been made over the last

two decades. For example, automobile repair shops have installed sophisticated diagnostics equipment that can identify, in seconds, nearly all the problems that can cause an automobile to malfunction or break down. Problem identification is rapid, efficient, and precise and virtually all guesswork has been eliminated. Given the extremely high capital investment that is immobilized in modern manufacturing processes and the consequent high cost of downtime, even a small reduction in the time it takes to diagnose malfunctions would be enough to justify investment in automated diagnostics systems.

3. *Train operators to do minor repairs.* Equipment operators can be trained and given the responsibility to do minor repairs. Operators become more motivated because their expertise has been expanded and their job has been enriched by the addition of a completely new task. The necessity to learn a new skill makes the job more varied and challenges the employee to excel. The company gains by the fact that maintenance personnel are liberated to focus on the more demanding and critical repair jobs that require a level of expertise that is beyond what operators can be expected to master. Operators, partly due to more training and partly due to experience gained while they are doing minor repairs, become more knowledgeable about the equipment and can thus operate them more competently and diligently. The waiting time to get equipment running after a breakdown is cut substantially. Experience has shown that the time spent waiting for maintenance personnel to begin repairs accounts for up to 80 percent of the total downtime. Apparently, better maintenance craftsmanship makes for better operator craftsmanship, and once more, improvement feeds on itself.

4. *Documenting and analyzing the pattern of equipment failure.* Malfunctions and breakdowns, for the most part, follow a predictable pattern over time. Invariably, a few predictable causes account for 80 percent or more of the time lost due to breakdowns. Knowledge of these critical causes can be used to implement measures to prevent them and to reduce the time it takes to repair the resulting breakdowns. More specifically, the critical causes can be analyzed and evaluated to give maintenance people insight into how breakdowns caused by them can best be corrected. Training and practice sessions should be designed and undertaken to make maintenance personnel proficient in repairing the few critical breakdowns that tend to recur. Each critical cause should be described in detail, and as many illustrations as possible ought to be used so that its true nature, effect, and behavior can be completely understood by maintenance personnel. Alternative methods for repairing each critical malfunction or breakdown should be studied and evaluated, and the best method must be documented fully. A video camera can be a useful tool for illustrating each critical cause and the best method and procedure for correcting it. Maintenance personnel must be trained to master the exact nature of each

cause and the accepted method and procedure for repairing it. The process to improve overall equipment effectiveness should target both the breakdowns and malfunctions so as to eliminate them wherever possible, and the methods and procedures for correcting them when they do occur.

In order to be able to establish the pattern of equipment failure and to isolate the dominant, critical causes, the company has to create a maintenance data base that records and keeps track of breakdowns and malfunctions over time. Every time a machine malfunctions or breaks down, the facts on its nature, cause, the parts involved, the operating conditions, the product being manufactured, the operator in question—his or her training and experience—and all other pertinent information, should be systematically recorded. With time, periodic analysis of the data base will reveal the pattern of dominant causes and what countermeasures can be implemented to prevent their recurrence. The same analysis provides the information base for taking action to improve the efficiency with which the company repairs the breakdowns that cannot be eliminated for the time being. Only a handful of companies have any credible maintenance data base that can be used to derive meaningful failure statistics. Traditionally, a malfunction or breakdown is not a noteworthy event and does not deserve any attention, except where it throws the plant into a crisis. But in companies that are trying to drive downtime to zero, every breakdown and malfunction is a significant event, an experience that must be evaluated, analyzed, learned from, and used to give fresh momentum to the improvement effort. Machine reliability and efficiency are driven closer and closer to 100 percent, as the causes of malfunctions, breakdowns, process variability, and reduced efficiency are diagnosed, identified, and removed. The relationship between the maintenance data base and progress toward zero breakdowns, malfunctions, and process variability is shown in Figure 11-7. The data base generates the information that is required by any meaningful and systematic action to push machine efficiency to 100 percent. A rich maintenance data base that is exploited so as to give insight into the pattern and causes of failure, and used to evaluate alternative actions to eliminate losses in equipment effectiveness, moves maintenance management from the domain of hunch and ill-founded conventional wisdom and converts it into a vehicle for pursuing competitive excellence.

MANAGING TO ACHIEVE ZERO BREAKDOWNS

Corrective maintenance is far from the ideal state for a company that is seeking competitive superiority. Breakdowns are waste and the repairs done to correct them are also waste. Improved breakdown maintenance must be

FIGURE 11–8 **The Maintenance Data Base: Vital Relationships**

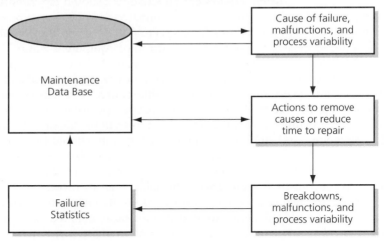

viewed only as the lesser evil when compared with the breakdowns themselves. The highest level of breakdown repair efficiency is attained when there are no breakdowns to repair. Corrective maintenance, despite the fact that some managers see it as inevitable, is caused by breakdowns, which, when removed, automatically eliminate the need for repairs. The requirement, then, is for a management process, tools, and mechanisms that will rigorously seek to reduce breakdowns to zero.

The foundation elements of such a management process and its supporting tools and mechanisms are shown in Figure 11--8. A few fundamental conclusions can be drawn from the conceptual frame. Foremost in the corporate arsenal to attain zero breakdowns are the corporate culture and value system that put a premium on excellence, the deep desire to reach for perfection that gives impetus to the search for competitive superiority, and the managerial or organizational attitude which define all waste as evil. The managerial philosophies and organizational attitudes are once more seen to be paramount to the process, fueling it, and generating the requisite momentum to sustain it over the very long haul. Total productive maintenance, although it has radically changed management thinking about maintenance and breakdowns, and is an important set of weapons available to the company that wants to eliminate breakdowns, is not sufficient to achieve that critical goal. In fact, TPM is a natural culmination of the corporate culture and value system, the drive to search for perfection, and waste elimination.

TPM fits naturally in and can only be effectively implemented by a company that has taken the time and invested the resources to cultivate the supporting corporate culture and value system, attitudes, and philosophies. It is perfectly normal that TPM was invented by a few world-class manufacturing

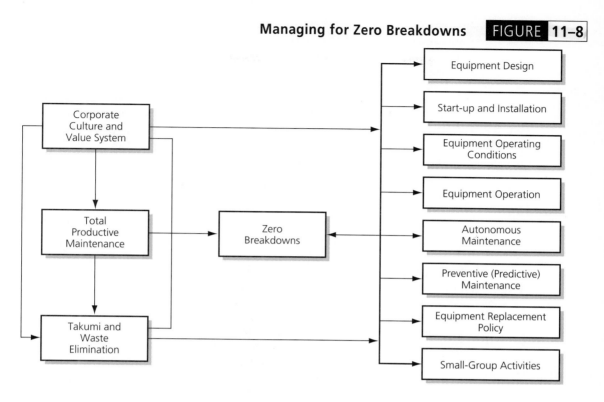

Managing for Zero Breakdowns   FIGURE 11–8

companies and is being rapidly adopted by others and by those that are on their way to attaining world-class status. Managers in these world-class companies are rarely shocked by the foundation TPM concepts and always find them in perfect harmony with their thinking. One can safely say that all the elements of TPM were invented by the best manufacturing companies in North America, and TPM only provided the conceptual frame for linking and putting them together systematically and cohesively.

The concrete decisions, practices, and methods to reduce and eventually eliminate breakdowns are implemented by lower level management and executed by production, maintenance, and engineering people. However, as evidenced by Figure 11-8, the bedrock corporate attitudes and philosophies upon which they stand or fall are shaped and promulgated by top management. The view adopted here, then, is that top management has both final and major responsibility for the level of breakdowns experienced by the company, even though breakdowns and malfunctions may appear to be inconsequential, operations-related events that are remote from top management concerns. Indeed, breakdowns and malfunctions develop into a major hidden problem because top management views them as remote and inconsequential and assumes no responsibility for their elimination. Top management involvement in corporate efforts to reduce breakdowns cannot be done at the level of the day-to-day, nuts-and-bolts actions that have immediate impact on the level of breakdowns and malfunctions, but their intervention and leadership are as critical. Top management intervention to build and nurture the right corporate attitudes and philosophies shape the holes within which the nuts-and-bolts actions must fit. Otherwise, actions by lower level managers, personnel, and technical people are tantamount to trying to fit a round peg into a square hole. The corporate culture and value system provides the framework for specific programs to eliminate breakdowns.

Figure 11–8 identifies eight specific action programs that aim at eliminating breakdowns within the framework provided by the corporate culture and value system.

Equipment Design

Design robustness is to a machine what the human genome is to the human body. Inherited genes predispose a person to particular diseases and largely determine the frequency with which he or she will be afflicted with major or minor illnesses. They are also a major factor in longevity. Design robustness, analogically, has a decisive impact on the frequency and severity of breakdowns and malfunctions and the outer limit of equipment useful life, all other things being equal. The pattern of equipment failure and the associated costs are basically set at the design stage, and substantially determine how many maintenance resources will have to be invested thereafter so as to counterattack or nullify the weaknesses in design. Life cycle studies have repeatedly shown that up to 70 percent of total life cycle costs are set at the design stage, so that subsequent production and maintenance activity can only affect the remaining 30 percent in any significant way.

The impact of design on breakdowns and malfunctions becomes patently obvious during equipment start-up, where most failures are caused by weak or defective components. When one considers that the start-up period for complex machines—that is, the time that it takes to bring production up to about 90 percent of the machine's rated output—can exceed 12 months, then it becomes evident that design robustness affects overall equipment effectiveness, substantially. In order to reduce breakdowns and malfunctions, one must start with robust, vigorously tested, and debugged designs. Subsequent maintenance effort can only serve to drive overall equipment effectiveness closer and closer to the limit set by the design. The maintenance system must be designed and executed so that the equipment operates close to that limit, and then it can surpass it by finding ways to strengthen the given design.

The relationship between design robustness, overall equipment effectiveness, and total life cycle costs suggests that maintenance concerns can be beneficially integrated into equipment design decisions in three important ways. First, when equipment is bought from outside sources, their evaluation and selection must explicitly take maintainability, reliability, and maintenance costs into account. All too often, equipment selection is based on investment and production costs alone with no consideration given to downtime, setup, and other maintenance-related costs. Equipment evaluation and selection policies and procedures must be designed to solicit and incorporate the perspective and advice of those responsible for maintenance. Investment costs are but a small fraction of total life cycle costs, so the latter should be the best basis for evaluating equipment economics. Second, maintenance should be planned, executed, and controlled to detect weaknesses in equipment design and to implement programs to eradicate them. The company that is able to uncover and correct design flaws in equipment bought from outside has made a giant leap forward in maximizing overall equipment effectiveness. This gives the company a defensible and sustainable advantage over competitors who use the same equipment. In one case, a company reduced its in-process defect rate from 11 percent to 6 percent by eliminating a design weakness in one process. The maintenance data base referred to earlier in conjunction with small group activities to be discussed later on, are the major mechanisms by which design weaknesses are uncovered and corrected. Moreover, projects that are specifically chosen to eradicate design weaknesses in purchased equipment are the most fruitful way for a company to start developing an in-house capability in designing and building manufacturing equipment. Third, weaknesses in design that reveal themselves during equipment operation and maintenance provide understanding as to how the equipment can be totally redesigned so as to build a new more robust machine. At that level, maintenance concerns become an integral part of internal process development, manufacture, and in the implementation of an innovation strategy

As a company successfully completes more and more projects that are chosen to eradicate design weaknesses, it builds the internal confidence and technical expertise to develop, design, and build its own major processes.[4] Internal process development and manufacture is the highest level of mastery of process technology and represents a natural evolution from internal design improvement activities. Companies should consider very seriously the option of designing and manufacturing their major process technologies, because it fosters the company's technical capability and generates strong symbiosis between engineering, production, maintenance, and marketing. The natural organizational interaction and interfunctional coupling that take place during internal process development and manufacture encourage the development of managerial and organizational skills that are vital to both product and process development. Projects bring many functional groups together and require a free information flow for them to succeed. This promotes mutual understanding and trust, ensuring that the concerns of all functions are taken

---

[4]See for example, S. C. Wheelwright, "Japan—Where Operations Really Are Strategic," *Harvard Business Review,* July–August 1981.

into account when equipment is being designed. The equipment can be designed with full knowledge of operating conditions so that weaknesses that cause breakdowns, malfunctions, and process variability can be eradicated or nullified at the design stage, the best place to manage for zero breakdowns.

Efforts to eliminate or strengthen design weaknesses in existing equipment and to produce new equipment designs that will minimize breakdowns exploit and nurture the strong symbiotic relationship that can exist between maintenance and design engineering. Insight and information developed during both preventive and corrective maintenance prove to be invaluable in designing breakdown-free equipment. Design activities must utilize both the maintenance data base and the experience of production and maintenance people as vital inputs into the equipment development and manufacture process. Similarly, and this is a rather crucial point, the intimate knowledge of the equipment design—the specific design characteristics, its performance during prototyping and testing, known component failure rates, mean time between failure and operating requirements and conditions (specifications)—can be used to formulate a master plan for maintaining the equipment all through its life cycle. This same information can also be advantageously used to plan and manage equipment installation and start-up more effectively.

When management succeeds in nurturing and exploiting such a symbiotic relationship between equipment design and maintenance, it has put in place a powerful mechanism for deriving strategic competitive advantage from maintenance. Indeed, maximum advantage is derived from maintenance not when it is used to repair or prevent breakdowns in existing equipment, but when it is used to design breakdowns out of the process altogether. Such symbiosis between maintenance and design cannot be created or effectively exploited if the company is not engaged in internal process development, design, and manufacture. Symbiosis, whether biological or social, requires the existence of at least two entities. Little opportunity exists to create and exploit symbiosis between equipment design and maintenance if the two functions do not exist within the same corporation. The leading world-class companies in Germany and Japan have fully understood the conditions for and power of symbiosis and consequently do much internal design and manufacture of process technology. Internal design magnifies the strategic leverage that can be derived from maintenance. The Japanese world-class companies in particular are distinctive in the resources they devote to internal process development. North American equipment suppliers continue to look on in amazement when a Japanese user buys a machine from North American sources, increases its reliability far beyond expectations in two or three years and can design and build an improved version for its own uses within five to seven years. According to Wheelwright[5] and Jaikumar,[6] internal process development and manufacture is one way Japanese

---

[5]S. C. Wheelwright, "Japan Where Operations Really Are Strategic," *HBR,* July–August 1981.
[6]Ramchandran Jaikumar, "Postindustrial Manufacturing," *HBR*, November–December 1986.

companies use manufacturing operations to create overwhelming competitive advantage on world markets.

In order to maximize the free flow of information between equipment design, maintenance, production, and marketing, the equipment design team should be multifunctional in nature. Particular care must be taken to ensure that production and maintenance people are adequately represented on such a team and that their views are heard and incorporated into the design. Moreover, the design team should be required to evaluate the maintenance requirements and implications of the design before it is finally approved.

Start-Up and Installation

Breakdown frequency is normally high during start-up and stabilizes thereafter at a much lower level. Most breakdowns and malfunctions that occur during the start-up phase are due to poor start-up planning and inadequate equipment testing and debugging. Errors made during installation and failure to adequately train operators carry over into the start-up phase and cause breakdowns and malfunctions. The fact that breakdowns decrease dramatically once the equipment has been in operation for a few months means that the villain is not the basic equipment design, but inadequate start-up planning, control, and management, generally. Start-up problems are particularly severe when the equipment in question is highly innovative or when the company that bought it has not historically been aggressive in adopting radical process innovations. Both cases suggest that experience and know-how play a key role in minimizing breakdowns and malfunctions during start-up, and that start-up and installation can be managed to reduce the level of breakdowns and malfunctions.

Equipment debugging, installation, and start-up take much more time than most managers allow for them. Maintenance people are put under pressure to meet very optimistic start-up dates, and, unfortunately, most cut corners to meet the deadlines. This effectively means that some debugging and operator-training activities are done during productive use of the equipment, with the consequence that breakdowns and malfunctions are abnormally high. One simple way to avoid this is to allow more time for debugging, installation, and operator training.

Supporting documentation for machine installation, operation, and maintenance must be complete, clear, and error free. Documentation must be meticulously audited by a specially designed audit team comprising maintenance and engineering people and operators. A complete training program for operators must be designed prior to start-up and every precaution should be taken to ensure that all operators become thoroughly familiar with all equipment operating features. Workers should know how to competently use the equipment before start-up actually begins. Companies that pay attention to start-up achieve major reductions in the time it takes to bring output close to the rated capacity of the equipment.

Equipment Operating Conditions

Maximum overall equipment effectiveness and 100 percent efficiency can only be envisaged when the physical factory environment is nearly perfect. Excessive noise and heat and even minimal levels of dirt and dust impact visibly and measurably on machine performance and are known to cause breakdowns, malfunctions, and undue process variability. Particularly in the modern factory where equipment is very sophisticated, fine tuned, and extensively equipped with highly sensitive and delicate electronic or electro-mechanical control devices, dust and dirt can cause defects in products and cause machines to break down. One can cite case after case where an automatic control device was triggered into action by excessive heat, noise, or dust, causing a machine to stop uselessly. Nearly every manager in a plant that extensively uses automatic devices for signaling malfunctions or stopping machines that are not functioning properly can give many examples where dirt, dust, and other problems in the physical factory environment cause the control devices to fail, leading to severe breakdowns. The automated or automatically controlled machine functions best when the factory is free from dust and dirt.

Despite its immediate and direct impact on breakdowns, malfunctions, and process variability, a dirty or disorganized plant impacts on equipment effectiveness and breakdowns in much more surreptitious but profound ways. Dirt, dust, and general plant disorganization reveal management laxness, the willingness to accept less than perfect performance and operating conditions. Tidiness is the mirror image of discipline, orderliness, and the search for perfection. Untidiness and disorderliness show up in plants where managers and the workers, of course, accept the status quo and do not pay attention to the small, seemingly inconsequential things like good housekeeping. Management theory is only now reluctantly accepting the simple truth discovered decades ago by the world's best-managed companies, that the journey toward excellence in manufacturing must quickly involve concerted efforts to master the details of factory management. The search for global or even national competitive superiority is nothing but a futile exercise if a company cannot motivate and train its employees to maintain a clean and orderly factory environment. Zero breakdowns and malfunctions call for dust free, orderly factories. There is a strong relationship between management's ability to maintain ideal operating conditions and its capacity to manage for zero breakdowns, even if the relationship is indirect and one has to probe deeper than the surface to uncover it.

The parlor factory concept discussed earlier symbolizes and operationalizes the push for perfect equipment operating conditions. It also shows that *Kaizen* and the search for perfection must infiltrate every managerial and operating task, from the most complex to the most simple. How much Kaizen influences prevailing management attitudes toward the physical factory environment indicates how deeply the roots of manufacturing and competitive excellence have penetrated into the corporate value system. Managers who are pushing hard to transform the physical plant environment into a parlor factory are concomitantly, even if unsuspectingly, cultivating operating and management discipline. By that very process, they are also inculcating Kaizen into the work habits of their employees. Craftsmanship in production as in any other human endeavor involves mastering the details of one's craft. Employees who have been trained to be acutely sensitive to the small things like dirt, dust, grit, and general disorderliness will very easily see the big quality problems and other forms of waste. In any event, when a company has pushed hard enough and long enough to eliminate defects and malfunctions, it will enter into a stage where further improvement can only come from technological breakthroughs or painstaking fine tuning. Management cannot rely on breakthroughs alone to sustain continuous improvement, because these are uncertain and rare. Kaizen and Takumi (the search for perfection) will ultimately bring the company into the fine tuning stage, where all major breakdowns and malfunctions have been eliminated and where the production process will be either perfectly stable or will exhibit minor variations. The capacity to focus on the details will then prove to be an invaluable asset in the drive to eradicate minor malfunctions and small process variability. The parlor factory concept and its implementation cultivate the technical and human discipline and attitudes that give the company the wherewithal to pursue continuous improvement during the fine tuning stage and long after the pool of revolutionary projects has been exhausted. Zero breakdown maintenance will inevitably take a company into that critical fine tuning phase.

Equipment Operation

Machines do not break down or malfunction unless they are used. Equipment operation brings humans and machines into close interaction, except in the very rare cases where the manufacturing system is completely automated. The human factor is once more omnipresent and dominates the relationship and the results. Breakdowns are sometimes caused by poor equipment operation. Craftsmanship embodies the capacity to use the essential tools of the craft professionally and competently. One cannot dissociate the craft from the tools that are used by it. The machines are the tools of the production crafts. A surgeon's competence is entirely revealed by the way she or he uses the scalpel. A neophyte surgeon knows a scalpel superficially and has little understanding of the intricate ways in which it can be used. She or he uses that vital tool clumsily and makes many errors. She or he must learn how to use the scalpel on cadavers and not live human beings. An experienced surgeon, on the other hand, knows the scalpel inside out and is proficient at using it in many delicate surgical procedures. Holding a scalpel comes naturally to the mature surgeon and she or he uses it with finesse and effortlessness. The mature surgeon makes few mistakes.

The ability to operate equipment flawlessly and professionally is an important test of production craftsmanship. All the skills developed by the worker must eventually culminate in the capacity to use the equipment perfectly to make a perfect product. Equipment that is operated expertly is less likely to break down, malfunction, or display undue process variability, because operator error as a source of breakdowns has been removed. Proper equipment operation also pays off in terms of better quality, lower scrap rates, higher efficiency, lower operator fatigue, and less work related accidents. However, the key point is that how well all operators use the equipment indicates how much the company has mastered the nuts and bolts, the brass tacks of its manufacturing technology. Technological competence serves very little competitive purpose if it remains lodged at the top and also in the research, development, and engineering departments. Technology is deployed to competitive purpose when it becomes embodied in the skills and expertise of those who use machines to make quality products. Technology must be pushed down from the corporate ivory tower, from the glamorous R&D laboratories, and onto the factory floor where it comes alive in the hands of ordinary workers as they use equipment with expertise and competence.

Workers must know their equipment completely. They must be experts at using it and must be able to quickly and accurately interpret its operating signals that may indicate that there is a malfunction. They have to be brought to the point where they are so closely acquainted with the operating dynamics of the equipment that they develop a sense for when it is operating optimally or not. Experience is the best teacher in this regard, but it must be bolstered, accelerated, and refined with formal and on-the-job training. Even if a company recruits the best available technicians and tradespeople, only a few will have the self-motivation to push themselves to master the equipment if there is not a formal corporate personnel development program that is designed to promote operator craftsmanship. Top management cannot leave the development of operator skills to the vicissitudes of happenstance. The best craftsmen, left to themselves, will eventually become rusty, complacent, and mediocre. Lethargy tends to set in where there is not concerted top management action to rejuvenate and sharpen already acquired skills and to rekindle the desire to learn new ones. Equipment operating methods need also to be documented, formalized, tested, and improved on an ongoing basis, while employees must be constantly trained and retrained to master them. Worker qualification is not a once-in-a-lifetime affair, but a permanent activity to test and evaluate whether operators are maintaining or increasing their mastery over the manufacturing process.

| Steps in Implementing Autonomous Maintenance | TABLE 11–3 |

Step	Activities
1. Initial cleaning	Clean to eliminate dust and dirt mainly on the body of the equipment; lubricate and tighten; discover problems and correct them
2. Countermeasures at the source of problems	Prevent cause of dust, dirt, and scattering; improve parts that are hard to clean and lubricate; reduce time required for cleaning and lubricating
3. Cleaning and lubrication standards	Establish standards that reduce time spent cleaning, lubricating, and tightening (specify daily and periodic tasks)
4. General inspection	Instruction follows the inspection manual; circle members discover and correct minor equipment defects
5. Autonomous inspection	Develop and use autonomous inspection checksheet
6. Orderliness and tidiness	Standardize individual workplace control categories; thoroughly systemize maintenance control • Inspection standards for cleaning and lubricating • Cleaning and lubricating standards in the workplace • Standards for recording data • Standards for parts and tools maintenance
7. Full autonomous maintenance	Develop company policy and goals further; increase regularity of improvement activities; record MTBF analysis results and design countermeasures accordingly

Source: Nakajima, 77.

Autonomous Maintenance

Workers who have mastered their equipment are ready to assume more responsibility for keeping them in perfect working condition. Nakajima refers to this as autonomous maintenance and outlined seven steps to be followed in implementing it, as shown in Table 11–3. Autonomous maintenance prevents breakdowns and malfunctions because it integrates some important preventive maintenance into the operating responsibilities of workers, thereby preventing breakdowns at the source. Workers are likely to sense whether something is going wrong with the equipment while they are operating it and can adjust or intensify the preventive maintenance activities to deal with suspected causes of malfunctions and process variability. The search for causes and equipment operation are one and the same continuous process. Autonomous maintenance has a positive impact on worker motivation because it enriches the job by broadening the range and depth of operator skills and by increasing their responsibilities. Workers come to have more control over their work life. Furthermore, autonomous maintenance increases and exploits symbiosis between equipment maintenance and operation. Operators who have to care for their machines understand and operate them better. They come to appreciate the fact that they will have a smoother, less stressful work life, if they maintain the equipment well.

Predictive Maintenance

The next best thing to designing a machine that will never break down or malfunction is to be able to predict when it is likely to break down. Predictive maintenance tries to predict when critical components are likely to fail so that they can be removed before they cause the equipment to break down. Predictive maintenance is systematic, periodic maintenance which aims to prevent breakdowns, while minimizing maintenance that is performed without precise knowledge as to the pattern of breakdowns over time.

The whole predictive maintenance program hinges on the ability to forecast component failure rates, mean times to fail, and the maintenance requirements over time, that is, how rapidly the condition of the equipment deteriorates with use. Equipment and component performance history and data generated by periodic maintenance audits provide the information needed to establish a maintenance profile for each machine. The maintenance data base is the reservoir where all the necessary data are kept. Forecasting maintenance requirements is not an exact science, but the passenger airline industry has demonstrated that it is possible to have reasonably accurate forecasts and to use these to plan a maintenance program for the equipment. The more complete the maintenance data base and the longer the period it covers, the more precise will be the forecasts of mean times between failure (MTBF). As the data base matures, the company can progressively shift from preventive maintenance based on rules of thumb to a more refined (optimized) predictive maintenance program.

Equipment Replacement Policy

No matter how much prevention is done, machines will age. Preventive maintenance slows down but cannot arrest aging. The equipment will eventually have to be replaced, because after a few revamps, it will start to become increasingly unreliable. Moreover, incremental or revolutionary technological change will catch up with even the best maintained equipment, placing the company in a relatively disadvantageous competitive position compared with those competitors who have already adopted more innovative processes. The decision of whether to replace equipment can have strategic implications that are not captured by standard financial calculations models such as the capital asset pricing model (CAPM) or discounted cash flows. North American managers tend to overemphasize the financial and ROI calculations to the detriment of nonquantifiable, competitive considerations, such as the quality impact of new processes and the impact of frequent investment in new processes on the company's ability to evaluate, adopt, and master new technology. Equipment replacement policies in North America, because they rely heavily on financial analysis, have had the effect of delaying investment in strategic process technologies and have left North American companies burdened with obsolete equipment technologies. Many mature industries have suffered irreversible declines in market share which are directly attributable to wrong equipment replacement policies. For example, the steel industry in North America has over the last ten years experienced rapidly declining market share to competitors from Japan and South Korea. It is interesting to note that only 20 percent of North American steel production capacity uses the relatively new continuous casting technology, while the corresponding figure for Japan is 70 percent. Continuous casting machines combined with electric arc furnaces can produce high-quality steel at a substantially lower cost, while simultaneously allowing smaller scale, focused mills, called mini-mills, to be used.

Archaic financial accounting principles, questionable maintenance policies, and a management accounting system that took a simplistic approach to performance reporting and control, have combined to grossly distort equipment replacement policy in North America. Financial accounting places equipment on the books at cost, "in accordance with generally accepted accounting principles." The accounting profession has stubbornly resisted efforts to account for machinery and equipment at replacement cost, although inflationary pressures and technological change cause book value to substantially diverge from replacement value of assets with long useful lives. The very high "depreciation cost" of the new equipment compared with the old equipment tends to discourage replacement of the latter. One often hears the comment that "we have a cost advantage because our equipment is fully depreciated." What some managers tend to forget is that a more reliable, more efficient new machine can easily wipe out the depreciation cost advantage of an older, poorly maintained one. Furthermore, maintenance policies that emphasize breakdown correction rather than prevention lead management to believe that high levels of breakdowns are normal. When this happens, it is difficult to detect the abnormally high downtime rates that are associated with equipment aging. Top management has lost a vital cue that can indicate that the equipment should be replaced. Finally, the performance reporting system, as discussed earlier, grossly understates the costs associated with breakdowns in the rare cases where companies attempt to measure them.

Most North American companies are caught in an obsolescence trap where an inadequate maintenance system accelerates aging while the replacement policies delay replacement. Management ends up keeping older, ineffective equipment for much longer.

There are fundamentally two reasons to replace existing equipment. The first is that the equipment has reached the end of its useful life and thus its effectiveness cannot be improved or kept steady by a solid zero breakdown maintenance program. Companies that have successfully implemented zero breakdown maintenance will detect very quickly when the equipment is worn out. Machine unreliability will become abnormally high despite the countermeasures that are applied by the zero breakdown maintenance program. There will be a discernible, steady upward trend on the bathtub curve, giving rise to increased downtime, more malfunctions, abnormal process variability, higher defect rates, production bottlenecks, capacity shortages, negative maintenance cost variances, and all the other ills associated with a higher than expected breakdown rate. When the expected breakdown rate is zero or near zero, any increase will be easy to detect, given the fact that its effects are so pervasive. All these factors provide the incontrovertible evidence that the equipment should be replaced, even if payback and ROI calculations show otherwise. The financial calculations are probably wrong and based on false assumptions if they contradict the signals that are emitted from the heart of the production system. The decision to replace equipment is an easy one for a company that has achieved significant progress toward zero breakdowns, zero defects, and zero inventories.

Second, management can replace existing equipment so as to establish a beachhead in an emerging but potentially strategically important new technology. In such a case, the equipment is replaced before it has aged irreversibly, but the strategic contribution of the new technology is judged to more than offset the additional investment burden that it imposes. The competitive potential of the new technology is likely to revolve around critical success factors such as quality, flexibility, product differentiation, and long-run reductions in overall cost. It is important that management look at any potential cost advantage with a long-term perspective, since even the most promising new equipment technology will likely produce a short-run cost disadvantage. The new technology must be understood, mastered, and refined—even further improved in some cases—before any significant overall cost reductions can be expected to take place. This is the central point behind the manufacturing progress function or learning curve. The company has to learn the new technology and master its managerial and operating exigencies such as human resource recruitment, training and development, process control nuances, and maintenance planning, control, and execution before any significant accumulated learning can exert downward pressure on overall cost. Certainly, the necessary accumulated learning is not likely to take place before the equipment has been in operation for a few years.

Financial analyses are likely to provide little help in evaluating the decision to adopt a new technology for strategic reasons. There are too many imponderables and the perspective too long term, causing the most educated assumptions and the most rigorous financial analyses to be little more than wild guesses. Top management can only rely on its vision of how the market and competitive situation will evolve, its general understanding of how the new technology will impact on the task of production, and the best available competitive intelligence relative to how leading competitors view the technology, in order to decide whether to adopt it or not. This is the entrepreneurial dimension of production and the old financial models stifle rather than unleash its power. The successful implementation of zero breakdown maintenance, zero defects, JIT, and other tools of superior performance manufacturing, obviate the need for any financial analysis when deciding to replace equipment.

Small Group Activities

Zero breakdown maintenance is equipment maintenance done for systematic improvement in overall equipment effectiveness. Breakdowns respond excellently to mind and creative power, a distinctively human trait. The power of all must be brought to bear in organized, systematic fashion on maintenance problems. All employees, but particularly those from production, maintenance, and engineering, must be mobilized in the search for solutions to the problems of breakdowns, malfunctions, and process variability. The best and proven way to do this is to have small group activities that concentrate on maintenance. Small groups bring ideas for improvement from all sources and involve workers in the drive to maximize overall equipment effectiveness. Maintenance small group activities will invariably overlap with other small group activities in quality and elsewhere, which promote cross-fertilization of ideas and solutions. The maintenance small group activities communicate the message that maintenance is an employee responsibility and encourage employees to search for creative solutions.

MAINTENANCE, PROCESS DESIGN/ OPERATION, AND ZERO DEFECTS

It should be clear by now that there is a strong relationship between zero breakdown maintenance, TQC, and zero defects. The maintenance system is one more weapon that management can use to amplify or complement the TQC process and to drive the company toward zero defects. The critical relationships are shown in Figure 11–9. Zero defects will be attained when quality is designed or built into the process, all work is done right the first time,

FIGURE **11–9**   **Maintenance and the Zero Defects (ZD) Program: The Vital Links**

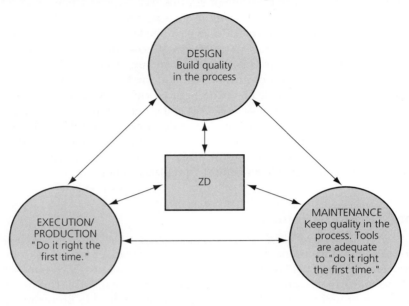

and the maintenance system both keeps the quality in the process and ensures that the equipment (tools) are adequate to "do it right the first time."

IMPLEMENTING ZERO BREAKDOWN MAINTENANCE

The concepts and ideas upon which zero breakdown maintenance is based represent a radical departure from conventional thinking. The implementation of programs to achieve zero breakdowns and malfunctions call for revolutionary changes in manufacturing strategy and policies, organizational structure, and management processes. Zero breakdown maintenance is one aspect of the changes that are required to convert manufacturing into a major strategic weapon in the corporate competitive arsenal. Its implementation should be approached as such.

Waste Elimination and Takumi

Any meaningful attempt to manage for zero breakdowns must recognize that breakdowns cause waste and are due to imperfections in the production system. Initial efforts to implement zero breakdown maintenance must focus almost exclusively on building total corporate awareness that all breakdowns are waste, impinge on overall corporate competitive performance, and must be put into the corporate conscience. Waste consciousness must be heightened and it must be broadened to include breakdowns and malfunctions. The mechanism for achieving this are varied, but top management's deliberate efforts to communicate a new vision of breakdowns and to persuade employees that they must be eliminated is vital.

Top management's efforts to sensitize the organization to the fact that breakdowns are waste can be bolstered by reasonable data on the costs associated with breakdowns. Even crude cost estimates will be enough to drive the point home. Employees can be shown how downtime reduction will eventually impact on the competitive performance and overall financial health of the company. The figures that result from a breakdown cost analysis should be made available to all employees and should be widely discussed. The dollar amounts are likely to convince even the most skeptical employees that some actions to reduce breakdowns must be undertaken.

Formulate, Adopt, and Publish a Zero Breakdowns Mission

Once top management is confident that all employees view zero breakdowns as necessary, a corporate mission that establishes zero breakdowns as the goal should be formulated. Like most other things in management, maintenance must be mission driven and oriented. The mission expresses management's vision of how far and how fast the company should go in reducing breakdowns. It also challenges all employees to think long term and to push as hard as they can toward the goal. The mission communicates the idea that breakdown reduction is a key corporate competitive priority and indicates that top management will support all valid efforts to eradicate breakdowns and malfunctions. The mission must be broadcast throughout the company and there should be special activities designed to evaluate the extent to which all employees understand its significance. All departments must be encouraged to document what the mission means for the company and for the department concerned. Specific activities must be designed to thoroughly inculcate the mission into the mindset of all employees. Inculcation is successful when each employee comes to view the corporate mission as their own personal mission, that is to say, every employee must come to wholly accept it as desirable, necessary, and good.

Implement Specific Zero Breakdown Programs

The initial actions to change the corporate direction zero-in on philosophies and attitudes. Once these are reasonably in place, specific actions need to be

FIGURE 11–10   **Elements of the Supplier–Partnership Concept**

Stage	Step	Details
Preparation	1. Announce top management decision to introduce TPM	Statement at TPM lecture in company; articles in company newspaper
	2. Launch education and campaign to introduce TPM	Managers: seminars/retreats according to level General: slide presentations
	3. Create organization to promote TPM	Form special committees at every level to promote TPM; establish central headquarters and assign staff
	4. Establish basic TPM policies and goals	Analyze existing conditions; set goals; predict results
	5. Formulate master plan for TPM development	Prepare detailed implementation plans for the five foundational activities
Preliminary Implementation	6. Hold TPM kick-off	Invite clients, affiliated, and subcontracting companies
TPM Implementation	7. Improve effectiveness of each piece of equipment	Select model equipment; form project teams
	8. Develop an autonomous maintenance program	Promote the Seven Steps; build diagnosis skills and establish worker certification procedure
	9. Develop a scheduled maintenance program for the Maintenance Department	Include periodic and predictive maintenance and management of spare parts, tools, blueprints, and schedules
	10. Conduct training to improve maintenance skills	Train leaders together; leaders share information with group members
	11. Develop initial equipment management program	MP (Maintenance Prevention) design; start-up equipment maintenance; LCC (Life Cycle Cost) analysis
Stabilization	12. Perfect TPM implementation and raise TPM levels	Evaluate for TPM prize; set higher goals

Source: Nakajima, 55. Reproduced with permission.

implemented. The step-by-step action plan proposed by Nakajima that aims to implement TPM provide a good basis for action implementation. This is shown in Figure 11–10. However, it is appropriate to point out here that unless the bedrock concepts upon which zero breakdown maintenance rests are well in place, TPM implementation will likely fail. If specific action programs are not being successfully implemented on time and with expected results, top management should seriously question whether the right corporate attitudes are in place. There should be a constant going back to deepen the integration of the bedrock concepts into the corporate culture and value system. Since the bedrock ideas are common to TQC, JIT, and all other waste elimination efforts, the constant going back reinforces the foundation concepts and all improvement programs collectively benefit. Again, one sees that one improvement program feeds on another to form a near perfect symbiosis that permanently drives improvement in manufacturing performance. A kind of organizational controlled nuclear reaction is unleashed by the search for perfection and Kaizen.

Conclusion

The pursuit of manufacturing excellence and the cultivation of competitive advantage from production, particularly in the context of increasing competition brought about by globalization, require that maintenance be conceived of and managed as a strategically useful set of activities. Maintenance is strategic because it is an important source of profits, can be used to bring about significant reductions in overall cost and response time, and can increase quality. In addition, sound maintenance management policies and practices are absolutely essential to the attainment of the key objectives of other strategic manufacturing programs such as TQM, JIT, SPC, MRP-II, robotization, FMSs, and waste reduction in general.

The decision to manage maintenance for strategic impact and as a source of competitive advantage flows from the demonstrable premise that the problems associated with traditional maintenance management policies and practices are operationally and strategically very costly. These policies and practices which emphasize correction instead of prevention also rationalize high levels of breakdowns. They also make it impossible for a corporation to adopt and aggressively pursue a zero-breakdown mission, and are the root cause of the six big losses that result in equipment being used at less than half their potential. Companies that succeed in extracting competitive advantage from maintenance, implement management policies and practices that place overwhelming emphasis on the total prevention of breakdowns and malfunctions. Moreover, these companies adopt and actually pursue a zero-breakdown mission, aim for 100 percent overall equipment effectiveness, and use maintenance to bolster the competitive benefits of other strategic manufacturing programs. TPM is currently the most complete, tested, and logically rigorous approach to maintenance management that can be implemented by companies that want to reap strategic advantage from maintenance.

Case for Discussion

ADVANCED PHARMACEUTICAL, INC. (API)

In 1989, top management at API was considering a plant expansion to cope with increased demand. The previous year, 1988, the company operated at 97 percent of capacity even though the stated policy was that a tight-capacity situation existed when capacity utilization reached 85 percent of normal. The sales forecast for 1989 anticipated a 15 percent increase and the company expected to cope by working overtime. However, sales for the first quarter of 1989 had increased by 25 percent. The union contract set a ceiling of 20 percent on overtime and the plant was already working two shifts. An extension to the plant could not come on stream before one year, and the company's major customers were already complaining about long lead times, back orders, and missed deliveries.

Historical Development

API was a small U.S. manufacturer of pharmaceutical products that was founded in 1969 by Mr. Peter Calvin, a pharmacologist. The company's foray into the pharmaceutical market started with the formulation and production of a generic antacid which was its only product for the first eight years of its existence. In 1977, the company added another generic product to its product line with the formulation and production of a drug to treat hypertension. Sales had grown from $650,000 in 1973 to $7.0 million in 1979, with profits of $630,000 that year.

The segment in which the company competed offered customers non-branded versions of major drugs, but at much lower cost. Generics were often priced 30 to 40 percent lower than their branded equivalents, because companies like API avoided the high R&D testing, trial, and approval expenditures that were involved in the development of brand name products. Despite the obvious cost advantage, the rising cost of medical care and the fact that all generics went through the FDA's approval procedures, generic drugs had not captured a healthy share of the pharmaceutical market. Physicians and patients still saw generics as of inferior quality and the "innovative" pharmaceutical companies spent heavily on product promotion and marketing. In some cases, marketing expenditures were as high as 30 percent of sales. Moreover, the "innovative" pharmaceutical companies always found ingenious ways to reformulate their products and to ward off competition from the generics. API entered the pharmaceutical market at a time when most experts believed in the "promise of generics." That promise had largely remained unfulfilled, and in 1978, API actively started looking for ways to enter the branded segment of the market.

The company got a major break in 1982, when it signed a licensing agreement with a Swedish pharmaceutical manufacturer to be the exclusive licensee for a very effective cardiovascular drug that had never been tested or marketed in the U.S. market, but which had been widely accepted and proven effective in Europe where it held 60 percent of the market for the treatment of angina. Testing and reformulation of the drug for the U.S. and, eventually, the North American market was completed in August 1983, and the company started to ship the product in November of the same year. The company allocated $1.2 million to promote and support the new product, and within one year, sales had reached $5.8 million. API experienced phenomenal growth thereafter, and total corporate sales reached $106 million 1988. From 1984 to 1988, the company struggled to keep capacity abreast of demand, first by maximum overtime with one-shift operations, then implementing two shifts and pushing overtime to the maximum with two-shift operations.

Maintenance Policies at API

During the period of exponential increases in demand, API management, like most other companies, paid little attention to maintenance. Machines were repaired when they broke down, and even then, shortcuts were taken in an effort to keep the equipment running and uptime high. Preventive maintenance was kept to a bare minimum and accounted for 5 percent of the total time spent on maintenance and 3 percent of the total maintenance budget. Production workers operated the equipment and plant and maintenance personnel insisted that the latter execute all maintenance activities, even if workers could easily and quickly fix most of the causes of machine breakdowns and malfunctions. Maintenance personnel often went through the process of diagnosing the causes of failure and malfunctions, despite the fact that the vast majority of these were evident to the operators. Production workers were quickly coming to see breakdowns as a means of getting a much needed break from a hectic production schedule.

API did not keep any record of what machines broke down and why. Maintenance personnel contended, however, that experience had taught them what machines caused the most problems and what was the nature of these. The accumulated experience of workers did not in any way influence either machine maintenance or replacement policy nor policies on the type and level of spare parts inventory.

The maintenance staff of six people reported to a maintenance manager, who himself occasionally did some maintenance work when an emergency arose. A recent analysis[7] had shown that a machine breakdown occurred every 1.5 hours, on the average, and took 0.8 hours to repair. The mean waiting time for machines to be available, once they had broken down, was therefore about 2 hours and the utilization rate of the maintenance staff was about 54 percent. The in-plant defect rate was 8 percent and 50 percent of these were directly attributable to poor maintenance, and breakdowns accounted for 12 percent of the plant's capacity and 90 percent of these could be eliminated by an effective maintenance policy. Lost production time due to poorly executed changeovers was 0.5 hours per changeover, of which there were two per machine per 8 hour shift. Slowdowns before and after repairs resulted in another 2 percent loss in production. There was evidence that a sound maintenance policy could extend the life of productive equipment by about 20 percent.

Two months ago, Ms. Kelly Roberts, vice-president of manufacturing, wanted to assess the effect an increase in preventive maintenance would have on productivity losses and temporarily hired two repairmen to do preventive maintenance work after the second shift. Surprisingly, breakdowns had decreased 25 percent during the period. Roberts wondered whether this meant that the API should change the way it managed maintenance, what that change should be, and what would be the impact on motivation, quality, productivity, and the capacity crisis API faced.

Discussion Questions

1. How is the pharmaceuticals market likely to change over the next ten years and how are these changes likely to affect API?
2. Is there a strategic role for manufacturing in a company like API? Describe the manufacturing role and how the production system will have to change to contribute to the company's competitive position.
3. What is the role of maintenance in API's manufacturing strategy? Are you satisfied that maintenance is currently being used to competitive advantage? If not, what changes would have to take place before it is?
4. How do the current maintenance policies affect API's ability to serve its customers?

---

[7]This analysis is based on the wellknown queuing models. According to the basic model of queuing theory.

Length of queue, including machines being repaired, $L_s = \lambda/(\mu - \lambda)$
Length of queue, excluding machines being repaired, $L_q = \lambda^2/(\mu(\mu - \lambda))$
Waiting time in the system, $W_s = \mu/(\mu - \lambda)$
Waiting time in the queue, $W_q = \lambda/(\mu(\mu - \lambda))$
Utilization rate of the maintenance crew, $P = \lambda/\mu$

where, λ = number of breakdowns per hour
         μ = time to repair a breakdown per busy repairman

5. What is the financial impact of maintenance?
6. What actions would you take if you were API's top management?

References

Claire, Frank V., "The Weakest Link: JIT and Maintenance Management," *P & IM Review,* February 1986.

Nakajima, Seiichi, *Introduction to TPM: Total Productive Maintenance,* Japan Institute for Plant Maintenance, Cambridge, MA: Productivity Press, Inc., 1988.

Wheelright, S. C., "Japan—Where Operations Really Are Strategic," *Harvard Business Review,* July–August 1981.

Managing for Superiority in Customer Service: Customer-Driven Business Planning

We have seen that superior and continuously improving customer service is a competitive imperative brought about by accelerating globalization. Companies today must create the capability to execute higher and higher levels of customer service. Even though all companies are concerned about service, few try to execute it to perfection. The difference between excellent and average run-of-the-mill companies lies in four basic facts:

1. Mediocre companies see service as a means of appeasing the customer when the product is substandard or when they have lost their competitive edge. Excellent companies see service as a must, a competitive requirement on which there is to be no compromise.
2. Mediocre companies view service as servitude, as a constraint, as something you get rid of when market conditions permit you to. Excellent companies view service as a constant, as being one of the reasons for being in business.
3. Mediocre companies look at service as responding to the whims and fancies of the customer. Excellent companies look at service as understanding and responding to the real needs of the customer.
4. Mediocre companies do not have a clearly defined service strategy. Excellent companies have a service mission and the organization, culture, and structure to enable them to pursue that mission.

DIMENSIONS OF CUSTOMER SERVICE

There are some critical dimensions of customer service that must be realized by any company that wishes to deploy a service-oriented strategy:

1. Stay close to the customer in order to understand his or her real needs and to be able to incorporate them in one's view of the business. The real needs include the right product, quality, quantity, time, and information.
2. Within limits, be in a position to reschedule quickly in response to real customer needs. The ability to solve the customer's problems when exceptional situations arise is a key aspect of service. Special requests are part of the customer's changing needs. This puts a premium on flexibility.
3. Keep lead times competitive. For the customer, money has a time value. As companies move to implement just-in-time concepts, the competitive value of time increases.
4. Keep the customer informed of critical events that jeopardize the company's ability to deliver lead time promises. The response time for vital information on the part of the customer must be short. Information must be of high quality.
5. Maintain consistent and predictable performance according to customers' expectations and suppliers' promises. Superior service means a very high level of on-time delivery that is predictable in the sense that the customer can plan his or her operations once the promise is made by the supplier. This would require that service be constantly high for the entire product line made by the company. In that case, crises are few and the company can give reasonable performance even through crisis situations.
6. Monitor the cost of customer service. There is a cost to customer service. The goal in the management of service is to keep executing with finesse and improving the service system so as to reduce the cost. Reductions in the cost of service can be used to create more strategic leverage by providing increasing levels of service at comparable cost. Excellent companies have reduced service performance to an art thereby being able to provide more for less.

The Cost of Customer Service

These costs are often hidden because of the way service has been traditionally conceived of and managed. One cannot talk of improvement in service without getting some handle on what costs are imposed on the company by its execution or nonexecution. Traditionally, the cost of service has been buried in inventory and capacity, and costs of nonperformance are hidden because there is no service performance measurement and reporting.

The three most important costs of service are

1. Inventory
2. Excess capacity
3. Lost sales or low equipment availability (equipment that is down because parts are not available) and stock-outs.

A company which tries to assure high levels of service by increasing inventory investment is not really solving the service problem, but is instead throwing money at it. Because inventory hides problems, the organization will in fact be worse off with such a strategy. Moreover,

- The cost of service increases rapidly, because the requisite inventory increases much more rapidly than the service level.
- The service level (product availability) is usually frozen at 70 to 75 percent.
- Inability to quickly replan and reschedule leads to spotty performance.
- There is not a proactive, planned, anticipated response to the market.
- A lot of buck-passing goes on because there is not an agreed-to set of numbers and clear responsibility, authority, and performance measurement and review.

It is costly to pursue increasing levels of service by investing in inventory. Such a strategy does not manage service but moderates the negative impact of inability to execute service. Inventory covers the problems created by a poorly executed service strategy.

The cost of service is also sometimes hidden in excess capacity. When companies cannot effectively match supply and demand and competitive forces create the need to maintain (or reduce) lead times and back orders, the usual response is to increase capacity. The evidence is that the inability to manage capacity so as to synchronize production with demand is widespread in North American industry. Published statistics show that capacity utilization in North America averages 78 percent. For the vast majority of companies, productive resources are "fully" utilized when they are operating at 80 percent of capacity. The following are the consequences:

- Cost of capacity is high.
- Capacity utilization of 60 to 70 percent.
- Illusion of flexibility.
- Waste of capital resources.
- Inability to manage capacity so there is crisis when demand is higher than historical levels.
- A lot of expediting, back orders, and customer appeasement.

Probably much more significant than either inventory or capacity is the cost of lost sales due to poor customer service. This cost cannot be objectively appraised. However, some managers believe that every incident of poor customer service is communicated to about 20 different customers via word of mouth. This would tend to suggest that a company's reputation for poor service can be achieved very quickly.

The management of customer service requires the effective management of the throughput of resources as a pipeline that integrates purchasing, production, and marketing. It requires the smooth flow of information from marketing to production and to purchasing, and a coordinated flow of materials and goods from purchasing to production and then marketing. Service is substantially managing a throughput of information and materials to and from the customer and across the spectrum of business activities. The following implications are evident:

- Linking key functions. All the organizational (business) functions must be coordinated tightly so that they operate as a single business unit pursuing a common goal or objective. Communication and cooperation need to be extensive and intensive. There must be a common set of numbers for decision-making purposes.
- Effective management of service. A company is effectively managing service when it builds a service culture and designs organization structures and programs to execute service. The aim is to deliver with less resources.
- Forcing service competence. There is no padding created by excess capacity and inventory, because this simply switches costs without reducing them. Service competence means that costs are being reduced as the causes of poor service are being identified and eliminated.
- Purchasing and production are market and customer driven, or are oriented toward totally satisfying user needs.

The philosophy that better service can only come at the expense of higher inventory levels and more capacity availability is a vestige of the traditional order point/order quantity approach to managing material availability. In the order point approach, stock-outs are viewed as being inevitable, because they are thought to be produced by demand unpredictability or errors in sales or usage forecasts. Therefore, the order point system has evolved classical strategies for protecting against stock-outs. These strategies vary, but the most prevalent are as follows:

1. Safety or buffer stocks.
2. Lead-time padding, (i.e., adding a certain number of periods to the lead time, over and above its expected normal length).
3. Overstating future demand or usage, just in case demand is higher than anticipated.
4. Having standby suppliers in case normal suppliers cannot respond to requirements on time.

These are all costly strategies. Besides they do not attack the service problem at its root. As a prelude to evaluating MRP-II as a strategic service management system, there is need to probe the order point system so as to discover its systemic and operating shortcomings.

The Order Point System

The basic system was developed in the 1920s in the United States. It was designed as a tool to replenish materials that have been depleted from inventory. The fundamental parameters of the system have not changed since the 1920s. This is enough to lead one to suspect that the order point system is outdated. It was never intended for complex materials environments or to exploit the computer. The order point system was basically an effort to simplify the calculation of order points and economic order quantities (EOQs).

The order point (OP) system makes some crucial assumptions that permit computation of the key inventory control parameters. The major ones are the following:

1. Instantaneous delivery. Materials are assumed to be delivered in the lot sizes ordered. The maximum inventory is thus equal to the EOQ.
2. All materials are controlled independently of each other.
3. Continuous usage. Materials (products) are used in roughly equal amounts, day-by-day, over the entire planning horizon.
4. There are two costs associated with inventory.
   a. Inventory holding cost
   b. Ordering/set-up cost
   The system, in trying to compute the EOQ, evaluates the trade-off between these two costs. These behave systematically as a function of the EOQ.

FIGURE 12-1 **The Behavior of Inventory-Related Costs**

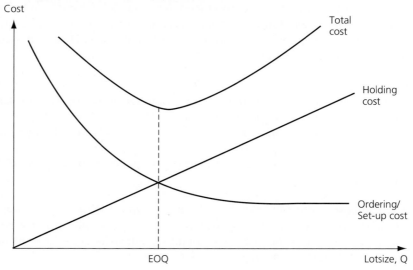

Figure 12-1 on page 426 shows how costs are assumed to behave as a function of the lot size.

5. Independent demand. One stock keeping unit (SKU) behaves independently of others. Under the OP system, every SKU is managed as a separate entity. The relationship between items is not exploited in an effort to increase the level of control. In effect, this assumption greatly simplifies calculation of the decision parameters (order point and order quantity). Any other assumption would make EOQ and OP calculation very difficult.

6. Optimize costs. The main objective of the OP system is to optimize the direct, quantifiable costs of inventory (order/set-up cost and holding cost).

The order/point order quantity (OPOQ) system tries to manage product and material availability by answering three questions, namely:

1. What to order?
2. When to order?
3. How much to order?

Based on the above assumptions, the behavior of the inventory level over time is shown in Figure 12-2. The assumptions and basic questions, when answered, provide the information for controlling the system. The critical assumptions outlined earlier were used to simplify computing the lot size (how much to order?) and the order point (when to order?). These questions are answered by setting appropriate quantities for the EOQ and the order point. The order point system is designed to control the quantity aspect of materials and not time. Order point systems are basically blind to time.

The parameters of the order point system control the efficiency with which materials flow through the company. What to order monitors the level of each individual material. When to order estimates the level of inventory that will exist during the lead time for replenishment. As such, it controls the level of inventory during the latter part of the ordering cycle. Since the order point usually incorporates some estimate of safety stock, it also indirectly affects the absolute level of inventory. In fact, the typical response to stock-outs in such a system is to increase the safety stock, thereby pushing the maximum inventory beyond the level of the EOQ.

The "how much to order" question is dealt with mathematically by assuming that the company is pursuing the objective of rigorously optimizing total inventory holding and ordering/set-up cost on an annual basis. The basic assumptions were selected to permit computation of the EOQ. Figure 12-2 shows the order point system with the safety stock impact highlighted.

The two basic computations for the order point system are the EOQ and the order point. The EOQ is given by the following well-known formula:

FIGURE **12–2**　**The Order Point Schematic**

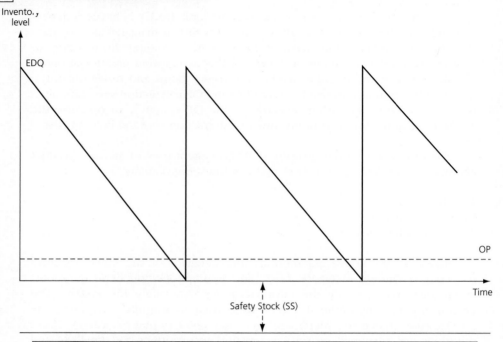

¹Maximum inventory (without safety stock) : EOQ
²Maximum inventory (with safety stock) : EOQ + SS

$$EOQ = \sqrt{\frac{2 \times D \times O}{h}}$$

where

D = Annual demand (usage)
O = Order processing or set-up cost per order (set-up)
h = Inventory holding cost per unit per year.

The order point is based on the lead time. It is the level of inventory that will cover usage or demand during the lead time. To illustrate the calculations, consider the following data for product XYZ:

Annual demand (D) = 8000 units
Ordering cost = $150
Unit cost = $120
Annual holding cost = 30% of unit cost
Lead time (L) = 1 week

Then,

$$h = .30 \times \$120 = \$36$$

$$EOQ = \sqrt{\frac{2 \times 8000 \times 150}{36}}$$

EOQ = 258 units
Weekly demand (d) = 8,000/52 = 154
Order point (OP) = Ld
= 1 × 154
OP = 154 units

The ordering policy for this material using the order point system is to order 258 units each time the inventory level reaches 154 units.

Consequences of the Order Point System

Despite its widespread use, the order point system has some very serious consequences that make it an ineffective tool for managing materials and inventory, in a context where high service levels are sought. The problems with the order point system are often hidden by the very high levels of inventory that it creates. This is so because of the following reasons:

1. *Reactive system.* The OPOQ system is reactive, in the sense that control action is triggered on the basis of a historical fact that the material is at its OP. The action is determined by the simple fact that inventory is depleted. Every other action is a deviation from the system as designed.
2. *No coordination.* The system does not coordinate purchasing, production, marketing, end users, logistics, quality, and engineering.
3. *Replenishment of depleted inventory.* The system replenishes depleted inventory with no regard as to the causes of such depletion or the need to replenish. In that sense, OPOQ is quantity driven, with no regard to the crucial variable, time.
4. *No planning system.* Because it does not incorporate forecast- or anticipated-use information continuously in the decision to order or not to order, the system falls far short of the requirements of a planning system. There is not a replanning capability in the OP system.
5. *Very high obsolescence.* The wrong materials are frequently bought in wrong quantities. Need reevaluation is not a continuing aspect of the system.

FIGURE 12–3 **The Concept of a Systemic Stock-Out**

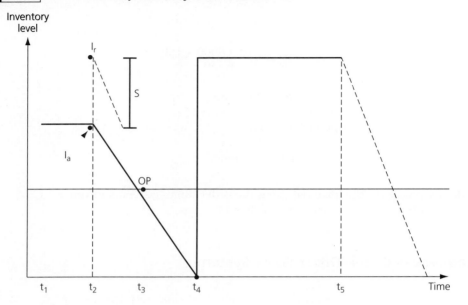

6. *Very low customer service or high inventory.* Customer service in an OPOQ context is quite low because the operation of the system generates stock-outs over and above those caused by demand and timing uncertainty. This is referred to as systemic stock-outs because they are caused by the wrong action being suggested by the operation of the system. Figure 12–3 illustrates the concept of a systemic stock-out. These are caused by the inability of the OPOQ system to handle demand patterns that are discontinuous or highly cyclical. At time t1, the system indicates that there is no need to reorder, because actual inventory, Ia, is much higher than the order point, OP. But because the end product that uses this particular material is scheduled for production at t2, sudden withdrawal of Ir units will cause a shortage of S units. The material consumption will be so intensive that the system will not have time to replenish the depleted inventory in time to avoid a shortage. A shortage occurs at time t2, even if the actual inventory is close to its theoretical maximum when the series of events that culminate into a systemic stock-out are triggered. The situation is completely reversed between periods t4 and t5. The system replenishes the inventory depleted up to t4 even if the product that consumes the material is not scheduled for production before t5. Materials are kept uselessly in inventory from period t4 to t5.

Dependent SKUs   FIGURE 12-4

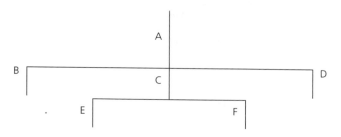

The OP system also generates stock-outs because of its inability to manage dependence of SKUs. The idea of dependence derives from the factual observation that certain SKUs are required only when the items in which they are used are being produced. This is represented by a structure like the one shown in Figure 12–4. In that case, SKUs B, C, and D go into A. If we manage B, C, and D independently of A, then we create a very low service level for A. For example, suppose we manage B, C, and D to achieve service levels of 90 percent. Because the production of A requires all three of B, C, and D, the resulting service level for A is $.9 \times .9 \times .9$ or 73 percent. It is easy to see that the service level for A deteriorates very quickly as we increase the number of parts that go into A. The OPOQ system, by assuming away dependence, makes achieving a high service level for A very difficult.

7. *High levels of inventory.* The usual reaction to stock-outs in the OP system is to increase the safety stock. As discussed previously, this causes an increase in the level of inventory. In addition, the system also causes inventory to increase because of the inability to handle discontinuous and cyclical demand patterns. Referring to Figure 12–3, one observes that the system will replenish the depleted inventory with an order placed at t_3, to arrive at t_4. However, the material is not needed until t_5. Because the system does not plan materials based on future usage (needs), it keeps unnecessary inventory from t_4 to t_5. Note that the extra inventory does not contribute anything to service.

8. *Incapacity to deal with fluctuating demand or usage.* The OPOQ system controls materials based on a fixed order point. Where demand or usage varies over time, the static order point causes stock-outs when demand or usage is higher than average and overstocks when demand is lower than average. The data below illustrate fluctuating demand or usage. It is necessary to have a system that can dynamically plan materials based on changing forecasts or orders for products and parts.

Annual demand (usage)	2600 units
Average quarterly demand (usage)	650 units
Demand during peak period (quarter)	1000 units
Demand during low period (quarter)	300 units
Average weekly demand	50 units
Lead time	4 weeks
Order point	200 units
Coverage, i.e. weeks demand covered by the order point	
1. Period when use is normal	4 weeks.
2. Period of peak usage (shortage)	2.4 weeks
3. Period of low usage (overstock)	8 weeks

MRP-II was developed to eliminate the operating, structural, marketing, and strategic inadequancies of OPOQ Systems. Subsequent discussion will deal with the basic elements of a customer and strategy-driven operations planning system and with the MRP-II approach to business and companies that are achieving superiority in customer service.

Operations Planning and the Strategic Management of Customer Service

A company's competitive environment is constantly changing. New competitors enter the market and established companies may exit or shift resources away from some niches and toward others. Technological innovation results in new or improved products and services being brought to the market or may alter the way in which existing products and services are marketed. Supply and demand conditions in input markets and innovation by suppliers may change input costs, lead to supply rationing, reduce the attractiveness of existing sources of supply, and jeopardize the viability of a company's procurement strategy. Most changes in a company's competitive environment are predictable and every company must respond to these. Planning refers to the process of mapping out the set of deliberate anticipatory actions and decisions that, when implemented, constitute a viable response to changes in the competitive environment. A plan is today's actions and decisions that are designed to deal with future events. The need for planning comes from the realization that decisions take time to implement and that appropriate responses to future events must be formulated and implemented ahead of the events that these decisions are designed to deal with. Planning is germane to and has long been recognized as one of the fundamental functions of management.

Operations planning is an integral part of the overall business planning system. It is the process of evaluating alternative courses of action for satisfying anticipated or forecasted market demand for a company's products or services and of choosing an appropriate set of actions to be implemented by the manu-facturing/operations functions. Because planning is fundamental to manage-ment, all companies engage in some form of operations planning. However, four features characterize the approach that competitively superior or world-class manufacturing companies use to plan operations. First, these companies use customer requirements and corporate and manufacturing mission to drive the operations planning system. They do so by formulating key requirements to be met by operations planning which derive directly from valued customer requirements and from corporate and manufacturing strategy. The operations planning system and processes are thus also dedicated to the creation of value for the customer and to the execution of manufacturing and corporate strat-egy. Second, superior performance companies set out to design and imple-ment planning systems that are mission oriented and customer driven. The operations planning system does not evolve haphazardly as occurs in most companies. Instead, the components of the planning system are deliberately chosen to facilitate the strategic planning of operations and the attainment of strategic goals. The logic of the system is clear and it can be easily explained on the basis of strategic priorities. The significant parameters of the planning system, its logic, major building blocks and the way it is used have all been specified, evaluated and deliberately chosen with competitive intent. More-over, the planning system is continuously refined and improved but always with full knowledge and clear understanding of competitive requirements, the role of the operations planning system in meeting these and how changes to the system affect and are affected by the corporate and manufacturing mis-sions. Contrary to most companies, world-class corporations plan their plan-ning systems. What we notice when we observe the superior performers is that they impose on the operations planning system the same competitive and managerial discipline that they use to extract superior execution performance from the factory. The rationale for this hard-nosed approach to operations planning makes sense. If increasingly tougher market conditions make it nec-essary for manufacturing plans to be executed to near perfection, then these same conditions must of necessity dictate that the planning system be capable of generating, to near perfection, the plans that guide the manufacturing sys-tem. The operations plan is a road map for the execution system. If the road map is wrong and shoddy, then the journey can at best be tedious and haz-ardous and the destination will likely never be reached.

Third, superior performing companies view the planning system and the formulation of sound operations plans as another means of pursuing total quality. Operations planning is part of the total quality effort because it increases order-liness, signals potential problems early and guides the search for their solutions or prevention, brings rigorous thinking and forethought to bear on the execu-tion system, decreases fire fighting, and reduces waste of resources. Finally, superior performance companies effectively integrate the operations planning system with the execution system and with marketing by providing integrative mechanisms; improvement teams, cross-departmental and cross-functional

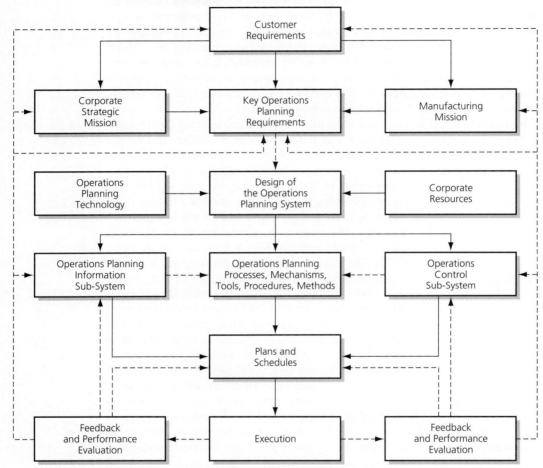

FIGURE 12–5 Customer Driven Operations Planning in Competitively Superior Companies

planning groups, frequent meetings, corporatewide planning policies and procedures—creating a free flow of information between marketing, operations planning, and the execution system; establishing an effective and efficient control system and mechanisms for evaluating execution performance; providing constant feedback to the operations planning; and building a solid information system, which is capable of generating the best possible, realistic factory-based information to the operations planning unit.

Figure 12–5 shows the basic elements of an operations planning system that is driven by customer requirements and by corporate and manufacturing strategy. Customer requirements, the corporate strategic mission, and the manufacturing mission are synthesized into a cogent set of key requirements that should be met by the planning system in general and the operations planning system, in particular.

These operations planning requirements include:

1. Performance evaluation criteria that are strongly influenced by the operations planning system such as target service levels for finished products and parts, customer lead times and their reliability, inventory levels, and turnover and capacity utilization.
2. Timeliness of plans and schedules.
3. Rapidity of replanning and rescheduling when business conditions or supporting information change.
4. Quality of planning information, both with respect to the market and the manufacturing/operations system. Planning information should be timely, accurate, realistic, and as complete as possible.
5. Quality of information provided to customers and to suppliers, particularly the speed of response to customer and vendor requests, and the quickness with which potential problems are identified, diagnosed, and communicated to customers, vendors, and internal users.
6. Use of advanced, state-of-the-art but proven planning concepts and technology.
7. Capability to optimize the use of productive resources or to choose the most attractive plans and schedules.
8. Degree of control and monitoring of the execution system.
9. Capability to stimulate and motivate continuous improvement both in planning and scheduling and execution.

As a whole, these key requirements define and express how the operations planning system will be used to support and execute a strategy that seeks customer service superiority.

The key operations planning requirements become an integral part of the planning system and their pursuit becomes a normal or natural part of operations planning activities when they are used as a major input in the design of the operations planning system. That is to say, the system is deliberately designed to pursue a set of strategic manufacturing objectives expressed as the key operations planning requirements. In order to be classified as a tool of corporate and manufacturing strategy, a system must, at the very minimum, be designed with deliberate strategic intent. The key operations planning requirements provide the strategic rationale for the choice of design elements, sharpen the evaluation of design alternatives, and greatly increase the potential for using the system to execute corporate and manufacturing strategy priorities. The specification of key operations planning requirements and their incorporation into the design of the system eliminate the usual, piecemeal evolution of the operations planning system that exists in most companies and instead give strategic purpose and competitive potential to a company's operations planning activities.

Figure 12–5 also presents the operations planning system as being composed of three parts: the operations planning information subsystem; operations planning processes, mechanisms, tools, procedures, and methods; and the operations control subsystem. These three parts or subsystems operate in tandem to produce the plans and schedules to be executed by the manufacturing operations function. Feedback based on actual performance during execution ensures that the whole planning process responds to actual events that are taking place on the factory floor, thus increasing the degree to which plans and schedules are realistic and executable.

Capacity Planning

Designing and operating an operations planning system that is driven by customer requirements and corporate and manufacturing strategy is the first phase of the management process that uses the planning system to implement a high performance customer service strategy. Capacity planning is also one of the critical phases of that management process. Capacity planning computes long-term capacity needs, evaluates alternative actions for increasing, decreasing, or shifting capacity from one geographic location to another, and selects an option to be implemented by the manufacturing/operations function. Capacity planning modifies the level and structure or form of the company's physical capacity and tries to achieve the best possible balance between capacity and demand consistent with the company's competitive priorities and desired market position. Capacity planning is an important activity in the strategic use of the manufacturing/operations function to attain superiority in customer service for the following reasons:

1. It directly and significantly affects the company's market position. The amount of physical capacity relative to demand influences the company's market share, partially determines its flexibility to respond to fluctuations in market demand, and constrains its ability to aggressively or offensively use capacity to preempt or discourage entry into the market by new competitors or to neutralize the efforts of established ones to gain market share. A company that has a capacity shortage has very few, if any, attractive options for warding off rivals that are bidding for the excess demand. Its only options, in the short run, are to increase the lead time it offers to its customers or to increase its reliance on subcontractors or other competitors. Both these options increase the attractiveness of alternative sources to its customers. The only credible and defensible option, in the long run, is to increase capacity, which reinforces the point that a capacity shortage invites competitors to launch a competitive assault on a company's market

position. The fact that it takes a significant amount of time to change the level of physical capacity means that a company that has some excess can use it to attract customers away from competitors that have a shortage. It can do so by implementing one or more of the following actions:

- Offer potential customers superior service in the form of shorter and more reliable lead times.
- Help potential customers to reduce cost by delivering products punctually and in small quantities.
- Stimulate its demand by reducing prices since the reduction in revenues are partially or total offset by economies of volume, dilution of fixed costs, the economic and strategic advantages of a larger market share, and the long-term returns of an expanded customer base.
- Maintain the level of service to existing and new customers by using the excess capacity to create the flexibility to respond to short-term unforeseen increases in demand.

2. It avoids excessive capacity overages or shortages, thus minimizing cost while maximizing the potential to give customers competitive and reliable lead times.

3. It can use the capacity plan to push for economies of scale and of capacity by adding capacity in appropriate chunks.

4. Sound capacity planning chooses the form (structure) and geographic dispersion of plants so as to exploit factory focus by systematically adding capacity in small scale, segmenting targeted plants, and locating these as close to the market as is justifiable on the basis of economic and competitive factors.

5. Capacity plans can be formulated to exploit and enhance whatever innate design-based flexibility that the manufacturing system may possess. Generally speaking, manufacturing flexibility refers to the capability of the production system to change from executing one set of tasks or activities to another and to effectively respond to changes in demand, customer requirements and other market and competitive conditions at minimum cost and disruption to the production process. The capability to change capacity and the supporting plans adds to overall competitive flexibility and ensures that execution flexibility is exploited in an orderly fashion, because capacity plans give the manufacturing system a clear road map as to the nature, magnitude, and direction of such change. Flexibility in the formulation and implementation of capacity plans keeps the production system responsive to changing customer requirements and market demand. In a global market where companies are likely to be managing a network of plants, the capability to quickly add capacity in the amounts needed, when and where necessary, to retire capacity quickly in declining markets, and to shift it from one location to another is undoubtedly an important competitive skill.

Major Decisions in the Strategic Deployment of Capacity

Companies that are managing capacity for strategic impact demonstrate consistency in three areas of decision making. These are:

1. The level of capacity the company will have relative to market demand and the timing of capacity additions or reductions.
2. The form or structure of the company's overall capacity, that is, whether it will be lodged in a few large plants as opposed to many small ones.
3. The geographic dispersion of plants.

The level of capacity: A company can adopt one of three different postures in deciding how much capacity to provide relative to overall demand. One option is to systematically choose a level of capacity that is somewhat lower than demand, thereby forcing a tight capacity situation. Companies that adopt such a capacity policy attempt to minimize capacity related costs by keeping investment low and capacity utilization high. They force competence in the use of physical facilities and push the operations function to search for ways to maximize progress on the learning curve. Moreover, they minimize the risk that plants will operate at below breakeven levels and depend on superior performance on other factors such as quality, cost, and innovation to compensate for longer and less reliable lead times. Except where the company has overwhelming superior competitive competence in other areas valued by customers, it faces the continuing risk that it may lose market share to more aggressive competitors, particularly those that achieve near parity in the areas of its competitive superiority. In addition, a tight capacity situation reduces production system flexibility and leaves the company very vulnerable to unpredictable surges in demand.

A second option favored by some companies is to provide a level of capacity that is somewhat in excess of demand with consequences that are the opposite of those discussed above. Capacity related costs are relatively high but the company reaps benefits such as greater flexibility, higher levels of customer service—high service levels for parts and end products, shorter and more reliable lead times—and an ability to deter competitors from attempting to gain market share at the company's expense. Moreover, these companies can periodically use aggressive pricing strategies—pricing at the margin—to stimulate the demand for their products, increase capacity utilization, and gain some reduction in unit costs as a result of diluting fixed costs over a larger volume. Japanese companies have demonstrated particular acumen at entering a market with excess capacity and subsequently using it aggressively to gain market share at the expense of their North American and European rivals. Companies that, as a matter of manufacturing and operations strategy, keep capacity somewhat in excess of demand employ patient capital, and sacrifice short-term margins for long-term higher market share and the competitive advantage that derives therefrom. These companies are customer service driven and place a premium on their capability to respond to unforeseen changes in the market and competitive conditions. They know that customers value a vendor that can respond effectively to special requests and unpredictable increases in demand. Therefore, they set out to design production systems that are innately flexible and that pursue flexibility as a matter of strategic priority. The excess capacity they deploy is merely one more way of building the capability to execute that strategic priority.

The third option, and the one that most companies prefer, is to have just enough capacity to satisfy demand. This option would be the ideal one when all costs and other competitive advantages and disadvantages are considered, except for the following paramount considerations:

1. Its effectiveness greatly depends on the company's ability to accurately forecast long-term market demand and competitive conditions, an almost impossible task.
2. Except if the company can change its level of physical capacity quickly, it is vulnerable to opportunistic assault on its market share by competitors when unpredictable bulges in demand cause a capacity shortage.
3. The company is constrained to increase or decrease capacity in relatively small chunks and sometimes at less-than-optimum scale levels. What the company gains in terms of the lower cost associated with high rates of capacity utilization, it may lose as a result of operating plants that are smaller than the optimal economic scale. However, multiplant companies can mitigate this effect and add or decrease capacity in optimal increments or decrements because they can distribute the change in capacity over a large number of plants. For example, a company that has 20 plants operating at close to 100 percent capacity experiences a 5 percent reduction in overall capacity utilization by building an additional one. It can therefore support a small, marginal erosion in capacity utilization in the short term by building a larger one if that is necessary to reach optimal economic scale for the additional plant.

The timing of additions to capacity is closely related to the issue of the level of capacity relative to market demand. Companies can adopt three policies with respect to the timing of capacity additions:

1. Anticipatory response. The company adds capacity well in advance of the materialization of market demand and on the basis of long-term market forecasts. Companies that adopt that posture hope to appropriate the increase in market demand or a substantial portion of it, hopefully, one that is appreciably higher than their current share of the market. They are

able to debug the new facilities early and reap a time advantage on the learning curve and can use these advantages to offset the higher cost of low capacity utilization. Moreover, these companies can use the timing of capacity expansion to create an illusion of excess capacity, thus discouraging competitors from expanding their own capacity. However, an anticipatory response, because it is based on long-term forecasts of market demand, imposes substantial risks on a company since forecasts may not materialize.

2. Punctual response. In this case, the company adds capacity about the time that there is enough market demand to operate the new facilities at breakeven levels. There are no particular risks or advantages to this posture. Nevertheless, the company suffers some loss of flexibility and deterioration of customer service during the time that it is using existing facilities to satisfy the additional demand up to the breakeven point for a new facility.

3. Reactive response. The company adds capacity when enough additional demand already exists for operating the new facility at target profitability levels. The company eliminates all risk that demand will not materialize. However, it gives competitors ample time to preempt the market and, in fact, helps them in doing so during the time that it is waiting for demand to materialize and consequently suffers a huge loss in flexibility and substantial deterioration in customer service. Very few companies or competitive situations can justify systematically adopting a reactive response to the market.

The Structure of Overall Capacity

A company can structure its capacity in different ways, each having its own strategic consequences. Capacity can be structured along two important dimensions: the size, and therefore number, of manufacturing plants and how intensively they will be exploited. Companies have the option of deploying capacity in the form of many small scale plants or they could deploy it in the form of a few large scale ones. Moreover, companies could decide, as a matter of policy, to exploit plants on a one-shift basis or they could operate them using two, or even three, shifts. The following competitive ramifications are important determinants of the choice of capacity structure:

1. Large plant operated on a one-shift basis. Large plants allow the company to reap economies of scale in production. One-shift operation gives the company upward flexibility to respond to large increases in demand, since capacity can be doubled with no addition to the physical plant. However, the downside is that the production system is located far from a large percentage of the market with a commensurate loss in customer service, since lead times are relatively long. The company also loses much downward flexibility to bring capacity in line with large decreases in demand. Companies that use large scale production units will have difficulty deploying a

focused strategy because each large plant must serve more than one market segment, except where the market niche is large enough to justify large scale manufacturing units.

2. Large scale plant operated on a two-shift basis. This structure has the same consequences as the one-shift option. In addition, it has the disadvantage of making it difficult for the company to adjust capacity upward when demand increases substantially. The company loses some upward flexibility because when demand requires more than two-shift operations, it must build additional, large scale plants.

3. Small scale plants operated on a one-shift basis: The advantages of this approach to structuring capacity are impressive. They include:

   • The company can rigorously deploy a focused strategy. It can specialize its plants by market segment and can give each a clear mandate for executing the competitive requirements of that segment. Furthermore, market segmentation can be pushed to the maximum extent that is competitively useful and such differentiation can be easily accommodated by a network of small plants.

   • Capacity can be adjusted closely to demand and can be added punctually because it can be built in small chunks. The company can increase its production volume steadily and progressively, one small plant at a time, with minimum or no disruption to the core network. Similarly, the company can retire capacity in an orderly fashion and can shift it from one location or market segment to another, almost imperceptibly to its competitors. It is relatively easy to keep capacity in balance with demand, thereby maximizing capacity utilization. The structuring of capacity as a set of small scale plants increases overall competitive flexibility because it facilitates the adjustment of production to demand and makes it much less difficult for the company to enter new market segments or abandon existing ones.

   • The company can maximize learning and factory-based innovations in processes, methods, systems, and techniques. These can also have a positive effect on product innovation as the factory develops insight as to how the product should be designed for ease of manufacture, low cost, and low manufacturing generated product defects. Each factory can be managed as a center for innovation and experimentation, and a large number of plants increases the chance that novel solutions will be found. In addition, it is easier and much less risky to test unproven ideas, products, processes, and systems in an actual factory environment because only one or two of these factories need to be used as a test site.

   • A network of small scale plants provides a solid basis for internal benchmarking and for comparative performance evaluation and analysis.

4. Small scale plants operated on a two-shift basis. This capacity structure has all the characteristics of the third structural type discussed previously. However, the company loses some upward flexibility, since additions to capacity will require it to build new facilities.

The Geographic Dispersion of Capacity

Companies that have multiplant operations must also decide whether capacity will be concentrated in one or a few geographic areas or whether it will be geographically dispersed. The greater the number of plants, the greater the necessity for the company to deliberately decide on the geographic dispersion of plants. Consequently, the deployment of a capacity structure that uses a large number of small scale plants requires a concomitant decision and policies on the geographic dispersion of capacity.

In some industries, the economics of transportation, ease of access to high quality transportation facilities and the nature of the production process—that is, whether it adds or reduces bulk or volume and, therefore, whether it causes logistics related costs to increase or decrease—exert major influence on the decision to geographically concentrate or disperse capacity. Industries where the production process significantly adds to the volume of the product and raw materials are widely available or can be brought in efficiently by a high quality transportation system, tend to locate manufacturing plants close to the market and capacity is thus geographically dispersed. Bottling plants for soft drinks, alcohol distilleries, breweries, and petroleum refineries are clear examples of these industries that add volume in the production process and that have geographically dispersed capacity. On the other hand, industries that significantly reduce volume or bulk during the production process tend to locate plants and capacity close to raw material sources and capacity will be concentrated or dispersed depending on the variety of raw material sources that the company can economically exploit. Metal processing, forest products, and hydroelectricity generation are all examples of industries where the production process significantly reduces bulk and that are located close to raw material sources. The case of hydroelectricity generation is a particularly glaring example where massive amounts of water, which is very expensive to transport, are transformed into very light electricity.

Although the search for a cost advantage is an important factor that influences the decision to geographically concentrate or disperse capacity, there are other strategic factors that come into play. These factors are particularly significant in the case where the company's capacity is deployed in the form of small scale production units, which buttresses the notion that strategic decisions support and feed on each other in companies that are achieving superior competitive performance.

1. The decision to deploy capacity in the form of small scale production units that are geographically dispersed puts the company, but particularly the manufacturing function, close to the market and the customer. Customer service, in the form of shorter and reliable lead times, speed of response to special customer requests, the accurate understanding of customer needs, and the speed of transmission of valued customer information, is high. Moreover, the manufacturing function can more easily detect, understand, translate, and respond to emerging market requirements and trends.

2. Geographic dispersion of capacity in the form of small scale production units means that the company can designate some of these as international production centers (IPCs), thus bringing into being a set of strategic manufacturing units (SMUs) that help it reap some of the advantages of focus and specialization, since SMUs have responsibility for spearheading the company's competitive efforts in specified product markets. But these international production centers also link into corporatewide technology, resources, and expertise whether they be general or product-market specific, giving them the capability to harness all corporate competitive skills that are relevant to their product-market requirements.

3. The deployment of capacity in the form of a network of small scale plants that are reasonably geographically dispersed, also gives a company the potential to improve the execution of its procurement strategy and to derive greater competitive leverage from its supplier network. The company can build a network of vendors (suppliers) that includes the best global sources at the same time that it uses local or emerging sources in areas where they can give performance that is superior to the global ones. It can spot potential emerging, competitively useful local sources early and can nurture privileged relationships with them.

Capacity structures that use many, small scale production units prevent a company from reaping the full benefits of economies of scale. But they also have what are incontestably significant strategic advantages that more than likely compensate for the disadvantages that derive from diseconomies of scale. Except in industries such as petroleum refining, metal processing, and chemicals where economies of scale are so important as to constitute an overwhelming competitive advantage, capacity structures that use small scale production units, particularly when these are geographically dispersed so as to be located close to a company's markets and customers, are likely to be the competitively superior alternative. Increasingly, innovations in process technology, robotics, and the refinement of the technologies at the core of flexible manufacturing systems (FMS) are systematically reducing the optimum scale of manufacturing plants. Moreover, improvements in management practices, information technology, and the greater ability to manage distant operations across national and cultural boundaries fostered by globalization and the growth of the global corporation are allowing companies to effectively spread capacity over a wide geographic area. Even companies that traditionally deployed very concentrated capacity structures, because of very radical economies of scale, are increasingly finding it feasible and competitively beneficial to have some form of dispersed capacity structure. Often, they are doing so to unbeatable competitive advantage. The huge, integrated and geographically concentrated steel mills are finding it very difficult to effectively compete against the geographically dispersed, region-based mini-mills that have capitalized on the electric arc furnace and continuous casting to reduce the optimal scale of steel operations. The large, integrated steel companies must eventually become networks of geographically dispersed and competitively versatile mini-mills, if they are to escape being driven out of the steel market entirely. Some of these mini-mills are so small, with capacities as low as 50,000 tons per year of raw steel output, that they are best referred to as micro-mills. More and more automobile manufacturers are deconcentrating their capacity structures and are building smaller plants that are spread out all over the world and closer to their markets and customers. Even Boeing, a company that historically has a highly concentrated capacity structure that made a lot of sense because of the nature of the product and the production process—a very large product, made to rigorous quality specifications, and using a production process that is at the same time highly automated and manual—will have to find ways to locate some forms of capacity closer to its customers.

The conclusion is evident. A company will have a difficult time staying close to its customers and giving them superior service, if it does not find ways to locate some capacity close to them. Once more, one sees that it is not enough for the marketing function to be close to its customers. The manufacturing function must be close to them as well and must deploy all resources, including capacity, in the creation of superiority in customer service. Marketing cannot be close to customers if production is not also close to them.

The remaining activities in customer and strategy driven business and operations planning are best considered within the MRP-II approach and philosophy to production and materials planning and control.

WHAT IS MRP-II?

MRP-II was developed to eliminate the operating, structural marketing, and strategic inadequacies of OPOQ systems. Subsequent discussion will deal with the basic elements of a customer and strategy-driven operations system and with the MRP-II approach to business and operations planning.

The MRP-II Framework

Figure 12–6 presents a comprehensive framework of the vital MRP-II planning and control processes. The following is a short description of each of the major building blocks of the framework.

Business Planning
The MRP-II planning process is triggered by top management estimates and expectations of dollar sales, aggregate profits, and cash flow for the business as a whole. In most companies, this activity coincides with the annual financial budgeting process. While companies generally do not use the general

The MRP-II Framework FIGURE 12–6

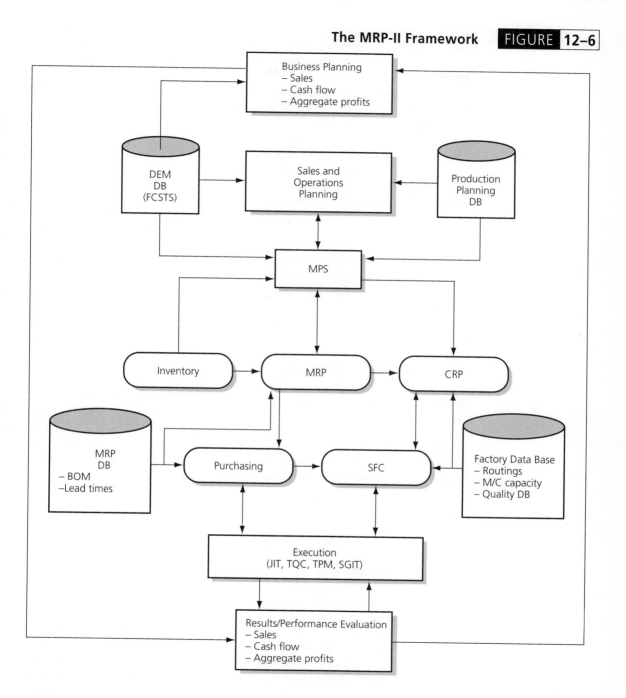

financial budget to plan lower level business activities, MRP-II pushes the company to incorporate the business plan into lower level plans. This is the necessary first step toward building a total integrated planning system.

Sales and Operations Planning

This planning subsystem develops an aggregate plan of sales and production rates for each family of products or product lines, so as to meet the financial targets that come from the business plan. The sales and operations plan converts sales dollars into product line sales and then chooses production plans to meet the budgeted sales, aggregate production costs, and gross profits.

Master Production Scheduling

The master production schedule (MPS) programs actual production rates of deliverable end items so as to meet customer or distribution orders. The MPS is both a plan and a schedule, and is the crossover point in the process that converts the general business plan into concrete and detailed production and materials schedules. The MPS is at the heart of the MRP-II process and is a crucial activity for companies that are dedicated to customer-service superiority. As we shall see later, higher level plans such as the business and sales and operations plan look forward to the MPS, while the lower level plans and schedules look back to the MPS.

Demand Database (DEM DB)

Business planning, sales and operations planning, and master scheduling all rely on forecasts of sales or demand. Demand management provides the up-to-date, reasonably accurate forecasts that are required by the company's planning activities. Forecasts are stored in the demand database which is linked to the planning and scheduling processes that require them. One of the first step toward putting customer service in production and materials planning and control is to use good forecasts to trigger the business planning process.

Production Planning Database

In addition to forecasts, sales and operations planning and master scheduling use factory-based information such as standard costs, machine capacities, and standard times per unit of output. This supplementary information is stored in the production planning database.

Material Requirements Planning (MRP)

MRP-II uses the MPS to compute and plan the materials needed for future end item production that is programmed in the master schedule. MRP is in fact the MPS expressed as lower level material requirements. The MRP database links material requirements to MPS end item production. The bill of materials (BOM) gives what materials (and in what quantities) go into making one unit of each finished product. The BOM is used to compute how much of each material is needed to support the MPS. Materials plans are temporally synchronized with the MPS by way of the lead times. Materials can thus be planned to arrive on time so as to support master schedule activity.

Capacity Requirements Planning (CRP)

End item production planned in the MPS and parts production scheduled by MRP consume capacity. The MPS and MRP are valid and realistic if there are enough human resources and machine capacity to execute them. CRP estimates the capacity required to execute the MPS and MRP. The key data for doing this are routings and machine center capacities. Routings show what operations are required to make a product and what is the time per piece at each operation. Machine center capacity shows total human resource and machine hours available at each machine center for each week in the planning horizon.

Shop Floor Control

The purpose of shop floor control (SFC) is to build a schedule that shows projected start and finish dates for each customer or production order at each machine center. SFC gives the basic information that is necessary for controlling the plant to a rigid time schedule that is driven by customer due dates.

Execution

The execution subsystem actually performs the factory work that executes customer or production orders. MRP-II is not a system for executing work, but instead it plans work to be executed by the factory. More and more worldclass manufacturing companies are using the principles and tools of TQC, JIT, TPM, and SGIT to design, operate, and drive the execution subsystem.

Performance Evaluation

MRP-II is also a replanning system. Production and materials are continually being replanned and rescheduled so as to keep the MPS and customer promises valid and realistic. Performance measurement, evaluation, and reporting at all levels of the planning and control hierarchy generate the feedback which signals the need for replanning and rescheduling. In MRP-II, performance measures emanate directly and naturally from ongoing planning, control, and execution activities. Most companies do not have a performance measurement and reporting system that is germane to their planning systems. In these companies, performance measurement and reporting is a separate activity that is done periodically and on an ad hoc basis. The measures do not flow from the planning system but are extracted from it by a supplementary set of activities undertaken by the accounting department. Where this is the case, performance evaluation and reporting is limited to broad indices of financial performance. MRP-II, on the other hand, integrates performance measurement and reporting that is appropriate to each level in the planning system. Financial performance measurement and reporting close the planning and control loop and give feedback for reformulating or updating the business plan.

Distinctive Characteristics of MRP-II

The basic concern in MRP-II is to develop plans for the delivery of components and parts that link into higher level plans such as the sales and operations plan and the master production schedule. The critical word is "link." The OPOQ inventory management systems do not link with other production and materials planning and control activities. As a matter of fact, classical inventory management "delinks" materials scheduling and master scheduling by creating buffers to absorb uncertainty. The order point system decouples the subsystems of production and materials planning and control such as demand management, master scheduling, and shop floor control. In the classical approach to materials management, these functions are managed separately and are kept distinct. MRP-II deliberately couples master scheduling, materials scheduling, and shop floor activities so as to integrate all the business functions in the pursuit of excellence in customer service.

The notion of a master schedule that drives the service system is foreign to classical order point inventory management. But in MRP-II, the master schedule is critical. Orders are launched, replanned, and rescheduled to meet the requirements of the master production schedule. The dominant concern is to manage the master production schedule so as to keep it valid and realistic and to execute the marketing priorities of the company. Because of the need to meet the master schedule, MRP-II is a forward-looking planning and scheduling system. The idea of anticipating materials needs is not new to material management. Looking forward to schedule materials is central to project management. The raw data to MRP-II are plans, forward-looking schedules, and forecasts. The whole flow of materials, parts, and production schedules is being driven by the MPS.

MRP also links production to the customer. In the classical inventory management philosophy, production and materials planning and control are shielded from the customer. The management of customer service is seen as a marketing problem, not a production one. MRP-II puts customer service within the responsibility of production planners and schedulers. Managing the master schedule is managing customer service, since the former is formulated on the basis of orders for deliverable items. Keeping the master schedule valid means knowing which order is important, which can wait, and which must be delivered with no change in delivery promises. This means having the right priorities. MRP-II manages the priorities created by the MPS. Setting delivery promises means knowing production capacities, volume of back orders, lead times for critical materials, the loadings of major machine centers, and the flexibilities of production and materials delivery schedules. In MRP-II, customer service is the major objective. It shows the planner the real priorities.

There are six key issues in MRP-II:

- Getting an agreed-to set of forecasts that describe realistic expectations of the market.
- Knowing the real priorities of the master production schedule, materials delivery schedules, supplier constraints, and shop floor realities and how these impact on the customer's requirements.
- Knowing the degree of flexibility in all the schedules and capacity plans.
- Synthesizing all these into a valid and realistic master schedule.
- Keeping the schedules and plans valid by rescheduling and replanning. (MRP-II is a production planning and control system that reacts to uncertainty by rescheduling and replanning.)
- Cutting the planning horizon into small planning buckets (time periods) to make updating and rescheduling repetitive (i.e., building a replanning reflex into the system). If you plan on a monthly basis, you are replanning 12 times a year; on a weekly basis, 52 times a year.

In a real-life production system, priorities are always changing. Customers change their delivery dates, machines break down more often than anticipated, suppliers sometimes have problems adhering to delivery promises, and demand forecasts are wrong. The manager must juggle all these factors to arrive at new priorities to be met by the master schedule. Scheduling production is literally an act of keeping the production system working on the critical customer orders first and delivering the right materials at the right place and the right time and in the right quantities. With MRP-II, managers can easily identify the critical items of the master schedule and the critical supply orders to produce them at the critical times.

MRP-II manages the PMPC system on a time-critical basis. The important thing is to make the master schedule happen at the right time and in no more time than is absolutely necessary. To do this, orders for materials must be launched at the right time and shop floor activities must deliver work-in-process and parts, also at the right time. The management of production activities on the basis of time is not new to management since it is the essence of the project management techniques such as PERT and CPM. It is also central to the old Gantt charts that are so widely used to control machine centers. MRP-II brought the emphasis on time to the shop floor and integrated it into all the service management activities of the company.

The dominance of the time factor in MRP-II is one reason why it contrasts with the order point system. The latter manages quantities, and even when time is used, it is buried into order point-calculations. MRP-II uses time directly and visibly. The ability to manage the scheduling system in order to deliver the right materials, at the right place and the right time, is what makes MRP-II potentially powerful. It means that no idle materials are held, which reduces the investment in inventories. Eighty percent of the inventory in a typical plant or warehouse are materials that will be needed two, three, or even six months hence. One major goal in MRP-II is to prevent this from happening by relating materials purchasing and scheduling to the end item schedule (MPS), and keeping both these schedules valid.

Business resource management with hard numbers is another distinguishing feature of MRP-II. One of the distinctive characteristics of the traditional order point order quantity system (OPOQ) is its high tolerance for errors in estimating demand, costs, and production levels. EOQ models are robust, in the sense that large errors in estimating critical parameters have very small impact on final decisions. In managing an OPOQ system, crude numbers based on the manager's guesstimates will do, partly because of model robustness and partly because of the incidence of buffering. Managing production planning and control with MRP-II, on the other hand, calls for "hard" numbers and generates "hard" numbers in return. If it is impossible to get the figures right, as is sometimes the case in estimating demand, then a higher level decision must adopt a scenario alternative that filters a set of hard numbers down to lower levels. This is the role of sales and operations planning, a critical MRP-II front-end process, as we shall explore subsequently. For example, an estimate could place a reasonable range on demand that goes between 10,000 and 15,000. But somewhere in the organization, someone must have the authority to say exactly where in that range the master schedule will operate, so that production planners can develop plans that show precise quantities of materials to support the master schedule. MRP-II is resource planning and control with "hard" numbers.

Independent/Dependent Demand

These comments lead to consideration of a very powerful concept in MRP-II. The range of demand of 10,000 to 15,000 for the end item is management's best guess of what it could probably sell in the market. The company can try to influence the market, but in the final analysis, one can only take what the market will give. Until management decides which demand level it wants to choose as its market objective, subsequent production and materials planning and control activities are at worst paralyzed, and at best confused. That is to say, the decision as to what materials will be needed, when and in what quantities, *depends* on a higher level decision that establishes the market objectives. Similarly, the orderly schedule of shop floor activities, the capacity plan at key machine centers, and the rescheduling of customer orders, *depend* on the master schedule decision. The demand for the end item is relatively *independent* of the production planning and control decisions that are being made on a day-to-day basis. The end item—master schedule item—is an independent demand item. Items such as parts, subassemblies, components, and labor that feed the master schedule are dependent demand items. Actions to manage these must of necessity await clear signals and decisions at the level of the MPS.

This distinction between independent and dependent demand is not an academic exercise; it is at the heart of what MRP-II is all about. If some lower level decisions depend on higher level ones, one must see the resource management system as a network of decisions that are linked through space and time. A way must be found to effectively cascade decisions from top to bottom and back up. It makes very little sense to try to decouple a set of decisions that are naturally coupled. What is more important is to effectively manage the interfaces where decisions made at different levels systematically impact on one another. In essence, MRP-II tries to tie lower level decisions on order launching and shop floor scheduling to higher level decisions such as aggregate capacity planning (sales and operations planning) and master production scheduling. Rather than spend energy to decouple, one should spend time making the coupling smoother. The processes for achieving this are germane to MRP-II.

So MRP-II is a way to effectively plan the business from top to bottom and make sure that every decision gets transferred up and down the planning structure with a set of hard numbers on what orders, materials, capacities, and production activities are required, when, where, and in what quantities. To do this, you need to have rapid and efficient information gathering, storing, processing, and retrieving. You also need very efficient communication, feedback, and performance evaluation processes. Marketing, production, materials, quality, and others must work together as a team to manage the resource planning and control system. One must therefore recognize that the effective execution of the management processes that are at the base of MRP-II are much more important to the company's ability to attain superiority in customer service, than the mechanics and techniques of MRP-II. The corporate culture and value system also provide the organizational framework, the foundation principles and philosophies, for effectively exploiting MRP-II for competitive advantage. Corporatewide customer orientation and consciousness harness all functions in the company's thrust to reach distinctiveness in customer service. The delegation of responsibility for customer service to all functions and measures taken to make all organizational units accountable to the customer forge consensus and team spirit, which are necessary conditions for successful exploitation of MRP-II.

The key MRP-II concepts can be summarized as follows:

1. Comprehensive business planning.
2. Integrated business planning.
3. Top-down planning.
4. Bottom-up replanning.
5. A service management system.

6. Proactive, market-driven planning and scheduling of marketing, purchasing, materials, production, and distribution.
7. Management of and by the database.
8. Computer-facilitated business planning and control.
9. Managing customers, materials, production, and distribution on a *time critical basis.*

BUSINESS AND PRODUCTION PLANNING IN MRP-II

The planning function is germane to any business, whether or not it is systematically executed. Business planning is essential because the lead time for executing activities geared toward serving the customer is often longer than the lead time the customer allows for their execution. Competitive pressures operate in such a way as to allow the customer more leverage over the lead time than the individual company. Except in the purely design–to–order or engineering–to–order business, short- and intermediate-term planning are inescapable. Even in engineering–to–order businesses, physical capacity plans must anticipate market conditions, since capacity availability can be used to aggressively exploit the market. Moreover, engineering–to–order businesses must plan on the short- to intermediate-term basis so as to be able to produce to a rigorous time schedule.

In a make-to-stock company, the basic short- to intermediate-term goal of business planning is to enable the company to put the necessary resources in place to respond to anticipated market conditions. Execution of customer requirements cannot be done efficiently if the resources have not been put into place in advance. Therefore, the MRP-II process tries to link estimates of market requirements to actual execution of customer orders in a systematic way. Figure 12–7 shows the major building blocks of the MRP-II business planning process in schematic form.

Business Planning

The business plan, in the context of MRP-II, refers to the set of processes that culminate into a pro–forma statement of dollar sales, aggregate profits, and cash flows. Depending on the complexity, depth, and breadth of the product line, business planning could project sales and financial performance by product line, product group, or even individual products. Of course, the greater the level of disaggregation in the business plan, the more focused can be top management's activities to subsequently control achievement of the crucial business objectives over the planning horizon.

The Business Planning Process  FIGURE 12–7

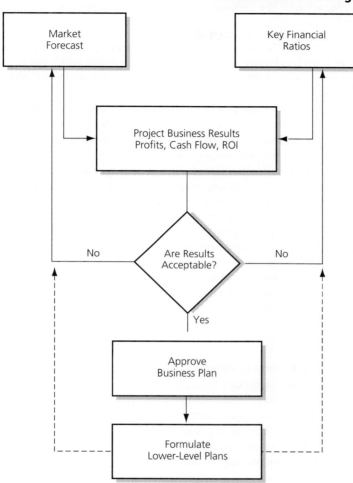

The business plan is a forecast of general business activity and top management's expectation as to what the company ought to achieve in order to maintain or enhance its financial health and competitive position. To the extent that reasonable forecasts of sales, cash flows, and profit levels fall short of the adopted plan, management is transmitting a powerful signal that it expects increased effort to stimulate market demand and increase productive efficiency. The typical time frame for business planning is one to two years, with a rolling yearly update. The plan is usually broken down into monthly or quarterly time buckets.

The Business Planning Process

A brief explanation of the fundamental aspects of the process shown in Figure 12-7 follows:

1. *Market forecast.* This is usually expressed in aggregate dollars, based on historical sales levels and adjusted for current market conditions.
2. *Key financial ratios.* These are derived from analysis of the most recent financial statements of the company. Some important ratios are cost of goods sold, sales and marketing, administrative, R&D and other expenses, and net profit, all expressed as a percentage of sales.
3. *Projected gross margins, profits, and cash flows.* Taken as a group, these measure the financial performance of the company.
4. *Evaluation of first cut projected financial performance.* One important aspect of the business planning process is the part that deals with the decision of whether or not to accept the business plan. At this stage, one can envisage alternative actions that would bring projected financial performance in line with management's expectations. Alternative actions can try to stimulate market demand or improve business efficiency by focusing on the major financial ratios.
5. *Proceed to next planning phase.* The acceptance of the business plan and its crucial assumptions is but the first stage of the total business planning process. The process must include ways to ensure that the data generated by the business plan are incorporated into lower level plans and execution programs.

MRP-II and the Business Plan

MRP-II both uses and facilitates business planning activity. Business planning is a front-end MRP-II phase which serves to prepare the company to meet customers' needs and to anticipate broad actions that are necessary to achieve basic financial goals. The initial forecast used to do the business plan, although it is general, is used as a benchmark for more specific forecasts that are then used to formulate the second stage in the planning hierarchy, the sales and operations plan.

The business planning process is improved by MRP-II as follows:

1. The forecasting system which is a vital aspect of the lower level MRP-II process improves business forecasting at the top management level.
2. The key financial ratios used to project business performance are more accurate.
3. Simulation of the business plan so as to arrive at conclusions as to what sales levels and/or efficiency indices (the ratios) will make the business plan feasible, can be both intensive and extensive.
4. MRP-II provides the ability to quickly monitor performance according to plan on a continuing basis. The business plan can be reformulated on the basis of current, accurate information.

TABLE 12–1

Period	Sales	Cost of Sales	Gross Profit	Production	Inventory*
1st Quarter	$6,000	$2,400	$1,800	$2,000	$2,600
2nd Quarter	7,000	2,600	3,400	2,000	2,000
3rd Quarter	9,000	3,100	5,900	3,000	1,900
4th Quarter	6,000	2,400	3,600	2,000	1,500

Note: Figures in thousands of dollars.
*Beginning inventory = $3,000

5. Disaggregation of the plan is easy because MRP-II keeps a reservoir of data that can be exploited to this end. Historical product-mix data are updated continuously so that dollar sales at the corporate (divisional) level can be used to arrive at sales by product line or group.

MRP-II brings top management into sales, operations, and materials planning by making the business plan an input in other planning activities. Table 12–1 shows what a business plan could look like. The format and vital information vary from company to company. The main point is that the plan projects (budgets) the company's expected financial performance.

SALES AND OPERATIONS PLANNING

Nature of the Plan

It is usually difficult to change the level of physical capacity of the production system over the short run. Even when capacity can be changed over the intermediate term by redeploying and transferring production employees, a minimum amount of time is required to put all the necessary resources into place. The basic point is that changing capacity takes time. This lead time for changing capacity depends on the degree of flexibility of the production system. In the case of systems like refineries and steel mills, one has the maximum level of capacity rigidity.

The problem for resource planning is that customers impose lead-time requirements that are shorter than the time needed to change capacity. Such is the case where production is made on a strictly-to-stock basis. Resources cannot be planned on the basis of customer orders, since the acceptance of these orders assumes that the resources are in place to execute them, or better yet, that the goods are available or will be shortly. The link here between the ability to accept orders for on-time delivery and the planning process is evident. So, one must plan capacity over three, six, or even twelve months, on the basis of forecasts. The primary objective of sales and operations planning is to plan capacity needs beyond the lead time imposed by customers but without modification in the level of physical capacity. This activity is also called production planning or aggregate planning. In the make-to-order or engineering-to-order environment, the SOP plans capacity to enable the company to negotiate competitive or acceptable lead times during order promising. Even if forecasting is difficult, the SOP is necessary to maintain good customer service. It is an integral part of any budgeting process.

Usually, the unit of measurement for purposes of sales and operations planning (SOP) is the product family or group. Aggregation at the level of product families makes forecast errors more tolerable, since these errors at the individual product level tend to offset each other when aggregated by family.

The second objective of SOP is the "optimization" of productive resources to respond to the sales forecast over a six to twelve month planning horizon. During this time frame, the actions that can be validly undertaken include:

1. Redeployment of production personnel. The decision to double shift is one that ought to be taken using the SOP process.
2. Overtime or undertime.
3. Increase/decrease of finished goods inventories.
4. Increase/decrease of the order file or back orders, which necessarily implies an increase or decrease in customer lead times. Once more, we see that a crucial service variable, the lead time, is directly affected by the SOP process.

The key to SOP is to increase or decrease necessary resources on time so as to avoid deterioration in customer service, while minimizing production cost, as much as possible. We will also see subsequently that there is a direct relationship between the production plan and the master production schedule (MPS) for end items.

The SOP Process

The logic of the SOP has three parts. The first deals with the necessity to allocate available capacity across broad product families. Such allocation culminates into specification of the basic production rate for each product line so as to meet the sales forecast. The second element of the logic relates to the choice of the mix of resources to generate the production rate. The third part of the logic tries to simulate alternative plans so as to select the "best" strategy for responding to variable market forecasts. Application of the three parts of the logic is summarized in Figure 12–8.

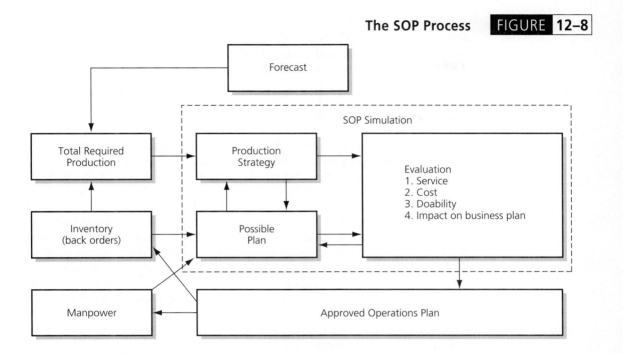

The SOP Process FIGURE 12–8

Forecast

Demand management plays a vital role in the SOP process for two reasons. First, the whole SOP process is designed to respond effectively to market forecasts. Where forecasts are not available, there is no feasible way to systematically respond to the market in a make-to-stock business. In the absence of the forecast, the company's response to the market is haphazard, tentative, and based on guesswork. Systematic business planning is *always* based on a market-driven forecasting system. Second, the forecast is the only exogenous data that are introduced into the SOP process, all the others being under the control of the company. If the sales and operations plan is going to be wrong, it is likely because of bad forecasts. Clearly, then, much emphasis needs to be placed on the efficient, continuous, and rapid generation of sales forecasts. The monitoring of forecast accuracy as an input of the forecast improvement process becomes a necessity. Forecasts will always be wrong, but there is a need to keep forecast error to a level that is judged acceptable by all parties concerned about SOP.

Experience shows that it is probably more important to develop strong consensus on the estimates of market demand than it is to have smaller forecast errors. SOP must envisage mechanisms for timely generation of sales forecasts and for periodically bringing production, materials, and marketing together to agree on market demand. If this is done, what start as sales forecasts per se become an objective to be aggressively pursued by the business.

This point needs to be emphasized. The first major goal of SOP is to transform what are purely sales forecast data into market-demand objectives that can mobilize the planning and control functions of the company. When this is done, there are no *wrong* forecasts in the traditional sense.

SOP Policies and Procedures

SOP involves bringing together the key functional groups so as to develop strong consensus on a set of numbers that are crucial to the whole business planning process. Steps must be taken to ensure that the process is executed regularly and punctually and that differences in points of view are ironed out before proceeding to the execution phases. Consensus aids execution in important ways. Obviously, then, the SOP process must be formalized, mandated, and scheduled on a permanent basis so that it becomes part of the way of doing business in the company and is incorporated in the planning routine. The way to achieve the kind of formalization that is necessary to SOP is to have a set of clear SOP policies that are well documented, communicated, and adhered to. The form and degree of elaboration of these policies will vary with the company. However, the policy statement must envisage frequent follow-up action to evaluate adherence to the procedures laid out, particularly early on in implementation of the SOP process.

THE MASTER PRODUCTION SCHEDULE

Role of the MPS in MRP Logic

The logic of material requirements planning (MRP) starts with the master production schedule (MPS). So one must first understand the basics of the MPS to understand the MRP logic. As a definition, we can say that the MPS is a production plan that specifies the level of end item production to be met by the production system, on the basis of firm orders received or firm forecasts approved by top management. Key characteristics of the MPS are as follows:

1. It is formulated with end items and not components. It shows the level of end item production, typically those deliverable to the customer. In some instances the various options that exist at the end item level are numerous, so it is not possible to plan for end items. The MPS, in that case, is formulated on the basis of production modules. This is very evident in automobile manufacturing. However, service parts are treated as end items.
2. The basic input into the master schedule are firm orders received or firm forecasts approved and adopted. Forecasts that are not adopted as firm can

be used to do a look-ahead and result in a tentative master schedule. The role of these latter forecasts and MPS is to provide anticipatory information to the master scheduler and to top management. They are not a critical input to MRP-II.

3. The master production schedule is formulated on the basis of weekly time buckets. A time bucket is the smallest unit of time into which the entire planning horizon will be divided. One year has 52 weekly time buckets.

4. The MPS horizon is long enough to do replanning.

The Role of the MPS

Since the MPS is formulated on the basis of end items, it is the critical phase at which production and marketing interact to provide customer service. The MPS is really a synthesis of the demands and needs of marketing with respect to customer service and order due dates and target lead times, and the capacity constraints, production costs, and raw materials availability of production. One sees why the MPS is critical to MRP-II. If we accept the fact that customer service is a dominant concern of any company, then the MPS becomes the one critical planning objective of the production function. Every other decision in production and materials planning and control should be geared to making the MPS happen. When production has not achieved the master schedule, the immediate consequence is that the order backlog increases. Customers are waiting, because the MPS incorporates the due dates for orders. Of course, a second consequence of not achieving the MPS is that production may have to be accelerated, resulting in nervousness, production inefficiencies, and reduction in quality levels. This is why the MPS is so often used as a critical aspect of the evaluation of the production function. In an effectively managed MRP-II system, the MPS drives the production and materials planning and control (PMPC) system. The MPS is the moving target for material requirements planning (MRP), purchasing, capacity requirements planning (CRP), shop floor control (SFC), and schedule execution. As such, it gives focus to management of the PMPC system. Since the MPS is so vital to the PMPC system, it must be formulated on the basis of sound management principles:

1. It is the result of negotiation between marketing and production in an atmosphere of mutual trust and comprehension.

2. It is realistic, in the sense that every one involved should agree that it is achievable, even if it is a difficult target.

3. It does not change often, and certainly not in the last crucial weeks of the MPS planning horizon when it is difficult to change the supporting decisions. One must remember that in a PMPC system based on MRP-II, all changes to the MPS reverberate down to the shop floor and may even involve changes in capacity plans.

4. All decisions and events that have repercussions on the MPS, such as the actual level of downtime—versus the planned level—the level of

work-in-process, and anticipated materials shortages, must be promptly and unambiguously communicated to the master scheduler.

In the make-to-stock context, the effect of the MPS on lead times is not obvious. However, nothing changes qualitatively, since nonperformance of the MPS would lead to serious depletion of inventory levels which will eventually impact directly on end item availability and lead times for subsequent periods. If inventory levels are such that nonperformance of the MPS is not critical to customer service, then the cost of the latter is much too high and is not recognized due to a poor performance evaluation system. The only thing that really changes when one goes from the make-to-order to the make-to-stock context is that in the former one programs customer orders directly into the MPS while in the latter it is warehouse replenishment orders that are scheduled. Customer orders consume warehouse orders in a make-to-stock company.

The MPS and Just-in-Time Production

The above discussion leads to the conclusion that a strong relationship exists between JIT production and master schedule management. The MPS is planned and executed to keep inventories at the targeted level, or to reduce them to the lowest level that production system constraints such as set-up times and manufacturing lead times make possible. By controlling the backlog (order file), the MPS determines the effective lead time that the company can give to its customers. The MPS matches production with actual orders or short-term forecasts, and therefore influences how much anticipatory production the company actually does. A master schedule that is based only on customer orders contains no anticipatory production, while one based entirely on forecasts results in all production being done on an anticipatory basis. The sales and operations plan is the planned level of anticipatory production but the MPS is actual anticipatory production. In addition, load leveling, a fundamental JIT prerequisite, is planned in the SOP but executed in the MPS. Level loads invariably mean level master schedules. Keeping the MPS realistic, from the capacity requirements viewpoint, means that the plant is scheduled according to the capacity of the bottleneck operation. The principle that the MPS must be always kept realistic and doable has the necessary fallout that capacity is balanced throughout the plant and that production can be synchronized.

Timing materials to arrive in small lots and just in time requires that the end item master schedule be planned in small lots. By implication, also, the MPS must be well planned and tightly controlled to prevent it from shifting too much or too often. Purchasing and component manufacturing cannot synchronize buying and parts production with the end item requirements if the master schedule is not reasonably firm. The backward scheduling logic on which MRP-II is based means that the MPS must be known with a high level of predictability before purchasing and production of lower level components can be done just in time.

Driving PMPC with the MPS

Companies that are using MRP-II to its fullest strategic potential, use it as part of a larger corporate arsenal for pursuing service superiority. They also use MRP-II to help build the right production and materials planning and control climate for reducing inventories with JIT. The MPS assumes a key role in that regard, and it drives the production and materials planning and control system. Driving the PMPC system with the MPS is not automatic. The MPS will be the motor of production and materials planning and control, if it is conceived of, planned, controlled, and executed for that purpose. The critical principles that must be adhered to in order for the MPS to drive the PMPC system are as follows:

1. Every aspect of the business must be made to focus on the MPS and must have critical MPS-related objectives. This makes the MPS all pervasive.
2. Define the MPS in strategic terms. Everyone with important management responsibility must be aware that the MPS is a strategic weapon. Service must be understood to be a strategic objective.
3. Have a clear, consistent coherent set of MPS policies that have been evaluated and approved by top management. This is the first signal that the company is serious about the MPS.
4. Evaluate and report on MPS performance intensively and extensively. Measures such as late deliveries to customers, back orders, and stock-outs capture the essence of the role of the MPS in a service driven company.
5. Plan the MPS to facilitate pull production. The plant should be level loaded to the capacity of the bottleneck operation, and the MPS should be frozen as much as market requirements permit.
6. Use the MPS to make delivery promises to the customer. This puts customer service right at the heart of production and materials planning and control.

MPS STABILIZATION

Business planning using MRP-II usually requires that serious thought be given to stabilizing the MPS, as much as possible. This should not be done in the name of production efficiency only, because there are powerful marketing reasons why it should be done. In fact, the primary reason why the MPS should be stabilized lies in the fact that it can be achieved with a high level of consistency and predictability, thereby making order promises and warehouse replenishment schedules firm. MPS stabilization removes a critical source of uncertainty relative to delivery promises.

One should point out that MPS stabilization does not mean that the schedule does not change but rather that very few changes should occur within the time frame that is absolutely necessary to execute it. One must recognize that there is a limit to how much schedule change flexibility can be built into a production system. Schedule changes which force the production system to operate beyond its innate and built-in flexibility have negative effects on quality and efficiency and compromise customer service. Set-up or changeover times and the length of manufacturing lead times are critical constraints that affect the plant's ability to adapt to schedule changes. Short set-up times result in short manufacturing lead times. Reduction in set-up times causes production lot sizes to shrink which in turn reduces queue times. The empirical evidence is that queue times account for up to 90 percent of manufacturing lead time. Thus, shorter set-up times eventually show up as shorter manufacturing lead times, and both determine how frequently or quickly the MPS can be practically changed.

What emerges from the above discussion is that MPS planning and control and JIT production, although they can be done independently as stand-alone systems, also have strong, mutually beneficial effects. As JIT reduces set-up times, lot sizes, and manufacturing lead times, it also makes the production system more flexible for handling MPS changes. Similarly, better MPS planning and control contribute to load leveling, MPS stabilization, and the synchronization of production and materials purchasing. These are necessary conditions for implementing the pull scheduling logic and Kanban which are core JIT concepts. Because JIT reduces set-up and manufacturing lead times, it increases scheduling flexibility and therefore contributes to improving customer service.

The problems caused by frequent changes to the MPS can be quite severe. Because the MPS drives the production and materials planning and control (PMPC) system in MRP-II, all changes to that schedule cascade down the planning structure and reverberate all through the business planning system. What may appear to be only a few minor changes may make MPS manageability and controllability practically impossible to achieve. We emphasize that this is no justification for not changing the MPS, but it is a powerful reason to set guidelines for and limits to such changes. Ultimately, how often and how radically a company changes its MPS will be dictated by the market and not by master scheduling guidelines designed to make things easy for manufacturing. If competitive conditions and customers require that the company change its MPS frequently, then management must give the plant the tools and capabilities to plan, control, and execute a fast changing MPS.

MPS Example

The following example in Table 12-2 gives the general format of the MPS. The calculations are self-explanatory except for the following:

1. Projected inventory (period n) = projected inventory (n – 1) + MPS (n) – (greater of forecast (n) or customer orders (n))
2. MPS = action to meet the forecast or customer orders
3. Available to promise (ATP)
   a. For week 1, ATP = actual inventory + MPS – (sum of customer orders until the next MPS)
   b. For every other week, ATP = MPS – (sum of customer orders until next MPS)

MPS Report   TABLE 12–2

		Week									
		1	2	3	4	5	6	7	8	9	10
Forecast		50	70	20	95	30	30	60	70	80	80
Customer orders		60	40	15	20	—	—	—	—	—	—
Projected inventory	90	80	10	40	5	25	45	135	65	135	55
Available to promise		40	—	35	40	50	50	150	—	150	—
Master schedule		50	—	50	60	50	50	150	—	150	—

Realistic Order Promising

A realistic and valid MPS is based on disciplined order promising. Companies that are managing production and materials so as to meet customer lead times consistently and predictably are using the MPS to do order promising. The available-to-promise calculation that is produced in the MPS report is used for that purpose. Figure 12-9 shows the vital relationships between the MPS and order promising in companies that are managing for superior customer service.

Evidently, and contrary to popular belief, production should not be the sole custodian of the MPS. The master schedule is as vital to marketing as it is to production. It must be planned, controlled, and executed to satisfy the priorities and constraints of both functions. Marketing contributes to effective MPS planning and execution by basing all order promises on information contained in the master schedule. The MPS must therefore be highly visible to marketing, in general, but particularly to those responsible for order promising and lead time negotiation.

FIGURE 12–9   **Order Promising in a Service-Oriented Company**

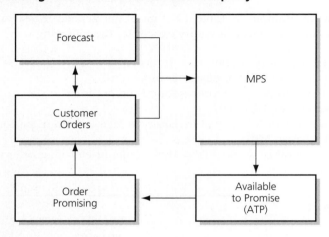

MASTER SCHEDULE POLICY

Defining MPS Policy

Policy with respect to the master schedule is basically the same as in other areas of the business. The idea of policy in management is to give clear guidelines to those who have to execute the activities that permit the company to satisfy its customers. In formulating policy one recognizes that it is impossible for top management to continuously supervise and give direction to subordinates. Therefore, policy statements are issued that express top management's desire or orientation in a particular area of decision making.

Master schedule policy is the set of guidelines and instructions issued by management that say how critical aspects of master schedule management should be viewed and dealt with. The master schedule policy of the company sets the decision parameters around master production scheduling activities and suggests ways for executing the MPS. It clearly identifies what MPS issues are more or less important, which ones are left to the discretion of subordinates, and which should be dealt with according to the specifications of top management.

The Purpose of MPS Policy

The first major reason for a master schedule policy derives from the cross-functional nature of that activity. We have said before that the MPS receives vital information from both marketing and production and materials planning and control. The formulation and execution of the MPS are PMPC activities that call for heavy interaction, coordination, and cooperation between marketing and production. Because of this, there are many potential areas of conflict and misunderstanding between marketing and production when the MPS is being formulated and implemented. In the absence of clear policy statements that specify how grey areas will be dealt with and which of the functions has responsibility for and authority over what aspect of MPS formulation and execution, conflict is likely to be dysfunctional and to result in poor MPS performance.

We have also said that a prime goal of the MPS is customer service. This is a dominant concern of top management because of the importance of customer service to the strategic position of the company. The execution of the master schedule gives the company the chance to support a customer-service oriented strategy. Top management cannot leave the performance of the MPS to chance. As a matter of fact, the sound management of the MPS involves making it happen predictably. Failure to realize the goals of the master schedule should be the exception in a service-oriented company. The master schedule policy is top management's major input in the formulation and execution of the MPS on an ongoing basis.

Master schedule policy is also needed because lower level managers can neither envisage nor thoroughly understand the top management concerns vis-à-vis the master schedule objectives of the company. Being far from the center of the competitive and strategic realities of the business, they have an operational as opposed to a strategic focus. Yet the MPS is a strategic weapon of the company, and must be viewed, managed, and executed with a strategic perspective. The master schedule policy incorporates the strategic perspective into the formulation and execution of the MPS.

Finally, a master schedule policy simplifies master schedule management. With clear policy guidelines to follow, the master scheduler is not left to grope in the dark or to second guess top management's intentions. With a precise notion of the critical issues and priorities, decision making is swift, efficient, and focused. The formulation of a master schedule policy is a clear sign that top management has thought of the vital master schedule issues as they confront the company and has tried to develop a systematic response to these.

Customer-driven business planning culminates in a market-derived master schedule. The remaining phases of customer-driven business planning and control validate the master schedule, keep it realistic, and liberate material, human resources, and machine resources at the right time and in the right quantities so as to execute the MPS. In order for business planning and control to be completely driven by the customer, all activities that are lower than

Conclusion

the MPS in the MRP-II model (Figure 12–6) must keep customer due dates and orders visible. The remaining MRP-II activities will incorporate the master production schedule as their critical inputs and will focus totally on MPS validation and execution.

Case for Discussion

GLOBAL PHARMACEUTICALS CORPORATION (GPC)

Top management at GPC had met to evaluate the progress of MRP-II. The evidence pointed to a successful project. Inventory turns increased from 2.8 prior to MRP to 3.6 currently, while average lead times had decreased to 3 from 3.5 weeks. Capacity utilization had remained constant despite an 8 percent increase in sales volume and on-time deliveries increased from 72 percent to 90 percent. Some among the top management group were still not convinced that MRP-II could have much impact on the company's competitive position.

GPC was a large pharmaceuticals manufacturer with annual sales of $3.5 billion in fiscal 1989. The company was present in almost every therapeutic segment of the market and spent about 12 percent of its sales on R&D. It operated 30 plants worldwide and had research facilities in the United States, Canada, United Kingdom, Germany, and Australia. Net profit margins averaged 9 percent and promotion and marketing expenses consumed 27 percent of every sales dollar.

GPC put strong emphasis on quality. The president of the company, Mr. Len Jairod, the first president to have come from manufacturing, liked to remind his staff that unconditional quality was a condition for survival in the industry: "Without quality, you simply cannot be in this industry." The production process was simple, but the meticulous control of quality and the maintenance of sound manufacturing practices were essential.

GPC had always emphasized customer service. In 1976, it created a separate customer-service department to handle all customer complaints and concerns. The response to the new department was very positive and in 1988, it started to solicit feedback from customers on how they rated GPC on product performance, price, and customer service, relative to other manufacturers. The surveys showed that customers were dissatisfied about lead time length, back orders, late shipments, and delivery of wrong items. While GPC's rating was fair, the whole industry received a low rating. Top management saw this as a signal that there was competitive leverage to be gained by implementing systems and policies that could make dramatic improvements in customer service.

Before Mr. Jairod became president, GPC's decision-making processes had clearly been dominated by the marketing function. Although marketing tried to cooperate with other functions as much as possible and a kind of consensus decision making existed, all top managers knew that, "when push comes to shove, marketing will have its way if it wants to." Some important corporate players downplayed the significance of manufacturing in an innovative pharmaceuticals company by pointing to the fact that production cost for most products accounted for less than 25 percent of sales. Mr. Jairod's promotion to president had come as a surprise to many and some interpreted it as a radical shift in corporate strategy.

Mr. Jairod constantly reminded his team that although production accounted for a much smaller share of the sales dollar at GPC than at most manufacturing companies, it still played a major role in quality, speed of new product introductions, speed of response to market and sales changes, lead time management and length, and customer service. Moreover, it was his point of view that even if generics manufacturers had heretofore been unable to capture a significant share of the market, they would eventually succeed and would exert downward pressure on prices. In his view, the days of 98 percent margins are practically over, and manufacturing would account for an increasingly higher percentage of the sales dollar. Most pharmaceuticals compounds were practically at the end of their patent protection. New products will no doubt continue to be discovered but they will account for an ever-decreasing proportion of sales. This made it necessary to entrench decision-making processes that emphasize consensus, cooperation, coordination, free flow of information and mutual support by all functions.

The MRP-II Project

In February 1989, GPC's top management decided that it was time to seek competitive superiority on customer service, particularly those aspects that were highly valued by customers and which would foster participation by those functions such as production and purchasing that were traditionally excluded from the execution of the company's customer-service priorities. The company also wished to reinforce the traditional role played by the marketing function. Management soon came to the conclusion that the implementation of a sound and complete MRP-II system was a critical step in any process to raise the strategic visibility and corporatewide performance of a customer service strategy. In April 1989, a top management committee was formed to spearhead the implementation of MRP-II throughout GPC. The committee selected GPC's New York plant as the first site to implement MRP-II because it was very representative of the company's manufacturing operations and was the first to embrace the new philosophy of consensus decision making. The plant steering committee was made up of the plant manager and her subordinates.

The plant steering committee took the following specific actions:

1. Training: The 260 plant employees received a total of 26,000 hours of MRP-II training, including 40 hours of hands-on training on a pilot MRP-II system whose database was updated monthly.
2. Project Manager: Bill Larson, manager of production planning was named MRP-II project manager. A believer in MRP-II, he had ten years plant management experience and a reputation as one who can get the job done.
3. MRP-II system specification: The steering committee created subcommittees in each department with the mandate to oversee the execution of department-specific MRP-II activities. Each subcommittee described its planning requirements and this formed the basis for specifying the entire MRP-II system.
4. Software selection: The MRP-II software was selected by the corporate steering committee. Each plant was slightly different, but management thought these did not justify individual software decisions and opted for software standardization and its attendant advantages. According to Bill Larson, the experience of other companies has shown that, within limits, software choice is not a decisive factor in the implementation and use of MRP-II.
5. Immediate goal—implement MRP: In addition to the standard database development and management modules, the committee decided to start with the basic management modules of Forecast Management, Sales and Operations Planning, Master Production Scheduling, Inventory Management, and Material Requirement Planning and Purchasing.
6. Project time, cost, and payback: The MRP phase of the project was expected to be completed in two years. Although the plant steering committee was aware that some companies were budgeting less than one year to implement MRP, the majority were of the view that it was better to start slowly to allow people to gain confidence, accelerating later on if the potential existed. Plant management advocated a prudent approach because that would encourage other plants to adopt MRP-II once a success was demonstrated. The project was expected to cost $450,000: Training $104,000 (26,000 hours at $40/hour), software $150,000, hardware $150,000, and other costs $46,000. The payback was expected to be one year based on expected inventory reduction and a holding cost of 25 percent.
7. Prerequisites: Management decided not to start to use MRP until bill-of-material accuracy was 99 percent, inventory record accuracy was 98 percent, and all personnel had thoroughly been trained on the pilot system.

Bill Larson monitored the progress of MRP-II implementation by holding weekly performance review meetings with the committees and by keeping track of a few key performance metrics. After 14 months the results were impressive. MRP had surpassed all performance goals. Bill asked for a meeting of the corporate steering committee to present his case for broadening the scope of the MRP-II project and for soliciting their reaction to progress so far.

1. What are the dimensions of customer service? What is the role of customer service in competitive strategy and advantage?
2. What is the role of production in executing a customer-service strategy?
3. Is GPC's top management justified in seeking superiority on customer service?
4. In what ways does MRP-II contribute to the execution of a customer-service strategy?
5. Has MRP-II implementation at GPC been successful so far? If yes, what are the factors that explain such success? If no, what would you have done differently?

Fogarty, D. W., J. H. Blackstone, Jr., and T. R. Hoffman, *Production and Inventory Management,* Cincinnati: Southwestern, 1991.

Plossl, G. W., *Manufacturing Control—The Last Frontier for Profits,* Reston, VA: Reston, 1973.

Schultz, T., "MRP to BRP: The Journey of the 80s," *Production and Inventory Management Review and APICS News,* October 1981.

Vollman, Thomas E., William L. Berry, and D. Clay Whybark, *Manufacturing Planning and Control Systems,* Homewood, Illinois: Richard D. Irwin, Inc., 1992.

Wight, Oliver, *Manufacturing Resource Planning: MRP-II, Unlocking America's Productivity Potential,* Essex Junction, VT: Oliver Wight Limited Publications, 1981.

13

Customer-Driven Production and Materials Scheduling

$\mathbf{M}$RP-II puts the customer at the heart of the production and materials scheduling system. The on-time delivery of customer orders is the number one scheduling priority. Although scheduling objectives such as machine utilization are also important, scheduling with MRP-II aims at meeting delivery promises made to customers. Objectives such as machine utilization and cost are optimized within the constraints imposed by customer due dates or concurrently with order promising, but not before. In order to put the customer into production and materials scheduling, MRP-II uses a realistic, market-derived MPS to drive the production and materials planning and control system.

A realistic MPS is one that is doable, that is, all the resources that are required to execute it are or will be available at the right time and in the right place. Materials are one key resource that MPS execution consumes. The role of MRP in the MRP-II system is to plan the production and purchasing of parts and components at the right time and in the right quantities to feed the MPS. MRP is thus one key phase of the MRP-II process. The MRP-II system uses the bill of materials (BOM), inventory, and lead time data to plan material requirements. These data will serve to link component production and purchasing to the MPS. Figure 13-1 shows the key elements of the MRP process.

THE MRP PROCESS

The Bill of Materials (BOM)

Simply defined, the bill of materials is the recipe for manufacturing the product. The bill shows what subassemblies make up what end items, what components or parts make up what subassemblies, and what raw materials go into what parts and in what quantities. It is the product structure. It shows how successive levels of the product are put together. The BOM shows both the physical structure of the product and how it is built or put together by operations. Consequently, it is both an engineering or technical and management document. One crucial interface between production and engineering

The MRP Process   FIGURE 13–1

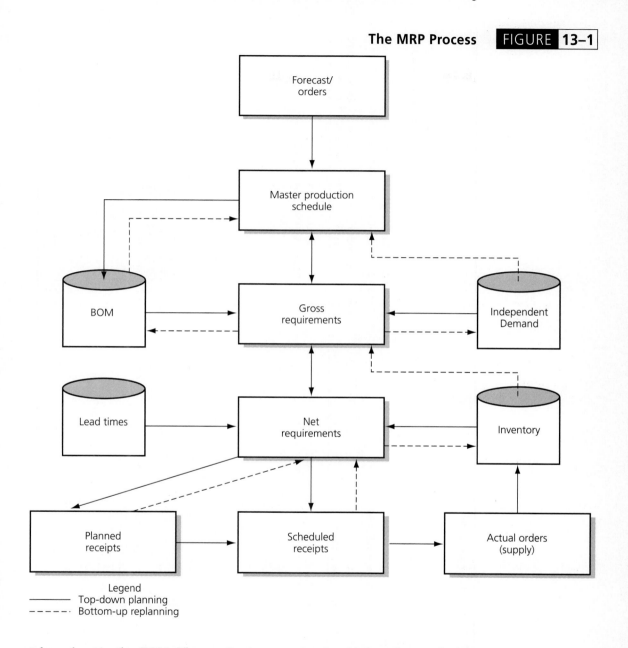

Legend
——— Top-down planning
– – – – Bottom-up replanning

takes place in the BOM. The continuing concern is whether the product is built or repaired according to specifications.

However, one must differentiate clearly between the BOM and the traditional engineering parts list. Going back to the recipe analogy used above, the

TABLE 13–1 Indented BOM

Parent Item No. X6011P1			Desc. Note PS R223-34 *			Date 14/02/89 Oper Msh			Time 9.08.26 Page 1 Production Database		
						Batch Qty. 46,980,000	Std. Lot Size 46,980,000	Std. Yield 46,980,000	Item Type 1 Unit Meas. Ea.		

Rel. Level	Seq. No.	Component Item No.	Description	Note	Item Type	Quantity Per Batch	U/M	Waste Factor%	Effective Dates From	To
.1		P060050	BOTTLE 25 ML. ROUND AMB	CS 0603-2	3	46,980.000000	EA	3.000		
.1		P102234	.1% SOL25ML 8-282	CS 1024-1	3	46,980.000000	EA	2.000		
.1		P134450	PELL REDUCED D-955 355.6MM	CS 1382-2	3	16,536.960000	GM	.500		
.1		P134470	PELL POLYPRO PRINTED	CS 1347-1	3	26,590.680000	GM	1.000		
.1		P160231	CONT ONDULATED SOL	CS 1622-1	3	326.276100	EA	2.001		
.1		P170140	SEPARATOR HOR SOL	CS 1714-0	3	326.276100	EA	.994		
.1		P252230	DISPLAY	CS 2524-1	3	3,915.031320	EA	2.000		
.1		P552233	ETI .1% SOL25ML 2-4	CS 5512-0	3	46,980.000000	EA	9.000		
.1		S290040	DROP COUNTER 25 ML IRR		2	46,980.000000	EA	2.000		
.2		P2900040	DROP COUNTER FOR 25ML	CS 2904-0	3	46,980.000000	EA	2.000		
.1		S770200	COVER 20MM BROWN LINER IRR		2	46,980.000000	EA	4.000		
.2		P770200	COVER 20MM BROWN LINERLESS	CS 7710-0	3	46,980.000000	EA	4.000		
.1		W6011MU	/DROPS	MFC 121.11	2	1,174.500000	LT	2.000		
.2	1	A113990	HYDROCHLORIDE, USP	0084402	4	1,174.500000	GM	2.069		
.2	5	C106430	EDETATE DISODIUM, HS		3	1,174.500000	GM	2.069		
.2	10	C107850	DIBAS. SOD. PHOSPH. (HEPTAH.) USP		3	2,642.625000	GM	2.069		
.2	15	C107180	MONO. SOD. PHOSPH. (MONOHYDR.) USP			2,912.760000	GM	2.069		
.2	20	C101980	SODIUM CHLORIDE, USP		3	221.500000	GM	2.069		
.2	25	C107930	BENZALK. CHLORIDE SOL.		3	669.465000	GM	2.069		
.2	30	C107290	PURIFIED WATER, USP		*0	1,174,500.000000	GM	2.069		

engineering parts list is a list of ingredients. The parts list simply details all the components that are required to make a product, with no regard to structure. The BOM is the whole recipe, the list of ingredients and all the logical sequence of instructions that show how to go from ingredients to the final dish. So, while the oven (process specifications) is not part of the list of ingredients (parts list), it is an integral, rather decisive part of the recipe (BOM). In order to develop sensible BOM data, one has to know both the physical composition of the product and how it is built by operations.

The BOM is thus a critical input to MRP. Using the BOM, one can determine what quantities of each material will be needed to support the MPS. When the BOM is used to calculate the quantity of each part that is required to produce the production schedule, the process is referred to as MPS explosion, because as one goes from end items to the raw materials, the number of inventory items increases dramatically (explodes). Table 13–1 gives the details of BOM for a personal hygiene product. The reader can come to appreciate the extent and value of the information that is contained in a BOM, and how it can be used to manage both materials and production planning and quality.

Quality and the BOM

Data accuracy is important to the management and operation of an MRP-II system. Information errors can be generated at the level of the BOM, since it is used to explode the MPS and arrive at the materials requirements plan. Managing the BOM should focus on making it valid, accurate, and up to date.

BOMs become plagued with errors because either management policies for keeping them error free have not been specified by top management or because the policies are not being adhered to.

Three common sources of error are:

1. Engineering changes that alter product specifications and components that are not quickly and punctually incorporated in the BOM. Changes to products that are not updated in the BOM often show up as double errors—the wrong part is in but the right is out.
2. The evolution of scrap levels: The BOM should have an allowance for scrap. As scrap levels increase or decrease, the BOM should be adjusted to reflect the new reality. This is, of course, a vital quality control issue.
3. Rounding off errors. When requirements are fractional, one must be careful in rounding off. A .95 requirement, rounded off to 1.00, results in an overstatement of materials requirements of 5 percent each time explosion takes place. This could also have severe quality impacts.

Policies for Assuring Accuracy
Most BOMs must be 100 percent accurate. This is absolute perfection and is very difficult to achieve. However, 100 percent accuracy with respect to the

BOM means that all "quantities per" are within the margin of error specified by management policy or engineering specifications and that there are no unnecessary or missing parts in all BOMs. Therefore, how wide the margin of error tolerated for the "quantity per" for each item will determine how easy or difficult it is to have 100 percent accuracy. The following table shows two versions of the same bill.

Bill of Material—Product XYZ

	Bill A Q/P	Bill B Q/P
End item	1.00	1.00
Part #101	1.10 ± 10%	1.10 ± 20%
Part #102	2.10 ± 5%	2.10 ± 15%

Clearly, it will be easier to have 100 accuracy for the second bill. However, bill A may be more accurate than bill B in absolute terms. It is important to establish realistic policies that specify the margin of error that will be tolerated in the BOM database. Moreover, the quality specifications for the product must be rigorously consulted and respected.

Beyond this consideration, specific management policies should be established to control the absolute level of BOM accuracy. The most common are as follows:

1. *Engineering change management (ECM).* Policies need to be established that specify how design changes are to be incorporated into the BOM database. These policies include
   a. Clear identification of who has responsibility for approving engineering change notices (ECNs) for each product.
   b. Specifying methods for generating ECNs and for their communication.
   c. Identifying all documents that must be used to initiate and give effect to all ECNs.
   d. Clear identification of who has responsibility for entering ECN changes into the BOM database.
   e. Specification of maximum delays for approving ECNs that have been initiated.
   f. Specifying maximum delays for transmitting approved ECNs for entry into the BOM database.
   g. Specification of maximum delays for entering ECNs into the BOM database once they have been transmitted.

h. Development and implementation of an audit procedure for periodically verifying whether ECM policies are being adhered to.

2. *Effectivity dating.* All parts must be effectivity dated. This allows those responsible for managing BOMs to update the database as soon as ECNs are received, regardless of how far in the future the affected part is to be used. Omissions caused by inability to track a large number of ECNs are thus eliminated.

3. *Mass replacement.* Involves replacing a part number wherever it is used with a single data entry. Mass replacement reduces the number of ECNs and transactions required to make engineering changes.

4. *BOM auditing.* The BOM should be continually audited. A sample of bills is systematically extracted from the database at specified intervals and verified in detail. Sampling is done in such a way that all bills will be verified over a designated period, usually a year. BOM errors are promptly corrected and error margins are tracked. If too many bills are found to have errors or if the error margins are too wide, a crash program to audit all remaining bills should be launched.

It must be emphasized that the quality of the BOM database is a function of management policy and discipline and motivation of the people who are responsible for database supervision.

Impact of the BOM on Quality

Errors in the BOM data can cause defects. How rigorously a company manages quality will influence how severely it controls the BOM database and vice versa. The materials and process specifications that are an integral part of the BOMs are also central to quality control. The quality control department can make extensive use of the BOMs to audit quality and to assure that the product conforms to specifications as to materials. Errors in the BOM database show up as defects in three ways:

1. Wrong bills mean that the wrong parts will be issued to production or repairs and this will show up as defects. In fact, when the wrong part appears on the bill, it will almost always result in a defect.
2. Errors in quantities per very often cause defects, because this usually means that the wrong recipe is used to make the product. If the BOM overstates the quantities per, this produces waste of materials.
3. The scrap levels that are allowed for in the BOM reflect how well quality is being controlled. Progress toward better quality control should show up as reductions in scrap levels. If the allowance for scrap is frozen for a long period, then the company is not making much progress in defect removal.

The positive impact that a good, well-managed MRP-II database has on defect prevention provides more evidence that there is strong symbiosis between the programs, tools, and concepts that produce continuous improvement and superior competitive performance in manufacturing. MRP-II was specifically designed as a set of tools and organizational processes for planning and controlling the business, production and materials in pursuit of customer service superiority. On the surface, MRP-II and TQM have little in common because they have very different strategic missions. But when one peers deeper and looks at their fundamental processes and mechanisms, one discovers that there are strong relationships between them. TQM provides accurate data on defect rates and yields that are a part of the BOM database. Once these data are made available to the MRP-II system, its basic organizational and control processes maintain the integrity of the original data. In addition, the group problem-solving and consensus-building processes of TQM (small group improvement teams, SGIT) foster the mutual trust, cooperation and coordination between the business functions, a basic prerequisite to the successful exploitation of MRP-II.

Inventory Record Accuracy

The foundation MRP planning modules, such as the MPS and the material requirements plan, rely heavily on information generated by the inventory management system. MRP plans production and materials as if the supporting data on inventory levels, both projected and actual, were accurate. Errors in inventory records start by affecting the MPS and tend to worsen as the system executes the explosion process and plans orders for net requirements. Inventory record accuracy is a necessity for effective use of MRP-II. Inaccurate records cause users to lose confidence in the system and they resort to creating informal systems to circumvent the problems associated with the MRP-II system that is in place. The traditional requirement is that the inventory records must state the actual inventory level to within ±3 percent. That is, if a record indicates that the inventory level is 100 units, there should be a 98 percent chance that the actual inventory lies between 97 and 103 units.

The achievement of high BOM and inventory data integrity is primarily a management and human problem. The following schema in Figure 13–2 shows the factors involved.

Some practical guidelines can be followed to assure high database integrity:

1. Create the right climate for database management where users will be motivated to achieve very low errors rates.
   a. Assign clear responsibility for identifying, counting, and verifying inventory.

Factors Affecting BOM and Inventory Record Accuracy FIGURE 13–2

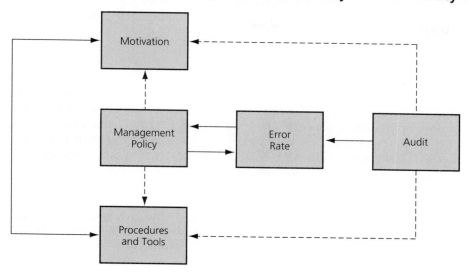

b. Give those responsible adequate tools for executing their tasks.

c. Measure periodically and according to a predetermined schedule, the level of record accuracy.

d. Constantly search for and remove causes of errors.

2. Record accuracy is a function of operating discipline, which can be increased by:

a. Constantly evaluating record integrity.

b. Establishing improvement objectives to be pursued.

c. Evaluating employee performance on record accuracy.

d. Rewarding and giving recognition to those who achieve target accuracy.

Cycle counting is the best available tool for controlling inventory record accuracy. It has four steps:

1. All SKUs (stock keeping units) are classified using ABC analysis according to the following, widely accepted parameters:

A items: 20 percent of SKUs that generate 60 percent or more of sales or budgeted material cost.

B items: 30 percent of SKUs that generate 30 percent of sales or budgeted cost.

C items: 50 percent of SKUs that count for 10 percent of sales or budgeted cost.

2. A fixed counting cycle is set for each class. All items in a class must be physically counted over the cycle set for the class.

3. Each week, the number of items set by the cycle for each class is counted, and the inventory records are corrected, if necessary.
4. If error rates are consistently too high, the counting cycle is accelerated.

Time Phasing

The next phase in the MRP process is time phasing. It involves synchronizing materials requirements at lower levels with materials requirements at higher levels in the product structure using the lead time. That is, time phasing goes forward through time (in the future), calculates the materials that will be needed to support the master schedule, and goes back in time from the master schedule due date to find out when the order for materials should be launched. The critical information for doing time phasing is the master schedule due date and the lead time for the material.

Because it starts with the projected due date and goes backward to find out when the material should be ordered, time phasing makes MRP a backward-scheduling system. This contrasts with the forward-scheduling approach of the traditional PMPC systems. The forward-scheduling system is best exemplified by the so-called cutting schedules of furniture and clothing manufacturers. In these systems, materials are ordered and work on an order is started as soon as possible, regardless of the due date for order delivery. A backward-scheduling system launches the order into production as late as possible so that the order is completed very close to its due date.

Backward-scheduling systems, because of the way they do time phasing, try to eliminate idle inventory. The master schedule due dates work to pull the other schedules and the materials through the plant. This contrasts with the forward-scheduling systems that push the materials and schedules through the plant. Thus MRP is a kind of hybrid scheduling system that is intermediate between the push scheduling logic used by the old "cutting" schedules and the pull logic of Kanban and JIT.

Gross-to-Net Explosion

Exploding the MPS involves calculating the quantities of materials that are necessary to support master schedule activity. One starts with the master schedule (level 0) quantities and using the BOM, calculates the quantities of each material at level 1 that will be needed to support the MPS. At level 1, all inventories are subtracted from the gross quantities required to arrive at net quantities. Then using the BOM information at level 2, one calculates the quantity of level 2 materials needed to support the net quantities at level 1.

The gross quantities at level 2 less any inventories existing at level 2 become the net requirements at level 2. Again using the BOM at level 3, the net quantities at level 2 are passed on to level 3. The process continues until the lowest level is arrived at. This process is called gross-to-net explosion. It is essential in calculating the right quantities of materials needed at each level to support the MPS. Gross-to-net explosion tries to eliminate inventories that may exist because prior plans were off target.

Lead Time and Its Management

The lead time is part of the MRP process called time phasing, which tries to release orders for purchased and manufactured items on time so as to meet the requirements of the MPS. The better this timing process is managed, the more leverage one can have on inventory reduction. Moving toward the pipeline concept means lead times must be tightly coupled, and reduced if possible, at all levels in the company. JIT delivery of purchased parts, manufactured components and finished products means that customer due dates are synchronized with purchasing and production activities using severely controlled lead times. The lead time is used to integrate procurement, production, and distribution with the delivery dates that customers request. The MRP process uses two types of lead time—purchasing and production. By tying supply orders for purchased and manufactured parts to the customer due dates of the MPS, MRP puts purchasing and production in customer service. Production and materials scheduling are thus effectively driven by market requirements.

Purchasing lead time is the time that is required to make purchased materials available for use, from the moment that a requirement exists. It has 12 components:

1. Recognition of need
2. Preparation of purchase requisition
3. Transmission of purchase requisition
4. Verification of purchase requisition
5. Supplier choice and negotiation
6. Preparation of the purchase order
7. Transmission of the purchase order
8. Receipt and scheduling of the purchase order by the supplier
9. Supplier queue time
10. Supplier production time
11. Transportation time
12. Dock-to-stock time

Dock-to-stock time refers to the time that elapses between receipt of the materials by the buying company and when the materials are in fact available for use. Pharmaceuticals manufacturers sometimes have long lead times because government regulations make it mandatory that certain materials be kept in quarantine for as long as six weeks, so that they can be tested for conformance to specifications. Usually, however, dock-to-stock times are hidden and are not accounted for when material requirements are being planned.

Production time is the time that elapses between launching of a production order and when the goods are available for shipment to customers. It can be further broken down into three parts:

1. Move time is the time required to transport parts from one process to the next, within the plant.
2. Transformation or production time refers to the time spent to actually build the product.
3. Queue time (Q-time) occurs when products are idle because either machine centers are unable to start processing them or because lot sizes force parts to wait their turn in a queue.

Q-time accounts for as much as 90 percent of the manufacturing lead time. Any effort to reduce manufacturing lead time must focus on eliminating the causes of Q-time. As will be seen subsequently, Q-time results from two basic factors:

- Poor input/output control that overloads machine centers
- Large lot sizes that cause products to wait in line for their turn to be processed on machines

Although the continuous improvement program should aim at reducing lead times, this should not be done at the expense of lead time firmness. Firm lead times reduce uncertainty and make it possible to have near-perfect synchronization between customer due date requirements and purchasing and production activities. Both MRP and JIT can be more advantageously exploited if lead times are firm. Stable, predictable, and shrinking lead times are necessary for successful use of JIT concepts and principles. Lead time stability and reduction are other objectives that are common to JIT and MRP-II.

The MRP Record

The information on the MPS, the BOM, lead time phasing and gross-to-net explosion, the inventory management database and purchase and production order management, come together in the MRP record. The MRP process culminates in a set of planned orders—production or purchasing—that satisfy the materials needs that flow down from the MPS and forecasts or firm orders for independent demand. The MRP record has five elements:

1. *Gross requirements.* The quantity of materials needed to satisfy the net requirements of the parent material as per the MPS plus independent demand (replacement parts, repairs) for the component.
2. *Scheduled receipts.* These are materials for which an order has been released.
3. *Planned receipts.* Materials that are planned for the future but an order has not been issued mainly because the appropriate time has not been reached.
4. *Available on-hand.* The amount left after requirements and safety stocks have been satisfied.
5. *Planned orders.* These are orders to be placed in the future to satisfy planned requirements. When the time to place an order has arrived and the order has in fact been placed, it becomes a scheduled receipt.

What emerges from this is that as the schedule is rolling through time, the status of items are changing and planned orders and planned receipt are becoming past due orders—if they are not placed as envisaged by the plan—or scheduled receipts, if the orders were placed on time.

A numerical example will be used to generate the MRP record for an assembled product and its parts. One needs the lead time information. These are given below:

MPS-Product (Z9620)	0 week
P9621-A	1 week
PP9621-B	1 week

The master schedule is needed to start the explosion and time-phasing process: The MPS is shown below.

MPS–Product (Z9620)

	0	1	2	3	4	5	6	7	8	9
Forecast		100	100	100	100	100	150	150	150	120
Cust. orders		100	120	80						
Proj. inventory	5	11	16	16	16	16	16	16	16	
Available to promise	5	6	25	100	100	150	150	150	120	
MPS		105	126	105	100	100	150	150	150	120

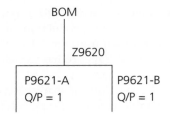

Material Requirements Plans

	Week									
	0	1	2	3	4	5	6	7	8	9
MPS (Z9620)		105	126	105	100	100	150	150	150	120

MRP (P9621-A)
Lead time = 1 week

	Week									
	0	1	2	3	4	5	6	7	8	9
Q/P = 1										
Gross requirements		105	126	105	100	100	150	150	150	120
Net requirements		55	126	105	100	100	150	150	150	120
Projected inventory	(50)									
Planned receipts			126	105	100	100	150	150	150	120
Scheduled receipts		55								
Planned orders		126	105	100	100	150	150	150	120	

MRP (9621-B)
Lead time = 1 week

	Week									
	0	1	2	3	4	5	6	7	8	9
Scrap = 5%										
Gross requirements		105	126	105	100	100	150	150	150	120
Net requirements		25	126	105	100	100	150	150	150	120
Projected inventory	(80)									
Planned receipts			133	111	105	105	158	158	158	126
Scheduled receipts		27								
Planned orders		133	111	105	105	158	158	158	126	

The computations that give rise to the tables will now be explained.

MPS: This is the action program, and gives the amount of finished items that must be produced in order to supply customer orders or forecast. In the make-to-order (MTO), or engineered-to-order (ETO) context, the actual MPS action program would be based on firm customer orders or firm planned orders (FPO). The FPO is an anticipated order that is not yet supported by a customer order but the company is highly confident that it will be. Where production is MTO or ETO, forecasts play a lesser role in planning the MPS. In any event, the immediate action-oriented MPS, the one that is being executed, is based on customer orders. Inability to forecast accurately is not a hindrance in these contexts, as far as MRP is concerned.

Projected inventory: For any week, projected inventory is computed as:

$$\text{Projected inventory (prior week)} + \text{MPS (for the week in question)} - \text{greater of forecast or customer orders}$$

Thus, for week two,

$$\text{Projected inventory} = (5 + 126) - 120$$
$$= 11$$

Available to promise (ATP):

$$\text{ATP (week 1)} = \text{projected inventory (week 0)} + \text{MPS (week 1)} - \\ \text{(customer orders for week one + customer orders for every week after week one until the next MPS)}$$

$$\text{ATP (week 2 and on)} = \text{MPS (week 2)} - \text{(customer orders for week 2 and every subsequent week until the next MPS)}$$

The Impact of Lot Sizing on MRP

So far, we have shown the lot-for-lot approach to MRP, that is, one lot of materials is produced or bought for each weekly requirement. The MRP record can also be modified to incorporate economic order quantities. Suppose the following data for part #P9621-A:

$$\begin{aligned}
\text{Ordering cost} &= \$150.00 \\
\text{Unit cost} &= \$\ 24.00 \\
\text{Inventory holding cost} &= \quad 30\% \\
\text{Inventory holding cost} &= \$\quad 7.20
\end{aligned}$$

Based on the MRP record for part P9621-A, the average weekly usage is 123. Annual demand is thus 6390 units. If we use the EOQ formula,

$$EOQ = \sqrt{\frac{2 \times 6390 \times 150}{7.20}}$$

$$= 516 \text{ units}$$

The modified MRP record appears below:

MRP (P9621-A)
Lead time = 1 week

					Week					
	0	**1**	**2**	**3**	**4**	**5**	**6**	**7**	**8**	**9**
Gross requirements		105	126	105	100	100	150	150	150	120
Net requirements		55					120				24
Projected inventory	(50)	461	335	230	130	30	396	246	96	492
Planned receipts							516			516
Scheduled receipts		516								
Planned orders						516			516	

It is possible to test which material plan is best from the point of view of cost. The comparison is as follows:

	First Plan Lot-for-Lot	Second Plan EOQ
Average inventory	0	268
Inventory holding cost	0	333 *
Total number of orders	8	2
Total ordering cost	$1200	$300
Total cost	$1200	$633

---

*Average inventory of 268 multiplied by the cost for 9 weeks at $7.20/year.

The EOQ approach cuts the cost by almost 50 percent. The results also show that as a company implements the core JIT concepts, it enhances the potential impact of MRP-II on customer service, inventory reduction, and

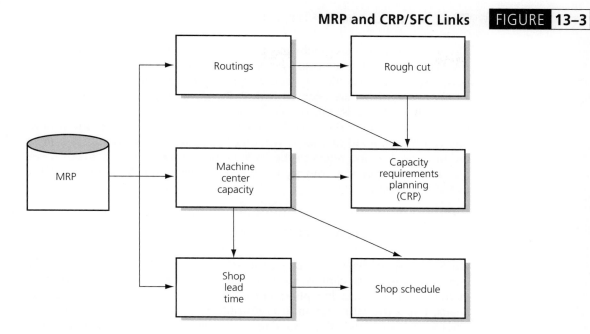

cost. The core JIT principles like single minute exchange of die (SMED) and single digit set-up (SDS) are used to drive set-up times and lot sizes down. MRP can schedule materials in increasingly smaller lots, thereby making lot-for-lot MRP economically feasible. SMED allows MRP to plan for both minimum ordering or set-up and inventory holding cost.

Other Aspects of MRP-II

The MPS due dates are valid and realistic if there is enough materials and capacity to execute all promised orders. MRP tries to ensure that the necessary materials are or will be in place. The other MRP-II activities, rough-cut capacity planning, capacity requirements planning (CRP) and shop floor control (SFC) test whether the plant is or will be able to execute the MPS. SFC in particular, builds work center schedules that are linked to the MPS due dates. The goal of rough-cut, CRP and SFC is to drive the plant schedule using customer required delivery dates.

Figure 13–3 shows the relationships between MRP, the machine center routings and shop lead times database, rough-cut, CRP, and shop floor control. All the information and plans converge to become the shop schedule that the plant must adhere to in order to meet customer due dates. The factory, in that sense, is the last link in the chain of activities that plan and execute customer delivery requirements.

Rough-Cut Capacity Planning

The whole idea behind rough-cut capacity planning is to test the feasibility of the MPS very early in the planning process and quickly. To do this, rough-cut develops resource profiles or standard set-up and labor/machine time per unit at work centers that are deemed critical. Rough-cut uses the information contained in the routings, but designates work centers that are likely to cause problems. By loading these work centers using the MPS at any point in time, one can have a good idea as to whether key resources are available to meet the forecast. Loading refers to the computation of total capacity needs based on set-up and per unit run times. Rough-cut gives quick diagnosis of the capacity situation.

Capacity Requirements Planning

Capacity requirements planning process computes the impact of all MRP items on all machine centers. CRP uses all the information generated by MRP including the MPS and time-phased material requirements to estimate capacity needs. Using the MRP system, it is possible to estimate what end items and parts are required and when. So, one can know when each work center must start working on each part. Using the routings data, CRP computes the capacity needed to execute each work order that is scheduled to arrive at each work center, given the lead time and due date for each part. The capacity requirements are computed for each work center designated in the routings. Basically, the only difference between rough-cut and CRP lies in the fact that the former computes capacity needs for work centers designated as critical, while the latter does it for all work centers.

Shop Floor Control (SFC)

MRP-II gives planning and control visibility for both customer and warehouse replenishment orders, or some mixture of the two. The planning and control function must provide for the necessary level of visibility right down to the factory floor. In many companies, the problem of visibility is particularly acute in the factory because the latter was not seen as an important link in the drive to improve customer service. Increased visibility of order processing means that the execution of these orders must be planned and controlled according to a time critical schedule that ties the plant schedule to customer due dates. Where plant schedules are effectively linked to customer lead time requirements, then the factory is being driven by the customer. The goal of shop floor control in an MRP-II environment is to specifically schedule the factory for customer order visibility and for achieving delivery promises with high consistency. In most companies, the factory is a black box, as far as customer order execution is concerned. Orders go in and management only hopes that they will come out in time to meet promised delivery dates. The scheduling system, in these companies, is not designed to focus on and continually monitor the progress of individual customer orders relative to a firmly promised due date. Production scheduling is not customer driven, so the result is missed deliveries and poor customer service.

There are four basic activities in SFC:

1. The development of start and finish dates for each order (work order) so as to meet the MPS due dates generated by MRP and SOP.
2. The preparation of the necessary shop paper—dispatch lists, job tickets—for facilitating execution of work orders.
3. The monitoring of the progression of jobs through the factory according to the "best" schedule, determined a priori.
4. The computation of job tardiness as an aid to priority scheduling.

Shop floor control does not execute jobs but provides the supporting information that aids smooth execution. As we shall see subsequently, this is the reason why it is desirable to integrate JIT with MRP-II, with MRP-II focusing on the planning function while JIT improves the execution. SFC uses data on the actual capability of the plant relative to set-up times, times per piece, and move and queue times to build schedules for work orders.

Start and finish dates for a job are substantially affected by how one views the capacity of work centers. There are two ways to load available machine and human resources, as illustrated in Figures 13–4 and 13–5.

1. *Infinite loading.* This approach assumes lead times for parts to be fixed. Time phasing of requirements could lead to the situation where particular machine centers would have to work at greater than 100 percent capacity utilization in order to keep the lead time constant. One relies on the planner to react to this information by rescheduling the start (due) date for parts in order to bring capacity utilization to less than 100 percent or to increase work center capacity so as to absorb the heavier load. Most MRP-II systems schedule on an infinite capacity basis. The approach may appear at first sight to be flawed. However, it is based on the principle that the due dates for requirements are firm and that a commitment to customer service requires the production system to respect the due dates as much as possible, by increasing capacity. Only when increases in capacity are not feasible or are too costly should one think of rescheduling. Infinite loading puts a premium on customer service.
2. *Finite loading.* The logic of finite loading loads jobs to 100 percent of capacity and uses that information to make delivery promises. Capacity utilization tends to be more stable than in the infinite loading approach, so

FIGURE 13–4   **Infinite Capacity Loading**

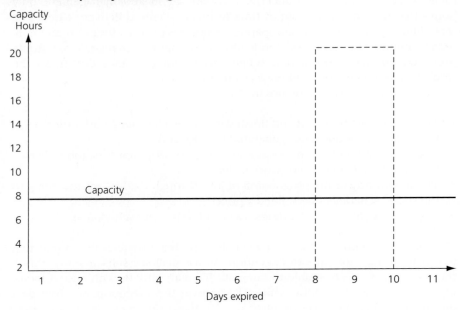

FIGURE 13–5   **Finite Capacity Loading**

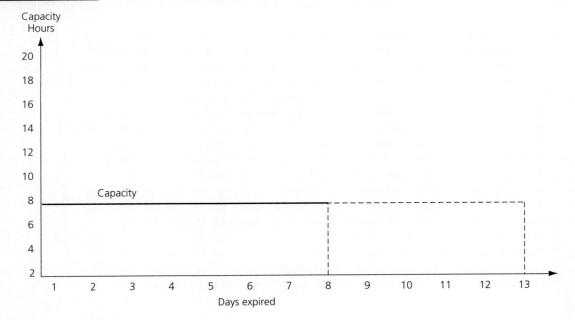

production efficiency is high. The trade-off is that the promised delivery date could be less than competitive. There is not a direct signal to release more capacity.

Job Lateness

The constant monitoring of the progress of jobs through the plant requires that some measure of job lateness be computed and reported on. In addition, job lateness must be computed at every stage in the process, on an operation-by-operation basis. In practice, two measures of job lateness are widely used:

1. *Past due.* This measure simply lists all jobs at a machine center that have not come out of the operation at the date planned. Although it is easy to compute, the quality of information provided leaves something to be desired since there is no attempt to measure the degree of lateness. When a job is late according to this measure, the scheduler must still answer the question "How late?" before rescheduling action can be evaluated and initiated.
2. *The critical ratio (CR).* This is an index of the degree of lateness and "earliness" of each job. The index is computed as follows:

$$CR = \frac{\text{time remaining for unfinished operations}}{\text{time remaining to due date}}$$

If the ratio is less than one, the job is early. A ratio of greater than one means that the job is late. By looking at this ratio, factory managers can know immediately which jobs should be given more or less priority. The full set of ratios are a measure of scheduling and shop floor performance, since they show what proportion of jobs are on time. If a good proportion of jobs are falling behind schedule as revealed by the CR ratios, it means that the plant will have difficulty meeting customers' delivery requirements if capacity is not increased.

As an illustrative example, suppose we have the following data relative to a part:

1. Lead time   10 days
2. Time per piece   0.5 hours
3. Work center   020
4. Standard lot size   80 units
5. Work center capacity 40 hours/week
6. Queue time   60%
7. Actual work order   80 units

The total production time for producing the work order is 40 hours (0.5 hours/piece × 80 pieces) or five days. The queue time percentage is 60 percent, so the length of the queue is 8 days, which means that work on the order cannot begin before day 8. The lead time is 10 days, so the entire 40 hours of production time must be terminated in 2 days (Figure 13–4).

Capacity utilization percentage in order to meet the 10-day lead time is 250 percent if one uses infinite capacity loading. This is clearly not feasible. One must either increase capacity at the work center to 20 hours a day or 100 hours per week or reschedule the due date. The second option is to reschedule and the impact is shown in Figure 13–5. The target delivery date increases from day 10 with infinite loading to day 13 with finite loading and capacity utilization is 100 percent. This brief example shows that the key to managing job timeliness is control—control and reduction of queue time and input/output control.

Queue time is a function of lot sizing and available capacity. The larger the lot size, the longer the queue time. So, the JIT drive to reduce lot sizes increases the company's ability to achieve efficient, on-time delivery by reducing the queue time. Typical queue times average 90 percent of manufacturing lead time. Move time is usually about 2 percent. So,

$$\text{Lead time} = \text{queue time} + \text{move time} + \text{production time}$$
$$= .9 + .02 + .08$$

If we cut lot sizes in half and input/output control manages available capacity well, we have the following situation:

$$\text{Lead time} = .45 + .02 + .08 = .55$$

The lead time has virtually been cut in half.

Input/Output Control

This concept refers to the need to load machine centers (input) to be less than or equal to available capacity. Overloading creates bottlenecks and increases queue time. To balance input and output, one must either reduce input, which means reducing the demand that marketing should seek to achieve (this is clearly an action of last resort in a service oriented company), or one must have timely increases in capacity. Rough-cut, CRP, and SFC all try to provide information for adding capacity on time.

Table 13-2 gives the routing data for a part. The MPS for week 8 is 30 units. Tables 13-3, 13-4 and 13-5 give the rough-cut capacity plan, the capacity requirements plan, and the shop schedule that derive from the MPS. The information contained in the shop schedule reveals that in order to meet the due date of the master schedule, work must start at operation 010 on 3/26. This same information can be used to monitor plant performance relative to the planned schedule. For example, suppose the work is completed at operation 010 on 4/15 instead of 3/31. Then, rescheduling action can be launched on 4/15 either to push the due date to 5/15 after negotiation with the customer or

| | Routing Data | TABLE 13–2 |

Part # Nat 00121
Std. lot size: 10

OPN.	SUT	RT/P	SUT/P	TT/P
010	4.0h	1.2h	.4h	1.6h
020	1.0	.8	.1	.9
030*	2.0	3.6	.2	3.8
040*	3.0	1.4	.3	1.7
			Tot.	8.0

| | Rough-Cut Capacity Plan | TABLE 13–3 |

MPS Week 8
: 30 units

Operation	030	040
Set-up hours	6.0	9.0
Production hours	108.0	42.0
Total hours	114.0	51.0

Note: Critical work centers for rough-cut capacity planning.

| | Capacity Requirements Plan | TABLE 13–4 |

	010	020	030	040
Set-up hours	12.0	3.0	6.0	9.0
Production hours	36.0	24.0	108.0	42.0
Total hours	48.0	27.0	114.0	51.0
Available hours	40.0	40.0	120.0	40.0
Capacity utilization	120%	68%	95%	128%

| | Shop Schedule | TABLE 13–5 |

Lead time (weeks)	1	1	1	2
Start date	3/26	4/2	4/9	4/16
Finish date	3/31	4/7	4/14	4/28

to accelerate the MPS through operations 020, 030, and 040. Using the SFC system in this way converts the factory into an instrument for executing customer service.

MRP-II IMPLEMENTATION: THE KEY SUCCESS FACTORS

The Traditional View of Success

Historically, corporate North America has had disappointing results in its efforts to implement MRP-II. As early as ten years ago, 90 percent of attempts to implement MRP-II failed. Today, even with the benefit of almost three decades of cumulative MRP-II implementation experience, failure rates of 70 to 80 percent are common. This is why very early in the history of MRP-II, managers became interested in understanding the factors that contributed to successful MRP-II implementation. But to understand these factors, it is necessary to define what is meant by success or failure.

The traditional way to measure success is to rate the MRP-II system using an A, B, C, D scheme. The classification uses a checklist that enumerates the criteria that are thought to indicate how well the MRP-II system is being exploited. By evaluating elements of the MRP-II system and allocating points to each item on the checklist, the global score or grade is calculated. Class A MRP-II users are those who, according to the traditional view, have succeeded excellently in implementing and using MRP-II. Class D users have, by definition, failed.

The ABCD classification scheme has some crucial flaws. First, because it designates a company as a Class A user but does not make continuous improvement, the key MRP-II concern, the ABCD checklist scheme causes managers to believe that they have achieved their ultimate goal. It builds a false sense of omnipotence and leads to arrogance. Many a company achieved class A status ten years ago became persuaded that they had achieved the ultimate MRP-II objective and stopped improving. Today, most of these companies are struggling to try to integrate the powerful JIT concepts into their supposedly class A MRP-II systems and are having major difficulties doing so. Second, the ABCD classification does not evaluate MRP-II performance relative to a strategic mission. Success or failure is obviously relative to the mission that has been carved out for MRP-II. However, most companies have not defined a clear, market-derived mission for their MRP-II systems. Because there is no strategic mission, MRP-II system evaluation by the ABCD checklist focuses on the nuts-and-bolts issues and the mechanics of MRP-II operation.

Our view is that the company must carve out a strategic mission for MRP-II. Therefore, success or failure ought to be judged on the basis of how well MRP-II executes its strategic mission. This means that

1. The mission must be clear at the outset.
2. The mission must be measurable.
3. Ongoing operation of the MRP-II system must generate the information necessary to monitor success on the strategic mission.
4. There must be a clear relationship between the design of the MRP-II system and the chosen strategic mission.
5. There must be constant monitoring of performance vis-à-vis the mission.
6. Continuous improvement of mission execution must be the central preoccupation of MRP-II system design and an ongoing feature of MRP-II operation and enhancement.

The basic mission of MRP-II is customer service. Regardless of the mechanics of the MRP-II system or the computer software that provides the horsepower for information processing, MRP-II succeeds to the extent that the bedrock concepts and core culture and values that are the cornerstone of competitive excellence and world class operations are well in place. Moreover, MRP-II must be specifically designed and operated to give the company the competitive capability to continuously improve customer service.

The Key Success Factors

Evidently, there is a difference between success in managing the MRP-II introduction project, that is, how well the initial implementation is done and success in ongoing exploitation of the MRP-II system. The two are related, since a badly managed introduction project reduces user confidence and demotivates users and managers, causing them to psychologically withdraw from MRP-II. An MRP-II implementation that drags on well beyond the time frame budgeted for it, costs much more than anticipated, and is generally out of control, leads to a poor organizational climate for subsequent MRP-II exploitation. Although a smooth and efficient implementation is no guarantee that the MRP-II system will be effectively used, a botched introduction project invariably results in failure to effectively use MRP-II.

Although the specific difficulties and problems vary from company to company, there are a few conditions that are now recognized to have a decisive impact on implementation success. These conditions can be summarized as follows:

1. *Respect for people.* The MRP-II system will be operated by people and it will place some new and rigorous demands on them. The time must be taken to inform people on all facets of the project, very early in its development. The users must be involved in the process as much as possible. Their concerns must be responded to fairly and as quickly as possible. If the groundwork is well done, MRP-II can be a powerful motivator

because it challenges the abilities of people and exploits their desire to learn and grow.

2. *Strong backing from top management.* The delegation of the necessary authority for smooth and rapid introduction of the MRP-II project and the allocation of the necessary resources, is the responsibility of top management. Unless top management gives the project full support, others are likely to put stumbling blocks in the way of project implementation. The primary task of the person initiating the project is to convince top management that it is a valid one.

3. *Relating MRP-II to the competitive position of the company and generating some hard estimates of probable financial returns.* The task of getting top management support is made much less difficult if the project initiator can show how MRP-II will help the company compete. Top management will also be excited about the project if initial investment analysis shows solid probable return on investment.

4. *Formation of project teams.* When the initial idea has been accepted, management of the project must be delegated to a project team. This aspect is vitally important, since there must be a group of people with primary responsibility for success or failure of the project. The choice of team members should follow three guidelines:

    a. All members should believe firmly in the validity of the project.

    b. They should, as much as possible, be people who command the respect of the whole organization, by virtue of a proven track record.

    c. They should be people directly affected by business planning.

    The mandate of the project team should be spelled out very clearly and communicated formally to all concerned.

5. *In-depth study of the distinctive characteristics of the company and of its particular situation.* One must avoid applying cookbook solutions. The most fundamental justification of a computerization project is that it contributes significantly to sound management given the company's own reality.

6. *In-depth study of the state of the art.* This helps avoid reinventing the wheel and allows the company to benefit from the experience of others and to avoid known pitfalls. Above all, one must avoid implementing a system that is outdated before it is operational. Subsequent modifications are costly in terms of money, time, and the morale of those implementing the project.

7. *Training.* It has been claimed that this is the critical key success factor. MRP-II is a new philosophy of materials management. Training minimizes the cultural shock associated with the introduction of MRP-II. Training must be done at all management levels.

8. *Need definition.* Very early in the process, one must think of the need. The more time that is spent evaluating and specifying the need, the less likely that there will be subsequent changes to project specification.

Every aspect of the system must be linked to an identified, clearly stated need.

9. *Implementation strategy.* There are two strategies (i) introduction by the "cold turkey" approach and (ii) step-by-step introduction. The latter is preferable. In that case, the whole system is implemented one module at a time, starting with the most simple.

10. *Project management.* As many project management principles as possible should be applied:

    a. Adoption of a project organization
    b. Definition of stages and development of time estimates
    c. Development of a project schedule
    d. Specification of milestones
    e. One must be frank to admit when the project is not going according to plan and to delay or even temporarily abort stages that are causing problems
    f. The designation of someone responsible for system sign-off.

Conclusion

At the base of all these factors is the corporate culture and value system. MRP-II is customer-driven business planning and control. The goal is continuously improving customer service. MRP-II puts production and materials planning and control in customer service. The real and crucial key success factors are customer orientation, deep customer consciousness, competitive spirit, and the other ideas that are the cornerstones of competitive excellence. When these foundation factors are in place, implementation and effective exploitation of the MRP-II system come naturally to the organization.

MRP-II succeeds in companies that use customer consciousness and the voice of the customer to forge interfunctional cooperation, consensus, and coordination. Whereas the order point order quantity techniques are somewhat immune to the absence of cooperation, MRP-II requires strong interfunctional cooperation for it to work. One of the distinctive features of MRP-II is that it integrates the diverse activities of the resource planning system and forces constant feedback between the major activities. In MRP-II the various subfunctions of business planning are locked together into a consistent unified planning system. Without an organizational climate that fosters cooperation and intense cross-functional communication, MRP-II is not likely to succeed. The introduction of MRP-II must be viewed as a major project in organizational change and adaptation that may call for the restructuring of tasks and responsibilities and a revolution in attitudes. For example, it has been observed that MRP-II results in the merging of purchasing with production control into a new materials function. The capacity to adapt to changing competitive conditions is the litmus test of a company's ability to implement and use MRP-II to strategic advantage.

Case for Discussion

GLOBAL PHARMACEUTICALS CORPORATION (GPC) (B)

Bill Larson had just presented his proposal for accelerating the implementation of MRP-II at the New York plant. A few top managers thought that inventory turns of 6.0, average lead time of 2.0 weeks, and on-time deliveries of 98 percent were overly ambitious objectives, but supported the direction in which he wished to go with MRP-II.

Justification for Broadening the Scope of MRP-II

While MRP had enabled the plant to make a marked improvement in business planning and control, significant problems still remained. The plant now had an effective tool for planning the master production schedule and had used it to drive purchasing thus ensuring MPS validity, as far as material availability was concerned. But plant management still could not systematically validate the MPS on the basis of capacity availability. No matter how well everything was done, products could not be shipped if capacity was not available. According to the master scheduler,

> We all have a rough idea of the plant's capacity and we use that crude information to make decisions. When we were operating at 70 percent of capacity that worked fine, but now we have probably gone beyond 95 percent capacity utilization. Bottlenecks, which were never a concern, are beginning to crop up all over the place. Without accurate data on these bottlenecks, we are lying to customers and to our regional warehouses, promising orders that we sometimes can't deliver. We find out too late that we can't deliver. We need to know in advance what operations are going to cause capacity problems so we can take action beforehand to deal with these.

Larson thought there was an even bigger problem

> Right now, the plant is a giant black box. Orders go in and we have no way of knowing with reasonable confidence when they are going to come out. MRP has given us visibility until things get into the plant. After that, we all hope that they will come out as planned. Execution must be visible to all the key players. There can be no control without visibility.

The Challenges in Broadening MRP-II

Most managers expected it would be easy to extend MRP to include capacity requirements planning, shop floor control, plant accounting, and performance evaluation. The data requirements would not be difficult to meet, since all that was needed were routings, production and set-up times, factory lead times, and overhead and labor rates at different operations. But some anticipated severe problems and resistance from plant personnel. The current system gave supervisors broad discretion in scheduling and expediting orders while a formal SFC system would require them to stick to the formal schedule. Supervisors made these decisions based on experience and that knowledge would be practically useless once the SFC and CRP databases had been set up. Lack of visibility and accurate data meant that hardly anyone could question the decisions made by supervisors, but SFC and performance evaluation based on MRP-II would enable management to evaluate the soundness of all decisions.

A particular sticking point with some managers was the volume of shop paper that would be generated by the SFC subsystem. Some believed that work orders and job tickets to monitor and control the execution system would number in the hundreds per day, which would require the addition of at least three more schedulers. For the past three years the company has been singing the virtues of employee empowerment, the lean production system, and the reduction of waste due to bureaucracy. The additions to MRP seem to run counter to these basic values.

Reevaluating the Potential

Larson was also concerned that some top managers viewed the MRP-II goals as being too ambitious. He decided to gather some data upon which to base firm conclusions. There were 120 different end items made in the plant and seven different production lines: three for tablets, one for capsules, two for liquids, and one for ointments. Each line processed two batches per day and he figured that the plant needed about 14 days of safety time/stock in order to have a well-planned schedule and an orderly response to the market. He wondered what that meant in terms of target overall inventory turns.

Although there were 120 end items, there were really only seven basic routings. The average number of operations per routing was five which meant that the plant needed about five job tickets to track and report on each work order. Larson estimated that each job ticket and each job order would take about two and five minutes respectively to manage. He would need to hire some more schedulers at an annual salary of $30,000 each, but could the reduction in inventory and a holding cost of 25 percent justify the cost? Moreover, since implementing MRP, master schedule delays caused by shortages of purchased items had declined from 40 percent of all delays to only 10 percent currently. This seemed to say that poor capacity planning and control of the schedule on the plant floor now accounted for the lion's share of late or missed shipments to customers. The company had already made dramatic gains in customer service, capacity utilization, and inventory turns and a few plant managers were questioning whether the additional impact of further improvement was worth the effort.

Larson decided to study the situation closely in preparation for the next meeting of the plant steering committee.

Discussion Questions

1. Evaluate the justification given by Bill Larson for extending MRP-II at GPC. Are these justifications well-founded? What other reasons would you propose?
2. How easy do you think it will be to broaden MRP-II at GPC? What are the potential pitfalls and how could they be avoided?
3. Evaluate the statement that "The plant is a giant black box." Is that state of affairs prevalent in industry? What are its effects on customer service? How can MRP-II correct it?
4. Are the concerns raised about the impact of MRP-II on the volume of shop paper justified? What are the advantages and disadvantages of doing shop floor control with MRP-II?
5. What actions should top management take concerning Larson's proposal?

References

Aherns, Roger, "Basics of Capacity Planning and Control," APICS 24th Annual Conference Proceedings, 1981, pp. 232–235.

Berry, W. L., T. Schmitt, and T. E. Vollman, "Capacity Planning Techniques for Manufacturing Control Systems: Information Requirements and Operational Features," *Journal of Operations Management* 3, 1, November 1982.

Melnyk, S. A., P. L. Carter, D. M. Dilts, and D. M. Lyth, *Shop Floor Control,* Homewood, Ill.: Dow Jones-Irwin, 1985.

Wallace, T. F., *MRP-II—Making It Happen,* Essex Junction, Vt.: Oliver Wight Limited Publications, 1985.

Managing Change in Manufacturing Strategy

O ver time, the typical production system implements many changes, but few of these can be considered to be strategic in nature. We consider change in manufacturing to be strategic change, if it conforms to one or more of the following criteria:

1. The change is explicitly undertaken to make the production function meet the exigencies of a new corporate strategy or strategic mission.
2. If the corporate strategy does not change, there must be explicit recognition that the production function is failing to carry out its strategic mandate. Hence, all changes that try to endow production with the wherewithal to execute its known strategic mandate would classify as change in manufacturing strategy.
3. The change is explicitly undertaken to respond to a known and significant actual or potential competitive threat or to exploit an emerging opportunity.
4. The change is undertaken so as to more deeply entrench the company's competitive position by creating and delivering greater discernible value to the customer. The additional value delivered must be shown to influence customer buying behavior.

NATURE AND PURPOSE OF STRATEGIC CHANGE

In general, the purpose of strategic change in manufacturing is to endow the company with a competitively useful production system and the wherewithal to use it to create or increase the company's competitive advantage. The goal is to enable the production function to execute or better perform its strategic mission.

Strategic change in manufacturing can come from four different areas, as shown in Figure 14-1. Change could be revolutionary in that it radically and quickly alters one or more of the four areas of manufacturing strategy. The deeper one reaches into the base of the pyramid, the more likely it is that successful change will require a strategic revolution. For example, change in culture and values is invariably revolutionary in nature because flaws in corporate

FIGURE 14–1   **Strategic Change in Manufacturing at Four Levels**

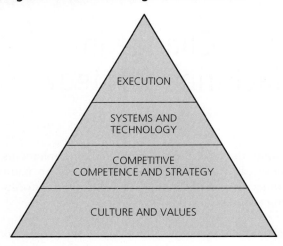

culture and values do not become apparent early in the life of a corporation. They usually come to the fore when the company arrives at an impasse caused by one or more of the following factors:

1. The company has grown substantially and is about to change from a local to a national competitor or from a national to an international one.
2. The fundamental nature of competition has been altered, for instance, when a market becomes global in scope.
3. The company has made a major acquisition and must impose its culture and values on the acquired company or must absorb the latter's culture and values.

Like corporate strategy, manufacturing strategy rests on a foundation of culture and values. If the culture and values are appropriate, then one can envisage small and progressive changes in the other elements of manufacturing strategy. One can speak of strategic evolution only if these small changes are numerous enough and follow a clear, consistent pattern over a prolonged period of time. We need to emphasize that strategic evolutions are feasible only if the foundation culture and values are strong and appropriate.

Managers who wish to undertake and implement change in manufacturing strategy must accept three important premises:

1. The production function is critical to the company's ability to compete.
2. Production must be driven by clear competitive priorities.
3. The customer must be at the heart of everything that is done in production.

How the manufacturing function can be changed to create competitive superiority, the basic components of strategic change,[1] and the premises on which it is based are well illustrated by the strategic turnaround in the late 1970s of Toyo Kogyo, the Japanese manufacturer of Mazda cars. Prior to the mid-1970s, the company was a relatively small but innovative, growing and profitable player in the world automobile market. The company was known for its line of cars based on the rotary engine and a very aggressive engineering and design organization. Toyo Kogyo took rotary engine technology well beyond the frontiers even dreamed of by its original creators. The company had carved out superior competence in that market niche and it was apparently destined to dominate the segment of the market where rotary technology was crucial. However, rotary engines had one weakness that was to prove damaging to Toyo Kogyo. These engines have very low fuel efficiency ratings compared with conventional engines.

Before the mid-1970s, neither fuel efficiency nor environmental safety was a critical consideration for automobile manufacturers. But, the OPEC oil embargo of 1973 and 1974 coupled with increased demands for environmental protection meant that these became key issues in the mid-1970s. In 1975, the Environmental Protection Agency (EPA) gave Mazda cars a very poor rating on both fuel efficiency and pollution emissions. The result was that by 1976, sales of Mazda cars in the United States declined drastically. The pressure to produce fuel efficient and environmentally safer cars meant that the company would have to anchor its product strategy more on conventional engine technology and less on the rotary engine, and it responded promptly to that challenge.

But the company did much more than this. Top management at Toyo Kogyo also recognized that it takes much more than good product technologies and designs to compete effectively. It is true that quality must be built into the product design to the maximum extent possible. However, the product will correspond to the intent of designers and engineers only if manufacturing faithfully builds it to the specifications. Product specifications are much more than physical or chemical tolerances such as +.0001 inch. Behind these formal specifications lie a host of assumptions on worker training, attitudes, discipline, production methods, craftsmanship, supervision, and work environment, to name only a few, that determine the ability of manufacturing to produce the specifications. The quality that is built into the product design can and is all too often eradicated or adulterated during production. Suppose one were to take the workers and supervisors from a Lada factory and transfer

---

[1]Wickham Skinner *Manufacturing: The Formidable Competitive Weapon* (New York, New York: John Wiley and Sons, 1985), and S. C. Wheelwright, "Japan—Where Operations Really Are Strategic," *Harvard Business Review* (July–August 1981). See also, Toyo Kogyo Co. Ltd. (A) (682-092), Harvard Business School Case Services, Harvard Business School, Boston, Mass. 02163.

them to a Mercedes Benz plant to produce Mercedes Benz cars designed by Daimler-Benz. Would the resultant products be Mercedes Benz cars? Not likely or at least not without an astronomically high scrap rate and prohibitive cost even for a Mercedes Benz. It would take at least ten years of training before these workers and managers could learn to faithfully produce a Mercedes Benz automobile.

Management at Toyo Kogyo also knew that the U.S. automobile manufacturers were not at all dependent on the rotary engine but were nonetheless increasingly succumbing to Japanese competitive pressure. While the oil embargo, stiffer environmental controls, and the dramatic shift in consumer preferences that these provoked were causing havoc with Toyo Kogyo, Japanese manufacturers such as Nissan and Toyota were flourishing. Toyo Kogyo's poor performance relative to Nissan and Toyota on key operating parameters, such as defect rates, inventory turns, productivity, manufacturing cycle time, and cost per automobile, had nothing to do with the product technology or design that it used. Instead, the company's performance on these crucial operating parameters was traced directly to basic weaknesses in the way it designed and operated its manufacturing system. Toyo Kogyo could not compete successfully partly because it had a product technology that was now inappropriate to the new market and also because its production system was outdated and could not execute the new market requirements on quality, cost, delivery, and flexibility. Nissan and Toyota flourished because they had manufacturing systems that were performing to more stringent market requirements and even leading the industry in tightening these. Consequently, strategic change at Toyo Kogyo required not only large scale overhaul of its product line but also change in the production system design and how it was exploited.

Strategic change at Toyo Kogyo both dictated and depended, to a large extent, on changing the production function so as to give it the capability to meet the emerging competitive requirements. The company formulated a vision of what a new, competition-driven production function would look like and labeled it the new production system, NPS. The most urgent goal of NPS was to reduce inventory by 50 percent and to increase quality and reduce cost and manufacturing lead times. NPS, once implemented, would have the following characteristics:

1. Statistical quality control (SQC)
2. Statistical process control (SPC)
3. Small group improvement teams (SGIT)
4. Three month, frozen master production schedule
5. Synchronized production flow
6. Cellular manufacturing
7. JIT delivery of materials from suppliers
8. Set-up reduction

9. Pull production
10. Small lot production
11. Kanbanized production
12. Load leveling
13. Multiple worker skills and increased autonomy
14. Mixed model processing
15. Single-source purchasing and supplier partnership
16. Automatic stoppage (Jidoka) systems
17. The pursuit of zero defects
18. Short cycle manufacturing
19. Increased automation
20. Computerized production scheduling

The mission would be Kaizen, that is, the continuous elimination of waste.

By 1980, both elements of Mazda's competitive strategy—a new product line and the new production system—were substantially implemented and saved the company from financial collapse. The company continues to improve and refine its production system along the lines envisaged in the mid-1970s and is now a viable competitor in an even more competitive and global car market.

Toyo Kogyo is only one of many examples of companies that have successfully implemented strategic change in production. A growing number of North American companies are achieving results that are as impressive. Harley-Davidson came back from the brink of bankruptcy to be a respectable and growing competitor by implementing total quality management and adapting JIT manufacturing to its domestic operations. Xerox made major strides in implementing TQM, statistical process control, JIT, and other programs of continuous improvement and was able to improve a dangerously eroded market share. Xerox pioneered the use of benchmarking to search for and evaluate industry-best practices and to motivate continuous improvement in quality and cost.

Impediments to Change in Manufacturing Strategy

People are the agents and subjects of change in strategy. The implementation of major change in manufacturing requires that either people change or that they be motivated to change the skills, practices, process technologies, systems, and methods that are used to execute critical competitive requirements. Attempts to change manufacturing strategy succeed or fail largely because of the way management deals with the human element. We have observed that managers who are good at implementing change in manufacturing strategy are excellent people managers and deal effectively with the concerns, fears, apprehensions, and misunderstandings of employees vis-à-vis the contemplated change. The barriers to changing manufacturing strategy issue from the human psyche and manifest themselves as basic sociological and psychological processes. The following six factors stand out as major barriers to change in manufacturing strategy.

Habits

Skills and ways of operating that have developed over many years become deeply ingrained habits. Change is sometimes so rare that the "new" practices of yesteryear become precious to those who have mastered them. Employees do things in a particular way because they have always done them that way. Old habits die hard, and so, change must break old habits and instill new ones.

Attitudes

The established ways give predictability and security. Change, on the other hand, generates instability and insecurity. People fear change because they are not confident that they can adapt to the new situation and cannot fully evaluate the consequences of the new way of thinking and doing. Radical change makes precious skills and knowledge obsolete and, if not properly managed, can destroy an employee's sense of self-worth. Some employees are suspicious of management's efforts to change things because managers are not always forthright about their intentions and the consequences of change. Every employee can produce a case, real or imaginary, where there was a hidden agenda behind changes proposed by management.

Apathy

Many employees unconsciously block change simply because they withdraw psychologically and emotionally from the situation or are just not excited by it. Some employees, and particularly direct production workers, are indifferent to management efforts to change the way manufacturing operates because they do not believe they can make a difference. Apathy blocks change because apathetic employees do not invest the necessary emotional and psychological energy to change themselves or their work and to contribute positively to the change process. They become deadweight for the organization.

Disruptiveness

Production systems, in the absence of constant innovation, eventually reach steady state. Subsystems, machines, processes, and functional subunits fit together to form a logical, intertwined whole. Change disrupts the equilibrium and, if not properly managed, can disorganize the entire system. For example, we have observed a tendency for manufacturing performance to deteriorate on nearly all fronts during implementation of major systems such as MRP-II and JIT. People avoid and resist change because they are looking for order and normalcy in all they do.

The Corporate Power Structure

The successful deployment of an effective manufacturing strategy requires the active cooperation of the other business functions. The integrated and eclectic nature of the production task means that the implementation of important manufacturing decisions calls for supporting action programs in other parts of the business. Because these decisions affect the company's ability to perform its most fundamental competitive requirements, that is, quality, cost, delivery time, and flexibility, they have profound consequences beyond manufacturing.

Active cooperation is not usually forthcoming. Historically, cultivated mistrust and dysfunctional approaches to conflict resolution by the exercise of sheer power rather than through consensus building have poisoned the climate for interfunctional cooperation in most companies. Traditional denigration of production and the low status of manufacturing in most companies enfeeble production's ability to get other functions to cooperate fully in implementing change. Managing production for strategic impact invariably means that the corporate power structure must be realigned to reflect the new competitive realities. Structure follows strategy. However, functions that possess and wield much power tend to resist changes that erode their power base. Those on whom the existing corporate power structure confers high status have an interest in preserving the status quo.

A small, but rapidly growing Canadian pharmaceuticals manufacturer decided to introduce MRP-II. The company had cultivated an image as a "marketing" company, which in reality meant it was sales and promotion driven. Sales and promotion expenses accounted for 24 percent of total sales. All vital signals suggested that the marketing group wielded enormous power. The last four presidents had a background in sales and the vice-president of marketing was paid 25 percent more than his manufacturing counterpart. The MRP-II project management team knew that full and active cooperation of the marketing function was vital to successful MRP-II implementation. They took steps to ensure that marketing people were well represented throughout the project management organization and undertook extensive education and information sessions for marketing personnel. They defined a corporate strategic mission for the project that put customer concerns at the heart of MRP-II when they defined the MRP-II mission as the constant improvement, to near perfection, in the execution of customer service. They saw MRP-II introduction as providing the company with a powerful tool that could help in planning and controlling the business so as to give customers firm and reliable delivery promises. Furthermore, they understood that MRP-II implementation could improve the execution of the company's strategy to provide superior customer service because it would give the capability to track customer orders through the planning and execution system. The company could provide customers with timely feedback on the status of their orders, information that customers value tremendously, particularly when orders could not be delivered as originally promised.

Marketing people saw things differently, however. Over the years, the marketing function came to view itself as the sole, legitimate custodian of customer service, and most other functions shared that perspective. Marketing people saw customer service as a marketing responsibility and could not see how other functions, particularly production, could have significant responsibility for serving customers. They came to the conclusion that MRP-II introduction would allow manufacturing to encroach significantly on an area of important marketing responsibility. They feared that this would materially reduce the power and status of marketing to the benefit of production.

MRP-II introduction also called for the marketing function to make the following changes in the way it managed customer service and how it operated.

1. Marketing would have to provide a 12 month rolling forecast by product line, instead of the 1 year forecast of dollar sales that it had traditionally provided. Forecast performance would be measured and reported on monthly.
2. Every month, marketing people would have to meet with production and purchasing personnel to agree on the sales and operations plan for the next three months. All subsequent changes to the plan would have to be approved by the sales and operations planning committee. Historically, production was required to produce whatever marketing thought it could sell.
3. All changes to the master production schedule to accommodate special orders or accelerated delivery promises would have to be approved by a designated person, such as the production manager or vice-president of manufacturing. Traditionally marketing demanded and got changes made to the master schedule when and as often as they wished.
4. Order promises had to be made on the basis of information contained in the master production schedule. Newly accepted orders had to respect the available-to-promise information generated by the master production schedule report. Sales people had, by contrast, accepted as many orders as they could close, with little regard for whether production could produce the order as promised.

From the perspective of the marketing function, MRP-II would decrease marketing power, prestige, and influence and would require changes in behavior that would constrain the freedom of marketing people to serve the customer as they saw fit. They suggested that they would be required to work harder so that production people could have an easier time. Marketing substantially delayed implementation of activities for which it had prime responsibility, such as forecast management and sales and operations planning. They put lower level marketing managers to represent them on the MRP-II project team. These managers did not have the authority to bind the marketing function to key project management decisions.

After 15 months of training, there was very little change in traditional marketing behavior to conform to the exigencies imposed by MRP-II. Marketing people continued to view customer service, promise orders, request changes to the master schedule and approach forecasting sales as they had historically done. The consequence was that the project fell two years behind schedule. Top management reduced its commitment and the resources that it devoted to MRP-II. The project team downsized the original, totally integrated MRP-II concept and adopted the less ambitious goal of implementing material requirements planning. Three years after the company launched the MRP-II project, it still did not have a credible material requirements planning system. The balance of corporate power remained basically unscathed.

Performance Measurement and Compensation

Decisions that implement change in manufacturing strategy tend to produce results over the long term. Worker training to cultivate craftsmanship, investment in the development of appropriate values and attitudes, and the implementation of systems and innovative process technologies are investments in the long-term competitive viability of the enterprise. In the short term, a production system could show quite unfavorable financial results, precisely because it is investing in the future. The performance measurement and compensation system in place in most companies ignore this fact and reward managers for producing short-term favorable financial results. Managers have been known to delay or postpone investment in long-term improvement and sacrifice the long-term health of their business units so as to meet the short-term financial targets imposed by top management.

The process of changing manufacturing strategy must identify and deal with these crucial change barriers. Managers that are unusually successful in managing the change process conceive of and implement action programs to eliminate the factors that impede change.

PATTERNS OF FAILURE IN CHANGING MANUFACTURING STRATEGY

Triggering Mechanism

Managers generally initiate change in manufacturing strategy when the evidence becomes overwhelming that internal operations are not performing to their expectations. Persistent losses, significant decreases in market share, productivity, on-time delivery, and machine utilization or abnormally large increases in cost, defect rates, and volume of back orders are the factors most likely to focus management attention on the need for change in manufacturing strategy. Sometimes, the message that manufacturing may not be executing its competitive mandate is driven home by published reports that indicate that the internal operations of major competitors are performing much better. Information on competitive manufacturing performance becomes available rather haphazardly and rarely as a result of serious, systematic efforts by mangers to monitor competitors using such approaches like benchmarking. Partly due to this, managers tend to disbelieve published data when they show that competitors are doing substantially better than one's own company. Managers are driven into action only when published information speaks loudly and unequivocally over a long period and particularly when internal performance measures show that wholesale deterioration has taken place.

A company should react to these internal indices. However, one must question the quality of its market and competitive intelligence and its closeness to its customers when these internal indices constitute the major triggering mechanism for changing manufacturing strategy. Managers who rely heavily on these internal indices almost never change elements of the production system that are not giving problems. Changing manufacturing strategy is tantamount to solving the problems uncovered by the internal reporting system and which management perceives are thwarting the achievement of expected operating results. Strategic manufacturing change is unduly reactive because the basic forces to which a company should strategically respond are at work in the market and industry long before internal indices reveal that performance has substantially deteriorated. For example, a new major process technology being contemplated by a competitor would have to be conceived of, researched, developed, designed, pilot tested, debugged, implemented on a large scale, and refined before internal indices would show a substantial deterioration in a company's relative cost or quality position attributable to the new process. For most major process technologies, the time between the process technology concept and its impact on operations could be easily 10 to 15 years. A company could not make up for that time disadvantage except through a massive and concerted effort to catch up. That is why most companies are forever trying to catch up to the industry leaders when it comes to implementing strategic change in manufacturing. And as soon as managers think they have bridged the gap between their companies and the leaders, they find they have as much catching up to do because basic competitive forces are constantly at work and the leaders are always anticipating and continually responding to them. This is a very important reason why competitive benchmarking must be used cautiously. By the time a benchmarking study reveals that there is a significant gap between a company's performance and that of its competitors, the latter could be two or three steps ahead in the strategic game.

Action Oriented and Execution Focused

Managers rarely change manufacturing strategy in response to anticipated or even incipient changes in the market or industry. Manufacturing strategy change focuses on the evident operating problems and is action oriented, that is, it deals with the doing part of strategic change to the detriment of the thinking, attitudinal aspects. Major changes in the manufacturing function such as the allocation and deployment of capital resources and production system structuring aim to improve the execution aspects of manufacturing strategy. Change seldom tackles the more fundamental cultural, value-bound, philosophical, and policy dimensions that provide the framework within which successful execution can take place. The bias for action means that top management easily sees manufacturing strategy implementation as a problem that is better handled by manufacturing managers, particularly those at the middle-management level. Consequently, top management has the propensity to delegate the task of changing manufacturing strategy to the lower echelons. Without the appropriate thinking, leadership, and nurturing that only top management can provide, change in manufacturing strategy takes much more time to bring about and usually does not reflect the market and competitive concerns that are central to corporate strategy.

Manufacturing strategy is responding more to changes in manufacturing practices and newly created management systems and tools than to changes in the market and corporate strategy. At any point in time, manufacturing strategy more accurately reflects the tools, systems, practices, and technologies that are available than what is required by competitive conditions or by changes in corporate strategy. For most companies it is mainly due to coincidence that the tools and practices implemented also serve the needs of corporate strategy. Partly because the available practices and systems are created by the leading, superior performers—Black and Decker pioneered the development of MRP-II, Toyota single-handedly developed JIT, Xerox pioneered the formal application of benchmarking—they are likely to contribute some competitive benefit to most companies that apply them. This phenomenon camouflages the fact that most companies do not use these tools and practices with any deliberate and clear strategic intent.

Rather than manufacturing strategy dictating the pace of change in practices, tools, systems, and technology, it is the latter that are dictating the pace of change in manufacturing strategy. Therefore, the customer gets what manufacturing can give rather than the production function giving what the customer wants. Manufacturing strategy is not stimulating innovation in manufacturing practices, instead it is innovation in manufacturing practices that is stimulating or pulling manufacturing strategy. When confronted with a competitive problem, managers choose a solution from the available pool of practices and technologies instead of creating the tools that are necessary to meet the competitive challenge. The result is that companies generally trail the market requirements and only a few are developing the practices and technologies that enable them to meet anticipated and incipient market exigencies. Just as corporate strategy should dictate the pace of technological innovation, so also should manufacturing strategy dictate the pace of innovation in process technology, practices, and production systems.

Affinity for "Brick and Mortar" Decisions

Manufacturing executives have a tendency to couch manufacturing strategy in terms of process technologies, machines, and systems. They are at ease with the "hard" stuff, the physical and tangible, what Skinner refers to as the brick and mortar or structural elements of manufacturing strategy. They have a tendency to either avoid or deal superficially with the "soft" or fuzzy aspects of manufacturing strategy such as culture and values, attitudes and philosophies. For most mangers, change in manufacturing strategy is mainly a matter of changing the configuration of the production system by the implementation of new or improved machines, process technologies, and systems.

Additionally, these managers assume that change in manufacturing strategy has taken place once the production system has been reconfigured. Dependence on systems implementation to effect change in manufacturing strategy is so prevalent that many managers view the system as the solution.

The failure to deal adequately with culture and values when changing manufacturing strategy derives from two related phenomena. Culture and values are people embodied which means that changing them requires that people change. Some managers trivialize how difficult it is to change people and assume that human beings are completely malleable. They also assume that people can and will change as long as they see the need for change. Their efforts to change the corporate value system concentrate on demonstrating the need for change and informing and persuading employees that change must take place. These managers rely heavily on group discussions, speeches, and formal policy pronouncements to persuade employees to change and to point to the direction in which they should change. Once they have communicated the need for change and have pointed the direction of change, they assume that the critical aspect of the change process has been implemented and whatever else is required to complete the change in values can be easily taken care of by lower level managers.

Other managers rightly assume that culture, values, and attitudes, precisely because they are people embodied, are tough to change. Values and attitudes develop and concretize over long periods of time. They define what is important and what is not, for the individual. They regulate his or her behavior on a daily basis by defining what is right and acceptable. They give the person a sense of self-worth vis-à-vis others. In order to change corporate culture and values, management must bring most employees first to question and reject current habits and ways of thinking and doing and then to adopt new ones. Usually, the habits and ways of thinking have been proved right because they produced some measure of success for the company and were in times past reinforced and promoted by top management. People do not easily abandon ideas and principles that have produced good results and that have become dear to them, particularly when the alternative ways of thinking and behaving have not been confirmed by their significant personal experiences. Culture and values may be defined by top management and reinforced and enforced by the corporate rewards and punishment system but they can influence how work is done only if they are internalized and become the personal property of the worker. Most managers who understand how difficult it is to effect substantial change in culture and values tend to avoid such change because many attempts to do so result in employee resistance, backlash and sometimes overt and covert rebellion. A handful of managers painstakingly and doggedly work at creating and inculcating appropriate values because they know that culture and values are the foundation upon which the pillars of strategy stand or fall. Change in manufacturing strategy must deal with the value set held by employees.

By contrast, brick and mortar decisions or systems solutions tend to be neat and are logical. Their logic, on paper at least, can be evaluated to see if they make sense, and they invariably do. Systems solutions appeal to the logical, rational managerial mind. Moreover, systems solutions are relatively easy to implement, if by implementation one means that a particular machine or system is physically in place. The expected results are usually visible and measurable and actual results can be used to gauge relative success or failure in implementing the system. Managers can use the results to drive the implementation which makes systems solutions congruent with the results-oriented behavior that characterizes management practice in North America. In addition, brick and mortar decisions or systems solutions are closer to the execution level of manufacturing management so they usually only require top management in most companies to approve the budget, give some organizational support to those operating managers that are responsible for implementing them, and to evaluate the results. The implementation of systems solutions is easily delegated to lower level managers. But, you can change systems and machines without changing strategy and strategic change does not necessarily mean that systems must change. Manufacturing strategy deployment takes place at many different levels and in many ways and production system configuration is only one of them.

Middle-Up, Middle-Down Change Management

Top corporate management is prone to rely on systems and brick and mortar solutions when attempting to change manufacturing strategy and they have a penchant for delegating the responsibility for doing so to middle level managers. This is not to say that production system configuration is not an important strategic issue or that there are not valid systems-based solutions to some complex manufacturing problems. On the contrary, some very powerful management systems such as total quality management, just-in-time (JIT), manufacturing resource planning (MRP-II), flexible manufacturing systems, and total productive maintenance, have been developed over the years and their implementation is a necessary part of any effective manufacturing strategy. However, North American corporations have generally failed in their efforts to implement these systems and those that have succeeded are seldom able to use them to their full competitive potential. TQM and JIT are a thorn in the toe for most manufacturing companies in North America. MRP-II, which was designed by a few U.S. pioneers more than 25 years ago, still causes problems for companies that try to implement it and most that have MRP-II are not using it effectively.

The problem is that top corporate management has so totally delegated the authority for implementing these systems that it has also delegated the initiative. When we look at the major systems or approaches to manufacturing that are available, we find that the initiative to bring these innovations into the company almost always comes from middle management, that is those below the vice-president-manufacturing level. Moreover, these are usually not brought in response to any explicit improvement mission formulated and promulgated by top corporate management. It is the initiative to bring these systems in that often stimulates top management to seek improvement in specific competitive factors such as quality, lead time, and cost. The absence of top management initiative coupled with failure on its part to nurture appropriate corporate culture and values make the task of implementing major manufacturing management systems doubly difficult for middle managers.

Leadership responsibility and authority for strategic change rest at the top of the organizational hierarchy. Top management controls the reward and punishment system that is a powerful mechanism for steering the corporation in new directions. Influence and courageous and visionary ideas more naturally flow from top to bottom. It is tough for top management to be totally and psychologically committed to projects that it is not instrumental in creating or that did not emerge from its role as leader of the organization or as the ultimate custodian of corporate strategy. It becomes easy for corporate management to withdraw its support, whether intentionally or otherwise, for projects when the expected results are somewhat disappointing. The widely held idea that top management commitment is critical to the successful implementation of systems such as MRP-II, TQM, and JIT recognizes that the initiative and leadership usually do not come from top management and that commitment is not natural.

Middle-up, middle-down change management is also difficult because it creates a credibility problem for middle managers. They have to persuade top management to embrace projects whose relationship to the company's competitive mission are not evident to that group. But lower level employees are reluctant to cooperate with middle managers until top management becomes involved in a major system implementation project. Middle managers become literally squeezed in the middle, hamstrung by top management apathy and psychological detachment and the low level of mobilization it engenders in operating level employees. It is not surprising, therefore, that most attempts at implementing major manufacturing management systems such as JIT, TQM, and MRP-II fail either partially or totally.

Frenetic Pace and Results Driven

Managers undertake major change in manufacturing strategy when they are faced with incontrovertible evidence that the competitive positions of their companies have deteriorated substantially. Sometimes, by the time management is stimulated into action by internally generated signals or measures, the damage inflicted on a company's competitive position is irreparable. For example, North American automobile manufacturers tried to mount a credible strategic manufacturing response to Japanese competition, years after widely published evidence convincingly showed superior Japanese performance on quality, cost, productivity, and product and process innovativeness. Analogously, the North American television producers were driven into action long after Japanese superiority in television production was universally confirmed and acknowledged. In the case of automobiles, the damage done may prove to be irreparable, while for television sets, North American producers have been all but wiped out.

Faced with the prospect of losing their markets either substantially or totally, top management puts undue pressure on manufacturing people to implement major change and produce results quickly. The pace and magnitude of change is often unbearable for middle level managers. One company became finally persuaded that foreign competitors had achieved competitive superiority on all fronts. The evidence produced over eight years showed that foreign competitors were achieving landed costs that were 30 percent lower. Defect rates for the North American company were six parts per hundred versus one part per hundred thousand for major foreign competitors. The company was quoting a 12-week lead time to customers and had an on-time delivery record of 70 percent. By contrast, foreign competitors were quoting a 10-week lead time and were delivering on time 98 percent of the time, despite a much longer transportation time. Top management demanded a crash program to eliminate the gap. Manufacturing responded with an action plan that required the company to implement JIT, TQM, and MRP-II in three years. Experience tells us that implementing any one of these systems properly could easily take three years of concerted effort, backed by solid top management involvement. Once the project was approved, manufacturing was on its own.

Top management designed performance measures to enable it to monitor the implementation. The pace was so frantic that one veteran said that "it made your head spin." The company chose to start by implementing MRP-II and after approximately 12 months of frantic work at an unrelenting pace, the results were starting to look good. Lead time went from 12 to 9 weeks and on-time delivery performance was approaching 95 percent. By the middle of the second year, however, lower level managers could not keep up the pace and employees started to resist because they were spending a disproportionately large share of their time on the MRP-II work. Employees were beginning to see the MRP-II project as stressful and a disruption to their accustomed ways of doing things. Burnout among the middle-management group was so widespread that both the plant manager and the MRP-II project manager resigned by the end of the second year. Top manufacturing management's attempt to muscle the project through in an effort to meet the deadlines and results set by top corporate management so shocked the employees and lower level managers (supervisors) that they strongly resisted any attempt to launch the TQM and JIT phases of the project, effectively killing it. The initially attractive results deteriorated rapidly and 30 months after the project was launched, the company was a poor MRP-II user and is still losing market share to foreign competition.

High-intensity programs that aim to arrest a badly deteriorated competitive manufacturing position are likely to fail because of the following reasons:

1. Changing manufacturing strategy is usually a long-term process that is best managed as a continuous process of steady improvement. Moderate improvements in quality, productivity, and cost that are sustained over long periods are the proven way to change a company's position.

2. High-intensity programs do not allow enough time for changing culture, attitudes, and habits and for building corporatewide consensus on the new manufacturing strategy and supporting improvement program. In the absence of consensus, too much time and energy are dissipated muscling projects through and dealing with dysfunctional conflict. Change is sought by the exercise of power and not by way of legitimate influence.

3. Managerial burnout is widespread because managers cannot sustain the heartrending pace that is called for. Manufacturing strategy change takes place in a crisis atmosphere where fear of failure causes key players to become defensive and protect their reputations.

4. There is heavy emphasis on the production of short-term results and to monitor performance metrics. Managers tend to use window dressing to make the results look good and to be preoccupied with the numbers instead of evaluating whether change is taking place.

5. Managers tend to favor projects that are likely to succeed and produce quick, measurable results instead of giving priority to programs that have the largest long-term, strategic benefits even if results may be slow in coming. There is broad consensus among managers in North America that when large-scale change in manufacturing strategy is being implemented, the initial improvement projects should be those that have a high probability of success and are likely to produce quick, measurable results. The reasoning is that success breeds the desire to succeed. While this approach

has positive motivational effects, the down side is that it leaves employees and lower level managers with the wrong impression that change will be very easy and they feel deceived when they have to tackle the more difficult projects. In addition, early emphasis on results gets managers addicted to the numbers and they continue to place emphasis on the metrics, even when they are not appropriate.

6. Top management becomes disappointed and tends to withdraw its support for projects later on when manufacturing fails to maintain the exceptionally favorable initial results. High-intensity change produces initial measurable results that cannot be sustained. Initial excitement quickly gives way to disappointment and frustration.

Manufacturing strategy change is best managed as a steady process that seeks moderate, sustainable improvements in manufacturing performance over the long haul and is propelled by a corporatewide competitive mission of continuous improvement. Change should be progressive, evolutionary, and continuous and should seek to keep the production function performing the competitive exigencies of a changing market and competitive situation. Change should also be proactive and anticipatory and improvement should be sought even if there is no visible and confirmed need for it because competition operates to make change necessary, even if the need is latent. Strategic revolutions become necessary from time to time, but they should be avoided, if possible. Evolutionary and continuous change vitiates the need for strategic revolutions. Change should focus, first and foremost, on the foundation elements of superior manufacturing performance, culture, and values, because projects to improve competitive competence are molded and energized by the culture and value system.

SUCCESSFUL CHANGE IN MANUFACTURING STRATEGY

Changing Culture and Values

As we said before, culture and values are people embodied and changing them requires changing people, a very difficult task. It is made doubly difficult by the fact that to change people, the manager must either be the model that he or she can present to subordinates or must first change himself or herself.

In an organizational setting, people change in response to leadership. Therefore, the chief executive officer must come to embody the entire value set that gives the company its distinctive makeup. The CEO's behavior, actions, and preferences must accurately reflect the values that he or she wishes subordinates to cultivate. The chief executive officer must be exemplary and must be the symbol of what the company stands for in thought, word, and deed. Moreover, as Robert D. Haas of Levi Strauss and Co.[2] has so poignantly reminded us, the entire cadre of managers and supervisors must come to internalize and project the company's culture and values in all they do. The first task of the chief executive officer is to blend the company culture and values into his or her person while the second task is to coach all managers to put them in theirs. Everyone in a position of authority must project the corporate value set as he or she exercises leadership, and executes responsibility. Managers, including the chief executive officer, should never compromise on values or show favoritism or too many exceptions to the rule. Over time, values become weakened by inattentive exceptions to the rule that are smoothed over as being insignificant.

Executives who are effective at changing the basic values and culture of their companies focus on the following five key issues.

Articulate Culture and Value Set

The chief executive officer needs to develop a succinct vision of the competitive situation and the company's mission in the marketplace as a basis for evolving and communicating an appropriate set of values. The factors in the competitive environment and the marketplace that make old values inappropriate and new ones necessary need to be fully understood and explained. One needs to explain why old values do not and cannot be made to work. One also has to show why and how old values hamper the employee and how the new ones will enhance personal growth and development. People can be altruistic, but major changes are more readily accepted if they enhance a person's self-worth.

Target the Authority Structure

The chief executive officer should train and direct all those in leadership positions to incorporate the new values. Managers sometimes unconsciously behave in a way that is detrimental to the company's aspirations. Behaviors that are destructive of new values should be pointed out, analyzed, and critically evaluated. Behaviors that are supportive of the new value set should be highlighted and the fundamental lessons they teach should be extracted and propagated throughout the managerial group. Positive behavior patterns should be held up as examples for employees to emulate.

Implement Group Processes

The group process inculcates and refines new values and corresponding behaviors. Small groups that meet regularly remind employees of the new values and enrich the pool of examples of both proper and improper behavior.

---

[2]"Values Make the Company: An Interview with Robert Haas," *Harvard Business Review* (September–October 1990).

Groups prevent the individual from feeling isolated and build a sense of shared fate, "We are in this together." Moreover, groups encourage the discouraged because employees can see that they are not alone in the learning process and they understand that they are not the only ones making mistakes. Change in culture, values, and attitudes take place more effectively, quickly, and less painfully in a group setting.

Action Program

The ultimate goal of culture and values is to influence how people think through and do work. Employees will find ample opportunity to test new values in the normal course of doing work. Nevertheless, the process of integrating the new value set into operating tasks and responsibilities can be accelerated if specific action programs for doing so are designed and implemented. The idea is to put employees to work quickly to solve real problems on the basis of the new value set.

Performance Evaluation and Compensation

The new values should show up in how people are evaluated. A company that seeks to create customer consciousness in the factory, for example, needs to find ways to measure the contribution that factory employees are making to customer satisfaction. It needs to identify behaviors or results that reflect customer consciousness and measure and report on these. Employees that exemplify the values that the company cherishes must be rewarded accordingly. It is easy to overlook the core values that are driving the company and to reward the visible, easily measurable, and popular accomplishments.

A worker on the packaging line who doublechecks the label on a bottle of medication to make sure that it is properly placed demonstrates much more concern for the customer and deeper customer consciousness than a marketing manager who accepts an order when he knows that the probability is high that it won't be delivered on time. Most companies overlook the worker on the production line but compensate the marketing manager with a healthy bonus when sales increase in the short term. A company that wishes to change its values needs to change the reward and recognition system to eradicate the old values and reinforce the new.

Changing Superior Competitive Competence and Strategy

The culture and values, systems and technologies, and the particular ways in which they are used by the execution system all merge to create superior competitive competence. As these are successfully changed, the particular competitive competence inexorably changes. The critical consideration is to pick the competence that the company wishes to nurture and to focus all improvement efforts on that skill cluster.

FIGURE 14–2   **Strategic Intentions versus Strategy in Fact**

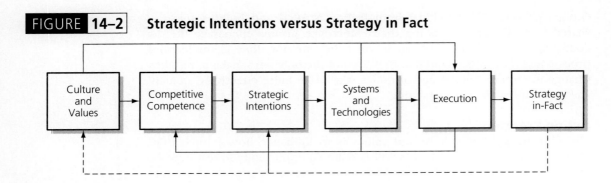

Strategic change is both easy and difficult to bring about, depending on the perspective that one adopts. One ought to differentiate between strategic intentions and strategy in fact. What managers generally refer to as strategy are in reality strategic intentions. The analysis of the competitive situation, evaluation of the company's and competitors' strengths and weaknesses, the selection of appropriate market niches, the picking of a generic strategy, the broad allocation of resources, and the structuring of the organization are all dimensions of strategic intentions. For a company to achieve the strategic intentions, it must create the necessary competitive competence which must in turn be effectively exploited by the execution system. Companies always achieve a competitive position in fact and it is usually different (inferior) than the intended competitive position. Figure 14-2 shows the relationship between the various elements of manufacturing strategy and also highlights the difference between strategic intentions and strategy in fact. It becomes evident that changing strategy in fact may require, at the minimum, fundamental change in the execution system and could call for more radical change in culture and values, competitive competence, and systems and technology. The goal in implementing strategic change in manufacturing is to make the executed strategy conform closely to strategic intentions. If the culture and values and the competitive competence are weak or poorly developed, then the company will fail to achieve its strategic intentions, although it may "succeed" for some time.

Strategic Change in Systems and Technology

Systems and process technologies vary widely in scale, complexity, and competitive impact, and not all changes in systems and process technology qualify as strategic change. So as to qualify as strategic change a system or process technology must radically alter the company's ability to perform one or more of the key success factors by which it seeks to carve out its competitive position. Or, it must substantially improve the efficiency with which the company performs one or more of its key success factors. How much improvement would be necessary so as to qualify a change in systems or process technology as strategic must be judged in relation to the market. Customers must perceive that they receive significantly more value to the extent that they are more entrenched as customers of the company or they are willing to switch their sourcing. Management must also be able to trace customer loyalty or switching directly or indirectly to superior performance attributable to the system. For example, Federal Express Corporation's single-hub sorting of small packages would qualify as a strategic change in system because the company's ability to attract and retain customers was due to its fast and reliable delivery and its ability to trace lost packages. The company's superior performance compared to its major competitors was directly traceable to the single-hub and mechanized-sorting operations that it had in Memphis.

An individual change in system and process technology may not have enough impact to qualify as strategic change. It could instead be part of a larger system or process technology the implementation of which would significantly enhance a company's competitive position. Individual small changes in systems and process technology must fit into an overall logic or pattern of improvement in manufacturing performance before they can be deemed to be change in manufacturing strategy. On the basis of these criteria, implementation and subsequent continuous enhancement of systems, such as manufacturing resource planning, flexible manufacturing systems, and CAD/CAM, in industries that compete on product innovation or in design-intensive industries of the make-to-order or engineered-to-order category, would qualify as strategic manufacturing change. Implementation of total approaches to manufacturing design and management, like total quality management, just-in-time, total productive maintenance, also constitute change in manufacturing strategy since experience shows that they radically improve performance of competitive factors such as quality, cost, delivery-time length and reliability, production system flexibility, and innovation, and that they also have the philosophy of continuous improvement at their core.

Managers who successfully implement change in systems and technology with strategic impact and with clear strategic intent use an approach that has seven elements.

Accumulation and Dissemination of Knowledge

Companies should not reinvent the wheel but they should also avoid applying cookbook solutions. Managers must have reasonably deep knowledge of a system or technology before they can evaluate its usefulness to their companies. Superficial understanding causes managers to arrive at hasty and ill-founded conclusions as to the merits of a particular system or technology and also leads to underestimation of the difficulties involved in implementing it. Profound knowledge allows managers to question the premises and assumptions upon which a proposed system or technology implementation is based. It also allows them to understand the philosophy behind the system to see whether it meshes with their company's corporate philosophy. The complete logic of the system or technology must be laid out so as to expose what it does, how it works, and why it produces the results attributable to it.

The conditions that must be met for successfully implementing the system or technology and for exploiting it to its full competitive potential must be thoroughly understood. The organizationwide impact of the system and the results that can be expected must be specified using real-life implementations. In the case of systems or technological innovations developed internally, evaluation using empirical data can be based on pilot studies or limited-scale applications using one or two plants if the company has multiplant operations. Knowledge is the basis for mastering the technology and for eventually improving or even replacing it with a better process.

Evaluation of the Internal Environment

A system or technology may be good for a company but the organizational climate may not be right for its smooth implementation. The internal environment may be hostile to the basic requirements of the system. Every system or technology incorporates basic philosophies, underlying principles, performance priorities, and supporting practices and makes crucial assumptions as to values, attitudes, and operating discipline. A system or technology cannot be effectively implemented and exploited to its full competitive potential unless the internal climate or operating environment provides the requisite support system. A poor industrial relations climate or employee or management resistance to innovation may make it unwise to embark on a new system implementation at a particular point in time. The potential barriers to implementation need to be identified and described and actions to eliminate them should be defined and evaluated. The potential levers that could be used to facilitate implementation should be identified and tactics for using them should be described and analyzed. The peculiarities of the internal workings of the company must be known, their impact evaluated and ways of accommodating them should be elucidated. The nature and sources of fear should be identified and measures should be taken to drive out fear. Where there is fear of change, innovation and change compound and provide rationalizations for harboring fear. Any major system or technology will have some adverse consequences that could be used by those who oppose change to justify their position. Change is normal for those who are not afraid of it and when they do innovate, the results usually confirm to them that they were right not to have been afraid. The labor force must be involved in and used as a catalyst to sustain the change. All misconceptions, apprehensions, and concerns should be fully dealt with openly and frankly. Commitment to defend the vital interests of all employees affected by the change backed by a guarantee of resources to train and prepare employees to adapt to the new system or technology are usually minimum conditions for overcoming fear.

There are exceptions, but a poor internal climate usually points to weak and poorly developed culture and values. A company that has a solid core of values is always ready to undertake change and innovation. Making the climate right may frequently require doing the groundwork to design a strong value set and to weave it into every facet of the organization. Previous discussion underscored this as the most fundamental task of the management of change in manufacturing strategy. Attempts to implement large-scale, integrated management systems, or process technologies often start the process of healthy change in culture and values. MRP-II made many companies realize how important it is to integrate production into the process of managing customer service and how intensive cooperation and coordination of marketing, production, and procurement were a necessary part of the process. Companies that had trouble implementing MRP-II came to see how interfunctional conflict and mutual distrust hamstrung their ability to execute a competitive strategy based on customer service and some took positive steps to foster cooperation between marketing and production. One company mandated monthly meetings between senior managers of both functions and started a program whereby managers of each function spend time—up to one year— working in the other function. North American companies that tried to introduce JIT, with its heavy emphasis on supplier partnership, came to understand how critical it was to build strong, cooperative relationships with suppliers. Evidently, then, systems can trigger change in culture and values, but it is far better for a company to continuously nurture the culture and values that will enable it to absorb new systems and technologies quickly. Those that do will always enjoy a competitive edge from the implementation of new systems and technologies. The odds clearly favor companies that are very open to new systems and technologies because the difficulties they encounter when implementing these help detect deficiencies in culture and values quickly and continually.

Top Management Involvement

We have said before that the initiative to implement major systems and process technologies usually comes from middle management. However, the successful implementation of large scale and integrated systems and technologies requires large commitments of organizational and financial resources backed by a network of organizational support systems. In most cases, only top management has the power and authority to commit the corporation on such a scale. Top management needs to be involved in projects that implement major changes in systems and technologies. Involvement is much more than approval of the necessary funds and the declaration of noble top management intentions relative to a project. It includes the participation by top management in the planning, execution, and continuous review of the project in a way commensurate with its role and responsibility as custodian of the company's competitive health. No amount of rhetoric can substitute for top management's active participation in bringing a system or process-technology project to fruition. The more top management participates in project definition, planning, and execution, the more lower level managers and employees are likely to commit time and energy to ensure that the project is successful. Top management involvement is critical to the success of major changes in systems and process technology.

Top management is more likely to commit itself to the project if those who initiate it clearly show the relationship between the system or process technology and the company's market and competitive requirements. The system must be given an objective that ties into the company's strategic mission. How the system contributes to the creation or sharpening of superior competitive competence should be clear to all. In other words, the system or process technology should either give the company the ability to perform customer-valued activities that it is not currently performing or improve its performance of existing activities. Moreover, top management is more prone to commit to a system or process technology that either exploits the existing culture and values or reinforces them. For example, we have observed that the companies that were quick to adopt MRP-II were those that had a long history of emphasizing superiority in customer service as part of their overall competitive strategies. Top management in these companies saw MRP-II as a way to exploit the existing culture and value system and also to entrench it more deeply into the organization.

Involve All Those Affected Directly and Indirectly by the System or Process Technology

Systems cannot be imposed on workers by an external, detached authority. The idea of turnkey systems is anathema to a people-oriented philosophy of management and betrays poor understanding of the intimate relationship that users develop, over time, with the systems they use. Workers should be proprietors of the systems and machines they use. This is easier to bring about if they are active agents and partners in the implementation. Those who impose systems almost always neglect concerns that are important to the worker, and which are not evident to the expert, and also thwart the effective and creative use of the system.

The following guidelines encourage and solicit worker involvement:

1. Integrate the implementation into existing small-group processes by delegating specific, clearly defined tasks to small-group improvement teams. Also use groups to encourage workers to spell out their grievances, concerns, fears, and suggestions for designing the system or making the implementation smoother. Where group problem solving processes are not in place, use the project as a major catalyst for starting SGIT. People participate better as members of a group than as individuals.
2. Show the relationship between the job and the system or process technology. The worker should understand how the system or process technology

will affect the work to be done and what new skills, attitudes, and techniques he or she will have to master. Systems and process technologies should be implemented as ways to improve work and quality, not as mechanisms for eliminating jobs.

3. The implementation plan should emphasize advantages to the worker such as training for the future, need to remain competitive, and quality of work life. Disadvantages and risks should be presented frankly and honestly and plans for dealing with these ought to be hammered out. The worker must be presented with facts as to, why on balance, the change is the right thing to do from his or her point of view. When the facts are laid out clearly and boldly, workers come to understand that technological change is necessary to remain competitive, create jobs with a future, and increase quality of life and of work life.

Systems or process technology implementations that do not involve the worker rarely succeed in the long run. Worker involvement eventually makes people open to change and reinforces culture and values based on innovation and continuous improvement. Absence of worker involvement fosters fear, suspicion, and apprehension and eventually leads to resistance to technological change. Once again, when management nurtures appropriate values, change is easy to manage and the changes themselves reinforce and refine the value set.

Training

Companies that do not compromise on training are infinitely more successful at implementing new systems and technologies than those that do. Training has been called the key success factor of the key success factors of systems implementation. Training is vital to successful change in systems and technology because of the following reasons:

1. It shows concern for people. Extensive and intensive training is top management's guarantee to employees that it wants to deal with their concerns.
2. It benefits the employee personally. Training has several motivational effects. First, the employee is motivated by self-interest since training increases his or her marketability. Second, training taps the higher level needs such as self-esteem and self-actualization. Third, employees are generally influenced by what they perceive as the company's altruism toward them.
3. It drives out fear since it is a guarantee that employees will receive the know-how to deal with changing technology.
4. The company can use the training program to eradicate dysfunctional attitudes and to instill positive ones.

5. The training program, in conjunction with group processes, can be used to shape the core company values. In fact, the company's core values should always be integrated into all training programs.
6. It builds craftsmanship. One key goal of any training program should be to create and maintain employee mastery of all facets of the job. Consequently, training builds confidence, prepares employees to undertake more and higher levels of responsibility and thereby enhances employee involvement in the improvement effort.

Identify and Evaluate Alternative Designs

A company can dovetail a system to its peculiar requirements without sacrificing the integrity of the basic technology. Supposedly standard systems can be enhanced, simplified, and otherwise reconfigured so as to correspond better to a company's operating requirements. However, a company should avoid inventing ways to be different as a pretext for having tailor-made systems. The peculiarities that justify custom built systems or process technologies must be significant and must derive from the company's unique and fundamental values and culture and from the distinctive way it competes in the marketplace. Most companies that implemented custom-built MRP-II systems, for example, got into trouble with them because they grossly underestimated the cost and time involved. If systems development people are given free rein, they can find a thousand special features to design into a system. Only a few such features will materially add to the system's operational or strategic usefulness. The evaluation of alternative system or process technology designs should focus on operational and competitively significant features. Managers that have a solid track record in managing strategic change in systems and technology focus on the following six factors when evaluating alternative systems or process technology configurations:

1. *Technological integrity and potential to perform the task for which the system or process technology is conceived.* The design should be technologically sound and should incorporate the state-of-the-art but tested technology. Moreover, all the design features should have the dominant purpose of facilitating the performance of the system specific task.
2. *Value forming and culture reinforcing.* The particular design must be superior to the others in terms of its potential to exploit corporate culture and values and to reinforce the value set. For example, a company that places strong emphasis on superior customer service should favor an MRP-II system design that has an elaborate and sound order-promising, scheduling, and tracking (reporting) logic. A company that emphasizes low cost, on the other hand, should select a design that has strong cost and inventory control features, such as cost analysis, variance reporting, planned inventory levels, ABC analysis, and inventory-level monitoring.

3. *Simplicity.* All things being equal, designs that are simple and user friendly are preferable to those that are not. Managers who are people oriented choose systems and process technologies that are as simple and user friendly as possible.

4. *Integration.* The closer systems come to full integration, the broader their effect and thus the more substantial is their competitive impact. CAD has more impact when integrated with CAM and the two linked with Computer Numerically Controlled (CNC) machines or with robots by way of a computer can improve costs, quality, flexibility, lead time, and speed of new production innovation in competitively very significant ways. MRP-II linked with bar coding has much more impact on production and material planning and shop floor control than either system taken alone. Integration eliminates duplication of tasks, effort, and information and maximizes the value of information by allowing it to be used in many places simultaneously. Integration creates and exploits symbiosis between systems and technologies. Chosen designs should push integration to the limit allowed by current technology and should be evaluated for the potential to promote integration in the future.

5. *Financial considerations.* Criteria, such as return on investment and payback, while important, are not a decisive factor in the decision to implement a new system or process technology. In a few leading companies, managers use financial calculations mainly to meet corporate capital budgeting requirements and not to rigorously evaluate a system's attractiveness. The view these managers adopt is that if on the basis of solid information on competitive trends, requirements and the innate strategic value of a system, the latter is attractive, then the financial results will necessarily follow. Innovation and systems change cannot ignore the financial criteria but the latter should not be used to block or delay innovations that competent managers agree have competitive value.

6. *Project management* Large-scale strategic changes in systems and process technology are better managed as projects. Indeed, companies that are successfully deploying effective product and process innovation strategies use matrix organizations extensively. The matrix structure permanently integrates the more rigid and hierarchical divisional or functional organization with the more fluid and ad hoc project structure, where influence and authority are exercised horizontally.

Several factors explain why managing changes in systems and process technology as projects give superior results. First, projects have a definite beginning and end and a clearly defined package of interrelated activities. The change process has a clear focus and responsibility and accountability can be clearly allocated. One should note, however, that authority relationships tend to overlap and are typically fuzzy. Second, projects give flexibility because any change of any size can be managed as a project, although that form of organization is usually used for large-scale changes. Projects can be started, accelerated, decelerated, and dismantled as the situation demands, without significant change in the normal functional structure. Change can be implemented with minimal disruption to the usual routine. Projects infuse entrepreneurship and momentum for change into the organization, thus keeping it adaptable.

Third, projects enable management to control the change process because they have specific time, budgetary, and quality objectives. Management can control the pace of change by controlling the tightness/looseness of the project time and cost budgets. Fourth, projects reinforce group processes because they are by definition group-based activities. Fifth, projects are a major training ground for managers with promise. Managers who are given project management responsibilities learn to manage change and exercise leadership on the basis of consensus. In addition, managers learn to deal with ambiguous authority relationships and to rely more on referent power and the authority of expertise and less on the authority conferred by hierarchical position. These managers come to understand and exploit the dynamics of the informal organization. All these are invaluable skills for any manager who increasingly has to deal with flat and fluid organizations, where change and ambiguity are widespread and where semi-autonomous, empowered work groups permeate the organization.

Successful project management is based on six key principles:

1. Select a project manager who, by virtue of performance and status, commands the respect of those directly involved in the project. The project manager should be a champion of the system or process technology change.
2. Break the project into smaller, more manageable subprojects that can be delegated to project teams.
3. Establish a project plan, schedule, and budget using well-known techniques such as PERT and CPM.[3]
4. Identify all project tasks and responsibilities and delegate these to specific individuals.
5. Design and implement a performance evaluation and review mechanism for monitoring and controlling progress by selecting appropriate measures based on time, cost, and quality. Project-development milestones for reviewing progress should also be specified and adhered to.
6. Use small-group processes as much as possible to solve ongoing project management problems. Project-related group activities present ideal

---

[3]PERT (program evaluation and review technique) and CPM (critical path method) are well-known and widely used techniques for project scheduling.

opportunities for constantly reminding people of the project's objectives and how they relate to the overall strategic mission and improvement effort. How the project fits into the broader long-term competitive scheme and the nature of market competition should be constantly kept in focus.

Beyond the Project Champion

Most companies have embraced the idea that the existence of a capable champion is crucial to the success of product, process, or system-based innovation or continuous improvement projects. Companies that emphasize the role of the project champion have identified the following personal qualifications that contribute to the success of an innovation or continuous improvement project:

1. Commitment to and belief in the value of the project
2. Excellent technical competence
3. Strong people-management and negotiation skills
4. High visibility and credibility in the organization that is the result of a solid track record of concrete achievements
5. A sponsor at the top management level who supports the project champion
6. The ability to communicate the project's mission, goals, advantages, requirements, and constraints to all functional groups involved in its implementation
7. A broad organizational and market perspective

While the champion undoubtedly makes an important contribution to the success of an innovation or continuous improvement project, his or her role must be placed in the proper organizational perspective. Capable champions, unlike apples, do not grow on trees. Why is it that some companies are consistently able to attract, retain, and improve the caliber of a constant stream of capable project champions, while most seem to have much difficulty doing so? Why is it that a project champion may fail in one company but go on to succeed brilliantly in another, even if the projects involved were basically the same? How is it that in some companies project champions enjoy their role and the challenges that come with it, while in others they face frustration after frustration and often leave the company discouraged and demotivated? The successful companies have recognized that beyond the direct, visible, and highly touted roles played by the project champions lies the very hard work of developing an adequate number of people to play that role and the internal environment where they can flourish and, in the process, contribute their part to an innovative, continuously improving company.

These few companies that are at the frontiers of competitive excellence view the project champion in a radically different way. They see the capable project champion as a natural culmination of managerial processes that cultivate superior human resources, the champion being only one such resource. Although the project champion plays an important role in the successful management of innovation and continuous improvement projects, the managerial actions that first develop or attract capable champions and then use them to manage innovation are much more fundamental and decisive. The traditional focus on the champions per se assumes that the managerial actions that develop and use them effectively are either the same in most companies or matter little. But, the world's best competitors view them as decisive and as the factor that distinguishes the low from the superior performing competitors. Champions usually do not have the authority to change the fundamental culture and values of a company and how it views, develops, and deploys human resources. That is why they need to have sponsors to help them get commitment to their projects at the top management level. For if it takes champions for innovation and continuous improvement projects to succeed, and some companies are consistently better than most at doing so, then it stands to reason that the true mark of distinction is not the project champion but the managerial actions that develop and use him or her.

The companies that are successful in using champions as agents of strategic change, innovation, and continuous improvement have an internal culture and management policies that give superior results in:

1. Indentifying, attracting, developing, and retaining people who can be capable project champions
2. Listening to champions and giving them the opportunity to influence the change or innovation process
3. Supporting champions with the requisite resources, leadership, and authority
4. Recognizing the champion's contribution and reinforcing it with appropriate rewards
5. Allowing champions the opportunity to champion

These companies are open to ideas and influence from lower and middle management. They have cultivated an internal culture and value system that encourages entrepreneurship and risk taking, pushes hard for success but not overbearing on those who fail from time to time. In fact, they provide the social and psychological support that helps champions survive the shock of failure. They are quick at spotting talent and at nurturing people to give their best.

That which determines the success of project championship in managing innovation and change is behind the project champion, expertly interwoven in the corporate culture and value system. It comes from the profound conviction on the part of top management that superior competitive performance ultimately comes from the development and deployment of superior human resources at all levels in the organization. Endowing the company with such human resources is one of the most fundamental tasks of top management.

Postimplementation Considerations

A system or process technology implementation is not complete unless it anticipates and deals with postimplementation issues such as system enhancement or process-technology refinement and improvement. For instance, once a new process technology is implemented, the project group should deal, in broad terms, with issues such as how to push improvement on the manufacturing progress function. Small group improvement teams should identify and exploit these improvement opportunities, but it makes for continuity of purpose, if broad guidelines are spelled out by the project team. This also keeps a clear vision on continuous improvement as the key mission. One major consideration with the implementation of any new system or technology is how to make it stick, that is, how to make it become a normal part of the way a company operates. For example, the ultimate goal in adopting JIT is not to implement it per se, but to make the company a JIT company. JIT or MRP-II or total quality management companies derive substantially superior results from them than companies that simply implement JIT or MRP-II or total quality management.

Companies that succeed in making new systems or process technologies part of the normal way of doing things implement the following actions:

1. Define all the operating requirements of the new system or process technology and put these into the job descriptions of all those who use, maintain, or support the system or process technology. Evidently, new job descriptions need to be written for all jobs affected by the system or process technology.
2. Build a summary plan for enhancement and improvement of the new system or process technology and delegate all items in the plan to existing small group improvement teams.
3. Formulate and activate a plan for ongoing employee training and development. Such a plan should specifically deal with the skills required to use the new system or process technology effectively. If an ongoing training plan exists, reformulate it to incorporate the requirements of the new system or process technology.
4. Define and apply minimum competency levels, as regards the new system, when hiring new employees. Design a training program for new recruits who do not meet the minimum competency requirements.
5. Design and use performance metrics for continuously reviewing results produced by the system or process technology.

The incorporation of a new system or process technology into a company's modus operandi should not be left to happenstance. Management has to take steps to ensure that the new system is used as anticipated or better. Old habits die hard. Top management has mastered the change process when a new way of doing things exists.

The Execution System

Strategies are designed to be operationalized. The execution system makes the difference between noble strategic intentions and strategy in fact. Strategic change, to be fully complete, must show up as different or improved ways of performing day-to-day activities in the production system. All critical success factors are substantially or partially brought to fruition in the production system. Culture and values, competitive competence, and systems and technology build the potential to realize strategic intentions in the production system. Therefore, all the mechanisms for changing manufacturing strategy, which prior discussion dealt with, also change the execution system. The remaining issues deal with the problem of how to ensure that manufacturing actually does what was decided at the top management level and that day-to-day operations closely mirror the strategic plan and intentions.

Supervisory Styles and Skills

Supervisors are a vital link between strategy and operations. Supervisors must be thoroughly immersed in the culture and values that set the company apart. Mechanisms for selecting supervisors with the potential to motivate and lead work groups in the direction set by strategic plans are a vital component of the execution system. Continuous and thorough training of supervisors based on a well thought-out, rigorously tested training program designed to hone supervisory skills and shape supervisory styles is essential to the operationalization of strategy. The performance evaluation and reward system should be specifically designed to reward supervisory behavior that is in accordance with and reinforces the pursuit of competitive goals.

Worker Training

Workers should be constantly trained, first to create and then to maintain craftsmanship. Companies that are achieving competitively superior levels of quality and productivity have solid training programs for sharpening worker skills and creating the appropriate discipline and attitudes. The training program should aim at developing all work-related skills from the most sophisticated to the most mundane. Training for craftsmanship means that skills that have already been mastered should be refined and improved using refresher courses or training programs.

Communication System

Strategic plans, intentions, and decisions need to be transmitted to the execution system. Top management needs to be kept informed of problems and challenges encountered by the execution system. A communication system that provides for multiple links between top management and operations is one important way to ensure that strategy is being effectively deployed in the production system. Every company that is making strategic plans and intentions happen in day-to-day operations also has a communication system where a two-way free-flow of information between top management and operations is the norm. These companies have designed elaborate and efficient formal communication systems that make extensive use of mandated group sessions for information exchange, periodic reports, newsletters, and performance review sessions. They also make heavy use of the informal system such as plant tours and open-door policies for impromptu exchange of information. In short, top management knows what is going on in the plant and operating employees know where top management intends to take the company.

Performance Measurement, Feedback, and Reporting

The strategic mission has meaning for the production worker only when it is translated into operating goals to be pursued through the normal performance of daily work. All employees, small groups, and production units should be given operating and measurable goals that derive from the strategic mission. Employees should be brought to understand how the company's overall strategic mission depends on how well they perform relative to the operating goals. Operating goals and objectives should be formulated to incorporate continuous improvement. Feedback and reporting mechanisms inform management as to how well organizational units and individuals are executing their operational goals, and ultimately, their responsibilities that are related to the company's strategic mission. A compensation system that rewards those employees and units that produce superior performance on the strategically derived goals reinforces commitment to the strategic mission and motivates appropriate action in day-to-day operations. A company that is pursuing quality superiority must give all employees quality-derived goals and objectives and must compensate them on the basis of quality achieved.

Organizational Processes for Continuous Problem Solving

A production system fails to improve and to execute the strategic mission of the company because operating problems are left unsolved or are covered up. Most companies do not have in place mechanisms for quick problem identification analysis and solution. Usually, small operating problems are symptomatic of deeper, companywide problems that block the achievement of competitive superiority. For example, abnormal levels of machine downtime usually indicate deep-rooted, dysfunctional attitudes relative to preventive maintenance, poor quality philosophies, attitudes and policies, archaic and inappropriate performance evaluation and compensation systems, and deep organizational conflict between production and maintenance. Operating problems that are left unattended to also eventually develop into crises before they attract management attention. The point is that companies that are serious about building competitive superiority pay close attention to ongoing operating problems and have installed organizational processes for identifying and solving them punctually. The preferred mechanisms for doing this are self-management, small group improvement teams (SGIT), and worker empowerment. These concepts will be presented in the following section.

SELF-MANAGEMENT, SGITs, AND WORKER EMPOWERMENT

Theory X and the scientific management movement spearheaded by Frederick Taylor and their assumptions that workers are lazy, irresponsible, lack managerial abilities, and are motivated solely by the pursuit of economic self-interest, have left a terrible legacy for managers of industrial plants in North America. They gave rise to management styles and philosophies that caused apathy, lack of interest in the job, low motivation, absence of pride of workmanship, low productivity, and the stifling of worker creativity. Modern corporations tend to put a low value on factory work which is viewed as the domain of the unintelligent, uncreative masses. The military, rigid hierarchy that supposedly assures maximum social and economic control of the worker reflects the management philosophies that theory X and the scientific management movement insidiously propagated. Most managers subconsciously manage on the basis of the archaic assumptions and principles of the scientific management movement, even if they preach otherwise. These assumptions run counter to the basic social and political philosophies of freedom and democracy and deny the true human spirit. Human beings are designed and born to be free. Except if the design of the human species is radically flawed, and it is difficult to argue that it is, then human beings are born with the capacity to be free moral agents. Free moral agency implies responsibility, autonomy, rationality, and empathy.

Self-Management

In a certain sense, the very concept of management as promulgated by so-called management thinkers, which is understood and practiced by managers in most companies today, is predicated upon the idea that people must be managed because they cannot manage themselves. It views the manager as an external agent who directs, coordinates, organizes, and controls others, that is, the people who work under him or her. This is true to some extent. Managers do direct, coordinate, organize, plan, and control the work of others. Moreover, to bring objectivity to bear on a problem or situation, the manager must be able to detach from it and take a view from the "outside looking in." But, effective managers become integral parts of the groups they manage. They must meddle with the situation, immerse themselves totally in it, in order to identify, empathize with, understand, and lead the group.

The ultimate challenge in management today is to create an organizational situation where people can use the innate ability they have to manage themselves. The organization has to find ways to tap the latent need that people have to seek autonomy, responsibility, and self-actualization. Workers are yearning to show that they are creative and can be trusted to act in the best interest of their companies while pursuing their self-interest. Companies that tap into that potential succeed in unleashing the most powerful competitive weapon in any corporate arsenal. The flatter organization is a by-product of self-management. Less external control means greater span of control which leads to less hierarchy. Autonomy and responsibility mean more power for the worker to exercise creativity and to take action to improve how the work is done.

Self-management pushes decision-making authority and leadership responsibility down to the level of workers who perform operating tasks. It is total employee involvement, job enrichment, and worker empowerment all in one. It builds mutual trust and confidence because for it to work, management must trust the worker and demonstrate confidence in his or her leadership and creative abilities. Workers invariably reciprocate by trusting management and readily supporting their initiatives. Self-management restores the self-esteem of workers and rebuilds pride of workmanship which are essential to pursuing quality superiority and continuous improvement. Self-management goes hand in hand with the development of worker craftsmanship because no one can meticulously work toward the mastery of an individual craft, any craft, unless driven by an inner need and able to exercise a great deal of control over his or her personal development.

Self-management is based on six core principles:

1. Corporatewide, competitive excellence requires and is built on individual excellence. Michael Jordan could not have won alone but the Chicago Bulls could not have won without Michael Jordan or someone like him. Wayne Gretzky alone cannot win the playoffs, but the Kings cannot win without Wayne Gretzky or someone with equivalent abilities.
2. A manager cannot know the job—its requirements, constraints, problems, nuances—better than the employee who does it day after day.
3. Competent, thoroughly trained and motivated employees do not need supervision.

4. No manager can manage or lead an employee who does not want to be managed or led.
5. A manager cannot manage an employee, in respect to planning, controlling, and executing the job, better than the employee can manage himself or herself.
6. Creativity and leadership skills are widely distributed in the general population.

The evidence that ordinary workers can manage their work and even make bold and creative suggestions for improving the company is widespread. Toyota receives about one million suggestions a year from its employees, most of whom are factory workers, on how to improve its operations. Thirty-nine percent of these are accepted and implemented. Canon, the camera and copier manufacturer has similar results. Volvo, the Swedish car manufacturer, has been practicing worker involvement and work group autonomy for decades with impressive increases in quality and productivity. Dofasco, the Canadian steel manufacturer has been reaping sizable benefits in cost reduction and improved quality and productivity from its suggestion program for decades now. U.S.-based companies, like Xerox, Ford Motor Company, Levi-Strauss, and IBM, have all benefited substantially from giving workers greater freedom and latitude in designing, planning, controlling, and executing their work. The point is that if the manager, as a human being, can manage others, then the ability to manage is a human trait that cannot simply vanish when one becomes a factory worker. If a human being cannot manage his or her own work, then, inescapably, he or she cannot manage others. The proof that human beings can manage themselves lies in the fact that they can manage others.

Small Group Improvement Teams (SGITs)

Organizational work is group work. Organizations function because of cooperative effort. Groups or teams facilitate the accomplishment of work because of many reasons. First, human beings are gregarious, biological entities. They have social needs and want to be loved and appreciated. Groups motivate their members by providing the opportunity for people to satisfy their social needs. Second, groups give a sense of security. The group is more powerful and has more bargaining strength than the individual. Third, groups facilitate social exchange by providing significant others with which one can undertake social exchange. Fourth, groups teach, correct, compensate, and otherwise increase the social and technical skills of the individual. As the old proverb goes, "As iron sharpens iron, so shall one individual sharpen another." Fifth, groups or teams provide for continuity because the team easily outlasts the individual.

Little doubt exists that the team has much more creative and performance potential than the individual. The challenge is to tap that potential by building high-performance teams. These have three fundamental characteristics: cohesiveness, clear goals, and true leadership.

Cohesiveness

The team is superior to the individual if it functions as a single unit, free of dysfunctional conflict. Members must be strongly attached to the group and they must show willingness to sacrifice their own personal goals and interests so as to advance those of the team. Cohesiveness assures that the "many" operate as "one," thus magnifying individual potential and effort. Cohesiveness is a function of the following factors:

1. *Shared values, common culture.* It is shared values that make for individual attractiveness to one another. People stay together and show solidarity, if they value the same things and have the same priorities. As management molds the organization to internalize the corporate value set, it also increases the potential to build cohesive work groups.
2. *Unity of purpose and direction, common mission.* Teams must exist with purpose. The more individuals share the purpose and mission and agree on the direction, the more they are likely to want to come and stay together. The goal or mission pursued by the group must be seen as valuable to all members to make it worth working together. The goal must be more important than individual goals or must contribute significantly to the personal goals of the members.
3. *Rewarding experience.* Members must benefit materially, emotionally, psychologically, or otherwise from being a member of the group. There must be fair, significant social exchange that can take place only in the group.
4. *Reward system.* The team must have a great deal of control over the rewards that flow to each member. Rewards give the team the power to change and enforce group norms and to give positive reinforcement for acceptable behavior in the team.

Clear, Measurable, Challenging Goals

The goals being pursued need to be clear to all members and there must be some way to measure and evaluate progress. The goals must challenge the team and members and there must be some way to measure and evaluate progress. The goals must challenge the team, and members need to see that these goals are beyond the individual but within reach of the team. Frequent review of team performance on these goals keeps these in clear view and provides feedback for continuing or changing action plans.

Leadership That Leads

Leaders impact on the team by incorporating the key values in their own behavior, clarifying, and communicating goals and missions, motivating the

TABLE 14–1	Individual Result	Team Result
Number of employees	100	100
Number who improve	1	100
Average individual improvement	2%	2%
Overall impact	.02%	2%
The power of all	100 times	

team to action, and administering the rewards. They also create the opportunity for members to influence the direction of the team, thereby adopting team goals as their goals. Leaders also challenge the team and may even instill a sense of destiny. Leadership that leads has to be legitimate, which means that there is broad consensus that the leader is the right person for the job. Legitimacy is assured either because the leader is a deserving person designated by higher management or because he or she has cultivated group support by demonstrating capacity to lead.

The Power of All

Cohesive teams exploit symbiosis and complementarity. Nature's full human potential is in the group or team. Because nature endows every individual only partially, no worker can be superior to the team, overall. Suppose a football team had 12 of the best quarterbacks in the sport. They would never win a game, except perhaps against a team that had 12 of the best runningbacks available. Twelve excellent quarterbacks or runningbacks equal 1 excellent individual player and 11 mediocre ones because the 11 surplus excellent quarterbacks are not worth much to a football team. A winning football team needs excellent quarterbacks, runningbacks, and people to fill all the other positions that make up the team. An excellent quarterback covers the weaknesses of the runningback, that is, he or she makes up for the fact that the runningback has little quarterback expertise. This is the power of all. In the group or team, one individual's talent covers and makes up for another individual's deficiencies. Table 14–1 shows how team effort amplifies individual effort. The team gives superior results, even if there is no symbiosis. Improvement is multiplied by a factor of 100, when the whole team improves. Symbiosis assures that the final result of teamwork will be even more favorable. The team, therefore, is a socially engineered work unit that creates the super, ultimate worker which nature does not provide. Consequently, superior manufacturing performance requires the company to build and use cohesive work groups throughout the manufacturing function.

Implementing Self-Management through SGITs FIGURE 14–3

1. Formulate, communicate and inculcate an appropriate vision and philosophy of the role and place of human resources in the enterprise.

2. Formulate, communicate and implement a corporate policy on SGIT's and the role of the worker.

3. Define a mandate for implementing SGIT's and delegate it to a project manager and marshal the necessary resources to do so. The mandate must include full implementation of the corporate policy.

4. Put together project management team and train its members extensively and intensively on team building and problem solving processes and on the relationship between SGIT's and the foundation corporate culture and values.

5. Implement initial training program to motivate interest and to explain key SGIT concepts. Initial training should emphasize:
   a. Competitive demands
   b. Top management support
   c. Quality of work life
   d. No loss of jobs
   e. Commitment to prepare workers
   f. Advantages to the worker of team skills, craftsmanship and the foundation corporate values and attitudes upon which self-management through teams is based.

6. Arrange for key workers (opinion leaders) to do tours of companies using SGIT's or to receive published information on these.

7. Create teams and select team leaders.

8. Formulate areas of responsibility that will be progressively delegated to teams.

9. Develop team training programs that are value and attitude forming, culture reinforcing and that develop problem solving skills.

10. Design performance evaluation, reporting and reward system for monitoring performance (progress) and for compensating high performance teams.

11. Launch first team problem solving projects in which each team starts to identify and select a problem to work on.

12. Design broadcast system for disseminating information on team performance and progress throughout the company.

13. Identify and deal promptly with on-going problems.

14. Broaden areas of responsibility and continue as per (9) above.

Figure 14-3 outlines some guidelines for implementing self-management through improvement teams. One will note the preponderance, once more, of the culture and values system. Change in manufacturing strategy and the pursuit of constantly improving quality, cost, delivery time, and productivity must inescapably change or nurture the value set upon which all aspects of manufacturing performance stand or fall.

Conclusion

Strategic manufacturing change, that is, keeping the company competitively well positioned, the creation and sustenance of superior competitive competence, continuous improvement, Kaizen, and the search for perfection, is a never ending process. Change, while it is painful and unnerving, must anticipate and plan for further change. If strategic change is undertaken for continuous improvement, and we have argued that it is, then that change must plan more continuous improvement. In a very real sense, all management is the management of change because change is the quintessential thing in every field of human endeavor. The fossil record of corporate evolution is layered with the remains of organizations that worshiped stability and tried to resist change. Those that are carrying the robust genome of corporations fit to survive are those that learned to live with, adapt to, and even exploit change to their advantage.

Case for Discussion

NORTH AMERICAN PAPER PRODUCTS, INC. (NAPP)

Ms. Brenda Schneider, mill manager of the British Columbia plant of NAPP's fine paper division and her management team, saw 1988 as a milestone in their efforts to save the plant. One year ago, corporate top management had served notice that the plant would be shut down unless there was measurable and substantial progress in its efficiency. The BC mill's productivity was 25 percent lower than its sister mill located in Ontario and its cost per ton of paper was 22 percent higher. In an effort to rejuvenate the mill, divisional top management had terminated the former manager who had come up from the production ranks and had replaced him with Schneider who was a business administration graduate with a major in finance.

There were many who opposed the choice of Schneider for that task, but top management stuck to its guns. Privately, however, Schneider thought that her chances for success were slim in the face of what was obviously a daunting task. She had never managed a mill before, and she had never even worked in one. All she had going for herself was a good dose of humility, a capacity to work hard and to learn fast, and an ability to work with people. She hated to fail and was determined to do all she could to save the mill. After all, jobs were at stake and there were 94 heads of families who depended on that plant for their livelihoods. Unemployment in the town was above 11 percent and any further job losses would be devastating to the community.

Schneider and her mill team had gone to work quickly to try to come up with a workable plan. After three months of gut-wrenching work, they came up, with the mill's version of the Manufacturing Excellence Project (MEP), a top management initiated, revolutionary philosophy and approach to managing the plant that would leave no stone unturned and which would be driven by five critical objectives promoted within the plant as "1/2 in 2," "1 in 1," "1 in 2," "2 in 2," and "3 in 2." Translated, these meant "increase productivity by 50 percent in 2 years," "decrease set-up time to 1 hour in 1 year," "cut lead time to 1 week in 2 years," "decrease defective products to 2 percent in 2 years," and "increase inventory turns threefold in 2 years."

The union had virulently resisted MEP at the outset. The local shop steward, the president of the union local, and the national union president had all served notice that they would fight MEP to the end. They saw MEP as a sinister plan to cut jobs, decrease wages, and weaken the union. Moreover, the union was going to use MEP as an example of what they thought would happen to Canadian jobs under the proposed North American Free Trade Agreement (NAFTA), and were going all out to use NAPP to rally organized labor's opposition to NAFTA and to give a much needed boost to a flagging membership. After tough negotiations and in return for a guarantee of no layoffs, the union adopted a wait-and-see attitude to MEP and cooperated in the initial phases of the project. That proved the value of MEP, and Schneider decided that she should press ahead. But she now realized that its implementation would be one of the toughest challenges that she had ever faced.

The Company, Its Market, and Strategy

From its humble beginnings as a one paper machine, 20 employee company, NAPP had grown to be a diversified, vertically integrated $4.0 billion Fortune 500 corporation in less than 40 years. The company produced a wide range of personal hygiene products such as towels, napkins, disposable diapers, sanitary pads, and tissue paper. Like all other companies its size in the paper-based products segment of the personal hygiene products market, NAPP was a vertically integrated company that produced most of its own requirements from lumber to the final consumer products that it manufactured. The company owned the rights to large tracts of timber that were harvested and converted into chips in its own chip-making plants. The economics of transportation dictated that these chip-making operations be located close to the timber tracts. Chips were then converted into pulp in the company's own pulp mills, but the company also bought pulp as needed from other pulp and paper manufacturers. Pulp was shipped to paper mills where it was converted into pulp paper. The output of the mills were shipped to plants that made the final products sold to customers. These plants were generally located close to the company's principal markets.

Although the pulp and paper industry was dominated by some very large, integrated companies, the existence of a substantial number of viable, nonintegrated companies ensured a healthy competitive environment. The smaller companies existed by focusing on particular market segments such as newsprint, pulp production, and the production and marketing of high-quality, fine papers in bulk. Paper making could be divided into distinct phases thus permitting companies to focus both by process and by product. Vertical integration did offer cost advantages, but nonintegrated companies could overcome these by being specialized and maintaining lean, short-cycle operations. The smaller companies also had the reputation of being more quick to adopt new concepts and techniques that promised to boost productivity.

NAPP competed in every significant segment of its industry. A segment was targeted for entry if the company's share of the overall market, when projected on that segment would support a minimum economic-scale plant. The company always entered a new segment, with an economic-scale plant and relied on normal demand growth or better than average market share to achieve economic scale operations. The company maintained a better than average growth rate by striving to give the maximum quality and service at lowest possible cost.

The company also tried to capture the advantages of focus, small scale, and specialization by dividing its operations into largely autonomous business units, some organized by process and others by product. Timber harvesting and chip-making operations were organized as autonomous business units of which there were 5. These in turn fed 5 autonomous pulp-making operations. The pulp-making operations fed a total of 12 paper mills that were specialized by paper grade. Two of these mills produced the fine papers used by the company for making consumer products such as facial and soft tissue towels. The plants that were at the final stages of the conversion process were specialized by market segment and geographic area. For example, the company had 5 plants across North America that produced diapers for 5 different regional markets, the U.S. Southwest, the Midwest, the Northeast, the South, and Canada. The company transferred products between the process-based divisions and from these to the product-based divisions at cost plus 20 percent. Divisions had some latitude in deciding which sources within the NAPP organization they would use, but could not source from outside except if there was a capacity shortage for the materials that they needed. Top management was of the view that such an arrangement enabled the company to exploit the advantages of both focus (specialization) and integration.

The Changing Competitive Situations and Their Effects

Prior to the 1970s, paper-based, personal-hygiene products had grown in line with the rise of the standard of living and general population growth in North America. In the early 1970s, however, three changes took place that dramatically altered the size and growth prospects of the industry. The first was the development and wide acceptance of female personal hygiene products, the most notable of which is the disposable sanitary pad. That latter product led to a slew of other similar products that catered to the unique needs of women. Second, the continued entry of women into the labor force not only increased expenditures on personal care products, but also made ease of use and disposal mandatory. The paper-based personal-hygiene products were uniquely suited to the needs of a growing and prosperous class of working women. Third, the development and wide acceptance of disposable diapers allowed companies to enter a whole new market. The reality of large numbers of women in the labor force combined with the obvious advantages of disposable diapers combined to create a large, new, and profitable market for companies like NAPP.

The double-digit growth rates of the 1970s and mid-1980s were coming to an end, and there were few developments in sight that would stimulate demand like the major breakthroughs of the early 1970s. Moreover, growing concern for the environment was causing a shift in demand away from the nonbiodegradable disposable diapers and sanitary pads and bleached paper products that generated the bulk of the growth experienced by the industry during the 1970s and 1980s. A few pioneering companies were successfully marketing products that were both biodegradable and unbleached and well ahead of most large integrated companies. There was the prospect that competition in NAPP's traditional markets would intensify which would put severe downward pressure on prices and margins. Keeping costs low and increasing productivity, for long a major concern of paper products manufacturers, would become a key priority.

Fine Paper Products, Mill #1

Mill #1 was the oldest of two fine paper mills that produced fine paper for the Canadian division of NAPP. Built in the 1930s, the mill had earned a solid reputation within the entire NAPP corporation as a low-cost producer of the finest quality paper. All mill managers, before Schneider, had risen from the ranks of production because, in the words of the last mill manager:

> You can't manage this place if you do not understand the nuts and bolts of paper making. You have to be tough with the workers and the union and assert your authority. Otherwise they will dictate to you how to run the plant. I run my mill the way I see fit and the union had to get used to that.

Workers at Mill #1 were among the highest paid manufacturing sector workers in British Columbia. A series of labor disputes over the years had given rise to an industrial relations climate that many characterized as tense at best and downright warlike at worst.

Union and management had come to be deeply suspicious of each other, and the union resisted the introduction of new technology because "it will eliminate jobs." The mill had never had a significant change in process technology in nearly 30 years while management often accused the union of blocking innovation and change and creating restrictive work rules. One of the sore points was the number of job classifications that were mandated in the collective agreement. There were 22 in all, and the union was determined to force management to respect all of them. Coupled with a high rate of absenteeism this made production scheduling extremely difficult.

That reputation for quality continued well into the 1970s, until NAPP built another fine paper mill in Ontario, whose capacity was three times that of Mill #1. The Ontario mill incorporated the latest process technologies available in the industry and made extensive use of advanced computer technology for controlling the paper-making machines and for fine tuning the production process. Most notable was the use of feedforward statistical process control (SPC) for producing paper to very tight tolerances. Mill #1 made limited use of feedback SPC using a software package that was designed in 1972. Since then, considerable progress had been made in isolating and modeling the operating variables and conditions that affected the quality of paper that came out of a machine, and the sensors that were installed on the machines for capturing and transmitting the data to a computer had improved dramatically.

Mill #1 could meet all quality specifications, but at high cost since defects were about 7 percent of the mill's output of $25 million valued at transfer prices. By contrast, Mill #2 achieved a defect rate of less than 2 percent and its productivity averaged 52 tons per paper machine per day compared to 35 tons for Mill #1. Product changeovers at Mill #2 took two hours compared to an average of six at Mill #1 and a typical production run of 60 tons. Before 1985, mill management did not attach much importance to this and the prior mill manager thought that low set-up times did not matter because "We can drive the set-up time per unit to near zero by scheduling long runs. In fact, I can save money by having fewer set-ups and fewer set-up people."

Pressures were also coming from another source. The mills that were quicker than Mill #1 in implementing MEP were already reaping the benefits. One in particular was already doing 360 product changes per year compared to only 30 just two years ago. That same mill was completely recycling 96 percent of all defective products as opposed to 15 percent when it launched MEP. These results made Mill #1's performance visible to top management.

The Manufacturing Excellence Project (MEP)

The push to come up with programs like MEP at the plant level had come from top management who was anticipating a tightening of the market as the high growth era of the 1980s came to an end. Top management was pressing for a substantial and overall increase in efficiency as the most viable means of defending the market share gains of the 1980s and keeping profitability high. Every division was expected to come up with a plan for improving individual plant operations but starting with the older plants. Each plant, in turn, had to produce its version of the divisional plan taking into account the specific situation of the plant. In general, MEP called for implementation of the following actions:

Human resources. Increase the level of training and responsibility of all production workers and facilitate the development of more consensus decision making. Implement SGIT throughout the plant and design performance evaluation and compensation systems that increase employee commitment to improve productivity.

Process technology. Within a negotiated time frame, all plants must have the most effective but proven process technologies available to the industry. Thirty percent of all measurable savings from other areas of improvement will be earmarked for the upgrading of new process technologies.

Manufacturing cycle times. There must be a concerted effort to decrease cycle times to the lowest achievable in the industry with the available technology. Programs, concepts, and tools, such as JIT, MRP-II, and SMED, should be implemented on an accelerated basis.

Quality. Defects should be reduced to near zero. All SPC programs should be updated, enhanced, and their use broadened to reach every process in the plant, without exception to scale, complexity, age, or phase of the manufacturing operation. Full-scale studies of process-operating conditions should be launched and the results used to implement feedforward SPC within a negotiated time frame. Full implementation of all TQM philosophies, concepts, policies, tools, procedures, techniques, and methods must be achieved within a compressed time frame.

Maintenance. Specific actions must be implemented to raise the profile, visibility, and strategic value of maintenance by the faithful application of all TPM principles, philosophies, and methods. This should start with the design and implementation of a rigorous preventive maintenance program and the complete, sustained training of all maintenance personnel.

Staff. All staff must be cut to the bare minimum. The number of people reporting to a top, middle, and lower manager in the plant, must be no less than 9, 12, and 20, respectively.

Brenda Schneider had been given a clear mandate. She was to come up with a version of MEP for the plant, get it approved by divisional management and implement it. She took the first four weeks of her new assignment getting a feel for the plant and the key people that she could use for MEP. After about six weeks, she had selected her team and went to work on developing MEP for Mill #1. The team worked feverishly for three months only to see its first plan rejected by divisional management as being not ambitious enough. The second plan, which was accepted by divisional management, cut the time frame for implementing MEP from five years to four and tightened the targets by 25 percent. Schneider and her team went to work implementing MEP, focusing first on training and SGIT. After much initial resistance, she was finally getting some cooperation, or a semblance of it, from the union. However, the union was still balking at a proposal by Schneider to give some financial incentives to workers for improving productivity and reducing waste. Mill #1 management thought that workers would react more positively if 20 percent of all cost savings were returned back to them. Management still had not decided whether the incentives should reward group or individual performance. The next phases would be difficult, but Schneider was wondering whether the early successes were a harbinger of spring or merely the calm before the storm.

Discussion Questions

1. What are the outstanding features of NAPP's competitive environment?
2. What is NAPP's manufacturing strategy? How would you characterize its response to the competitive situation?
3. What are the major forces that are dictating the need for change both at the corporate level and specifically at the level of Mill#1?
4. What are the major barriers to strategic change at Mill #1? How would you characterize the way that Brenda Schneider has handled the situation so far?
5. What actions would you recommend to Schneider to increase the chance for success of MEP?

References

Kaplan, Robert S., "Must CIM Be Justified by Faith Alone?" *Harvard Business Review,* March–April 1986.

Leonard, Barton, and William A. Kraus, "Implementing New Technology," *Harvard Business Review,* November–December 1985.

Marucheck, Ann, Ronald Pannesi, and Carl Anderson, "An Exploratory Study of the Manufacturing Strategy Process in Practice," *Journal of Operations Management,* 9: 1, January 1990.

Meredith, Jack R., and Marianne M. Hill, "Justifying New Manufacturing Systems: A Managerial Approach," *Sloan Management Review,* 51, Summer 1987.

Platts, R. W., and M. J. Gregory, "Manufacturing Audit in the Process of Strategy Formulation," *IJOPM,* 10: 9, 1989.

Skinner, Wickham, *Manufacturing: The Formidable Competitive Weapon,* New York: John Wiley and Sons, 1985.

Wheelwright, S. C., "Japan—Where Operations Really Are Strategic," *Harvard Business Review,* July–August 1981.

Index